HONOR KILLING

Also by David E. Stannard

Death in America (Editor)

The Puritan Way of Death:
A Study in Religion, Culture, and Social Change

Shrinking History:
On Freud and the Failure of Psychohistory

Before the Horror:
The Population of Hawai'i on the Eve of Western Contact

American Holocaust:
The Conquest of the New World

David E. Stannard

HONOR KILLING

How the Infamous "Massie Affair"
Transformed Hawai'i

VIKING

VIKING

Published by the Penguin Group

Penguin Group (USA) Inc., 375 Hudson Street,
New York, New York 10014, U.S.A.
Penguin Group (Canada) 10 Alcorn Avenue,
Toronto, Ontario, Canada M4V 3B2
(a division of Pearson Penguin Canada Inc.)
Penguin Books Ltd, 80 Strand, London WC2R 0RL, England
Penguin Ireland, 25 St. Stephen's Green, Dublin 2, Ireland
(a division of Pearson Books Ltd)
Penguin Books Australia Ltd, 250 Camberwell Road, Camberwell,
Victoria 3124, Australia (a division of Pearson Australia Group Pty Ltd)
Penguin Books India Pvt Ltd, 11 Community Centre,
Panchsheel Park, New Delhi – 110 17, India
Penguin Group (NZ), Cnr Airborne and Rosedale Roads, Albany,
Auckland, New Zealand (a division of Pearson New Zealand Ltd)
Penguin Books (South Africa) (Pty) Ltd, 24 Sturdee Avenue,
Rosebank, Johannesburg 2196, South Africa

Penguin Books Ltd, Registered Offices: 80 Strand, London WC2R 0RL, England

First published in 2005 by Viking Penguin, a member of Penguin Group (USA) Inc.

1   2   3   4   5   6   7   8   9   10

Copyright © David E. Stannard, 2005
All rights reserved

Illustration credits appear on page 467.

CIP data available.

ISBN 0-670-03399-5

This book is printed on acid-free paper. ∞

Printed in the United States of America
Set in Dante
Designed by Francesca Belanger

For Susan Rabiner

Contents

A Note on Language

The spoken Hawaiian language is one in which a slight shift in pronunciation may indicate a major difference in meaning. To communicate this in writing it is now conventional to insert one of two symbols in certain words. The first of these is an *'okina* (what appears to be a backward and upside-down apostrophe), indicating a glottal stop, such as the hesitation in the middle of the English-language exclamation "oh-oh!" The second symbol is the *kahakō* (in English, the macron), which is a dash placed over certain vowels to signal that they should be stressed. The potential for misunderstanding in using these marks incorrectly is illustrated by the words *kou* (your), *ko'u* (mine), and *ko'ū* (damp, moist).

Use of the 'okina and the kahakō—although now commonplace in English-language Hawai'i newspapers, government documents, and other writings—is of fairly recent vintage. This book focuses on an era when those symbols were not in use, and when quoting material from that earlier time I have left the original spelling intact. Thus, among other examples, the name of the islands is sometimes given as "Hawaii," while at other times it appears as "Hawai'i." In addition, Hawaiian words are italicized only the first time they are used.

Three other conventions should be noted. First, the Hawaiian language does not use the letter "s" to indicate the plural; instead, the particle *na* is added before a word. However, it is common for English-only speakers, when using occasional Hawaiian words, to pluralize them by adding an "s." I have done that here. Second, in Hawai'i, the word "Hawaiian" refers solely to the indigenous or native people, not to everyone who happens to live in the islands. And third, the word *haole* is the everyday term for Caucasians. In fact, it refers to anything foreign—as in foreign lands (*'āina haole*) or certain introduced plants—but since Europeans and European Americans were the first non-natives to settle in the islands, the term also was applied to them. The nineteenth-century missionaries called themselves haoles, as have white people ever since. Only in very recent years have some new arrivals expressed resentment over use of the term, believing that it implies disparagement. It does not.

D.E.S.

Introduction

T his year, like the year before it and the year to follow, about seven million people will vacation in Hawai'i, more than six tourists for every resident. They will be enticed by the beaches and mountains of pristine natural beauty and by the famous climate of endless summer. The people will attract them as well—sufficiently exotic in appearance to satisfy a desire for something foreign, but American enough in language and style to provide a sense of comfort and security.

Those seven million travelers will be lured by what the islands' Visitors Bureau aggressively promotes as an earthly paradise, an Eden where "the spirit of aloha"—an aura of loving welcome—is everywhere. But what the Visitors Bureau never mentions is that for the first half of the twentieth century, most of those famously friendly and multihued people of paradise lived under the authoritarian rule of an openly white supremacist oligarchy.

During that time the islands' economic life was in the grip of a handful of local corporations with tightly interlocked directorates. The same few white businessmen met periodically to decide which of them, or their subordinates, would be the next governor. Their selection was then conveyed to the president of the United States, who made the appointment. Hawai'i was an American colony (the official term was "territory"), and voting for their governor was not a privilege enjoyed by the islands' inhabitants, 80 percent of whom were native Hawaiians or Asians.

This was a political arrangement envied by outsiders of a certain stripe, people like Army Major (ultimately General) George S. Patton. Patton was a frequent visitor to Hawai'i, and a close friend and polo partner of the islands' most powerful business leader, Walter S. Dillingham. Their racial views had much in common. Even in the aftermath of the Holocaust, Patton would write that he regarded Jews as "lower than animals . . . a sub-human species without any of the cultural or social refinements of our time." For his part, Dillingham believed—and so testified before Congress—that God had made the white race to rule and the colored to be ruled. It was as plain as "the pig-ment in the skin," he said, adding that when a white man is "asked to go out in the sun and work in the canebrake, away from the tropical breeze, you are subjecting [him] to something that the good Lord did not create him to do."

Patton and Dillingham had enjoyed a lively correspondence for years. With the onset of the Depression, they began expressing deep concern re-garding the future of American politics. In one exchange of 1932, Patton complained about "the total lack of balls and backbone evinced by our rulers." At least "in Hawai'i you can start a dictatorship and hold on for a while," he wrote, "but here that much to be desired form of government can hardly be put into effect."

For most of Hawai'i's people Patton's "much to be desired form of gov-ernment" had long been their everyday reality. Federal investigations prior to World War II routinely compared conditions on the sugar and pineapple plantations to slavery or involuntary servitude. In 1920, when half the terri-tory's adults labored for an average of less than eight cents an hour, a report by the U.S. Department of the Interior described their lives as driven "by the biting lash of necessity . . . in the spirit of the slave." A decade and a half later a director of the National Labor Relations Board observed that workers in Hawai'i lived "more like slaves than free people. . . . They have no chance to change their jobs or get away from their present environment. They speak and mumble in undertones." His report concluded that for the majority of the population, Hawai'i was the very "picture of Fascism."

Even California's right-wing Republican power broker and confidant of William Randolph Hearst, John Francis Neylan, after numerous visits agreed. He described "what the white race has done to the kindly [native] people" of Hawai'i as a matter of "everlasting shame to the Caucasian." And he called plantation agriculture in the islands a "system of peonage" that was "a dis-grace to American civilization."

In the towns outside the plantations—and in Honolulu, the only true city in the territory—conditions were less oppressive, but only marginally so. The most desirable neighborhoods were racially restricted, and the majority of Asians and Hawaiians lived in slums or tenements or shantytowns. The news-papers were flamboyantly reactionary, adamantly opposed to any and all ideas that smacked of liberalism, including antilynching laws. Not surpris-ingly, in such an environment, of seventy-five men executed for crimes in the islands since the early nineteenth century, only one was white—a foreign sailor who jumped ship in 1906 and then murdered, decapitated, dismem-bered, and disemboweled the son of a prominent white family. All the remaining seventy-four put to death by the government were Hawaiian, Chinese, Japanese, Puerto Rican, Korean, or Filipino.

In contrast, since the late 1950s the political environment in the islands has been as progressive as that of any state in the country. Hawai'i has strict gun control laws, no death penalty, and a statewide (rather than municipality-based) public education system. It was the first state to legalize abortion, the first state to pass the Equal Rights Amendment, the first state to establish near-universal health care, the first state to mandate domestic partnership benefits to same-sex couples, and the first state officially to declare its opposition to federal antiterrorism laws that compromise civil rights and civil liberties. It has one of the nation's highest minimum-wage rates, it is among the most unionized states in the country, and it has the most equitable tax structure of all the fifty states.

During the past forty years the people of the islands have elected and re-elected five governors. Of the first four, one was Irish in ancestry, one Japanese, one Hawaiian, and one Filipino, all from impoverished or working-class backgrounds. The fifth and current governor is an unmarried Jewish woman, and a Republican, in a state that is overwhelmingly Democratic and less than 1 percent Jewish. Not surprisingly, visiting dignitaries never tire of saying that ethnic and race relations in the islands are a model of what, in the best of worlds, they one day might become in the rest of the country.

In truth, social conditions are far less rosy than that, especially for Hawai'i's native people. And recent decades have demonstrated that corruption is a disease that afflicts liberals as much as it does anyone else. But there is no denying that what happened in the islands during the course of just twenty years, from the 1930s to the 1950s, was an astonishing reversal. In terms of the speed and totality of changed ethnic fortunes and political ideology, it may be unrivaled in American history.

Equally remarkable is the fact that pivotal in that turnaround was a connected series of racially charged events—a white woman's allegation that she had been raped by a gang of native men, a kidnapping, a murder, and two sensational criminal trials—that together focused the world's attention on justice in Hawai'i for months on end during 1931 and 1932.

This book tells that story—of racism, violence, and gross abuse of power—in a city that became an ethnically divided powder keg; but it was far from a local story. It was headlined on the pages of newspapers from San Francisco to New York and London to Sydney. In the spring of 1932 alone, the *New York Times* ran almost two hundred stories on the tumultuous happenings in Hawai'i. The *Chicago Tribune* called it "one of the great criminal cases of modern times." Day after day, the Hearst newspaper chain printed a boxed message on the front page of its papers in San Francisco, Los Angeles, Atlanta, Washington, Boston, New York, Seattle, Detroit, and a dozen other cities, urging readers to pressure Congress to place Hawai'i under direct military rule so that "the honor of American womanhood" might be protected "from the Hawaiian rabble."

During this same time, millions tuned in nightly to hear radio newscasters ominously describe how no white woman was safe from marauding gangs of brown-skinned rapists on the streets of Honolulu. And why the lynching of a native Hawaiian who had not been convicted of any crime was, in the words of media celebrity and news commentator Floyd Gibbons, a justifiable act that "rid this world of probably as abysmal a brute as ever befouled it."

In a twelve-month period that witnessed the Olympic Games in Los Angeles, the kidnapping of the Lindbergh baby, the transatlantic flight of Amelia Earhart, the Veterans' Bonus March on Washington, the election of Franklin Delano Roosevelt, the imprisonment of Al Capone, the Japanese invasion of Manchuria, and the worst days of the Great Depression, the astonishing tale that unfolded on a small tropical island in the Pacific was voted by Associated Press editors one of the top world news events of the year—and the single most important criminal trial in the country.

Not surprisingly, magazines like *True Detective* and *Startling Detective Adventures* exploited the drama with lurid cover stories on the "Hawaiian Horror," providing readers with "a complete account of the most atrocious outrage ever experienced by a white woman." But at the other end of the journalistic spectrum the tone was only slightly more sedate. On the day that the second of two raucous jury trials finally reached its denouement, with still one more stunning turnaround, the California Bar Association journal, the *Recorder*, observed that "no trial in recent years, within the territorial limits of the United States, has received so much attention." The *Recorder* then went on to explain why this was so and, in the process, to justify revenge murder—honor killing—as every "red blooded" American's right. It also lamented what it regarded as the central issue hovering over the trial: the "disgrace" that in Hawai'i "a mongrel race now threatens white supremacy."

The legal case was the last great battle waged by the most famous criminal attorney in American history, Clarence Darrow. It also was the setting for what the *New York Times* would describe as the most dramatic moment in any of Darrow's courtroom struggles. A published review of his career at the time—one that Darrow himself clipped and saved—noted that with the famous Scopes "Monkey" trial, in which he battled William Jennings Bryan in the sweltering summer heat of Dayton, Tennessee, "Darrow received greater notice than at any other time in his life, except when he went to Hawai'i as counsel in the Massie case, which attracted world-wide attention." Indeed, in his memoirs Darrow himself devoted more space to the Honolulu trial than he did even to the infamous Leopold and Loeb case, the first of America's so-called trials of the century.

Upon Darrow's death in 1938, his friends gathered to honor the man who had tirelessly advanced so many progressive causes. They wrote essays and poems to praise his legacy of support for blacks, the poor, the underprivileged, the oppressed. His major trials were discussed and celebrated—except one. No mention at all was made of the world-renowned case he had tried in Honolulu only six years earlier. And since then, unlike Darrow's many great contributions to American legal lore, it has faded into obscurity. Because in this one, win or lose, he was on the wrong side.

The story of what became known everywhere at the time as "the Massie case" has been told before, in several straightforward journalistic accounts, as well as in a few melodramatic (and wildly inventive) fiction and film renditions. This is not surprising, as it has all the elements of myth. A pampered young woman, apparently martyred at the hands of a gang of bestial thugs. A socialite mother who will stop at nothing to avenge her daughter's shame. A dethroned native princess quietly doing battle on behalf of the most wretched of her people. A cabal of corrupt military leaders and businessmen, determined to imprison innocent men in the name of law and order, and incidentally to further their own fortunes. And a chorus of voices, many millions strong, calling for blood. Little wonder that *Time* magazine later called it "the case that had everything."

But what these versions have ignored is the rich historical backdrop to the story, and more important, its remarkable aftermath. A century and a half of unbridled greed by some, and unbounded suffering by others, finally was brought to a head in two criminal trials, in two crowded courtrooms, on one of the most isolated islands on earth.

Today, most people who know what happened during those fateful months regard the events as a tragedy and a scandal. That it was. But out of those courtrooms, and out of the events that surrounded them, there also emerged numerous acts of bravery by people whose names and life stories have faded into obscurity. They include the falsely accused and unyielding victims of a witch hunt, the editor of a small daily newspaper, a handful of attorneys, a single determined judge, and a random collection of jurors. They came from various racial and ethnic backgrounds. They were rich and they were poor. But when it was over they had one thing in common. In the face of nationwide racial hysteria, they had confronted and defied direct threats to their safety, their social status, and their financial well-being by some of the most powerful forces in the United States. And because of their actions, and those of others who followed, before long an entire society was turned around.

In addition to everything else, then, this is a tale of unfaltering courage by a few in the face of overwhelming intimidation. However much it is rooted in the past, it is a story with a powerful message for the present.

Nothing but Trouble

Today, Ala Moana Boulevard, on the south shore of the island of O'ahu, is a busy six-lane divided thoroughfare that emerges from Waikīkī's western end and sweeps along the coastline for several miles toward downtown Honolulu. It curves between tall oceanfront hotels and sleek high-rise apartment buildings, overlooks yacht clubs and beach parks, and passes huge shopping malls boasting scores of restaurants and hundreds of shops with names like Gucci, Cartier, Chanel, Neiman Marcus, Armani, Christian Dior, Ralph Lauren, and Versace.

But before World War II, Ala Moana Boulevard was Ala Moana Road—or simply "Beach Road" to most people—a narrow, unlighted, badly paved, and rarely used bypass that took those who bumped along on it to Kewalo Basin, a depressed waterfront area where fishing boats unloaded their catch and occasional late-night revelers tried to sober up on fish chowder at the wharfside Kewalo Inn. A city dump lay some distance down the road on one side of the docks. An old and abandoned animal quarantine station squatted on the other side. In between, the deserted landscape was dense with un-tended coconut, mango, kiawe, and ironwood trees, and with overgrown tangles of bushes and weeds.

At a little before one o'clock on the Sunday morning of September 13, 1931, a car carrying a young man and two middle-aged couples along Ala Moana Road toward the Kewalo Inn slowed and then stopped. The car's headlights, cutting through the pitch-black night, had illuminated the figure of an elegantly dressed woman walking alone in their direction and waving to them. As she approached the car the people inside noticed that the woman's mouth was swollen, and one of her cheeks was reddened and scuffed. The driver of the car reached over and rolled down the passenger window. The woman, squinting in the dark, peered inside. "Are you white people?" she asked. They said yes. "Thank God," she replied. Then she opened the front door and climbed in, directing them to drive her home.

Less than twenty-four hours later nearly everyone in Honolulu had heard the shocking tale of a young navy officer's wife who had been gang-raped by a carload of native Hawaiians. And until the day that they died the people in the car who rescued her never forgot the night they met Thalia Massie. It was the beginning of the most astounding year of their lives.

Few who knew Thalia would have predicted that she might change the course of history, even in one small corner of the world, or that her name and face would come to adorn the front pages of newspapers and magazines from coast to coast and around the globe, symbolizing for tens of millions the purity and vulnerability of white American womanhood. Thalia herself would have ridiculed the notion. Sarcasm was her shield against the world.

Not that Thalia didn't want to be famous. She basked in publicity when it found her, and then briefly and vainly chased it when it began to melt away. Fame is a common enough ambition, after all. But in her case the quest also ran in the family, accompanied by a conviction that self-indulgence without consequence was a birthright.

Thalia Massie's father was a slim, handsome, blue-eyed man named Granville Roland Fortescue. Commonly known as "Roly," he was the illegitimate son of Robert Barnwell Roosevelt, Teddy Roosevelt's wealthy and powerful "Uncle Rob"—a "lusty and raffish" man with a "love of the limelight," says one Roosevelt biographer. Robert Roosevelt also "was a bit lax in his morals," writes a second observer, "living a remarkable double life, keeping another woman and ultimately an entire second family in a house only a block or so distant" from his official family residence in New York.

That "other" woman was Minnie O'Shea, who gave birth, out of wedlock, to three of Robert Roosevelt's children; Roly was born in 1875. Minnie always claimed that her offspring had been fathered by a conveniently deceased (and thoroughly fictitious) husband named Robert Fortescue, so she called herself Mrs. Fortescue and gave that last name to her children. But everyone in the Roosevelt family knew that the children's father was Uncle Rob.

Minnie finally married Robert Roosevelt in 1888, upon the death of his first wife, Elizabeth. Although the true paternity of thirteen-year-old Roly and his siblings could never be acknowledged, the rest of the Roosevelt clan accepted them into the family. Roly made the most of it. After high school, Yale was his first stop, but he was expelled for a prank that involved firing a gun dangerously close to the head of a sleeping fraternity brother. The University of Pennsylvania was next. There he tried out for the football team and was rejected, so he assaulted the coach, hospitalizing him for three days. Pennsylvania officials seemed more impressed with Roly's family connections than the Yale administration had been. Not only was he allowed to remain in residence, but the coach was overruled and Roly was made a member of the team— becoming a letterman during Penn's undefeated season of 1897.

Then, in 1898, adventure beckoned. Roly signed up for duty in the Spanish-American War. Serving as a "Rough Rider" alongside cousin Teddy, he was wounded in action at the battle of San Juan Hill. This tale of heroism, for which he was awarded a Purple Heart, became an important chapter in subsequent Fortescue family lore. The official record was less celebratory, describing his injury as a "slight bullet wound in foot," obtained while functioning as his renowned cousin's personal orderly.

During his three-month stint with the Rough Riders, Roly had been part of its patrician contingent known as the "Fifth Avenue Boys" or "gentlemen rankers." These were fifty or so young and white Ivy League thrill seekers who, despite their entry-level enlisted rank, joined the officers aboard ship on the way to Cuba in feasting on three-course meals served by black waiters in a luxurious and private dining saloon. Meanwhile, the 430 Indians, cowboys, miners, dockworkers, and lumberjacks who made up the rest of the regiment, and who did most of the fighting and most of the dying, were left on deck to eat meals of hardtack, beans, and meat that was so rotten it was finally thrown overboard. Social rank, as well as military rank, had its privileges. As a loyal acolyte who always addressed his cousin as "Colonel," Roly was assured of special treatment for as long as he remained under Teddy's protective wing.

While Teddy, seventeen years Roly's senior, was serving as governor of New York, having been elected to that office less than ninety days after returning home from Cuba, Roly shipped out for the Philippines. In opposition to the 1898 American takeover of their country from Spain's colonial rule (the same year that the United States seized Puerto Rico and Hawai'i), the Filipinos rose up to resist. Three years and more than two hundred thousand Filipino lives later, the rebellion by a "jumble of savage tribes," as Teddy put it, was finally quelled and an American occupation force was installed.

From there Roly moved on to become U.S. military attaché with the Japanese army during the early part of the Russo-Japanese War. The astounding victories of the Japanese on both land and sea sent shock waves of doubt through the headquarters of Western political and military leaders, stunned that a major European power had been humbled by a small Asian country. Roly came away from his experience with the Japanese convinced more than ever that they were a fundamentally "insincere, treacherous, and inscrutable" race.

Roly's tour in the Far East was uneventful. But while his name had not appeared in the press during his time in the Philippines or Japan, it did—repeatedly—upon his return home. In news stories that ran from coast to coast throughout 1905, Lieutenant Granville Roland Fortescue, a recent graduate of the Army Staff College, was named as one of the chief culprits in a sensationally sordid divorce trial. The case focused on the heavy drinking and sexual escapades of Mrs. Grace Viola Taggart, the wife of U.S. Army captain Elmer S. Taggart and an independently wealthy mother of two children. Claiming that Mrs. Taggart, the daughter of the former president of the Chicago Board of Trade, had made a habit of carousing and sleeping with Roly Fortescue and other men, Captain Taggart not only sued his wife for divorce, but sought both child custody and alimony from her. These were revolutionary ideas at the time.

An eager public devoured the salacious and occasionally bizarre details that emerged in courtroom testimony—Mrs. Taggart was accused of using her considerable influence, when her husband complained of her behavior, to have him locked away in an army mental ward, allegedly a deranged victim of "the Philippine climate and drink." In the end, the court found in favor of Captain Taggart, but turned its most withering criticism not on his wife, but on Roly and one other man. During the course of an extraordinary six-hour reading of his verdict, the judge denounced the two men at length, blaming them for Mrs. Taggart's immoral behavior and saying that, henceforth, they deserved to be treated universally as "social outcasts."

By this time, however, Roly's cousin Teddy had been living in the White House for four years—the twenty-sixth and youngest-ever president of the United States—and Lieutenant Granville Roland Fortescue was serving, in the words of one magazine, as the president's "military aide and master of social ceremonies." It was a job that, among other duties, entailed being the athletic president's sidekick, partner on horseback, and sometime punching bag. Roly—whom Teddy called "an adventurous and eager little fellow"—regularly was seen sporting black eyes and bruised knuckles after being summoned to a boxing or fencing lesson with his brawnier cousin.

If, at times like this, being Teddy's aide-de-camp had its downside, the benefits made it all worthwhile. The Taggart divorce trial was a case in point. Roly simply ignored it. While the accusations and denunciations were front-page news from New York to San Francisco, he and Teddy were busy attending a Rough Riders reunion in Texas, followed by a wolf hunt (killing seventeen wolves between them) in Oklahoma. In the Washington circles that mattered, Roly was a minor celebrity, a dashing and virile and eligible young military officer with family ties to the nation's pinnacle of political power.

Nevertheless, the conclusion of the Taggart trial did turn out to be something of a family embarrassment. A month after the judge had excoriated Roly from the bench, the secretary of war accepted the young lieutenant's resignation from the army. But as luck would have it, seven months later his father died, leaving him an inheritance of thirty thousand dollars. That was less than one-sixth the amount Robert Barnwell Roosevelt left to his legitimate sons, John and Robert junior, but it was the equivalent of nearly six hundred thousand dollars today.

Before long, Roly was traveling the world, from the jungles of the Amazon to the cabarets of Berlin, spending his money with little apparent concern that it might ever run out. It was on a warm August morning in 1907, he later wrote, when—at age thirty-two—he at last found his calling. The sun was streaming in through the windows of his suite at the Hotel Splendide in Aix-les-Bains, France. A "soft-footed valet" was arranging his "golf suit, shirt, and tie for the day," while "a deft-fingered waiter was setting the breakfast table, serving *café au lait, brioche,* a single soft-boiled egg." On the table with his meal was a blue envelope, a telegram from a friend informing him that the *London Daily Telegraph* was looking for a correspondent to report on a new colonial war in North Africa.

Nine years earlier, at San Juan Hill, Roly had met Richard Harding Davis, the first of that era's glamorous, swashbuckling war correspondents. Famous for wearing Savile Row suits and patent leather boots even in the thick of battle, Davis almost single-handedly had made matinee idols out of practitioners of his profession. Soon, young men with reputations to build—including the likes of Winston Churchill in South Africa—were flocking to sites of colonial conflict and filing breathtaking news stories about their adventures. Roly jumped at the chance to join them and headed off to Morocco. Before long his demonstrated fearlessness under fire once again, as in Cuba, brought him widespread recognition as a hero. At least according to his memoirs.

With the war ending, and his bank account dwindling, Roly returned to Washington. There, in 1910, he met and married twenty-six-year-old Grace Hubbard Bell, described in the *New York Times* as "a woman of distinction and beauty" who, like her fiancé, had "scores of friends in high places." Their wedding was heralded as one of Washington's social events of the season.

One of Grace's grandfathers was Gardiner Greene Hubbard, the scion of a wealthy Boston family, the first president of the Bell Telephone Company, and a founder of the National Geographic Society. Her father was Charles J. Bell, a cousin of Alexander Graham Bell and a millionaire Washington banker and financier in his own right. While growing up, Grace and her brother and sister, Robert and Helen, divided their time between a mansion on Connecticut Avenue in Washington and, in the summer, her grandfather's eighteen-acre estate named Twin Oaks, complete with a twenty-six-room "country house," on Woodley Road near Rock Creek Park.

Brother Robert liked to describe how, as children, they and their governesses were piled into horse-drawn carriages and driven "in state" from one palatial residence to the other. They were not the only people whose arrival at Twin Oaks deserved that description. Royalty from around the world visited the Woodley Road home in the late nineteenth century, including Hawai'i's Queen Lili'uokalani in 1897. Gardiner Hubbard was a supporter of the queen, and an adviser while she was in Washington seeking support following a coup in the islands instigated by American interests. Between stays at the old Shoreham and Cairo hotels, Lili'uokalani was a guest at the Hubbards' country house, as her niece, Princess Ka'iulani, had been on an earlier occasion. Helen, Grace, and Robert were teenagers at the time, and the queen's visit was said to have been a highlight of their young lives.

"Grace would have been President if she had been a man," her father often said. From early childhood she had been a top student in her classes at Washington's Mount Vernon Seminary and, her classmates would later remember, the leader of every endeavor in which she took part. On the evidence of her youthful behavior hers might have been an interesting administration. She and some friends once stole a trolley car "and ran it all over town," a journalist later recalled, and another time "joined hands and roller skated down Pennsylvania Avenue, refusing to move for any traffic until they had everything tied up." These and more were just madcap pranks, as she and her family saw it, and as the authorities reluctantly agreed. Like Roly, Grace's pedigree shielded her from reproach.

Grace debuted in Washington society in 1902. She soon became known as an accomplished golfer and horsewoman, and an expert at bridge. Five years later, while vacationing in Mexico, she met and became engaged to Count Gaston de Ramaix, said to be one of King Leopold of Belgium's inner circle of advisers. On the eve of the planned fall wedding, however, Grace called it off without explanation, creating what the New York and Washington press called a "social sensation."

A year and a half later those same newspapers carried the story of her engagement to retired army captain Granville R. Fortescue. When their wedding was held in June, only three weeks after the engagement announcement, the *New York Times* praised the "delightful informality" of the wedding on the lawn of the Bell estate in Washington. Eight months after that, on Valentine's Day of 1911, Thalia was born. In 1912 she was joined by a baby sister named Marion.

Funded by wedding gifts and other family largesse, Roly and Grace's extended honeymoon seems to have been idyllic. Though they traveled widely, they maintained a home in Washington until 1913, when they decided to move to London. There, Roly reestablished his ties with the *Daily Telegraph*, and by the summer of 1914 he and a very pregnant Grace were traveling around Europe with their two daughters and assorted servants in tow. In Belgium, a week after Austria's Archduke Ferdinand was assassinated—the event that would soon trigger World War I—Grace gave birth to a third daughter, Helene.

But this was no time for the distractions of parenthood. Roly was again going to be in the thick of things as a war correspondent. As he recalled in his autobiography, he rented a private trolley car and loaded it with "my wife, the two week old baby, two other girl children, a nurse, fifteen pieces of heavy baggage, and innumerable small odds and ends from suit cases to boxes of milk bottles." The trolley took them to Ostende, where they all, except Roly, piled aboard the channel steamer and headed for London.

On August 3, according to him if not to history, Roly single-handedly broke "the news that stunned the world": Germany was about to invade Belgium and declare war on France. For the next year, he would follow the conflict through Belgium, France, Germany, Austria, Serbia, Russia, Romania, and Turkey. And Grace would be by his side. Leaving three-year-old Thalia, two-year-old Marion, and two-month-old Helene in London with friends, in September she joined Roly in Paris on the adventure of their lives. Often, according to him, it was Grace who led seasoned male correspondents into situations of great danger that they might not have risked on their own. Just as frequently, however, they appear to have whiled away their nights at Maxim's or the Café de Paris.

By the spring of 1916, the Fortescues were back in Washington. A year later, with the United States now at war with Germany, Roly reentered the army as a major, was shipped off to France, and in late 1918 became a casualty of a gas attack at Montfaucon. After a brief hospitalization, he returned home. Cousin Teddy had just died. It was time to settle down.

Roly was now in his early forties, Grace was thirty-five, and the three girls ranged in age from seven to four. He was a man of consequence, he believed, and he had expended enough energy during the past twenty years for any one life. From then until his death in 1952, Roly wrote some short stories, a few unproduced plays, and his autobiography, and dabbled briefly as a magazine fiction editor. But he flatly refused to pursue any occupation that might bring in steady income for the family. The money from his father's will was long gone, but he insisted that there was more where that came from, a family inheritance or two that would take care of everything if only Grace would be patient.

From then on, whenever Roly's or Grace's name appeared in the press, usually on the society page, their address was listed either as "Twin Oaks," the Hubbard-Bell mansion in Washington where they had been married, or "Wildholme." Wildholme was one of several houses on a 256-acre estate in Bayport, Long Island, that had been purchased by Roly's father in 1873. As with most of his money, however, Robert Barnwell Roosevelt had left his property, including the estate, to his legitimate sons. And it was they who allowed Roly and Grace and the girls to settle in there on occasion and to act as if they owned the place.

Throughout the 1920s, to most outside observers, the Fortescues were living to the fullest the sumptuous lives their combined families' wealth had granted them. But it was an illusion of affluence. While relatives helped out from time to time, paying for the girls' tuition at costly private schools and permitting the Fortescues to stay for extended periods at their homes, Roly continued to refuse all opportunities to earn a living. Grace, whose socialite parents were still alive, was reduced to charging friends and neighbors for bridge lessons in order to keep her own family from falling into arrears.

If the outside world was taken in by their pose as prosperous gentry of the leisure class, those possessed of the most sensitive antennae for social distinctions—the gardeners, caretakers, and maids at the family residences in Washington and Bayport—were not fooled. Roly—or "Major Fortescue," as he insisted on being addressed—was "dissolute, lazy, and a heavy drinker," recalled the wife of Emil Anderson, the Twin Oaks gardener, in a 1932 interview. The Andersons by then had lived on the estate for more than two decades. Added the spouse of Ernest Bouché, Wildholme's gatekeeper since 1909, the Fortescues "lived like low class foreigners" when they were in residence, "except when they had visitors."

Everyone who knew them from this vantage point, including the town taxi driver in Bayport and a former governess at Wildholme, commented on Grace and Roly's "eccentric" behavior, their constant bickering over money, and their frequent separations. Grace avoided seeing friends from before her marriage "because she could no longer afford to be one of them," Mrs. Anderson reported. At one point, when Thalia was nine or ten years old, Grace took the three girls and went to live in England for a year—where she again paid her way by giving bridge lessons—but then she returned and reconciled with Roly.

Nothing changed after the reconciliation. When neither of the two estates was available to them, Roly would take a room at a men's club in Washington or Manhattan (he remained a member of the Chevy Chase and Army and Navy clubs), while Grace would move into a hotel or an apartment with whatever savings she had scraped together. In 1928, so one landlord in Washington later remembered, Grace rented an apartment for $130 a month, then had to move out after requesting an extension on the rent because the apartment's cost proved beyond her means. As for Roly, his only source of income by then was his military pension of $180 a month.

It is not clear how aware the girls were of their parents' dire financial situation. As boarding-school children, they rarely saw Grace or Roly except at Christmas and during the summer months, when the family was house sitting at either the Roosevelt or Hubbard estate. When the girls were to stay with them, the Fortescues never seemed able to afford the expense of traveling to pick them up, or of paying an adult to accompany the children. So, much to the consternation of the household help at Twin Oaks and Wildholme, Grace would arrange for the girls to be sent by train—even when "still quite young," Mrs. Anderson said—and they "traveled alone with identification tags pinned to their clothing to show where their destination was."

At one time, Grace and Roly somehow came into possession of a Shetland pony that pulled a carriage in which the girls liked to ride past the servants' quarters "with their noses up," recalled Wildholme's caretaker. The Fortescues finally decided they could no longer pay for upkeep of the pony, however, and gave it and the carriage away—much to the satisfaction of the recipients, an Irish family that worked on the property.

Events like this, and the disapproving household gossip they must have overheard, may well have suggested to Thalia, Marion, and Helene that their parents were living a lie. On the other hand, as children they led remarkably insulated lives, growing up in the company of genuinely wealthy relatives or away at expensive private schools. Thalia's education began with tutors in Paris and a convent school in Belgium, then continued at academies in Virginia, Washington, and Manhattan. The Hillside School in Norwalk, Connecticut, followed, and finally she attended the National Cathedral School for

Girls in Washington, famous for its exclusivity (it is the sister school to St. Albans School for Boys) and for the sprawling fifty-seven-acre wooded campus on which it sits.

But whether or not they believed Grace and Roly's pretenses, the Fortescue children in time adopted their parents' display of self-importance and ancestral entitlement. They were not without their own resources; one girl was especially known for her brains, another for her beauty. Marion was an excellent pupil who was sent to study at Oxford. Helene was quite attractive and wanted to be a rich and famous actress, so she married (and divorced) Julian Reynolds, heir to the Reynolds aluminum fortune, and wound up performing starlet roles in a dozen Hollywood films. Only Thalia, the oldest of the three, seemed unlikely to attain her goals. Though reasonably intelligent, she was no scholar. Oxford was out. And while, like Helene, she aspired to an acting career, her looks and her bearing posed an insurmountable barrier.

As a young child, Thalia was pleasant enough in appearance, often described as healthy and robust. Even those who were most reproachful of her parents, including the Andersons of Twin Oaks, enjoyed Thalia's company. Mrs. Anderson described her, in contrast to her sisters, as "quiet and homelike," with "a very nice character," attributing her subdued and retiring nature to the fact that she was "quite stout" and thus avoided making friends. But as a fourteen-year-old boarder at the Hillside School, Thalia was diagnosed with a thyroid condition. According to both her doctor and the school principal, she became extremely "high strung" and suffered from palpitations and shortness of breath. These are all common symptoms of hyperthyroidism. She also began losing weight, another symptom of the disease.

Then something else happened. Her eyes began to bulge and protrude. This condition, known as exophthalmos, is a response to inflammation of the eye muscles. Among people with a thyroid disorder, exophthalmos is caused by overactivity of the thyroid gland and occurs only in those with a specific form of hyperthyroidism known as Graves' disease. It is especially common among young females. As it did with Thalia, the exophthalmos sometimes leads to a visual impairment known as strabismus, or misaligned eyes. In Thalia's case, the strabismus took the form of hypertropia, meaning that one of her eyes had a mild upward deviation. Although the severity of Thalia's strabismus waxed and waned—sometimes the deviation was pronounced, at other times her eyes looked almost normal—as a consequence of it she began walking with a slight stoop, her head tilted down and to one side. Among people thus afflicted, this is an involuntary and commonplace way of compensating for the blurred double vision that is caused by the optical misalignment.

Before the 1940s, when radioiodine was found to be an effective treatment, people with Graves' disease were liable to develop sufficient damage to the optic nerve to drastically reduce their overall vision. And Thalia's vision was indeed impaired, whether the cause was Graves' disease or something else. In addition to the depth-perception problem caused by strabismus, as her family physician once noted, she was so nearsighted that without her glasses Thalia "practically couldn't see," even in broad daylight.

During her second year at the Hillside School, Thalia's health became so fragile that she had to drop out. Her grandparents brought her back to Washington and, in 1926, enrolled her in the National Cathedral School for Girls. But Thalia's behavior was now becoming increasingly erratic. The employees and neighbors of the Long Island estate where the Fortescue girls spent vacations began complaining about their "running wild," with no parental supervision at all. "They had an old Ford and an old Dodge," the estate gatekeeper, Mr. Bouché, said, and Thalia would drive one or the other recklessly along nearby town and country roads, her two sisters holding on for dear life.

But what bothered the nearly sixty-year-old man the most, he said, was that all three girls, by now in their early to mid teens, seemed to enjoy "running around naked" on the estate, "paying no attention" to his presence, and even seeming to taunt him with their "loose mannerisms." They did the same thing with young men, he said, who used to gather openly on railroad tracks above one of the estate's lakes where the girls were known to go swimming in the nude. Added Mrs. Bouché: it was only a matter of time before Thalia would get "more than she bargained for."

By the summer of 1927, sixteen-year-old Thalia had become "a drawling, insipid, cigarette smoking radical," in the words of one disapproving neighbor. She was also drinking heavily, recalled a close cousin, who added that Thalia seemed to enjoy being "extremely immodest in her actions in front of young men." She was estranged from her father—neither of them any longer approved of the behavior of the other—and her mother, according to Mrs. Bouché, "was too busy playing bridge and gambling" to bother with Thalia or her sisters.

Then, abruptly, Thalia seemed to change once again. Sometime during her year at the Cathedral School in Washington, she met a twenty-two-year-old Naval Academy cadet named Thomas Hedges Massie. At five feet five inches tall when he stretched, Tommie, as he was always called, was barely the same height as Thalia. But, as his Annapolis classmates remembered him in their yearbook, he always seemed "at ease in a drawing room," a quality that made him an ideal suitor for a daughter of the Fortescues.

Tommie was graduating that summer, and Thalia invited him to take a postgraduation leave and visit her at Wildholme. He did, and they fell in love. Though Tommie's immediate family was situated on a far lower rung of the social ladder than the Fortescues, he was nice looking and acceptably solvent, while the extended Massie clan enjoyed some prominence in his home state of Kentucky. If nothing else, should the two of them marry, Tommie would provide a respectable means for Thalia and her father to put permanent distance between one another.

Thalia and Tommie spent much of the summer of 1927 together at the Roosevelt estate. Tommie's sardonic personality seemed a perfect match for Thalia's, and each of them delighted in goading the other into the sort of pranks that must have reminded Grace and Roly of their own youthful larks. One day they thought it would be funny to make believe they were poor, so they spent an afternoon in the nearby town of Patchogue, selling pencils on a street corner. Another escapade attracted more attention and inadvertently illustrated what had long been glaringly apparent—that the Fortescues had grievously erred in naming their daughter after Thalia, the Greek muse of comedy.

One evening Thalia and Tommie, back in Patchogue and looking for something to do, noticed an unattended baby carriage in the lobby of a movie theater. In that more innocent time and place it was a local custom for parents attending a movie to leave infants in the theater lobby, numbered tags attached to their carriages. If a baby began to cry, an usher would go into the theater and call out the carriage number, summoning the parents to come out and comfort their child. As Thalia and Tommie walked past the theater lobby, they decided to take one of the sleeping infants and hide it, leading its parents to think their child had been kidnapped. All in fun, of course.

Not surprisingly, the parents in question (a "screaming and shouting" Italian couple, Tommie later would recall with distaste) were not amused when they discovered their baby was missing. They frantically reported the apparent kidnapping to the police, who promptly found and arrested the culprits. But when later that night the local magistrate saw the last name of the young woman who was standing before him, he quickly dismissed the case, calling their offense a mere "parlor trick."

To the household help who knew them well, the Fortescues may have been poseurs, but to others they were not a family to be trifled with. Nor, it seems, was Thalia the only daughter to have inherited her parents' strange sense of humor, with its air of invulnerable privilege. A few years later her sister Helene stole a butcher's truck and drove it home from a party, airily dismissing the theft as a practical joke when police later traced the missing vehicle to her. On another occasion she summoned a large number of family and friends to what she announced was her wedding in upstate New York, only to inform them, after an elaborate ceremony, that it all had been a joke.

Thalia's wedding, however, would be real. A month after the kidnapping incident, the announcement of her engagement to Tommie was given prominent play in the *New York Times*. And two months after that, on Thanksgiving Day, they were married in the nation's capital, at the Bethlehem Chapel of the Washington Cathedral. A large photograph of Thalia, holding an armful of roses and lilies of the valley and draped in her "robe de style of white satin trimmed with net and pearls," dominated the opening page of that Sunday's *Washington Post* Society section. The reception was held at Twin Oaks, and the couple was showered with expensive wedding gifts from the Bells, the Hubbards, the Roosevelts, and—to a lesser extent—the Fortescues.

By all accounts Thalia and Tommie were happy, as well they should have been. It was the best time ever in the nation's history to be young, white, and well connected. The economy was booming. Routine Wall Street investments were doubling or tripling in value in only a year or two, while a $5,000 purchase of RCA stock set aside in 1921 would have been worth an astonishing $1,098,000 in 1929. In that time, not surprisingly, the number of millionaires in America more than quadrupled, while the government graciously helped out by slashing their taxes. Throughout the decade per capita income for all Americans increased by 9 percent, but for the rich it grew by 75 percent, finally reaching the point where the most affluent 1 percent of Americans possessed 83 percent of the country's liquid assets. Never before in the history of the United States had so few people controlled so much of the nation's wealth, nor have they since. Optimism reigned: it seemed like the good times would go on forever.

True, the Ku Klux Klan, with as many as five million members, also was enjoying itself, marching en masse in white hoods and robes through the streets of Washington in 1925. And wildcat strikes were shutting down coalfields throughout the West as miners joined the worldwide protest over the executions in Massachusetts of the Italian anarchists Sacco and Vanzetti. And the popular black leader Marcus Garvey was in the process of being deported as an undesirable alien. And ominous clouds of political unrest and military adventurism were hovering over China and Japan. And, with the benefit of hindsight, anyone who looked closely at the nation's economy could have seen that unregulated and skyrocketing speculation in the stock market (in 1927 alone more than eighteen billion dollars in new stocks were floated) was not being backed by anything close to sufficient assets.

But those were not the sorts of things people like Thalia and Tommie thought much about. This was the era of the flapper and the Ziegfeld Follies, a time when comics like Eddie Cantor had the entire nation rolling its eyes and singing songs like "My Mammy," "Yes, We Have No Bananas," and "Makin' Whoopee." It was the era of the mah-jongg fad, of marathon dance contests and flagpole-sitting competitions. Daredevil stunts of every sort filled the front pages of newspapers; Jean Lussier went over Niagara Falls inside a giant rubber ball and lived to tell about it; Harry Houdini survived for ninety minutes underwater in a sealed casket (and then died a few months later, on Halloween).

In 1927, the year of Thalia and Tommie's marriage, Charles Lindbergh became the first man to fly an airplane across the Atlantic from New York to France. "Lucky Lindy" found thousands of people waiting for him at Le Bourget Airport near Paris and an ecstatic half million letters and seventy-five thousand telegrams waiting for him when he returned home. His feat started a craze called the Lindy Hop, which joined the Charleston and the Black Bottom on the list of dances performed into the night in speakeasies across the country.

The year 1927 was also when Babe Ruth of the New York Yankees hit a record sixty home runs in one season, sending sportswriters into paroxysms of eloquence while describing nothing more than the flight of a batted ball. "Upward and onward, gaining speed and height with every foot, the little white ball winged with terrific speed until it dashed itself against the seat of the right-field bleachers, more than a quarter of the way up the peopled slope," wrote a *New York Times* reporter of one home run hit by what he called "His Majesty the Babe."

As the economy quietly overheated, sports in America—like bread and circuses to the Romans—became bigger business than ever. Two months before Thalia and Tommie were married, the second Dempsey-Tunney boxing match in Chicago drew more than one hundred thousand spectators, while tens of millions listened on the radio. The $2.65 million in gate receipts for the fight established a record that would not be broken for half a century. Two days after Thalia and Tommie's marriage, the Army-Navy football game attracted seventy thousand fans in New York. It too was broadcast to millions from coast to coast—followed by the regularly scheduled Hawaiian music show.

Even religion was a hot growth commodity. In 1925 adman Bruce Barton, America's leading popularizer of both business and spirituality, had achieved authorial superstardom with a book, *The Man Nobody Knows*, solemnly declaring Jesus Christ to have been both "the most popular dinner guest in Jerusalem" and "the most successful advertising man in history." The next year Aimee Semple McPherson, the celebrated faith-healing evangelist who preached her message from the million-dollar, five-thousand-seat Angelus Temple in Los Angeles, mysteriously disappeared from a California beach, only to turn up a month later as the alleged victim of a kidnapping and the actual perpetrator of an international sex scandal. Perhaps it is not surprising, then, that the most popular movie of the following year was Cecil B. DeMille's biblical extravaganza *King of Kings* (for which Bruce Barton served as consultant), or that the book then stirring up angry discussion across the country was Sinclair Lewis's *Elmer Gantry*, about a corrupt, religion-peddling con man.

It was a remarkable year, 1927, in a remarkable, if often frivolous, era. A perfect time for people like Thalia and Tommie to embark on a marriage. Only Robert Roosevelt Jr. disagreed. Thalia's uncle, Roly's older half brother—one of the acknowledged, legitimate sons of Robert Barnwell Roosevelt—owned Wildholme, the house in which the Fortescues stayed on the family estate.

Robert junior, then in his sixties, had met Tommie Massie that summer of 1927, and he liked him. He was out of town, however, when the engagement was announced and plans for the wedding were set in motion. Had he been around, those who knew him said, Robert would have tried to prevent the marriage. Tommie, he believed, was too fine a young man for the likes of Thalia. He was convinced that she was destined for nothing but trouble.

Four years later, and five thousand miles away, Robert Roosevelt Jr.'s fears would be realized.

Paradise of the Pacific

Immediately after the Massies' marriage, Tommie was assigned to chemical warfare school in Edgewood, Maryland. The young couple found a small apartment just outside the base. Neighbors said they appeared to be happy and in love. From Maryland, Tommie was transferred to Boston, where he joined the crew of the newly commissioned aircraft carrier USS *Lexington*.

In 1928 the "Lady Lex," as its officers dubbed the ship, was moved to the West Coast by way of the Panama Canal. The events of the Massies' lives during this time have left few facts—only rumors. Typical of them was one concerning Thalia joining Tommie during the *Lexington*'s stopover in Panama on its way to the West Coast. By the time the ship left the Canal Zone, heading to its final destination in California, stories were spreading among the crew about Thalia "running around with various men—in fact, with almost any man who looked prosperous and clean," one former naval officer recalled. Close friends of the couple also later claimed that Thalia "had been in a sanitarium somewhere in the east" not long after she was married. But these unconfirmed stories only surfaced several years later.

Better documented is the fact that sometime during the first year or two of her marriage Thalia became pregnant, and then lost the child. The details are unclear, but difficulty in successfully carrying pregnancies to term—like Thalia's vision problems, her nervousness, and her increasingly volatile personality—was a condition known to be associated with untreated Graves' disease.

Other than Thalia's failed pregnancy, among the little that is known with any certainty about the Massies during these years is that, while stationed in San Diego, Tommie applied for submarine school and was accepted; he transferred in January 1930 to its training center in New London, Connecticut. Upon graduation in May of that same year, he was assigned to duty with Submarine Squadron Four at Pearl Harbor in Hawai'i. As the Massies prepared to depart for the islands, friends and family congratulated the couple on their good fortune. An extended second honeymoon in one of the world's most beautiful places awaited them.

By 1930, Hawai'i had become an American playground for the wealthy, an unspoiled "Paradise of the Pacific," to borrow the ubiquitous cliché from hundreds of magazine articles and books now extolling the virtues and special lure of the islands. Even the staid *New York Times,* in a 1927 editorial, rhapsodically referred to Hawai'i's famously "balmy climate and sapphire sea, a paradise of flowers and entrancing ladies playing ukuleles." It was an idyllic vision—one that had been carefully created, packaged, and launched a dozen years earlier.

In retrospect, the timing seems incongruous. On March 3, 1915, D. W. Griffith's *The Birth of a Nation,* far and away the most popular and technically accomplished motion picture of its era, opened in New York. Exploiting the deepest racial fears and hatreds of white Americans, the film depicted black men as uncivilized and wild-eyed rapists, portrayed mulattoes as dangerously wily and scheming villains—who, like their black half brothers, lusted after white women—and celebrated the Ku Klux Klan as the savior of the country.

Before its first run in theaters was complete, and despite protests and boycotts by the NAACP and other black organizations, Griffith's film had grossed more than sixty million dollars at the box office. This was at a time when reserved seats for its exclusive opening night cost all of two dollars, a sum that publicists and entertainment writers found staggering.

At the same time that *The Birth of a Nation* was shocking or outraging audiences everywhere with its portrayal of African Americans as menacing beasts, in San Francisco people were pouring through the gates of the Panama-Pacific International Exposition to be charmed and entranced by brown-skinned Hawaiians. A year earlier Hawai'i's territorial legislature had appropriated one hundred thousand dollars—the equivalent of nearly two million dollars in today's money—to establish a Hawaiian pavilion at the San Francisco exposition, the latest in a series of world's fairs that had been attracting the curious to various cities since the 1870s. That one hundred thousand dollars was equal to what the competing San Diego exposition was spending on all its ethnology and archaeology exhibits combined.

Visitors to both the San Diego and San Francisco expositions were disappointed by many of the so-called ethnic village displays. In San Francisco the Africans, although touted as "thin, black, and hollow-cheeked wanderers from Somali land," were deemed too civilized to hold the public's interest, so their exhibit was closed down in a matter of weeks, its performers deported by U.S. immigration authorities. A part of the Chinese exhibit was considered by some inappropriate for the opposite reason: it was too barbaric, featuring a "chamber of horrors," with replicas of opium dens and other notorious Far Eastern folkways. Following objections from the Chinese consul and local Chinese merchants, it also was closed down. The Hawaiian exhibit, on the other hand, was a smash success as the centerpiece of what fair publicists called the "Joy Zone."

Flower-bedecked, grass-skirted hula dancers of both pure and mixed-race Hawaiian ancestry enthralled San Francisco fairgoers—almost nineteen million of them during the exposition's ten-month run—as did the Hawaiian musicians' delightfully dexterous plucking and strumming on a variety of stringed instruments, including what appeared to be a tiny guitar. Adapted from the Portuguese *braguinha,* brought to the islands by sailors from Madeira, the instrument was called by the Hawaiians a *'ukulele,* literally "jumping or dancing flea," because of the speed with which the musicians' fingers flew across the strings. "The ukulele has become very popular since the opening of the Hawaii Building at the San Francisco Exposition," reported the *New York Times* in September 1915, adding that "the thing makes a sweet jingle somewhat as fetching as the melody of mandolins." So fetching, in fact, that the Hawaiian performers "have infected visitors with a desire to possess the instrument," said the *Times,* "and they are being imported from Hawaii and manufactured on a large scale in this country."

Soon musical-instrument makers throughout the nation were turning out facsimiles of ukuleles by the hundreds of thousands—and stamping them "Made in Hawaii," to the consternation of island manufacturers. One song in particular, "On the Beach at Waikiki," became a national sensation, closely followed by "I Lost My Heart in Honolulu." The latter tune, immediately touted as "a syncopated classic," told of

> One wond'rous night
> One wond'rous maiden
> Down on the glist'ning coral sand
> I just held her hand, understand.
>
> Oh! Midnight scene of tropic splendor
> Undreamed of dreams, love glances tender
> Had I a thousand hearts to lose, I'd lose them all
> In Honolulu.

In 1916 the Ziegfeld Follies and at least seven other Broadway companies mounted productions featuring scenes of the islands, inevitably including erupting volcanoes and dancing "hula hula" girls. That same year, recordings of what purported to be Hawaiian melodies outsold all other popular music in America, with the Victor recording company alone releasing 146 different Hawaiian records. Hawaiian singers appeared out of nowhere from coast to coast (one writer said that most of them "hail from Sunny Italy and get by with the assistance of a little grease paint"), performing songs that had never been heard in the islands. "The Yaka Hula Hicky Dula," a string of nonsense sounds that bear little resemblance to Hawaiian, was an especially big hit, introduced by Al Jolson in a Broadway musical on the life of Robinson Crusoe.

At first most of the new so-called Hawaiian songs were Tin Pan Alley parodies and novelty numbers, or tunes with mildly suggestive lyrics, such as "When My Honolulu Lady Does the Honolulu Dip." ("It's such a fascinating movement, like the rolling of a ship.") Many told of men who left for Hawai'i and never returned, although a minority opinion was expressed in "The More I See of Hawaii the Better I Like New York." But before long the novelty songs were surpassed by what came to be called *hapa-haole* music—literally, "half-Hawaiian half-white" melodies that were largely sentimental songs of love and yearning, accompanied now by steel guitar. (It was said that actress Mary Pickford, a frequent visitor to Hawai'i, used a recording of Hawaiian steel guitar master Sol Ho'opi'i to get her in the mood for a movie scene in which she had to weep on cue.)

By the mid-1920s romantic neo-Hawaiian music was all the rage in America. College students everywhere, with or without raccoon coats, were strumming ukuleles and singing "Honolulu Moon," "Dreamy Hawaii," "Hawaiian Butterfly," "Blue Pacific Moonlight," and "She Sang Aloha to Me," while Hawaiian music shows could be heard nightly on radio stations throughout the country. "Little Brown Gal" ("in a little grass skirt, in a little grass shack, in Hawaii") later became a special favorite of radio performers, as did "Honolulu Baby" ("Where'd you get those eyes/and that dark complexion, I just idolize?").

Hollywood film crews, meanwhile, seemed to be camped out permanently on the beach at Waikīkī, cranking out movies with titles like *Passion Fruit, The Black Lily, The White Flower, The Bonded Woman, His Captive Woman, Hula,* and more. *Hula* was made in 1927 and starred a young Clara Bow, that era's famed "It" girl. Like all films of the time, *Hula* was a silent. But unlike any others, it opened with its star swimming nude (though partially concealed by foliage) in a rural island stream. The accompanying panel read: "A Hawaiian Isle—a land of singing seas and swinging hips—where Volcanoes are often active and maidens always are."

Tourist traffic to Honolulu began a steady climb. Many of those expectantly striding down the gangplank upon arrival were unmarried men and women in search of what the music and the films and the gossip had promised. As was their custom, nubile Hawaiian women and handsome young men did their best to be accommodating. So much so, in fact, that soon the beaches were filled with frolicking white women and dark-skinned "beach boys" whose jobs ostensibly involved handing out towels and setting up umbrellas and beach chairs, while providing directions and sightseeing tips.

Beginning in the 1920s, and for years to come, guidebooks suggestively evoked Waikīkī beach life. "An eastern lady of fashion" is described in one brochure lying "prone beneath the sun while a smiling Hawaiian youth anoints her back and legs with coconut oil . . . [as] nearby another bronze boy kneels over another fair visitor, kneading and manipulating the muscles in the soothing and relaxing Hawaiian massage." When riding their surfboards, these same young Hawaiians, in the words of another tourist brochure, "remind you of flying fishes . . . clad only in the briefest of trunks, their fine bodies gleaming like polished bronze." Photographs in magazine advertisements promised female vacationers to the islands that young (and invariably "bronze") Hawaiian men were available to teach them how to swim and surf and paddle outrigger canoes.

Local authorities began to get nervous. One distinguished and disapproving native Hawaiian matron spoke for many when she criticized "the laxity of the white women to observe proprieties," and warned that their "looseness of manner" could lead to trouble:

> They lie there on the beaches, half nude, while the boys are rubbing them with coconut oil. . . . These women come from prominent families with lots of money. They come down here and seem to go crazy for the time being . . . getting a marvelous thrill out of these beach boys. . . . A white woman is made to feel that unless she has met a beach boy at Waikiki, she has lost half the thrill of the tropics.

Fifty years earlier, during a time when increasing numbers of white prostitutes were traveling to the islands to entertain sailors from whaling ships and other vessels, authorities required each arriving unattached woman to "satisfy the sheriff that she is not coming for improper purposes." In the

1920s, fearful of scandal, local people would have been forgiven for thinking along those lines again. Their concerns were not unfounded. Beach boys would later recall how they met arriving ships and "sized up the girls that came in," telling one another "that one up there with the blue dress, that's mine, okay?" As for the vacationing women, one of them remembered her first surfing lesson when she was nineteen: "Can you imagine what it was like for me, going to a Catholic school on the mainland, to have a man take me surfing? To sit on top of me, on the back of my legs? The thrill I had. Skin to skin. In the water." In such situations, said one beach boy, all it took was a little "lomi lomi [Hawaiian massage] of their legs and shoulders—they could lose their bathing suit just by you rubbing them."

Most of the early tourists were well-heeled, and many were celebrities. If it wasn't the Fords or the Rockefellers or the Du Ponts, it was Mary Pickford or Douglas Fairbanks, Charlie Chaplin or Babe Ruth—even, occasionally, the likes of the maharaja of Indore or the Prince of Wales—disembarking from crowded cruise ships in Honolulu Harbor, along with servants, piles of steamer trunks, and more than a few Hudsons and Stutz Bearcats for driving around the remote and mountainous island roads. Or around town, especially to its mysterious, unsavory areas. As one beach boy told an interviewer years later:

> They'd bring their cars down from the mainland . . . big cars—limousines. And they'd have the [chauffeur] drive it. And all these [beach boys] sit there with their bare feet and everything. They're riding these things through town. . . . I used to take tourists slumming in Chinatown . . . go to the bars and the nightclubs and all these dinky tenement places. And Tin Can Alley, Corkscrew Lane. . . . You know, back of the alleys. And they enjoyed it. We did that quite a bit.

So grateful were some tourists for this sort of special treatment that they paid beach boys to visit their mainland homes for parties. One brought a group of them over for the World Series. Plutocrat Alfred Bloomingdale, upon his departure from the islands, gave his Buick to a beach boy in appreciation for his services.

Dignitaries need proper accommodations, so the luxurious oceanfront Royal Hawaiian Hotel was built in 1927, followed a few years later by the equally posh Halekulani Hotel, both of them joining in Waikīkī the older, though also lavish, Moana Hotel, along with a collection of smaller resorts and recently built mansions for Honolulu's resident white (or *haole*) elite.

The Royal Hawaiian quickly was nicknamed "the Pink Palace," since its four hundred large rooms and suites were contained within a bright pink Moorish-style stucco facade. The hotel owed its architectural influence primarily to Hollywood and the current Rudolph Valentino–inspired fad for things Spanish; its appearance was no more Hawaiian than were the pseudo-Chinese costumes worn by its baggage handlers.

There was more than a touch of the islands' heritage at the hotel's opening night, however, which was launched with a huge pageant featuring a fleet of Hawaiian outrigger canoes, each of them carrying torch- and spear-bearing Hawaiian warriors in full regalia who were greeted on shore by lei-bedecked native princesses representing all the islands. A celebration of the "romance and glamour which still remain from the far-gone days of kingdoms and tribal principalities," said the next day's special edition of the *Honolulu Star-Bulletin*, the opening events provided viewers with a "haunting" ceremony, thrillingly "colorful and semi-barbaric."

But there was nothing barbaric in what the Pink Palace, like no other hotel anywhere, soon provided for its guests: their own luxury cruise ship, the *Malolo*—almost three-quarters the length and half the gross tonnage of the *Titanic*, with seven decks, two theaters, a swimming pool, a gymnasium, and space for 650 well-to-do and pampered passengers to stretch out for their nearly weeklong voyage to the islands. It was the fastest and most expensive ship yet built in the United States. In addition to the cost of the cruise, a month's lodging and board at the Royal's finest suites could run upwards of two thousand dollars, at a time when American attorneys and physicians earned an average of barely five thousand dollars a year.

Throughout the 1920s upper-crust tourist money in the islands flowed as freely as the bootleg champagne. Prohibition may have been in force, but it never meant much in free-living Hawai'i. Like its sugar and pineapple, the image of the islands had become a commodity, marketed far and wide. And with notable success: between 1922 and 1929 the number of tourist arrivals, and expenditures, more than doubled.

Doubling as well during the 1920s was the number of haoles now living in the islands, not just visiting. Overwhelmingly the new arrivals were military personnel, including navy men and their dependents, like Tommie and Thalia, along with civilians from the mainland recruited to work at Pearl Harbor and other nearby bases.

The Hawaiian Islands, though barely two-thirds the size of Vermont, are strategically situated 2,500 miles from California and 3,800 miles from Japan, a country with military ambitions that had grown alarmingly grandiose in recent years. As the most densely populated nation in the world, without sufficient resources to support itself, Japan had already ruthlessly subordinated Korea to its rule. But Korea was not enough. With military training compulsory in its schools and its own sense of manifest destiny rapidly growing, Japan's imperial gaze swept across East Asia and the Pacific. Famously, the Chinese province of Manchuria came into view. Less famously, so did Hawai'i.

Although both Japanese and American authors had for years written fictional accounts of a Japanese attack on the islands, since the dawn of the 1920s top officers of the Imperial Navy had engaged in serious discussion of possible invasion scenarios. Outraged by a series of American diplomatic insults, including the 1924 Exclusion Act barring Japanese immigration to the United States and its territories, Japanese admirals were now producing and publishing hypothetical strategies for assaulting and occupying Hawai'i. One book by a Japanese navy commander described the islands as nothing less than "the Waterloo, the Verdun which will determine victory or defeat in a Japanese-American war."

The United States had seized Hawai'i in the late nineteenth century, reducing the islands from a sovereign nation to an American possession. America's military had been a presence ever since. Now that U.S. Pacific Fleet maneuvers and war games included among their fictional premises a Japanese invasion of the islands, however, a rapid buildup of army and navy personnel in and around Honolulu began in earnest. By 1930 the island of O'ahu was home to the greatest concentration of American soldiers and sailors anywhere. But the expectations and attitudes the military men brought with them to Hawai'i were far different from those of the thousands of affluent and pleasure-seeking tourists who had been frolicking on the beach at Waikīkī for the past decade.

For an American soldier or sailor sent to Hawai'i at this time—virtually all of them white—the experience was similar to that of a European posted to the colonies. The islands were owned and controlled by the United States, but they were a "territory," not a state. The overwhelming majority of the population was nonwhite, Asian or Hawaiian, as was the entirety of the low-paid workforce laboring in the fields of the sprawling sugar and pineapple plantations. In contrast, a small and wealthy white minority controlled the economy and lived in a style of opulence that most officers and enlisted men had never before encountered.

It was bad enough that almost half the islands' residents were of Japanese ancestry, precisely the people the U.S. armed forces would be fighting in the event of a war. But to then come upon white women and Hawaiian men—and white men and Hawaiian women—playing on the beach and swimming together, and more, was something that not only some Hawaiian matrons found inappropriate. One recently arrived haole woman made the point without ambiguity:

> I was raised in the South. If my old Negro mammy should come here I would hug and kiss her—but the Negro belongs in his place. I can't endure the Hawaiians. I go in swimming at the beach to cool off, but I begin to boil when I see how some of the white women act up with Hawaiian men who take them out on surfboards. My boy has a Hawaiian friend at school. I try to appeal to his pride to induce him to choose another pal. I do not want any half-breed grandchildren. The mere thought of it makes me boil.

This was a new turn. For nearly a century and a half the natives of Hawai'i had enjoyed a special place in the European and American imagination. Since the time of their first encounters with Hawaiians, Westerners had regarded them, along with the Tahitians, as somehow distinct from other dark-skinned people they had met during their voyages of discovery. Early accounts of eighteenth-century adventurers returning from the South Seas repeatedly compared the Hawaiian Islands to the mythical Greek "Blessed Isles," celebrated by Hesiod, Pindar, and Homer as lands where the weather is perfect and "Oceanus breathes ever with a West wind that sings softly from the sea." The new blessed isles were said to be little different from the ancient ones. Work was rare and leisure plentiful, while the beautiful and friendly people devoted most of their energies to sensual pursuits, posing little threat to the power of the newcomers.

Although political upheaval and the tragedy of introduced epidemic disease had long since chipped away at that idyllic image, the mystique never fully faded, kept alive as it was in the works of countless travel writers and such popular authors as Mark Twain and Robert Louis Stevenson. Since the time of the 1915 Panama-Pacific International Exposition, island promoters had played relentlessly on the theme of the Hawaiians as a people of paradise— kind, generous, playful, romantic, exotic—with the islands portrayed as a conflict-free world where everyday barriers of race were somehow transcended. Wealthy and cosmopolitan tourists delighted in the fantasy, reinforced in music and film. The military men who were sent there, along with their families and the inevitable camp followers, emphatically did not.

Well aware of how different Hawai'i was from the segregated or homogeneous towns in which most American soldiers and sailors and their spouses were raised, and of the everyday challenge living in the islands was likely to pose for them, local military commanders prepared written guides for incoming personnel. The guide for navy officers described the weather, the room rates at different hotels, and the cost of food and clothing and cars. It also provided information on private schools, noting their tuition, reputation, and racial profile. (Mid-Pacific Institute's tuition was two hundred to three hundred dollars, and it "compares favorably with schools of its type on the mainland. Its students are, however, for the most part, Orientals.") Tips on hiring servants were given. ("The servant problem is the same here that it is everywhere. The majority are Japanese—some are good and some are not.") Normal rates of pay for household help were provided. ("General servants with a knowledge of cooking ask from $10 to $15 per week.") And finally, the guide recommended eight neighborhoods "in good sections of the city," and supplied a range of rental costs for each of them.

One of the communities was called Mānoa Valley. It was a place, a visiting reporter from Chicago would soon write, with "fine old fashioned homes, set in deep acres of gardens and flowers that bloom the year round, homes with the prim touch of New England about them, or the magnificence of the old South." It was also the most expensive and exclusive neighborhood on the navy's list. So when Tommie and Thalia Massie arrived in Honolulu, that was where they made arrangements to find a house. It wasn't easy. The homes higher up in the valley were far beyond their financial reach, but one section of lower Mānoa was filled with bungalows on small lots that were popular rentals for young navy officers and their wives. At least four other military couples lived on their same street, while a dozen more had settled into the surrounding two or three blocks.

In Hawaiian the word *mānoa* means both "vast" and "deep." But among those most familiar with the valley it was far more than that. For centuries Mānoa had been home to Hawaiian royalty, its cool breezes a refuge from the hot, dry flatland of Waikīkī spread out below. Almost a hundred years prior to the Massies' arrival, a visiting English naturalist named Frederick Debell Bennett climbed to its dramatic ridgeline and joined with everyone else who had ever seen it by pronouncing Mānoa "unrivalled in beauty":

On three sides it is bounded by continuous mountains, luxuriously wooded to their summits, while the fourth opens to a view of the wide and distant ocean. . . . The view of this valley from the surrounding hills is at all times impressive, but some of the effects produced upon its landscape by the lights and shades caused by the capricious atmosphere of a mountainous region are often such as to elicit from the observer an expression of rapture. It is impossible to convey an idea of the scenic beauties displayed, when a cloud passes its shadow slowly across the vale, obscuring, but for a moment, the brightness of a meridian sun; or when a local shower spans the plains with a gaudy rainbow; or when a mist descends upon the lowlands and veils them in obscurity, until again raised by the breeze it rolls over the hills, gradually unfolding the beauty of the lands beneath and restoring them to their brightness.

Finally, at a loss for words, Bennett conceded defeat: "The sublime effects produced upon a spot like Mānoa by these simple and natural causes," he concluded, "must be seen to be appreciated." Bennett, of course, attributed the beauty he had seen and felt to the vicissitudes of nature. Hawaiians had a different explanation.

According to ancient legend, a young woman named Kahalaopuna lived in Mānoa and was so beautiful that rainbows followed wherever she went. Kahalaopuna was the daughter of a chiefess named Kuahine and a chief named Kahaukani. One day a jealous would-be lover killed Kahalaopuna. So great and so inconsolable was her parents' grief that they were transformed—her mother into the light rain that falls like tears in the valley every afternoon, her father into the valley's softly moaning wind. And to this day, the rain in Mānoa is called the Kuahine rain, the wind in the valley is the Kahaukani wind, and together they re-create the rainbows that had been their daughter's constant companion, and that still color the sky almost daily.

It was 1833 when Frederick Bennett made his way deep into the wooded hills and glens of Mānoa. Hawai'i was still an independent nation, and for every haole living in the islands there were more than three hundred Hawaiians. The most powerful person in the kingdom was an imposing woman named Ka'ahumanu, the widow of King Kamehameha, who maintained a summer home in the cool highlands of the valley. Now, as the Massies were moving into a Tudor-style bungalow on a secluded and quiet lane, it was June of 1930. In the intervening century, although Mānoa had remained the blissful home of the island's elite, much had changed.

The islands bristled with signs of the ongoing military buildup, and haoles were now almost as numerous as natives, many of whom lived in abject rural or urban poverty. But even when their populations were combined, including members of the military, haoles and Hawaiians amounted to barely one-quarter of the population of the islands. Most people were immigrants or the children of immigrants—from China, the Philippines, and especially Japan—brought to Hawai'i over the preceding half century as plantation workers.

In the early 1920s, the English writer W. Somerset Maugham described a trip he had taken to Honolulu. "I could hardly believe my eyes," he said of the street scenes he encountered, especially "the unimaginable assortment of people." After portraying the different groups—including "the Americans, ignoring the climate, [in] their black coats and high, starched collars"; the Hawaiians, "pale brown, with crisp hair," and wearing nothing but "a shirt and a pair of trousers"; the "Japanese . . . neat and trim in white duck," with their children "in bright coloured frocks, their little heads shaven, look[ing] like quaint dolls"; the "Chinese men . . . fat and prosperous," and their women "enchanting with their tightly-dressed black hair, so neat you feel it can never be disarranged"; and "the Filipinos, the men in huge straw hats, the women in bright yellow muslin with great puffed sleeves"—he marveled at the overall picture:

> It is the meeting-place of East and West. The very new rubs shoulders with the immeasurably old. And if you have not found the romance you expected you have come upon something singularly intriguing. All these strange people live close to each other, with different languages and different thoughts; they believe in different gods and they have different values; two passions alone they share, love and hunger. And somehow as you watch them you have an impression of extraordinary vitality. Though the air is so soft and the sky so blue, you have, I know not why, a feeling of something hotly passionate that beats like a throbbing pulse through the crowd.

Somerset Maugham delighted in the city's exoticism. Others did not, including many residents of Mānoa Valley. Fortunately for the sensibilities of its comfortable inhabitants, Mānoa was a manicured, wealthy, and almost entirely white suburban enclave. Racially restrictive covenants in real estate transactions made sure it would remain that way.

It was the same in other exclusive white neighborhoods throughout Honolulu, and on the other islands as well. Years later an editor of the *Ho-*

nolulu Star-Bulletin described his wife's upbringing at this time on the Kona Coast of the island of Hawai'i, the so-called Big Island: she and her parents had lived "in a restricted, haole, well-to-do atmosphere," he said, where "the Japanese and Hawaiians were thought of as servants and nothing else." As with the Japanese maid the Massies employed soon after moving in, most of the Asians and Hawaiians seen in and around Mānoa were domestics or day laborers—hired help.

Like the other young military wives then being transferred to the islands, Thalia had every reason to anticipate that her stay would be the stuff of dreams that all the movie magazines and newspaper Sunday supplements had been writing about for years. Her own great-grandfather's *National Geographic,* now being run by her cousin, Gilbert Grosvenor, had devoted an entire issue to the islands, extolling the virtues of their "floral wonderland" while also displaying a requisite but tasteful sampling of scantily-clad native girls and brown-skinned seminaked young men.

But Thalia and Tommie arrived in Honolulu at the worst possible time. In 1930 and 1931, across the country more than 3,600 banks had collapsed, bringing $2.5 billion in deposits down with them. A record-shattering 54,640 businesses failed during those same two years. The impact on Hawai'i was inevitable. Following the stock market crash, the number of visitors to the islands fell by 15 percent almost immediately. Before long it would be down 50 percent and still declining. The sand and the water at Waikīkī remained pristine, the climate was as balmy as ever, but the guest rooms and banquet halls of the opulent beachfront hotels were growing increasingly empty.

Even in New York tourism was plummeting. In 1931 the Savoy-Plaza Hotel lost more than a million dollars in just nine months. Seeking to entice old customers, the elegant Ritz sent out hundreds of personal letters to past guests, vainly imploring them to return. The Pierre and the Waldorf slashed room rates to six dollars a night. The Essex House had its grand opening with much fanfare and an advertised rate of three dollars per room or five dollars for a suite. But still no one came. If cash-strapped tourists were shunning New York, the metropolitan heart of America, why would they travel to Hawai'i, an expensive five-day sail across 2,500 miles of open ocean?

The plain fact was that the only class of people Thalia had ever known, or ever wanted to know, had almost stopped visiting the distant island paradise where she lived. And without them, the excitement over being transferred to Honolulu quickly wore off.

■ ■ ■

At nineteen years of age, Thalia found herself trapped in a humdrum marriage and a tediously sedate neighborhood on a remote island in the middle of the ocean. Day after day she was expected to do little but attend luncheons or teas with other officers' wives. Considering herself of higher social stature and far more cosmopolitan than they, she simply refused to participate in what she regarded as the older wives' wasteful pastimes. Tommie's consternation—since many of those women were his superior officers' spouses—had little effect on Thalia. She preferred, as she was happy to tell anyone who would listen, to devote her free time to less boorish activities.

A pattern of behavior, almost a ritual, soon established itself. Grace Fortescue, still listed with her husband Roly in the New York Social Register's "Blue Book" at his family's Bayport address, had made some appropriately genteel contacts for their daughter and her husband in Honolulu. The first dinner party invitation came from Mr. and Mrs. Derek Perry, wealthy world travelers whose home in the city's exclusive Pacific Heights neighborhood overlooked all of Honolulu and the coastline below. Thalia was not impressed.

According to Mrs. Perry, within minutes of arriving for the party intended to welcome her to the islands, Thalia demanded a drink and began prowling the house, making critical comments about it at every turn. When the others settled into a game of bridge and light conversation, Thalia took a book from a shelf and sat off by herself, reading. At dinner, Thalia "proceeded to criticize everything her husband said, told obscene stories, and finally left the room," tracking down, in due course, the Perrys' liquor supply. They later found her, Mrs. Perry said, "in the kitchen, sprawled over the table, completely out."

Living next door to the Massies was a twelve-year-old girl who grew up to become the territorial governor's daughter-in-law, Ruthie Judd. Years later she would recall "skating on the road on a weekend, or playing roller skate hockey" in the street, when Thalia, "who was a drunk . . . would come to the door [mumbling incoherently] . . . 'you kids.' I can remember it so vividly . . . because she drank so much. God, she was a bitch! She had a very nice husband, though we rarely saw him."

The former owner of the Mānoa house the Massies rented, a man who "came to know them pretty well" in 1930 and 1931, described Thalia as "a heavy drinker, in fact they both were, and I have seen her stewed many times." Her other behavior at the Perrys' became part of a pattern. Even the Massies' closest friends during their stay in Honolulu—people who supported them through all the turmoil to come—upon reflection painted the same portrait of Thalia. A prominent local physician who spent a lot of time entertaining and playing water polo with the Massies informally diagnosed Thalia as possessed of "a peculiar complex": she did not make friends easily, and "if she did not like anything, no matter what it was, she would not hesitate to say so." Another self-described "good friend" and frequent dinner companion of the couple, the general manager of a title company, was more specific:

> Mrs. Massie was not at all liked and was very unpopular among the Navy set. She was a very peculiar woman and extremely outspoken. If she saw a woman wearing a dress she did not like she would not hesitate to tell her it was a terrible looking thing. She would hurl all kinds of insults at people regardless of who or what they were or how little she knew them. She would even criticize the hostess when she was invited out to dinner, the manner in which things were served at the table, things inside the house, and the house itself.

Other acquaintances and neighbors commented on Thalia's custom of coming to the front door or walking around in the yard half naked—"looking like a prostitute," said a man who lived a few houses down the street. In a phrase, "she craved attention," as one couple put it.

That was when she was in a good mood. When in a darker frame of mind, some said, she displayed "a cruel streak." She would occasionally attack Tommie in front of guests, sometimes "grabbing his arm and biting him viciously." When gatherings were held at other people's houses, Thalia would often become irate about something during the middle of the party and stalk off into the night alone. On one occasion, when invited guests to the Massies' home were a half hour late for dinner, they found that Thalia had bolted the front door and refused to allow them in. Before long Tommie was almost perpetually drunk, those who knew the couple said, and raucous parties at their house frequently ended with the police—called out by neighbors who were unaccustomed to such things—having to quiet matters down.

It was no better when the two of them were alone. "Mr. and Mrs. Massie drank and quarreled," and often violently cursed one another, recalled their maid, Beatrice Nakamura, adding that when Tommie was away on sea duty Thalia frequently entertained men who were friends of the couple. One was a fellow naval officer, known to Beatrice only by a nickname, "Red Fig." The other was a young man about Thalia's age who was a college student and the son of a high-ranking military official. When Tommie was gone it was not unusual for one or the other to spend the night—in one instance an entire week—or for Thalia to go to the beach with one of them and not return for several days, something the neighbors also noticed and discussed among themselves.

None of this could remain private for very long. As a nationally popular observer of the island scene wrote in *Hula Moons,* a book published in New York that year, in multiracial Honolulu "the whites form a village within the city," and within this village "almost everyone knows everything about everybody":

> The newspapers publish the news, while the word-of-mouth carries the gossip, scandal, conjecture and rumor which make up three-fourths of the conversation. . . . Honolulu loves its dish of scandal; it keeps itself thoroughly misinformed about the private life of its public figures at all times. Anyone who thinks he gets away with anything there just doesn't know his Honolulu.

The local phrase for this rumor mill was (and still is) the "coconut wireless." And as the coconut wireless circulated ever more salacious rumors about Thalia, Tommie's humiliation and outrage grew. As did his drinking. An older, civilian couple who had befriended the Massies, Mr. and Mrs. Nelson Pringle, increasingly served as Tommie's sounding board. Mr. Pringle was a former navy officer who now worked for the afternoon newspaper, the *Star-Bulletin.* Twice Tommie spent the night at their home in ʻĀlewa Heights, a good distance away, after a quarrel with Thalia. On another occasion he stayed with them for a week.

According to the Pringles, Tommie was frustrated, angry, and embarrassed by Thalia's behavior—by the fact that "she was lazy and lay abed at all hours," that she was "careless of her personal appearance and did not seem to care whose feelings she hurt or who she offended," and that "she was constantly endeavoring to make Mr. Massie jealous by talking about other men." During the time that he spent a week with them, the Pringles said, Tommie "was in such bad condition owing to the behavior of his wife, that he couldn't sleep and walked the floor all night—in such bad condition that it was necessary to give him a sedative without his knowledge as he was keeping others awake."

Tommie's response to Thalia's conduct was not always so passive, as on the night when he followed Thalia around Diamond Head while she rode in a car with another naval officer. When he finally caught up with the couple, according to a policeman's report, Tommie punched the other navy man, then slapped Thalia and dragged her away.

Apparently bored with everyone and everything around her, Thalia was determined to live a life of unfettered fun and independence. But the last thing she wanted was a divorce—which was what Tommie was now threatening. She had no real friends in Hawai'i. Or anywhere else. She dreaded returning home to her parents, especially to her father. And she knew nothing about supporting herself. So time and again, she would promise to make amends and try to do something useful.

Her first effort at rehabilitation occurred in the fall of 1930. Thalia enrolled in a freshman English class at the University of Hawai'i, walking distance from where they lived. With her prestigious educational background at posh private schools—compared with the presumably low standards at what was, literally, the most provincial public college in the United States—the beginning English course should have been easy. Instead, she flunked it. The following semester she registered for an introductory Spanish course, having previously studied the language and received high grades at the Hillside School in Connecticut. She failed the Spanish class, too. Within a year after arriving in the islands, then, and after taking just two college courses, Thalia was placed on academic probation, allowed to register for further classes only after making a special petition to the university administration.

During the same time that Thalia unsuccessfully was attempting to enrich her mind, she made an effort to expand her creative horizons as well. She wrote poetry, even publishing in a college quarterly a sonnet, "On Approaching Blindness," about her poor vision and the day she believed drawing near "when I shall feel darkness folding soft / . . . to shield me from the sun, too bright aloft." She also tried acting in community and on-base theater productions. But again, to her disappointment, she found the local talent superior to her own. To make matters worse, when she pressured Tommie into joining her in the cast of one production, he promptly—on opening night—forgot his lines. His nonperformance on stage seemed symbolic of everything that was happening to their marriage.

After two failed tries, Thalia decided not to bother anymore with the university. She also soon abandoned her efforts to become a poet or an actress. By the spring of 1931 she had other things on her mind. She was pregnant again. At first she tried staying at home for the duration, but the monotony became intolerable. She decided to find a job. With no particular talents and no training (and in the middle of the Depression), she counted herself lucky when she was hired by the Atcherley Advertising Service to sell novelty promotional items. During late May and early June, Thalia went door to door in a small business district trying to convince shop owners to buy cigar lighters embossed with the names of their stores or companies. After two weeks she had made one sale and called it quits.

By then it was clear that Thalia's pregnancy was going as badly as everything else. Her blood pressure began to soar. Abnormally high levels of protein were detected in her urine. She suffered from headaches, depression, and a worsening of her already poor vision. Her hands began to swell, then her face. Her weight increased far more than it should have. Then, in midsummer—well into the latter part of the pregnancy—she was diagnosed with preeclampsia. Soon after, she lost the baby.

Even today preeclampsia is a serious and debilitating condition that can affect one in twenty women. In Thalia's case the symptoms lingered after the pregnancy ended, especially the weight gain and the depression. She became more irritable and caustic than ever. And that drove the wedge between her and Tommie even deeper. Apparently, as their maid would in time suggest, and as both Tommie and Thalia later intimated in trial testimony, it put an end to their already atrophied love life.

In frustration and bewilderment, Thalia sought counseling from Dr. E. Lowell Kelly, a twenty-five-year-old assistant professor of psychology at the University of Hawai'i. Kelly had received his doctorate from Stanford, and would soon move on to the University of Michigan. Years later, after his research had been greeted with international acclaim, he was elected president of the American Psychological Association. What eventually made Kelly's reputation was a twenty-year longitudinal analysis of marital compatibility among three hundred couples. As he sat down to speak with Thalia, he was in the process of designing that project.

The Kelly Longitudinal Study, as it became known, was based on a battery of standard psychological inventories, plus a questionnaire of Kelly's own design. Like the standardized inventories, Kelly's survey began with multiple-choice questions. Unlike the others, though, his form elicited information on Thalia's parents and their relationship, her courtship with Tommie, their financial situation, their relationships with friends, and the number of children they hoped to have, if any. The questions went on for pages. They asked about drinking and quarreling. In one section specifically designed for wives, the queries pursued the subject of sexual adequacy, compatibility, and faithfulness—and asked the subject, if she could change anything about her husband, whether she would change his "weight," his "height," the "size of his sexual organ," and more. A great deal of the document focused on sex, and then finally on the topic of overall marital happiness.

Kelly's own questionnaire, as distinct from the others in the battery, also left several pages for its subject to write down in longhand her most intimate thoughts and feelings. Thalia poured out her soul, focusing in detail on what she regarded as Tommie's coldness and cruelty of late, and her own lack of affection for him. Kelly used the questionnaire as the foundation for the counseling sessions to follow, but after several meetings, as he later recalled in a private letter, he decided that Thalia's "personal and emotional problems" were beyond his competency. "I became convinced that she was in need of psychiatric treatment and so advised her husband by telephone," he wrote. "Shortly thereafter, Mrs. Massie cancelled a scheduled appointment stating that her problems were no longer so serious."

That was the final time Professor Kelly ever spoke with Thalia. He filed away the questionnaires she had filled out, along with the pages containing her longhand comments. Like Thalia, he no doubt expected that nothing would ever come of their sessions together.

It was now August, soon after her pregnancy had terminated. She was at her weakest and most vulnerable, and then Tommie announced that they were through. He wanted a divorce. Thalia pleaded with him, saying she would do anything to keep their marriage together. At last they agreed to a compromise. In good military fashion—and in a manner that revealed his judgment of his wife's immaturity—Tommie drew up a formal written plan that placed Thalia on "probation" for three months. During that time, as friends who witnessed the document recalled, Thalia had to "mend her ways, or be sent home to her family."

It was the low point of Thalia's young life. Her marriage was empty and loveless, but she clung to it in desperation. It was all she had. Her attempts at education and work had been failures, she had no talent or training or money, and she was unwelcome in her parents' home—wherever that might be at the moment. Still wanting nothing to do with the other officers' wives and their mundane activities, Thalia nonetheless promised Tommie that she would try.

No longer daring to venture out with other men or have them over when Tommie was away, Thalia stayed home by herself, waited on by her maid, Beatrice. Before long almost the only time she ventured outdoors was in the late afternoon, with her dog, Prince, in tow, for long brooding strolls along the quiet tree-shaded streets of Mānoa, which, like everything else in Hawai'i, she now despised.

At one time the movie theaters of Waikīkī had offered Thalia some distraction. But in the end, they too must only have made matters worse. In response to declining theater attendance following the onset of the Depression, Hollywood turned up the heat on explicit violence and sex, hoping to lure back straying customers. Murder, mayhem, and excitement were all the rage in the new talking pictures, with Jimmy Cagney emerging as a star following roles as a bootlegger, a con man, and a gangster in films like *Sinner's Holiday,* *Doorway to Hell,* and *Blonde Crazy.* In a gambling film, *Smart Money,* Cagney worked with another newcomer, Edward G. Robinson, who had burst into prominence with his own controversial gangster films, *The Hole in the Wall,* *The Widow of Chicago,* and *Little Caesar.* Even Al Capone claimed to be shocked by these underworld fictions, declaring them "bad for young people" and urging that they be "collected and dumped in the lake."

But complementing every Cagney and every Robinson there were at least several female stars—Joan Crawford, Janet Gaynor, Clara Bow, Ruth Chatterton, Constance Bennett, Marlene Dietrich, Carole Lombard, Greta Garbo, Marie Dressler, Norma Shearer, Jean Harlow, and others—who were doing things on-screen that were even more shocking, things no film actress had ever done before. In movie after movie, from Shearer's Oscar-winning performance in 1930's *The Divorcee* ("If the world permits the husband to philander, why not the wife?" read the film's advertisements) to Bennett's 1931 *The Common Law* (in which she portrays a nude model after abandoning her male roommate), young female film idols were portrayed as unmarried mothers, kept women, prostitutes, or just hedonistic libertines—who happily get away with it.

One of the lesser stars of that era was Dorothy Mackaill, who vacationed in Hawai'i regularly and finally retired to the islands. She had written a year earlier of impressionable female moviegoers like Thalia:

> In order to be sophisticated, fledglings turn to their primer, the movies. Who has the good times, the swell clothes, the boyfriends, the excitement, all the breaks? Why who but the Connie Bennetts ... the Crawfords, even the Mackaills. And why? ... Not because we are portrayed as "nice girls" sitting at home with the old folks or practicing the piano. No, because ... we are smoking, drinking, dancing, being made love to, getting in and usually out of ... passionate situations.

"None of the old taboos . . . mean a damn to us," Mackaill concluded. Neither, for a time, had they meant a damn to free-spirited Thalia Massie. But now, at the risk of losing her marriage and being cast adrift unless she changed her ways, Thalia had agreed to be bound by the constraints of middle-class morality. The joys expressed and the liberties taken by those screen sirens, to say nothing of their fame, were only bitter reminders of the unnoticed, unloved, and empty life she was living—among inferiors—more than two thousand miles from nowhere.

3 Something Awful Has Happened

Saturday evening, September 12, started out warm and muggy. It is called "kona weather" in Hawai'i; from time to time in late summer or early fall the naturally cooling trade winds die down and the air becomes heavy and still. The new moon was only two days old. Barely a faint sliver in a shrouded sky, it disappeared entirely when night closed in.

Because of the nearness of the equator, dusk passes quickly in this part of the tropics, the transition from day to night occurring almost like the closing of a curtain. At eight o'clock it had already been dark for an hour. Dinner over, Thalia was in the back bedroom of their Mānoa bungalow, dressing for a party. Tommie was in the living room, preparing drinks for some navy friends and their wives who would soon be dropping by. Thalia and Tommie had disagreed earlier, after he returned home from work to tell her of a "tea party"—meaning a drinking party—that some of the officers had arranged for that evening at a nightclub on the outskirts of Waikīkī.

As always, she had not wanted to attend. If they had to go somewhere (and they might as well, since staying home meant listening to the Boys from Dixie followed by the Melody Sisters on the radio), even the movies would be preferable. The entertainment section of the afternoon newspaper, after announcing Loretta Young's recent filing for divorce, enthusiastically recommended the shows at two movie theaters in Waikīkī. *Little Caesar* was playing, with a Mickey Mouse cartoon and Laurel and Hardy's *Laughing Gravy*, at the Hawaii Theater, while the Princess Theater was showing Clara Bow's romantic comedy *No Limit* ("She Gets Her Man, But Is He Worth the Price?"). Either of them would be better than another drunken night with Tommie's navy friends. But Thalia's marriage was now in the balance. She agreed.

After Thalia had signed the probation agreement, a little of the old confidence had returned to Tommie's smile and his walk. But it was decidedly tentative. Four years earlier, after graduating in the bottom third of his class at the academy, Tommie had caught what appeared to be the break of a lifetime, marrying into what he thought was enormous wealth, glamour, and power. With in-law connections that others could only dream of—millionaire corporate directors on one side, the blue-blooded family of a former U.S. president on the other—his success in the military and beyond seemed guaranteed. Tonight, however, as he set out the glasses and the ice, and the bottles of beer and bootleg liquor, Tommie had lingering doubts that his marriage would last even the few remaining months of the year. Whatever her behavior of the moment, Thalia was still Thalia.

In the next room, Thalia silently selected her clothes for the evening, determined to show the other wives how a person of sophistication was supposed to dress. If nothing else, she would be noticed, although doing so was not as easy as it had once been. Even though her parents, despite their pretenses, never had any real money, Thalia and her sisters had grown up largely in the care of their grandparents and other genuinely affluent and generous relatives. She had never wanted for anything. But now Thalia and Tommie had to make do on his salary as a junior officer in the submarine corps. It was sufficient to pay the bills, but not much else. And it was at times like these, when dressing for a party, that Thalia was most acutely reminded of her reduced situation.

Take her slip, for instance. It was cotton, a fabric women of her upbringing would never have put on under the elegant ankle-length silk gown and jacket she planned to wear. Or her girdle. The attached garter to which she hooked her stockings had been badly torn a while ago and she'd had to have it resewn. In the past she would simply have thrown it away. Four years ago, on the day her wedding was announced, a wire service story reported that American women were spending millions of dollars more on silk stockings than men were on their entire wardrobes. But times had changed—even for Thalia.

Of late, despite her youth, Thalia's girdle had become an unfortunate necessity. The abnormal weight gain during and after her pregnancy had not yet dissipated. She put on a flowered "slipover" or "step-in" with delicate ribbon shoulder straps, the cotton slip, and then a long green silk dress with a white top and a matching green silk jacket with brown fur trim on the elbow-length sleeves. She had picked the dress up from Uyeno's Cleaning Shop ten days earlier and it still smelled faintly of naphtha. Finally, she fastened a necklace of jade beads about her neck, slipped into a pair of alligator-skin pumps, and pinned her light brown hair back with a faux tortoiseshell barrette. Just a few more minor decisions to make. Selecting a green brocade handbag embroidered with butterflies and pomegranates, she paused to consider what to put inside it. Lipstick, mirror, powder, a package of cigarettes—Lucky Strikes—

and a box of matches. Glasses? No. She would not be driving tonight, and whenever possible she avoided being seen in public wearing glasses.

Thalia joined Tommie in the living room at just about the time their guests showed up—two fellow officers, Jerry Branson and Tom Brown, and their wives, Jean and Mary Ann. The two men, especially Branson, were showing the effects of the alcohol they had consumed with dinner at the Browns' house before driving over. Branson and Tommie had been friends and drinking partners since their days at the academy. If Tommie's record there had been less than stellar, Branson—who graduated 564th in a class of 579—made Tommie appear a genius by comparison.

For most of the next hour or so the couples chatted and drank home brew and a bootleg liquor known as 'ōkolehao. In Hawaiian the word means "iron bottom," a double entendre originally referring to the round shape of the pot still in which it was made and a translation that always was good for some cocktail party humor. Universally referred to as "oke" by navy men, it was a raw and potent moonshine concoction made locally from various substances, such as rice or pineapple or sugar by-products, or the root of the Hawaiian ti plant. On the nearby wooded hillside, one of the largest stills in Honolulu was then operating day and night, catering to the substantial thirst of Mānoa's naval community.

The group finally decided to drive down to the party at about 9:30, though some would remember the time differently. They had all had plenty to drink. But not enough. They packed up some flasks of oke to take with them, leaving behind a kitchen sink overflowing with empty beer bottles and glasses still smelling of whiskey, or so said a subsequent police report.

Tommie drove one of the cars, the tan Model A Ford that he and Thalia had purchased a year earlier, while the Bransons and the Browns piled into the one Jerry was driving. At one point, in the midst of the crowded Saturday night streets, Tommie lost control of his vehicle and it banged into another car. But the damage was slight, the driver of the other car was unconcerned, and the Waikīkī party was waiting, so they hurried along.

Their destination was the Ala Wai Inn, a two-story frame building designed to resemble a Japanese teahouse, but with a dance floor in the middle that flowed out onto what was advertised as "the largest open-air pavilion in Honolulu." It was located on one of the banks of the Ala Wai Canal, created less than a decade earlier as part of the Honolulu business community's plans to turn Waikīkī into a world-famous tourist resort.

The area inland from the beach was once a wetland, fed by streams running down from the mountains through the Mānoa Valley rain forest, and stretching for almost as far as the eye could see. The land had been engineered by Hawaiians as early as the fifteenth century into an elaborate system of terraces, ponds, and waterways that they filled with extensive plantings of taro (the Hawaiians' primary subsistence crop) and other produce, as well as fish and shellfish. At the end of the nineteenth century, Asian immigrants added rice, watercress, and lotus flowers to the mix of crops. But the prospect of building hotels on hundreds of acres of land that could be reclaimed from half a millennium of agricultural use was more than the chamber of commerce could resist. So the farmers were evicted and a two-mile-long canal, said to have been second only to the Panama Canal in construction costs, was dug. Seventy-five million cubic feet of earth were dredged, and the mountain streams and waterways were diverted into the ocean.

The result of this massive project was a new—and dry—Waikīkī, built largely on landfill and dubbed by developers the Gold Coast, an exclusive square mile of land facing the ocean on one side and surrounded on two others by what amounted to a moat. While there was entertainment to be had at Waikīkī's extravagant and exclusive resorts, most young navy officers were dissuaded from taking advantage of it by the prospect of spending a week's salary for the privilege. Instead, they tended to while away their weekend evenings at modest bars and clubs on the periphery of the district. The Ala Wai Inn was their latest discovery. A dinner and dance on Saturday nights, starting at seven o'clock, cost $1.50. The dance alone, from 9:00 p.m. to 1:00 a.m., was fifty cents.

Throughout the week the inn was filled with Honolulu residents of every race and ethnicity, but Saturday nights of late had become Navy Night—and that meant that almost all the patrons were white. There were no rules in force declaring the place off-limits to everyone else, but simple discretion on the part of Hawaiians and Asians did the trick. As one writer returning from the islands would soon remark in an article in *Harper's:* "One need only talk for five minutes with the average naval officer—who for some unaccountable reason is usually a Southerner—to realize that he is straining at the leash to put Hawaii's brown and yellow peoples in their 'place.'" In light of that, it clearly was the better part of valor for non-haole men to avoid the Ala Wai Inn on Navy Night.

As with most rules, there were exceptions. Joe Freitas was one. Half Hawaiian and half Portuguese, diminutive and outgoing, Joe was the popular doorman at the inn—popular with the military customers especially because he knew how to be both jocular and properly deferential. Ostensibly his job was to greet the guests, but his more important task was keeping an eye out for police officers and liquor investigators.

Joe was not concerned that the Massies, the Bransons, and the Browns might be law enforcement officials. The men were in mufti, in Hawai'i a type of white linen suit that marked them as navy officers as surely as their uniforms would have. But however they were dressed, in their swaggering, outspoken manner they reeked of military almost as much as they did of alcohol. And since Joe's responsibilities also included making sure that no trouble broke out, he decided to keep an eye on them.

As Thalia went on ahead, Tommie stopped briefly to banter with Joe. Each found the other vaguely familiar, and at last they realized they had once met at the boxing matches that were held regularly at central O'ahu's Schofield Barracks, then the largest U.S. Army base in the world. Boxing was extremely popular in Hawai'i in those days, the excitement heightened by interracial contests that regularly pitted military men against Hawaiians. After some discussion of past and upcoming fights, Tommie tossed Joe a wave and followed Thalia and the rest of his party into the inn.

It was jammed with more than three hundred people. Seating was arranged in semicircles on two levels, partially surrounding the dance floor and the bandstand. Upstairs, there were private rooms that could be reserved in advance. Biggy's Orchestra, moonlighting from its usual Saturday night engagement at the Alexander Young Hotel, was raucous and loud. This may have been Honolulu, but the orchestra catered to its customers' musical tastes, and tonight those were decidedly not Hawaiian. On the crowded and stifling dance floor, and spilling out onto the broad canal-front pavilion, bodies pressed and jostled against one another, men and women sipping from glasses and flasks filled with 'ōkolehao as they performed the latest dance numbers brought over from the mainland.

With each passing moment, Thalia regretted having given in to Tommie's pleas that she accompany him to the party. Pushing through the crowd, she made her way to a table on the grassy area near the water. Tommie joined her there, along with the Bransons, the Browns, and several other couples. But soon he was drawn into conversation with a group of men. As others also began drifting away, Thalia was left in the company of the Pringles, the couple that had taken Tommie in on the occasions when Thalia's behavior had become more than he could bear. The Pringles knew every detail of the Massies' troubled personal lives, and they had always sided with Tommie.

Thalia decided to move upstairs, where she went slowly from room to room and table to table, stopping to sit and talk for a while, and have a drink with people she knew, occasionally looking around in annoyance for her absent husband, expecting him to join her.

He was nowhere to be seen. At gatherings like these, he rarely was. Although the officers almost always brought their wives and girlfriends to such parties, before the night was through the festivities inevitably became occasions for all-male rituals. These were warriors in training, and a special breed of warriors at that. Not only were females extraneous, but too much of their intimate presence threatened to compromise ceremonial demonstrations of manhood.

They were not at war, but navy lives were hardly stress free. Every day the Pearl Harbor submariners took primitive, cramped, diesel-powered steel tubes to the bottom of the sea, never knowing for certain if they would return to the surface. Many hadn't. The first tragedy of the diesel submarine era had occurred just outside Honolulu Harbor sixteen years earlier when the F-4 sank in three hundred feet of water. All 19 men aboard suffocated or drowned. Since that time, seven navy submarines (or "sugar boats," as their crews liked to call them) had sunk in waters from Panama to San Clemente, and 110 men's lives had been lost. In just the last six years, two of the prides of the fleet—the S-51 and the S-4, the most recent design then in use at Pearl Harbor—had gone down. Sixty-six men died in those two accidents alone.

In recognition of the dangers they faced, the navy provided all submariners with bonus pay and an extra dollar for each dive they took, up to a maximum of $15 a month. In Tommie's case, that was on top of his monthly salary of $240. The bonus money was little more than symbolic. Theirs was a private world, one of rough-and-tumble, in which difference in rank and other normal protocol mattered far less than it did among crews of the surface fleet. And so, on evenings like this, as the alcohol steadily took its toll, distinctions between us and them—between males and females, between men who faced death routinely as part of their work and other men—became more clear-cut, just as the difference between bravery and bravado became harder to distinguish.

Soon after Thalia departed for the upstairs rooms, Tommie, who was the engineer aboard the S-43, caught up with his partner Tom Brown. Then, on the edge of the dance floor, they bumped into another shipmate, James "Red" Rigby, who was entertaining anyone who would pay attention with the sorts of wild stories and other antics that had made him famous, or infamous, at navy parties. (It was said that he once pulled on Jimmy Durante's nose to see if it was real, a story endlessly told to assured gales of laughter.) Unlike the other officers, Rigby was wearing a dark suit that night.

Tommie decided to stay with Rigby and his friends, while Thalia, one floor up, fumed. He did stop by occasionally to check on her, even getting in a dance or two. But then he quickly returned to his buddies downstairs. Without informing his own spouse, Rigby by now was inviting all within earshot to a gathering at his Mānoa home, a few blocks from where the Massies lived, once the Ala Wai festivities ended. Monte Rigby, Red's wife, was livid when she learned he had invited the Massies. Later she would admit to police investigators that she didn't like Thalia and had once told her so, bluntly saying that Thalia had made "many enemies" during her time in the islands, and that "she was hurting her husband's career." Then, at around 11:30, something occurred that became central to the rumors and speculations about that night's events.

Thalia had finally settled into drinking and conversation with a group of men and women in a crowded private room upstairs. There was not enough seating for everyone, and Thalia was among those standing. When she entered the room someone introduced her to those she didn't know, one of whom, the wife of Ralph Stogsdall, skipper of the submarine S-26, was named Josephine. Presumably showing off her eclectic knowledge of history—in this case the stereotype of Napoleon's first wife as flighty and frivolous—Thalia said, "Oh, Mrs. Stogsdall: Josephine without brains!" Thalia was the only one who thought the remark funny, although Mrs. Stogsdall smiled. Later she would have her revenge, describing Thalia to an interviewer as "not a good-looking woman . . . considerably round shouldered," adding that "in speaking [she] was caustic in her remarks, rolled her words and wobbled her mouth."

Stogsdall himself was probably the drunkest person in the room, as was his custom. When he got up to go to the men's room, Thalia slipped into his seat. Upon his return he demanded it back. Thalia refused to relinquish it. They began to argue, with Mrs. Stogsdall—the only one among the group who wasn't drinking—urging her husband to let it go. But finally he regained possession, prompting Thalia to say he was "no gentleman." He replied with a casual dismissal, describing Thalia as a "louse"—a word that, in the slang of the day, could mean a tramp. Thalia reached down and slapped his face, hard.

In the quiet that immediately followed, slowly, one by one and two by two, people began excusing themselves, preparing to head home. Someone suggested it might be a good idea to bring Tommie back upstairs to try to calm Thalia down. Before long, there he was, Josephine Stogsdall recalled, "sort of weaving in the doorway." When the last of the group in the room finally left, Tommie was sitting with his wife, talking to her. Downstairs, the music and the party continued.

The next time anyone at the inn recalled seeing either Tommie or Thalia it was close to midnight. Tommie had reassembled his friends, the Browns and the Bransons, suggesting they head somewhere for a nightcap before going on to the party at the Rigby house. Thalia was nowhere to be found. Some in the group were under the impression that the band stopped playing at midnight, but their spirits were rekindled when they found out they still had another hour of music to go. It was all the invitation Jerry Branson needed. Substantially drunker than almost anyone else, he soon was up on the bandstand, waving his arms as if leading the orchestra. Then he was down on the dance floor with his shoes off, demonstrating something that vaguely resembled a tap dance. Next, he was lying in the same spot, feigning exhausted unconsciousness, as the raucous crowd around him loudly and in unison chanted a count to ten.

Exasperated, the Browns and Jean Branson decided to leave Jerry in Tommie's care. They headed home together in the Bransons' car, no one giving much more thought to Thalia's whereabouts. That included Tommie. He was used to this sort of thing, and he assumed that she had found a ride home. More than an hour later, with the party finally breaking up at a little after 1:00 a.m. and the orchestra playing "Home, Sweet Home," he at last tried calling her. As some friends who were with him at the time would testify, Tommie told them "he was trying to get his wife, Thalia, on the phone as he wanted to prove to her that he had looked for her, since she always accused him of not doing so." No one answered at his home, so Tommie and Jerry Branson climbed into Tommie's car and drove back up to Mānoa in search of early-morning fun at the Rigbys' place.

They arrived there sometime before 1:30, only to find no one in the house other than the Rigbys' maid and their children, all sound asleep. Massie and Branson were early for the party, not realizing that everyone else had decided to make a first stop at a popular restaurant named the Barbecue Inn. But the front door was open, so they decided to go inside. Jerry flopped down on a couch on the lanai and soon was drifting off to sleep, while Tommie went rummaging in the kitchen for some food, awakening the maid as he did so. It then occurred to him to try calling Thalia at home once again. The next thing Branson knew, Tommie "was making considerable noise, walking about the house, turning off lights, slamming the door, and going out and starting his car."

Thalia, meanwhile, had left the Ala Wai Inn, alone and on foot, just before midnight, later explaining that she was bored and needed some air. Joe Freitas, the doorman, recalled seeing her leave. He also remembered that she stopped at the entrance to chat for a minute with a young local musician, and that Thalia had initiated the conversation, calling out to him by name. Then they separated and she walked slowly down Kalākaua Avenue in the direction of the beach.

Kalākaua Avenue is named for King David La'amea Kalākaua, the last king of Hawai'i, nicknamed "the Merry Monarch" because of his revival of Hawaiian music, dance, and other traditions after a half century of their suppression under American missionary influence. Kalākaua died in 1891, but it was fitting that the street named after him was, forty years later—as it is today—the main thoroughfare running through Waikīkī, the heart of Honolulu's entertainment district.

Thalia had to cross a small bridge that spanned the Ala Wai Canal before making her way along the wide boulevard, which was lined with coconut trees, date palms, and abundant shower trees, thick with delicate pink and white and yellow blossoms. Then, according to her own recollection, she turned right, off Kalākaua and down a smaller street known as John Ena Road. She was walking on the right side of the street, headed *makai* or toward the ocean, past a row of low-rise wooden buildings that housed small shops and fast-food stands. Streetlights illuminated the roadway much more brightly than on Kalākaua Avenue, and most of the business establishments were still open because across the street from them was a popular bandstand that didn't close until midnight on weekends.

The bandstand was on the site of an amusement park that had recently been destroyed in a fire. Renamed Waikiki Park, all that remained of the original was the public dance hall, an open-air pavilion with a large mirrored globe that hung from the ceiling and turned continuously, reflecting a cascade of brightly colored lights across the dance floor.

The park's rules required that the orchestra stop playing a few minutes before midnight. When Thalia walked past the park on this Saturday night, she later recalled, there was no music playing. Alice Aramaki, who worked in her father's barbershop on John Ena Road, directly across from the dance pavilion, lived with her sister in the back of another shop next door. Alice, a quiet young Japanese woman, had kept the barbershop open late that night, since it was not uncommon on weekends for men to stop in for a haircut almost until midnight. After it appeared certain there would be no more customers, she cleaned up and locked the door just before twelve.

As the music across the street died down and people began streaming out of the dance pavilion and climbing into cars in the parking lot or heading for something to eat in the nearby concessions, Alice stood in the front part of her sister's open-air store, leaning against an icebox, watching the crowd disperse. It was a habit of hers, but this time she noticed something unusual. Amid the boisterously talking and laughing crush of casually dressed local people passing by, there was, she later said, "a rather fat" young white woman in an elegant fur-trimmed green gown walking slowly, "with bowed head," on the sidewalk directly in front of her. Alice was standing only about a dozen feet away as Thalia passed by. White women dressed like that were a rare enough sight in this neighborhood at this time of night for Alice immediately to take note of it, but so too was the appearance of a haole man in a dark suit with an open-neck white shirt, like the one she noticed walking a few feet behind Thalia. She estimated the time at about ten to fifteen minutes after twelve.

Others witnessed a similar scene. Mr. and Mrs. George Goeas had been attending the dance, and once it was over they walked to their car and drove a short distance down John Ena Road, close to where Alice Aramaki was standing, before deciding to stop at a roadside saimin (Japanese noodle) stand for a bite to eat. At about 12:10 a.m., as they waited in the car for their order to be delivered, George later testified, a man and a woman walked past the car:

> I noticed a white woman walking with her head bent down, and the way she walked seemed as if she was under the influence of liquor. About a yard and a half from her we saw a white man following directly in the back of her. He kept this pace for about twenty-five yards and from there on I could not see as there was a store blocking the view. . . . [The man] was bare headed and wore a dark brown suit. He looked like a soldier to me. . . . It seemed kind of funny to see a white woman walking in that kind of condition and I noticed the way she held her head down and it made me think they had a quarrel or something.

Mrs. Goeas added a much more detailed description of the woman and her dress, making it certain that the person they had seen walking by was Thalia Massie. George Goeas held a cashier's position at the Dillingham Insurance Company, a subsidiary of one of the most powerful corporations in Hawai'i. He would live to regret having identified Thalia that night.

Neither Alice Aramaki nor Mr. and Mrs. Goeas knew Thalia's intended destination as she passed them. All they could say was that she was walking in the direction of the ocean. That could have meant she was going to Fort DeRussy, straight ahead, and its nearby private armed forces beach. Or she could have been headed for one of the small and inexpensive hotels, the Ikesu or the Niumalu, which were on the next block, both of which had nightclubs attached. It also might have meant she was on her way to "Submarine Alley," a cluster of ramshackle cottages on an unpaved lane near the water that was a "risqué area" frequented by navy men, as one former resident described it, quickly adding, "I wouldn't say prostitutes or anything, but loose." Or Thalia may simply have been wandering, with no specific goal in mind. Wherever she was headed, and whoever was close to her side, however, she was moving amid a crowd of people far different from those she had left behind at the Ala Wai Inn, and a crowd much more typical of Honolulu in those days—whatever the travel brochures and navy manuals described. But no one who watched Thalia passing by had any reason to fear for her safety. Honolulu had an extraordinarily low incidence of crime in those years. As one prominent haole attorney observed at the time, any lawyer who tried to make a living in Honolulu by specializing in criminal law "would starve to death—unless you classed bootlegging as a crime." As for the sexual assault of white women by Asian or Hawaiian men, it was literally unheard of, never having happened even once in more than a century of white settlement in the islands.

Mr. and Mrs. Eustace Bellinger and their neighbors, Mr. and Mrs. George William Clark, and the Clarks' son, George junior, had spent most of the evening playing cards at the Bellingers' home not far from Diamond Head. As 12:30 approached, Mrs. Clark suggested they call it a night, but before heading home she offered to take them all out for something to eat at the Barbecue Inn, the same restaurant that the Rigby party would be going to a half hour later. When they arrived there, however, it was too crowded for their taste, so they decided to try the Kewalo Inn on Ala Moana Road, stopping along the way to get some gas.

As they neared Kewalo Basin, at about ten minutes before one o'clock, a young woman stepped into the headlights of their car and gestured for it to stop. For a fleeting moment Mrs. Clark thought the woman looked like the Clarks' nineteen-year-old daughter, Ramona, who had gone out with friends earlier that evening. Relieved to see that it was not her, Mrs. Clark became alarmed again when she saw the woman's condition. "Her face about the lips was badly swollen," she later told the police, "and she had a mark on her cheek which might have been caused by a ring."

In his police testimony, George Clark Sr. recounted that Thalia told them she had been to a party in Waikīkī. "She had left the party about midnight because someone at the party had said something to her that peeved her," he recalled Thalia telling them, "so she went for a walk and fresh air." He continued:

> She said she went along Kalakaua Avenue until she came to the pink store . . . at the corner of Kalakaua and John Ena Road. After she had gone down the road a short distance she said a car drove up behind her and two men jumped off it and dragged her into the car. When she cried out for help they punched her on the mouth and held their hands over her face to stifle her cries. She then said they drove her down the Ala Moana Road until they came to a clump of trees and drove in there.

Eustace Bellinger confirmed the Clarks' memory of what had happened, adding that Thalia said there were "five or six Hawaiian boys" in the car that picked her up, and that they "had beaten her up and thrown her out of the car." He recalled, as did the others, that Mrs. Clark then suggested they take Thalia to the police station or to a hospital, but Thalia adamantly refused, asking them simply to drive her home. Bellinger also remembered something the others didn't mention. He was the driver of the car, and he said that after he stopped, Thalia approached and stood next to the passenger-side front door. She was speaking, but they couldn't hear what she was saying because the roadway was dusty and the windows were rolled up. After Bellinger leaned across and lowered the window where she was standing, Thalia—now no more than a few feet away from them at most—looked inside and still had to ask if they were white people.

The ride to the Massie house in Mānoa took a little longer than it might have because Bellinger was unfamiliar with the neighborhood and made a wrong turn or two. Along the way, George Clark Sr. asked Thalia if she had been standing in the road very long. No, she replied, theirs was "the first car to come along after she came out of the woods," he later told the police. Mrs. Clark finally asked what everyone else in the car was wondering. As she delicately put it: "Have you been hurt in any other way?" But Thalia "said no," Mrs. Clark reported, "and asked us not to ask any more questions as her jaw hurt so badly."

The Clarks and the Bellingers had no reason to doubt Thalia's claim that she had not "been hurt in any other way," because, as Mrs. Clark later recalled, "we all noticed her evening gown seemed to be in good condition." Still, as they pulled up in front of Thalia's house at 2850 Kahawai Street, at twenty or twenty-five minutes past one o'clock, young George Clark Jr. resisted his mother's suggestion that he accompany Thalia to the front door. She was, after all, a navy officer's wife. And the reputation of navy men was such that "I did not think it advisable" to walk her to the house, he said later, "as her husband might take a shot at me."

According to Thalia, just after she walked in the door Tommie called from the Rigbys' nearby house, where he and Jerry Branson had gone to continue the night's partying. This time Thalia answered the phone and, Tommie later recalled, cried out to him: "Something awful has happened. Come home."

When Tommie arrived, only a few minutes later, he said he found Thalia wearing a nightgown. She was crying as he entered the room, and immediately began describing to him how she had been kidnapped and beaten by a gang of Hawaiians. Then she added something she had not told the Clarks and the Bellingers. Her abductors, she said, had dragged her through the dirt and into some bushes and, despite her furious resistance, had violently raped her six or seven times. As Tommie later told a jury of eager listeners: "She was in a total state of collapse and broken down from sodomy."

Although Thalia protested vigorously, Tommie insisted on calling the authorities.

4 Thalia's Story

In the fall of 1931, Honolulu's police headquarters was a sight to behold, if not one to inspire much confidence. The main room was small and dingy, reeking of cigarette and cigar smoke, with battered wooden desks and file cabinets scattered here and there. Other offices and rooms, equally unimpressive, filled the first two floors of the old and nearly abandoned Kapiolani Office Building. Although this was only temporary housing for the department while the regular headquarters was being renovated, there were more than a few citizens—particularly those living in places like Mānoa—who would have agreed that the dilapidated setting accurately reflected the current state of law enforcement in the city.

The Governor's Advisory Committee on Crime, formed in response to complaints by some of Honolulu's leading lights, had released a 192-page report only seven months earlier. While noting that concerns were greatly exaggerated—the current crime rate actually was far lower than it had been a decade earlier—the report did point to certain deficiencies in the police and prison administrations, including the fact that the city had only one police-man for every eight hundred residents—half of what elsewhere at the time was considered a minimum. The police were also underpaid and almost entirely untrained.

During the previous few years, to bolster the numbers, almost anyone who applied for a job was hired, including people with criminal records. One new detective was a former bank officer who had served time for embezzlement, while a recently hired ambulance driver had been in prison for manslaughter. Eight out of ten policemen had never been to high school, and more than one-third of the force had less than three years of police experience. One result of all this, as the Honolulu newspapers delighted in pointing out, was occasions when patrolmen fled at the sight of a burglar's pistol (guns were rare in the islands in those days) or brought along muscular friends as bodyguards when engaged in what they feared might be a dangerous pursuit.

The famous exception was Charlie Chan—or Chang Apana, as he was properly known. Physically almost the exact opposite of the way he was portrayed in the movies, Apana was a small and wiry man who chain-smoked, wore a Panama hat, and carried a whip instead of a gun. While vacationing in Waikīkī in 1919, the novelist Earl Derr Biggers heard of the extraordinary exploits of a fifty-year-old Chinese detective who specialized in busts of opium dens and gambling parlors. It was said that he had single-handedly arrested as many as forty people in a single day. Biggers sought out Apana, interviewed him at length, and in 1925 published *House Without a Key,* the first in a series of Charlie Chan novels. This was followed by dozens of films with plots that bore roughly the same resemblance to Chang Apana's actual adventures that the white actors who portrayed Charlie Chan bore to a real Chinese. In any case, to many of the city's luminaries, Chang Apana was the exception that proved the rule.

In 1931, Honolulu had a crime rate roughly equal to that of Appleton, Wisconsin, or Cedar Falls, Iowa, today, but many haoles with influence insisted that it was a very serious problem indeed. And they placed the blame on the police force, observing that for decades the force had been staffed largely with native Hawaiians—a practice they now were determined to end. Many of the newest recruits were non-Hawaiian, as were high-level staff replacements such as the current chief of detectives.

In partial support of the haole community's criticism of Hawaiian policemen, a U.S. Justice Department report on law enforcement in the islands found that while Hawaiians possessed most of the attributes necessary for success in police work, on one measure they consistently came up short. Hawaiians, the report said, were "uniformly conceded to be inherently of a kindly, generous, forgiving, and easy-going nature" and generally were disposed "to help an accused person rather than to prosecute such a person." What the report failed to note was that Hawaiians were also incorrigibly individualistic, notorious for their unwillingness to go along with a group if they thought the group was wrong. All these characteristics would soon make an apparently straightforward criminal case very complicated.

When the telephone rang at police headquarters on early Sunday morning, September 13, it interrupted the silence of a typically uneventful night. A few drunks had been apprehended and given a place to spend the night, but that was about all.

The only noteworthy exception had occurred about an hour earlier, at 12:45, when a large and formidable Hawaiian woman named Agnes Peeples barged into the station to report that she had been assaulted following a near accident at the intersection of King and Liliha streets, less than a mile away. Mrs. Peeples's haole husband, Homer, had been driving their 1924 Hudson home from a party at a friend's house near Fort Shafter, Mrs. Peeples reported, when they entered the intersection at the same time as another car carrying several young men. After the two vehicles swerved to avoid each other, they screeched to a halt and the occupants exchanged angry accusations. One thing led to another, and Mrs. Peeples and a Hawaiian man in the other car, possibly a teenager, got into a shoving match. She wound up scratching his neck and punching his face, while he cuffed her on the ear, before calmer heads separated them and they drove off in opposite directions.

Although Mrs. Peeples, by her own description, seemed to have got the better of the altercation, when she discovered that her ear was bleeding she ordered her husband to drive to police headquarters. There she filed assault charges against the man who had hit her. She didn't know his name, but she had written down the car's license plate number—58-985—and had observed that it was a relatively new "light-tan"-colored touring car.

The officer to whom Agnes Peeples reported this incident, Cecil Rickard, was a locally born haole who had joined the police force just over a year earlier and been assigned the job of station house radio dispatcher. Rickard dutifully wrote down all the information Mrs. Peeples provided. She was not seriously injured, and she and her husband had obviously been drinking—she later described her condition as "neither drunk nor sober" but "feeling good"—so he didn't regard the matter as especially important. Still, it was the major event so far at the station house that night, and Mrs. Peeples told him that she was now going to the emergency hospital to have her ear examined. Also, Rickard and Agnes Peeples knew one another. So after checking with a superior officer, Rickard broadcast a short version of the story to the three police cruisers on duty that were equipped with radio receivers. He told them to be on the lookout for a car with the license number that Mrs. Peeples had provided. Then, after a half hour or so had passed, Rickard began checking the license plate files of the traffic division for the name and address of the owner of the car in which Mrs. Peeples's assailant had been riding.

Officer Rickard was still going through the files when, at 1:47 a.m., the station house telephone rang. It was answered by Captain Hans Kashiwabara. On the other end a soft-voiced man with a halting manner of speech and a southern accent, Tommie Massie, "very calmly" told Kashiwabara that a woman had been assaulted—"by a man," the voice on the telephone said—and requested that the police send investigating officers to his home in Mānoa Valley.

Captain Kashiwabara immediately called the detective bureau upstairs, where Detective John Jardine, who was in charge of the bureau during the night shift, answered the phone. Kashiwabara told Jardine of the call from Mānoa and asked him to send some men to investigate. Since Jardine was alone in the office at the time, he had Rickard contact one of the radio-equipped patrol cars and direct its officers to drop whatever else they were doing, including looking for the car with license number 58-985, and head directly to the address Tommie Massie had given them. The radio call was taken by Detectives George Harbottle and William Furtado. The address was only a few minutes away. They drove at high speed up University Avenue and into the winding, narrow streets of Mānoa.

As Harbottle and Furtado approached the address they had been given, they noticed another police car parked down the street, and they pulled up alongside it. Inside they found a police officer, William Simerson, and William Gomes, a private guard who worked for the wealthy residents of Mānoa as a night watchman. A third man in the car—drunk near the point of unconsciousness, his hair disheveled, his clothes rumpled and unbuttoned—was Jerry Branson, whom Tommie had left behind, semiconscious at the Rigbys' deserted house, when Thalia answered Tommie's phone call and begged him to hurry home.

After Tommie left, slamming doors as he went, Branson had bolted awake and found himself alone in unfamiliar surroundings. In confusion, he wandered out into the night. Although in those days the Honolulu Police Department did not assign officers to regular beats, an exception was made for Mānoa, home to many of the island's wealthiest and most powerful business leaders. Officer Simerson, a tall, corpulent, and imposing Hawaiian (whose nickname, of course, was "Tiny") had been assigned the Mānoa beat that evening. Sometime after 1:30 a.m., he and Gomes encountered Jerry Branson—besotted, unkempt, in white linen trousers that were belted but open at the fly, a white suit jacket thrown over one shoulder—stumbling around by himself outside the homes of Honolulu's haole upper class. They thought it prudent to ask him some questions.

As an officer in the United States Navy, and a white southern gentleman to boot, Branson resented the interrogation, telling Simerson and Gomes that what he was doing was "none of their damn business." That was just the beginning. Identifying himself to Simerson as the head of the navy shore patrol, he threatened to "get" the Hawaiian policeman if he didn't release him immediately. Simerson replied skeptically, saying that if Branson really was in the shore patrol he would know better than to insult a police officer. He put Branson in his car and drove to the nearest call box, where he sent for a police wagon to transport Branson downtown.

To Harbottle and Furtado, Branson presented the perfect picture of a suspect. Furtado directed Simerson and Gomes to transfer Branson to his car while they waited for the paddy wagon, and for Gomes to keep an eye on him while he, Harbottle, and Simerson talked to the Massies. Meanwhile, downtown, Detective Jardine was troubled. Although Captain Kashiwabara reported that the man who called in the request for help seemed calm, and the word "assault" was broad enough to mean anything, any report of violence at this time of night from Mānoa was something to be handled with particular care.

John Jardine was only twenty-nine years old, but he had been on the police force for most of the preceding decade. As a teenager he had taken a job at a lumber mill outside Seattle and then signed on as an oiler in the engine room of a transpacific freighter. His parents were immigrants from Portugal, and John had been born and raised in a tough neighborhood near the Honolulu waterfront, where his father worked as a coal passer.

In the plantation era, when social class, ethnicity, and race often served as substitutes for one another—and custom identified the Portuguese as nonwhites—Detective Jardine was, by virtue of his ancestral and personal background, well attuned to the islands' social nuances. And he sensed trouble in the phone call from Mānoa. When two more detectives, Frank Bettencourt and George Nakea, returned to police headquarters at about two o'clock, Jardine directed them to join Harbottle and Furtado at 2850 Kahawai Street in the heart of Mānoa Valley.

As the second team of Bettencourt and Nakea was racing toward the address they had been given, Detectives Harbottle and Furtado, accompanied by Officer Simerson, entered the Massies' cottage and made a discovery that startled them. Simerson had been to the Massie house before, called out by irate neighbors complaining of fighting and noise. Thinking they had now been sent to investigate a simple one-on-one assault case, they were unprepared for the story that unfolded.

The victim, dressed in a nightgown and lying on a couch in the front room, sobbingly told the investigators that she had been to a party with her husband and friends at the Ala Wai Inn earlier that evening. At around midnight she had decided to go for a walk and get some air, when suddenly a car pulled up alongside her and four or five Hawaiians jumped out and pulled her inside. After punching her in the face and driving to a remote spot near the waterfront, the men dragged her out of the car and into some bushes. Despite her struggles, they then took turns raping her six or seven times.

The policemen were astounded. Although Detective Harbottle had been on the police force for less than a year, Furtado was a veteran. So Harbottle stood to the side as Furtado began to question Thalia more closely, taking notes as he proceeded. In his report Furtado observed that "there was blood dripping from her top lip . . . and her hair was all mussed up," something confirmed by Harbottle and Simerson, but that none of the passengers in the car that had transported Thalia from Ala Moana Road to her home in Mānoa would later recall having noticed. Tommie, the officers noted, clearly was drunk, while Thalia—although she had obviously been drinking—was fairly lucid.

Knowing that haoles—especially recently arrived military people—often had difficulty telling Chinese, Japanese, Filipinos, and Hawaiians apart, Furtado asked Thalia how she could be certain that her attackers were Hawaiian. She assured him she knew the difference between Hawaiians and Asians. On the other hand, she said, the moonless night was so dark that she had not seen their faces well enough to describe them individually or even to identify them if she saw them again. What Thalia didn't say was that without her glasses, even with a full moon, she was blind as a bat.

Furtado then asked her if she might recognize her assailants' voices if she heard them again, and she said she might. There was one other thing Thalia volunteered might be of help: she thought one of the men had been referred to by the others as "Bull." But at the time "Bull" was a common term of address among local working-class men, the equivalent in later years and other places of "Mack" or "Brother" or "Bro." To policemen who knew the ways of the streets in Honolulu, that would be of no help at all.

What about the car? Could she identify it? Not really, she replied, except that it was an old car, a Ford or a Dodge maybe—perhaps inadvertently naming the same two cars she had at one time driven around the family estate on Long Island. Also, it was dark colored, possibly black, and it must have had a torn cloth top, she said, because she could hear it flapping in the wind. And the license number? Again, she said, it was so dark that she could hardly see anything, certainly not the numbers on a license plate.

By this time the other two detectives, Bettencourt and Nakea, had arrived on the scene. They took over questioning Thalia while Furtado stepped out into a hallway. Using the Massies' telephone to call police headquarters, he updated Detective Jardine on what was happening, telling him that the reported assault had turned out to be a gang rape of a young navy officer's wife by four or five Hawaiians. On the telephone Furtado and Jardine discussed the possibility that the men who had earlier clashed with Mrs. Peeples might also have assaulted Mrs. Massie. For his part, Jardine immediately concluded that they had to be the same men. The two women had independently identified their assailants as Hawaiians, a rare enough occurrence by itself, but on top of that both incidents involved a handful of men riding around in a car, and the assaults had taken place within an hour of each other. Taken together, it had to be more than coincidence.

Furtado and Jardine agreed that Jardine himself should become part of this increasingly volatile investigation, so he and another officer, William Seymour, checked out a police car and drove up to join the growing throng at the Massie house. First, though, Jardine told Officer Rickard, the station house radioman, to contact Chief of Detectives John McIntosh, apprise him of the situation, and have him come down to headquarters as soon as possible to interview the victim when they brought her in. Then he asked Rickard if he had tracked down the name and address of the owner of the car that had been involved in the assault on Agnes Peeples.

Rickard said he had just found it. The car with the license plate number that Mrs. Peeples had reported was a light tan 1929 Model A Ford, registered to a Miss Haruyo Ida, who lived at 1409-A Cunha Lane. Although Jardine did not yet know that Thalia had just described a car very different from that as the one her attackers had been driving, he still was surprised to hear Rickard's report. An unmarried Japanese woman owning the car that he now was certain had been involved in an attack by a group of Hawaiians on two women in the past couple of hours was not what he had expected to hear. But he told Rickard to send some officers out to the Ida woman's house to investigate anyway.

Thalia was now undergoing her second round of questioning, this time by Detectives Bettencourt and Nakea. Again she repeated—with increasing annoyance—that she would not be able to identify the men who had assaulted her, except perhaps by their voices. Nor did she have a clear recollection of what the car looked like, except that—as she had told the other officers—it was an old car, a Ford or a Dodge, dark in color with an apparently torn and flapping cloth top. But, again, she had no idea what the license number was.

Officer Simerson, who had been observing from the sidelines thus far, then joined in. He asked Thalia to try hard to recall even one number from the license plate, saying that all Honolulu plates had five digits, and just one or two would help. But his prodding was to no avail. She had not even seen the license plate, Thalia said. Meanwhile, following his telephone conversation with Jardine, Detective Furtado took a moment to lean over and whisper reassuringly to Tommie that they already had suspects in the case. As Furtado later recalled, he then told Tommie about the men who had been involved in the fray with Agnes Peeples and the car they were tracking down as a result of that assault.

When Jardine arrived, he stood back and observed the increasingly chaotic scene. Thalia was angry and frustrated, having been asked and having answered the same questions over and over again. And Tommie "appeared to be little more than half-conscious . . . under the influence of liquor he had drunk at a party they had attended earlier that evening." Deciding that at that moment Tommie was "hardly a rational man" and that Thalia had told them everything she knew—which was next to nothing—he suggested they take Thalia to a hospital emergency room to get medical attention for her facial wounds and for an overall examination. "I had in mind, of course, the necessity of a vaginal examination by a doctor to establish some kind of solid facts about the story of the rape," he later explained. But Thalia started shouting, "I don't want to go! I don't want to go!" Jardine, later describing her as "half-hysterical," appealed to Tommie for help, and Tommie successfully coaxed her into going to the hospital after wrapping her in a blanket and guiding her out the front door.

By now the setting on the lawn and street outside the Massie home was a tumult of confusion. The Rigbys had finally returned home with their friends the Pringles, prepared to party all night. Noticing the commotion outside the Massie house, they walked over to investigate. There they met another navy couple from the Ala Wai party, Lieutenant A. W. "Doc" McKechnie and his wife, who had driven up to Mānoa for the supposed after-hours gathering at the Rigbys', but were attracted instead by all the activity at the Massies' place. Several carloads of other navy couples who had been headed for the Rigbys' party were there as well.

Someone hearing of trouble at Lieutenant Massie's house had called the navy shore patrol. They too were on hand, looking for something to do. So was a crowd of neighbors. Disturbed by the noise and seeing the lights, they had come from blocks around, prying police officers, the navy men, and one another with questions about what was happening. No one seemed to know for certain. But suppositions soon turned into rumors—rumors that, in some minds, quickly solidified into fact. And one fact on display for all to see was a drunk and disheveled white man, semiconscious in a parked police wagon: Jerry Branson, still waiting to find out what the authorities were going to do with him. Another fact quickly made its way through the crowd. Thalia Massie had been beaten and raped. One neighbor, a woman, shook her head in doubt, saying with disgust that Thalia was "goofy."

Tommie and Thalia were escorted to the police car that Detective Jardine and Officer Seymour had driven to their house. As she walked past the parked paddy wagon, Thalia, surprised to see Branson inside, poked her head in the window and asked, "Jerry, what are you doing here?" It was one more piece of odd behavior to those gathered around. The car carrying the Massies and the paddy wagon carrying Branson pulled out and headed down the hill toward the hospital, leading a caravan of police vehicles and the cars of curious onlookers—the Rigbys, McKechnies, Pringles, and others—that followed close behind.

It was now just past 2:30 a.m. Back at police headquarters, Officer Rickard had located a patrol car to send out to Cunha Lane and investigate the connection between the assaults on Agnes Peeples and Thalia Massie. Going on Detective Jardine's conviction that the assailants in both cases had to have been the same men, Rickard openly broadcast that information to any and all who were within hearing distance of the department's radio-equipped patrol cars. The car assigned by Rickard to head out to Cunha Lane was driven by Detective John Cluney, a forty-year-old former used-car salesman, born in Honolulu, who had joined the police force eleven months earlier. His partner, five years younger than Cluney, was Thurman Black. Born and raised in California, Black had worked for the Matson steamship lines before deciding to stay in Honolulu, having learned that they were hiring policemen, no experience necessary. He too had been on the force for less than a year.

If neither of the two detectives heading out to Cunha Lane had much experience in law enforcement, at least Cluney knew something about the neighborhood where they were headed. And although it was less than four miles from there to the hills and tree-lined streets of opulent Mānoa or the glamour of Waikīkī, it may as well have been another part of the world. Calcutta, perhaps, or so some would say.

5   Hell's Half Acre

Cunha Lane was both a street and a neighborhood located to the west—the 'Ewa side, it is called in the islands—of downtown Honolulu. Named after E. S. Cunha, a sailor on a whaling ship in the 1860s who remained on to establish one of the city's most celebrated saloons, it marked the spot where two traditional districts, 'A'ala and Pālama, joined together. 'A'ala is a Hawaiian word meaning "fragrant," while Pālama designates a sacred site where, in ancient Hawaiian times, young women of royal lineage were kept apart from men until they were deemed ready for a conjugal ceremony with a selected young chief. Although it might have been difficult to convince newcomers of this in 1931, these districts, situated between two valleys, Kalihi and Nu'uanu, were once prized farming and pasture lands. They were separated from the ocean only by a small section of the district of Iwilei.

About six hundred years earlier the Hawaiians had realized that, although they would never cease to be open-sea fishermen, given that the islands were surrounded by the largest ocean in the world, there was a more efficient way of maintaining the supply of everyday seafood. They began constructing high rock and coral walls curving out into the ocean and back again, rising from the seafloor to just above the high-tide line. Built into the walls were small sluice gates that allowed young ocean fish to enter and feed on the rich coastal nutrients, but did not permit them to exit the walls once they had grown to maturity. The Hawaiians called these structures *loko kuapā* or *loko ku'i*, man-made saltwater fishponds. In time hundreds of them—O'ahu alone had nearly two hundred—interlocked into huge networks that ringed the circumference of each of the major islands. Ranging from a few acres to a square mile in size, they provided the Hawaiians with almost effortless access to an ever-replenishing supply of seafood. But few of these aquaculture farms anywhere rivaled those on the southern coast of O'ahu, from Waikīkī to Pearl Harbor, and including the reef-protected waters at Iwilei.

As whaling ships and large merchant and naval vessels began showing up in the islands during the nineteenth century, the channel to the Iwilei coastline was seen as the perfect location for a major harbor and waterfront district. Within a few years the character of that entire part of Oʻahu had changed forever. The fishponds and much of the reef were destroyed, and the coastal villages were replaced with cheap lodging houses, grog shops, and brothels. The transformation was emblematic of all that had been happening in Hawaiʻi for half a century. In that short time more than a thousand years of island history was nearly obliterated.

No one will ever know with precision when the first humans arrived in Hawaiʻi, but it was close to two thousand years ago, well before the birth of Muhammad or the fall of the Roman Empire. The initial inhabitants appear to have come in large double-hulled oceangoing canoes that were powered by sails, voyaging from the Marquesas Islands, 2,400 miles to the southeast. For the dozen or more centuries that followed, before the arrival of outsiders from the West, the Hawaiians lived in a seclusion that was consonant with their home, the most remote populated islands on earth.

In a benign environment, with no serious contagious diseases, the population grew steadily, reaching something on the order of eight hundred thousand by the late eighteenth century. By that time, almost every valley and plain on each major island contained plantations, many of them intricately irrigated, that supplied the population with so much food that a third of every year was set aside for religious ceremonies and harvest festivals, while all but the most essential labor was prohibited. In the world outside, however, epidemics had raged for millennia—from smallpox and tuberculosis to plague, influenza, and a host of venereal infections. Although those diseases wreaked havoc on all the continents, in the wake of their destruction they left survivors with varying levels of immunity. It was an immunity they carried with them in the pestilence-laden ships that wandered into Hawaiian waters in 1778.

The Hawaiians were astonished at the sight of the strange-looking vessels with their tall masts and square rigging, and at the appearance of the pale-complexioned and oddly dressed men who sailed them. The British were equally overwhelmed at the unexpected discovery of high islands in their path—larger than almost any thus far encountered, with mountains soaring more than thirteen thousand feet above the ocean waves—and of hundreds of thousands of people who greeted them in unguarded friendship.

Today the event that is most remembered in British and American textbooks about this historic moment is the death of Captain James Cook, the leader of the expedition. But at the time Cook's second in command,

Captain Charles Clerke, wrote that the killing of Cook was the result of nothing more than "an unfortunate string of circumstances." And he feared that it would overshadow the fact that the Hawaiians had treated the British with a "hospitality and benevolence" that was "without precedent in other countries."

One specific form of that hospitality was described in detail by a young ship's surgeon. The young women of Hawai'i "spend most of their time in singing and dancing," he wrote, and "as to modesty it is not to be looked upon as a Virtue or the want of it as a Vice among these people. Brought up from their youth in the most unbounded Liberty both of Words & Actions the beautiful Nymphs of Owhyee make that which is the chief object of their pleasure the general Subject of their discourse, & feel no Shame in inviting you to their Embraces." He later noted that "we live now in the greatest Luxury, and as to the Choice & the number of fine women there is hardly one among us that may not vie with the grand Turk himself."

But for the Hawaiians those generous embraces proved fatal. The crews aboard the two British ships were infested with syphilis and gonorrhea, diseases to which the islanders had no previous exposure. They spread like wildfire through the population, as did other contagions left behind by subsequent explorers. As year followed upon year, deaths from the imported diseases climbed rapidly. Births came to a standstill. The population began a steady collapse. By 1820 it was down to about 200,000. By the early 1830s it was barely 130,000. By the mid-1850s it was less than 70,000. By the 1890s it had fallen below 40,000.

While the indigenous population was withering away during the course of the nineteenth century, small numbers of European and American settlers were moving in. The first among them to come as a group were Protestant missionaries. They arrived in 1820 and set up mission stations throughout the islands, but their godly endeavors were short-lived. Within less than two generations the missions disbanded, and many of the leading missionary families turned their attention to business.

The Hawaiians had demonstrated the rich potential of the islands' soil, but their immense plantations now lay abandoned and overgrown. For centuries those lands had provided sustenance for a population that, at its peak, was ten times larger than the number of people inhabiting Hawai'i in 1850. But those who were eyeing the land for its agricultural possibilities were not interested in sustenance. They were seeking cash. After persuading the Hawaiian monarch to convert the land tenure system from common usage rights to fee simple ownership—except for large portions to be owned by the crown and ali'i (native aristocrat) families—haole entrepreneurs swept in and purchased vast tracts on which to grow sugarcane for export. Others found a different path to becoming landed gentry. They married Hawaiian women of ali'i blood, acquiring their property and producing subsequent generations of mixed-race haole-Hawaiian nobility.

But sugar and later pineapple plantations required labor, massive amounts of it. In the absence of an adequate and acceptably submissive native workforce, the plantation owners turned to Asia. The first imported field workers were Chinese, but so great was the need for laborers that by the mid-1880s the Chinese constituted nearly a quarter of Hawai'i's population. As the plantation owners' official newsletter editorialized at the time, such a large number of workers from any single national ancestry threatened "a danger of collusion among laborers"—in a word, unions, of one sort or another. The plantations shut down the Chinese supply line and turned elsewhere.

First the owners brought in Portuguese immigrants, but they were not available in sufficient numbers, and—like the Hawaiians—they openly resisted the tyrannies of plantation life. As for the plantation owners' subsequent attitude toward the Portuguese, it was ably expressed by an executive secretary of the Hawaiian Sugar Planters' Association. He referred to them as "besprinkled with a considerable amount of the swarthy blood of the Moors . . . and not at all the same as the Nordic or fair skinned races." In fact, he said, the Portuguese were no different from the "millions upon millions of low grade, undesirable, non-assimilable scum" who in recent years had migrated to the United States from the rest of southern Europe.

Labor recruiters decided to return to Asia. Soon huge annual allotments of Japanese "contract" laborers—essentially indentured servants with specified terms of work obligation—were arriving to work on the plantations. The numerical and ethnic transformation of Hawai'i's population was dramatic. Throughout most of the century following the arrival of Captain Cook and his men in 1778, the population of the islands had been in sharp decline, although Hawaiians still constituted more than 90 percent of the residents, with haoles and some Chinese making up the rest. After a reversal of the decline with the importation of Chinese laborers in the late 1870s and 1880s, in the sixteen years between 1884 and 1900 the overall population of the islands almost doubled, from 80,000 to 154,000. During that short time the proportion of Hawaiians fell from 55 percent to 24 percent. The proportion of Chinese fell from 23 percent to 17 percent. The proportion of haoles and Portuguese fell from 21 percent to 19 percent, of which only 7 percent were true haoles, that is, "Nordics" or "Anglo-Saxons." And the proportion of Japanese rose from 0.1 percent to 40 percent.

If the plantation owners had been worried about labor collusion among the Chinese when they represented 23 percent of the population, they grew more fearful than ever when confronted with the far larger and growing numbers of Japanese. But there was little they could do about matters because by the turn of the twentieth century Hawai'i had become a part of the United States, which had banned Chinese immigration in 1882. An effort to diversify the workforce eventually brought in workers from the Philippines, but only much later, and by 1920 they constituted only 8 percent of the population.

Out of perceived necessity, the haoles decided to form a political alliance with the Hawaiians. It was a very unlikely alliance because in 1893 those same white sugar planters had collaborated with a rogue American minister to the islands in landing U.S. Marines and seizing the government from the Hawaiian monarchy. Unwilling to use violence as a means of resistance against the most powerful nation in the world, for five years the deposed Queen Lili'uokalani and thousands of Hawaiians and others asked the president and Congress for a reversal of the coup that had stolen their government from them. Encouraged by U.S. president Grover Cleveland, who decried the overthrow as an illegal "act of war" against a friend and ally, more than 90 percent of Hawaiians signed petitions seeking restoration of the government. But the leaders of the revolt were active as well, pressuring Washington to annex the islands as a U.S. possession. In 1898 Congress gave the Hawai'i sugar planters and their allies what they wanted. Then, two years later, the islands were made a territory of the United States, with the federal government seizing for itself nearly two million acres of land. The *Honolulu Gazette,* a newspaper owned by a key leader of the coup and the future owner and publisher of the *Honolulu Advertiser,* welcomed Hawai'i's new political status by proclaiming that "if color is to rule any subdivision of American territory, that color will be white."

But an unexpected consequence of being made a territory was the U.S. constitutional requirement that citizenship and the power to vote were mandated for all adult males who had been born in the United States, regardless of race. That definition excluded Asian and Portuguese laborers who had been born in foreign countries, but since Hawai'i was now a part of the United States it included most haoles and all Hawaiians. Not only did Hawaiians outnumber haoles by more than three to one, but they were experienced and talented in the political arts. The recently overthrown government that had reigned in the islands for the better part of the nineteenth century was a

European-style constitutional monarchy, with a hereditary king or queen, but also with a strong elected legislature. It had negotiated numerous treaties with other countries, was a recognized nation throughout the world, and boasted a literacy rate far higher than that of the United States.

Although territorial status called for a governor who was appointed by the U.S. president, all other offices were elective, including the post of non-voting delegate to Congress. In the first elections held, Hawaiians swept into power under the banner of the Home Rule Party and elected as their congressional delegate a European-educated native Hawaiian nationalist.

The leaders of the haole business and political establishment, all of them Republican, were apoplectic. But because the appointed office of governor—and along with it all the patronage power of classic colonial rule—was theirs, they were not without leverage. Negotiations ensued, and in 1901 the haole elite struck a deal with the Hawaiian leadership. In return for the Hawaiians running more "reasonable" candidates for the key congressional post—that is, candidates friendlier to the haole perspective, Republican candidates—the haoles agreed to have the governor fill most civil service positions with Hawaiians.

For the following two decades and on into the early 1930s, although by then they represented barely 15 percent of the swelling population, Hawaiians held half the elective, judicial, teaching, and government clerical jobs in the territory. They also constituted more than 65 percent of the officers in the Honolulu Police Department. At least for the time being.

While a certain number of Hawaiians were well taken care of by the 1901 agreement between the haole and Hawaiian political leaders, many were unaffected by it, having long ago established small farms in remote areas or moved into the city of Honolulu, where they found mostly menial work. As for affordable housing, there were pockets of it here and there, including the streets and back alleys of Chinatown.

Meanwhile, almost all the Chinese and Japanese contract laborers who had arrived in the islands in the late nineteenth century deserted the plantations as soon as their work obligations expired, or as soon after that as they could afford to leave. The field labor was backbreaking, the wages next to nothing, and the living conditions abysmal. If they didn't return to their home countries or move on to the West Coast, as many did, most of them settled into the islands' capital city. There they found small ghettos populated by people of their own race and ethnicity, or—in the footsteps of numerous Hawaiians—they took to living in Honolulu's poor and densely populated Chinatown.

Then, in 1899, Chinatown became the focus of the city's last great nineteenth-century epidemic, bubonic plague. The authorities decided to fight it with fire. They believed that unhygienic conditions had caused the plague and that controlled "sanitary fires" would be the best cure. But one of those fires burned out of control, destroying a dozen square blocks of the district where more than four thousand Chinese, Japanese, and Hawaiians lived. Most of them were then removed to the nearby districts of ʻAʻala and Pālama, where, without any possessions, they took up residence in hastily constructed quarantine camps, which evolved into tenements.

The glee with which Honolulu's major newspapers greeted this disaster did nothing to quell suspicions that the fire had not been an accident. One of the *Honolulu Advertiser*'s headlines happily declared the fire "Almost a Clean Sweep," while its editorial page campaigned for the construction of a new Chinatown on the far outskirts of the city. The burned-out area should be converted into a park and "a white man's business quarter," the paper urged, adding that "we would rather see the Asiatics pressed back than the owners of Honolulu's most beautiful and stately homes."

Then, in the late teens and early twenties, during and after the massive Ala Wai dredging project, designed to create a glamorous new beachfront tourist area, large numbers of Hawaiian and Asian residents of the old Waikīkī and neighboring districts were forced to find inexpensive housing elsewhere. Those who had farmed in the huge wetlands of Waikīkī and surrounding areas first tried to find land in the island's rural communities, and some did. Others decided to build makeshift shacks out of discarded wood and cardboard, and to live in an area known as Squattersville, near the waterfront. But for most, the obvious places for relocation were the districts of ʻAʻala and Pālama, the already congested communities inhabited by those people of varied ancestry earlier displaced by the Chinatown fire and by Hawaiian families that had lived and farmed in the area since before anyone could remember.

By the early 1920s ʻAʻala and Pālama and the environs immediately surrounding them were, by every statistical measure, the most impoverished, depressed, and crowded neighborhoods in Honolulu. They contained nearly a third of the city's population. They were almost entirely non-haole. And it was here that the most notorious gambling parlors and opium dens were to be found, along with numerous "taxi dance" establishments that catered to sailors and the laboring classes, especially recent Filipino immigrants, who were still overwhelmingly male.

In response, Honolulu's political leaders designated that part of the city as the most fitting locale for a variety of institutions—including a settlement house, an orphanage, two schools for wayward boys and girls, the city's insane asylum, the territorial prison, a hospital dedicated to the care of people with leprosy, a garbage incinerator, and the grimy and smelly Honolulu gasworks. With its large, captive, and powerless population, private developers decided that this also would be an excellent place to build fertilizer plants, a soap works, tanneries, a slaughterhouse, and a number of pineapple packing plants, which contributed their own unique, sickly-sweet smell to the area's overall stench of sulfur, manure, and animal carcasses.

If this generally was regarded as the worst section of the city in which to live, one area within it was especially worthy of note because in some ways it was the hub of this part of town. Although it had a Hawaiian name— Kauluwela—it was not a traditional district, but one of several recently created census tracts carved out of overpopulated A'ala and the northwest part of downtown. In Hawaiian the word *kauluwela* has two meanings, "colorful" and "swarming." Both of them aptly described this gathering place where indigent Chinese, Japanese, Filipinos, Portuguese, Koreans, Puerto Ricans, and Hawaiians lived under conditions of crowding and degradation equal to that of any city anywhere.

Within Kauluwela, and bordering it, was a collection of small neighborhoods with names like Hell's Half Acre, Buckle Lane, Tin Can Alley, Cunha Lane, Mosquito Flats, Corkscrew Lane, and Blood Alley that were known as the worst of the worst. They had been that way for years, at least since the Chinatown fire at the turn of the century. In 1911 a visiting journalist who had previously reported on slums and corruption and racketeering in New York and Chicago declared flatly that "for downright overcrowding and unsanitary conditions . . . Honolulu has some of the worst slums in the world."

A decade later, after a newspaper exposé had described one swarming tenement house in which "pestilence and death are everyday familiars" (its 430 residents, on a single floor, were provided with a total of seven bathtubs and five tiny kitchens) the editor of the *Honolulu Star-Bulletin*, R. A. McNally, decided to take a look for himself. Accompanied by a group of the city's leaders, he discovered that the neighborhood known as Hell's Half Acre actually was about six acres in size, into which "are jammed together in reeking, tepid tenements and squat shacks, probably 2,000 persons at a conservative estimate." That made for a population density double that of Calcutta or the most crowded districts of Hong Kong today.

"In that district there is not one passageway large enough to admit the entrance of a vehicle," McNally wrote. "It is a labyrinth of winding lanes, or to be exact, pathways through which the tide of humanity surges from the bowels of interlocking tenements and squalid one-room shacks, resembling sheds. . . . As one penetrates the maze of wooden structures whence issue a Babel of unintelligible gutturals from foreign lips, the scene unfolds even more degradation. The whole atmosphere breathes contamination, moral and physical."

Following such revelations and a flurry of accusations and counteraccusations, proposals and counterproposals, matters soon returned to normal. And ten years later—while Tommie and Thalia Massie were just settling into their bungalow high up in Mānoa—a team of sociological investigators conducted yet another investigation of Hell's Half Acre and its neighboring communities of Cunha Lane, Tin Can Alley, and the rest. In terms of "squalor, crowded living conditions, apparent lack of sanitation, insidiousness, and vulgar practices," the team reported, "these areas are on a scale comparable to the slums in cities of the Orient." Even Hollywood was impressed with the reputed odiousness of this part of town, later promoting on posters and marquees an especially tawdry film, Hell's Half Acre, as a true-life story ("actually filmed in Honolulu") set in the neighborhood famed as "the Toughest Spot in the Wide Pacific."

Like Hollywood's screenwriters, Honolulu's privileged whites thought they knew all about these places, or at least all they needed to know. And partly they were correct. By every conventional index, these were the city's primary sites of vice and social decay. Yet, despite the neighborhoods' poverty, intense crowding, and lurid nicknames, they appear to have bred remarkably little violence.

According to social workers, each ethnic group had its own distinct pathology. Hawaiians had the highest rates of "juvenile immorality" (as measured by instances of single parenthood); the Chinese were the most frequently arrested for narcotics offenses (primarily old men smoking opium); Filipinos were identified with gambling; and the Japanese dominated the field of casual prostitution. Suicide rates here were among the highest in the city. (White parts of town with high military populations also had elevated suicide rates—and more organized prostitution.) More venereal disease was reported here than elsewhere. And the vice most associated with young people—"petty thievery of milk from the back porch or a chicken from back-yard coops," in the words of one 1930 crime study—also was more common in these parts of town than in others.

But there was much more to these congested places than vice and petty crime. While it was true that most of the people forced to live in such communities were desperately poor, the great majority of them worked. Tenements and tiny ramshackle houses existed side by side with larger homes and plots of farmland that produced fruit, vegetables, and even sugarcane, sometimes with a single ancient water buffalo on hand to pull the plow. Small pig farms were dotted here and there. Of those who didn't have land or farm animals, many—especially Filipinos—worked from dawn to dusk in the nearby pineapple canneries, where a tray boy in the 1920s earned five cents an hour. Hawaiians worked on fishing boats and at the waterfront as stevedores. The Chinese operated small retail establishments, while the Japanese dominated Honolulu's building trades and commercial fishing.

Decades later, despite the desperate poverty of their early years, former residents of these neighborhoods invariably had fond memories of growing up in those times. In interviews conducted during the 1980s, they recalled that their families were too poor to afford anything beyond the barest necessities, if that, but they also told endless and often humorous stories of family and communal sharing, to which every generation was obliged to contribute. Chinese boys apprenticed in their uncles' tailor shops. Teenage Hawaiians dove for coins tossed by tourists from arriving cruise ships. Japanese girls trained to be teahouse geishas.

Other girls, primarily Hawaiian and Portuguese, found that jobs in shabby dance halls, where they entertained lonely men for a few cents a dance, paid better than positions as waitresses, maids, or cannery workers. And although some "taxi dancers," as they were called, were prostitutes, most of those were older haoles, professionals from the mainland who followed the troop ships and used taxi dancing as a cover. The younger local girls commonly arrived at the dance halls wearing freshly ironed dresses and accompanied by chaperones—their mothers—much to the disappointment of many a paying customer.

Almost half the population of these teeming quarters had not been born in Hawai'i, and many adults were unable to speak a common language or understand one another's cultural habits. But across the divide, when the work-day was finished, they sat outside and played music or games of chance, like the Hawaiian card game *kēkake* or the fast-paced Chinese fan-tan, or wagered on the neighborhood lottery, a numbers game known as *chee fa*. Others, who could not read, sat in small circles listening to those who were literate reading the news aloud from that day's Chinese-, Japanese-, Filipino-, Korean-, Hawaiian-, or English-language newspapers. And old men, mostly Chinese, threaded their way through the crowded streets carrying long, heavy sticks laden with bananas for sale, or offered for a pittance homemade dim sum— including the spicy pork-stuffed dumplings that the Hawaiians called *mea'onopua'a*, literally "delicious pork things," in time simplified to the popular island treat *manapua*.

Children and teenagers, meanwhile, did what children and teenagers do everywhere. But here they had to do it before eight o'clock, when the curfew siren sounded from the waterfront's Aloha Tower. Ignoring the curfew not only invited chastisement from parents or relatives or neighbors, it also risked running afoul of the whip-carrying curfew police who prowled these districts in large black Dodge and Buick sedans. Whenever they arrived on the scene after dark, young people could be seen scattering in every direction.

On special occasions the Japanese living in these neighborhoods pooled their meager resources and held traditional *bon* dances. The Hawaiians had luaus. The Portuguese celebrated Holy Ghost festivals. There were Buddhist ceremonies and Catholic rituals, baptisms and weddings and funerals. But whichever event was happening at any particular time, increasingly there were people from other races and nationalities on hand to join in, however remote their ancestral backgrounds.

When the people of these slums had been plantation workers, the owners and overseers used the traditional tactic of divide and conquer to crush efforts at unionization. First they segregated the housing of their workforce by race and nationality, and then they deliberately sowed interethnic enmity and distrust by pitting one group against another. Workers performing the same tasks were paid different wages, depending on their countries of origin, and when work stoppages were attempted, higher-paid strikebreakers from rival nationalities were brought in as replacements. A united front of all plantation laborers was the haole elite's worst fear. But so far, worker solidarity had been averted. During the 1920s, after several incidents of major violence against would-be strikers had left the fledgling unions weakened and more splintered by race than ever, labor peace—on management terms—became the enforced order of the day among more than sixty thousand plantation workers. By the end of the decade the only people in the islands with union contracts were a handful of plumbers, carpenters, and barbers—all of them haole be-cause their unions excluded nonwhites. With a broken and submissive work-force, plantation owners reaped enormous harvests of sugar and pineapple, harvests that in past years could hardly have been imagined.

When immigrant ex–plantation workers and their families first began moving into Honolulu, they tended to replicate the race and nationality boundaries that had been imposed on them by the plantations, forming self-segregated communities within the city. "Little Tokyo," "Azores of the Pa-cific," "New Canton"—or, more colloquially, "Pake [Chinese] Patch"—were some of the names used to describe their neighborhoods. Each of these groups generally kept to itself, having learned on the plantations to distrust the others. Each one also attempted to preserve its values and culture with after-school language classes and by insisting on strict traditional discipline for its emerging younger generations.

In these ghettos social and political entanglements with outside groups were avoided. And for good reason. Coupled with the poverty—in 1920 Japa-nese residents owned an average of less than ten dollars in real property per person, less than 0.5 percent of what the typical haole owned—there was the fear. At that time well over half the working Japanese population remained plantation laborers, while the other leading occupations were house servants, geishas, day laborers, and subsistence farmers. Even among those who now lived independent lives in the city, working as fishermen or retail clerks, the fierce intimidation of the plantation experience had created a lingering timid-ity in the face of authority.

This was reflected at, among other places, the ballot box. On the planta-tions, workers who insisted on voting were handed a slate of acceptable can-didates by field overseers—or lunas, meaning "bosses" in Hawaiian—as they entered the polling booth. Inside the booth, the pencil for marking the ballot hung from a string tied over the Republican side of the ballot. From outside the booth the lunas could see if the string moved away from the Republican column—and if it did, there would be consequences. Workers had lost their jobs and their homes for displaying Democratic inclinations.

Habits of mind that were formed under those conditions remained pres-ent among many workers long after the plantations were behind them. Al-though few Filipinos were yet eligible to vote, throughout the 1920s the great majority of Japanese who were eligible did not even bother to register. Only once, in 1922, did a Japanese candidate run for a seat in the legislature. He lost.

Things were different among the Hawaiians and the Chinese—the Hawaiians because of their long political experience as the indigenous people of the islands, the Chinese because, for most, the brutal and bullying world of the plantation was well behind them. As the 1920s were drawing to a close, 26 percent of the Chinese who were American citizens had registered to vote, the same percentage as among haoles, while the figure for Hawaiians was 38 percent. In contrast, for the Japanese it remained less than 6 percent—but 6 percent of what was far and away the largest ethnic group in the islands. And waiting in the wings were more than seventy-five thousand Japanese, virtually all of them U.S. citizens by birth, who were under the age of twenty. That easily exceeded the number, for the same age category, of haoles, Hawaiians, and Chinese combined. To the Japanese that was a promise; to others, it was a threat.

It is not surprising that most haoles considered the growing ranks of Japanese to be a political menace. Even in the early 1920s, in anticipation of a time when Japanese voter strength would be ascendant, some in the haole leadership began lobbying Washington for a complete takeover of the government. They urged the imposition of what was called a commission form of government, one similar to the one then in place in the District of Columbia. It would have had no legislature and no elected officials at all. Governance of the territory would be wholly in the hands of Congress, administered through an executive directorate composed of one or more federally appointed officials—except that in the case of Hawai'i, those officials would include high-ranking military officers. Decisions on every law and every tax dollar collected would be made by those admirals or generals and other appointees. It would be a system of quasi-military oligarchy, short of martial law, but not by much. And it was a measure of the haoles' xenophobia that so many of them preferred it to democracy with the prospect of significant Japanese voter influence.

But haoles weren't the only people fearful of Japanese power. There was little love lost between many Japanese and Chinese—or most other nonwhite immigrant groups, each of which kept guard over its own hard-won turf. The Chinese had lived in the islands longer than the Japanese; they had intermarried, mostly with Hawaiians, and become successful businessmen. Because of the Chinese Exclusion Acts, they remained relatively few in number—and thus politically unthreatening to whites. If some Japanese would later confess to resentment over the socializing they observed taking place between Chinese and haole elites, while they themselves were often regarded by both groups with disdain, the Chinese were equally vexed at what they perceived as Japanese pretensions of superiority because of Japan's ongoing and successful military adventurism in China.

As for Hawaiians, they too were concerned that increased numbers of Japanese voters, who thus far were casting most of their ballots for Republicans, would further diminish the Hawaiians' already waning political influence, which was shifting to the Democrats as their old compromise with the Republican haole elite unraveled. From one side, the Hawaiians felt themselves under pressure from a haole population that was growing by leaps and bounds—a growth that was accompanied by an especially virulent form of imported racism never before seen in the islands. And now, from another side, there were the Japanese, regarded by some as the most standoffish and insular of all island ethnic groups. As a measure of that insularity, throughout the 1920s the interracial marriage rate for Hawaiians was close to 50 percent and that of haoles and Chinese close to 20 percent; for Japanese it was less than 3 percent.

Then, in 1930, the first two successful Japanese candidates for office, Democrat Andy Yamashiro and Republican Tasaku Oka, were elected to the territorial legislature. Haoles were outraged. Since the earlier call for a commission form of government had fallen on deaf ears in Congress, the extremist but influential white Taxpayers League of Honolulu began a campaign for a simpler and more direct solution to the problem: Washington should, by fiat, limit the right to vote in the territory to haoles.

For their part, Hawaiians were less outspoken, but they were worried. Of Yamashiro's and Oka's elections, "the people thought this was a landmark . . . that this surely was the end of Hawai'i," recalled the former head of a private school for Hawaiian children. Added Princess Abigail Kawananakoa, the would-be heiress to the islands' empty throne, the Japanese were only part of the problem. Hawaiians, she said in a 1932 interview, increasingly were apprehensive that they were being "crowded out of their home" by all the growing Asian immigrant populations:

> We [Hawaiians] must live here, we cannot go to China, we cannot go to the Philippines, we cannot go to Japan. . . . I have nothing but admiration for the Chinese and the Japanese and the Filipinos, but this is our home, and everybody is crowding us out of our home. . . . It is a desperate situation.

But if fear and interethnic tension persisted among the elites of most ethnic groups, as well as among the poor who had suffered directly under haole economic and political domination—thus keeping them alienated from one another even after the threatening presence of the plantation overseer was only a distant memory—for a growing number the times were changing.

It began with young people in the foul and disreputable back alleys of places like Hell's Half Acre. Local business and political leaders may have found the conditions in those neighborhoods repellant, but for sociologists they were fascinating. The slums of Honolulu seemed a unique locale for evaluating some grand theories that had been worked out in seminar rooms at Yale and Columbia and the University of Chicago. And while those theories have now long since been discarded, the information generated in testing them remains telling.

One thing the sociologists considered especially noteworthy was that the most racially integrated and egalitarian groups anywhere in Honolulu were teenage gangs that were beginning to gather in the most run-down and derelict areas. In sections of town where a single nationality—be it Hawaiian, Chinese, or Japanese—was overwhelmingly dominant, there appeared to be little crime, but also little intercultural understanding or support, and little resistance to established authority—haole authority.

The reverse was true in the most impoverished neighborhoods of all, places like Tin Can Alley, Hell's Half Acre, Cunha Lane, and the others into which a vast collection of humanity had been driven in recent years, without regard for race or ethnicity. "Apparently one of the most effective melting pots for the races is the crucible of crime," explained a sociologist, in academic language typical of the time, "for once having been purified of the restraining dross of a distinguishing culture and tradition, the individual mingles freely with others of his emancipated kind."

While single-race or single-nationality ghettos tended to remain conservative and tradition-bound, Hell's Half Acre, Tin Can Alley, and Cunha Lane were not ghettos, but slums with a multiplicity of ethnic groups. As such, wrote one investigator, they were places "characterized not so much by the absence of moral codes and restraints, as by the conflict of a number of distinctly different cultures and values, none of which is taken very seriously by the second generation." Ironically, this writer concluded, "Americanization, in the sense of the break-down of the traditional, primary group controls and the individualization of behavior, proceeds at an unusually rapid pace in such areas."

This, as much as the Japanese threat, was the haole elite's worst nightmare. After striving mightily for decades—on the plantations and in the streets of Honolulu—to prevent ethnic coalitions from forming, coalitions that might be able to resist the haoles' power as no single race or nationality could, here that very thing was incubating in the part of town that they had made a human dumping ground. As one law enforcement study concluded:

> Many of the second and third generations of certain of these races [Portuguese, Japanese, Chinese], born in Hawai'i and educated in the Hawaiian schools, will not accept work upon the plantations, . . . cannot secure other employment, and are consequently idle much of the time. [With young Hawaiians] they congregate on street corners, in the numerous pool rooms, and in other like places. . . . Some of them possess low-priced automobiles and, acquiring gasoline from mysterious sources, can be seen frequently driving lazily around the city. For the most part these gangs, so called, are not of the organized type, so often found in mainland cities, nor are they of a vicious or dangerous character. They are described more accurately as loiterers, or at the worst as hoodlums. They present, however, a difficult and an increasingly serious problem in police administration in Honolulu.

The precise difficulty presented by such admittedly nonviolent and unorganized groups was not specified in the report, but it didn't have to be. Everyone in the city knew what it was: these collections of young men, of varied races and nationalities, were behaving in ways that a southerner, describing blacks, would have called "uppity." They were insolent, brash, and openly unwilling to defer to whites as their parents and grandparents had done. They were, in a literal sense, insubordinate. And although there was nothing political in their activities and their general behavior, it took little imagination to envision the long-term political consequences if such social rebelliousness by nonwhite youths went unchecked.

For a hint of those possible consequences, in fact, all one needed to do was recall what Saturdays and Sundays once were like in 'A'ala Park, a small triangle of open space near Hell's Half Acre and Tin Can Alley. There, during the early 1920s, hundreds of listeners, some said thousands, had gathered regularly to hear the fiery speeches of Japanese, Filipino, and Hawaiian labor organizers. Such resistance to unbridled white power had been dealt a crippling blow with defeat of the union movement in the mid-twenties. But had the blow been fatal?

From their homes in the uplands of Mānoa Valley, the islands' top business leaders could gaze down upon the Gold Coast of Waikīkī, with its already tested promise, and make plans—once the Depression finally ended—of turning all that sunshine and surf into even more wealth than they already possessed. Then they might look west, toward the horizon beyond downtown, where the festering tenements of Kauluwela and Pālama—Buckle Lane, Blood Alley, Cunha Lane, Tin Can Alley, Hell's Half Acre, and all the rest—were located. That, they now knew, was where the trouble lay.

6 Arrest

It was ten minutes to three on Sunday morning when Detectives Cluney and Black arrived outside 1409-A Cunha Lane, an old plantation worker's cottage in a poor, densely populated, and decaying neighborhood on the fringe of Hell's Half-Acre. Cluney shone a flashlight on the Model A Ford parked alongside the house. As expected, the license plate read 58-895. Like the cottage and the small patch of yard in front, the tan car (Cluney described it as "yellow") was well kept.

At the front door Cluney knocked. Inside, he could hear voices, speaking in Japanese. He knocked again, calling out "Tantei," the Japanese word for detective. The door finally opened. Two young women in nightgowns stood in the doorway, an elderly woman behind them and off to the side, looking frightened. Gesturing toward the side of the house, Cluney said he wanted to see the boy who had been out driving that car.

"It's kind of late," one of the younger women protested. Cluney said he didn't care how late it was, he wanted to see the boy. She hurried into the rear of the house.

A minute or two later a small man appearing to be in his late teens or early twenties, looking groggy and still half asleep, emerged from a back bedroom, wearing a T-shirt and struggling to button up a pair of dressy pinstriped trousers. He asked what was going on.

Cluney first demanded his name. It was Shimotsu—Shimotsu Ida—but everyone called him by his haole name, Horace, or his nickname, "Shorty." Cluney wanted to know if he had been out driving his sister's car earlier in the evening. The young man hesitated, then said no, he had loaned the car to some friends. Who? Cluney asked. What were their names? Again Ida hesitated, then said he didn't know.

The detective didn't have to be a mind reader to know this was a lie. Neither did the young man's older sister, Haruyo, who turned to the policeman and pleaded with him, saying that their father was dead and Horace was the only male in the family. It would break their mother's heart if he was in serious trouble. That was no concern of Cluney's. He was taking her brother in for questioning. But he did agree to allow the young woman and her sister to follow behind in her car as they drove to the station.

While waiting for the girls to dress, Cluney used the Idas' telephone to call downtown and tell headquarters that he and Detective Black were bringing in the driver of the car that was involved in the assaults that had occurred that evening. When Ida's sisters at last were ready to leave, Horace put a lightweight suede jacket on over his T-shirt and followed the policemen out to their car.

As Cluney and Black's police car, followed by Haruyo and Chiyono Ida in the Model A, made its way back to headquarters, a much larger procession to the same destination was beginning to form across town. Thalia had been at the emergency room for almost half an hour, first examined by a nurse, Agnes Fawcett, then by the physician on duty, Dr. David Liu, while Tommie and the friends and neighbors milled around outside with the police.

Two radio cruisers were parked in the street, alongside the porch on which Thalia's friends were gathered and chatting, next to the open jalousie windows of the examining room where she had been taken. The cars had receivers but no transmitters, so any messages sent from headquarters had to be returned by telephone or from a police call box. But the absence of immediate replies did not prevent an excited Officer Cecil Rickard from broadcasting a running commentary—at least three messages in those thirty minutes—on the progress of Detectives Cluney and Black in tracking the car with "license number 58-895" to its owner's home on Cunha Lane.

As Rickard later recalled verbatim on the witness stand, his radio message identified the men in the car with that license plate as responsible for an "assault on a young woman on the corner of King and Liliha Streets," meaning Agnes Peeples. But anyone not fully briefed on the night's events—and that included most of those gathered outside the hospital—had every reason to think the victim referred to on the police radio was Thalia.

The radio messages blaring from the police cars were easily heard from fifty feet away, with Officer Seymour later adding that "several members of the Massie party" listened to the broadcasts with interest and talked about them at length. One of the Massies' acquaintances who had accompanied them to the hospital, Lieutenant McKechnie, remembered that one of the detectives also told them they had the license plate number of the car Thalia's assailants had driven. Red Rigby's wife, Monte, recalled that Tommie's friend Nelson Pringle and a neighbor, Navy Lieutenant Michael Russillo, joined McKechnie and several detectives in discussing the license number and its importance. Then one of them, she thought it was Pringle, came over and told her and her husband all about it.

Inside, Nurse Fawcett and Dr. Liu were too busy examining Thalia to pay much attention to the chatter outside. Fawcett helped Thalia undress and prepare for the examination, at the same time inquiring as to what had happened. Thalia explained, and the nurse asked if she would be able to describe the men or recognize them, but the answer was still no. Fawcett, who was from Australia and just getting accustomed to Hawai'i's racial complexities herself, then asked Thalia: "Are you sure they were not Filipinos or some other nationality?" As she had with the detectives at her home, Thalia replied: "Oh, no. I know the difference." The men who had raped her were Hawaiian, no question about it, Thalia said—although, Fawcett recalled later, Thalia added that "it was dark" and she wouldn't now be able to identify them.

Fawcett looked Thalia over, making note of the fact that she saw no marks or bruises of any sort except on her face. As for the vaginal area, she said she found no evidence of rape. In fact, she noted, Thalia was "clean as a new pin."

Dr. Liu was more conventionally clinical in his report. After mentioning that Thalia "had an alcoholic breath" and "was under the influence of liquor," his notes said that on her face there was "marked swelling of the upper lip," with her "right cheek markedly swollen, left cheek moderately swollen." Although he did not conduct a careful examination of her entire body, those were the extent of Thalia's injuries as far as he could detect. There was no apparent trauma anywhere below her waist. He found no semen in her vagina, but she told him she had douched before coming down to the hospital. As for genital injury: "Vaginal examination of hymen was old, lacerated at 5 and 7 o'clock position. No other abrasions or contusions noticeable."

When later asked if it was possible for there to be no vaginal injury at all if she had been "dragged into a car," forced into "the brush," and raped six or seven times, as Thalia said had happened, Liu acknowledged that the question had troubled him. He asked a senior physician for his opinion and was told that it was indeed possible. She was, after all, "a married woman [and] the vagina opened quite a bit."

Before returning her to the police, Liu asked Thalia if she had seen the car's license plate or would be able to recognize her assailants if she saw them again. As with the police interrogators and Nurse Fawcett earlier, she said no to both questions: "It was too dark," she replied. During his discussion with her, Liu recalled, she broke into tears from time to time. Finally, the examination complete, he told her she was free to go, and despite the alcohol and the ordeal she had been through, Thalia "got right up and walked away," something that surprised the doctor.

Outside, the confusion over Jerry Branson's role in the unfolding affair at last was being cleared up. Tommie talked to Detective Jardine and explained that Jerry had been with him all night until Tommie called home from the Rigbys'. When Thalia, on the phone, told Tommie what had happened, he left Branson and rushed home. Obviously, it was impossible for Branson to have had anything to do with the assault on Thalia. Jardine seemed satisfied, but he wanted Jerry and the others who were on hand to accompany him to police headquarters anyway. So when Thalia appeared in the hospital doorway, they all began piling back into their cars.

Down at the station house, only a half dozen blocks away, Captain John McIntosh, the head of Honolulu's detective bureau, was waiting for them.

John Nelson McIntosh had been born nearly fifty years earlier in the village of Trim, county Meath, to the northwest of Dublin in Ireland. Like many poor and adventurous young men then living in one corner or another of the British Empire during that great imperial age, he responded to the call of duty as soon as he was old enough to carry a gun. In early 1901 he arrived in South Africa as part of Her Majesty's colonial forces—the newly formed South African Constabulary. The Boer War appeared to be ending, with the British on the threshold of victory over Dutch settlers of the Transvaal and Orange Free State, and the Home Office had decided it needed a constabulary to maintain postwar order among the defeated Boers.

Unlike other Irish volunteers who had gone to South Africa to fight the British as part of Ireland's overall anti-British and anticolonial struggle, McIntosh took the side of the English. But he and his fellow policemen got a good deal more than they bargained for. Predictions of the Boer surrender turned out to be premature, and they found themselves impressed into fighting a scorched-earth guerrilla conflict for the ensuing year. During that time they also helped supervise the incarceration of 136,000 Boer internees in concentration camps—a fifth of whom, including more than 22,000 children, died from disease and starvation. An even larger number of Zulu and Xhosa natives died in similar, but segregated and more harshly run, British prison camps.

The war finally ended in 1902. McIntosh stayed on as a member of the constabulary, which then acted partly as a police force and partly as an occupying army, overseeing the Chinese laborers who joined the Boers, Africans, Indians, and "coloreds" chafing under the British regime. The response of the

British to the hatred they encountered everywhere was to employ what even members of Parliament routinely decried as "methods of barbarism" in maintaining the peace.

With the dissolving of Her Majesty's South African Constabulary in 1907, young John McIntosh found himself out of a job. But he had a solid and hard-earned education in the brutal ways of colonial peacekeeping. So he moved to New Zealand and joined that country's national police force, the successor to the Armed Constabulary that had fought a series of bloody wars of colonial conquest against that country's Māori natives.

McIntosh served with New Zealand's police bureau in various capacities, from mounted policeman to head of a police district, for thirteen years. With the end of the First World War, and a slashing of police budgets in New Zealand, McIntosh decided to return to South Africa and continue his police career. But he had a brother living in Hawai'i and decided to pay him a visit first. It was 1921. Following in the footsteps of many visitors both before and since, McIntosh was seduced by the islands and decided to stay. But in this new setting, what kind of work might a colonial policeman with twenty years' experience in subduing and controlling Boer, African, Chinese, Indian, and Māori subjects find suitable for his talents and training? The answer soon became obvious. He hired on as a plantation field overseer, a luna, at 'Ewa Plantation, near Pearl Harbor, on O'ahu.

It was a propitious moment for a man of McIntosh's background to find such work. A year earlier 'Ewa Plantation was one of six plantations on the island simultaneously shut down by a strike of Filipino and Japanese field laborers. At the time the average wage for male workers was seventy-seven cents per ten-hour day, fifty-eight cents for women—a wage that had not risen since before World War I.

The haole business community saw the 1920 strike as itself a war of sorts—a race war, a war to test the mettle of civilized white society. As the *Honolulu Star-Bulletin* editorialized, the question posed by the work stoppage was simple: "Is control of the industrialism of Hawai'i to remain in the hands of Anglo-Saxons or is it to pass into those of alien Japanese agitators? . . . The American citizen who advocates anything less than resistance to the bitter end against [the] arrogant ambition of the Japanese agitators is a traitor to his own people."

Describing the strike as "anti-American," the president of the Hawaiian Sugar Planters' Association announced that the owners would crush it, "no matter what the cost or how long it takes." A decade earlier the celebrated

American journalist Ray Stannard Baker had visited the islands and written an extraordinary series of articles on what he had seen there for the *American Magazine*. He observed, "The more the planters' interests can keep the workers struggling and fighting among themselves for places to work, the larger the profits of the business." Faced with a racial coalition of Filipinos and Japanese, the planters resorted with a vengeance to what Baker described as "the wisdom of Napoleon's motto: 'Divide and you dominate.'"

The plantations brought in thousands of Portuguese, Hawaiian, Chinese, and Korean strikebreakers, paying the Hawaiians and Portuguese four dollars a day and the Chinese and Koreans three dollars. That was four to five times what they had been paying the striking Filipinos and Japanese. The Koreans in particular possessed a deep historical enmity for all things Japanese, so it was not difficult for the sugar planters to coax them into signing an edict justifying their strikebreaking. It read in part: "We place ourselves irrevocably against the Japanese and the present strike. . . . we are opposed to the Japanese in everything."

The planter oligarchy then bribed the Filipino union leader into pulling his laborers off the picket lines. In doing so he publicly proclaimed that he now realized the strike was nothing more than a Japanese plot "to cripple the industries of the Territory of Hawaii in the hope that they may be taken over by an unscrupulous alien race."

The plantations lost nearly $12 million in breaking the 1920 strike, but in the end they regarded the lost profits as a necessary and successful investment. Four years earlier, on another island, plantation managers had agreed to give workers small cash bonuses at the end of the year. Some of the recipients, so impoverished that they had never before seen a dollar bill, threw the paper money away in disgust or thought it was scrip for exchange at the plantation store. Others, though, pocketed the bonuses and immediately clambered aboard ships bound for Honolulu or California. It took months for the plantations to rebuild their workforce, but they had learned their lesson: never allow workers any opportunity to accumulate even small amounts of cash. The laborers' perpetual impoverishment was the single thing that prevented them from escaping the cruelties of plantation life.

In a second strike, in 1924, on the island of Kaua'i, Filipino workers armed themselves with pistols and cane knives against threatened violence. The sugar planters called out police and National Guardsmen, who set up rifle squads and machine guns on the banks of a river above the strikers' encampment. Soon sixteen strikers and four policemen lay dead and the strike was broken. After this, immigrant plantation workers were given literacy tests. Those who could read and write were regarded as potential trouble-makers and sent home. There would be no further organized opposition to the plantation ruling class for more than a decade.

John McIntosh's time as a plantation luna was sandwiched in between the strikes of 1920 and 1924, a time of particular bitterness, rancor, and humiliation for the field workers. After two years he let it be known among people of consequence that he had twenty years of work experience on the colonial police forces of South Africa and New Zealand. Honolulu's sheriff, Charles Rose, promptly came calling.

Ascending through the police ranks in record time, within a few years McIntosh was promoted to captain and made head of the detective bureau, replacing a Hawaiian named David Haʻo, who was forced out to make room for him. This failed to sit well with most of the other detectives, who had more seniority and, like Haʻo, were not white. They also resented the fact that McIntosh insisted on looking over their shoulders as cases progressed, constantly intervening as an arrest or an interrogation was imminent and taking it over for himself or one of his more favored, and almost invariably haole, assistants. Other, smaller things grated on them as well, such as his refusal to pronounce Hawaiian names—their names—correctly even after a decade of living in the islands.

McIntosh ignored criticism of his harsh treatment of nonwhite subordinates and criminal suspects, and of his grandstanding and open contempt for Hawaiians. On the contrary, he happily admitted to anyone who cared to know that he had not attained his position by the conventional route; rather, as he told one interviewer, "I was put there by the business interests and the politicians." And put there to control a force largely staffed by what he liked to call a bunch of "useless dumbbells."

One of those people so contemptuously dismissed by McIntosh was Detective George Nakea, a seven-year veteran of the police department, a Hawaiian, and—besides Detective Jardine—the ranking officer among those to whom Thalia Massie, at her home in Mānoa, had repeatedly told the story of being beaten and raped by a gang of vicious natives. But Nakea was far from a useless dumbbell. He harbored a disdain for McIntosh, openly dismissing him as a drunk and an incompetent, that more than matched McIntosh's disparagement of him.

■ ■ ■

The police cruiser driven by Detective John Cluney, and carrying his partner Thurman Black and the assault suspect Horace Ida, pulled up outside police headquarters at 3:05 a.m. Haruyo and Chiyono Ida followed behind them in the tan Model A. The Massie party already was on its way to the same station house from the hospital emergency room. Cluney told Ida's sisters to park their car and wait downstairs. Then he and Black led Ida upstairs to the detectives' assembly room. Cluney expected McIntosh to be waiting for them there, but he was nowhere to be found. Only the radio officer, Cecil Rickard, was on hand to greet them. Cluney told Black and Rickard to keep an eye on things while he went to locate the captain.

Ida, waiting silently to see what would happen next, was the only person in the room who did not know he was there as a suspect in two assaults. Detectives Cluney and Black had told him nothing, intending to let Captain McIntosh systematically link the crimes and make the accusation during his interrogation. But Rickard, not apprised of this strategy, could not contain himself. While Cluney was going from office to office in search of McIntosh, Rickard asked Ida (as Rickard later recalled) "if he had assaulted that white woman." Ida was stunned and replied that he and his friends had been out driving around earlier in the evening, but had not had anything to do with a white woman. When Rickard pressed him, Ida admitted that he and his friends were involved in a near accident with the occupants of another car, and that one of his companions "had struck this Hawaiian woman," but he insisted that he knew nothing about any white woman.

A few minutes later Cluney returned and led Ida into McIntosh's office. The chief of detectives joined them and began his questioning. He planned to start slowly, trying to get Horace to give him the names of the other men who were with him that night, then take him through the lesser of the two assaults, the one involving Agnes Peeples, and finally to the attack on Thalia Massie. But the interview was hardly under way when it was interrupted by a burst of loud, boisterous conversation and laughter from the first floor. The Massie party had arrived at headquarters. Surprised at the navy officers' high-spirited behavior, in light of the situation, the policemen were annoyed to find themselves the targets of the navy officers' jokes. To avoid a confrontation, they decided to retire to another part of the station house.

McIntosh said he would talk to Thalia first, then get back to Ida, who was led away as Thalia was being escorted up to McIntosh's office. While the Massies' friends and neighbors remained downstairs, the police officers and detectives who had accompanied the Massies to the hospital, as well as others returning from their shifts, were gathering in the dayroom on the second floor. McIntosh called two of them aside, Claude Benton and Percy Bond, and directed them to take a drive along Ala Moana Road to the place where it appeared from her earlier statements that Thalia had been assaulted, and to look for any evidence of a crime. He then told Detectives Jardine and Nakea to drive back to the Massies' house with Tommie and retrieve the dress and other clothing Thalia had been wearing that night. He wanted each garment professionally examined for evidence.

As with the brief conversation between Rickard and Ida, no third party witnessed the questioning of Thalia by Captain McIntosh. It was just the two of them, with the door to his office closed. According to McIntosh's account, he and Thalia had "a conversation for ten or fifteen minutes" before he decided to take a formal statement from her. He started things off by simply asking her to recount what had happened that night. At first she responded almost precisely as she had to the questions of the various detectives at her home two hours earlier, and to the inquiries of the nurse and the doctor at the hospital to which she had been taken.

McIntosh scribbled notes, putting down the time the interview began as 3:30 a.m. He later compiled those jottings into a formal report. According to his notes, Thalia told him she had left the party at the Ala Wai Inn sometime between 12:30 and 1:00 a.m. In his subsequent report, her time of departure was changed to "around midnight." From the inn, she said, she had walked along Kalākaua Avenue, then down John Ena Road, where "a car drove up behind me and stopped":

> Two men got off the car and grabbed me and dragged me into their car. One of them placed his hand over my mouth. When they got me into the back seat of the car they held me down between them. They were Hawaiians. I begged and pleaded with them to let me go. I struggled to get off the car and away from them and they kept punching me on the face. I offered them money if they would take me back to the Ala Wai Inn. They asked me where the money was. I told them it was in my pocketbook. They grabbed my pocketbook and found I had no money in it. They were driving along the Ala Moana Road all this time heading towards town. I really don't know how far they drove me—maybe two or three blocks. They drove the car into the undergrowth on the right hand side of the road, dragged me out and away from the car into the bushes and assaulted me. I was assaulted six or seven times.

McIntosh asked: "You mean they raped you?" Thalia replied: "Yes." He pressed her on the matter of her assailants' ethnicity and she said again that they were Hawaiian. So far this was nothing different from what she had told anyone else. But then, McIntosh claimed, he asked her: "What was the license plate number, do you know?" And Thalia—who for the past two hours had told everyone else who had asked her the same question that she could not even see the license plate because of the extreme darkness—calmly said: "I think it was 58-805. I would not swear to that being correct. I just caught a fleeting glimpse of it as they drove away."

It was, of course, a fleeting glimpse that was only a single digit different from the number—58-895—that had been broadcast repeatedly to the police cars that had carried Thalia from her home to the hospital and then to police headquarters. Only one number short of identical to the number communicated to everyone gathered around the police radio cars parked outside her examining room at the hospital emergency ward. And only one numeral different from the one McIntosh well knew was the license plate number on the car that Horace Ida had been driving that night.

At this point McIntosh got up, opened the door to his office, and called for Detective Cluney. When Cluney entered, McIntosh asked him to show him, but not say aloud, the license plate number of Horace Ida's sister's car, the car that had been involved in the earlier assault that evening on Agnes Peeples. Cluney had written the number down before driving out to the Ida house, and he proceeded to dig a crumpled piece of paper out of his pocket. He handed it to the captain, who took it and then, with a smile, pointed to a number he had written on the blotter on his desk, the number he later said Thalia had given him. Except for one digit the two numbers were identical. McIntosh told Cluney to bring Ida into his office.

As soon as Horace Ida walked into John McIntosh's office for the second time that evening, McIntosh wheeled on him. Pointing at Thalia's bruised and swollen face, he said, "Now look at your beautiful work!" Thalia, still without her glasses, and having just told McIntosh, as she had everyone else, that she was certain her assailants were Hawaiian, gazed at the diminutive Japanese man they had brought before her. Officer Cluney later reported that "she nodded her head once or twice, and looked at Captain McIntosh as if to imply that this was one of the men who had assaulted her." Then she asked Ida: "Where are the other boys?"

Ida turned to the two policemen pleadingly. "I didn't do it—I didn't see this woman," he said, vigorously shaking his head. "I didn't do nothing to her."

Thalia kept her eyes fixed on the young Japanese man, looking him up and down. She asked him a few more questions, including whether he knew someone named "Bull." Ida replied in the negative, continuing to glance from one police official to the other as if seeking help.

McIntosh dismissed Ida, telling Cluney to hold him on suspicion of kidnapping, assault, and rape. At this point Officer Benton arrived at the office, returning from his inspection of the purported rape scene. Although it was still dark outside, he and Officer Bond had used flashlights to search the area Thalia described as the site of her assault. He had with him a box containing a pocketbook mirror, a handkerchief, an empty bottle smelling of whiskey, two cigarette packages, and some matches. Thalia identified the mirror and one of the packs of cigarettes as hers. Benton then went into the detectives' room and wrote up a report on what he and Officer Bond had found at the rape scene.

It was now around 4:00 a.m., and McIntosh had been on duty all day and much of the night. He called for a police cruiser to take Thalia and Tommie home, after assuring Tommie that they had one suspect under arrest and expected to pick up the others before long. He ordered another car to drive Horace Ida's sisters back to their house, after he had their car impounded. And then he sat down to think through what he should do next.

There already was little doubt in his mind, or in that of anyone else who was aware of Thalia's story, that this promised to be Hawai'i's most explosive criminal case ever—the first one in history involving the rape, by Hawaiians, of a white woman, and a navy officer's wife at that. As Honolulu's chief of detectives, McIntosh had to be sure his investigation reached the quick conclusion that the islands' leaders, those who had placed him in this position of responsibility, would expect and require.

Officer Benton finished typing up his report, dutifully listing all the items he and his partner, Bond, had found at the scene. No mention was made in the report of any tire tracks.

Rush to Judgment

Ateam of detectives continued to grill Horace Ida. Adamant that he knew nothing about an assault on a white woman, he resisted giving up the names of the men who had been with him on Saturday night. Detective Jardine recalled Ida's stubbornness, attributing it to a delinquent's code of honor acquired in the tough neighborhood in which Ida had grown up. But "when police pressure is strong enough," Jardine said, anyone will talk. He added, without elaboration: "Believe me it was getting strong that night."

During the course of his stonewalling—which he later admitted was an attempt to protect his friends from possible assault charges in the Peebles incident—Ida found himself caught in several small lies, including one that would come back to haunt him. After several hours of harsh interrogation he finally broke, telling police the names of his companions. They then took him to a cell, where he fell asleep on an unpadded bench, using his rolled-up suede jacket as a pillow. Horace had been living in Los Angeles until recently, and that's where he had bought the jacket.

Luciano Machado, a thirty-two-year-old seven-year veteran of the police force, was the obvious detective to send out and apprehend the men Ida had named. Like them, Machado—who was Hawaiian, Portuguese, and Spanish—had grown up in the area around Pālama and 'A'ala, and he was a familiar face to most everyone there. Known by his nickname, "Big," Machado also played guitar in a Hawaiian band and was married to one of the most popular singers in the islands, a woman who one day would become a legend in Hawaiian music circles, Lena Machado.

The people of the neighborhood trusted Luciano. He was also regarded by almost everyone on the force as an excellent investigator. The sheriff, who was not shy about rendering harsh judgments, concurred, calling Machado "one of the best detectives we've got." Machado did not return the compliment. He was one of many on the force with little regard for his bosses, criticizing their favoritism and the way they enforced the law. Time and again he and other officers complained that they had arrested people who turned out to have friends in high places, only to find the charges dropped without investigation. Machado also regarded McIntosh as a racist, and he freely complained about the captain's crudely bigoted language and behavior.

Because he knew what Machado thought of him, McIntosh hesitated to give the detective the assignment. But no one else was as likely to return so quickly and successfully with the men in tow. Not only was Machado an experienced and competent detective, familiar with the part of town where the suspects lived, but he was Hawaiian. If others found fault with Hawaiians as police officers because of their open, generous, and easygoing manner, those same characteristics were associated with Hawaiian lawbreakers. Statistics revealed that Hawaiians engaged in little serious criminal activity other than bootlegging or gambling and the minor fistfights that from time to time followed a night of drinking. But on the rare occasions when Hawaiians did commit serious crimes they were well known for confessing their guilt to friends, family, and the authorities with almost no encouragement or prodding.

This was especially true when the person doing the interrogating was another Hawaiian. Someone like Big Machado. And when Machado heard the names of the other suspects that Ida had provided, he knew exactly where to find them.

Honolulu was a sports-obsessed city in the early Depression years. To the outside world the islands were best known for producing Olympic-medal swimmers such as Duke Kahanamoku and Buster Crabbe. But among locals it was boxing and barefoot football that filled the arenas and the athletic fields with cheering fans. Until 1929 boxing had been illegal, though matches held in supposedly secret locations drew hundreds of spectators, and open gambling on a fight's outcome was a part of the entertainment. With legalization, the sport drew even larger crowds every week to arenas throughout Honolulu and on the military bases. Barefoot football (which derived its name and its most elementary rule from the fact that many of the poorest island residents did not own shoes, thus creating an athletic tradition out of necessity) was a sport with dozens of teams organized into regional leagues. Although the games originally sprang up spontaneously among teenagers and young men, after a time the Honolulu Recreation Commission stepped in to sponsor the leagues, reasoning that they were a way to keep unemployed youths busy and out of trouble.

Now into their ninth season, the games attracted enormous crowds. Albert Chee, a local Chinese sportswriter, obviously proud of his command of American sports-page hyperbole, explained why:

For pure and unadulterated action these shoeless wonders know no equal. Besides spills, thrills, and chills, these gladiators of the white chalked arena are capable of displaying superb skill in the art of passing, punting and intricate plays, not to mention the tackling, which is fierce, to put it mildly. As someone has previously remarked, they all but bite one another's ears off.

League play had just opened the previous week, and two of the four names on the list Horace Ida had given the police as his Saturday night companions, Joe Kahahawai and Ben Ahakuelo, were good football players. Both were Hawaiians who lived in or near Hell's Half Acre. Both were also boxers, although Ahakuelo was far more accomplished and better known in both sports. During football season his name appeared in newspaper sports pages every week, as the leading runner for a team that always contended for the league championship. "Headed by 'Flash' Ahakuelo, the sensational performer of last year," read a story in that week's *Honolulu Advertiser,* "the Kakaako Wildcats are ruled a slight pre-season favorite" in the senior conference.

It was late morning on a typically sunny September day, the cooling trade winds having returned during the night, when Detective Machado pulled up in a police car across from the Kauluwela School athletic field and went looking for the rape suspects. In addition to Ahakuelo and Kahahawai, Horace Ida had named two others—Henry Chang, who was Hawaiian-Chinese, and David Takai, Japanese—as the men he had been out with the previous night. Neither Chang nor Takai were athletes, but Machado was certain that on a Sunday morning at this time of year they would be out watching their friends play football. It was what Machado himself would have done that day if the choice had been his.

No doubt, Tommie Massie also would have preferred to be out in the sunshine enjoying a football game. When the Massies' maid, Beatrice, showed up for work that morning she found the house's shades drawn, Thalia shut up in the bedroom, and Tommie visibly hungover and irascible. Her presence annoyed him and he sent her home early. At the police station the night before, Tommie had tried telephoning his squadron's commanding officer, Captain Ward Wortman, to tell him what had happened and to ask for his help. It was three o'clock in the morning when he called, and Tommie was obviously drunk. Wortman hung up on him. Then Tommie tried calling the skipper of his submarine, Leo Pace. Pace's wife, Peggy, answered the phone and told Tommie to try again the next day.

So he did. When he finally reached Pace at midmorning and soberly informed him that Thalia had been the victim of a gang rape by a carload of Hawaiians, Pace came right over, with Peggy by his side. Tommie also called Lieutenant Commander John Porter, the navy physician who had treated Thalia during her pregnancy the past summer and who was the Massies' regular doctor. Porter pulled up in his car shortly after the Paces' arrival. Leaving Thalia in the care of Dr. Porter and Peggy Pace, Tommie and Leo drove out to Pearl Harbor to speak with their commanding officer.

Ward Wortman was a hard-drinking, hard-charging, chain-smoking officer with decades of experience dealing with sailors in the toughest ports of call in the world. An 1899 graduate of the U.S. Naval Academy, and captain of the Navy football team that year (he scored their only touchdown in a season-ending loss to Army), Wortman had spent most of his life in the military. Though relaxed and easygoing with military personnel, he had an open and visceral contempt for most civilians, and a particular animosity for those who weren't white.

When Tommie and Leo told him what had happened to Thalia, Wortman exploded in outrage. He also immediately realized that the men under his command would share his reaction once they heard what had happened—which they soon would, if they hadn't already. And despite his anger, he knew that his first responsibility was to the squadron. He picked up the phone and called the submarine base duty officer: all leaves and liberty were to be canceled, by his order, effective immediately. Enlisted personnel were confined to the base until further notice. Wortman himself would have been happy to lynch the men who had perpetrated this crime against Massie's "kid bride," as he put it, but he was not about to allow his sailors to run loose in Honolulu in search of the rapists. If nothing else, it appeared to be unnecessary. Tommie told him that the police already had one of the thugs in jail and expected to pick up the others later that day.

After Tommie and Leo left to return to their wives, Wortman went straight to the office of the naval commandant, Admiral Yates Stirling, the top military official in the islands.

On the way home, Tommie decided to take a detour into Honolulu to cable Thalia's parents. They were living apart again, Roly at a club in Manhattan, Grace at a hotel on Long Island, where she was organizing an anti-Prohibition campaign. Tommie sent a message to Grace, telling her that Thalia had been beaten by some local hoodlums and was under medical care, but not telling her about the sexual assaults.

Back in Mānoa, meanwhile, Dr. Porter had examined Thalia and decided that her jaw might be fractured. He thought she should be sent to the hospital to have it looked at, but he was uncertain. Thalia was resting comfortably and did not seem especially bothered by any other injuries. So he arranged for a second opinion. "I had another doctor come down and have a look at Mrs. Massie's jaw to see if my diagnosis was correct," Porter later testified, "and, in his opinion, he didn't think she ought to go to the hospital."

After the other physician left, Dr. Porter decided to trust his own judgment. Although he seriously doubted that Thalia had been raped—a doubt he would express only privately, a long time later—he was genuinely concerned about her facial injury. He made arrangements for her to be admitted to Queen's Hospital, downtown. A gift of the Hawaiian monarchy in 1860, intended to provide free medical care for the poor, by 1931 Queen's had become—as it is today—Honolulu's major medical facility, for those who can afford it. Before heading for the hospital, though, Thalia had to deal once again with the police.

While Detective Machado was busy looking for four young men on a football field in Kauluwela, Captain McIntosh showed up at the Massie house. He arrived in Haruyo Ida's Model A Ford, the car her brother Horace and the other suspects had been in the night before. Driving the car was a patrolman named Henry Sato, who had arranged to have the car jump-started by mechanics at the Universal Motors dealership because no one at the police station could locate the key. McIntosh also had with him a barrette and some green beads that two more officers had found while inspecting the crime scene after dawn. Thalia identified the items as hers.

Then McIntosh asked her to step outside to examine what he called "the suspects' car." It was parked at the curb, and she slowly walked around it, finally nodding her head. Yes, she said; although she couldn't be certain it was the very car in which she had been abducted, "it was a car like that."

Only eight hours earlier, Thalia had repeatedly told a succession of police officers and detectives that the men who had kidnapped and raped her were driving an old car, a Ford or a Dodge, one that was dark colored, maybe black, and had a torn and flapping cloth top. A new, light-colored Model A Ford was now parked in front of her house; an old Ford would have meant a Model T, since that was the sole car Ford had produced until just three years earlier. Between 1908 and 1928 Ford had produced about sixteen million

Model Ts. Almost all of them were black, and none of them looked like the Model T's replacement, the Model A. Everything about the two cars, including their method of operation, was different. Acceleration on the Model T was done by means of a hand throttle on the steering column, and gear shifting (which made a loud and distinctive "tranny whine") was done by foot pedals. In contrast, the Model A used a modern foot accelerator, clutch, and brake, combined with a manual gearshift. From inside or out—even by just listening to them in operation—it was impossible to confuse the two. And Thalia well knew this, since she had driven a Model T on the estate at Bayport and now owned and operated a Model A herself—a Model A, in fact, that looked almost exactly like this one, down to its light tan color and its pristine condition, including a tight cloth top with no sign of rips or tears.

McIntosh accepted and noted Thalia's identification of the car Horace Ida had been driving as similar to the one she had been abducted in the previous night, although he now knew of her earlier conflicting testimony. After having Sato check the inside of the car for any items that may have belonged to her, and finding nothing, the captain thanked Thalia and then directed Sato to drive him back to the station. But along the way he decided to take a detour and look at the crime scene on Ala Moana Road.

No one else was there when McIntosh and Sato arrived at the abandoned animal quarantine station where Thalia said she had been raped, and where her beads and various items from her purse had been found. It had rained that morning and the ground was still damp. At McIntosh's urging Sato drove Haruyo's Model A back and forth across the dirt clearing. By the time they left a few minutes later the car's distinctive tire tracks were imprinted clearly in the mud.

Out in Kauluwela, at the football game, Detective Machado had found all but one of the men he was after. Since Ben Ahakuelo's team wasn't playing that day, he was at a practice at Atkinson Park across town. But Chang, Takai, and Kahahawai were there, and had been for some time. They all were in their early twenties, about ten years younger than Machado, and they had known him for most of their lives. So when he waved to them and hailed for them join him, they had no hesitation in doing so.

David Takai was slim and quiet, Henry Chang more rawboned and outgoing, but Joe Kahahawai was the one who stood out. Taller and more powerfully built than the others—close to six feet tall and about 180 pounds—Kahahawai was classically Hawaiian in both bearing and manner, his striking appearance contrasted by the fact that he was extremely quiet and soft-spoken.

After Joe was born, in a rural part of Maui on Christmas Day in 1909, his parents moved to Honolulu. Before long, they were divorced. Although he was raised by his mother and a stepfather, Joe remained close to his father, a streetcar motorman. Attributing his shyness to his country roots, Ben and Henry and the others he grew up with in Kauluwela frequently kidded him about his *kua'āina*, or countrified, personality. After elementary school, Joe accepted a scholarship to St. Louis High School. Because of the requirement that all St. Louis students wear uniforms, Joe now took a second round of ribbing from his friends: anyone who dressed like that had to be a *māhū*, they said—a homosexual.

Joe's mother, father, and stepfather were devout Catholics and had been delighted when he received the scholarship. But then, as now, St. Louis was a local football power and Joe had been recruited because of his ability to knock people down, not for his academic skills. He played on the line, wore number 38, and thereafter proudly displayed an engraved ring identifying him as a member of the class of 1928. Like everyone else, though, his plans for the future dissolved with the stock market crash of 1929. Joe wound up with odd jobs here and there, including working at the docks. He also boxed for money from time to time, under the name Joe Kalani, at various military barracks and other venues. Throughout most of 1931 he was undefeated, fighting as both a professional and as a member of the 298th Infantry Division of the National Guard.

Although he'd had some minor scrapes with the law, as had most of the boys and men from his neighborhood, Joe was generally known to be easygoing. But he did have a temper, once punching a drunk and breaking his jaw because the man refused to stop kicking a dog. The most recent incident, and the only one for which he had been arrested, involved using his fists during an effort to collect on a debt. Although he had been charged with robbery and assault, a jury had acquitted him of the robbery charge, but only, fumed the prosecutor, because one influential juror—"a loud and boisterous Portuguese," the prosecutor said—was also a St. Louis High School alumnus who admired Joe as a football hero. On the assault charge he received a thirty-day suspended sentence. As a member of the National Guard, Joe had a reputation for staying in the barracks at night, studying, and keeping his gear cleaned and in shape while others were at the movies or partying. Of all his friends, he was the least interested in women.

Simply because he was big and dark and quiet, his friends said, there were those who thought Joe was stupid. They were wrong. But another common suspicion about him was correct: Joe had little regard for haoles, especially those in the military, ever since one of them had murdered a close family friend named William Kama three years earlier. Kama, a police officer and a Hawaiian, had been called out to break up a fight between a few local men and some soldiers who were looking for women in the wrong part of town—Hell's Half Acre. When Kama and his patrol partner, a Hawaiian named Sam Kunane, approached the melee, one of the soldiers pulled out a pistol and shot Kama in the head, killing him instantly. He then turned the gun on Kunane, shooting him in the chest and critically wounding him. Both officers had been operating undercover and were dressed in civilian clothes, but no one denied that they had held up their badges as they approached and identified themselves as police officers.

After demanding jurisdiction, as was routine in such cases, the army court-martialed the admitted killer, reduced the charge to manslaughter, and found him guilty after deliberating for barely an hour. The soldier had been on leave from a transport ship heading for the Philippines at the time of the shootings, and his defense amounted to a plea of self-defense. When he shot the two men he had not believed they were officers, he said, because he had never before heard of such a thing as a "colored policeman." As one of his attorneys explained, this was a case of a young man "led into a hell hole of iniquity," who did nothing more than shoot "two black men" as they approached him in what he regarded as a threatening manner. He was shipped out of the islands to be imprisoned on the mainland, and—rumor had it—eventually had his sentence reduced. To Joe and his family, nothing better illustrated the deep-seated contempt that haoles had for Hawaiians. Even their policemen's lives were worth next to nothing.

Machado informed the three men that he had to take them in for questioning about the assault on Mrs. Peeples the previous evening. Sheepishly, Joe admitted that he was the one Machado was looking for. He had been drinking and lost his head when the large Hawaiian woman, who also had obviously been drinking, shoved him in anger and then scratched his neck after Joe shoved back and hit her. Takai and Chang had nothing to do with it, he said. They had dropped Takai off before it happened, and Chang had been seated in the back of the car and never even got out. As they climbed into the police cruiser the three of them joked about the incident, obviously not taking it very seriously.

And what about the haole woman? Machado asked the question casually as he drove them toward police headquarters. At that, they laughed even louder, apparently thinking he was joking. What haole woman? He wasn't joking, he said, he was very serious—and he pressed them on the subject. They were adamant. They knew nothing about a white woman. Finally, as they pulled up in front of the station house, Machado turned to each of them and said it would be a lot easier if they just told him the truth now—to "give him a break," he said, and themselves as well. They insisted that they didn't know what he was talking about. But they were no longer laughing.

Inside police headquarters Machado and the three men were met by Captain McIntosh, who was backed up by a small phalanx of officials, including Navy Lieutenant Commander Richard Bates, who was head of the shore patrol, two more navy men, and two detectives. McIntosh wanted to interrogate the suspects, but he thought Thalia should identify them first. He directed the two detectives—Arthur Stagbar and Thomas Finnegan—to get a police wagon and take Chang, Takai, and Kahahawai, along with Horace Ida, to the Massie home immediately. The three naval officers accompanied them in a separate car.

One of the complaints frequently lodged against McIntosh by the Hawaiian and other non-haole detectives under his command was that in high-profile or other important cases, he often removed nonwhite detectives from an investigation they had begun and replaced them with hand-picked haoles. What was happening now conformed to that pattern. Other than John Jardine, none of the detectives who had worked the case the previous night—almost all of them non-haoles—would play a further leading role in the investigation. Nor would any other nonwhites, on a force that was overwhelmingly Hawaiian in ancestry. Instead, Thomas Finnegan (like McIntosh, born in Ireland and relocated to Hawai'i a decade earlier) and Arthur Stagbar (a German American from Oshkosh, Wisconsin) had been assigned the task of parading the suspects before the victim.

In Mānoa, Thalia was getting dressed to go to the hospital when the police and shore patrol cars pulled up outside her house. Detective Finnegan and Commander Bates went inside to prepare her for the procedure they had planned. First, as Finnegan recalled, he told Thalia that they "had some suspects in regard to her case"—"some men to be identified as her assailants," he later rephrased it—"and wanted her to look them over and see if she could identify any of them." He also asked her "to have a talk with them, as she had stated she could identify them by their voices." But he cautioned her not to make comments about any of them until after he had led them away.

They settled Thalia into a chair in the living room, glasses in her lap, and drew all the curtains to simulate the darkness of the previous night. Stagbar led Joe Kahahawai, Henry Chang, David Takai, and Horace Ida into the room, in that order. Thalia, sitting "six or seven feet" away from them, began her questioning with Kahahawai, asking him if he was Hawaiian, where he had been the preceding night, and whether his nickname was "Bull." He replied matter-of-factly, answering yes regarding his ancestry, no to the inquiry regarding a nickname, and generally displaying "no perceptible reaction and no hesitation in answering her questions," Finnegan would later testify. The others responded to Thalia's questions in the same manner—Chang ignoring his part-Chinese ancestry and identifying himself as Hawaiian, Takai and Ida as Japanese, and all of them saying they had attended a dance at Waikiki Park on Saturday night. Finally, Thalia stood up, put on her glasses, and looked the men over more closely. Then she indicated to Finnegan that she was finished, and he had Detective Stagbar take the men back outside.

Having told the police and hospital staff earlier that all her attackers were Hawaiians, Thalia identified the first two men questioned, Joe Kahahawai and Henry Chang—the two who, in response to her question, had said they were Hawaiian—as among the men who had beaten and raped her. "Positive and without a doubt," recalled Finnegan. Horace Ida had replied to her question about nationality by saying that he was Japanese. But Thalia had seen Ida up close in Captain McIntosh's office the previous night, dressed in the same clothes, including his distinctive leather jacket, and at the time McIntosh had identified him as a suspect. On Ida, Thalia now wavered, saying that she thought he was one of the men who attacked her, but wasn't certain. As for Takai, whom she had never seen before, who said he was Japanese, and who didn't look remotely Hawaiian, Thalia said he definitely was not one of her assailants.

Detective Finnegan had come on duty only a few hours earlier and hadn't been told that Thalia had previously claimed that all her attackers were Hawaiians. Consequently, he was puzzled by the disparities in her identifications, since Kahahawai, Chang, Takai, and Ida—while strongly denying that they knew anything about an assault on a white woman—all admitted they had been together for the entirety of the previous night. How could Thalia's identification of them have varied so much? It seemed obvious that if they had been together the whole night, either all of them had participated in the rape or none of them had. Since she "gave no particular reason" for the evidently clear distinctions that she found among the four men, Finnegan said, he was tempted to ask her for details—apparently not considering the possibility that Thalia thought she was participating in a conventional police lineup, with actual suspects mixed in with nonsuspects. But "owing to her condition," Finnegan said, he and the others decided against questioning her any further.

One thing neither Finnegan nor anyone else commented on, at least for the record, was the extraordinary equanimity that Thalia had just displayed. Calmly questioning the suspects who had been brought before her, even stepping forward to inspect them at close range, she showed no emotion at all in identifying at least two of them as the men who had kidnapped, beaten, and repeatedly raped her less than twelve hours earlier.

It was late Sunday afternoon. Finnegan and Stagbar returned with the four suspects to police headquarters while the Massies headed to Queen's Hospital. McIntosh had the men assigned to separate cells where they couldn't communicate with one another. Now all that was left was the arrest of the fifth suspect, Ben Ahakuelo.

Back at Pearl Harbor, throughout the ranks, the troops were in an uproar. It hadn't taken long, once they discovered they had been confined to the base, for the sailors to learn why. The wife of one of their own officers had been sexually assaulted by a carload of natives. From there the details were imagined, and the more horrific the fantasies, the greater likelihood they had of being believed. More than three decades later one of those sailors—one who would become deeply involved in the violence to come—remembered what was said to have happened to young Thalia Massie as though it had been just yesterday:

> Well, they violated her in every respect and there are only three orifices on the human body. And they kicked her and broke her pelvis and they bit the nipple practically off one of her breasts. . . . They broke her nose. Blackened both of her eyes, of course. On her face was a perfect imprint of a rubber heel, where they stomped on her.

By midafternoon Admiral Yates Stirling had not yet heard the wild rumors that were circulating among his men. But he was as outraged as they were, whatever the details. The commandant of the Fourteenth Naval District had been told by the commander of the Pearl Harbor Submarine Base, Captain Wortman, that Thalia had been beaten and raped "by a gang of half-breed hoodlums on the Ala Moana." Wortman, who had checked with the police, added that they already had suspects locked up in the city jail.

That was enough for Admiral Stirling. He had met the victim, he later re-called, describing her as "demure, attractive, quiet spoken, and sweet . . . the daughter of prominent people in the Eastern States, raised in a cultured American home." And her assailants, he was told, were "dark-skinned crimi-nals." If the police already had them, there could be no doubt as to their guilt. Nor was Stirling's preferred punishment—"to seize the brutes and string them up on trees"—any worse than they deserved.

The admiral did not feel this way about all such cases. During the past five months in Honolulu at least two men under his command had sexually assaulted Hawaiian women. In one instance, in late June, a sailor had broken into the home of a fifty-seven-year-old grandmother and attacked her while she was sleeping. Twelve weeks earlier, after a teenage Hawaiian girl had fought off a rape attempt by a thirty-seven-year-old sailor near Diamond Head, the man choked her, smashed her head against a stone wall, and beat her with the starter crank from an automobile. Both men were apprehended by local police—the second one while fleeing with blood smeared on his face and shirt—but the navy, as always, demanded jurisdiction. There is no record, in either case, of punishment having been meted out.

To Stirling, though, the attack on Thalia Massie was an entirely different matter. If his "first inclination," as he said, was to lynch the monsters who had committed such a ghastly crime, that reaction would have come as no surprise to those who knew him. On one of his earlier duty assignments, in the Philippines, that is what he certainly would have ordered done. Stirling loved to boast of the indiscriminate killing and general despoliation he and his troops had carried out there years earlier. It was a scorched-earth cam-paign, killing the people they encountered and then destroying the land and livelihoods of those who happened to survive. Along one stretch of river, he wrote in his memoirs, "we burned the villages; in fact, every house for two miles from either bank was destroyed by us. We killed their livestock: cattle, pigs, chickens, and their valuable work animals, the carabaos. It seemed ruth-less; yet it was after all war, and war is brutal."

Stirling, who had been in Hawai'i for a only a year, looked like a man play-ing the part of an admiral in a Hollywood movie: in his early sixties, tall, ram-rod straight, hair graying at the temples, an aquiline nose, and piercing blue eyes. He acted as though he were performing as well. Believing that Hawai'i's proper role in the scheme of things was to be America's "Gibraltar of the Pa-cific," Stirling was publicly dismissive of the idea of civilian rule in the islands. "Self-government in Hawaii is a menace to the nation's naval security in the Pacific Ocean," he asserted, "and the sooner curtailed the better for the nation." There was no question in his mind that the "polyglot population in the Islands" should be held under the strict rule of a commission government—which, in the present situation, meant that he would have been the autocrat in charge. As for the unfortunate "constitutional law which gives the right to become citizens to all who by accident of birth in the Islands can call themselves Americans," it was nothing but a "dangerous" ideology propounded by "enthusiastic priests of the melting pot cult."

For the sake of preserving "the prestige of the whites" in the islands, Stirling said, the official response to this current outrage against a young white woman had to be "quick action . . . and adequate punishment." The maximum penalty for rape at the time was life imprisonment at hard labor. He ordered a staff car to pick him up and take him directly to the governor's mansion, 'Iolani Palace, the former home of Queen Lili'uokalani.

The governor was Lawrence Judd, a descendant of missionaries who had arrived from upstate New York a hundred years earlier. In the mid-nineteenth century Judd's grandfather made political history in the islands by engineering a political scheme known as the *Māhele* (meaning "to divide, to cut into parts"), which enabled white settlers to acquire huge tracts of land for sugar plantations and, in the process, make tens of thousands of Hawaiians homeless and landless. After that, like most Hawai'i missionary families turned wealthy business owners, the Judds sent their sons to Yale. Lawrence's father had been in the class of 1862 and his four brothers were also graduates. Lawrence himself attended the University of Pennsylvania for three weeks (during which time he managed to get himself inducted into the Phi Kappa Psi fraternity) before dropping out and taking a series of odd jobs in New York. Soon, though, in the spring of 1909, he was lured back home with the promise of a position with Alexander and Baldwin, one of the largest and most powerful corporations in the islands.

Since the 1880s sugar production in Hawai'i had been growing rapidly, while the number of corporations that controlled the industry was contracting at almost the same rate. Bit by bit small, independent plantations were being taken over by their "factors," the companies that handled their supplies and financing. By 1920 the average plantation was eleven times larger than in 1880, and a handful of sugar factors—known as the Big Five—now controlled 94 percent of production. Alexander and Baldwin was one of the Big Five. So was Theo. H. Davies & Company, to which young Lawrence Judd moved after just a few years, at a higher salary plus a share of the profits. Though not endowed with an excess of intellect, as he happily admitted, Judd did have a talent that proved extremely valuable in the business world. He could take and carry out orders from superiors without batting an eye, thus lending the imprimatur of the Judd family name to endeavors favored by the corporate and political elite. Once that talent became known, Lawrence Judd found himself being guided carefully along a most rewarding career path.

When World War I broke out he enlisted in the army. He was promoted from buck private to second lieutenant in three months—and then, in short order, to captain and then to major. Serving his entire tour of duty as a supply officer in Hawai'i, Judd kept in touch with his civilian employer "by making weekend visits at intervals," he later recalled, and seeing to it that Theo. H. Davies & Company—for which he was still employed as a buyer— got whatever supplies it needed from the military. With the "war business booming, I shared in the rapidly rising profits of the firm," he acknowledged, candidly adding that on reflection he wasn't sure whether this was "strictly ethical."

Ethical or not, it impressed the people who mattered. Soon after being mustered out of the army, Judd was summoned to a meeting of the top business leaders in the islands. He was told that his next task was to run for the territorial senate. Protesting that he knew nothing about politics (in his autobiography Judd is always being surprised by these serendipitous turns of events) he was told to "leave the decision on your qualifications to your elders." So he did, and "by some quirk of circumstance," he would later write, he "led the ticket in the general election."

Judd spent most of the 1920s in the territorial senate. Having done with alacrity whatever he was directed to do by his "elders" during those years, in March of 1929 he was called to the office of the territorial governor in 'Iolani Palace. There the outgoing governor, Wallace Rider Farrington, told him that he had been selected to be the next governor. As always, Judd protested, saying that, at forty-two, he was too young for the job. And, as always, his modesty was ignored. A week later President Hoover made the appointment, sending his name to the U.S. Senate for confirmation. When Judd inquired about going to Washington for the confirmation hearing, he was told "not to bother," he said. There would be no need for a hearing.

Judd's inauguration took place three months later, and the first thing the new governor did was invite the heads of the Big Five and Hawai'i's other large corporations to his office. One by one, he asked them what they wanted. Lower taxes and reduced government expenditures was their unanimous recommendation. If that was what they wanted, that was what they would have. And, as he wrote in his memoirs, not surprisingly "the legislature gave us what Hawaiians call *kōkua,* complete cooperation."

Two years later Governor Judd was in Hilo, on another island altogether, when Admiral Stirling came calling, unannounced, at 'Iolani Palace. When word reached him that the admiral demanded his presence, and the subject to be discussed was the gang rape by Hawaiians of a young navy wife, Judd knew that this time it was he who would be extending the kōkua. In addition to the huge army and navy payroll that was spent in Honolulu each month, and the large number of civilian workers employed by the armed forces, Admiral Stirling soon was to make public the navy's upcoming expenditures on construction at Pearl Harbor. It would total just under two million dollars—around twenty-three million dollars today—a genuine "boon to Oahu," as the *Honolulu Advertiser* would say in a praiseworthy editorial. With sugar, pineapple, and tourism now declining, the navy was becoming the islands' economic lifeline.

Immediately, Judd hurried back to O'ahu. He was met there by Stirling, Commander Bates of the shore patrol, the mayor of Honolulu, and the city's district attorney. Many more such meetings would take place in the days, weeks, and months to come, some of them large and public, others small and secret. But this one set the tone for all that were to follow.

The admiral was used to giving orders. The governor was used to taking them. Before long, a full-bore prosecution of Joe Kahahawai, Ben Ahakuelo, Henry Chang, Horace Ida, and David Takai was under way.

Later, the Honolulu sheriff would say they all had acted "prematurely." And the governor subsequently lamented the fact that "from this beginning were to come blasted careers, ruined lives, tragedy, and death." But for the moment no one was thinking that far ahead.

8 Making News

When he had no other place to stay, Ben Ahakuelo lived with his mother on a crowded little side street named Frog Lane, just across from the Kauluwela School athletic field where Kahahawai, Chang, and Takai had been arrested on Sunday morning. Ben arrived home from football practice that afternoon to discover the tiny cottage surrounded by police officers. They told him they had to bring him in—charges unspecified. He asked for some time to clean up before being taken into custody. He was calm. It wasn't the first time he had been arrested, and the tough-talking twenty-one-year-old, who labored on the docks as a stevedore when work was available, was not about to betray any sense of intimidation. "I was all dirty from playing football and wanted to wash up and change clothes, but they wouldn't let me," he later complained. The police took him down to the station the way they found him. As they led him in, he recalled, "I saw all the brass from the Navy, and I looked at these people and said, 'What the hell is going on?'"

Of the five young men arrested that day for the assault on Thalia Massie, Ben Ahakuelo was by far the most self-confident, pugnacious, and best known. In addition to his accomplishments on the football field, which got his picture in the sports pages frequently at this time of year, his portrait—bare chested, fists cocked—adorned newspaper advertisements as well as posters for upcoming fights that were tacked on storefronts and telephone poles throughout the city. Ben was the best lightweight boxer in the islands, and his face was more familiar to sports fans than those of most politicians. Only five months earlier he had represented Hawai'i at the national AAU championships in New York. And even in the big city he made an impression, though not entirely for his pugilistic prowess. As a reporter for the *New York Herald Tribune* later recalled:

> Ben Ahakuelo is known in sporting circles in New York as a member of the Hawaiian boxing team which competed in Madison Square

Garden in New York last April in the national amateur championship tournament. . . . [He] received the plaudits of boxing fans on the opening night of the tourney, April 27, when, after outpointing Irving Johnson, of the 3rd Corps Area, United States Army, in three rounds, he hung a lei around his opponent's neck. The following night his friendly gesture was forgotten and he was knocked out after forty-six seconds of the second round by Steve Salek, of Boston, who eventually was runner-up for the title.

Unlike other boxers, Ben insisted on performing barefoot, even in Madison Square Garden. It was said that young women found that particularly alluring. And unlike his friends, who also were arrested that day, he didn't plead his innocence. Instead, he ridiculed his accusers. When John McIntosh, the chief of detectives, told him he was being held for the rape of a white woman the previous night, Ahakuelo dismissed the notion as absurd, telling McIntosh that he had been at Waikiki Park, dancing with white women all night, implying that he could have slept with any of them if he had wanted. And when they took him to the hospital for Thalia to identify him, he refused to stand mute for her inspection. After Thalia sat up in bed and asked him if his name was Bennie, as the police had told her, he replied with both arrogance and sarcasm. "No," he said, slowly drawing the words out, "it's Benjamin P. Ahakuelo."

Whether because of confusion, fatigue, or—as she later claimed—an excess of painkilling drugs, Thalia did not identify Ben as one of her attackers that evening. The police brought him back to the jailhouse and McIntosh assigned him a segregated cell anyway. At this point the victim's testimony didn't matter. Like David Takai, whom Thalia also couldn't identify, Ahakuelo admitted that he had been with Chang, Ida, and Kahahawai all night. That was enough for the chief of detectives.

After all, less than three years earlier, when they were eighteen years old, Ahakuelo and Chang had been arrested and charged with an almost identical criminal offense—the gang rape of a teenage girl. And they had done time for it.

The incident happened outside Kauluwela School, near Hell's Half Acre, on the night of March 22, 1929. For some months prior to then, recalled Mrs. Joseph Tyssowski, who ran a Catholic mission house in the area, the unlighted and unguarded school grounds had become a third-rate lovers' lane for neighborhood teenagers. Early in the evening "the girls and boys would tell their parents they were going to church," Mrs. Tyssowski said, "and at 8:30 or 9:00 they would return home." Often, it was later than that. And during the hours that they were away from home, at least some of those pious teenagers never set eyes on the church, but instead spent the time kissing and fondling in remote corners of the athletic field, in the darkness behind the school.

Rose Younge, a Chinese girl, was one of those Mrs. Tyssowski had in mind. With her family she had arrived in Hawai'i a few years earlier. She was seventeen years old in 1929, and seemed to have adjusted well to life in the islands. So well, in fact, that she was out with friends almost every night, supposedly either attending church or going to this or that teenage girls' club meeting, and then getting home late.

On this particular Friday night, having told her mother that she was going to a club function, Rose met up with sixteen-year-old Harry Baty, and they retired to a quiet spot behind the school. While Rose and Harry (and several other couples) were making love in the shadows, a dozen or so teenage boys were whiling away the evening on the school steps, playing music and, as local slang had it, "talking story." After a time, Harry Baty came walking out from behind the school, alone. He had a conversation with some of the boys on the steps, and then another young man walked back to where Harry had been. As the night wore on, one by one, six of the sidewalk troubadours—following brief negotiations—had sex with Rose.

During the next few days word began spreading around the neighborhood of what had happened. When confronted by her mother and an aunt the following week, Rose admitted that she had slept with the boys. But she embellished the story a bit, claiming that at ten o'clock, on her way home from the club meeting, she had been attacked and dragged behind the school, then was bound, gagged, and raped by the young men who had been loitering on the school steps and sidewalk. Naturally, the aunt called the police and reported the crime—and the police promptly rounded up and arrested eight suspects, all of them either Hawaiian, Chinese, or Japanese. Among them was Ben Ahakuelo. Two others were friends of his from early childhood, Akau "Henry" Chang and Edward "Buster" Seki.

The next day the front pages of the local dailies carried the story of the young girl who had been assaulted by what had now grown to "thirteen gangsters." After having "her arms pinioned and her mouth gagged," reported the *Honolulu Advertiser*, she was raped repeatedly and then "left in a semi-conscious condition" in the schoolyard. Since the major thoroughfare closest to Kaluwela School was Vineyard Street, the press quickly dubbed the accused youths the Vineyard Street Gang.

Honolulu society erupted in outrage. Although there had been only three indictments for rape, and one conviction, during the preceding two years in the city, the press raised the specter of a wave of youthful gangland assaults against girls and young women, insisting that drastic action be taken. Poring over every arrest—not conviction—for anything even remotely connected with sex, the *Advertiser* came up with a shocking "284 arrests for rape and kindred offenses" during the past four years.

It was a ludicrous figure obviously plucked from thin air. Even if those "kindred offenses" had included any and all discovered acts of consenting sexual activity among teenagers—which was prohibited, though rarely enforced, under the city's "immorality" statute—the number was nonsensical. But the newspaper didn't stop there. In a major editorial, it warned that unless something drastic was done, and done soon, this terrifying situation would "not be confined to Kakaʻako and Tin Can Alley," but "is going to extend to Waikiki; to Manoa; to Pacific Heights; and the aristocratic circles of Nuʻuanu Valley. It is going to invade the homes of leaders of business and society and the families of members of the legislature." The piece concluded by reporting that the *Advertiser*'s editor "recently conversed with the father of a decent white girl who had been raped in Honolulu." It noted ominously that "he has been practicing daily with a six-shooter with the intent to kill, on sight, the ravishers of his daughter when discovered."

This, like the nearly three hundred recent rapes and "kindred offenses," was pure fabrication. There was no such victimized white girl, nor any gang of "ravishers." But the editorial, and others like it, had their intended effect. As the legal machinery ground forward, indicting the so-called Vineyard Street Gang and setting a date for trial, large public meetings were held all over the city, most of them called by the wives of Hawaiʻi's leading businessmen. A series of demands was put forward to the territorial legislature, including the legalization of mandatory public whippings for those convicted of any sexual offense whatsoever. In signaling its support for such legislation, the *Advertiser* also chose to describe one of the attorneys who agreed to defend the accused teenagers as "a full brother to the most dastardly crime which disgraces civilization."

Within days of their introduction, the new laws were pushed through the territorial house and senate, though not without controversy. One senator, speaking in opposition, described what was now being called "the whipping post bill" as "barbaric" and "the child of hysteria," while the author of the house version of the bill came close to calling its opponents rapists themselves.

Meanwhile, the trial of the Vineyard Street Gang was just getting under way. Charges had been dropped against a number of the originally arrested young men, including Buster Seki. But Ben Ahakuelo and Henry Chang were among the six who remained under indictment.

During the days leading up to the trial, several ad hoc women's committees had organized a mass courtroom showing to demonstrate to the judge, the jury, and the entire city that they would not tolerate what they called a "soft glove" treatment of the accused. They need not have worried, given the judge who was hearing the case and the jury that had been seated. Though still in his thirties, Judge Albert M. Cristy was a moralistic, no-nonsense Harvard Law School graduate and the son of a Congregational minister who for years had headed up the Anti-Saloon League of Rhode Island. Impatient with judicial liberalism, Judge Cristy once denied an appeal based on insanity by dismissing such words as "paranoid" and "psychosis" as just so much "folderol." The twelve-man jury was composed of nine haoles, one Chinese, and two men of mixed haole-Hawaiian ancestry, all of them conservative, well-established members of the community.

But then, on the witness stand and before a packed courtroom, after at first repeating her account of having been raped, Rose Younge completely reversed herself. On cross-examination, when presented with discrepancies between what she had originally told the police and what she was now saying under oath, the young woman admitted that she had made up the entire story to counter the rumors that had been spreading about her. Contrary to what she first claimed, she now said that her "life was not threatened" in any way and that, had she chosen to do so, she could have walked away at any time. Further, after the boys had made their desires known to her, one by one, she had "consented to their proposals, naming conditions."

The jurors found themselves in a quandary. Although clearly there were no grounds for a rape conviction, the upstanding men of the jury wanted to send a message to the youth of Honolulu that such group sex activity was uncivilized and reprehensible, whether the female in question consented or not. After deliberating for just over two hours, they returned a verdict of not guilty on the rape charge—but guilty of "assault with intent to ravish." For nearly eighty years, since the establishment of the Hawaiian Kingdom's Penal Code of 1850, that had been the term used in local legal circles as code for attempted rape. Despite the fact that the alleged victim had just admitted under oath that no such crime had been committed against her, it was the best the jury could come up with on short notice in its determination to find the young men guilty of something.

The penalty called for in the law was anything from four months' to fifteen years' imprisonment, but the jury strongly recommended leniency. Judge Cristy accepted the jury's findings and recommendation, sentencing Ben Ahakuelo and his friends to the minimum four months in jail, noting that, with good behavior, they would be out in ninety days. He admonished the young men to use their jail time to rethink their behavior, then to straighten out their lives.

In a surprise to those in attendance, Cristy then turned his disapprobation on the press. Of them—although he was unable to prescribe jail time— he was less forgiving. He excoriated the editors of both English-language daily newspapers, the *Advertiser* and the *Star-Bulletin,* for printing news accounts and editorials that were patently prejudicial, "providing pre-trial publicity for statements made ex parte on the basis that the statements were true." Newspapers "should not create public opinion prior to a trial," he went on, adding that "what was rotten in this trial was the way the thing was handled by the newspapers before it got to the court. A hysteria was worked up over a case that was rotten, dirty, and disgusting, but was not the crime it was played up to be."

The next day the *Advertiser* defended itself against what it called Judge Cristy's "very clever" but "thoroughly unsound . . . piece of ill-temper," asserting that his criticism of the press "reflected no credit upon the intelligence or the judgment of his profession." In a lengthy editorial, the *Advertiser* also pointed out that the accused young men had, after all, been found guilty by the jury—"convicted of gang assault"—and that Cristy had sentenced them to jail as criminals. The newspaper's articles and editorials, in short, had been vindicated by the jury and by Cristy himself.

Rose Younge's family sent her back to China for a time, but two years later she turned up again in the criminal justice system. This time she accused a man of rape after he stole a pie and a bag of apples from her as she was walking home from the store. The authorities declined to prosecute. Ben, Henry, and the others, meanwhile, spent three months in the territorial prison. Soon the great uproar over crime began to recede. Without fanfare, the governor vetoed the whipping-post bill, saying it was "the product of a spur-of-the-moment desire to do something radical to correct an evil situation," but that in this case such legislation would "accomplish more harm than good." He also appointed an eleven-member Advisory Committee on

Crime to look into the territory's criminal justice system and the challenges it faced.

Two months later, the Conference of Social Workers of Hawaii held its annual meeting. During the time of fear that had recently gripped the city, conference organizers had delegated a special committee to focus on what they called "the crime wave in Hawaii" that was on everyone's mind. After poring over volumes of statistics dating back to 1915, the committee reported that conditions certainly existed for an upward surge in criminal activity: a 50 percent increase in population, including a surge in unmarried, and often homeless, men—conditions that traditionally fostered all sorts of crimes, but notably sex offenses.

It was with acknowledged surprise, then, that the committee found that the total number of arrests for all offenses, great and small, had actually diminished during this fourteen year period. The homicide rate had remained constant, it added, while "convictions for all types of sex offenses" had declined by almost 30 percent. As for juvenile delinquency, a separate committee charged with that investigation found that it too was on the decline. In fact, statistics showed that until the trumped-up convictions of the so-called Vineyard Street Gang, not a single young person had been incarcerated for any crime against a person, as distinct from property crimes, during the previous two years. All in all, the conference concluded drily, "this would hardly suggest that we are on the crest of a crime wave."

The governor's Advisory Committee on Crime later came to the same conclusion. "The evidence before this Commission," it declared in summary, "consisting of the unanimous opinions of judges, prosecuting officials, police officials, and juvenile court officials, and also the records of the courts, would indicate that there is no crime wave in this Territory."

The man who was behind the sensational and disingenuous *Advertiser* editorials throughout this affair would also play a major role in the Massie case three years later. His name was Raymond S. Coll.

Ray Coll had arrived in Hawai'i with his wife, Nan, in 1922. He was forty-six years old and had spent most of the past several decades writing for and editing newspapers in Pennsylvania and Arizona. When his last employer, the *Pittsburgh Dispatch,* was sold, Coll was offered a position as editor of the *Philadelphia Daily Ledger.* But first, he decided, he and Nan should take a trip around the world. Along the way they stopped in Hawai'i to visit some relatives. They were overwhelmed. "It was a beautiful spot," Nan later recalled, "a fairyland. . . . We were enchanted." Ray informed the *Ledger* that they would have to find another editor, since he and Nan would be staying in the islands permanently.

With his newspaper background, Coll had no trouble landing a job at the *Advertiser*. Hired initially as a reporter, within a few months he moved up to managing editor. Coll drove himself as hard as he did his staff, devoting the better part of most days, and many nights and weekends, to work. But if ever there was any question as to whether he was in, reporters for the *Advertiser* could always tell by peeking through the open door to his office to see if a battered old leather blackjack that he carried everywhere was hanging from the coat tree in the corner.

It was an affectation Coll had picked up during a stint as editor of a couple of papers in Bisbee and Douglas, Arizona, beginning in 1906. He hadn't lasted very long at either, only a few years, but he liked to reminisce about those rough-and-tumble days in the hinterlands, where he said he had acquired the habit of always being armed.

Bisbee and Douglas are small towns on the Mexican border that flourished briefly at the turn of the century because of the nearby copper mines at Morenci and Clifton. Bisbee, with a population of fifteen thousand when Coll lived there, boasted of being the most important town in the region. Although the number of its white residents was dwarfed by the sixty thousand Mexicans who crossed the border each year to work in the mines, as in Hawai'i it was the whites who ran things. And, again as in the islands, not just any whites. In 1903 a police officer in a neighboring town summed up the local attitude toward non–Anglo-Saxons by describing a gathering of people as a "pretty big crowd—mostly Mexicans, but a lot of Dagoes [Italians], Bohunks [Hungarians], and foreigners of different kinds—no whites at all."

There also was a substantial, if dwindling, number of Indians in the area. The Apache leader Geronimo had been born nearby and had conducted raids against the invading whites for years, until his capture in 1886. In fact, at the time of Coll's 1906 arrival in Bisbee, the old Indian warrior was still alive, an active octogenarian who had ridden his favorite horse in Teddy Roosevelt's inaugural parade the previous year, and he lived through Coll's tenure in Arizona. The Arizona-Mexico borderland at that time was as close to the Wild West as any eastern newspaper editor was likely to get in the twentieth century. Coll made the most of it.

Throughout his time in Bisbee and Douglas, his papers, the *Review* and the *Dispatch*, regularly printed warnings of Indian uprisings that conjured, in the words of one article, "visions of slaughter [that] blanched the faces of the more timid." Carrying the headline "Night of Terror," one particular story described a recent evening during which "children covered their heads under the bedclothes and women trembled, while men examined the old guns that were laid aside years ago." But then, almost with disappointment, the account concluded that it all was just a rumor. "No homes had been burnt in the night; no men had been slaughtered while defending their homes and families; no beautiful women had been dragged away to the mountains of Old Mexico as captives of the savage redmen." Still, it made page 2.

Stories about drunken Indians were routine fare in the *Review* and the *Dispatch* during Coll's tenure, and much was made at one point of a "strange romance" between an Indian man and a white woman in faraway Phoenix—"strange" simply because it existed. One story on the discovery of a dead white infant near Brewery Gulch acknowledged that "little attention would be paid to the affair" had it been a Mexican child, since Mexicans were in the "habit of burying their deceased offspring in some remote place, rather than bear the expense of a decent funeral and burial."

Under Coll, both newspapers often gave major front-page space to matter-of-fact accounts of lynchings that had occurred a thousand miles away. Chinese, who had been brought in as laborers in the 1870s and now mostly were merchants, were referred to as "Chinks." And then there was the matter of the black minister in Douglas, the Reverend G. T. Bell, who wanted to send his children to the public school. Writing in the *Dispatch*, Coll attacked the minister and his family, contending that "it is impossible for negro and white children to attend the same school rooms without friction . . . [because] when a white child is thrown in contact with a negro child invariably the white child feels humiliated." He continued: "Some people may get up and shout about social equality of the negro until they are blue in the face, but when it comes down to the fine point ninety-nine out of a hundred of them are simply talking theory and the one hundredth ought to be deported to Africa."

Since the Arizona courts had not made it sufficiently clear that racial segregation was the law of the land, Coll wrote in another editorial, the subject should be brought before the district court, "and if segregation is not held legal there, it ought to be made so by the legislature." Perhaps coincidentally, in the midst of this series of commentaries, Coll ran a large front-page story headed "Three Negroes Are Lynched," about a mob killing in the small Tennessee town of Tipton.

There may be little that is remarkable about these articles and editorials in the context of their time and place. But they reveal something about a newspaper editor who spent most of his career on the East Coast while yearning for and occasionally finding jobs on the frontier, an editor who, in 1922, showed up in Hawai'i, the most remote American frontier of all, and settled there for good.

In certain respects, life in the Arizona-Mexico mining towns resembled life in Hawai'i. In both places a small white settler class ruled a conquered indigenous people and a much larger nonwhite immigrant population. In one case, tens of thousands of those immigrants toiled in copper mines, while in the other instance an equal number labored on sugar and pineapple plantations. And in both Arizona and Hawai'i the whites used dual wage systems and other tried-and-true colonial techniques, including straightforward brutality, to maintain social order and racial dominance.

But in Hawai'i, the relationship between natives and white settlers was infused with far more nuance and complexity than it was in Arizona, after a century of intermarriage and mutual accommodation to the realities of political power. Ray Coll had difficulty understanding this. For years, in interviews and private conversations, he would claim—against all evidence to the contrary—that Honolulu was "worse off than any other city as to sex crimes," and that this was because, with "its semi-tropical climate . . . the native girls mature very rapidly." The only way to deal with this and with the city's many other serious problems, he said, was to require more "Anglo-Saxons" on the police force and on juries, and to establish a commission form of government in which the military and the Big Five corporate elite run everything.

Once settled in as editor of the *Advertiser*, Coll became fast friends with two of the city's most powerful men: his publisher, Lorrin Thurston, and the islands' most influential businessman, Walter Dillingham. Among Hawai'i's magnates, few were as outspoken in their contempt for nonwhites as were those two. In the 1890s, Thurston had been the principal propagandist and agitator behind the overthrow of the monarchy, while Dillingham—though only twenty years old at the time—had been a member of the mounted division of the so-called Honolulu Rifles, vigilantes who were called out to suppress Hawaiian resistance.

For most of his adult life Thurston had believed in and advocated the disenfranchisement of the non-haole "ignorant majority of the electorate," as he called all nonwhites, while Dillingham lived in dread of the day that Asian immigrants might hold public office. Even half a century later, in 1980, Thurston's son proudly spoke of how the Dillinghams and the Thurstons had opposed statehood for Hawai'i because of fears that it would lead to a decline of unfettered haole control. Dillingham, the younger Thurston said, hated the idea of "a goddam Jap—to quote him exactly—[being] governor or members of the Supreme Court, or the other official government offices," adding, "and I hated it as much as he."

In addition to his friendships with Thurston and Dillingham, Coll openly courted the military. According to his wife, Nan, soon after their arrival in the islands, they were going to "all the admirals' parties and all the generals' parties," and were spending many nights at lūʻaus with the top political and business figures in the territory. The recreational behavior of these elites might have tried the patience of the sensitive, but fortunately that characterization did not include the Colls. One formal ball in honor of newly promoted General Douglas MacArthur, held at the elegant Moana Hotel in 1925, ended with a group of drunken men—including MacArthur—leapfrogging up the hotel's marble staircase. At other affairs, future general George S. Patton—who became Dillingham's best friend—was likely to command attention with a favorite party trick: standing on his head while drinking a tumbler of mixed scotch, gin, and bourbon. Conversation at such events often turned to the best, and most draconian, ways of dealing with Hawaiʻi's Japanese population (the "Orange Race," the military and their civilian friends liked to call them) once the inevitable war broke out.

Such hobnobbing paid off for the Colls. In time, money just seemed to flow their way. Somehow, a salaried employee of a newspaper with a circulation of less than twenty thousand found himself building a mansion on the most exclusive strip of beachfront property in Honolulu and welcoming six hundred guests to his and his wife's housewarming gala. Over time, he and Nan also maintained suites at the most luxurious hotels in Waikīkī.

But that was years later. In the 1920s, Ray Coll was just getting started in the islands. Among other things, he had an image to build. Before long, claiming that he had been targeted for a hit by Honolulu gangsters, Coll decided that his Arizona blackjack afforded him insufficient protection. He bought a German shepherd. She accompanied Coll everywhere, sleeping away most afternoons next to his desk. The blackjack and the guard dog complemented Coll's carefully groomed picture of himself as a man of action, a bare-knuckle, patriotic, old-school journalist not to be crossed. Fittingly, he insisted that everyone, without exception, call him by one name and one name only: "Boss." He remained editor of the *Advertiser* for nearly four decades—including a period of several years when the paper insistently claimed that labor unions in the islands were under the direct control of Joseph Stalin and the Kremlin—and when he died his newspaper's headline read simply, "'Boss' Coll Dies at Age 90."

Though short, Coll was sturdily built, with thick tousled hair and a powerful lantern-jawed face. His "penetrating blue eyes could be as cold as diamonds," observed a subsequent editor, adding that they also could "twinkle with tolerance and amusement." On the evidence of the stories told about him, tolerance and amusement were attitudes he reserved for a special few. For those convicted of crimes, he wrote in one editorial, there was no alternative to locking them up and throwing away the key. "The criminal mind is incapable of permanent reform," he wrote, just as "the shark is always the shark."

Charged with boosting the *Advertiser*'s circulation following major new investments in a printing plant, Coll embarked on a campaign that a subsequent editor of the same paper would, with understatement, describe as "lively," "sensational," and "scandalous." It involved, on the one hand, publishing gossip about drinking, gambling, and divorce among socialites, and on the other hand editorially charging that the police were in cahoots with imaginary Asian and Hawaiian underworld kingpins.

Any who might disagree with the newspaper's positions on these and other matters could ask to purchase space for airing their own views. While the *Advertiser* might or might not agree to sell the space, it openly refused to publish critical letters. As Coll explained editorially in 1923, the paper had no intention of "furnish[ing] free space in which to advocate principles or measures with which it is not in accord."

The *Advertiser* had long lagged behind the *Star-Bulletin* in circulation and revenue. Competing with the *Star-Bulletin* was difficult because it had been founded in 1912 by Wallace Rider Farrington, the sitting governor of Hawai'i from 1921 to 1929, and still the newspaper's majority owner when he died in 1933. Conflicts of interest did not much trouble the islands' power brokers of that era. But under Coll's aggressive and flamboyant leadership, the *Advertiser* quickly began closing the gap. Within six months of his taking the helm in 1922, circulation was up almost 40 percent.

Throughout the 1920s, the *Advertiser*'s offices had been located precisely where Honolulu's main police station was temporarily being housed, at King and Alakea streets. In early 1930 the newspaper moved into a newly constructed three-story Mediterranean-style building, complete with a large granite-floored lobby surrounding a fountain and an interior garden—the same building it is in today. But although the *Advertiser* and police headquarters were then more than a half mile apart, from the day after Thalia Massie claimed that she was raped until well into the following year there would in reality be no distance at all between them. So copious was the flood of information from the police to the newspaper that during the first of the two criminal trials to come, cross-examination at one point had to be halted while six missing police reports were sought—and only partially retrieved—from the *Advertiser*'s editorial offices.

The news of the rape of a young navy officer's wife had begun trickling into the *Advertiser* newsroom, and those of the other newspapers in town, early Sunday morning. The trickle soon became a flood tide. Telephone lines all over the city were buzzing throughout the day with reports from people who said they had spoken with one of the policemen on the scene in Mānoa, or with the medical team at Queen's Hospital, or with the witnesses who had gathered outside the Massie house well before dawn, or with anyone who knew anyone else who claimed to have information.

For the past year the *Advertiser,* which published in the morning, had been putting out a "bulldog" edition that appeared on the streets the night before. If Coll was going to get the story of Thalia Massie's rape into that edition on Sunday night, he would have to hurry.

Then the names of the arrested suspects appeared on his desk. One of them, Ben Ahakuelo, was known to every sports fan in the city for his heroics on the football field and in the boxing ring. But to Coll, Ben Ahakuelo and Henry Chang, another of the suspects, were also known for something else. Two and a half years ago Coll had put a lot of effort into getting them convicted of viciously beating and raping a teenager named Rose Younge. And now here they were again, charged with the very same crime. Coll would get a rare second shot.

9   Alibis and Accusations

I t was nearly seven o'clock on Sunday night and Chief of Detectives John McIntosh was ready to interrogate the suspects. They had been moved from their cells at the city jail to the police station's main assembly room. Under the supervision of Detective Jardine, they were kept apart and under guard, to be certain they could not communicate with each other. In his office McIntosh was joined by Griffith Wight, the deputy city attorney, and Henry Silva, an investigator for the city attorney's office. All they needed now was a stenographer. But they couldn't find one. At last they heard from Helen Rosario, a clerk with the police department. She knew shorthand and was willing to come down to the station, but couldn't be there for several hours.

McIntosh decided to begin without her. They could get the basic story from the men they had arrested, then go over it again for the record when Mrs. Rosario arrived. He told Jardine to bring in the first suspect, Horace Ida.

For the next few hours, without anyone taking notes, McIntosh, Wight, and Silva questioned each of the young men they had under arrest. What emerged was a very troubling story—especially for the prosecution.

Horace Ida, who was older than the others by a couple of years, had been born on Maui in 1907 when his immigrant parents worked there as plantation laborers. As soon as they were able to leave the plantation, his father, Torakichi, and his mother, Ai, moved to Honolulu with Horace and his two sisters in tow. Torakichi took a job on a fishing boat, while Ai stayed home with the children, including two additional daughters who were born in Honolulu. In the city the Idas initially lived in a tenement house on River Street, the neighborhood known as Tin Can Alley. From there, as soon as they could afford it, they moved to a small, shared cottage on the outskirts of Hell's Half Acre.

Horace went to Kauluwela Grammar School, where he met Joe Kahahawai, Ben Ahakuelo, and David Takai. He had known Henry Chang since their families lived close to each other on River Street. All of them attended Sunday school, taught by a Catholic missionary, and all of them—especially Horace—frequently got into trouble. Years later the missionary could still remember Horace "sitting in the back seats, nudging [the other] boys and smiling, making slurring remarks" when she talked to them about "the Virgin Birth at Christmas." This, combined with Horace's "profane language in the midst of games," caused her to send him home. He then proceeded to "take great delight in being leader of the boys and trying to pull them out of Sunday school."

Of the five boys, the missionary said, Henry Chang was second to Ida as a troublemaker. But like Horace's, Henry's misbehavior was nonviolent and far from felonious. The worst thing she could recall about Chang, and she admitted it was only a rumor, was that for a time as a teenager he reportedly stole some bicycles and dismantled them, selling the parts. Takai was the most "skeptical" of the group when it came to activities likely to get him in trouble, she said. His mother had died when he was very young and he was brought up by his father and two older sisters, both of whom worked as barbers. He had been taken to juvenile court twice as a boy, once for truancy and "disobedience to his sister," and once for fighting. For the latter offense he had to pay a five-dollar fine.

As for the remaining two, Kahahawai supposedly was the most easily led and Ahakuelo the most independent. "We were wild kids, fighting in the streets and going to dance halls," Ahakuelo later said about himself and his friends, before adding that that didn't make them rapists. But when told of that comment years later, a man who grew up with them—and now is a comfortably retired businessman in his midnineties—laughed and recalled that all those fights were weaponless playground battles with strict rules that were enforced by designated "referees." He compared them to what went on in the Bowery Boys and Dead End Kids movies of the 1930s and 1940s: harmless teenage slugfests.

If their world was not especially violent, however, everything else about it was impoverished and demoralizing, the missionary recalled. No one in the neighborhoods where they lived ever had enough money for decent food or clothing, or anything else. Housing was decrepit and desperately crowded, and on hot summer or early-fall nights it could be unbearable. Indoor plumbing was nonexistent. But on military paydays, or "whenever the fleet came along," she recalled, the streets came alive with activity. "Pimps and runners came right out on Vineyard Street and invited men down blind alleys," she said, and while ministers went out of their way to bring soldiers and sailors into their churches, prostitutes were known to walk in and "pull men right away from a religious meeting."

By the time Horace and the others were in their midteens they were cynical beyond their years and spent more time in pool halls than in school. After dropping out of two different high schools, one public and one private, Horace went to work doing menial jobs at several pineapple canneries and then at a gas station. In 1927, when he turned twenty, he realized that this was how he would spend the rest of his life unless he made some drastic changes. He had saved a little money, so he packed his bags and left for Los Angeles. The jobs there were not much better, but at least he could brag about the big city on his visits home.

A year after Horace left, at around Christmastime, his father and the entire crew of his fishing sampan, the *Daikoku Maru*, disappeared at sea. Weeks of searching followed before the local fishing community finally abandoned hope and held a memorial service for the men. Horace returned to Honolulu for the ceremony, but once the funeral was concluded he headed back to Los Angeles. Although he often mailed gifts home, he never seemed to have money to send. Then, in late August of 1931—a few weeks before Thalia's fateful night at the Ala Wai Inn—Horace arrived in Honolulu again, to spend some time with his mother, now nearing sixty, and his four sisters.

For the past year or so, Henry Chang also had been away from the islands. After being released from jail following the "multiple fornication" fiasco in Judge Cristy's courtroom, Henry decided to try out a new life in Alaska, where he worked in a fish cannery. But then his mother asked him to come home. She had put together sufficient resources to move the family to a small chicken farm in an area known as Moanalua Gardens, and she needed Henry's help to run the place.

On September 12, Horace's older sister Haruyo told him that she had been hired to work as a geisha, with a group of other young women, at a wedding party on the other side of the island. She offered to loan him her car if he would assure her that he would be careful with it. Haruyo had worked at numerous jobs for several years to save enough money to buy the nearly new Model A Ford, and she kept it in perfect condition. Excited about the opportunity to show off, Horace got dressed in his best Saturday night attire—a white silk shirt (they were all the rage in Honolulu at the time) and dark pinstriped trousers—and then began making the rounds in search of old friends.

His first stop was the Mochizuki Teahouse at Liliha and Kuakini streets, a few blocks away. The teahouse, where Haruyo worked from time to time, was one of more than a dozen such establishments in this part of the city. Because virtually all Japanese immigrants to Hawai'i in the late nineteenth century had been agricultural laborers, the initial ratio of males to females was extreme. One response to this situation was for male workers to send home for "picture brides." The establishment of teahouses with geisha girls was another.

As time wore on and more Japanese women settled in the islands (by 1930 almost half the Japanese population was female), the function and nature of the teahouse changed dramatically. There were still geishas, but instead of being formally trained women, imported from Japan and accompanied by chaperones, most of them were locally born hostesses who lived with their families. Although educated in traditional song and dance, by the late 1920s most geishas were young American citizens of Japanese descent who wore kimonos only when working—attire that tended to clash with their modern makeup and permanent-wave or marcelled hairstyles.

Whatever Horace expected to find at the teahouse on this Saturday night, apart from a little money that he borrowed, he was disappointed. So he got back in his sister's car and moved on to a predominantly Filipino speakeasy, where he bumped into David Takai, Ben Ahakuelo, and another friend from grammar-school days, Buster Seki. David was excited. As Horace had done, he was planning to leave for California in a few days, and in celebration he was buying the beer. Ben, who was twenty years old, said he would have enjoyed leaving the islands too, at least for a while, but his girlfriend was pregnant. They wanted to get married, but the young woman was Chinese and her mother was adamant that she was not going to marry a Hawaiian, especially one whose main claim to fame in life was as a football player and an amateur boxer. Still, legal or not, "I'm just the same as married," Ben would say, "and I'm not going anywhere."

After a while, Ben remembered a nearby party that was in progress. The beer would be free. And there would be good food to go along with it. The party was at the house of a politician, Sylvester P. Correa, the city supervisor who represented the district. It was almost directly across the street from where Ben lived. One of Correa's daughters, Beatrice, was getting married, and her family was holding a lū'au in her honor. Though not actually invited, Ben knew Correa's son, Sylvester junior, or "Doc," and was certain that he and his friends would be welcome at the party. So the four of them climbed into Haruyo Ida's car and headed over.

As is traditional at lū'aus, there was more food than could possibly have been consumed—including a whole pig roasted in an *imu,* an underground oven—and an equally inexhaustible supply of beer. As Ben later said, "we drank beer and had pig for a chaser." The food and the beer were good, and the people were friendly. But this wasn't exactly their crowd. So after half an hour they decided to drive across town to Waikīkī. The Eagles Club was sponsoring a dance at Waikiki Park that night, and that was the best thing Ben and David could think of as an affordable sendoff for David's upcoming move to the mainland. Dancing didn't much interest Horace or Buster, though—and Horace was having too much fun driving his sister's car—so they dropped Ben and David off at the dance and continued on in search of other companions.

By ten o'clock Horace had picked up and dropped off at the dance two more acquaintances, a couple of haole University of Hawai'i students he had met aboard ship on the way back from California, Arthur Castner and Ernest Christiansen. Then he brought a bored Buster Seki back to the Correas' lū'au. Unable to think of anything else to do, Horace went home. After talking briefly outside his mother's house with another friend, he considered his options. The night was still young. Haruyo's car was sitting out front. He decided to go back to the lū'au by himself.

The party at the Correas' place was no more exciting than it had been earlier that evening. Even Buster had left by then. But two more friends from Kauluwela School days had now arrived, Henry Chang and Joe Kahahawai, the Hawaiian football player and boxer, who was a friend of the Correa family. When Horace told his two new companions that Ben and David were at the Waikiki Park dance, Henry and Joe suggested they join them there. So once again, Horace drove across town, arriving outside the park at about 11:30.

The dances at Waikiki Park always ended at midnight, but Joe and Henry were more interested in catching up on things with Ben and David, who were inside, than they were in dancing. So the time didn't matter. The admission fee did. Neither of them had any money. But it was common practice for people leaving the park near closing time to give their ticket stubs to anyone hanging around outside, thereby letting them in free. And as it happened, a friend of Henry's was just then leaving the dance with his girlfriend, so they handed over their stubs and Henry and Joe started to go inside to search for Ben and David. First, however, after Horace introduced them, they stopped to talk for a few minutes with the two university students, Castner and Christiansen, who had decided to leave the dance early and were walking across the parking lot.

After the other four men separated, Horace was left alone again, standing guard over his sister's precious car. The musical chairs continued a short while later, when Joe returned, feeling sorry for Horace, and gave him his ticket stub so that Horace could enjoy some of the last-minute fun inside while Joe made sure that nobody touched the shiny Model A.

At last, the dance broke up. At a little after midnight the five young men—Horace Ida, David Takai, Henry Chang, Joe Kahahawai, and Ben Ahakuelo—considered what to do next. The options were no more attractive than they had been from the start of the evening, so they decided to give the lūʻau at the Correas' place one last try before calling it a night. They drove off, heading *mauka*—toward the mountains—and away from the beach.

Although the gathering at the Correas' house was the most appealing of the limited options they could think of at the moment, especially since the beer and food were free, they remained open to suggestions. So when a Ford roadster in front of them, with its top down like theirs, and filled with five young people from the dance, started waving to them and calling out Ben's name, he waved back and asked Horace to pull up alongside. The driver of the other car was Tatsumi Matsumoto, who went by the nickname "Tuts" and had known Ben for almost ten years. Earlier at the dance, Ben and Tuts had asked the same girl to dance simultaneously, then engaged in some good-natured disagreement as she walked off to dance with someone else. Maybe Tuts or the others knew of a party going on somewhere.

They were on Beretania Street, a wide thoroughfare, driving slowly past the Honolulu Academy of Arts and a park named Thomas Square, when one of the men in the other car, Robert Vierra, decided to impress the two females in his company by jumping onto the running board of Horace's car. The cars remained side by side as he bummed a smoke and Ben and his friends asked their new passenger where he and his group were headed. The answer was uninspiring, so after Vierra hopped back onto the running board of the roadster and rejoined his friends, Horace continued on to the lūʻau.

It was close to 12:30 when they arrived at the Correas' house, to find the party was over and all the food and the beer were gone. After chatting briefly with Sylvester's son Doc, Ben and Joe returned to the car, where Horace, Henry, and David were waiting.

With nothing else to do, and with his mother's place just across the road and football practice scheduled for the next morning, Ben said good night to his friends and walked home. David agreed it was time to call it a night. He lived a few blocks away, at Liliha and King streets, on the other side of the Kauluwela School playground. It was about 12:35, then, when Horace dropped David off and pulled out across the intersection, directly into the path of an oncoming 1924 Hudson driven by a middle-aged white man.

As the cars swerved to avoid one another, a female passenger in the Hudson shouted to Horace to watch where he was going. Joe, who was sitting up front beside Horace and feeling his alcohol, shouted back, saying something to the effect that if the damn haole would get out of his car Joe would teach him a thing or two. Both cars screeched to a halt and their doors flew open. The first person out of the Hudson was not the driver, however, but his wife—a tall, powerfully built, and angry Hawaiian woman, Agnes Peeples.

Horace and the others had no idea what was about to hit them. Agnes, her daughter would later recall, was "built like a Sherman tank." After divorcing her first husband, but before meeting and marrying Homer Peeples, she had kept food on the table for her family by making bootleg beer and selling it. Her old car was a familiar sight as it pulled up regularly at the back door of the Eagles Club and similar establishments with her three children sitting atop cases of homemade brew that were crammed into the rumble seat.

Joe stepped in front of Agnes as she was getting out of the car and she shoved him. He replied by hitting her on the ear and knocking her backward. She replied to his reply by grabbing his throat with her left hand and scratching it while punching him with her right fist.

At this point, as a few spectators began to gather, the drivers of both cars ushered their respective combatants back inside the vehicles and drove off in opposite directions. Horace dropped Henry off at his place, drove Joe home, then headed home himself.

After finishing up with the last of the suspects, McIntosh, Wight, and Silva—later joined by Sanford Wood, the United States attorney—discussed what they had heard. There were only two real discrepancies among the men's stories, and they were minor. One of them concerned the route Ida had taken after leaving the dance. Henry, David, Ben, and Joe recalled following the same sequence of roads on the way to Thomas Square, while Horace's recollection had them taking a different street at one point. But this was easily explained by the fact that a few months earlier, while Horace was in Los Angeles, a new connector road had been completed. His unfamiliarity with the area could easily explain why he thought they had taken one street, while the others said they had taken a different one.

The other discrepancy concerned Horace's unique suede jacket. When initially questioned early Sunday morning, Horace told the police he was dressed the same way he had been all night, including the jacket he had on at the time. Now he said he hadn't been wearing the jacket earlier on Saturday night and had only put it on when Detectives Cluney and Black came to his mother's house to arrest him. The other men said either that Horace was not wearing that or any other jacket when they were driving around, or that they could not recall with certainty whether he was or wasn't.

In contrast with these trivialities, there was clearly one huge problem in hanging Thalia's rape on the five men: they simply wouldn't have had time to do it. Leaving the Waikīkī dance at five or ten minutes after midnight, and arriving at the Correas' house at about 12:30, left insufficient opportunity for them to have committed the crime. During those twenty or twenty-five minutes, they had been seen by Tuts Matsumoto and his friends driving toward the mountains and then down Beretania Street—the opposite direction from where Thalia said she and her attackers were headed at that very moment. They could not possibly have circled back, driven across town, kidnapped Thalia, taken her to a remote location, raped her repeatedly, and then made it to the Correas' house by half past twelve. Merely driving those six miles or so nonstop through the city's streets would have been difficult in the short time available to them.

They also couldn't have done it after leaving the Correas' place, because only fifteen minutes later, at 12:45, Agnes Peeples filed her complaint at the police department, identifying a car with their license plate number as the one with which she and her husband had just had a near collision. That car was heading *makai*, in the general direction of the ocean, not away from it, as would have been the case if its occupants had just raped Thalia on Ala Moana Road. And only five or ten minutes after Mrs. Peeples's complaint was lodged with the police, Thalia flagged down the car near Kewalo Basin that picked her up and took her home. So the suspects also couldn't have kidnapped and raped her after the run-in with Homer and Agnes Peeples.

If these five men hadn't done it, though, who had? They were the only suspects. At this point, with no other leads having surfaced, it was highly unlikely that any others would turn up. And to let Horace, Ben, Joe, Henry, and David go, and thus fail to get a conviction in a case such as this—especially after Thalia had now positively identified Chang and Kahahawai as among her assailants—was unthinkable.

As the chief of detectives, the deputy city attorney, and the others were talking the matter over, Mrs. Rosario—the stenographer—finally showed up. It was after ten o'clock. The *Honolulu Advertiser*'s bulldog edition for Monday morning had just hit the streets, and it had all the earmarks of editor Ray Coll's brand of journalism.

Across the top of the front page was a huge banner headline, "GANG ASSAULTS YOUNG WIFE." Several sensational subheads and the story below described the kidnapping, the "terrible beating," and the sexual assault "six or seven times" on "a young woman of the highest character . . . a white woman of refinement and culture" by a gang of "fiends" with previous criminal records, including rape. Various city officials were quoted in the story—the mayor, the sheriff, and the district attorney—and they assured the newspaper that the victim had provided police with a description of the automobile in which she had been abducted. (The *Advertiser's* next edition added—as did the *Star-Bulletin* later in the day—that she had "had the presence of mind to make a mental note of the number of the automobile as her attackers drove off after assaulting her.") The article closed with Chief of Detectives John McIntosh saying that "the men being held by police will be taken before the victim in an effort to positively identify them." Obviously, although all this had been written well before the suspects were questioned, there could be no doubt as to their guilt. Anyone who read the newspapers could see that.

McIntosh asked Mrs. Rosario to get out her stenographer's pad. He then told Detective Jardine to bring the suspects in for questioning once again—official questioning this time. As Mrs. Rosario later testified in court, she then faithfully recorded every question and every answer—at least, she said, "those they told me to put down." According to one of the defendants, David Takai, during this interrogation Deputy City Attorney Griffith Wight called him a liar when he described, as before, the man from another car jumping onto their running board as they drove past the Academy of Arts and Thomas Square. It was an incident that, if confirmed, would have placed them far from the scene of Thalia's abduction at just the time that she claimed it was taking place. Wight then ordered Mrs. Rosario to not record what Takai had just said.

Nor did she record Wight's effort to get Ida to confess by telling him, falsely, that the police had discovered some green beads belonging to Thalia on the floor of his sister's car. Obviously, Wight said, they had fallen there during the struggle. Horace replied that if there were beads on the floor of the car they must belong to his sister, because he had never seen that haole woman before.

Days later, after Mrs. Rosario had typed up each suspect's statement, the police brought the documents to the men for signing. Takai was not the only one who found discrepancies. Joe Kahahawai found some too, including an assertion he had not made claiming that Horace Ida had worn his suede jacket when they were out that night. Joe signed the document, but only after crossing out the material that had been inserted without his approval.

For the rest of the week, things moved quickly. As he had promised the press, McIntosh brought all the suspects except Takai—who Thalia had said was definitely not one of her assailants—to Queen's Hospital. Although Thalia had already identified Kahahawai and Chang as among the men who beat and raped her, the two of them continued to deny everything. Knowing of Hawaiians' reputation for confessing to crimes under almost no duress at all, McIntosh said he thought they might break down and admit their guilt once they saw the bandaged and bedridden condition of the victim. The chief of detectives was accompanied by two police officers and by the same men who had joined him in interrogating the suspects on Sunday night, including Griffith Wight, who would prosecute the case. They met and spoke with Thalia and Tommie before bringing the suspects, one by one, into her room.

When Ida entered, McIntosh told him to walk up close to Thalia and then turn his back and sit down. She claimed to have been thrown into the rear seat of the kidnappers' car, and since Ida was driving she would have seen him from that position. McIntosh had instructed Ida to wear his suede jacket to the hospital, and he now suggested that Thalia reach out and touch it. She did, then "pulled back as though the thing was repulsive to her," the chief of detectives later testified.

Thalia's cheek was bruised and swollen. It turned out that whoever struck her had fractured her jaw. Playing on this, McIntosh introduced each of the suspects the same way he had greeted Horace Ida when he was brought in to face Thalia at the police station early Sunday morning. "Look at your handiwork," McIntosh would say; "aren't you proud of it?" Whereupon Thalia, on cue, would add: "You did it, you can't deny it."

Ida and the others, however, did deny it—each in his turn saying he didn't know what she was talking about. Everyone in the room remembered Ben Ahakuelo's denial as being especially, and typically, forceful. "Oh, yeah? I don't know you and I don't know anything about it," he said—doing so, McIntosh remembered, "with a sneer and a leer." At that point, one of the policemen recalled, Tommie Massie leaped to his feet and seemed to be "making an attempt to strike" Ahakuelo, while Ben crouched into a boxing stance, prepared to fight back.

A few more accusations and denials flew back and forth, and the suspects were returned to their jail cells. Before long, Thalia would begin remembering numerous and remarkably detailed facts about her assailants that had previously eluded her. These included the recollection that one of them had been wearing a suede jacket similar to Ida's and that another had a gold tooth—just like the one she had seen in Ben's mouth during his verbal exchanges with her and with Tommie in the hospital. She now also said that she might have left the Ala Wai Inn earlier than she had thought, perhaps around 11:30.

If these were odd bits of evidence the prosecution planned to use in building its case, they provided scant reason for optimism, because almost everything else that emerged in the days to follow worked in favor of the defense. In response to press reports, witnesses began showing up at police headquarters. Alice Aramaki was among the first, reporting that she had seen a woman matching Thalia's description walking past her father's barbershop on John Ena Road at about ten minutes after twelve on Saturday night. She added that Thalia appeared to be drunk and was being followed by a white man in a dark suit.

George Goeas then telephoned the police to report that he and his wife had seen a young white woman in a long green dress walking a little farther along the same street, near the spot where Thalia said she had been abducted, at about 12:15 on Saturday night. After Goeas then visited the station and told his story in the presence of a police stenographer, McIntosh and Wight drove out to the Goeases' house and took a statement from Mrs. Goeas. Like her husband, she noted that the woman they saw appeared to have been drinking and that she was either being followed, or was accompanied by, a haole man who was wearing a dark suit.

Three young men—Robert Vierra, Tatsumi Matsumoto, and George Silva—arrived involuntarily, having been rounded up by the police. The suspects had named them as the men in the car they had driven alongside on Beretania Street the night before. The three witnesses confirmed that they had been at the Eagles Club dance and had seen Ben Ahakuelo and the other men there until just after closing time. Although Ahakuelo and Matsumoto had known each other for years, Ben was familiar to the others as well because of his athletic celebrity. And Vierra had distantly known Takai and Chang for some time. Along with two young women, Margaret Kanae and Sybil Davis, they also confirmed that they had been in the car that rode alongside the one that Horace Ida was driving as it passed the Academy of Arts and Thomas Square at around 12:15 or 12:20. They remembered that Vierra had jumped from their car to the other one to bum a cigarette.

When fifteen-year-old Mina (short for Wilhelmina) Correa was questioned, she confirmed that the accused men had been at the wedding lū'au for her sister on Saturday night, and that they had returned later to ask if there was any beer left. She had told them no, and they had gone on their way. Mina did not recall what time that was, but her older brother Sylvester junior ("Doc"), who was twenty-one, put it at a little before 12:30. He had gone out briefly at midnight to drive a guest home, then returned twenty or twenty-five minutes later to help Mina clean up after the party. That was when Ben, Joe, and the others showed up. Sylvester recalled talking to them for a few minutes before Ben walked home and the others drove off.

The stream of witnesses continued. Some came in on their own after reading newspaper accounts and realizing they might have something to contribute. Police investigators tracked down others, following leads suggested by Thalia's story or those of the accused men. The couple who had given Kahahawai and Chang their ticket stubs for the dance at about 11:30 were located. Others said they had seen Ahakuelo and Takai at the dance until, and a little after, it closed at midnight. Agnes Peeples's police report, showing that she had been in a fight with Joe Kahahawai between 12:35 and 12:40, was already on the record. But she was brought in anyway, and confirmed the timing and the location. The Clarks and the Bellingers, who had found Thalia between 12:50 and 1:00 walking on Ala Moana Road—a good distance from where Agnes Peeples had her run-in with the suspects—showed up to describe their encounter with the victim.

But if the parade of witnesses was causing the case against the accused men to disintegrate, it was no more damaging to the prosecution than the complete absence of any physical evidence showing that Thalia had been raped at all. The car the men had been driving that night was dusted for fingerprints. There were plenty, but none belonged to Thalia. Nor was there any indication of a struggle in the car, or any evidence—such as prosecutor Wight's bogus green beads—suggesting that Thalia had ever been in the vehicle. Dr. Thomas Mossman, the assistant city and county physician, examined the suspects and their clothing at the City and County Emergency Hospital. Like Thalia, their genitals showed no sign of trauma. Neither their outer clothing nor the underwear they had worn that night contained blood or semen stains.

Next, doctors at the Queen's Hospital Laboratory scrutinized Thalia's gown, slip, girdle, stockings, and other undergarments. No semen was found anywhere, and while there was some blood on the white upper part of her green dress, it amounted to only a few spots near the shoulder, where drops from her cut lip apparently had fallen. One more small stain appeared on the lower part of the dress, and the doctors cut out a patch of the garment for microscopic examination, but it turned up negative for either blood or semen. Even more remarkable, Dr. Mossman later said, was that Thalia's clothing was neither torn nor wrinkled, and appeared almost as if it had just come from a dry cleaner—which it had. Nor were her shoes scuffed in the slightest. Needless to say, none of this supported Thalia's claim that she had been pulled out of a car, dragged through the dirt to a clump of bushes while struggling to free herself, and raped a half dozen times.

Then there were the tire tracks at the scene of the crime. On Monday morning, the day after Chief of Detectives McIntosh had taken Haruyo Ida's car across the wet ground of the site where Thalia said she had been attacked, two police officers revisited the area. One of them, Claude Benton, had asked the department's identification officer, Samuel Lau, to go with him to the place where the attack had occurred and to photograph any tire tracks that might be there. Benton had been one of the first two policemen on the scene, sent there by McIntosh while he was interviewing Thalia early Sunday morning. In his report on that visit, Benton had said nothing about tire tracks. But now, he told Lau, he had seen some. He also suggested they drive there in Haruyo Ida's car and bring her brother Horace along to confront him with any evidence they might find.

Lau loaded his camera and some white powder into the Model A. The powder would be used to highlight any tracks that he might want to photograph. But when they arrived at the scene they discovered that McIntosh had neglected to have it sealed. Various police and press vehicles had during the past thirty or so hours obliterated any clear tire tracks that might once have been there. Benton, however, led Lau to the one tire track—well off to the side, by itself—that was pristine. He told him to photograph it.

After thinking about it for a moment, Lau refused. He had heard that McIntosh had been a passenger in Ida's car when it was driven to the scene of the crime the day before, and he asked Benton if he could assure him that McIntosh hadn't made the tire track in question. Benton could give him no such assurance. Deciding that he wanted no part in what he suspected was an effort to plant evidence, Lau put his unused camera back inside the car, and the three of them returned to police headquarters.

If the prosecution's case was in trouble, no one whose reading of the press was limited to the *Advertiser* or the *Star-Bulletin* would have known it. Although there was a direct flow of information from McIntosh's office to the editors of both newspapers, neither of them ever published any information that might possibly get in the way of a guilty verdict. Thalia's name would not be mentioned in either paper for several months, but within three days of the assault all of the accused men's police mug shots, along with their names and addresses, appeared routinely and were given prominent display. The mayor was quoted as saying he would provide extra funds to bring in private investigators to guarantee a conviction, but the city and county attorney—Griffith Wight's boss—assured the press from the start that no outside assistance was necessary. "The prosecution has a clear case against the defendants," he announced, "and enough evidence to warrant a conviction."

As it happened, soon after Thalia made her claim that she had been raped, two other Honolulu women filed similar charges with the police. The court dismissed one of the cases almost immediately—with the prosecutor's consent—as frivolous. The other case was that of a twenty-year-old woman who reported that she had been attacked by a man while they were out picking flowers together on the Pali Road in Nuʻuanu Valley. Both the accuser and the accused were Japanese, meaning that in normal times nothing much would have been made of the matter in the haole community or the English-language press. But in the aftermath of this case, members of the League of Women Voters, claiming that it was further evidence of a city awash in sexual assaults, were demanding the right to carry firearms. And editor Ray Coll was writing in the *Advertiser* that Honolulu had become a place of absolute terror for women.

"Even among the cannibals of New Guinea or the aboriginal blacks of North Australia womanhood is safer than in this enlightened American territory," Coll wrote in a large editorial headed "Something Must Be Done." As for the recent assault on the young navy wife—certain, as he was, that the police had arrested the right men—he added that "the perpetrators . . . are local youths, not transient thugs," and he suggested that "a small army of special deputy sheriffs" be sworn in and sent to patrol the neighborhoods where such "loafing morons" and "half-baked youths" lived.

The only outspoken exception to this call for the summary conviction of Thalia's accused assailants was a Japanese-language newspaper named the *Hawaii Hochi*. In a city with more than a dozen newspapers, publishing in half as many languages, the *Hochi* and another Japanese-language paper, the *Nippu Jiji*, boasted almost as many daily readers as did the *Star-Bulletin* and the *Advertiser*. Both the *Hochi* and the *Nippu Jiji* also had English-language sections that were read primarily by the growing number of second-generation Japanese, or nisei, who spoke Japanese, but whose written knowledge of their native tongue was shaky. Other readers included Hawaiians, who had lost their newspapers—and to a large extent, their language—when Hawaiian was banned from use in schools or any official venues in the wake of annexation. Neither newspaper had many white readers, other than those associated with labor organizing.

The *Hochi* had been founded as a solely Japanese-language publication in 1912 by Kinzaburo Makino, an immigrant from Yokohama and the son of a British wool merchant and a Japanese mother. He started the newspaper for the sole purpose of agitating on behalf of Japanese plantation laborers and against the sugar barons. Known as Fred Makino among haoles, he was easy to spot in his everyday uniform of Panama hat, white suit, white shoes, bright-colored bow tie, and large cigar. The Japanese consul, embarrassed by his behavior, referred to him as "a low-class charlatan . . . of mixed-blood, notorious for being irresponsible." The *Advertiser* attacked his newspaper as "rabid," saying it needed to be "muzzled like a mad dog" and "exterminated." Knowing that he must be doing something right, Makino reveled in the criticism, and in 1925 he decided it was time to expand his influence by adding an English-language section to the paper.

To edit the English section Makino selected George Wright, a rough-hewn former labor organizer in his midfifties. Wright had been a professor of chemistry and physics at Allegheny College in Pennsylvania, then a mining engineer in Nevada and California, before moving to Hawai'i in 1917. Once settled in the islands, he took a job as a machinist at Pearl Harbor and immediately proceeded to stir up trouble by organizing a citywide labor council, publishing a labor newspaper, and generally doing whatever he could to offend and antagonize leaders of the sugar industry. An outspoken advocate of multiracial labor coalitions, Wright was attacked in the haole press for being "a renegade white man" who lent "his considerable cleverness and white man's intelligence" to such subversive endeavors as aiding the strikes of Japanese and Filipino plantation workers in the early 1920s. Inevitably, he was fired from his job at Pearl Harbor, and almost immediately he took over at the *Hawaii Hochi*. He and Makino were a match made either in heaven or in hell, depending on your politics.

Wright named his part of the paper the "Bee" section because it was intended to sting. And on September 15, the same day that the *Advertiser* and the *Star-Bulletin* were starting their front-page campaigns against the men accused of raping the unnamed white woman of refinement and culture, Wright printed a small news item that raised a series of important questions and introduced what, for months to come, would be a persistent and critical minority voice.

Why, asked Wright in that first article, were prosecutors apparently uninterested in the fact that there were witnesses who placed the accused men far from the scene of the assault at the time it supposedly was occurring? Did this not suggest, he said, "an apparently water-tight alibi" for the defendants?

Why could the police find no evidence of the alleged victim having been in the car driven by the accused men, or of damage to her gown, especially "if the struggle had been as intense as the woman claimed"? Why did the woman show no injuries, when examined by physicians, "except the bruise to her face which was caused by the blow that fractured her jaw"? And who was the white man seen following the victim "down Kalakaua Avenue to John Ena Road, where she is said to have been kidnapped"?

That was only the beginning. Two days later, after the *Advertiser* and the *Star-Bulletin* printed the names and addresses of the alleged rapists, the *Hochi* countered by publishing Thalia's name, noting that she was the wife of Navy Lieutenant Thomas Massie. From then on, as the mainstream English-language dailies pursued their efforts to convict the accused men, Wright's "Bee" section of the *Hochi* repeatedly raised questions that no one else was asking in public. These included, a few days after the arrests, how it was that Thalia could so clearly identify her assailants to one group of policemen only hours after she had told other officers that it had been too dark to see anything. Or "how Mrs. Massie happened to remember the number of the automobile the next morning after she had denied that she remembered it the night of the alleged assault."

True to its name, George Wright's "Bee" annoyed and stung the *Advertiser* and the *Star-Bulletin* with regularity. Immediately after Ray Coll's lengthy "Something Must Be Done" editorial appeared, Wright published an even longer piece in the *Hochi* entitled "Why Get Hysterical?" Arguing that merely saying "something must be done" only "beclouds the issue and arouses blind passion," Wright asserted that "this paper regards the crime of rape as the most vicious and horrible offense of which human beings can be guilty." However, he continued, when confronted with such a crime the public "requires calm and careful thinking," not "hysterical outbursts that tend only to . . . create irresponsible blood-lust." Then, after providing a list of still more serious problems with the evidence in the Massie case—problems that no other newspaper ever mentioned, before or after—Wright concluded by asserting that "something is being covered up." While "this newspaper . . . will not tolerate any laxity of prosecution, neither will it tolerate any frameup or any attempt to railroad these young men to prison or to the gallows."

Clearly George Wright had his own sources in the police department. And Wright's sources included the rank-and-file officers and detectives who had first interviewed Thalia—the non-haole members of the force who had been cut out of the investigation as soon as McIntosh had taken it over.

The trial would not begin for another eight weeks. In that time, two completely different accounts of what happened to Thalia Massie on Saturday night, September 12, made their way through the homes and streets and workplaces of Honolulu. Which rendition people believed depended in large part on the newspapers they read. And what they read was a consequence of who and what those people were. Unlike the world of the plantation, where nonwhites of different nationalities and races were pitted against one another to prevent solidarity, the split in opinion that now was emerging cut right down the middle—haoles on one side, almost everyone else on the other.

10   Taking Sides

Ben's mother didn't have a telephone, but she knew where to find one. And she knew the person to call.

Aggie Ahakuelo, who lived modestly on the fringe of Hell's Half Acre, was among the city's poorest people. Princess Abigail Wahiikaahuula Kawananakoa, who divided her time between a mansion on Pensacola Street in Honolulu and a luxurious beach home at Mālaekahana on O'ahu's windward coast, was among its wealthiest. Her official signature read, simply, "Princess." And at this particular moment she was making preparations for an elaborate reception to be held at her home the following night for King Prajadhipok and Queen Rambai of Siam, along with their traveling retinue.

The king and queen, on the way home from visits with Emperor Hirohito of Japan and U.S. president Herbert Hoover, had just arrived in the islands aboard the SS *Empress of Canada*. They were greeted by a welcoming armada of one hundred airplanes from the Eighteenth Wing of the Army Air Corps and the navy's Pearl Harbor Fleet Air Base. At the princess's mansion, the reception included Governor Judd, Honolulu's Mayor George Fred Wright, business tycoon Walter Dillingham, and scores of other civilian and military dignitaries. The press later described the royal couple's arrival:

> The driveway was lighted with blazing Hawaiian torches and by each stood a Hawaiian youth dressed as a warrior of olden days in *malo* [loincloth] and feather cape and bearing a spear. Boys similarly dressed lined the entrance, where the royal pair were greeted by a welcoming *oli* [traditional chant], and formed an aisle across the lanai for their entrance to the drawing room, where they received the hundred and fifty guests invited for the evening.

That was just the reception line. Press accounts went on to describe the vast home itself, filled with flowers and brightly colored feather *kāhilis*— large standards symbolic of royalty—and the guests dressed in silk, satin, and velvet, all the men wearing red sashes over their tuxedos and the women bedecked in jewels. Hawai'i's King Kalākaua had visited Siam a half century earlier and been decorated by the reigning monarch of the time. Now, although politically powerless since Queen Lili'uokalani's throne had been seized by American troops in 1893, Princess Kawananakoa was returning the gesture. Clearly, when the telephone call from Mrs. Ahakuelo of Hell's Half Acre was announced, the princess had other things on her mind.

But she took Aggie's call without hesitation. It was not because she knew her. She didn't. And it wasn't because Aggie, as a girl, had been a dancer in Queen Lili'uokalani's court. Princess Kawananakoa knew nothing about that. The princess spoke with Mrs. Ahakuelo because, despite the enormous gulf of affluence and social rank that separated the two women, it was her obligation to do so.

Hawai'i's European-style royalty was founded in the early nineteenth century, modeling its external trappings on what the leading families of the islands had seen during visits abroad, especially to England. But the islands' political structure had been steeply hierarchical for many centuries before then, although power throughout the archipelago was not centralized under a single monarchical figure. Instead, each island was ruled by hereditary chiefs known as ali'i, whose honorific rank and stature varied. Ancestry was part of what determined a chief's rank, but so too did his recognized mana, or spiritual power. And mana was achieved, in large part, by the evident prosperity of the commoners—the maka'āinana—who lived under a chief's rule. Since maka'āinana were free to move from place to place and live under the chief of their choosing, it was in each chief's own interest to provide well for his people. Doing so not only increased the number of subjects under him, and thus his material wealth, but that in turn elevated his reputation among other ali'i as a possessor of spiritual power.

Although the ravages of introduced disease and consequent political upheaval did much to change Hawaiian cultural norms following European contact in the late eighteenth century, one characteristic of social life that endured was the expectation, by rulers and ruled alike, that ali'i were obliged to care for the common people. Sometimes this caring was symbolic, as when Princess Kawananakoa—like Queen Lili'uokalani before her—visited the isolated leper settlement at Kalaupapa on the island of Moloka'i to offer comfort to the native sufferers of Hansen's disease, the last of the great scourges to have been brought to the islands. At other times the assistance was more tangible, and that is why almost all of Hawai'i's major trusts and private charitable institutions—in support of public parks, museums, education, health care, and more—were created by bequests from nineteenth-century Hawaiian royalty. The most prominent example today, although it remains only one of many, is the estate of Princess Bernice Pauahi Pākī. Established upon her death in 1884, its income was designated solely for education, particularly for indigent Hawaiians—and it is now valued at more than six billion dollars, making it one of the largest private charities in the world.

Princess Abigail Kawananakoa was approaching the age of fifty. A widow for more than two decades, she was a woman of fabulous wealth. She had been educated in California, married a nephew of Queen Kapiʻolani, traveled the world, been accorded a place of honor at the London coronation of King George and Queen Mary, and was a prominent figure in New York and Washington social and political circles. A conservative Republican activist (for years she had been the party's national committeewoman for Hawaiʻi), as a young woman the princess had been praised for her beauty wherever she went. Recently, however, she had grown so large that when her limousine pulled in front of the most expensive shops lining the beachfront at Waikīkī, it was a signal for clerks to emerge and begin parading their finest wares along the sidewalk for her consideration. Her size made it too difficult for her gracefully—and regally—to emerge from the car and inspect items in the stores.

But corpulence was not the princess's only problem of late. Her children also had become a major worry. One of her daughters, now twenty-six years old, had been abandoned by her husband and subsequently decided that she was unable to care for their five-year-old daughter. On this weekday afternoon, while planning the imminent gala to honor the king and queen of Siam, Princess Kawananakoa was in the midst of negotiations for the legal adoption of her granddaughter. Another of the princess's children, her only son, apparently cared nothing for the obligations that accompanied his royal bloodlines. A famously irresponsible yachtsman and playboy, he seemed to be perpetually in trouble with the law. In years to come, one young woman would die in an automobile accident caused by his reckless driving, while a second would be killed during an argument at a drunken party in his home. He served time in the territorial prison for the second offense, after pleading guilty to manslaughter.

It was in her role as the last living symbol of Hawaiʻi's deposed monarchy that Princess Kawananakoa took Aggie Ahakuelo's telephone call that September day. But it was as a mother of two troubled children, as much as anything else, that she listened and offered her help.

The son of the distraught woman who was pouring out her story on the telephone might well be guilty, the princess knew, and if so his crime was horrendous. But she also knew, as did everyone who was born in the islands or had lived there for any length of time, that such behavior was so out of character for Hawaiians that no precedent for it could be recalled. Beyond that, the princess was fully aware of the virulently anti-Hawaiian and anti-Asian attitudes of the people who had been arriving in Honolulu of late, white people from the mainland—military and civilian alike—who were bringing their prejudices to bear on every aspect of island life.

Princess Kawananakoa consoled Mrs. Ahakuelo and urged her to remain calm. She would call a friend of hers, she said, a prominent attorney, and ask him to investigate the situation and, if possible, to represent the accused men. After hanging up, she put in a call to one of the most influential and respected legal figures in the territory. His name was William H. Heen.

Like everyone else, Bill Heen found it almost impossible to say no to the princess, just as others found it difficult to say no to him. Born in 1883 to a Chinese father and a Hawaiian mother in a small town on Maui, Heen seems to have succeeded at everything he attempted in life until, after Hawai'i became a state in 1959, he failed in an effort to be elected to the U.S. Senate at age seventy-six. But in 1931 he was a vigorous forty-eight. After graduating from Hastings Law School in San Francisco, Heen had returned to the islands and opened a private practice. He soon crossed to the other side, however, becoming county attorney and then the territory's deputy attorney general, earning a reputation for aggressive prosecution of graft and corruption cases. His success at the bar and as a leader of the fledgling Democratic Party led President Woodrow Wilson, in 1917, to appoint the thirty-four-year-old as judge of the First Circuit Court. No other non-haole had ever held such a post. But, although for the rest of his life he was always known as Judge Heen, the role of impartial arbiter was too passive for his tastes. He resigned the post in 1919 and from then on alternated between private practice as a defense attorney and various prosecutor positions.

Heen was the only elected Democrat in the territorial senate, a fact that did not prevent him from being selected by its members to chair the Judiciary Committee. Not that he won every battle in that office. In the term just ended he had failed in an effort to pass "antiflogging" legislation that would have prohibited the corporal punishment of prison inmates. The bill had been crafted in response to the death of a Hawaiian youth, William Keawe, at the Wai'alae Training School for Boys, following an officially administered beating. Another bill that Heen introduced and that was defeated would have opened jury duty in the territory to women. But in both instances the defeat was only temporary. As in much else that he did, William Heen was on the right side of history.

After talking with Princess Kawananakoa, Heen took some time to plan his approach to the assignment she had just given him. He had no desire to get caught up in the futile defense of a collection of patently guilty thugs and rapists. His interviews with the suspects would be tough and confrontational. He also was keenly aware of the explosive racial atmosphere that already surrounded the case and that inevitably would grow more intense as the trial date approached. Since the alleged victim was white and the defendants were all Hawaiian or Asian, while he was half Chinese and half Hawaiian, it wouldn't hurt to have a haole attorney working with him. The obvious candidate was a man named William Pittman. Even apart from his legal skills, which were formidable, Pittman perfectly fit the ideal profile of a white defense attorney in a case such as this.

To begin with, William Buckner Pittman, or Bill as he was known to everyone, hailed from Vicksburg, Mississippi. A proud descendant on his mother's side of Francis Scott Key, the author of "The Star-Spangled Banner," Pittman was a white-haired fifty-five-year-old with a smooth round face and prominent jowls to go along with a slow drawl and a very quick mind. He and his older brother, Key Pittman, had left the South as young men. Bill received his legal education in the state of Washington, then practiced there and in Nevada and California before turning up in Honolulu in 1915. His brother stayed on in Nevada, becoming a successful politician and, beginning in 1913, one of that state's two United States senators.

Although he never achieved his older brother's fame or notoriety (which included an allegation that, upon the senator's death on election eve in 1940, his supporters kept his body on ice in a hotel bathtub until the votes were counted), Bill Pittman was a colorful character in his own right. And, like a certain breed of white southerner even in those days, he possessed a deep and powerful hatred of racism.

As Heen remembered years later, the two men, both successful former prosecutors, interrogated the suspects one after the other, aggressively cross-examining them on detail after detail. Ida, Takai, Chang, Ahakuelo, and Kahahawai had been kept in separate cells since their arrests and had not had the time or opportunity to compare stories. But they were adamant in what they said and consistent in the telling. Heen and Pittman were convinced that the five men were innocent. They decided to take the case.

Across town, Walter Dillingham erupted in anger when he learned the identity of the attorneys who would be defending what the haole newspapers now routinely were calling the "gangsters" who had severely beaten and raped the young "white woman of refinement and culture" who also happened to be a navy officer's wife. Some of Dillingham's largest construction, shipping, and other contracts, worth many millions of dollars, were with the navy. Admiral Stirling was his good friend. He would not allow those "beasts," as he called them, to walk free just because they had somehow arranged to be represented by the best attorneys in the islands. And Walter Dillingham was accustomed to getting his way.

Dillingham had been born in Honolulu on April 5, 1875, the son of Benjamin Franklin Dillingham, a former Massachusetts sailor who had stayed on after a voyage to the islands and established a small hardware store in Honolulu. The store soon grew into the Pacific Hardware Company, the first of the older Dillingham's rapidly expanding corporate enterprises. Others would include the Oʻahu Railway and Land Company, which provided Oʻahu's largest sugar plantations with quick market access and maximum profits. Walter may not have been born into wealth, but throughout his childhood and youth he had observed closely as his father built the multimillion-dollar Dillingham Corporation, finally joining his younger brother Harold in taking the reins upon their father's death in 1918.

Long before ascending to the helm of the family firm, however, Walter had made a name for himself independently in sports, business, and politics. An avid horseman and polo player, he was handsome, lean, and muscular, standing well over six feet tall. His parents had sent him to Massachusetts for high school, and he stayed on to study at Harvard. Although he left Harvard after two years to return to Hawaiʻi and work in various family enterprises, his would-be class of 1902 never forgot or ceased to honor him. At its twenty-fifth reunion in 1927, the class notes described Walter as being to Hawaiʻi what plutocrat J. Pierpont Morgan was to New York.

By that time Walter Dillingham had become the single most powerful man in the islands. It was his Hawaiian Dredging Company that had promoted and then secured the contract for creation of the Ala Wai Canal, thus laying the foundation for the new tourism mecca of Waikīkī. But not before the firm bought up hundreds of acres of real estate in the area, real estate that would skyrocket in value once the project was complete. Part of that land served as the grounds for Dillingham's huge estate, La Pietra, on the lower slopes of Diamond Head. Counting the tennis courts, the swimming pool, the servants' quarters, the horse barns, and the villa itself—but not the land— the cost upon completion in 1922 was just under $350,000, the equivalent of about $4 million today. It was only because of his connections that he was able to build it so cheaply. At one point, during the midst of the Depression, Dillingham calculated that just two of his companies, the dredging and contracting firms, had earned roughly $61 million since their founding. But by then his business interests also included ocean and air transport, mining, ranching, finance, vast real estate holdings, and much more. He served as a director of half a dozen of Hawai'i's largest corporations and maintained his own lobbyists in Washington to be certain that federal legislation served his will. Of course, he did much of his own lobbying as well, routinely bringing influential national business leaders and politicians to the islands, where they would be honored guests at La Pietra.

Dillingham also was the longtime vice chairman of the American Defense Society. Founded in 1915, two years prior to the U.S. entry into World War I, the society's program of action ranged from permanently abolishing the teaching of the German language to the internment of people it decided were "enemies within our gates." (William Randolph Hearst was among those found to fit that description.) In the aftermath of the war the ADS evolved into an evangelically white supremacist, adamantly militarist, and all-purpose superpatriot advocacy group. It called for suppression of such supposedly subversive magazines as the *Nation* and the *New Republic,* and it exposed the likes of Charlie Chaplin and Will Rogers as Communist agitators.

In addition to Dillingham, the society's most noteworthy officers included Madison Grant, the leading scientific racist of that era and a man who, in his best-selling book, *The Passing of the Great Race,* called for the forced sterilization "of those who are weak or unfit," including "the diseased and the insane and extending gradually to types which may be called weaklings rather than defectives and perhaps ultimately to worthless race types." In the early 1930s, Grant and his associates formed a mutual admiration society with Nazi Germany's leading racial ideologues, proudly embracing and publicly endorsing one another's ideas.

But this was all grandiose stuff. At the moment, Walter Dillingham had more local and mundane matters occupying his attention. Specifically, bad publicity, the sort of publicity that could come from a national spotlight shining on Hawai'i and illuminating a case of criminal violence by nonwhite reprobates against a navy officer's wife. Privately, Dillingham would write, he and "many whites, as well as Hawaiians" doubted that the men arrested were guilty. This was because three of them were Hawaiians, "a peace loving people," he wrote, whose "sex relations have been more social than brutal . . . and of whom court records here show they have been particularly free from the stigma of rape." Nevertheless, there were far larger and more important matters at hand than the guilt or innocence of a handful of lower-class "gangsters," as he persisted in calling them.

Putting down his morning newspaper, Dillingham picked up the telephone and called the head of the Honolulu Chamber of Commerce, for some years a position he himself had held. Together, the two men then arranged for an emergency meeting of the most influential men in the territory. They included the governor of Hawai'i and the mayor of Honolulu; Admiral Stirling; Captain Wortman of the Pearl Harbor submarine base; the local army commander, General Briant Wells; the city and county attorney and his chief prosecutor, Griffith Wight; the Honolulu sheriff and the chief of detectives, John McIntosh; the editors of the two English-language daily newspapers, the *Advertiser* and the *Star-Bulletin,* plus the publisher of an English-language weekly, the *Honolulu Times;* and, according to Dillingham, "twenty of the leading businessmen of the community, including two ex-Governors."

From the start, there was disagreement among those who attended. Griffith Wight, who had interrogated the suspects alongside John McIntosh and would be leading the prosecution of Thalia Massie's alleged assailants, had impressive academic credentials. Born in St. Paul, Minnesota, in 1890, he had attended prep schools before entering Yale University, graduating in 1912. He also was a graduate of Stanford Law School. But fifteen years had intervened between his Yale and Stanford degrees, time spent in the family lumber business and the U.S. Army. It was the army, in fact, that had taken him to Hawai'i following World War I, and only after his discharge in 1924 had he entered Stanford. As a result, although he now was forty-one years old, he had earned his law degree only four years earlier and had worked as Honolulu's deputy city and county attorney for less than two years. Stirling, in particular, regarded Wight as a boy who had been given a job that required a man's experience. He wanted the city fathers to hire a private team of attorneys to take over the prosecution.

In his judgment of Wight, Stirling was correct. Wight's excellent education said more about his family background than about his intelligence or his legal skills, but he adamantly insisted that he was up to the task. The young prosecutor really wanted this case. It was the opportunity of a lifetime. His boss was the city and county attorney, James Gilliland. In other locales the district attorney would often seize the chance to handle a trial of such magnitude himself, given the attention it was certain to attract. But Gilliland was thoroughly beyond his depth as the head of the city prosecutor's office. The position was an elective one, and he was a popular, glad-handing politician, but not much else.

For the past several years, powerful forces in the community had been demanding a change in the way the office of city and county attorney was selected: they wanted it to be filled by appointment, not election. If that sentiment prevailed—as seemed likely, and soon—someone of Griffith Wight's background and experience was a natural candidate for the job. But first he had to show off his talents, and there was unlikely ever to be a better stage than this one. No matter what Stirling said, Wight would not step aside. And, privately, he determined that he would win the case, no matter what he had to do. Compromising with Stirling, he said he would be willing to accept the offered assistance of the territory's attorney general, Harry Hewitt.

A second compromise was struck. Wight would remain in charge of the prosecution, with help from the attorney general's office, but in addition money would be raised to bring in confidential outside assistance. As it turned out, few local attorneys were eager for the opportunity to take on Heen and Pittman. And as time passed, and word of the accused men's alibis leaked out, the case for the prosecution began looking weaker by the day. It took more than a month for the prominent firm of Thompson, Beebe & Winn finally to agree to work with the prosecutor behind the scenes. On October 27, a confidential letter of agreement from senior partner Frank E. Thompson to Dillingham noted the firm's willingness to assign one of its partners, Eugene H. Beebe, to "assist in the preliminary work and in the prosecution of the five defendants." It further stipulated that, for a retainer of $2,500, "Mr. Beebe will have such assistance from all the members of our organization as he may require to prepare the case for trial," although the actual courtroom work would be conducted by prosecutor Wight.

Around Honolulu, Frank Thompson was known as a fixer, someone people in power could rely on to get things done. It was Thompson, as the attorney for the Hawaiian Sugar Planters' Association in 1920, who had bribed a Filipino labor leader into calling off a strike. He also still served as an undercover go-between, conveying information on potentially troublesome people—especially Japanese—from plantation office files to army and navy intelligence on O'ahu. And unlike Dillingham and Stirling, Thompson was confident that, with their combined efforts, they could secure a conviction of the men Thalia had accused of raping her.

But the weakness of the case and the limited experience and ability of the prosecutor weren't the only worries Admiral Stirling expressed at the Dillingham meeting. His other main concern, shared by everyone else in the room, was the publicity the trial was certain to generate. On the one hand, just as the city fathers were determined to send a harsh message to the increasingly restive youth of places like Hell's Half Acre, Stirling wanted to be able to report to his superiors in Washington that the thugs who assaulted Lieutenant Massie's wife had received quick and certain justice. But he had no desire for the image of his command to suffer in the interim, and bad news at any time was difficult to control and could easily cause embarrassment.

The businessmen in the room had the same misgivings. Whether it was the effect that news of an assault by natives and Asians on a white woman might have on the already weakened tourist industry, or on southern senators who had never been friendly to island sugar interests, publicity about the case could do nothing but harm to Hawai'i's economy. The politicians at the meeting agreed, allowing to go unspoken another worry of particular concern to them: the fact that powerful interests in Congress had for years been aching for an excuse to impose a commission form of government on the islands, an eventuality that would mean the end of their jobs and their influence.

Something had to be done to keep things under wraps, all agreed. Admiral Stirling announced that he had the perfect solution: they should hold what he called "a closed trial," thereby preventing the prying press and public from learning anything about it. Others, briefly, thought that a good idea. But Hewitt, the territory's attorney general, patiently explained that any such proceeding would be illegal because the Sixth Amendment to the United States Constitution explicitly requires that "in all criminal prosecutions, the accused shall enjoy the right to a speedy and public trial." Even in the unlikely event that they should be able to pull off such a gambit, the attorney general warned, it would unquestionably be grounds for reversible error on appeal. This only strengthened Stirling's conviction that, like the granting of citizenship to nonwhites, the placing of Hawai'i under the protective umbrella of the U.S. Constitution and its laws had been a grievous mistake.

Again, a compromise was arranged. Stirling, Dillingham, Governor Judd, and the others would use their considerable influence with the press to throw a blanket of silence over the trial and everything leading up to it. There was no way to muzzle the local press, but the editors who were present agreed, as Dillingham later wrote, "to use their best efforts to correct the gossip obviously inspired to bring about sympathy for the defendants . . . [and] by editorials to counteract the work of the scandal mongers." This was a reference to George Wright's editorials in the *Hawaii Hochi* cautioning against hysteria and warning that a "frame-up" was in the works. Beyond that, however, all efforts would be made to prevent news of the affair from reaching beyond the islands, at least until it could be announced that island justice had been swift and sure—that the rapists had been caught, convicted, and sent to prison, most likely for life.

This would not prove difficult. Communication with the outside world was slow and inefficient in those days. The Hawaiian Islands are the most isolated inhabited landmass on earth, and telephone and radio service between Hawai'i and the continent was not scheduled to be in place until the end of the year. Moreover, Dillingham had long ago mastered the art of broadcasting two public messages—one, as he put it, for "home consumption" and another "in correspondence with people on the mainland . . . with Congressmen and others"—as he had done a decade earlier with the contentious issue of Asian labor and immigration. Collectively, the power of the assembled politicians, businessmen, editors, and military leaders was enormous. In no time at all the wire service representatives in Honolulu agreed to suppress stories on the case until it was successfully closed. It was, as Stirling would say, a matter of national security.

One final bit of business required the attention of the assembled men. The prosecution needed every scrap of incriminating evidence it could assemble between then and the time of the trial. Nothing should be overlooked. Agreement was unanimous on putting together a fund of five thousand dollars to be used for reward money or for gathering information useful to the prosecution. Soon after the meeting was held, a display advertisement appeared in local newspapers offering a home for sale, with four bedrooms, a three-car garage, and large servants' quarters—on an acre of beachfront land in the exclusive neighborhood of Kāhala—for sixteen thousand dollars. By that measure, a five-thousand-dollar reward should generate a good deal of interest.

11 Grace and Tommie

Thalia's broken jaw was not healing as quickly as had been hoped. Although released from the hospital ahead of schedule, for weeks she claimed to require seclusion at home, saying that the pain made her attendance at grand jury proceedings impossible. In fact, she did not make herself available to the grand jury for another month, and when she appeared, according to the *Star-Bulletin*, "her head was swathed in bandages and she was unable to walk unassisted to the courtroom."

During that same intervening month, according to their maid, Beatrice Nakamura, Thalia actually appeared much healthier than on the day of her grand jury appearance. She had no difficulty in walking, and while her broken jaw had been wired, her head was hardly swathed. Apparently her condition had taken a sudden and dramatic turn for the worse on the morning of her grand jury testimony. By that evening, however, she was back to her old self. She and Tommie drank a little less than before, but they continued to bicker and argue almost to the point of violence in Beatrice's presence, with one or the other occasionally stalking out of the house, heading for somewhere else to spend the night. Although they continued to sleep in the same bedroom, Tommie and Thalia now occupied separate beds.

In early October Thalia's mother, Grace Fortescue, arrived in Honolulu accompanied by Thalia's youngest sister, Helene. Grace was understandably worried about her oldest daughter's condition, but not to such an extent that she neglected to have studio photographs of herself and Helene, along with a press release, sent on ahead so that Honolulu's newspapers would note the arrival of the women. The press release identified Grace as a Washington socialite, a niece of Alexander Graham Bell, and the wife of Granville Roland Fortescue, a cousin of former president Teddy Roosevelt and one of his San Juan Hill Rough Riders. It further noted that Helene Fortescue was scheduled to make her Washington debut the following season, and that the two women would be staying with Mrs. Fortescue's daughter and son-in-law,

Navy Lieutenant and Mrs. T. H. Massie, during their stay in the islands. All in all, a proper society page notice.

The Massies' bungalow on Kahawai Street was charming, but small. With the addition of Grace and Helene, and with Beatrice around for most of the day, conditions bordered on the claustrophobic. But there was no alternative. Grace, as usual, had no money, despite her public pretenses. It was either stay with Thalia and Tommie or return home—and Grace quickly decided that she liked Honolulu. She immediately contacted and introduced herself to Walter Dillingham, who invited her to his and his wife's palatial home, modeled and named after the villa outside Florence where they had been married in 1910. They assured Grace that they would do everything possible to assist Thalia at this difficult time.

Before long Grace was lunching at the most exclusive country clubs, taking hula lessons, and going lawn bowling with her newfound friends from O'ahu's white upper class. But back in Mānoa, in between entertainment opportunities, Grace was worried. Thalia had confided to her that she had not menstruated since before the night of the assault, which had happened a month ago. On the off chance that Thalia might be pregnant, Grace arranged to have her admitted to the Queen Kapiolani Maternity Hospital so that a preventive dilation and curettage might be performed. Thalia was in the hospital for two days. Surgery was performed on the second day, and the results on the medical report showed that her uterus was not enlarged and the curetting proved "meagre" and "negative." She wasn't pregnant.

The only noteworthy thing about Thalia's hospital stay was Grace's behavior. When she discovered that some of the nurses on duty were Asian or Hawaiian, she stormed in to see the administrator and insisted that only white nurses be allowed into her daughter's room. It was a demand those at the hospital had never heard before. Thalia herself did not especially mind the presence of nonwhites, the nurses reported. In fact, according to a haole nurse named Helene Tromlitz, Thalia took advantage of her multiracial maternity ward surroundings to inquire about something she had always wondered. Is it true, she asked, "that Chinese women are built crossways?" In a subsequent interview, Nurse Tromlitz said she assured Thalia that it was not true—then volunteered to the interviewer that "none of the nurses at this hospital believe she was raped," an assessment confirmed by the nursing superintendent.

Meanwhile, Grace had now taken to holding dinner parties. At one of them, the naval officer known to Beatrice Nakamura as "Red Fig" (his name turned out to be Rudolph Fink) was in attendance. He was the same man who in the past had spent nights and weekends with Thalia while Tommie was away at sea. At this party he was introduced to Thalia's strikingly attractive younger sister Helene. Before long, according to the maid, Red Fig and Helene had become "very friendly, and they went camping for about a week together, I don't know where." Helene was only seventeen at the time, but that was a year older than Thalia had been when she was married.

Much as she enjoyed staying with Thalia, Grace soon realized that her dominating presence in the small house was taking a toll on everyone. She had begun "scolding" Thalia "for not doing more work about the house" and for sleeping too much, Beatrice later reported, while Tommie soon was speaking with none of them, except when he was arguing with Thalia. Finally, Grace sent a wire to her stepmother in Washington, asking for some money. Her father had died two years earlier, leaving her and her siblings several hundred thousand dollars each in Bell Telephone stock. But it was not yet convertible into cash. When the money from her stepmother arrived, Grace went in search of a furnished house to rent for Helene and herself.

It didn't take long to find one. By the end of the month, just two weeks before the trial was scheduled to begin, Grace and Helene moved into a furnished cottage of their own at 2754 Kolowalu Street, a walk of several blocks to where Tommie and Thalia lived. Although almost all Mānoa's residents by then were white, there were some exceptions, most of them Hawaiians whose families had been in the valley for generations. To Grace's chagrin, one such person turned out to live almost directly across the street from her.

The woman's name was Mary Ann Malu'ihi Perry Koloa'amakai'i. She had been born in 1872 on her family's sixteen-acre dairy farm, when agriculture was still common in the valley. Now close to sixty years old, "Aunty Mary Ann," as she was known to everyone, had lived for decades in an old house on a large piece of property that was thick with ancient fruit trees. She was famous for the lū'aus that she held from time to time, to which all her neighbors automatically were invited, and for her habit of regularly bringing large baskets of papaya, avocado, and other fruits and vegetables to families who lived nearby. According to the published recollections of Mānoa residents from that era, Aunty Mary Ann was "one of the uncrowned queens" of the valley, esteemed by all for "her warmth, love, and hospitality."

But not by Grace Fortescue. As Mary Ann's granddaughter Mina explained, "Grandma was a dark-skinned Hawaiian lady," and when she attempted to present her new neighbor with "a nice basket of offerings, [Mrs. Fortescue] received her very coldly, almost as though invisible, and Grandma came home very hurt." Grace could not understand what a woman of Mary Ann's color was doing in this upscale white community, and she never tired of calling the police to complain of the multiracial neighborhood gatherings at Mary Ann's home. As a newspaper reporter later pointed out, following a lengthy interview with Grace, she seemed unable to understand that "Hawaiians are not related to the Negroes," which explained, he said, why she persisted in referring to them as "niggers."

In this Grace was far from alone, at least among military personnel and their families. To most haole newcomers Hawaiians were only lighter-hued versions of the blacks they had left behind in the States. There, the rules of American apartheid made race a simpler matter. Blacks were expected to know their "place," a stipulation that was enforced with particular vehemence in the South should a black dare call a white man by his first name or presume to look a white woman in the eye. Over the years, many blacks had been lynched for offenses that often were no greater than these.

Racial tension had, of course, been a reality of life in the islands for many years. But the play of competing political interests, especially between old-time haoles and Hawaiians, had masked its harshness. What was happening now, and what Grace and Admiral Stirling and others represented, was different. It began during the first year of the military buildup, 1919, outside the Hotel Blaisdell in downtown Honolulu, when hundreds of sailors and Hawaiians engaged in a brawl that would become emblematic. It was occasioned, wrote one newspaper account, by a group of sailors "applying the term 'nigger' to two natives who were seated on their doorsteps playing ukuleles."

The casual use of that epithet was a habit the army and navy men refused to break. Even a dozen years and numerous racial skirmishes later—some of which resulted in deaths—a former Honolulu newspaper editor who had moved to New York described the everyday bearing of the soldiers and sailors in Hawai'i as "truculent and arrogant." Writing in the *New York Herald Tribune* in January of 1932 about his sojourn in the islands, he recalled: "I have seen naval officers, in their colorful evening clothes, swaggering about the public rooms of the Royal Hawaiian Hotel as if they were in an occupied country . . . and have heard innumerable references to 'the niggers' from these soldiers, sailors, and their officers . . . a large percentage of whom originate in our so-called Southern states."

Old haole families, those who liked to describe themselves as *kama'āina*—appropriating a term meaning "children of the land" from the Hawaiians—frequently complained among themselves about the brusque and overtly racist behavior of the newly arrived whites. Ida Knudsen von Holt, with her husband Harry among the two oldest and wealthiest white settler families in the islands, put it plainly to one interviewer. "The Hawaiian does not feel anything about [the soldiers and sailors]," she said, "but the servicemen treat them as colored, and they're not colored." There was, after all, a long-established and complicated etiquette surrounding the way haole racial dominance over Hawaiians traditionally was enacted, at least in public. In private, things sometimes were different.

The same reporter to whom Grace described Hawaiians as "niggers," the *New York Times*'s Pulitzer Prize–winning Russell Owen, also recorded, years later, what he had been told by "one of Honolulu's prominent businessmen" after he had gained his confidence. "He confessed to me," Owen wrote, "that when he was a boy, attending the exclusive school for white children in Honolulu, he and some of his friends used to find it lots of fun to take some Hawaiian girl out on a dark road at night and rape her." Never with fear of prosecution, of course. In fact, although there was as yet no record of a Hawaiian ever raping a white woman, other than Thalia's recent accusation, there were numerous instances over the past hundred years of whites raping Hawaiians. Most of the white men, if captured, pleaded to reduced charges and received little punishment at all.

Sometime after renting her new house and settling in, Grace wrote to her stepmother, thanking her for the money and explaining that without it "our stay out here would be dreadful instead of really very pleasant. Had Helene and I had to stay in Thalia's little house, all cramped together, well really, I can picture nothing worse. Thalia is practically well now, but gets tired and therefore irritable very easily. Helene is slightly bored. Tommie is a perfect dear, but just about on the point of a nervous breakdown, and with my sweet and angelic disposition—can't you just picture the results if we were packed in a three room home for six months?" But if Tommie was on the brink of a nervous breakdown, Grace was only a part of the reason. Of late, his entire life had become a nightmare.

Tommie was born and spent his early childhood years in a small rural town in Kentucky named Winchester. Situated, its residents still like to boast, "in the heart of Daniel Boone Country," Winchester was an all-white enclave in the hills south of Lexington. Tommie's father owned a shoe store in town—Massie, the Shoe Man, it was called—at the corner of Main and Broadway. The family came from strict Christian roots, specifically a frontier denomination known as Disciples of Christ. Fiercely competitive with the

Baptists in nineteenth-century Ohio and Kentucky, the Disciples banned musical instruments, rejected affiliation with all organizations that were deemed "unscriptural," and had been led early on by an itinerant preacher named Raccoon John Smith.

Born on the fifth of March in 1905, Tommie grew up to be the pride of the Massie family, despite the fact that his piety was disappointingly subdued. After attending public elementary school in Winchester, he was sent to study at a military academy in the hamlet of Millersburg, on the eastern edge of Bourbon County, less than twenty-five miles away. Another student who attended that school several years later, and had the misfortune of being Jewish, has written about the experience. Millersburg Academy was run by "a bible-whacking martinet," he recalled, and "on the second day of school, the older cadets threw me on the floor to feel for my horns," since "primitive Southerners knew that Jews had horns. Things didn't get much better for the next two years."

Outside Millersburg, while Tommie was a student there, a black man named Grant Smith was accused of raping a teenage white girl. Neither the girl's age nor the rape charge turned out to be true, but that didn't stop forty men from lynching Smith, hanging him from a telephone pole on the Maysville-Lexington Turnpike. One local newspaper described with delight how "the moonlight shone full on the darkey" as his body swung slowly in the evening breeze.

Between the time of Tommie's birth and his departure to enroll at the Naval Academy, more than eight hundred black men, women, and children are known to have been lynched in the rural areas of ten southern states—Alabama, Arkansas, Florida, Georgia, Kentucky, Louisiana, Mississippi, North Carolina, South Carolina, and Tennessee. This is a rate of roughly one per week, year in and year out. Although Kentucky produced fewer lynchings during this era than most of the Deep South states, that was only because Kentucky had fewer blacks available for killing. When corrected for the size of its black population, Kentucky had the third worst lynching record in the country. And central Kentucky, where Tommie's family lived, was home to more such barbarities than any of the state's other regions.

In one Kentucky case that occurred when Tommie was young, a black farmer named David Walker was accused of insulting a white woman. That night a mob of fifty men surrounded his house and set it on fire. When Walker came to the door and pleaded for his life and that of his family he was shot dead. Then his wife appeared. According to a press report, "She held in her arms their infant child and begged the Night Riders for mercy. Disregarding her pleadings the infuriated mob opened fire and a bullet pierced the body of the infant in its mother's arms. A second shot struck the mother in the abdomen and she fell, still holding the dead body of her infant." The Walkers had four other children. One by one each of them was murdered that night.

Lynching—and all that it signified in terms of race and sexual honor—was an integral part of Kentucky culture, as it was in every other southern state. And while allegations of interracial rape, or other insults to white womanhood, were not the only charges that triggered mob violence, what one Little Rock newspaper asserted in a 1918 editorial, when Tommie was a teenage boy, would have resonated with most whites in Kentucky and throughout the South. Just let any black men cast their "lustful eyes on white women" and "seek to break down the barrier that has been between the negro and white man for a thousand years," it said, and whites would be neither "slow nor timid" in replying. "This may be 'Southern Brutality' as far as the Boston negro can see, but in polite circles, we call it Southern chivalry, a Southern virtue that will never die."

To grow up in the South during the early decades of the twentieth century was necessarily to be immersed in a culture of antiblack hatred and violence. There is no reason to believe that any of Tommie's family or friends ever participated in a lynching. But they didn't have to for the practice to affect them. That was a point made in 1929 by Walter White of the NAACP, a leader for years in the futile effort to convince Congress to pass antilynching legislation:

> Generation after generation of Southern whites . . . have had it constantly dinned into their ears from the pulpit and press, in the home and school and on the street, that Negroes are given to sex crimes, that only lynching can protect white women, that unmentionably horrible deeds can be prevented only through the use of extreme brutality. . . . One can estimate the long and difficult climb the Southern white child, living in an atmosphere where dissenting opinion is ruthlessly suppressed, must make to attain even a reasonably intelligent attitude toward lynching and the Negro.

From Millersburg Academy, Tommie made a step up in the world, transferring to the Porter Military Academy in Charleston, South Carolina, which advertised itself as a school that "combines high scholastic attainment and culture with strong incentive to Christian manhood." The first year Tommie was there, South Carolina was home to the lynching of six blacks—for murder, rape, and "being intimate with a white woman." And South Carolina had the second lowest rate of lynchings in the region.

Following three years away at school in Charleston, Tommie was nominated to be a midshipman at the U.S. Naval Academy by Kentucky senator Augustus O. Stanley. As with the previous institutions he had attended, Annapolis was a regimented all-white, all-male environment. During his time at the academy, Tommie developed a reputation among his classmates as a young man with a "cynical attitude" and a temper that he struggled—usually with success—to keep under control. He also was treated for headaches.

Part of the problem was frustration. Tommie had entered the navy hoping to fly airplanes. Four years in a row he applied for flight training, and four years in a row he was turned down—he was too short.

After marrying Thalia, and being stationed in San Diego on an aircraft carrier, Tommie made one final appeal. Having spent most of his life in military schools and academies, he had grown to hate the regimentation and routine that were everyday life on a navy surface ship. In making his flight school application this time, he formally requested a waiver of the pilot's height requirement. It was granted. Good news, since he had already passed all the aviation instruction skills tests. But then, after a psychological examination, he was found to be "temperamentally not qualified" for the job. In his personnel records the word "not" was written in capital letters. No specifics were provided. The submarine corps had different requirements, however, and that was when he applied for, and was accepted at, the submarine training school in New London.

Tommie soon discovered that he loved the life of a submarine officer—the informality, the easy camaraderie, the sense of being a part of something special. And the good times in Hawai'i, surrounded by friends from Annapolis and from submarine training school in New London—including classmates Doc McKechnie, Jerry Branson, Red Rigby, and others—began to make it look as though things would turn out better than he had ever expected.

But then there was Thalia. Their marriage had been difficult almost from the start. Each had hoped that Hawai'i would provide the cure. It hadn't. Things only got worse. And all their friends knew everything about it—the drinking, the fighting, and the other men. So did people who weren't their friends, but just barely knew them, neighbors like Lieutenant Hugh and Elizabeth Johnson, Commander Clinton E. Brain and his wife, and Lieutenant Michael and Christine Russillo. They all lived on the same street, within a few houses of Tommie and Thalia. So did Joe and Helen Cochran, and Charlie Gray and his wife, along with the Masons, the Caters, the MacMillans, the Raniers, and others—navy people whose homes were only a block or two away, and all of them intimately familiar with the problems the Massies had been having for months.

Now this. Thalia storming out of a navy party, as she tended to do more often than not, and winding up on the front pages, the center of a huge controversy. Only a month earlier Tommie had told her he wanted a divorce, but then decided to give her one last chance—a decision he now regretted.

Dr. Porter, who had treated Thalia during her pregnancy and examined her after the assault, and who knew her as well as anyone did, had taken Tommie aside after the police investigation started and urged him not to pursue legal charges against the accused men. Even if the police insisted, he said, Tommie should not let Thalia testify. Tommie probably didn't know what John Porter suspected: that Thalia had not been raped at all. Maybe Tommie wasn't sure himself. It didn't matter. They had to go ahead with the case. Porter pressed him, suggesting that the Massies allow him to intercede with Admiral Stirling and get the couple quietly and quickly shipped off to some other base, far away from the islands, someplace where no one had ever heard of them before. In addition to being a doctor, Porter was a lieutenant commander who had been in the navy for more than fifteen years. He was not without influence, and he could use Thalia's health as an excuse, telling the admiral that in his professional opinion she could not stand the stress of a trial.

But Tommie still said no. The fact was that Thalia was doing fine, perhaps better than at any time since they had moved to Hawai'i. He, Tommie, was the one who feared the trial that lay just ahead. Although his fellow officers and the enlisted men at the base appeared sympathetic, Tommie had heard all the rumors. That Thalia had been drunk and was beaten up by one of her navy lovers. That Tommie had broken her jaw when he arrived home to find her with another man. That Jerry Branson was that other man. That Thalia was a notorious publicity seeker, and the rape only a story she had concocted to draw attention to herself.

Then another rumor began circulating. This one suggested that Tommie would be subpoenaed as a witness at the trial—by the defense. Was it true? And if so, what did the attorneys who were defending the men who assaulted Thalia think they could get out of him that would be beneficial to their clients? Wasn't it improper to force a man to testify against his wife?

He had already testified before the grand jury, along with a handful of police officials and a dozen or so navy men and their wives who had been at the Ala Wai Inn that Saturday night. That had been easy. After all, the grand jury was provided with only the prosecution's side of the case, charged as it was with deciding solely whether there was sufficient evidence to warrant a trial. But the courtroom scene with defense attorneys on hand would be different.

Tommie contacted Captain Wortman and volunteered for sea duty while the proceedings would be in progress. That later would be held against him as well, with men at the base criticizing him behind his back for being absent from the courtroom—either because he apparently was too much of a coward to face his wife's assailants or because even he didn't think Thalia had been raped.

And maybe they were right. But for now, Tommie just wanted to get away. And no place was farther away than a submarine on the bottom of the ocean.

12 On Trial

I t took almost a month after their arrest for all the accused men to be released on bail. The prosecution had originally demanded $10,000 for each
of them. That was impossible and absurd, argued the attorneys for the
defense. They pleaded for a more realistic figure. After all, there was no way
for the defendants to escape the islands. The judge lowered the figure to
$3,500, but even then only Horace Ida's extended family and friends were
able to gather the 10 percent necessary to convince a bondsman to put up the
money. A week later, bail for the others was dropped to $2,000. One by one—
Joe Kahahawai was last—they were released.

Immediately, Admiral Stirling stormed into Governor Judd's office, demanding that bail be revoked and the men be returned to jail until their trial—
"which should be a short one," he said—had ended. Judd informed him that
the law entitled the accused to post bond and that there was nothing he or the
admiral could do about it. Stirling left as angry as when he had arrived, but not
before lecturing the governor on the racial deficits of the local population and
warning him, Judd later recalled, that as long as the defendants were allowed
to roam free "there may be trouble . . . there may be incidents."

The alleged rapists were arraigned on Saturday, October 17, and pleaded
not guilty. The newspapers, still describing them as "gangsters," expressed
surprise at their "self assured" and calm demeanor, as well as their "neatly
clad" appearance in court. Ben Ahakuelo was wearing a brown suit and a
"spotless" white shirt, said the *Star-Bulletin*. Horace Ida and Henry Chang
were similarly attired, while David Takai "was distinguished by a large pale
green satin bow tie." Joe Kahahawai had been unable to come up with a suit
or a flashy bow tie, but at least he wore a "freshly laundered shirt," the newspaper reported.

The attorneys had divided up responsibility for representing the five
men. Heen took on Ahakuelo and Chang, while Pittman handled Ida and Kahahawai. At first Takai, who had never been identified by Thalia as one of her

assailants, was represented by an attorney named H. E. Stafford. Stafford promptly arranged for a meeting between his client and the police at which he urged Takai to turn state's evidence against the other four. Prosecutor Wight assured Takai that charges against him would be reduced if he did so, since they had nothing to link him directly with the assault other than his admission that he had been with the others on the night that Thalia was raped. In addition to receiving a suspended sentence, the authorities assured him, he would collect the five-thousand-dollar reward money that the city fathers had raised. Since he had intended to leave for California shortly after that unfortunate September night anyway, he would now be free to board a steamship for the coast, with all that money in his pocket, as soon as he finished testifying in court against the others.

Takai refused. He had indeed been with the others on the night that Mrs. Massie said she was raped, he told the prosecutor, and he was certain that neither he nor any of the others had so much as laid eyes her. He would not fabricate a story to put the others in prison and save himself.

Attorney Stafford then decided that he didn't wish to represent David Takai after all. Telling the press that Takai had not paid him an agreed-upon fee, he withdrew from the case. Takai was lucky. In Stafford's place, the court appointed a young, locally born Japanese lawyer named Robert Murakami, who had graduated from the University of Chicago Law School in 1925.

Because of the name of the street where Thalia said the assault had occurred, the proceedings now were known informally as the Ala Moana Case. The judge who would be presiding over the trial was Alva E. Steadman, a thirty-seven-year-old native of Beresford, South Dakota, and a 1922 graduate of Harvard Law School, by way of Stanford University. Soon after arriving in Hawai'i, Steadman had married a member of the illustrious Cooke family and proceeded to move rapidly into the legal community's upper echelon. The Cookes had missionary roots in the islands tracing back to the 1830s and business connections dating to the 1850s. That was when the family patriarch, the Reverend Amos Starr Cooke, jointly founded a mercantile establishment named Castle & Cooke, which grew into one of the so-called Big Five corporations that came to dominate completely the economic life of Hawai'i. Despite holding predictable opinions that he was happy to share openly—such as his view that whites were "natural leaders" and therefore should always be placed in positions superior to those held by nonwhites— Steadman was regarded by many court observers as reasonably fair and honest on the bench.

The overheated political climate leading up to the trial would sorely test that reputation, as it had been tested only once before. Almost exactly three years earlier, Steadman had been the judge in what up to then was the islands' most notorious criminal trial ever. In that case, a deranged Japanese teenager named Myles Fukunaga had murdered the son of a prominent haole businessman. Steadman reduced the legally required ten-day psychological examination of the murder defendant to ninety minutes. The trial lasted two days, with the defense calling no witnesses, and Steadman delivered the sentence three days later: death by hanging. After a futile appeal based on his evident insanity (the appeal was argued by Robert Murakami, now David Takai's lawyer), Myles Fukunaga was executed. The entire process, from the arrest to the hanging, took six weeks. Later, Walter Dillingham said he thought of Alva Steadman as "a man's man in every way."

It also was no secret that Judge Steadman's in-laws were among the highly influential community leaders who badly wanted a quick conviction and a severe sentence for the accused men. One of the Cooke women had even campaigned openly for the whipping-post bill and other draconian punishments for sex offenders when Ahakuelo and Chang had been on trial two years earlier. And when Steadman began dismissing out of hand every pretrial motion presented by the defense—including a request for a bill of particulars stipulating precisely what crimes each of the men was accused of having committed—doubts as to his probable fairness in this case began to surface.

In fact, the only pretrial defense motion granted by Steadman was removal of the defendants' alleged aliases from the indictment. These included "Bull" for Kahahawai, which Thalia claimed was used by one of her assailants, but that no one had ever connected with any of the men. The supposed nickname had been inserted by prosecutor Wight.

Then, as if to confirm the worst fears of the defense team, on the eve of the trial Judge Steadman announced that this would be the last legal case over which he would preside. He had just been offered a lucrative position as general manager of the newly established Cooke Trust Company, a Castle & Cooke subsidiary, and he planned to accept it once the trial verdict was filed.

The trial officially known as *Territory of Hawaii v. Ben Ahakuelo et al.* opened on November 16, a Monday. It was unseasonably warm and muggy outside, a condition made worse indoors by the scores of spectators who squeezed into every seat in the courtroom, attempting to cool themselves with all manner of makeshift fans. Most of those who found seats were overdressed and heavily perfumed women from the city's leading families, some of whom had given servants time off to arrive early and hold places in line for them. Others, denied entry because of a lack of space, were left standing in the judiciary building's corridors or milling about on the courthouse grounds. Between 8:00 and 8:30 a.m. attorneys for both sides, all wearing white or tan tropical suits and removing their lightweight Panama hats as they entered the courthouse, began pushing through the crowd and making their way to the long counsel tables near the bench.

The Honolulu Courthouse was known officially as Ali'iolani Hale, the "House of the Heavenly Chiefs." It was built in the 1870s as the meeting place for the kingdom's legislature, and sported a palatial design, including Ionic columns and a cut stone exterior along with curved double staircases, stained-glass skylights, an octagonal rotunda, and inlaid marble floors.

Located directly across a wide, tree-lined boulevard from the royal palace that was eventually built in 1882, the imposing courthouse building, today housing the Hawai'i Supreme Court, has a large gilded statue of King Kamehameha standing in front of it. Kamehameha was the first monarch of the unified island kingdom, and in the eighteenth century he declared a law—now a part of the state constitution—guaranteeing all people of Hawai'i, especially women, children, and the aged, safe passage on roads and highways. To supporters of Thalia Massie, who were attending the trial on that warm November morning, the sentiment seemed more insulting than ironic.

As always in American court cases, the first order of business was jury selection. And as was often true in Hawai'i, certain aspects of the procedure were different from prevailing customs in the rest of the country. For one thing, the Organic Act of 1900 that established Hawai'i as a territory of the United States required that juries be constituted without regard to the jurors' race. This was consistent with the U.S. Constitution's Fourteenth Amendment guarantee of equal protection, but Hawai'i law contained an exception to the color-blindness rule. Unlike in the continental United States, juries composed exclusively of persons from any one race were expressly prohibited.

Throughout most of the nineteenth century very different legislation had been in force in Hawai'i. Since the early 1800s kingdom law stipulated that if both the accuser and the accused were either haole or native—the only recognized "races" in the islands at that time—all jurors in a trial must be of that same race. But if the accuser and the accused were of different races, the jury composition had to be half haole and half native. This was a version of the common-law mixed-jury tradition that dated to thirteenth-century

England, in earlier times primarily involving trials at which Jews or other "aliens" were defendants.

As the nineteenth century progressed in Hawai'i, it became evident to all observers of the islands' courtrooms that native juries were far stricter in judging other natives than haole juries were in dealing with haoles. In addition to banning this archaic jury system, territorial status in 1900 restricted membership on juries to literate, adult, male citizens of the United States. This meant, effectively, natives and "Anglo-Saxon" haoles. And haoles in the islands at that time were greatly outnumbered by natives. Thus, although the prohibition on single-race juries appears in retrospect to have been remarkably progressive, in reality it served largely to protect haoles, who only seven years earlier had overthrown the monarchy, from juries made up entirely of Hawaiians.

By 1931, however—although the law was still in force—the number of natives and haoles in Hawai'i was almost equal. Moreover, there were then large numbers of Chinese, Japanese, and still technically nonwhite Portuguese citizens eligible to serve on juries, while a rapidly growing proportion of the population was of mixed racial ancestry. Hawaiians and many longtime residents of all nationalities took this in stride. But the varied and sometimes apparently nondescript racial identities of Hawai'i jurors, at least among people accustomed to the conventional all-white juries of the U.S. mainland, especially in the South, would soon cause both confusion and outrage in the American press.

Along with understanding the local complexities of race, the best Honolulu attorneys knew something else about the assessment of potential jurors that outsiders found difficult to fathom: that race, while it mattered, was no more reliable a predictor of a juror's predilections than were social class and political affiliation. By statute, two jury commissioners, one Republican and one Democrat, were charged with providing names for the court's jury list "in proportion with the respective number of registered voters in each of the precincts." This meant not only that certain poorer precincts, with low numbers of registered voters, were underrepresented in the jury pool, but that there was good reason to believe that many jurors whose names were put forward had strong political opinions and were closely allied with one or the other major political party.

In confronting the pitfall of highly politicized jurors, defense attorneys had a distinct advantage because they were provided with twice as many peremptory challenges as were available to the prosecution. That is, they had double the number of chances to disqualify potential jurors without stating a reason for doing so. Because there were five defendants in this case, the defense could use up to thirty peremptory challenges, while the prosecution was limited to fifteen. Both sides used all of them, after grilling each prospective juror on all manner of things, including political connections and beliefs.

Jury selection dragged on for hour after hour, and on into the night, for two days, but at last a jury was impaneled. Racially, it was composed of two Chinese, two Japanese, one Portuguese, one "American" (meaning white Anglo-Saxon), and six who were a mixture of haole and Hawaiian. All of them were responsibly employed either by large corporations or by the city of Honolulu, and one was a retired police captain. Three of them worked for Big Five corporations. Except for its racial composition, the jury was typical. During the past four years, among all jurors serving in the Honolulu courts, and despite the Depression, 97 percent had been employed—more than half in executive or professional positions. But two-thirds had also been haole. In this case, with only one haole on the jury, Heen and Pittman appear to have taken race very seriously in using their peremptory challenges.

Well aware of the scrutiny he would be receiving in this, his final appearance on the circuit court bench, Judge Steadman went out of his way to instruct the jurors with care. He informed them that they would not be sequestered, but said they should avoid reading press reports of the case and ordered them to not discuss it with anyone. Moreover, he told them, the trial was not to be regarded as "a contest in oratorical skill." Rather, he said, it was a straightforward exploration "of whether the Territory can produce evidence sufficient to find these men guilty. As they stand now, they are presumed to be innocent." He then continued, with specific reference to the accusation that had been brought against the defendants:

> The charge in this case is rape. No offense is more serious. There is no offense in respect to which all respectable men feel such revulsion at the mere mention of the word. The duty of the jury, however, is to determine not whether rape is outrageous—because that is obvious—but what is the evidence. The jury must decide two things. Whether rape has been committed, and whether these defendants, or any of them, is guilty. If they, or one of them, is guilty, the jury must convict; if not, it must acquit. It is just that simple.

Of course, in reality it was far from that simple, especially because of Hawai'i's unusual, though not unique, legal requirement that in rape cases the prosecution had to produce corroborative evidence in support of its charges. Thalia's testimony by itself was insufficient, in the eyes of Hawai'i law, for a finding that the men were guilty. Among the states at that time, only Ohio and New York had similar restrictions on taking an alleged rape victim's word at face value.

Hawai'i law, which prohibited conviction in a rape case "upon the mere testimony of the female uncorroborated by other evidence direct or circumstantial," was an effort to prevent reversal of the burden of proof: that without a corroboration requirement of any sort—if only evidence of vaginal bruising or torn clothing—it inevitably falls to the defendant to demonstrate that he did not commit the crime. In this case, however, the corroboration rule ran head-on into an overheated political climate that was overwhelmingly favorable to the prosecution. Both sides involved in the Ala Moana trial knew that in this atmosphere, establishing a sufficient level of proof to convict the defendants would not be difficult. The jury was charged with weighing the veracity of a female victim who was young, white, socially prominent, and married to a United States Navy officer against that of defendants who were poor, unemployed, dark skinned, and of dubious social standing. Two of the five men had previous criminal convictions (however undeserved) for "assault with intent to ravish," while a third had been convicted of assault and battery.

Officially the defense needed only to demonstrate that the prosecution had not met its legal burden of proving guilt beyond a reasonable doubt. But in reality, by the time the jury retired to begin its deliberations, for the defense team to prevail it would have to have proved beyond a shadow of a doubt that its clients were innocent.

During jury selection, attorneys Heen, Pittman, and Murakami were particularly aggressive, as if to put the court on notice that they intended to contest the prosecution on every possible matter of disagreement. At one point, a prospective juror turned out also to be the bail bondsman for one of the accused men. While this clearly was grounds for automatic dismissal, defense lawyer William Pittman argued vigorously that it was inappropriate to dismiss a prospective juror simply because he had a "business" relationship with a defendant. After all, he pointed out, other potential jurors who worked for the telephone company, the board of water supply, and various private firms also had—or may have had—business connections of one sort or another with each of the defendants. Judge Steadman listened patiently and then dismissed the bail bondsman.

But in one area, at least, the attorneys for the defense made a calculated decision to proceed with caution. That was in their handling of Thalia. While it was the prosecution's burden to prove two things—that the crime itself had been committed and that the accused men were the culprits—the attorneys for the defense only had to establish that their clients did not commit the crime. Although Heen, Pittman, and Murakami had accumulated evidence strongly suggesting that Thalia had not been raped at all, they decided, as Heen put it in a private interview months later, that "it was not the inclination of anyone to embarrass Mrs. Massie any more than it could be helped."

There was also another and less chivalric reason for their decision. Thalia had been so thoroughly portrayed in the press as a fragile and brave martyred victim that the potential for backlash, among jurors as well as the larger community, posed too great a risk should the defense openly contend that she had been lying about everything from the start. Again, it was not the job of the defense to prove that Thalia had made everything up—especially since, at the very least, someone had punched her in the face with sufficient force to fracture her jaw—but only to demonstrate that the police had arrested the wrong men. That did not mean they would fail to raise doubts about Thalia's fundamental claim, but only that they would have to be subtle in doing so.

The defense reserved its opening statement until later, and the prosecutor, after a brief but fiery opening, called his first witness, Thalia. The next day's newspaper accounts of her testimony overflowed with sympathy. "A beautiful young woman, cultured and of gentle bearing, told a jury today the sordid details of an alleged assault on her body by five gangsters," was the way the Star-Bulletin's front-page story began. At one point, Thalia turned in the direction of "the youths charged with her assault," the article continued, and "her blue eyes met an array of ten brown ones as the accusations were spoken." With "her face scarred, her body bent and wracked by physical and mental anguish," the Advertiser added, "the girl faced bravely the ordeal in the crowded courtroom." Even the Hawaii Hochi, still the only newspaper that had reported any weaknesses in the prosecution's case, was impressed with Thalia's "tragic story . . . told through eyes blinded by tears."

Melodrama aside, Thalia's demeanor and her statements under direct examination by prosecutor Griffith Wight were very convincing. She was dressed conservatively in a dark suit, her hair tucked under a small matching hat. Calmly answering the prosecutor's foundational questions about her personal background and what she had been doing prior to the assault on the night of September 12, Thalia spoke in a soft, matter-of-fact manner. But when she reached the point of describing the kidnapping and the rape, she collapsed in tears, and Judge Steadman called a recess to allow her to compose herself.

When the examination continued, Thalia described what had happened with a clarity and vividness of detail that would have astonished the policemen who first interviewed her. Where once she was in the dark and unable to identify anyone, now Thalia said "it was not very dark" either where the men picked her up or where they took her. She claimed that she saw the men's faces clearly, and that she heard them address one another by their first names, and even by nicknames (coincidentally the ones that had appeared frequently in the press during the past two months). Thalia also recalled specific details about each of her assailants, including Horace Ida's suede jacket and Ben Ahakuelo's gold tooth. She proceeded to describe with amazing specificity the colors and types of shirts and trousers that each of the men had been wearing, all of which matched prosecution exhibits of the clothes worn that night by the men who now were on trial. While she did this, Thalia pointed out the defendants, seated in the courtroom, as the men who had kidnapped, beaten, and raped her—all except Takai, about whom she said she still had no recollection.

And now, as earlier in the presence of Chief of Detectives John McIntosh, she recalled within one digit of its actual number the license plate on Horace Ida's sister's car as the one she had seen driving away from the scene of the rape. And she identified Haruyo Ida's late-model tan-colored Ford—with no torn or flapping top—as the vehicle her abductors had driven.

Finally, and crucially, she now was absolutely certain she left the party at 11:35, not 12:00 as she had told the detectives and Captain McIntosh. Since Thalia and the police estimated that it took about ten minutes to walk from the inn to her place of abduction, that meant that Thalia could have been kidnapped as early as 11:45.

Prosecutor Wight elicited this information from Thalia smoothly. Her recollection was clear, her delivery perfect. Wight had no fear of contradiction. At the grand jury proceeding he had not called to testify any of the officers who had first spoken with Thalia. And he had no intention of doing so at this trial, nor of introducing the reports they had written.

Thalia's detailed accounting of the time and place of her abduction, along with her near-photographic recollection of the assailants' faces and clothing, was of central importance to the judge and jury in the case. But it was other graphic detail that, according to the press, most visibly affected courtroom spectators. Detail such as the sustained punching of her face by the football player and boxer, Joe Kahahawai, egged on by a "grinning" Ben

Ahakuelo, who repeatedly urged Kahahawai "to hit me again." Or how she cried and begged him to stop punching her—and when he didn't, how she started to pray out loud. Or how, once they arrived at the deserted and over-grown site of the former animal quarantine station, they pulled her out of the car and "dragged me some distance" before holding her down and re-peatedly raping her. From her initial claim of being raped six or seven times, Thalia had now settled on "four to six times." Chang, she said, had assaulted her twice, having told the others after they were through that "he wanted to go again." Yet, despite the terror and the pain, she insisted, through it all "I struggled as hard as I could."

If there was a dry eye in the courtroom at that point, there probably wasn't after Thalia began to tell of her pregnancy. When she was admitted to the Queen Kapiolani Maternity Hospital a month after the alleged assault, the dilation and curettage had been performed by Dr. Paul Withington. It was he who signed the postoperative report indicating that Thalia had not been pregnant. But Withington was a family friend of the Massies, and Wight had no intention of calling him to testify. So the prosecutor felt safe in elicit-ing from Thalia the assertion that some weeks after the assault "I found I was pregnant . . . and had an operation performed by a doctor." When Wight asked her how she could be certain the pregnancy was not a result of sexual intercourse with her husband, Thalia answered that "my husband and I had not had intimate relations" since the time of her last menstrual period prior to the rape, "nor have we had any since."

"So your pregnancy resulted from this attack?" Wight asked. "Yes," Thalia replied. Before closing his direct examination, the prosecutor intro-duced into evidence the clothing Thalia had been wearing on the night of the assault, along with the contents of her purse, recovered at the scene.

The examination of Thalia by prosecutor Wight lasted less than two hours, beginning just after ten o'clock in the morning and ending at a little before noon. William Heen was handling the cross-examination for the defense, and he would take a good deal more time. After a few preliminary questions, he requested a recess for lunch, and Judge Steadman adjourned until 2:00 p.m.

When Heen resumed his questioning of Thalia that afternoon, his de-meanor was polite but firm. He began by asking her about the time of night that she, Tommie, and the two couples who were with them had gone to the party at the Ala Wai Inn. "We went about nine or nine-thirty," she replied. That was insufficiently precise for Heen. Which was it, he wanted to know, nine or nine thirty? She wasn't sure. He quietly persisted: "Might it have been beyond nine-thirty?" Yes, she acknowledged, "I don't remember the exact time."

From the outset Heen was serving notice on Thalia that he was going to press her on details, whether or not they seemed important to her. The sympathetic exchanges with prosecutor Wight were over. Heen was also establishing for the jury the fact that Thalia was nonchalant and imprecise about matters of time—at least those matters of time that had not been well rehearsed with the prosecutor.

And so it went with minor topic after minor topic. How many people were in the group that gathered at her home before the party at the Ala Wai Inn? Were there both men and women in that group? How many were men and how many were women? Did you have dinner at the inn? Did you dance? Did you dance every dance? Did you have any refreshments? Alcohol? What kind? How much? And more—before suddenly circling back and asking: "When you say it was nine or nine-thirty, or perhaps later than nine-thirty, when you went to the party at the Ala Wai Inn, how do you recall it was about that time?"

Thalia replied that there was a clock in their house, "and I looked at it and said it was about time we left."

"Well then, when you looked at the clock and said it was about time to go, what time was it according to the clock?"

"Shortly after nine, as I remember."

"About how many minutes would that be according to your best judgment?"

"I don't know—between nine and nine-thirty."

"But you said shortly after nine."

"I mean between nine and nine-thirty."

And then Heen was back to asking how much liquor they had consumed and how many dances she had danced, before abruptly shifting gears again: "About what time was it that you left the Ala Wai Inn?"

"It was about 11:35."

"How do you recall that time?"

"Because some friends of mine left the dance at 11:30 and I left the party a few minutes after they did."

"Did you look at any clock or look at a timepiece so as to know that your friends left at 11:30?"

"No."

"Then how did you happen to know it was 11:30?"

"My friend told me later that she had looked at her watch and it had been 11:30."

"Several days later?"

"I don't remember."

"What is your best recollection as to that?"

"I don't remember."

"You don't know whether it was the next day or a week after?"

"No. I don't remember when it was."

Without ever raising his voice, Heen asked all these questions in rapid succession, leaving hardly a moment of silence between Thalia's answers and his next inquiry. It was a classic—indeed, a textbook—cross-examination.

Apparently sensing a trap, Thalia now simply failed to remember an astonishing number of things. Heen asked if the stores that lined John Ena Road, on which she had been walking when she said she was abducted, were open as she passed by. She didn't remember. What about cars, were there many of them on the street as she strolled along? Heen and most everyone else in Honolulu, including the jurors, knew that John Ena Road was always crowded with cars until well after midnight on Saturdays. And on that particular Saturday night, the park manager would testify, there were at least five hundred people at the dance. Thalia paused, then said, "I didn't notice any cars."

What about the dance itself—was it going on while she walked past the pavilion? Ten days after the incident she had told McIntosh and Wight that there was no music playing when she walked by the park, meaning that the dance, which ended at midnight, was already over. On the stand now, she gave an evasive, indirect answer, saying "at that time I didn't know the exact location of Waikiki Park and I didn't know it had an entrance on John Ena Road." In fact, the park's only entrance and exit were on that street, directly across from where she had been walking.

After a recess, Heen resumed the cross-examination. He led Thalia back to the story of the abduction, beating, and rape that she had earlier told in such detail and with such emotion. Thalia appeared more comfortable—for this she was prepared—and he allowed her to be expansive. She went over the same ground covered under prosecutor Wight's direct examination. Heen's questions were less aggressive than earlier, simply prodding her to continue and provide more detail. When the narrative reached the point where the assailants removed her from the car and took her to the bushes just before she was raped, Heen asked: "Did they drag you along the ground or hold onto you and force you to walk with them?"

"They were holding me and dragging me," Thalia answered. "I didn't exactly walk. They pulled me along."

"Were your feet dragging on the ground as they took you there?"

"Yes."

As the lawyer persisted, her tone became flat and unemotional, in contrast to the tearful way she had described the same events under questioning by the prosecutor. It was as if a caution flag had gone up. No doubt Thalia sensed in the attorney's voice a skepticism that five men who were merciless enough to commit such a brutal crime—and who were far from prying eyes, with no reason to hurry—would take so little time—twenty minutes, she claimed—to carry out their repeated assaults. And then, Heen asked, when the ordeal was over, "did you come right out of that place?" She had previously testified that after they finished, one of the men—Ahakuelo, she thought—had helped her up and given her directions so she could find her way back to the road, which was about 250 feet away. Then the car drove off into the night.

She now said: "I wandered around through the bushes and trees and finally came to the road."

"About how long were you wandering around in the bushes and trees?"

At this moment Thalia apparently realized the danger toward which Heen was leading her. The prosecutor had warned Thalia that time would be a central factor in how the jury decided the case. The more time she said was consumed by the repeated assaults and the events immediately preceding and following them, the more difficult it would be to fit everything into the limited window of opportunity. She had already shifted her estimate of when she left the party at the Ala Wai Inn from midnight back to 11:35, and confined her estimate of the time consumed by the rapes to only twenty minutes. Now she said abruptly that she had no idea how long she wandered in the bushes, and when Heen persisted she held firm: "I don't know."

For most of the rest of the afternoon, Heen led Thalia at a modest and unchallenging pace through everything that had occurred after the rape itself, from the point when she hailed the car containing the Bellingers and the Clarks on Ala Moana Road to her first two days in the hospital. Thalia's recollections were remarkably clear and precise in answering almost every question. The only exception, other than on matters of time, occurred when he asked a series of questions about the police officers who showed up at her home in response to Tommie's call for help. At that point she suddenly lost all recall of everything that had happened: "I was hysterical. . . . I don't remember much about it."

Not only did she not remember any questions the police had asked her at that time, but initially she denied that they had asked her any questions at all. Repeatedly, her responses were variations on "I don't remember much" or "My husband explained it all." That wasn't good enough for the defense attorney. He bored in now, picking up the pace, asking her if it was not true that she had told the police that all of the men who had assaulted her were Hawaiians? Hadn't she said to the officers that the only name she heard was the nickname "Bull"? Had she not told them it was too dark to identify any of her attackers? Wasn't it so that she had told the police she would be unable to identify the car in which she had been abducted? Prosecutor Wight objected, but Judge Steadman overruled him, and Heen kept hammering away.

Thalia alternated between denying that she had spoken with the police at all until her interview with Chief of Detectives McIntosh, and saying, over and over, "I don't know," "I don't remember what they said or what I said to them," or "I don't remember anything."

On the matter of the license plate number of the car the men were driving, Heen asked Thalia if it was true that she had told the police officers that she had never seen it at all. She denied this. Although according to her, she had taken the trouble at the scene of the crime to memorize the number, with the exception of only one digit, she now insisted, "I didn't think of the number until Mr. McIntosh asked me." The defense attorney continued without letup, and Thalia's last three words, just before court adjourned for the day, were "I don't remember."

The next morning, Thursday, Griffith Wight called Navy Lieutenant Commander John Porter, Thalia's physician. Porter had been the second doctor to see Thalia, after Dr. David Liu—who examined her at the hospital only two hours or so after the alleged assault, and who was not on the prosecutor's witness list. Dr. Porter had seen her about eight hours later, on Sunday morning at her home—then afterward, at the hospital—and Wight's intent was to have him describe in painful detail the extent of her injuries. Porter did not disappoint. Referring to a chart he had brought with him, he listed every blemish that he had found on Thalia's face and body when he examined her at the hospital on Sunday afternoon.

The main damage was to her face. Her jaw was fractured in two places, he testified, adding that "her right eye was practically closed, the right cheek was one mass of bruises where she had been hit, and there was considerable swelling of the nose and bleeding from the nostrils, both right and left sides." In addition, he mentioned some minor bruises on her body and an abrasion on her left ankle, all likely caused by her being hit or having fallen. But the facial injuries were by far the most serious of her wounds.

Wight asked the doctor if he had made a vaginal examination of Thalia. He said yes, and in answer to a follow-up question he said that her "vaginal opening is unusually large" because she had had a baby, "and it seems she was torn at that time." In light of that, Wight asked whether it was possible for "four to six men to have sexual intercourse with her without showing any result?" Anticipating what he would say in interviews months and years later, Porter was evasive: yes, it would be possible, he replied, adding that multiple intercourse (he was not asked about gang rape) "may or may not" have shown up in a medical examination.

Wight pressed on, asking about her condition upon entering the hospital on Sunday afternoon. He got more of an answer than he expected. In emphasizing the amount of pain Thalia's jaw was causing her at the time, Dr. Porter described how he had given her "several opiates" as soon as he saw her at her home, adding that he continued to keep her under those drugs during her stay at the hospital. As a result, he said, "she probably didn't know just what she was doing at the time."

Quickly, Wight steered the interrogation in another direction, closing by having Porter confirm that Thalia's jaw would never be the same, that "she will probably always have a little lump on that side."

On cross-examination, William Heen went through a few preliminary questions before picking up the matter of the opiates. When was it that he said he had administered the first dose? At her home, a little after ten o'clock on Sunday morning, Porter said. Heen didn't mention yet that this was before Thalia had made her first identification of her assailants.

After acknowledging that another doctor he called to Thalia's home had disagreed with the seriousness of his diagnosis, Porter answered in reply to a question that the next time he saw Thalia was in the hospital on Sunday afternoon. "Did it appear to you that she had been given some more opiates after the first treatment you gave her?" Heen asked. "Yes," the doctor replied.

The defense attorney wouldn't relent. When was the next time Porter saw Mrs. Massie? About seven or eight o'clock on Sunday night, during his regular rounds, the doctor said. "And did she appear at that time that she had taken her opiates according to the orders given by you?" Again Porter said yes. How frequently did she receive these opiates under his direction? Every four hours, or "as needed," the doctor answered, finally adding: "She got them frequently. I cannot say every four hours." And how long did this regimen continue? It continued for the entirety of her weeklong stay in the hospital.

"And you said you had to give her these opiates on account of her condition," Heen continued, "and that as you said on your direct examination, being under opiates, she did not know exactly what she was doing at that time?"

"From the time I saw her, from her nervous condition and so forth, she appeared dazed, sir, for four or five days."

"And she appeared to you, as you stated on your direct examination, that 'she didn't know what she was doing.'"

"Well, she didn't know what she was doing for the first four or five days, with the shock and so forth, and with the pain and with the opiates. I really don't believe she knew exactly what she was doing." Then, after a pause as if to evaluate for himself what he had just said, Porter added: "I still stick to it."

Pleased that he had compromised the credibility of Thalia's identification of her assailants, both at her home and at the hospital, Heen indicated that he was through with the witness.

What he didn't know was that Dr. Porter possessed far more valuable information. As her physician, and as a colleague and friend of Dr. Withington, who had performed the obstetrical surgery on her, Porter knew that Thalia had been lying when she testified that she had become pregnant following the alleged rape. And it was he who, many years later, would tell an interviewer that Thalia's eyesight was so poor that, without her glasses, she was nearly blind. She could not possibly have seen the men's faces and clothing as clearly as she had testified, to say nothing of the license plate number of a car speeding away in the dark. But Porter no doubt felt that he had volunteered more than enough information as it was.

The next people called to testify for the prosecution confirmed certain aspects of what was already well known, but they also posed further problems for the prosecution's crime scenario. First, George Clark described at length his riding in the car driven by Eustace Bellinger that picked Thalia up on Ala Moana Road on Sunday, September 13, at around one o'clock in the morning, perhaps a little earlier. Clark said that when Thalia climbed into the car he noticed that "her face was all puffed at the mouth" and "she said she had been beaten up by a gang of young hoodlums and left in the woods, as she called it, to get home the best way she could." Combined with what Thalia and Dr. Porter had said, Clark's testimony supported the prosecution's claim that someone had at least punched Thalia, and had certainly had time to rape her, if she left the Ala Wai Inn at 11:35 Saturday night and not at midnight. That window of almost an hour and a half was more than sufficient for the crime to have been committed. It was, however, reduced on one end by at least ten minutes—the time it would have taken Thalia to walk from the inn to the place where she said she had been abducted—and on the other end by roughly another half hour because of the Peeples incident.

Agnes Peeples was the next witness to testify. The prosecution needed her to explain how the license plate number of the car in which the defendants were riding had originally become known to the police. It was her assault complaint that had led to the arrest of Horace Ida, and then the four others. But she also complicated matters for Griffith Wight. Mrs. Peeples's run-in with the accused men had begun at about 12:35 and ended at 12:40, at most fifteen to twenty minutes before Thalia was picked up on Ala Moana Road.

The minutes on the clock simply were not adding up in Thalia's narrative: the absolute minimum time necessary for the men to drive from the confrontation with Mrs. Peeples to the scene of Thalia's abduction, then to the scene of the rapes—and to carry out the multiple assaults—was forty or fifty minutes, while there were at most twenty minutes available between the time Mrs. Peeples last saw the defendants and the time Thalia was picked up by the side of the road. Obviously, if the suspects had committed the crime, they would have to have done it before the Peeples encounter. And if it did happen before, given the approximately ten minutes required to drive away from the scene of the crime to the place where the Peeples incident happened, the assault on Thalia would have to have *ended* no later than 12:25. That left a maximum of forty minutes—from 11:45, the earliest, according to her own testimony, that Thalia could have been abducted, to 12:25—for the kidnapping, beating, and multiple rapes to have occurred. Although this was within the realm of possibility, there remained very little room for error in the story prosecutor Wight was laying out, and no room at all if the defendants—and Thalia—were seen elsewhere between 11:45 and 12:25.

Equally important, the two central charges—that Thalia had in fact been kidnapped and raped, and that the defendants were the men who did it—still rested for support solely on her testimony. And under cross-examination defense attorney Heen had shown that although Thalia's recollections were astonishingly clear on select matters, that clarity of recall vanished when confronted with almost anything else that had happened that night—especially regarding matters that might undermine her accusations. Finally, there was

Dr. Porter's testimony that Thalia was so drugged that she didn't know what she was doing on the very occasions when she identified the men now in court as her alleged assailants.

Prosecutor Wight hoped that the jury, in its sympathy for a young woman who doubtless had been beaten, would be able to sidestep, at least to some extent, the legal requirement for corroboration of a rape accuser's charges. But he also knew that even if the jury were to take most of her story on faith—that someone had beaten and raped her—he badly needed something to substantiate her claim that the police had arrested the right men. The explosive testimony of his next two witnesses, he was certain, would put to rest any lingering doubts.

He called to the stand Detective John C. Cluney, one of the two men who arrested Horace Ida at his mother's house early Sunday morning. After briskly taking the detective through his movements up to and including the arrest, Wight directed the questioning to a moment, after their arrival at police headquarters, when Cluney and Ida found themselves alone together. At that point, Cluney testified, "Ida said he admitted that one of the boys in his car struck Mrs. Peeples, but as far as the striking of this white woman he said he didn't know anything about it."

Wight paused to allow this to sink in, then followed with: "At that time, had you mentioned to him that a white woman had been struck?" Cluney replied: "I had not." Had anyone else told him? No, Cluney said—and Ida had not been out of his sight since the time he had been placed under arrest at his mother's house. The prosecutor turned the witness over to Heen for cross-examination.

Unless Detective Cluney was perjuring himself, Horace Ida had as much as confessed to participating in the assault on Thalia that night. There appeared to be no way for Ida to have known of the attack on a "white woman" unless he had been a part of it.

Heen, taken aback, stalled by asking Cluney to recall what time it was when he arrived at the Ida home—the same question Wight had asked and Cluney had answered only a few minutes earlier. Then, perhaps on a hunch or possibly because he knew something others didn't, he asked if Cluney had written a report on what he had seen and done that night. The detective replied that he had, but that he did not have it with him. Heen requested a break in the witness's testimony until Cluney retrieved the report. The court agreed. Cluney was excused temporarily, and after a recess the prosecution moved on to its next witness, police officer Claude Benton.

Benton and his partner, Officer Percy Bond, had been the first police officials to search the crime scene, only two or three hours after the assault had apparently occurred. Chief of Detectives McIntosh had sent the two men out early Sunday morning, while it was still dark, and Benton had returned to headquarters with various personal items that Thalia identified as having been in her handbag. But Wight was interested in something else. After having Benton describe how he and Bond had parked their police car outside the grounds of the former animal quarantine station and walked in using flashlights to illuminate the area, he got the officer to tell the court that he had then "discovered automobile tire tracks which had gone in there at a fast rate of speed."

It was muddy in parts of the open space near the old quarantine station, Benton recalled, and he could plainly identify the kinds of tires that had made the tracks. Immediately, William Pittman for the defense was on his feet, objecting that the police officer had not been qualified as an expert on tire tracks, and thus any conclusions he might draw were inadmissible. Judge Steadman overruled the objection.

Wight continued. "What type of tire marks were they?"

"There were three Goodrich Silverton cords and one Goodyear All-Weather," the detective stated.

"Could you tell from the marks which wheel had the Goodyear on?"

"The left rear."

Needless to say, those were precisely the same tires, on the same wheels, that were on Horace Ida's sister's car. Attorney Pittman continued to object—and to be overruled.

Wight then drew increasingly detailed testimony from Benton on the tire tracks he had seen, having him sketch a diagram of the site on a blackboard and describe how his and Bond's "very strong flashlights and the headlights of our automobile" had allowed them to see clearly in the dark. Later, Wight would attempt to qualify Benton as an expert witness because he had once worked in a tire store—but not before the policeman said he had written up a report on all this and turned it over to Captain McIntosh before quitting work for the night.

"Didn't you do something else?" Wight prodded the officer.

"The following morning, yes."

"That is what I mean, *that* morning, the *Sunday* morning."

Benton had not meant the same morning. He had spoken correctly when he said "the following morning"—Monday morning—but when Wight pressed him, he understood what he was expected to say. "Yes," he answered, "later in the morning."

And what had he done at that time, Wight asked, only "four to four and a half hours" after his and Bond's initial survey of the crime scene? He and another police officer, Samuel Lau, had taken Horace Ida—in Ida's sister's car—to the area where the assault was said to have been committed and where the tire tracks he had discovered were still embedded in the mud. There, Benton testified, they found that the tires on the Ida car "were identical" to the tracks left only hours before, obviously by the car containing the men who had raped Thalia Massie.

Wight asked Benton to repeat what he had said: "You say the marks of this car, left by car 58-895, and the former marks you had seen on the ground were identical?"

"Identically the same."

"Had any other car gone over these marks?"

"None over these particular marks."

"Did Ida say anything when you made this examination?"

"He was very quiet."

"Did he deny that they were the same marks?"

"He denied that he had been in there."

"Did he deny that they were the same marks?"

"He did not deny that. No, sir."

It was a dramatic moment. Wight had now elicited sworn police testimony that Horace Ida voluntarily spoke of an assault on a white woman before anyone had mentioned the fact of such an attack in his presence, and he had Ida—on Sunday morning, only hours after his arrest—unable to deny that the tires on the car he had been driving matched perfectly the tread marks earlier left by a car at the location where the rape had occurred. Back to back, the two police officers' accounts were devastating.

At this point, not wanting to lose his momentum, Wight turned to the judge and asked permission to take the jury to the scene of the crime.

13   For the Defense

Before packing up and visiting the crime scene, the court—in the presence of the jury—was treated to a lengthy peroration by defense cocounsel Pittman. He adamantly pressed Judge Steadman to instruct everyone that "the only object in visiting the premises with the jury is so that they may follow the Court intelligently, and the testimony from the witness stand." No testimony should be taken on location, he insisted—that is, no specific evidence pertaining to the case should be pointed out by the prosecutor— and he must be disallowed from "showing spots where he found the tire tracks or where he found these other things." Of course, that was precisely what Wight had intended to do, and he argued back, saying that with its objection the defense was attempting to hide things from the jury. Pittman erupted again, telling the judge that the last remark from the prosecutor was intended to prejudice the jurors, as was this entire scene-of-the-crime excursion. Judge Steadman said he would allow the location visit for the jury—and he would join it, along with counsel, clerk, and official reporter—but his instructions on how they were to behave outside the courtroom largely supported Pittman's demands.

More quietly than Pittman, Heen slipped in two separate requests. First, as long as they were going to the supposed crime scene, why not take the time to visit John Ena Road and Waikiki Park, where the alleged abduction had taken place? The judge agreed. Also, just as he had insisted that Detective Cluney retrieve a copy of his written report on what Horace Ida had told him at police headquarters following his arrest, Heen asked the prosecuting attorney for any written reports filed by Officer Benton regarding the tire tracks. Wight turned to Benton and, leading him as before, asked, "Did you make a report? You did not make a report of that case because you arrested no one, is that it?"

No, Benton surprisingly replied. That was not it. He had in fact made a written report, but at the moment he didn't know where it was. Heen had expected as much, so he used the occasion to ask as well about the police reports of the first officers to question Thalia, knowing full well that Wight had no intention of calling those men as witnesses or of locating their written statements. Wight said he had not seen the reports in question and knew nothing about them. Suspecting correctly that at least some of the reports were at the offices of the *Advertiser*—the police later claimed they had been sent there to be bound—Heen asked the court to have them sent over to him before proceedings resumed that afternoon.

When the afternoon session began, following the excursion to what were said to be the crime scenes, only a single report was made available to the defense. It was the one Officer Benton had written at four o'clock Sunday morning, after his and Bond's first visit to the site while Captain McIntosh was still interviewing Thalia. Heen quickly scanned the report, then put it aside and began his cross-examination.

After a few preliminary questions, Heen asked Benton to go to the courtroom blackboard and draw the tread of a Seiberling tire. Once he had done that, Heen began a series of detailed, technical inquiries. On the actual tire, how far apart are the grooves he had drawn? How deep are they? How many types of Seiberling tire are there? What about Goodyear? Will you please draw a diagram of a Goodyear Double-Eagle tire? How many grooves does it have? And a Goodyear Deluxe? The All-Weather? The Pathfinder?

And so on. Benton started out confidently, and did in fact have answers to most of Heen's questions. But soon he was forced to admit that his experience with tires had ended when he left his job at the tire store four years earlier—and the Ida car was only two years old. To everyone in the courtroom this seemed the point of it all: Heen was pushing this hard to expose Benton's limited familiarity with tires and tread design, thereby undermining his claim of expertise. And at last he had taken the officer to the outer extent of his knowledge.

But actually that was the least important part of what the defense attorney was doing. Even after Benton had acknowledged that he knew little about recently released tires, Heen kept pressing the policeman for details on tread design, grooves, and other markings on tire after tire after tire. Then suddenly he shifted to the fact that Benton had said in his direct testimony that the tire marks at the crime scene showed that the car making them had been moving fast. How could he tell that? From the dirt that had been kicked up, Benton said. What kind of dirt? Gravel. What kind of gravel, number four or number three? Was there even such a thing as "types" of gravel? Benton had no idea. Anyway, Heen went on, wasn't that area mostly sand, not gravel? Again, the questions focused increasingly on minutiae, while the policeman vainly tried to supply answers.

However shaky he had been in some of his answers, Benton had clearly demonstrated during this ordeal that he took the tire tread evidence seriously and that he considered it of great importance to the case. And that, not the policeman's knowledge of tires, turned out to be what Heen had been demonstrating all along. He then picked up the report the prosecutor had reluctantly given to him.

Upon your return from the scene of the crime, Heen asked the officer as he brandished the document, "you wrote out a report?"

"Yes, sir."

"Giving [Chief McIntosh] all your findings?"

"Yes, sir."

"Now, what did you find at this place?"

Proud to demonstrate his recall and his attention to detail, Benton enumerated his discoveries: "I found a ginger-ale bottle, muddy yet, with the odor of intoxicating liquor in it. I found two of boxes of matches, one Parrot brand and one Lancer brand. A package of Lucky Strikes cigarettes—maybe one or two had been used. And a ladies' pocket mirror, orange color."

Heen continued to draw Benton out, allowing him to demonstrate the care and professionalism with which he had retrieved evidence from the crime scene and how he had noted each and every one of his findings in the written report he had prepared. Then, finally, Heen read Benton's report aloud for the jury. It contained no mention at all of tire tracks. "Now, Mr. Benton," the attorney asked, "if you thought at the time you discovered those tire marks on those premises on Ala Moana Road that they were important evidence, why didn't you include them in your written statement?"

"I simply reported my findings to Chief McIntosh," Benton replied, not answering the question, "and I take orders from him."

"He told you not to put it in this report?"

"No, sir."

"Then why did you leave it out?"

"Because I merely reported my findings to him. Then this automobile came up. Upon investigation of these particular tracks and the tires that were on this particular car, it was followed through by other detectives."

"Is that the best explanation you can give?"

"To the best of my knowledge."

At this point, Heen let it go. Opaque and evasive as the officer's answer had been, it was what the attorney wanted the record to show: the police investigators had developed their interest in the tire markings at the place where Thalia said she had been raped only after they had the Ida car in their possession. He excused Benton, though he said he planned to recall him soon.

In redirect questioning, prosecutor Wight went back over various points in Benton's original testimony, gaining little new ground. But then, Wight once more pushed Benton to affirm that the follow-up visit he had taken to the scene in Haruyo Ida's car—when Horace Ida had admitted that the tire tracks in the mud matched those on his sister's vehicle—occurred at about eight o'clock on *Sunday* morning. That is, Wight said once again, only four or five hours after the officer's original on-site investigation, correct? Correct, Benton replied.

Heen then recalled Detective John Cluney, who had been excused earlier to retrieve his report showing Ida's self-incrimination, but Cluney now said he had been unable to locate his report. Heen turned to Wight and asked him if he had Cluney's report. Wight replied that there was no such report. There then began a three-way discussion among Heen, Cluney, and Wight. The result of it was a good deal of hairsplitting on the part of the prosecution as to what constituted a "report." Whatever it was, Heen wanted it. Wight refused to produce it. Heen pressed and Wight said he did not have anything that could properly be called a "report" from this witness. "And if one was made, I have lost it."

Judge Steadman, agreeing with the prosecutor that he was not obliged to produce what Heen was seeking, ordered the defense attorney to continue his cross-examination. Heen resumed his questioning, following the same pattern that he had with previous witnesses. He patiently and laboriously led Cluney through minute details of his earlier testimony before abruptly returning to the point at which Ida had supposedly admitted that he knew, without being told, about a white woman having been assaulted. "Did you put that down in your report?" Heen asked, referring to the document that the prosecution either had lost or refused to produce.

"I did not."

"Didn't you think it was important at that time—that that evidence was important at that time?"

"I knew it was important evidence."

Heen pressed. "And you didn't put it in your report?"

"I did not," Cluney replied. Then, for some reason, he continued: "I was instructed to keep it under cover."

"Who instructed you to keep it under cover?"

"I had a conversation with Mr. Wight."

"Did Mr. Wight tell you why you should keep that under cover?"

"He said it was good stuff."

"To hide?"

"I don't know what his intentions were."

After steering the discussion around to other matters, but always circling back to what Cluney had said about Ida's supposed near confession—and to whom and when he had allegedly said it—Heen established that Cluney had never told Captain McIntosh about the matter. McIntosh was Cluney's superior officer and the man in charge of the entire investigation. All official reports, Cluney acknowledged, were supposed to be given to him. But no, Cluney said, the only person he had told about Ida's comment was the prosecutor, Mr. Wight.

And when was that? Heen asked.

"About a month ago," Cluney replied.

"That would be about the nineteenth of October."

"About that time." In short, the detective was admitting, for more than five weeks after Ida had allegedly made this extremely damaging statement to him—a virtual confession—he had told no one about it.

"Did [prosecutor Wight] ask you about it?"

"No," Cluney answered, "I volunteered. . . . We just happened to be talking about this case and I remembered the exact statement Mr. Ida made to me that night."

It would be months after the end of the trial before the radio officer on duty the night of Ida's arrest, Cecil Rickard, would affirm that he had mentioned the assault on Thalia to Ida as soon as Ida was brought into police headquarters. He was alone with Ida at the time, while Cluney was walking around trying to locate Captain McIntosh. Thus, even if Ida had later mentioned "the white woman" to Cluney—which he denied that he had done—it would have had no bearing on his guilt or innocence. But at the trial Heen didn't know about Rickard's comment to Ida, so he did the next best thing. He destroyed Cluney's credibility.

After getting the detective to admit that he had neither included the alleged incident in his written report nor told anyone about this potential bombshell for more than a month after it had supposedly happened, Heen simply stood in silence and looked at the detective, apparently having decided that he had given Cluney all the rope he needed to hang himself. And Cluney, with that last improbable assertion about having "just happened" to remember Ida's "exact statement" while he was chatting with the prosecutor, had now obliged. Heen had also led the detective, whether Cluney realized it or not, to implicate the prosecutor in his fabrication, suggesting that Wight was a less than honest officer of the court, bent only on winning his case at all costs.

It was bad enough, as one of the defendants was later to recall, that "at the trial, all the big guys in town—the guys working for the big firms—came and sat in court and stared at the jury. . . . What they were saying with their eyes was that if this thing doesn't come out right you're going to get fired." But at night the jurors returned home to families and friends whose knowledge of the trial came only from newspapers. And as far as the *Advertiser* and *Star-Bulletin* were concerned—and were reporting in front-page stories—the prosecution was having its way at every turn with an inept and hopeless defense.

As Judge Steadman was calling the court to order on Friday morning, William Heen stood and addressed the court. Holding in his hand the previous night's edition of the *Advertiser,* he began: "At this time I feel it is my duty on behalf of my clients to call to the attention of the Court publications in the bulldog edition of the *Advertiser* of the last two days. . . ."

That was as far as he got before Griffith Wight leaped to his feet and demanded that the judge excuse the jury immediately. Steadman did so. Then Heen resumed. "In the last two issues of this newspaper there appeared headlines which amounted to comments on the evidence given during the trial of this case. Under the date of November 19, 1931, which appeared on the streets the night before, we have this headline: 'Woman's Story of Assault Unshaken Under Bitter Cross-Examination.' And in the following issue this headline appears: 'Defense Fails to Shake Damaging Evidence Offered in Attack Case.'"

Calling the coverage "intentional propaganda" that "borders on contempt of Court," Heen asked the judge to admonish the jury to disregard any information that might come to it by way of the press. Prosecutor Wight, of course, disagreed. He said the newspapers had a right to publish whatever they wanted—and anyway, their interpretation of events was correct. He then asked the attorney general of the territory, who was sitting next to him and advising him on the case, to further address the issue for the prosecution. To Wight's surprise, the attorney general agreed with Heen. In fact, he went further, saying that he believed that a newspaper's "drawing a conclusion as to the effect of testimony is improper," and that the judge should ask the *Advertiser* and *Star-Bulletin* "to desist from drawing conclusions, which are the province of the jury."

Wight quickly stood and started to complain about a prodefense comment that had appeared in the *Hawaii Hochi,* but Judge Steadman cut him off. He had no interest in telling any newspapers what they could and could not publish, the judge said. And he feared that "calling this matter to the attention of the jury" would only "accentuate it." But he agreed that the press reports were troubling. He said he would reiterate his charge to the jurors that they were not to read anything about the case in the newspapers, nor were they to discuss the prosecution or defense arguments with anyone other than their fellow jurors at the conclusion of the trial.

Wight's case was almost complete. He spent the rest of Friday examining the police officers who had taken the defendants to the Massies' home and to Thalia's hospital room, seeking her identification of them. Their testimony and Heen's cross-examinations were perfunctory. By late afternoon the prosecutor was ready for his final witness, Chief of Detectives John McIntosh, but Heen interjected that he still had some questions to ask Officer Benton about those tire marks. And he would like to finish that cross-examination before McIntosh testified. The judge agreed and said he thought it best to begin fresh with both men on Monday morning. Court adjourned for the weekend.

At nine o'clock Monday morning, November 23, Heen resumed his cross-examination of Benton. He began by returning to the subject of those tread-mark diagrams the policeman had drawn on the blackboard. Quickly, however, he moved to the question of precisely *when* Benton—accompanied by Horace Ida and another policeman, the photographer and evidence specialist Samuel Lau—had visited the crime scene in the Ida car and made the tire tread comparisons.

Benton stalled. Heen pressed. Finally, Benton admitted that it had occurred on Monday morning, not Sunday morning, as the prosecutor had coaxed him to say on direct examination. Thus, Heen asserted, it was not four hours or so after his initial nighttime investigation of the site—as Griffith Wight had put it, and Benton had agreed under oath—but was closer to thirty hours later, correct? Correct. Had he put together a report of that second trip, as he had of the first? No, Benton said, he had not written a report, but he did privately tell Captain McIntosh about what he had found. Was anyone else present when he spoke with McIntosh? No, there was no one else present at that time, Benton replied.

No witnesses to critical events, no written reports of extremely important findings—although he had laboriously typed out the details of his other discoveries, down to the brand names of recovered matchbooks and the number of cigarettes missing from a package. Was anything Benton said truthful? It was now immaterial. His entire testimony was tainted by the revelation that, with the prosecutor's assistance, he had willfully lied under oath about the day on which he had revisited the scene of the crime. Heen dismissed him.

Prosecutor Wight then called his final witness, the chief of detectives, Captain John McIntosh. His direct examination was a routine run-through of the accumulated evidence that allegedly showed the defendants to be guilty as charged. McIntosh responded to the prosecutor's questions matter-of-factly, describing as important the minor inconsistencies in the stories the accused men had told regarding their activities on the night in question and providing a close account of his initial interview with Thalia. Only at this point did the defense counsel intervene. As to that interview with Mrs. Massie, Heen asked, "did you make notes?" "I have the original notes made here at the time," the captain replied, reaching into his jacket pocket. "May I look at that, please?" said Heen, and before the prosecutor could object, McIntosh handed over a small notebook. Wight continued the examination as Heen flipped though the book's pages.

When it came time for him to cross-examine, Heen paid little attention to the scenario McIntosh had created under the prosecutor's guidance. Instead, he zeroed in on the fact that Wight had avoided asking the captain if Thalia had told him what time she had left the Ala Wai Inn and gone for a walk. In her courtroom testimony, Thalia had insisted that she had left the inn at 11:35, but McIntosh now admitted that she had told him, on the night of the assault, that she had left "at around about midnight."

Holding the notebook McIntosh earlier had given him, and feigning puzzlement, Heen asked: "It appears in your written statement that you took at that time, on page four of this book, you have this: 'Around 12:30 or 1:00 a.m. I decided to go for a walk and some air.'"

"If that's what is there, that's what she said," McIntosh answered.

Drawing the moment out, Heen repeated the question, got the same answer, then asked the captain if he wanted to read what he had written in his notebook: "I want you to see it," he said, in case "you might disbelieve my statement."

"No, I don't disbelieve. That statement is as she made it." If there was a contradiction between McIntosh's raw notes and his report on the interview with Thalia, it didn't matter. Neither helped Thalia's new chronology of events.

Heen then shifted his interrogation to a series of points, some minor and some not, where Thalia's recent testimony on the witness stand was at odds with what she had told McIntosh in his office two hours after she claimed to have been raped. And McIntosh, having seen what had happened to Cluney and Benton under cross-examination after they had tried to invent incriminating evidence, answered every question in an unhesitating and straightforward manner. Whatever his role in putting this rickety case together, the head of the detective bureau was a veteran of three decades with colonial police forces and a man who knew how to survive in a hostile environment where he did not have the upper hand. And that was precisely where he found himself now.

The captain now admitted that Thalia had described all of her assailants as Hawaiians. Also, McIntosh acknowledged that, other than the term "Bull," Thalia had never before mentioned any of the names or nicknames—including "Benny" and "Shorty," which was Ida's nickname—that, in court, she claimed to have heard the accused men calling each other. McIntosh further admitted that a thorough search of the car Thalia said the men had driven turned up no fingerprints that matched hers and no other evidence suggesting that she had ever been in the automobile. He also said that when Horace Ida was brought into his office and McIntosh presented Ida to Thalia as a suspect—only two hours or so after Ida had supposedly raped her—Thalia neither identified him as one of her assailants nor made any reference to the suede coat Ida was wearing. Both observations by her would come much later, after she had spent more time with police officials. She also said during that first interview, McIntosh recalled, that she "was not sure" if she would be able to identify any of her assailants if they were shown to her.

Before he was finished, Heen got McIntosh to say that in his interview with Thalia immediately after the attack on her, she was not able to describe the clothing worn by her assailants, although he had asked her about their clothes several times. This was in sharp contrast to Thalia's statements on the witness stand when she had described the men's clothing in great detail. Nor had she said anything to McIntosh about one of the men having a gold tooth, at least not until long after she had spoken with Ahakuelo in her hospital room and apparently noticed—or was told—that he had one. The captain also confirmed that when he showed her Haruyo Ida's car, Thalia had not identified it as the one that had been used in her abduction, saying only that "it was a car like that."

The defense attorney then moved to the subject of the policemen who first spoke with Thalia, asking: "Did you interview the officers who went up there to her home?" McIntosh said that he had. Did he get reports or written statements from them? Yes, he had. Where are their statements now? "In the hands of the County Attorney, Mr. Wight," McIntosh replied.

As he had done previously regarding the other reports and written material, Heen immediately turned to the prosecutor and asked him to provide the statement of Detective William Furtado, the first police official to interview Thalia. Wight refused, contending that such statements were privileged internal materials, prepared in putting together the prosecution's case. He was, he said, under no obligation to share them with the defense. The judge agreed, ruling that "there is no legal duty to produce" such materials. And at the time this case was being heard, Judge Steadman was correct. It was not until 1947 that the U.S. Supreme Court would clarify what constitutes "attorney work product"—private material that need not be disclosed—as opposed to what, in the Court's words, are "non-privileged facts hidden in an attorney's file" and "essential to the preparation of his case." Separately, it would be more than thirty years (in *Brady v. Maryland*) before the Court decided that it was an unconstitutional violation of due process for a prosecutor to suppress evidence favorable to the accused.

But the absence of solid legal ground did not prevent Heen from repeatedly interrupting the proceedings whenever the subject came up and asking for the reports. And asking for them, each time, in the name of the individual officer who had filed it—Furtado, Simerson, Nakea, Harbottle, Bettencourt, and more. In each instance, Wight refused to deliver the documents. And, as Heen intended, the jury had no alternative but to sit and listen to the exchanges. Only then would the defense attorney move on.

Presumably working on the principle that there was nothing wrong with beating a dead horse if there remained some benefit in doing so, Heen now asked McIntosh about Detective Cluney's discredited claim that Ida had mentioned an assault on a white woman before he should have known of it.

"I don't remember Cluney ever telling me anything like that. Not to me," McIntosh said.

Heen wanted to be sure. "Did he tell you anything like that later on?"
"No."

"Did he tell you anything like that *at all*?"
"Not at all."

"And you were Mr. Cluney's superior officer at that time?"
"I was."

Heen abruptly shifted gears, turning his focus to the gown Thalia had worn the night of the assault. Holding it up, he asked McIntosh if that was the dress he received from Mrs. Massie and sent out for analysis. The captain agreed that it was and, under further questioning, affirmed that the laboratory report indicated that no semen stains were found anywhere on the dress. Nor, he said in answer to a question, were semen stains discovered on the underwear of the accused men.

After a lengthy review of the process that had been followed in Thalia's identifying the defendants, Heen introduced one more topic not previously discussed. He began by asking McIntosh about people he had interviewed who had attended the dance at Waikiki Park on the night of the assault and others who had seen Thalia walking down John Ena Road at just after midnight. As McIntosh started to name the individuals with whom he had spoken, prosecutor Wight—who had avoided putting any of these people on the stand himself—leaped up and objected, saying, "These people are not witnesses and [the defense] cannot impeach them."

Judge Steadman agreed, telling Heen he was getting beyond the scope of the examination. Uncharacteristically, Heen did not protest. Instead, he called Thalia back to the stand for further cross-examination. Her mere presence as a return witness caused more of a stir than anything she had to say, because under Heen's low-key but persistent questioning she testified as she had for most of his previous interrogation. She was unhappy about having to take the stand again and, no matter what question he asked, now insisted that she remembered almost nothing about the night of the assault.

When she was at the emergency hospital, Heen inquired, had she spoken with the nurse? Yes. What was said? "I don't remember anything except she told me not to get upset." What had she discussed with the doctor who examined her there? "I didn't talk to him." When Heen would not let it go, Thalia remained adamant: "I don't remember telling him anything." In fact, by now Thalia was so committed to not recalling anything that when Heen asked her whether she had first been taken to the hospital or the police station, she once again—as though on autopilot—said she didn't remember.

Finally, Heen picked up the dress Thalia had been wearing the night she was attacked. He asked her to stand and hold the dress up in front of her to show how long it was. She did as he asked. "It reaches near your ankles?" Heen asked. "Yes," Thalia replied.

When Heen excused Thalia and said he was through, Wight initially told the judge he had another witness who had not arrived yet. Soon, however, he changed his mind and announced that the prosecution was resting its case.

■ ■ ■

The argument for the defense began with attorneys Pittman and Murakami both calling upon the judge for a directed verdict of not guilty. Murakami, who was defending David Takai, had the stronger case; Thalia had never identified Takai as one of her assailants, and the only evidence remotely linking him to the crime was his admission that he had been with the other men on the night in question. The judge denied both motions, and then Heen rose to address the jury with his opening statement.

The key to everything in this trial, Heen said, was timing. After describing for the jury, in detail, the whereabouts of the defendants during the entire night and early morning of September 12 and 13, he said he planned to show that they had had absolutely no opportunity to commit the crime. They had been under virtually constant public scrutiny, and nowhere near Thalia, from well before the time she departed the Ala Wai Inn almost to the moment the Clarks and the Bellingers picked her up as she walked along Ala Moana Road. Moreover, he would demonstrate that Thalia, too, had been observed during a critical portion of this time, and that if she had been abducted where and when she claimed under oath to have been, it was impossible for those she accused to have done it.

It had taken the prosecution just over three days, with twelve witnesses, to make its case. The defense would take a week and counter with fifty-two witnesses. The first was Tatsumi Matsumoto. He was followed by four others—Robert Vierra, Margaret Kanae, Sybil Davis, and George Silva—who had attended the Waikiki Park dance together. Two of them had independently encountered at least one of the defendants there between eleven and twelve o'clock on Saturday night. And all of them had seen the accused men in the parking lot about five or ten minutes after the dance ended at midnight, and again while driving along Beretania Street—far from the crime scene—at about 12:15 or 12:20 on Sunday morning.

As he wrapped up his direct examinations, Heen asked Matsumoto and each of the others if they had previously told their stories to the police or the prosecutor. Yes, was the answer, they all separately had discussed the night's events with both the police and the prosecutor. When? On Monday, the day after the arrests of the defendants. Police officers had shown up at the witnesses' homes (or in two cases at their university dormitories) that morning and brought them in for questioning and signed statements. This was barely twelve hours after the accused men had undergone their own interrogations at police headquarters. Heen had one more question. Had they seen or heard from Ahakuelo or any of the other defendants between the time of the car-jumping incident on Beretania Street Saturday night and their Monday morning police questioning? No, they all answered. The message to the jurors, in short, was that Matsumoto and the others, before giving their statements that confirmed everything the defendants said, had no way of knowing what the accused men had earlier told the police.

The parade of witnesses that followed, establishing the whereabouts of the accused men at every crucial moment on late Saturday night and early Sunday morning, was both extensive and varied. It included women and men, young and old, who had little in common except that they either knew one or more of the defendants, or they recognized Ben Ahakuelo because he was a prominent local athlete. They ranged from the young man and woman who had given their ticket stubs to Henry Chang and Joe Kahahawai at 11:30 to others who had seen the men after the dance ended at midnight.

Having accounted for the comings and goings of each or all of the defendants from well before the time Thalia said she left the Ala Wai Inn, until approximately 12:15 or 12:20 on Sunday morning, when the five people in Tatsumi Matsumoto's car encountered the men driving on Beretania Street, Heen now picked up the timeline from there. According to the testimony of the son of city supervisor Sylvester Correa, the defendants all showed up at his house at about 12:25. That was where the wedding lūʻau they had left earlier in the evening was being held, and they were returning to see if any beer was left. Correa—whose sister also took the stand to confirm his testimony— said he told them the food and the beer were all gone. So after standing around and talking for a few minutes, at about 12:30 they climbed back in their car and headed off. All except Ben, he said, who walked to his home on the next block.

There was no need to call Agnes Peeples to the stand, since the prosecution had already done that. Her testimony accounted for the defendants' whereabouts from 12:35 or so, immediately after they left the Correas' home, to 12:40, when she headed off for the police station to report the fight she had just had with one of the accused men.

As for Thalia's whereabouts during this time, Heen called three witnesses. First was George Goeas of the Dillingham Corporation. He and his wife had driven to Waikiki Park that Saturday night, as they did on most Saturday nights, and didn't leave until the music for the last dance had ended. They then walked slowly to their car, stopping from time to time to talk as the departing crowd moved past them, before driving a short distance down John Ena Road and deciding to get something to eat at a saimin stand. It was while waiting for their food to be delivered that Goeas first noticed a white man and woman walking past them in the direction of the beach. The woman appeared to be drunk, he reported, and it was difficult to tell if she and the man were together, because the man always seemed to be a step or two behind or in front of her. Goeas guessed that they were a couple that had had an argument.

Heen asked the witness to step down and attempt to imitate the way the woman had been walking. Goeas tilted his head to one side and stooped over the way Thalia always did, then walked very slowly toward the jury box. Back on the stand, he further described the woman who almost certainly was Thalia, and the dress she was wearing that night. Shown the dress from the courtroom exhibit, he said it appeared to be the same one the woman had on, and in answer to another question he said he was quite clear on when all this had happened: "About five to ten minutes past twelve."

As he had with most of the previous witnesses for the defense, Heen then asked whether Goeas had told any of this to the police or the prosecutor. Yes, indeed, replied the witness: "I read in the paper where this case happened, so I wanted to do my bit and try to see if this was the right party, so I went down and talked to Detective Jardine." After giving the police and the prosecutor his statement, Goeas added, he identified Thalia's dress—which they had brought out for him to examine—as identical to the one worn by the woman he had seen. It also was the same gown he had just been shown in court. Heen asked if, at police headquarters, he had signed a statement containing all this information. Oh, yes, Goeas said, "I signed four or five copies, I think."

Prosecutor Wight attempted to shake Goeas's testimony, but without success. In fact, the only thing of note that Wight received in return for his efforts was a second demonstration of the way Thalia had walked. "Like this, wobbling down like this," Goeas said as he got up, slumped forward, and again walked very slowly toward where the jury was sitting.

Mrs. Goeas was next. She confirmed everything her husband had stated, adding her own ambulatory demonstration, describing Thalia as "stooped . . . stumbling . . . and swaying a little bit" as she did so. The time, Mrs. Goeas said, was "close to ten past twelve when we first saw her." Again, Heen asked if she had told all this to the authorities. Yes she had, she replied. After her husband had gone to the station to report what they had seen, about five men—including Captain McIntosh and the prosecutor, Griffith Wight—had shown up at the Goeases' house. They questioned her and asked her to identify the dress now on exhibit as the one worn by the woman she had seen. "Yes," she said she had affirmed at the time, that was the very same dress.

Wight's cross-examination of Mrs. Goeas yielded as little as had his interrogation of her husband. The same was true of the next witness Heen called, Alice Aramaki. Although she had been born in the islands, Miss Aramaki required a Japanese translator to assist with some of her testimony. But what she said supported everything the Goeases had recounted, although Miss Aramaki had never met them. She was standing in her sister's store a short distance away from the saimin stand, after closing up her barbershop at midnight, she testified, when a woman fitting Thalia's description walked slowly past her, a white man following closely behind. Alice, too, imitated Thalia's walk. She put the time at "about ten or fifteen minutes after twelve." And she confirmed that soon after the story of the assault on the navy wife had broken in the newspapers, she told all of this to prosecutor Wight—pointing him out across the courtroom—and signed a written statement that he prepared.

Next, Heen recalled Captain McIntosh to the stand. He had some questions on two subjects, and he was brief and to the point. First, had McIntosh taken the Ida car into the crime scene prior to Officer Benton's supposed discovery of tire tracks at the site? Yes, McIntosh answered. When was that? On Sunday, the day before Benton claimed to have found the matching tread marks. Heen's second inquiry concerned the sworn testimony of Tatsumi Matsumoto and his friends who had seen the defendants on several occasions that Saturday night. The police and the prosecutor interviewed those young people barely twelve hours after the interrogation of the suspects. Who at that early stage of the investigation had informed the authorities that Matsumoto and the others were witnesses? McIntosh said he had no idea, but that it had been prosecutor Wight, not he, who had ordered that they be picked up for questioning.

Heen then stunned the courtroom and called Wight to the stand as a witness. As the surprised prosecutor took his seat, Heen bore in. How did he know to call Matsumoto and his companions as witnesses so soon after the arrest of the defendants? Wight was unsure, but said he thought one of the arrested men had mentioned them in his statement. Specifically which of the defendants had told him about their encounter with the Matsumoto car? Wight didn't recall. Heen tried coming at the question from several angles, but Wight insisted that he did not recall anything else.

It was not difficult to discern the message Heen was sending to the jury. If it hadn't been evident from previous witnesses' testimony, it was certain now that the prosecutor had known from the beginning of his investigation that there was solid evidence confirming the alibis of the men who had been arrested. Yet, rather than deal with that evidence honestly, Wight had tried to conceal it. Tatsumi Matsumoto, Sybil Davis, and the others who were with them that night provided only the first indication of this deception. In fact, from the very start, the prosecutor had compiled sworn testimony from most of the numerous witnesses who had been called by the defense, all of it demonstrating that the suspects could not have committed the crime. That was why Wight had not called any of those people as witnesses himself. But there was more.

The defense now called Joseph Kahahawai to the stand. Neither Heen's lengthy direct examination nor the prosecutor's equally long cross-examination elicited anything especially new or revealing. In answer to Heen's questions, Kahahawai simply described in detail where he had gone and what he had done on the night that Thalia claimed she was raped, and he stuck to that story despite Wight's repeated efforts to trip him up.

Near the end of the cross-examination, however, the prosecutor and the defendant briefly clashed. Wight asked about what Joe and his friends had been wearing that night. Joe replied in some detail. And was Horace Ida wearing a leather coat? No, Joe answered. This was important to the prosecutor, since it was almost entirely on the evidence of his distinctive suede jacket that Thalia had belatedly accused Ida. Wight pressed the issue: "Do you recall when you were questioned . . . that you were asked, 'After twelve o'clock when you left the dance hall, how was Shorty dressed?' And you said he had a leather coat on. Do you remember that?"

"That is what you put in there," Kahahawai replied.

"Not what I put in there," Wight countered, obviously taken aback and then immediately changing the subject, noting to the court that he wanted to correct a date he had used earlier. The two men then fell into confused squabbling over the date, and Wight finally directed his questioning to entirely different matters.

But on redirect examination Heen returned to the subject of the jacket and Wight's questioning of Kahahawai on the night of his arrest. Joe cleared up the confusion that the prosecutor had left hanging. Horace had indeed been wearing the leather jacket at the police station after his arrest on early Sunday morning, but not—as the prosecutor had asked—on Saturday night, when Thalia said she was attacked. Why, Heen asked, did Wight seem to think Joe had said in his written statement that Horace was wearing the jacket that night?

"Well, he put it in the statement, and then after I signed the statement I scratched it out."

Feigning puzzlement, Heen turned to the prosecutor and asked to look at Kahahawai's statement about the leather coat, "to see if it is scratched out." Wight conceded that it was. Heen insisted on seeing the document, and, reluctantly, Wight handed it to him. Heen glanced at the paper, then passed it to the court clerk, saying: "If the Court please, I offer this in evidence."

The next of the defendants called for the defense was David Takai. As he had with Kahahawai, Heen took Takai over the by-now familiar story of where he and the others had been and what they had done on the night in question. Over objections from the prosecution, Takai said that McIntosh showed him some green beads during his interrogation, saying they had been found in Ida's car, proving they had assaulted the navy wife. Not knowing that the chief of detectives was attempting to trick him, Takai had replied that the car was owned by Ida's sister and the beads probably belonged to her.

Takai also affirmed that while they were in jail, he and the other accused men had been kept apart and were not allowed to speak with one another. At another point, Heen got the prosecutor to stipulate that he had sought to have Takai turn state's evidence against the other defendants, offering him a suspended sentence, but that Takai had refused. And on the matter of Tatsumi Matsumoto and his companions traveling alongside Takai and the others as they drove along Beretania Street, Takai said that when he told the prosecutor and the chief of detectives about that on the night of his initial interrogation, they called him a liar.

As during his cross-examination of Kahahawai, when it was his turn to interrogate Takai, prosecutor Wight seemed not to know when to leave well enough alone. He asked the defendant why there was no mention of the Beretania Street encounter with Tatsumi Matsumoto's car in the first statement Takai had given in the stenographer's presence at the police station. The implication—although it made no sense in light of the testimony of Matsumoto and his friends, both in court and to the police only hours after Takai and the others had been arrested—was that Takai had invented the incident after being questioned by McIntosh and Wight. But Takai replied without hesitation: "I told you this matter and you told her [the stenographer] not to take it down."

Apparently surprised, Wight said: "*I* told her not to take it down?" After a brief back-and-forth of accusation and denial, Takai conceded that it might have been McIntosh who said it, not Wight. But, he insisted, one of the two had directed the stenographer not to record that statement. Wight moved on. However, at least some jurors may have remembered that several days earlier, the police stenographer had been on the witness stand. At that time, Heen had asked her if, during the interrogation of the suspects by McIntosh and Wight, she had recorded "every question and every answer." She had replied: "I think I did. Those they told me to put down I put down."

The last of the accused men to testify was Horace Ida. Again, most of his testimony was a lengthy narrative that went over the same familiar ground that Kahahawai and Takai had already covered. He too had been offered a deal if he would testify against the others, he said. In fact, as Walter Dillingham wrote at the time: "Every known pressure and influence has been brought to bear upon each and every one of the defendants to persuade him to turn state's evidence." None of it, he reported with disgust, ever came to anything.

The critical point in Ida's testimony came when Heen asked him about his visit to the crime scene in the presence of Officers Benton and Lau. He said the two policemen had taken him, in his sister's car, to the site on Monday morning, the fourteenth of September. Benton, who was driving, ignored numerous tire marks that were all over the place and headed directly for one, off by itself in the mud. He then ran the Ida car within a foot of the tread imprint and pointed out that the marks were identical. When asked about it at the time, Ida said he replied by saying: "It couldn't be [the tire mark from my sister's car] because I didn't come here that night and there are plenty of cars in Honolulu that have the same kind of marks." After more back-and-forth, the two policemen went off by themselves and had a long discussion that he couldn't hear, Ida said. Lau, the officer who had brought a camera with him, refused to photograph the tire marks, and the three of them packed up and returned to the police station. The witness was excused.

By now, the tire tread fiasco was an old story to the jury. But just to be certain, Heen called Officer Lau to the stand. He confirmed everything Ida had just said.

Only days before both the prosecution and the defense expected to rest their cases, the defense had effectively destroyed every attempt by the prosecution to present corroborative evidence showing that the accused men were guilty. The fraudulent tire tracks at the scene of the crime had been exposed as nothing short of willfully planted evidence. The claim by Detective Cluney that Horace Ida had, in effect, implicated himself in the assault on Thalia had been unmasked as equally fabricated. What remained to support the prosecution's case was Thalia's own remarkably detailed identifications of the men who had raped her, as well as her description of the car they were driving and the number of that car's license plate. When court resumed, the defense had plans to deal with that evidence. And that, they hoped, would be that. Unless, of course, the prosecution had something else up its sleeve.

As things turned out, it did.

14

"Lust-Sodden Beasts"

When Heen called Detective Frank Bettencourt to the stand, Griffith Wight exploded, angrily objecting to the policeman's being allowed to testify for the defense. Judge Steadman overruled the objection. There then began a procession of police witnesses. Some were upset at having been called and were hostile to Heen's questioning under direct examination. Others seemed eager to testify. But all of them told the same story about their interviews with Thalia at her home on the night of the assault.

Earlier in the trial, Heen had taken the jurors outside the courthouse to inspect Haruyo Ida's car, the same car, everyone agreed, into which the defendants either had or had not dragged Thalia and carried her away. Prosecutor Wight protested that the car had since been washed and polished, but that had no bearing on the fact that it was a fairly new, light tan Model A Ford that was in excellent condition.

On the witness stand Detective Bettencourt became the first policeman to testify that only two hours after Thalia's alleged kidnapping and rape, she had described her assailants' automobile as "an old, black Ford or Dodge." He added, under both direct and cross-examination, that Thalia had said all the men who attacked her were Hawaiians, but that "when I asked her if in the event we should find these boys she could identify them . . . she said no." Bettencourt further testified that he did not hear Thalia mention any names that the men had supposedly called one another. Nor had she been able to recall the license plate number of her abductors' car: "When I asked her if she took the car number down, she said 'no,' I didn't take any car number down."

The next detective to testify was George Nakea. His recollection of the interview with Thalia confirmed Bettencourt's account. Detective George Harbottle followed Nakea to the stand, with the same results.

Then came Officer William Simerson. His story matched that of the others, as did that of Detective William Furtado, who continued the litany. The only thing new he had to add concerned the repeated police radio broadcasts of the suspects' license plate number while Thalia was being examined at the emergency clinic. Everyone who was standing around waiting for her—including her friends as well as the police—had heard the number, he said.

Finally, Heen called his last police witness, Detective Luciano Machado. Although Machado had not been at the Massie house with the other policemen, he was the one who arrested three of the suspects, and he had been on hand when Thalia—on her second try—identified Ben Ahakuelo from her hospital bed. On direct examination, the detective testified that the suspects had been adamant about their innocence, even though he pressed them aggressively after picking them up. More important, he said that Thalia failed to identify Ahakuelo even the second time he was brought before her—until Captain McIntosh leaned over and whispered in her ear: "This is Bennie."

On cross-examination, Wight was unable to shake any of the police department witnesses. Since their collective testimony undermined almost everything of importance that Thalia had said, his only alternative was to attempt to discredit them, implying that they had conspired as a group to aid the defendants. Small differences in the police officers' testimonies, however, as well as major differences in their attitudes about having to testify at all, made the conspiracy theory less than credible. But just in case any jurors had doubts about the veracity of the policemen's accounts, Heen also called the nurse and the doctor who had examined Thalia and spoken with her at the emergency hospital. On each of the items that were central to the police testimony, and contrary to Thalia's claims, both Dr. David Liu and Nurse Agnes Fawcett confirmed the police witnesses' accounts.

By the time the defense was preparing to wrap things up, almost nothing of the prosecution's case was still intact. In fact, all that did remain was Thalia's completely uncorroborated, and repeatedly contradicted, courtroom testimony. Prosecutor Wight needed something—anything—beyond Thalia's accusations. And a week before the trial had opened, Detective John Jardine had brought it to him: four eyewitness accounts of her abduction.

On a morning in late October, while having his usual cup of coffee at the Green Mill Restaurant on Bethel Street near the police station, Jardine had been approached by an old friend with a tip. He said he knew four people who had been out together on the night that Thalia said she had been assaulted. They had been driving down John Ena Road at around midnight when they saw a group of men dragging a woman off the sidewalk and into their car.

Jardine reported the information to Captain McIntosh, who assigned him and another detective to investigate. They did, and later—years later—Jardine reported that he told his superiors, including prosecutor Wight, that the eyewitnesses' stories were confused and contradictory. But Wight believed there were ways to handle that. He would be selective as to which of the men he called to testify, and he wouldn't even do that unless it was absolutely necessary. Since Heen had just finished destroying virtually the entirety of the prosecution's case, that necessity was now at hand.

Both sides had finished presenting their cases in chief, and Wight was in the midst of recalling witnesses in rebuttal for the prosecution, people who had previously testified and who, for the most part, had nothing much to add. This is not uncommon, since the prosecutor is limited in the rebuttal phase of a trial to attacking issues and evidence introduced by the defense. Wight had just finished with Officer Claude Benton, failing once again to revive his moribund tire tread testimony, when he turned and called Eugenio Batungbacal.

As soon as they realized what the prosecutor was planning, the defense attorneys were on their feet, objecting that the time for this sort of testimony had long passed—it should have been presented during the case in chief—and the court should not allow it to proceed. Judge Steadman disagreed, overruling the objections and telling Wight to continue. But from the start, as Detective Jardine had warned the prosecution, Batungbacal was a less than impressive witness. His English was poor, and a translator could not be found on such short notice. The fact that he had a mouthful of chewing gum didn't help. The judge ordered him to remove it, and finally, weathering a continual barrage of objections from Pittman and Heen, the prosecutor got to the witness's testimony and to the reason why he had been called.

Sometime between 11:30 and 12:00 on the Saturday night that Thalia had been attacked, Batungbacal said, he had been driving with three of his friends along John Ena Road, outside Waikiki Park, when he observed "about four or five men with one girl." Two of the men appeared to be "holding the woman [and] they looked like they forced the woman . . . to the car." After passing by, the witness said, he turned his car around to head back the other way, but the woman and the men no longer were there.

That was it. Wight gave his surprise witness over to the defense. Heen took Batungbacal through far more detail than Wight had regarding what he and his friends had been doing that night, systematically turning the witness's story inside out. By the time he was finished Batungbacal had contradicted himself repeatedly as to the time the events in question had occurred and the matter of just what it was that he had seen. Before long, even the car the men on the sidewalk supposedly were taking the woman to had disappeared from the story. There was no car at all. How had the woman been dressed? He didn't know. What had the men looked like? He wasn't sure—their backs were turned. How exactly had the woman been walking? He didn't know how to describe it, but come to think of it maybe they weren't dragging her along. It sort of looked as though they were all drunk and maybe just "going together . . . to a party." And this woman, was she white? He didn't know. Heen pressed, and Batungbacal snapped back that she wasn't facing him, so he couldn't tell: "If she is facing me I tell you whether she is nigger or white or Portuguese."

It was late in the day. Heen turned to the judge and asked: "May we take an adjournment at this time? I can say that I am through now with this witness." It was an understatement. Judge Steadman agreed.

But the next day Wight, still not having learned when to leave well enough alone, was back with two of the other three men who had been in the car with Batungbacal. Their names were Roger Liu and Charles Chang. Wight elicited little more from them than he had from Batungbacal. The cross-examination went the same way as well. Heen got both men to say they did not get a good look at either the woman or the men who were with her—all of them had their backs turned—and on second thought, maybe they were not forcing her to do anything after all. As Liu eventually put it, after Heen asked him why he and his friends had not helped the woman if she appeared to be in distress, "I thought they were just a bunch of friends." Chang agreed, saying he didn't recall himself or the others even mentioning the incident that night, since there didn't seem to be anything "out of the way" about it. The people in question were just a handful among a lot of people walking and standing around after the dance had ended.

Wight did not call the fourth and final witness who had been in the car that night, James Low. But Heen, who by now was enjoying himself and had discovered the identity of the fourth man, did call him. By beginning this line of inquiry, Wight had opened himself to surrebuttal by the defense—that is, presentation of evidence that rebuts the prosecution's rebuttal evidence. Low turned out to be far more articulate and credible than the other three, and much more precise in describing what he had seen, which was why Wight had not called him.

Although his testimony agreed with the others that the woman's back had been turned, making it impossible to describe her, Low was certain that she was wearing a dress, perhaps blue, and that she "was walking like a drunken person . . . with her head down." Also, there were no men surrounding her or forcing her to do anything—but "there was a man following immediately behind her, about two or three feet." Both the man and the woman seemed to be heading toward a dark-colored touring car parked at the curb. As the car Low was in passed the couple, he testified, one of the men with him "made a remark that the man had grabbed her." However, by the time they had a chance to turn around and go back, the man and the woman were gone, and so was the car they had been walking toward.

As for just when all this had occurred, Low was certain that the dance had ended, and he put the time at about ten minutes past twelve. He also, when asked, went to the courtroom map of John Ena Road and took a great deal of care in locating precisely where the couple had been when he saw them. It was about 150 feet past the spot where Mr. and Mrs. Goeas and Alice Aramaki had seen a white man and woman—the woman appearing to be drunk, with her head down—walking in the direction of the beach. The location Low pointed out on the map was almost exactly where Thalia had been seized, according to her testimony. And all of them—the Goeases, Aramaki, and now Low—put the time they had seen her at between 12:05 and 12:15.

Was Thalia the woman James Low had seen that night? The context of his testimony, mingled as it was with that of the other men who had been in the car with him, raised as many questions as it answered. But one thing was certain. If it wasn't Thalia, this entire series of witnesses had done nothing to help the prosecution. And if it was Thalia, it had only assisted the defense. Because, if nothing else, it meant that she had left the Ala Wai Inn at the time she had originally reported to the police—"round about midnight"—and not 11:35, as she had said on the witness stand. More important, it further established her presence on John Ena Road, apparently in the company of a white man, just when the defendants were seen by numerous witnesses either in the dance pavilion parking lot or driving along Beretania Street, far from the alleged scene of the crime.

After Low's testimony, Wight and Heen called several minor and anticlimactic witnesses in rebuttal and surrebuttal. Then both sides rested. It was Monday, November 30, two weeks after the trial had begun. Closing arguments were scheduled for the next day.

The spectators' gallery was packed on Tuesday morning, with Judge Steadman having to insist repeatedly that everyone be seated. He ordered bailiffs to remove those who were standing in the rear, and then the huge doors to the courtroom were closed. It was 8:35 a.m. when Griffith Wight rose to address the jury. He promised them that his closing argument would be short, and it was. It also began at a high pitch and never wavered.

"This is one of the worst cases we have ever had," he began, reminding the jurors that "the complaining witness is only a young, inexperienced girl" who wanted nothing less than to be in this courtroom. Yet, "you saw what a clean, straightforward way she told her story. It was a horrible ordeal for her, but she went through it bravely and without exaggeration." Like all women, he said, she "has the right to walk on any street at any time, day or night," but when the victim attempted to do just that "she was assaulted by beasts." And not just any beasts, he added, but "lust-sodden beasts." The crime was committed very quickly: "with the lust of animals, they dissipated her and were gone. They're not angels, you know that," he shouted, whirling and pointing at the defendants, "no, they are more like devils." Finally, once they had done what they set out to do and had left her, ravished, "her strength was gone, she was exhausted—a mass of beautiful young flesh had been outraged."

Worse was yet to come, if such were possible, because "after the attack," the young prosecutor said, "she became pregnant. She didn't want the child. So she went under an operation and removed it." How do we know all this? We know, he said, because that is what the victim told us, in sworn testimony—testimony that had to be believed, Wight demanded, because the alternative would be "to brand her an unmitigated liar."

But, he insisted, they did not have to take only her word for it. There was corroboration for all of Thalia's accusations. She had marks on her body. Her jaw had been broken. A set of beads belonging to her, as well as items from her purse, had been found at the scene of the crime. She had remembered the license plate number of her assailants' car, and the fact that one of them had been wearing a suede jacket like the one that Horace Ida had worn. And finally, "the tire marks found [at the crime scene], which corresponded with the tire tread on the defendants' car should prove to every man on the jury that Ida's car was there that night."

Wight did not dwell on corroboration, however, and for obvious reasons. All that the best of it showed was that someone had punched and maybe beaten Thalia, probably at the place she described along Ala Moana Road. As for the suede jacket and the license plate number and the tire tracks, during the course of the trial they all had repeatedly been exposed as spurious evidence, most of it criminally planted. For Wight, though, evidence was not the foundation of his case. Thalia was—a young, vulnerable, inexperienced girl, as he had described her in his opening words. "Be men!" he at last exhorted the jurors, urging them to take a stand for virtue. After all, he said, if they would only put themselves "in the place of the husband of the twenty-year-old girl to whom this has happened," each of them certainly knew what he would do. "You would want to go down and shoot the men." Wight's summation lasted only thirty-five minutes, but it accurately reflected the mood of the navy and a large portion of Honolulu's haole community.

The first of the three attorneys to speak for the defense was Robert Murakami. Although he directly represented only David Takai, Murakami addressed the prosecution's case against all the defendants. He was very soft-spoken and his voice had been heard only a few times during the course of the trial. What the prosecutor had said about the crime of rape was correct, he began. "It is a terrible crime . . . and it is probable that Mrs. Massie was assaulted, either by a gang or by a man," reminding the jurors that Captain Kashiwabara, the policeman who took Tommie's call reporting the rape, had testified that Tommie said she had "been assaulted by a man." But either way, he went on, "we cannot be swayed by our passion and prejudice against the crime itself." The defense had shown beyond a reasonable doubt, he asserted—although the burden of proof rested with the prosecution—that "these were not the men who committed the crime." Indeed, he said, in obvious reference to the way Wight had conducted the trial, "I doubt that the prosecuting attorney, as a reasonable man, can honestly believe that these are the men."

Most of Murakami's presentation was a meticulous, step-by-step dissection of the time question. The prosecution had never, at any point in the trial, taken a clear stand on precisely when Thalia had supposedly been raped. That was because, the attorney said, "according to the prosecutor's theory, the time of the occurrence jumps forward and backward to meet the exigencies of his case." In fact, he said, the prosecutor did not have a single theory, but several. Murakami then clearly and simply explained for the jury each of the prosecution's various scenarios—and how none of them allowed for the possibility that the defendants could have committed the crime.

It made no difference whether the jurors believed that Thalia had left the Ala Wai Inn at midnight, as she first told the police, or at 11:35, as she testified in court. Either way, Murakami said, it was not "humanly possible" for the defendants to have done what the prosecutor claimed they did in the time now known to have been available to them. That was why the prosecutor, in desperation, had "attempted to put words in the mouths of [his own] witnesses" and "tried to prevent the officers who first investigated the case from testifying. But why? Was the prosecutor afraid of the truth, the whole truth, and nothing but the truth?"

Indeed he was, boomed William Pittman, speaking next for the defense, representing Horace Ida and Joseph Kahahawai, and taking the opposite of Murakami's surgical approach to closing argument. In their fear of the truth, he said, the prosecution had embarked on nothing less than a campaign to manufacture evidence, to withhold evidence, and to suppress evidence. Reminding the jury that the proper role of a prosecutor is to represent "the people" in seeking out the truth—not disingenuously to contrive a conviction through trickery and subterfuge—Pittman declared that "this entire case is a frame up."

He was just getting started. Wight and Murakami each had taken well under an hour to deliver their summations. Pittman, striding about the courtroom and filling it with a cascade of language thick with the accent of his Mississippi upbringing, would be on center stage almost twice as long as Wight and Murakami combined. And for openers, he told the jurors, he took a backseat to no one in his hatred for the crime of rape. He wished Mrs. Massie "really did know who assaulted her," he said, "because if she did I should like to see them rot in prison." Where he came from, he reminded the court, "they hang men, or burn them alive" for rape. "But there is a worse crime," he said, "one more heinous, and that is sending innocent men to the penitentiary . . . branded on their chests, 'You are rapists' . . . unfit to associate with human beings . . . unfit to crawl with reptiles." This became his constant theme for the two hours that he spoke: the reprehensible evil of the "frame up," a term he returned to again and again, applying it repeatedly to both the police investigation and the prosecution.

In fact, the only question Pittman left unanswered was whether his contempt was greater for the haole "rabble" who were "crying for blood," or for the "bungling" prosecutor, or for the entire police department's corrupt leadership. The haole rabble, a clear reference to the *Advertiser* and *Star-Bulletin* editors among others, were the easiest to dismiss—they were nothing more than "servile sycophants," he said, "the servants of an outmoded caste of people who rule Hawaii, even though they are unfit to rule . . . a small group of hypocrites, more anxious to satisfy the Navy than to seek justice."

As for the prosecution: "This case will destroy the confidence of the people in their government, when the prosecution deliberately suppresses evidence . . . forcing the defense to grope in the dark. This is a frame up. Remember when I asked Mr. Wight to see those [police] statements, and he said 'I won't show you'? Never in the history of twenty-five years of practice have I witnessed such a spectacle in a courtroom." It was the prosecution that should be found guilty, he said—guilty of using "flimsy" and "manufactured" evidence to convict five innocent men of the worst crime imaginable.

And the police? Begin with Chief of Detectives McIntosh, he said, the man who connived with an underling, Officer Benton, to plant the false tire tread evidence. "It was a deliberate scheme to send these boys to the penitentiary. Some action should be taken against them. . . . If the public cannot trust the guardians of the peace, what protection have the people?" Then there was the matter of Thalia's identification of the defendants as her attackers. How was that accomplished? Did the police put the suspects in a lineup with nonsuspects, as they should have done? No. They employed "fool methods" instead. "They brought the boys before Mrs. Massie and said, 'We have the boys we suspect and we want you to identify them.' Imagine a police department so covered with cobwebs as to depend on that type of identification . . . a procedure that has been discarded for fifty years" by other departments elsewhere. If the police only picked up a few popular detective magazines from time to time they would know that much, he said.

But not every man in the department was guilty of such dishonesty and ineptitude. On the contrary, "thank God we have on the police force such men as Nakea, Harbottle, Machado, Bettencourt, and Simerson," he said. "The public should be thankful to them for coming forward to do their part toward clearing these defendants."

And if Wight could challenge the jurors' masculinity, so could Pittman, warning them that they would "never have another night's peaceful sleep" if they sent the defendants to prison. "You cannot, if you are honest and upright men, convict these men—but you must, on your manhood, be brave and fearless and acquit them and do it promptly. If you convict them, you have got to have no conscience, you have got to have no soul, you have got to be cowardly." Then he softened: "I know these men are innocent," he said, "and I know this jury will not swerve from its duty of acquitting them."

Pittman had begun his closing argument at about ten o'clock and it was noon when he concluded. Heen would be the last of the defense attorneys to sum up his case, followed by the prosecutor's closing rebuttal. Judge Steadman called a recess for lunch, asking everyone to be back in the courtroom by 1:30. No one imagined that the case would not go to the jury at the close of the day.

Heen began by telling the jury he would take at least two hours with his concluding statement because "I do not propose to leave a stone unturned in my endeavor to prevent five innocent boys from being railroaded to jail." Despite evidence to the contrary that he had introduced during the trial but not belabored, he said he was "willing to assume" that Thalia had been assaulted. That was not the question before the court. What was before the court was her hopelessly contradictory accounts of just what had happened, and when and where it had happened—as well as her belated and, as he put it, "coached" identifications of her assailants.

It was the prosecution's obligation to prove guilt beyond a reasonable doubt, Heen reminded the jurors, and to provide corroborative evidence. "Evidence that Mrs. Massie was at the Ala Moana scene is not enough," he told them. "It must be shown that the defendants were there and committed the crime." But the prosecutor couldn't even say when the alleged crime had taken place. David Takai's attorney, Robert Murakami, had gone over Thalia's and Wight's contradictory time estimates in detail. But Heen hammered the point home, since this more than anything else proved his clients to be innocent.

Making his way through the evidence piece by piece, minute by minute, Heen insisted there was no possibility that the five defendants could possibly have committed the crime of which they were accused. One of the fundamental requirements for a finding of guilt—opportunity—simply did not exist. This, in and of itself, should settle the matter. But just in case it didn't, he then began to dismantle every other piece of evidence that the prosecution had presented. "We have proved beyond a doubt that some of the witnesses for the prosecution have manufactured testimony in this case," he said, referring to the bogus tire-tread evidence. "It was thus nothing for one of them to have whispered the [license plate] number to the woman." As for her supposed identification of the defendants as her assailants, he reminded the jury of "the doctor's testimony that Mrs. Massie was under the influence of drugs and 'did not know what she was doing' when she saw the defendants at the hospital." After at first being unable to identify them, "she obviously was drilled in her testimony by some of these detectives who want to see these innocent boys go to jail."

But as Heen was dismantling the prosecution's case, a low rumble of conversation began spreading around the otherwise hushed courtroom. James Gilliland, the city attorney, had just arisen from his seat at a bailiff's request and rushed out into the corridor. He returned a few minutes later, knelt beside the prosecutor's table, and had a whispered conversation with Griffith Wight, who then summoned another bailiff to deliver a note to the judge. After reading the note, at 3:30—following two hours of Heen's closing argument, and just as he was beginning to wrap things up—Judge Steadman interrupted the leader of the defense team and asked him to pause. As the courtroom cleared for a recess, Steadman requested that the attorneys for both sides join him in his chambers. There, waiting for them, was Detective John Jardine. He had found two more witnesses of great importance to the prosecution, he reported, and the judge wished to discuss the prosecutor's request that Heen suspend the remainder of his closing argument until after these witnesses could testify.

For two hours, spectators waited amid a swirl of rumors for court to resume. The judge and the attorneys finally emerged at 5:30, and Steadman took his seat at the bench. Calling the court to order, he announced an adjournment until the following morning. Then, addressing the jurors, he said: "Something has come up that was wholly unexpected. There is an intimation that we will have some further evidence—that we do not yet know." He continued:

> This is an unusual procedure, to have an adjournment after the argument commences. The usual procedure is that there shall be no separation of the jury after the argument has begun, but we feel that it would be an unnecessary hardship to cause you to go to a hotel for the night. We permit you to go to your homes with the particular request that you do not read the newspapers, that you do not discuss this case, or permit anyone else to discuss it in your presence. I wish to re-emphasize the former instructions of the court in that connection. I ask you to keep your minds open, and not to reach any conclusions. A high obligation rests upon you, and I trust you to fulfill it faithfully.

With that, the jury was dismissed and the attorneys returned to the judge's chambers. There is no record of what transpired there, but it is not difficult to imagine what the defense lawyers had to say. With few exceptions, throughout the trial Judge Steadman had overruled their most important objections—especially on their key charge that the prosecution was withholding crucial exculpatory evidence from them. Prior to the trial, he had denied their requests for bills of particulars stipulating precisely what the charges were against each of the defendants. This was particularly important in Takai's case because Thalia had never identified him as one of her assailants. And now this. It was outrageous. But the judge had ruled, and there was nothing to do except wait to appeal the case, in the event their clients were found guilty.

■ ■ ■

The next morning, at 8:30, Judge Steadman called the court to order, but not before holding a private session with Grace Fortescue in his chambers while Thalia waited outside in her car. As spectators settled into their seats, many of them were carrying special editions of the *Advertiser* or *Star-Bulletin*. For once, the *Star-Bulletin* outdid its main competitor: "Ala Moana Assault Case Halted, New Evidence Will Be Sought," read the paper's banner headline. And then, beneath it, in a succession of boldface subheads: "Another Woman Looms as Possible Witness . . . Was Seen at John Ena Road on Night of Assault . . . Prosecuting Attorney Sees Five Defendants on Trial as the Right Men."

Once everyone was settled, Steadman turned the proceedings over to the prosecution. Griffith Wight stood and addressed the jury to explain what had happened the previous day. "Yesterday afternoon, during Judge Heen's argument to the jury," he began, "we discovered new evidence that we thought was important. We wish to stipulate that this new evidence discovered during Judge Heen's argument—"

Heen stood and interrupted. "We will stipulate that some new evidence was discovered," he announced, "but we do not agree that it was important." Steadman then instructed the prosecutor to call his witness.

His name was George McClellan, a civilian employee of the Army Air Corps at Luke Field and a well-known figure in local sports. For years he had organized and managed football and boxing events, and he now frequently was seen in arenas and on athletic fields working as an official. On direct examination, which was brief, McClellan testified that he and his wife, Ramona—both haoles—had attended the dance at Waikiki Park on the night of September 12. This was something not hard to recall, he said, because they attended the dance almost every week. As usual, they had stayed until the end. Afterward, at a little after midnight and feeling hungry, they had walked together down John Ena Road to the saimin stand, where they stopped for a bite to eat.

McClellan then said that he had been wearing dark trousers and a dark blue sweater over a white shirt. "And how was your wife dressed?" Wight asked. "In a green evening dress," the witness replied.

That was the extent of the testimony, but in his rebuttal closing statement Wight intended to make much of it. If there was any possibility that it was Mrs. McClellan, and not Thalia, who was seen by the Goeases and Alice Aramaki (and perhaps James Low) walking down John Ena Road at a little after midnight, at least one tiny hole in the defense's otherwise airtight alibis for the accused men might open up. If Thalia had indeed left the Ala Wai Inn at 11:35, her abduction then could have occurred at almost any time after 11:45, when she would have arrived at the place where she said she was kidnapped, and not after 12:15, when she was only *thought* to have been seen on John Ena Road—and when a carload of eyewitnesses placed the defendants on Beretania Street, far away from that area. Or so Wight would argue. It wasn't much. There were, after all, witnesses who said they had seen the defendants at the dance and in the parking lot repeatedly between 11:30 and midnight. But at this point, it was all he had.

On cross-examination, Heen maintained his practice of taking far longer with the witness than Wight had on direct examination. Though obviously displeased that the judge had interrupted his closing statement just as he was reaching its conclusion, he worked slowly and carefully with McClellan. He asked about his background, his work, his community activities. He asked why he had not come forward earlier. (It turned out he had not come forward at all, but had been summoned by the prosecution after Detective Jardine had provided Wight with another of his last-minute tips from anonymous sources.) And then he asked the witness a series of questions about the dance on the night of September 12, including the name of the band that was playing and the names of any friends or acquaintances he and his wife had run into. McClellan's answers were remarkably clear and certain and accurate. On no question was his answer more precise than when he described once again in great detail every item of outer clothing he and his wife had worn on the night in question.

Then, picking up on McClellan's statement under direct examination that he and his wife attended the dances at the park almost every Saturday night, Heen asked him if they had gone to the dances during the month of October, in addition to the one on September 12. Heen ticked off the dates—October 3, October 10, October 17, and so on—as McClellan replied affirmatively each time. Returning to those dates, one after the other, Heen then asked him if he could remember the name of the band that was playing on that particular evening. Time and again, he could not. More important, he also could not recall the clothing that he and his wife had worn on any of those other occasions—in stark contrast to his precise and detailed recollections of what they had worn on the more distant night of the twelfth of September.

Heen indicated that he was through with McClellan. Wight's next witness was Mrs. McClellan, but she was ill and confined to the Tripler Army Hospital in Moanalua. There were cars waiting outside the courthouse, Judge Steadman announced. They would take the defendants, the jury, and the court recorder to the hospital, while he and the attorneys would make their own way there. Heen drove his car to the hospital. Mr. and Mrs. George Goeas and Alice Aramaki rode along as his passengers.

At Tripler, Ramona McClellan had been moved to a large recreation room to receive the judge, the twelve jurors, the five defendants, the attorneys, and assorted other court personnel. Seated in a wheelchair, she was sworn in, and Griffith Wight carried out his direct examination of her. Perhaps in deference to her condition, he was even briefer with her than with her husband. And in response to his questions, Mrs. McClellan confirmed her husband's testimony—that the two of them had gone to the dance that night, had walked along John Ena Road afterward, and that she had worn "a light green dress, very long."

When asked if he wished to cross-examine, Heen declined. Instead, he asked the bailiff to go out to the hallway and bring in the Goeases and Miss Aramaki. When they entered, he asked them to take a look at Ramona McClellan; then he indicated to the judge that he was finished.

Back in the courthouse at 11:15, Judge Steadman directed Heen to resume his closing argument. But Heen—perhaps aware by now that the more Griffith Wight spoke, the better it was for the defense—requested that the prosecutor reopen his own closing statement first, and establish the relevance of the McClellan testimonies. Surprised and unnerved, Wight agreed, but asked for a five-minute recess to prepare his remarks. When he did speak, he proceeded to further entangle his case in a web of absurdities. The best that can be said for his performance is that, for some unrevealed reason, he may have thought that confusing the jury would be a clever strategy:

> Mrs. Massie left the Ala Wai Inn at 11:30 o'clock on the night of September 12. This, however, is uncertain. There is no record to reveal at what hour she was picked up in an automobile and assaulted at Ala Moana. It is probable that the woman in green whom Miss Aramaki, a witness, saw on the night of September 12 and the woman who was seen followed by a man, may be two different persons. At least there were three women in long green party dresses walking along John Ena Road on the night of September 12. Mrs. George McClellan was another woman in green who walked on John Ena Road that night. That makes four women. . . . There are two theories, and both theories are probable. Either that the boys assaulted the woman between 11:35 and 12:30 or somewhere around 11:10 and 11:45.

Apparently satisfied with himself, Wight stopped there and the judge called a recess for lunch. Anyone who had been following the trial had to have been bewildered by the prosecutor's last remarks. Did he simply misspeak?

No, he was suggesting—in fact, he later stated it even more boldly—that Thalia may have been kidnapped twenty-five minutes before even she now said she had left the Ala Wai Inn. There were numerous navy officers and their wives who had placed Thalia there until at least 11:30, which was why she had been unable to revise her departure time to before 11:35, after first telling the police she had left at midnight. But now Wight was claiming that she might have been abducted and raped between 11:10 and 11:45, presumably to allow the defendants cleverly to return to the dance before it ended so as to create eyewitness alibis for themselves. The entire performance was bizarre.

After lunch Heen called several witnesses in rebuttal of the McClellans. One after the other, the Goeases, Alice Aramaki, and Harold Godfrey, the manager of the dances at Waikiki Park, took the stand.

It turned out that Mr. and Mrs. Goeas knew the McClellans quite well, and saw them frequently. If it had been Mrs. McClellan walking down John Ena Road that night they certainly would have recognized her. But no, it wasn't her. And the man with the woman they had seen wasn't Mr. McClellan, no question about it. Miss Aramaki, without a translator, was less than precise on such matters as the heights of the man and woman she saw walking past her sister's store that night. But of one thing she was positive: the woman she had seen that night was not the woman in the wheelchair at the hospital, Mrs. McClellan. And finally, there was Harold Godfrey. George McClellan had mentioned him as one of the people he and his wife knew well and had seen at the dance on September 12. Godfrey confirmed both of these statements. In fact, he said he had spoken with the McClellans several times that night. And when asked if he remembered what Mrs. McClellan had been wearing, he said yes—he was absolutely certain that she had worn a light cream-colored dress, not a green one.

When Heen at last did return to his closing statement, he was angry. Now that they all had participated in this long-winded, time-wasting, and silly detour, he began, what had they found? "What did this new evidence amount to? Nothing, so far as the prosecution is concerned. If anything, it helped the defense. The prosecution thought they had found something to pull them out of the mire. I told you yesterday that the prosecution was sunk. Well, they were sunk even deeper today.

"Now the prosecutor tells us 'there are two theories in the case,' maybe three. And they are all 'probable.' The prosecution is gambling with theories. If that's what Mr. Wight wants to do, let's shorten the case and get a pair of dice. There can be only one theory in this case," he continued, "and that is that Mrs. Massie was seized after midnight—if she was seized at all." And the accused men's alibis for the postmidnight period were as solid as they were for the hour or so before midnight: in both cases numerous independent witnesses had sworn that they saw them in times and places that made it impossible for them to have committed the crime.

But other crimes had been committed, Heen said. Officer Benton, for instance, had "perjured himself on the stand" when he was "caught red-handed in framing the tire evidence to send innocent men to jail." And Officer Cluney had "lied under oath" in his effort to put words in Horace Ida's mouth. Those two officers, and others who had behaved similarly, were part of a conspiracy driven by "the public clamor to crucify [the defendants] on a cross of prejudice and sentiment." Other officers had testified, however—testified for the defense. What about them? Bettencourt. Nakea. Furtado. Harbottle. Simerson. The defense attorney ticked off the names. "Are we to disregard the testimony of these witnesses—and every other one except the complaining witness— simply because they are Hawaiian, Chinese, Japanese, or Portuguese?" After reminding the jury of his detailed, point-by-point refutation of the prosecution's case before he had been interrupted the day before, Heen finally closed quietly with an unblushing reference to Providence and a plea that the jurors "be honest and courageous in reaching your verdict, and return a verdict of not guilty on your first ballot."

The last word was given to the prosecutor. "If anyone has been crucified," he began, "it is this lovely girl who crucified herself to protect other women of Honolulu." Thalia and Grace had absented themselves from most of the trial after Thalia's testimony on the first day, but they were there now, and Wight turned and pointed to them. "I cannot praise Mrs. Massie enough for her bravery in coming forward to testify in court," he said. "The assault will leave its stigma with her throughout her life."

It was a good opening, but everything that followed was largely a variation on the same theme. "Death is preferable" to what Mrs. Massie endured, he shouted, especially when it is endured at the hands of—he now turned to the defendants and repeated what had become his favorite term for them— "these lust-sodden beasts." And death was what these defendants properly deserved, "but unfortunately rape is not a hanging offense in this Territory." Most of the remainder of his summation was of a piece with his opening. And when he did attempt to deal with the evidence in the case, the prosecutor only revived already discredited testimony, such as the tire-tread marks, insisting against what everyone in the courtroom had witnessed, that "Officer Benton's testimony still stands unchallenged."

Yes, there was a police conspiracy, he said. But it was a conspiracy among those "traitors" in the department who testified for the defense. That was why no corroborative physical evidence was ever found. "Think of Officer Lau," he said, "a fingerprint expert who couldn't find one single fingerprint [of Mrs. Massie's] on that car. Why? Because he didn't *want* to find any." There was no doubt in his mind that the accused men were guilty, Wight said, and at last he had settled on a single theory to explain things. Unfortunately for him, it was the most outlandish of all the scenarios he had previously tried out: the defendants had kidnapped and raped Thalia before midnight, and then returned to the park in order to be seen by eyewitnesses who could then provide them with alibis. This, of course, fit none of the evidence that had been provided by anyone, including Thalia.

As his finale, Wight returned to his main theme. "What we call upon you gentlemen of the jury for is to vindicate Hawaii, to show that you will protect your women. Could you go home and look your mother or your wife in the eye if you failed to do your duty in this case? If you acquit you will announce to the world that our women must be kept at home, that we must go armed to protect ourselves from gangsters. . . . Show the world that here is a place where, above all things, we protect our women. . . . Stand together like the rock of Gibraltar for a true verdict and thus justify your manhood."

The next day, the *Advertiser* called it "a strikingly effective closing argument."

15 "The Shame of Honolulu"

I t was nearly nine o'clock Wednesday night, December 2, when the jury was given the case. Anticipating a quick verdict, hundreds of spectators gathered outside the courthouse, waiting with the defendants, the attorneys, and the press for the announcement of a decision. Three hours later, at midnight, Judge Steadman recalled the jurors, saying, "I take it from your silence that you have not reached a verdict." The elected foreman, William Brede, confirmed that to be the case. Urging them to get a good night's rest—they had started the day more than fifteen hours earlier—Steadman told the jurors their families were bringing fresh clothing to the Hotel Blaisdell, where they would be spending the night.

At eight o'clock the next morning the jury returned. They broke for lunch at noon. At 6:30 they recessed again for dinner. At a little after 10:00 p.m. they informed the judge that they were deadlocked and exhausted. Throughout the day and evening they had requested and received various excerpts of the courtroom testimony, most of it Thalia's. They had also asked for and been given a dictionary.

On Friday morning they began again. The newspapers were now printing special editions, counting the hours the jury had been out. By noon it was almost forty hours. At the close of the business day, with the weekend approaching, more people than ever began filling the courthouse grounds. Tempers flared. Some feared that the vicious rapists of a fragile young white woman might get off free. Others worried that five innocent young men were being framed into spending the rest of their lives in prison. The newspapers' lead articles all concerned the jury deliberations, but two of them also were giving prominent play to a story out of Maryland that more than a few readers found unnecessarily provocative. According to the United Press account, "Mac Williams, negro, who shot and killed his employer and then turned the gun on himself, inflicting a serious wound, was lynched last night. A mob of 4,000 took the negro to a public park where he was hanged. The leaders of the mob poured gasoline on the body and burned it."

Judge Steadman had ordered the jury foreman to destroy all ballots after they had been cast. But the jury room was cleaned every time the jurors went out for a meal, and soon word of a juror holdout began to make its way through the crowd and into the press. Dozens of ballots had been cast, the report said, and for almost two days the vote had stood at ten for conviction, two for acquittal. Now, late Friday morning, it had just shifted: eleven voting guilty, only one not guilty.

Of all those waiting on the courthouse lawn, the newspapers observed, the most relaxed appeared to be the defendants. They had found a spot beneath the statue of King Kamehameha and returned to it each morning, where they read the sports pages, conversed with one another, and spoke to well-wishers. When asked by reporters to explain their apparent nonchalance, they said they were innocent and trusted the jurors, and added that there was no point in getting upset about things that were beyond their control. Grace and Thalia waited in seclusion. Tommie, who had been sent on maneuvers at his request two weeks earlier, was still at sea.

As noon approached on Friday, Judge Steadman sent a bailiff up to take the jurors to lunch. But they sent him away, asking for another half hour. Minutes later, spectators gathering in the courthouse rotunda heard shouts coming from the jury room overhead, along with the noise of heavy furniture being dragged across the floor. The bailiff rushed to the judge's chambers and asked him to come quickly to the jury room. He did, bringing Griffith Wight, the prosecutor, and William Heen with him. As Steadman later stated for the record:

> The jury room was then opened and all jurors were standing. Most of them had their coats off for the sake of comfort, while separated by 10 or 15 feet two jurors did give evidence of belligerence and were in their undershirts and trousers. There was no evidence that any blows were struck, nor were there any signs of actual physical encounter. The court directed that the jurors immediately attire themselves properly. One juror did state that the trouble had been occasioned by the other calling him a provocative name. . . . After the two jurors had put their shirts and coats on I did speak a few remarks, the exact words of which I do not recall, but the tenor of which was that while I appreciated that in the course of any long trial and deliberation personal feelings are easily aroused, it was of paramount importance that jurors restrain their emotions and passions and keep them under control.

He then sent them all to lunch. Hoping that Chinese food might help calm their frayed nerves, some of the jurors suggested eating at the Honolulu Chop Sui House, so that was where they headed.

The attorneys for the defense were less easily placated. No doubt fearing that the rumors of an 11–1 jury poll were correct, Heen moved that Judge Steadman declare a mistrial. "In support of this motion we submit that the jury, after a prolonged session engaged in deliberating upon its verdict, has reached a point where at least two jurors have shown by their actions that they were about to resort to physical force," Heen argued. Things had reached such a pass, he added, that at least certain jurors were "no longer re-lying on the process of reasoning in determining their verdict in this case." Of course, what most concerned the defense was the possibility that its lone vote for an acquittal was now being physically intimidated into joining the others in a guilty verdict.

Prosecutor Wight vigorously argued against the motion for a mistrial, and the judge agreed with him. After lunch the jury continued to deliberate. Following dinner, and a drive up a picturesque mountain road to refresh them, they tried again to reach a decision. Shortly after their return they sent out for more blank ballots. But at ten o'clock they adjourned for the night, still without a verdict. "Many spectators were present to watch the men file out of the building," the *Star-Bulletin* reported. "All looked fagged and weary."

Saturday was more of the same, despite expectations among certain courtroom pundits. In those days high school football in Hawai'i was like high school football in much of Texas today—the most exciting game in town, which few people missed. And on this particular Saturday the championship game between Kamehameha and McKinley high schools was being held. If that lone holdout juror happened to be a football fan, many believed, he would fold before missing out on such a contest.

But throughout the day there was no news from the jury room. Finally, at nine o'clock Saturday night, Foreman Brede sent a note to Judge Steadman informing him that further deliberation was hopeless. A verdict could not be reached. Steadman assembled the jurors in the courtroom and told them he was rejecting the claim that they were deadlocked. He congratulated them on their efforts and their patience, but added that he did "not believe a more con-scientious group of twelve jurors can be obtained for a retrial of this case."

Telling the jurors to sleep late on Sunday morning if they liked, and offer-ing magazines and walks and automobile rides to clear their minds, Judge Steadman directed them to deliberate for at least one more day. He was giving them what since 1896 had been known as an *"Allen* charge"—referred to less formally by attorneys as a "dynamite charge"—a strong admonition to seek common ground and come in with a verdict. When he asked if any of them wished to examine any more of the evidence, they said no. When he asked if they required further instructions on the law, they sat in stony silence.

Several months later, in an interview with an official of the U.S. Justice Department, Judge Steadman said that he wanted the jurors to return a guilty verdict and that was why he kept them out as long as he did. But after another long day and night, at 10:05 p.m. on Sunday, he reluctantly accepted their insistence that the deadlock could not be broken.

The jurors had deliberated for more than ninety-seven hours, a record for any jury in the islands' history, and—contrary to rumor—they had not even approached a vote of 11–1 or 10–2 on any ballot. In fact, it turned out that they had cast scores of secret ballots and never came closer to agreement than a 7–5 vote one way or the other. The first and final votes were 6–6. Those who voted to acquit said they found especially disturbing the obvious efforts of the prosecution to manufacture, suppress, and falsify evidence. And none of them, whichever way they voted, had ever given any thought to the Kamehameha-McKinley football game.

According to the account in George Wright's English-language section of the *Hawaii Hochi,* "bedlam broke loose in the halls of the judiciary building following the discharge of the jury." No other newspaper reported that, but all of them carried one version or another of what he wrote next: "Some of the jurymen were the focus of the defendants, who rushed over to them and shook hands with them and profusely thanked them."

Admiral Stirling, for one, felt he knew what that was all about. The outward indifference of the young men while the jury was deliberating raised suspicions enough, but they were suspicions confirmed, Stirling and others thought, when reports surfaced about a retired police lieutenant taking the defendants out for drinks as soon as the trial was over. What had happened in the courtroom, Stirling later wrote, "was a stupid miscarriage of justice which could have been avoided if the Territorial Government had shown more inclination to sympathize with my insistence upon the necessity of a conviction. The defendants"—whom he later characterized as "cutthroats"—"were not men who should have been given the benefit of a reasonable doubt."

In Stirling's mind, the five accused men had clearly been guilty, but were let go because of their race. And the jury's composition and split balloting proved it. As he put it: "I was informed reliably that the vote of the jury began and remained to the end, seven for not guilty and five for guilty, the exact proportion of yellow and brown to whites on the jury."

In fact, there had been only one "white" man on the jury, as every local newspaper had reported since the start of the trial. Some of the others bore last names suggesting European ancestry, but all of them were part-Hawaiian, "mixed race" jurors of a sort Stirling usually dismissed as "mongrels." Moreover, the single haole juror on the panel later revealed that he had voted not guilty from the first ballot to the last. The three jurors who pushed hardest for conviction were Hawaiian, Chinese, and Japanese, and every member of the jury who subsequently discussed what happened during those intense four days of deliberation agreed on one thing: none of the voting and none of the debate had broken down along racial lines.

But Yates Stirling was a man rarely troubled by inconvenient facts, one of many things he had in common with Grace Fortescue. He regarded the failure to convict as a public shaming of the navy, just as Grace was humiliated by the failure of the prosecution to substantiate Thalia's accusations—accusations that were supposed to have put an end to what she called the "lying gossip and filthy stories" that had been whispered about her daughter. But because of the "crafty methods" employed by the defense counsel, she said, Thalia had become just another victim of Hawai'i's "half-breed natives" who regularly defied the law and, in so doing, "mocked one of the white man's most sacred tenets."

They would not get away with it, Grace pledged. And throughout her life, what Grace Hubbard Bell Fortescue wanted—with the exception of a hardworking husband—she usually got. The first thing she did was seek out Judge Steadman, who "had been considerate and kind to us during the trial," she later wrote in her memoirs, "begging him to put the defendants in jail." Steadman, according to her account, said he agreed that the men were a menace, but he informed Grace that there was nothing he could do. Under Hawai'i law bail could be denied only for capital offenses, which rape was not, and then only "when the proof is evident or the presumption great." Thus, the men remained covered by the bail terms predating the just-concluded trial.

As for Steadman's actual thoughts regarding the accused men, they were more complex than what Grace reported. Although admitting in a private interview that he would have voted for conviction, he added: "I would never have felt entirely right about it." In that, the judge reflected accurately the attitudes of many in the old-time haole community who wanted to see the expendable defendants put away in prison, if necessary for life, just to quiet things down—even if they doubted that the men were guilty. But whether they were guilty or not, at least until the conclusion of another trial, Ida, Ahakuelo, Takai, Chang, and Kahahawai would remain free on bail.

Grace, however, was just getting started. Supported by editorials in the *Advertiser* urging that "the defendants in the notorious assault case . . . be jailed pending a second trial," she asked Admiral Stirling to approach Governor Judd about the same matter. Judd was in Washington at the time, so Stirling had to content himself with dressing down the acting governor, Raymond Brown. His appeal was typically straightforward: the defendants "should not be allowed to contaminate the community with their presence," he said. Brown's reply was the same as Judge Steadman's. He told the admiral that the men had posted bond and could not now be jailed, but that authorities were doing their best to put together a retrial as quickly as possible. They had to be careful, though, because even those most sympathetic to the prosecution were warning that in a second trial the territory would be lucky to get off with a hung jury. The facts of the matter were clear-cut: without new evidence—solid evidence this time—there was no chance of a conviction.

Acting governor Brown had some concerns of his own that he then shared with Stirling. Although there had been no serious violence yet, minor incidents were breaking out everywhere between navy men and civilians. Just the previous night there had been a near riot because of a confrontation at the Black Cat Café on Hotel Street. In another part of town a sailor had been hit on the head and awakened to find his wallet missing along with his clothes. Elsewhere, navy enlisted men were said to be walking the streets brandishing firearms and homemade weapons and looking for trouble. Brown asked Stirling to help in cooling things off by beefing up shore patrols. The admiral replied that he would be happy to do so, on one condition. As he later recalled, "I insisted [the shore patrol] be given the same authority as policemen and could shoot to kill without being tried for murder." Brown declined the suggestion.

As the first few days after the close of the trial passed, it seemed as though no one in Honolulu could speak of anything else, regardless of the occasion. Addressing a long-scheduled banquet for the Honolulu Boy Scout Council, Walter Dillingham put aside his upbeat prepared text and railed against "the desperate crimes committed in our midst by gangsters and hoodlums." He was equally "disgusted and sick of the stuff that has been handed out" about the innocence of the accused men, he added. Later, Dillingham would privately admit that "in the minds of many people," and especially in light of "the weak and unconvincing character of much of the testimony," the defendants probably were not guilty. But he still believed the authorities "should have forced a conviction."

Dillingham also headed up a newly appointed emergency committee of the Honolulu Chamber of Commerce charged by business leaders with cleaning up the police department and seeking "legal and other assistance" in tracking down additional evidence that could be used in a second trial. Two months earlier the chamber had appropriated five thousand dollars for use in assisting the prosecution. That money was made available to coax confessions from the defendants, among other purposes, but was not publicly announced. Now, the day after the trial was over, the chamber voted to put up another five thousand dollars, this time as a publicly posted reward for information that would lead to a conviction.

The city and county attorney announced that prosecutor Wight was being released from all other responsibilities to concentrate full-time on preparing for the retrial. To assist Wight, the chamber directors hired their own attorney to head up a task force of handpicked police detectives, led by John Jardine. Their mandate was unequivocal: "To secure evidence dealing with the activities of the five defendants in the case." In two days the detectives had swept through what the chamber's report called "underworld haunts" and arrested nine men who were believed to have information on the case and on the whereabouts of the accused men on the night in question.

Among the prominent businessmen at the chamber's emergency meeting following the trial was Edward P. Irwin, a man Grace later singled out as one of her two or three strongest supporters and closest friends during her stay in the islands. He also was a longtime adviser to Dillingham, among other things preparing for him a 1921 report presented to Congress that described the Japanese in Hawai'i as "arrogant, insolent, domineering, and truculent." Because of their growing desire to be represented by unions on the plantations, the Japanese had become "a menace," the report said, and Congress should lend its support to big business in Hawai'i by making it easier to import cheaper and more tractable laborers from other places.

Irwin was a midwesterner who had arrived in the islands in 1906 and gone to work for the *Star-Bulletin*. Since then he had also worked for the *Advertiser* and for a publication named *Crossroads of the Pacific* before finally founding his own weekly, the *Honolulu Times*. Over the years, his temperament had made it difficult for him to hold on to salaried positions. The *Advertiser* fired him twice, on one occasion even announcing in its own pages that he had been terminated "for general unreliability and too frequent intoxication." During a brief stint as editor of that paper he was sued for libel several times and once wound up in a fistfight with a Hawaiian territorial senator, on the floor of the legislature, after the politician had called him a racist.

Despite the fact that Irwin's wife was Hawaiian, the politician was right. Irwin considered Hawaiians to be irresponsible and easily led, but he had a particular enmity for Asians. Time and again he would refer in print to the pathological "inner formation of the Oriental brain," and condemn mixed marriages between whites and Japanese, who—"with their flat features, protruding teeth, short legs" and overall "hostility to our ideals"—should be barred from living in the islands. No Hawaiians or Asians ought ever to be trusted to head important organizations, he once told an interviewer, adding that few nonwhites would mind such a prohibition in any case "because they have a natural tendency to look up to the haole." For this and other reasons, Irwin also was opposed to having anyone other than haoles serve on juries faced with "serious cases," and he supported a federalized commission form of government for the islands, in essence a dictatorship that would strip residents of all voting privileges.

At the moment, however, the newspaperman had more pressing issues on his mind. He and Grace agreed that what she called the "hush-hush policy" imposed by Dillingham and Stirling on outside news coverage of the trial had turned out to be a disaster. It had allowed slick defense attorneys and corrupt officials to operate with impunity in preventing a deserved conviction of the men Thalia had identified as her rapists. Clearly, external pressure on local authorities was necessary if ever there were to be justice. But how best to maximize that pressure prior to the retrial?

Eight months earlier the famous muckraking journalist Lincoln Steffens had published his autobiography. *Time* referred to it as "a meaty, marrowy, seasoned report on an active life which many a reader will envy." It sold well, especially among members of the press. In the book's humorous fourteenth chapter Steffens described in some detail "how to make a crime wave." It was really quite simple, he wrote. All a reporter had to do was file with great fanfare a steady stream of stories about minor, everyday crimes that normally were too insignificant to merit coverage. Years earlier, as a beginning police reporter, Steffens had done just that at the *New York Post*, he wrote, thereby creating an impression of a city under siege. As the *Post*'s circulation soared, editors at other newspapers demanded the same sorts of stories from their reporters. Soon the pages of all the city's newspapers bristled with accounts of genuine—but incidental—criminal activity. Panic over the fictional crime epidemic spread throughout Manhattan.

As Steffens confessed in his book, the crime wave that he had proudly created was entirely invented, although technically all the "crimes" had been real. There had been no increase at all in the city's actual crime rate, he wrote. "It was only the newspaper reports of crimes that had increased." The only "wave" had been a "wave of publicity."

In mid-October of 1931, just one month before the trial had begun, Edward Irwin had written a characteristically overheated editorial in the *Honolulu Times* decrying the effects of gangster movies on impressionable youth. At the time, Irwin apologized to his readers for relying on news reports from cities outside the islands to provide examples of the kind of criminal activity that could be expected to follow on the showing of such films. It couldn't be helped, he wrote: "we haven't here, in this small community, enough violence to answer headline purposes, so we're obliged to draw upon the mainland." But that was then. This was now. He decided to take a page from Steffens's book.

On Saturday, December 12—six days after the Thalia Massie rape case had ended in a hung jury—the *Honolulu Times* hit the streets bearing a banner headline, "The Shame of Honolulu." Even the title was taken from Steffens's famous book, *The Shame of the Cities*. The centerpiece of the issue was a large and inflammatory front-page editorial claiming that women in the city routinely ran the "risk of being assaulted and foully raped by gangs of lust-mad youths . . . foul, slimy creatures crawling through the streets and attacking the innocent and the defenseless." Irwin then printed page after page of the past year's news stories from all the local newspapers that seemed to validate his wild accusations.

Each of the articles was accurately reproduced and, if read with care, signified little. Most of them recounted rumors or at most reports of alleged misdemeanors that had been printed on the inside pages of the *Advertiser* or the *Star-Bulletin*. But atop the stories Irwin had appended his own bold and misleading headlines. "Alarming Array of Sex Crimes Crowds Few Months in Honolulu," "Police Prey on Women of the Underworld," and "Governess Is Assaulted" were typical. And through it all ran his serpentine commentary on "the danger of ravishment by bands of human beasts that lurk in the shadows of night in this the 'Paradise of the Pacific.'"

Of course, the people of Honolulu—at least those not on the lookout for reasons to be outraged—knew what to think of the shabby little tabloid, and shrugged off the sensationalism. But they were not the readers Irwin was after. In addition to his normal press run, he printed 3,500 special copies of the newspaper, all of them bearing a large stamp reading "Compliments of a

Navy Man on Duty," and had them delivered free of charge to the Pearl Harbor barracks and other island naval posts. Along with the newspapers was a note urging the recipients to mail the publication to their families and especially to their hometown newspapers on the mainland. Within days ships leaving Honolulu for the West Coast contained mailbags filled with copies of the *Honolulu Times*. They were addressed to hundreds of big-city dailies and small-town weeklies located in every state in the nation.

With each passing day following the jury's announcement of its deadlock, tempers in the city grew shorter. It began with a few navy wives who claimed they had been treated rudely, and even threatened, by Asian and Hawaiian teenagers. In reply, a group of enlisted men marched into the downtown area armed with containers of aviation fuel, only at the last minute deciding against an apparent mass arson. Elsewhere, a sailor drove a car outfitted with mounted machine guns into the center of a major intersection. He claimed to be the advance guard of a planned invasion of Honolulu that turned out to be a one-man operation—a drunken one-man operation. And on Wednesday, December 9, a crudely written message was found in the Chief Petty Officers' Mess at Pearl Harbor. Signed "The Kalihi Gang," it said, "We have raped your women and will get some more."

Later, even Admiral Stirling admitted that the note had been a hoax, probably perpetrated by the petty officers themselves. But in the meantime word of the threat spread rapidly among navy wives. In no time police and shore patrol telephone lines were jammed with calls from terrified women claiming to have seen suspicious dark-skinned men lurking about their homes. A neighbor of the Massies reported that a "very dark man, Hawaiian or mixture," had come to her house selling brooms. But most broom salesmen carried a variety of products, she said, and this one had very few, convincing her that he was up to no good. Across the street, only the day before, another officer's wife had peeked through parted curtains as an automobile driven by a Japanese man and containing "two girls of the geisha type" slowed in front of her house. One of the girls seemed to be writing something down. The woman quickly called the police.

Many of these navy wives were living alone for the time being. Their husbands, along with Tommie Massie, were at sea on maneuvers. Within hours of receiving news of the "Kalihi Gang" note, Rear Admiral George Pettengill, commander of the minecraft forces then operating in Hawai'i waters, wired the Pacific Fleet commander in Washington that conditions were unsafe for white women in Honolulu. Large-scale naval war games in the Pacific were scheduled to take place in less than two months. Normally, such major operations involved stops in the islands, and the wives of navy men accompanied the ships and vacationed in Honolulu during the exercises. But Pettengill, without authorization from Stirling, recommended to Washington that no wives be allowed to sail with their husbands during the upcoming operations. Conditions on the streets of the city simply were too dangerous.

When he learned of Pettengill's wire, Stirling informed the press that he had not known of it in advance, but "until the criminals who committed the Ala Moana assault are convicted and locked up, and until Honolulu is safe for women, I wouldn't think of going against Admiral Pettengill's recommendations." Later he would say that "since the five accused men were as free as air, I half expected, in spite of discipline, to hear any day that one or more had been found swinging from trees by the neck up Nuuanu Valley or at the Pali." In Hawaiian the word *pali* means "cliff." The one to which Stirling was referring is more than a thousand feet high and is only a short drive from downtown Honolulu.

The "Shame of Honolulu" edition of the *Honolulu Times* hit the streets and was delivered to military bases on Saturday morning. Its stories of dark-skinned "lust-mad" beasts lurking in alleyways fit perfectly with the "Kalihi Gang" letter. Hundreds of sailors who had been wondering what to do with themselves that weekend wondered no more.

As word began to spread on base of what was being planned, Stirling canceled all shore leave, but it was too late. Honolulu was swarming with navy men determined to teach the locals a lesson. One after another the police and shore patrol calls came in. A fight had broken out between navy men and Filipinos outside a pool hall near Liliha Street. A pitched battle was in progress between sailors and civilians across from the Alexander Young Hotel on Bishop Street. A clash of military and Hawaiian men had erupted at Fort and School streets. And more. Before the night was over at least eight riot calls were turned in to police headquarters, all involving groups of men wearing navy dungarees and nonwhite civilians.

Realizing that the home addresses of the men accused of raping Thalia had been printed repeatedly in the newspapers, police officials sent squads to stand guard outside their houses. But none of them were home. Ben Ahakuelo and David Takai were dancing at Waikiki Park, while the others were out with friends. Horace Ida, once again having borrowed his sister's car after dropping her off at a party where she was working as a geisha, was driving around with an acquaintance, watching the riots from a distance.

At about 9:30 Horace decided to stop at a speakeasy on Kukui Street. He had been there earlier in the week and sitting nearby at the time were several sailors in uniform. Before leaving, one of them who called himself "Primo" had come over to congratulate Horace on the jury's nonverdict. And now, on Saturday night, here was Primo again, pulling up to the speakeasy in a roadster containing four other men.

Horace was standing on the sidewalk outside the bar, talking with a handful of friends. When they saw the gun, everyone fled. But Horace didn't move quickly enough, and in a matter of minutes he was riding in the front seat of the car, squeezed in between the driver and another passenger. The man to his right was pressing a revolver into his ribs. Following behind were three other cars, all of them filled with sailors, some riding in rumble seats, others standing on running boards. The road they were traveling on led to only one place, the Nuʻuanu Pali with its sheer drop of almost a quarter mile to the valley floor below.

The man with the gun appeared to be the leader of the group. Wearing a black or dark blue civilian suit, he gave orders to the other navy men with the confidence of an officer. And he wanted one thing from Horace, and one thing only, he said: a confession to participating in the gang rape of Mrs. Massie. That, Horace replied, was the one thing he couldn't give him, because they hadn't done it. Fine. Then he was going to die.

As the procession of autos approached the Pali Lookout—a parking area near the cliff's edge, popular with daytime sightseers and late-night lovers—the navy men realized there was insufficient privacy for what they had planned. So they followed the winding path down the other side of the mountain, finally reaching a flat open area that was part of a dairy farm. There they pulled off the road and dragged Ida from the front seat of the first car.

The leader of the group ordered Horace to remove his shirt and turn around. The first blows he felt came from what seemed to be a thin leather belt, but soon others joined in with heavier belts, beating him on the back and shoulders with the metal buckles. When he went down they began kicking him, then someone hit him on the head with a gun butt. Repeatedly, they demanded a confession, but finally he feigned unconsciousness, and the beating stopped. Most of those standing around had no stomach for finishing the job. They started climbing into their cars and heading up the mountainside. The leaders of the group threw Ida's body into some bushes and joined the others for the drive back to town.

The next day's newspapers all carried large front-page photographs of Horace Ida's cut, bruised, and battered face and body. After the navy men's vehicles had left the scene of the attack, a passing motorist saw Ida and drove him to the closest police station. From there he was taken to police headquarters in Honolulu and then to the hospital. "He was severely handled," said a police spokesman, "and he is lucky to be alive."

Sunday night was quieter in Honolulu. There were a few minor incidents, the most threatening of which was when a group of sailors surrounded Ben Ahakuelo's home and pounded on the door, demanding to see him. The police broke up that incident, and Monday dawned with less violent—but no less intense—verbal confrontations common on street corners and in the daily press.

Japanese-language newspapers expressed outrage at what had happened. At least one of them likened the attack on Ida to an attempted lynching, reminding readers of the continued vigilante killings of blacks in the South and noting that such behavior was hardly a sign of "the white man's superiority." The *Star-Bulletin* expressed concern that the assault on Ida might lead to sympathy for him and his codefendants in a retrial of the rape case. And Raymond Coll's *Advertiser* blamed all the weekend's violence on the fact that the defendants were still free on bail. To emphasize its general stance immediately after the beating of Ida, the *Advertiser* also ran a front-page editorial cartoon depicting a dark-skinned, simianlike figure, labeled "The Beast," hunched forward, its knuckles almost dragging on the ground, while a gathering storm marked "Outraged Public Feeling" blew in its direction.

For his part, Admiral Stirling said he was pleased that the discipline he insisted upon from his men remained strong, as demonstrated by the fact that they had refrained from killing the accused man. This was despite the fact, he said, that as he was being beaten Ida had confessed to them that he and his friends had indeed raped Mrs. Massie. Ida denied that he had said any such thing, and people believed whichever claim they were predisposed to believing. Later interviewed by a staff writer for the *Chicago Tribune*, Thalia said she was certain Ida had confessed. "'Otherwise he might not have come back alive,' she says, smiling sweetly," he reported. According to her—but this was several months later—he had confessed and named Joe Kahahawai as the ringleader of the gang.

As for Ida's family, they issued a statement that appeared in all the newspapers saying they were proud of him for not falsely confessing even under extreme duress, describing such behavior as true *yamato damashii*. In literal translation the term means "Japanese spirit," but in actual use it referred to a warrior or samurai cast of mind.

With the exception of Princess Abigail Kawananakoa and several others, in the months since Thalia's explosive accusation, much of the social and political elite of the native Hawaiian community had been remarkably quiet, if anything allying themselves more with Honolulu's upper-class haoles than with working-class Hawaiians. Many of them appeared concerned and fearful that whites, painting with a broad brush, might regard them as sharing traits with the Hawaiian rabble, including the likes of Ben Ahakuelo and Joe Kahahawai. But now cracks began appearing in that self-protective edifice.

An organization known as the Native Sons and Daughters of Hawaii, through its "premier," Mrs. Emma Ahuena Taylor, held firm to that position, issuing a statement that might have come from the pen of Admiral Stirling. "Depraved mongrels are at large," read the proclamation of these ancestrally appointed native leaders, "while terrified women of refinement blush with shame at the thought that the onus of this disgraceful tragedy might be applied to the innocent, law abiding, and decent men of Honolulu through the obscenity of these brutes. . . . A naval officer's wife has been ravished by five beasts. . . . [We must] find the rapists and a jury of intelligent men to convict them. Show the navy that we are earnest."

Opposing them, the Hawaiian Civic Club, an equally prestigious organization of elected native leaders, issued a statement condemning Admiral Pettengill and the navy. A group of club members—one of whom, former Honolulu sheriff David Kaukaohu Trask, had served as Ahakuelo's attorney during his first trial two years earlier—regarded the rape accusation as a witch hunt from the start. Having now seized control of the organization, they issued a public statement saying that in Honolulu it was and always had been "safe for women to go about at any time, day or night, without fear of molestation." They also demanded that Admiral Pettengill retract his "unfair, unwarranted, and uncalled for statement that has besmirched the good name of our fair city and cast a reflection upon the Hawaiian people."

Almost lost in the furor were the comments of Princess Kawananakoa. Saying she was in "utter sympathy" with the victim of the alleged rape, who was being "sacrificed on the altar of merciless publicity," she also decried the violence against Horace Ida. "Whether the defendants in question are innocent or guilty will be established by due process of law," she continued. "We must be determined that there shall be no more of these disturbances and uprisings which tend to defeat the very purpose of the law: to bring order out of chaos."

Saturday, December 12, had been designated Marconi Day in much of Europe and the United States, the thirtieth anniversary of the spanning of the Atlantic Ocean by wireless radio. Now the Pacific was being tied in to what would someday be a worldwide network. Before the riots had broken out in the city that night, the celebration was especially joyous in Honolulu. The islands, finally linked by radio to the outside world, were able to participate in a ninety-minute program featuring a talk by Guglielmo Marconi himself. To mark the ceremony, local radio station KGU was given ten minutes of air time to carry a three-minute speech by the acting governor, followed by seven minutes of Hawaiian music—all of it piped into homes across the ocean, thousands of miles away.

In the days following, cablegrams poured into the Honolulu radio station from broadcasters throughout the nation, assuring the local manager, B. A. Rolfe, that the reception had been excellent. "Congratulations on a great show," wired the head of NBC in New York; "the music was fine and you sounded like yourself, only better." A week later announcement was made of a direct transpacific telephone connection. From then on, the press release said, "the radio telephone service will be open for business, by which one may speak from any telephone on Oahu, Kauai, Hawaii, or Maui to any telephone on the mainland, Canada, Mexico, and Cuba."

For local business and political leaders, who had hoped to profit from long-distance telephone connections, the opening up of direct communication with the mainland could not have come at a worse time. Since Admirals Pettengill and Stirling were now sending cables to Washington about purported conditions in the islands, and making those cables public, wire-service reporters in the city decided that the ban on the sensational rape case could no longer be sustained. Accounts of Saturday's street fights, and sensationalized accounts of allegedly unchecked racial and sexual violence in the streets of Honolulu, soon were appearing in newspapers and magazines and on radio broadcasts from coast to coast.

The theme of each report was the same. Datelined December 15, a United Press International article was the first to hit the front pages of the nation's newspapers. The story's opening sentence announced the unusual presence of military police on patrol in "this 'Paradise of the Pacific'" because of "fear of a racial outbreak." The body of the story described the September assault on Thalia, referred to as an unnamed U.S. Navy officer's wife who had been taking "a starry night's stroll on the famous beach at Waikiki, noted in song and legend." It went on to tell of her kidnapping and rape at the hands of "five hoodlums," and of her being left "broken and hysterical by the roadside." Despite her identification of four of the five assailants, the story said, the rapists had recently been released by a jury that refused to convict them. Consequently, the "motley assemblage" of residents in this "melting pot of the Pacific" were thrown into a "racial uproar which culminated in the American sailors, bitterly resentful at what they called a miscarriage of justice, taking the law into their own hands."

As things now stood, the article concluded, "ominous mutterings" could be heard "from Chinatown to the Japanese fishing colony on the waterfront, from the lavish mansions of green Manoa valley to the Filipino huts in the sugar cane fields. But no more than in the army barracks and naval stations where youths from Missouri and Kansas and Texas demand protection for white women." A follow-up UPI story told readers to be on the lookout for copies of the *Honolulu Times*—especially its editorial, "The Shame of Honolulu"—that "navy men are mailing out by the thousands."

Time was next with a story headlined "Lust in Paradise." It too described the islands' "motley population" and the rape of an unnamed young white woman, "the daughter of a gallant soldier, the granddaughter of one of the world's greatest inventors." In this "paradisaic melting pot of East & West" the inevitable had at last happened, *Time* said: "Yellow men's lust for white women had broken bounds." The story concluded by quoting Admiral Yates Stirling to the effect that he had the situation under control, but that "Honolulu may expect cases of assault upon women unless the better element gets to work to stamp it out."

For those who might have missed the newspaper and magazine coverage, Lowell Thomas—America's leading national news broadcaster—soon was on the air with his own commentary. It's "a bad situation in Honolulu," he ominously intoned. After the rape of the wife of an American naval officer and the release of her assailants, Thomas reported, "the gobs on shore were enraged, and went on a rampage." The city had been declared unsafe for the wives of American officers and all shore leave had been canceled, he continued, noting as an incidental sidelight that the nearby "volcano of Mount Kilauea has been erupting, with flames spurting two hundred feet above the summit."

As the uproar in the mainland press began spreading, pressure on the navy's leadership increased. Frantic wires flew back and forth, with Washington demanding more information and the island-based officers determined to protect themselves from criticism. Since no negative repercussions had followed from Admiral Pettengill's unauthorized letter to the Pacific Fleet command informing Washington of the unsafe conditions for navy wives in Honolulu, Captain Ward Wortman thought it was time to have his own say in the matter. Of all the high-ranking officers in the Pacific command, Wortman, the head of the Pearl Harbor Submarine Base and commander of Submarine Squadron Four, was the most hotheaded. Deciding that his communiqué deserved top priority, he bypassed the chain of command and addressed the cable to the secretary of the navy, Charles Francis Adams, with a copy to Admiral Stirling. Wortman wasted no time in getting to the point:

From: COMSUBRON FOUR
To: SECNAV

Assault on wife of submarine officer occurred twelve September. Horribly beaten. Repeatedly raped. Necessitated operation for pregnancy. Six weeks hospitalization. Five defendants brought to trial late November. Despite recognition of two men and admission of the five being in a car whose number was taken by victim at time, a mistrial was entered after jury out four days. Defendants out on bail . . . boasting openly in the city. On ninth December received in this command: "We have raped your women and will get some more." Signed, Kalihi Gang. . . . Officers wives have been driven to curb and vilely insulted while driving home. These events occurring on streets of city in broad daylight. Other disturbances after dark. . . . Complaining witness ill. Husband at sea.

Nearly every other sentence in the cable was a bold lie, but Washington didn't know that, and the reaction was instantaneous. Secretary Adams replied not to Wortman, however, but to his boss, Admiral Stirling. Adams directed Stirling to confer with Hawai'i's governor "as to the advisability of the fleet coming to Honolulu this winter. It would be extremely inadvisable to send it there if the conditions pictured by COMSUBRON actually exist," the secretary continued, "for it would be beyond the limits of human nature that some acts of personal violence did not occur."

By this time, Governor Judd had returned from his trip to Washington. He and Stirling met to discuss the situation. Neither was happy with what had come to pass, but each of them was faced with a different crisis. If the fleet were to bypass Honolulu during its upcoming maneuvers it would cost the islands untold millions of dollars. On top of that, the emerging reputation of Hawai'i as a place teeming with dark-skinned thugs and rapists could completely destroy the already weakened tourist industry. Judd had consulted with Attorney General Harry Hewitt upon his return and been advised that the reports about threats to navy wives now spreading throughout the country were gross exaggerations and even wholesale fictions. "The product of over-wrought imaginations" was how Judd later characterized them. Moreover, Hewitt belatedly informed the governor, a close reading of the evidence at the rape trial—what was suppressed as well as what was introduced—raised serious questions not only about the guilt of the defendants, but about what had actually happened to Mrs. Massie that night.

For his part, Stirling was determined to evade any responsibility for the turmoil. The way to do that was simple. Blame the civilian authorities. But first, denigrate the local population generally. As Governor Judd recalled their conversation that day, "Stirling seemed intent upon justifying his position that Hawaii was peopled largely by individuals of a very low class, whose presence was somehow or other Un-American and a danger to defense and a hazard to the womenfolk of the defenders." Stirling, in his memoirs, did not disagree, asserting that there was in the islands an "almost universal lack of sentiment against the enormity of the crime of rape," even in cases such as the one involving Mrs. Massie, where the proof against the perpetrators was "conclusive." Until that attitude was changed, the admiral wrote, "people must be expected to take measures to protect their women in their own way."

On another matter, Stirling had no comment. It concerned Judd's growing belief, as he put it, "that the Navy wanted complete military rule for Hawaii." Even the governor's staff had started to joke with him that the marines might be landing at any time, and that he and they would then be without jobs.

But if Admiral Stirling never directly informed Judd that he was eyeing the governor's mansion, he did everything possible to undermine Judd's authority in the nation's capital. Those efforts began with his cabled reply to Secretary Adams, with a copy to the chief of naval operations, Admiral William Pratt. The cable was a summary description, from his perspective, of everything that had happened since the night of Thalia Massie's alleged rape.

Admiral Stirling's wire was predictable, up to a point. He provided the standard navy account of what had happened to Thalia, followed by her positive identification of her assailants. He noted how the prosecutor who handled the case in court was inexperienced, despite Stirling's own efforts to convince Governor Judd "to obtain the best criminal lawyers available for the prosecution." He lamented the sorry state of the police department with its "vast majority of Hawaiians and mixed bloods," as well as the doubtful likelihood of "mixed blood juries rendering justice in cases involving rape because of apparent apathy toward the crime of rape." And so on.

But then Stirling dropped in something new. The previous day the Honolulu city and county physician had released his annual report. It was duly reported in the press, as it was every year at this time. During the past eleven months, the summary account said, the emergency hospital had handled 10,497 cases, including 5,650 industrial accidents, 1,021 physical examinations, 302 automobile intoxication tests, 192 insanity diagnoses, 114 autopsies, and 40 criminal assaults. The *Advertiser* led its report of the story that morning with the headline "Forty Assault Cases Here in Eleven Months," and Stirling promptly inserted that in his cable to Washington. He changed one word, however, converting the forty "assaults" to forty "rapes," and he added that "several cases convicted of rape were recently released by authorities on parole after four months imprisonment."

The next day Admiral Pratt sent his reply. So outraged was he by the contents of Stirling's cable, he wrote, that he was unwilling to send the fleet to Honolulu two months hence—not just the wives, but the entire fleet—"unless justice is done at the coming retrial and the police and hoodlum conditions are thoroughly cleaned up by local authorities." Pratt was astonished "that during the past year forty rape cases have been charged, and what is worse . . . that several men convicted of rape were released after four months confinement only." Then came the punch line: "American men will not stand for the violation of their women under any circumstances. For this crime they have taken the matter into their own hands repeatedly when they have felt that the law has failed to do justice." Many would read this as a license to lynch.

During much of the time that the flurry of navy cablegrams was in the air, while on the ground in Honolulu accusations and counteraccusations were the order of each and every day, Tommie Massie was once more away on sea duty. He had returned briefly after the end of the trial, but almost immediately headed out again as part of the pre-Christmas maneuvers then taking place in Hawaiian waters. Before leaving this time, however, he went to see Captain Wortman. He was worried about all the reports of navy women being threatened by local men, and he wanted Thalia to have some protection during his absence. Wortman agreed and sent an enlisted man, Machinists' Mate Albert O. "Deacon" Jones, to stand guard at the Massies' home.

Jones was a rough-and-tumble twelve-year navy veteran, a boxing trainer at Pearl Harbor during his off-hours. He was short and stocky and sported tattoos that ran the length of each forearm, a naked woman on one and a dagger on the other. On his left hand he wore a large gold ring decorated with the carved head of a dragon. A loud and boisterous storyteller, with himself at the center of most of his yarns, Jones hit it off immediately with Grace Fortescue. She said she considered him trustworthy and sympathetic. For his part, although Jones regarded Thalia as physically unattractive, with "the personality of the bottom of your big toe," he found Grace to be something truly special: a Washington and New York socialite with the soul of a sailor. "A wonderful woman . . . a tough old gal" was how he was later to describe her. "She would have made a hell of a good bosun's mate," he said. Before long Grace and Jones were playing bridge together as partners against Thalia and Helene.

As Grace later recalled, Jones "had lived many years in the South [and] he told me repeatedly of the horror the Ala Moana case had kindled in his squad." He also informed the three women that he was among those who had kidnapped Horace Ida only a week or so earlier. There was no doubt that Ida had confessed to being one of the rapists, he assured them, but such a confession— one that was the product of torture—would never stand up in court. Grace said that the local officials and private attorneys she had spoken with had told her the same thing. Yet, if it turned out that the police and the chamber of commerce investigators failed to turn up new evidence, it would take a confession from one of the men to get a conviction next time. There had to be a way.

Before departing for sea duty a few days earlier, Tommie had left a navy-issue .45 revolver with Thalia, but Grace feared that a single gun was inadequate protection for the three women. Deacon Jones told her he had just purchased a .32-caliber Colt automatic and several dozen steel-jacketed cartridges at the W. W. Diamond Company in Honolulu. He offered to take her there if she liked. Grace thought that a good idea, and soon Helene had her own .22 pistol while Grace was the proud owner of a .32-caliber Iver Johnson revolver and a box of twenty lead cartridges.

Both Grace's Iver Johnson and Jones's Colt were workaday guns, inexpensive and simple to operate. But each of them had earned fame of a sort among gun connoisseurs. An Iver Johnson .32 had been the weapon favored by the anarchist Leon Czolgosz, the assassin of U.S. president William McKinley, and by anarchist Gaetano Bresci, the killer of Italy's King Umberto I. Also, on the night of his arrest for allegedly participating in the murder of two men in the course of a robbery, another anarchist, Nicola Sacco, was found to be carrying a Colt .32. The .32 may have been a small-caliber weapon, but there was no doubt that it was capable of killing a man with a single shot, especially when fired at close range. At least by anarchists.

16 A Death in the Islands

Most first-time visitors find Christmas in Hawai'i a delightfully incongruous experience. Carols sung under banyan trees and coconut palms, to the accompaniment of ukuleles and steel guitars. A barefoot and lei-bedecked Santa Claus arriving at Waikīkī Beach not in a sleigh, but in an outrigger canoe. Exchanged greetings in shops and on street corners of "Mele Kalīkimaka"—"Merry Christmas" in Hawaiian. And all of it, in the absence of a rare winter tropical storm, bathed by sunny skies and balmy temperatures.

Prior to the advent of refrigerated container ships that now carry Christmas trees from the mainland to the islands, it was a custom for some families to grow potted Norfolk Island pines, native to the South Pacific, and bring them in the house to decorate with ornaments during the holiday season. The Massie-Fortescue household was no exception. The Massies' tree was located in the living room, and on Christmas morning of 1931 Thalia, Tommie, Grace, and Helene sat around it and opened their presents before going to lunch with other officers and their families at Pearl Harbor. Maneuvers were over and Tommie and the rest of the navy men now had some time to relax.

Since her arrival in Honolulu, Grace had been receiving monthly support checks from her stepmother, Grace Hubbard Bell. With Roly as hopeless as ever on matters of financial assistance, her stepmother's checks were all Grace had to live on, other than the money she now made playing bridge. In addition, Mrs. Bell had sent Grace a generous sum as a Christmas present, which she spent on a set of carved Chinese camphor wood chests. Grace already had picked out the places where she would put them when she returned to Wildholme in Bayport after the retrial of Thalia's assailants. The larger of the two would go in the green room, she said, the smaller one in the parlor.

Hawai'i, Grace wrote in a letter thanking her stepmother, was "really very amusing, and the climate is perfect. Warm but not hot, flowers everywhere, and the mountains so rugged & barren on one side & covered with queer trees and low shrubs on the other." She went on to describe her daily routine: hula lessons, followed by tea at the navy yard, while Tommie and his friends played badminton (or "babminton," as she put it) and deck tennis. At night it was games of bridge or dominoes or the movies. Her younger daughter, Helene, was taking painting lessons in the daytime four days a week, and in the evenings going to hotel dances and keeping company with several young navy suitors.

All in all, for Grace and Helene, the trip to be with Thalia in her hour of need had turned into a lovely sojourn in paradise. Even the aftermath of the post-trial violence and racial turmoil soon became a subject of whimsical humor among navy people. Grace was only one of many white women who armed themselves against imagined Asian and Hawaiian brutes lurking in the darkness. They had lined up by the dozens to purchase guns and acquire permits to carry concealed weapons. Admiral Stirling found the whole enterprise comical, especially the "not uncommon sight of ordinarily timid women proudly displaying their weapons to each other and challenging each other to pistol matches on the beach."

The only glimmer of worry Grace betrayed at this time concerned the outcome of a second trial. Although "the Chamber of Commerce has hired a lawyer and told him to spend any money necessary to get more evidence," she wrote to her stepmother, "they don't want to force a second trial until they are *sure* they can convict the men." Accepting Stirling's invented account of how the first trial's jurors had voted along racial lines, Grace believed that nonwhite jurors were predisposed against conviction by virtue of their race. "The citizens of Honolulu know that," she wrote, presumably referring to the white citizens of her acquaintance, "and want to be perfectly positive before bringing [the case] to trial again that they have absolute evidence—so that a jury will *have* to convict." Apparently she had little doubt that such evidence would be forthcoming, since she added that she was hoping to have the trial successfully completed by the end of February, allowing Helene and her to return to New York in March.

Others in the navy community shared Grace's equanimity during the holiday season. On New Year's Eve, Tommie and Thalia attended a celebration at the exclusive Wai'alae Country Club, hosted by Captain Wortman. All the submarine officers and their wives attended, and true to Wortman's reputation, it was what one officer described as "real falling-down party." The captain provided a fifth of bootleg whiskey for each person in attendance. The next day those at the party also were expected to call at Wortman's home for an open house to launch the New Year. They all did, but most departed quickly to return to their own homes and nurse their hangovers. Meanwhile, back in Washington, the army surgeon general had just filed his annual report on health conditions among American troops throughout the world. Those stationed in Hawai'i were deemed the healthiest of all.

The mood was more somber at the governor's mansion. Lawrence Judd had been kept busy throughout the holidays trying to put together an information package that would douse the media fires still smoldering throughout the country because of Yates Stirling's incendiary assertions about crime conditions in Honolulu. After an intensive review of court records by his aides, the governor learned that rather than the forty rapes Stirling had claimed for the city in 1931, there had actually been only one rape indictment all year, Thalia's. Every other sex offense was either an attempted assault (eleven cases) or consensual sex between minors, what informally was known as "sex under sixteen," Judd later wrote.

As for Stirling's tale of convicted rapists going free after four-month sentences, obviously the admiral was referring to the gratuitous convictions of Ben Ahakuelo, Henry Chang, and several other teenagers two years earlier for "assault with intent to ravish." In that case, however, even the judge had agreed that they had done nothing more than participate in consensual "multiple fornication," a practice that he found "disgusting" but not illegal.

All this would have to be cleared up, and soon, Judd knew. Tourism was certain to suffer even more than it already had if Stirling's broadsides were not corrected. And then there was the matter of the forthcoming fleet exercises. For Honolulu to avoid being boycotted by the navy, Judd would at least have to demonstrate good faith that the territory was carrying out reforms in the area of criminal justice. He met with his cabinet and ordered the creation of a temporary territorial police, under the command of the National Guard, to assist the beleaguered local police force. Then he began putting together a list of items that he would ask a special January session of the legislature to consider. They included making rape a capital offense, eliminating the requirement for corroborative evidence in rape cases, equalizing the number of peremptory challenges available to attorneys for the defense and the prosecution, and changing from an elected to an appointed police chief and prosecutor.

But as the holiday season unfolded, none of this was yet publicly announced. And Admiral Stirling remained busy, on Christmas Eve sending by mail an even more detailed account of the supposedly dreadful situation in Honolulu to his superiors in Washington, this time with inflammatory clippings of *Advertiser* and *Honolulu Times* editorials enclosed. Moreover, for every step Judd might take in the direction of mollifying his critics from the navy and from the higher reaches of the business world, condemnation awaited from other parts of the community.

In addition to the Hawaiian Civic Club's denunciation of Admiral Pettengill, the *Hawaii-Chinese News* now was demanding that the navy rein in the thugs in its ranks who had beaten Horace Ida, contrasting this "stupid mob mind" with "the American principle that a man is innocent until he has been proved guilty." In its Japanese-language edition the *Nippu Jiji* blamed the recent turmoil on the "racial feeling" introduced into the Ala Moana case by the *Advertiser* and *Star-Bulletin*, claiming that those newspapers would have ignored the entire affair if Mrs. Massie had been an Asian woman. And, of course, George Wright's "Bee" section of the *Hawaii Hochi* was the most colorfully outspoken of all.

Recently, the *Advertiser* had editorialized in favor of "death or emasculation for convicted rapists and death for robbery under arms," arguing that what Honolulu needed was "just one real man of action" and some "red-blooded leadership." In reply Wright attacked the *Advertiser* and its "bleating for 'red blooded leadership,'" saying that Ray Coll's newspaper "would sing hymns of adulation to any saber-rattling, swash-buckling Mussolini who rode roughshod over our Constitutional guarantees." In another piece Wright blasted the governor and other officials for failing to counter the admirals' lies about conditions in the city. Instead, they "cower under an incubus of fear," he wrote, "hiding their heads like ostriches in the sand, waiting till the trouble blows over." But it won't blow over, he said, cautioning that "the city and county government is sitting on a volcano."

Wright's prose may have been overwrought, but his warning was correct, and the volcano began erupting on New Year's Eve. It turned out that Ward Wortman's party for his officers at the Wai'alae Country Club wasn't the only New Year's celebration that got a little out of hand. So did the one at the territorial prison.

For years disciplinary conditions and oversight at the prison had been notoriously lax. The rare escapees were caught with little effort, since there was no distant place for them to run to on a largely rural island of barely six hundred square miles. And since the start of the Depression, the prospect of three meals a day and a roof over their heads further discouraged most otherwise indigent inmates from even considering escape. On the contrary, prison work crews in and around Honolulu—often completely unsupervised—hurried back at the end of the day, fearful of being locked out after six o'clock and thus missing dinner. The local citizenry knew and often laughed about the informality of the prison situation, and even that year's "Report of the Governor's Advisory Committee on Crime" made no mention of a need to tighten things up. It did, however, express concern over the paucity of reading matter, motion pictures, and religious instruction for the inmates.

Traditionally, prisoners and guards celebrated New Year's Eve the same way other people did. They drank beer and ʻōkolehao, sang songs, and made resolutions to do better in the months ahead. This year, as the night wore on and festivities continued, the alcohol ran low, so two inmates were sent out to buy more. Already drunk, and with money in their pockets, the temptation to stay away for the holiday weekend proved irresistible. Irresistible as well, for one of them, was a young white woman discovered asleep in her bed. Early Saturday morning, January 2, after spending New Year's Day driving around in a stolen car, Lui Kaikapu, a Hawaiian who had been serving time for burglary, broke into a home in the upscale neighborhood of Wilhelmina Rise. Finding the woman of the house still in bed, her husband having just left for work, Kaikapu raped her, tied her up, and then looted the house of valuables before driving off.

Arrested later that day, Kaikapu faced an outraged judiciary—outraged not only by the rape, but because he had provided Admiral Stirling and the rest of the navy brass with apparent proof of their spurious charges about crime and race in Honolulu. Kaikapu was indicted, tried, convicted, and sentenced to life imprisonment in less than twenty-four hours. Meanwhile, the newly appointed territorial police fanned out. Joined by an army of volunteers, they began tracking down the second escaped convict.

But none of that was sufficient for Admiral Stirling, or for a large constituency of other aroused citizens. On Tuesday, January 5, Stirling sent still another cable to Admiral Pratt in Washington. It reported on the "latest" rape of "a young white American woman" by a native man, and went on to urge Pratt to keep the fleet away from Honolulu during the forthcoming war games unless the governor met two conditions: a complete overhaul of the police force and a conviction in the retrial of the men accused of raping Mrs. Massie.

Despite having other weighty matters on his mind—in the fighting in China the Japanese military was now closing in on the city of Shanhaiguan just outside the Great Wall—Pratt replied to Stirling the next day. He ordered him to "make it very plain to Governor Judd that the fleet's movements now and in the future are dependent upon action and results, not upon intentions. The fleet will not remain in Honolulu for the contemplated visit and no liberty will be granted until the situation is cleaned up."

That same afternoon hundreds of people jammed the spacious Gold

Room of the Alexander Young Hotel in downtown Honolulu to form a new organization sponsored in part by the League of Women Voters. Calling itself the Honolulu Citizens' Organization for Good Government, the group was closely allied with Admiral Stirling's way of thinking and promptly drew up a list of demands including "the closing of bootleg joints and the sterilization of certain delinquents." Delegates from the group called upon Governor Judd the next morning. He was waiting for them, and was receptive to their message. Judd told the Citizens' Organization leaders of a lengthy cable he had prepared in reply to Admiral Pratt's most recent message, and that afternoon he sent it off.

The beginning of the governor's cable to Pratt was not quite what his visitors had in mind. It began by insisting that conditions in Honolulu were not nearly as bad as the admiral thought. Counting the assault on Mrs. Massie and the most recent one by the escaped prisoner, there had been only two indictments for rape in the city during the past twelve months, Judd wrote. In a follow-up message he appended a statement from the leading historian of Hawai'i, Ralph Kuykendall, asserting that, other than the Kaikapu case of the previous week—and pointedly omitting Thalia's accusation—"during at least a hundred years after the modern discovery of Hawaii there is, so far as I am aware, no authentic case of a consummated assault by an Hawaiian man upon a white woman." Judd then asked: "Can any other people justly claim a cleaner record?"

Knowing, however, that history would not be enough to change the admiral's mind, the governor resorted to outright pleading that the navy not curtail the fleet's activities during the upcoming maneuvers. With local newspapers now reporting that it would cost Honolulu merchants more than six million dollars if the fleet bypassed the city, Judd assured Pratt that he was calling an emergency session of the legislature to push through all the police and judicial reforms that the navy was seeking.

But one major problem still loomed: the retrial of Horace Ida, David Takai, Henry Chang, Ben Ahakuelo, and Joe Kahahawai. Chief of Detectives John McIntosh had just held a news conference to inform the press that, despite all the efforts of his office and of the investigation team put together by the chamber of commerce, no new evidence of value to retrial prosecutors had been uncovered. He didn't add, because he didn't have to, that this meant—at best—a repeat of the first trial's conclusion. Under Hawai'i law, after a second failed effort to convict, the men would go free.

■ ■ ■

With the merriment of the Christmas season now fast receding, Grace Fortescue was once again following news events closely. McIntosh's press conference was particularly worrisome. If no new evidence turned up, only a confession by one of Thalia's assailants could be counted on to bring about a conviction. Deacon Jones, the sailor who had guarded the house while Tommie was away, had assured Grace that Horace Ida had confessed under the duress of his beating. But when Tommie told that to Eugene Beebe, the private attorney who was working with the prosecutor's office—and with whom Tommie had become friendly—Beebe replied that even if Jones was telling the truth, such a confession would never hold up in court. As Tommie later explained, "Beebe said that no force was to be used and no marks should be showing."

Grace and Tommie began putting together a plan. Tommie had heard rumors that of the five defendants, Joe Kahahawai was the most likely to crack under pressure. If they could just get him alone, preferably with an independent witness on hand, they might be able to use the threat of violence, but not actual assault—no marks would be showing—to convince him to put a confession in writing. The form the threat would take was simple. Gunpoint. The difficult part would be getting him alone. How to even find him in the first place?

The next morning—the same day Admiral Stirling was sending his excited cable to the chief of naval operations—Grace drove down to the courthouse and spoke with a Mrs. Whitman, the clerk who had been most in evidence during the rape trial. Mrs. Whitman told her that although the defendants were free on bail, Judge Steadman had ordered them to report daily, but at separate times, to a probation officer in the judiciary building. Kahahawai's schedule called for him to show up at 8:00 a.m., she was told. From there, Grace went to the *Star-Bulletin* and picked up a news clipping containing a photograph of the young Hawaiian. The clipping also mentioned his address, so she drove there. It was "a tenement-house rabbit warren," she would later write, affording no opportunity to abduct him without someone noticing. The only chance would be to take him right in front of the judiciary building, employing some sort of ruse that would not arouse suspicion.

On Wednesday night, January 6, Grace took Thalia and Helene to the movies in Waikīkī, having arranged for Helene to spend the next few days at Thalia's home. They went to the Princess Theater to see *Dance, Fools, Dance*, a melodrama in which twenty-three-year-old Joan Crawford played a spunky young society woman turned newspaper reporter who goes undercover as a nightclub dancer to get the goods on a hard-boiled gangster, portrayed by

Clark Gable. Later that evening Grace wrote in a letter to her stepmother: "I wish you could have seen us returning from the movies after dark. I drove the car, Helene in the middle with her .22 and Thalia on the outside, her Army Automatic cocked & pointing out the window. We looked like an arsenal on wheels." After months of being at the mercy of the justice system, Grace was finding her way back to where she belonged: in charge.

The next day, Grace, Tommie, and Deacon Jones, along with another enlisted man recruited by Jones, Fireman First Class Edward J. Lord, worked out the details of what needed to be done. Jones knew where they could rent a car, a large dark blue Buick sedan. Tommie would drive it, disguised as a chauffeur in a gray suit, cap, gloves, and tinted goggles. Whether he pasted on a false mustache as well would later become a topic of some disagreement. Lord, dressed in civilian clothes, would cover the rear exit to the judiciary building with Massie's .45 service automatic in his pocket. Jones, also wearing a civilian suit, would cover the front.

If, as expected, Kahahawai departed the building through the main portico following his meeting with the probation officer on Friday morning, Jones would approach him and say in official-sounding tones that Major Ross, the head of the territorial police, needed to see him immediately, guiding him into the car. Once the Hawaiian was in the automobile, with Jones at his side, Tommie would drive the Buick up to Mānoa, saying they were going to Major Ross's home. There they would interrogate Kahahawai at the point of a gun in Grace's rented bungalow.

But who, other than the four of them, would serve as a witness to Kahahawai's confession? And how could they be certain Joe would get in the car? As to the first question, Grace thought she knew just the man. She had a note delivered to Ray Coll, the editor of the *Advertiser,* inviting him to be on hand at her home when Kahahawai would admit his guilt. Grace knew Coll, and this was just his sort of thing, to say nothing of the fact that the confession would be the scoop of a lifetime. As for convincing Joe to get into the car, they decided to put together a bogus police summons.

Grace sat down at her writing desk and, using a pencil and plain typing paper, carefully printed in block letters:

TERITORIAL POLICE
MAJOR ROSS COMMANDING
SUMMONS TO APPEAR
KAHAHAWAI, JOE

None of them realized that Grace had misspelled "Territorial," but they all thought it looked insufficiently like a summons to fool anyone. Grace noticed that morning's *Advertiser* on a corner of the desk, later saying that "a paragraph, just the right size to fill the space, caught my eye." She clipped it out and pasted it in the middle of the page. The text made no sense for the purpose intended—or perhaps for any purpose—but Grace didn't care, so long as it fit the space. It read:

> Life Is a Mysterious and
> Exciting Affair, and Any-
> thing Can Be a Thrill if
> You Know How to
> Look for It and
> What to Do With
> Opportunity
> When It Comes

But something was still missing, something that would make it look like an official document. Tommie remembered the diploma he had received in 1928 after completing his tour at the Chemical Warfare School in Maryland. It contained an embossed gold seal. He dug out the diploma and cut off the seal, and Grace pasted it in the lower right-hand corner of the document.

The finished summons was an absurd-looking forgery. But then, the entire enterprise was absurd. Tommie of late was drinking heavily again and experiencing extreme mood swings. One minute he might be agitated with excitement over the prospect of Kahahawai confessing; the next minute he could be in a deep depression. "There were times when I would go home and would like to have cut my brain out," he later said, adding that he was hardly sleeping at all, except on the nights when he gulped down sedatives the doctors had prescribed for Thalia months earlier. The sailors, Jones and Lord, seemed to have no sense of what they were getting themselves into. For good reason. When later asked by police if he had been sober while the four of them carried out this scheme, Jones answered: "I'm never sober."

In contrast, Grace knew precisely what she was doing, and she was loving every minute. If anything, the cryptic message she had clipped from the *Advertiser* and pasted on the fake summons applied to her, as she later acknowledged, describing it as "ironic." Opportunity had come along at just the right time, in the midst of the mysteriousness and excitement of the past few months, and now she was enjoying the thrill of knowing exactly how to handle it.

By Thursday evening, January 7, everything had been prepared for the following morning. Grace was to stand inconspicuously outside the front doors of the judiciary building and signal to Jones when Kahahawai emerged after his session with the probation officer. To be certain that she would be able to identify him, Grace had pinned the newspaper photo of the young Hawaiian man to the back of her purse. Now, just before retiring for the night, she decided to take one more look at it. As she recalled in her memoirs, assuming the urgent immediacy of the present tense: "I take his picture from my purse. Again I study that brutal, repulsive black face. . . . I read until I become sleepy. I go to bed about ten o'clock."

Ray Coll was not heard from the next day. The kidnappers would have to do without their independent witness to Joe Kahahawai's anticipated confession. Many years later Coll's wife would recall that he had been ill that morning and couldn't make it. Grace never mentioned the letter she had written to Coll, and neither did he, allowing it to be included in his collected papers only after his death. But Coll was there in spirit. That morning the *Advertiser* carried an editorial cartoon entitled "The Spectre That Confronts Honolulu." It depicted a raging and hideous semihuman beast identified as "Crime," with filed teeth and clawlike fingernails, tearing down a protective wall surrounding the peaceful island of O'ahu, a wall labeled "Respectability."

Out at Pearl Harbor, Admiral Stirling was getting ready for a midmorning meeting he had scheduled with Governor Judd. Although the tone of the meeting was certain to be contentious—Stirling was trying to pressure Judd into pushing up the date of the rape defendants' retrial—the admiral later recalled that his state of mind was conflicted. "It was one of those beautiful Hawaiian days that awakened one into a delightful sense of the joy of living," he would write, "and made one forget the very existence of sordid people whom a trusting Providence had permitted to exist on these heavenly islands."

Across town, Joe Kahahawai left early for his appointment with the probation officer, William Dixon. It was a long walk and he didn't want to be late. Two weeks earlier, on Christmas Day, he had turned twenty-two and things seemed to be looking up a bit since the end of the trial. Joe still lived with his mother and her second husband, but he was spending more time with his father these days. Joseph Kahahawai Sr. had implored his son to learn from the ordeal he had just endured at the hands of the law and turn his lackadaisical life around. Joe was trying. He dressed as well as he could for the meeting with Mr. Dixon, wearing a brown cap and one of his best shirts, a blue one that his mother had just washed and sewn some new buttons onto the night before.

Joe's cousin, Eddie Uliʻi, walked with him that morning. They arrived at the judiciary building at eight o'clock on the dot, paying no attention to the gray-haired woman sitting in a Durant roadster that was parked at the curb. Nor, as he and Eddie emerged from the building a little later, did Joe notice the same woman standing off to the side and signaling to a burly white man in a dark suit who was positioned on the other side of the circular courthouse driveway. But if Joe didn't see her, Eddie did, later saying that after he and Joe had "walked about fifty feet, and I looked back, the woman was pointing at us." In an instant the man in the dark suit was at their side, while a Buick sedan pulled up to the curb, driven by a man "wearing goggles," Uliʻi recalled.

At that moment Deacon Jones opened the rear door of the car and reached out to take Joe by the arm, saying: "Get in the car, Major Ross wants to see you." He waved the fake summons in front of him. Eddie later recalled that it contained an official-looking seal and that the man holding it was wearing a ring carved with the image of a dragon. Kahahawai complied with the directive, but he also called out to his cousin to come along with him. Jones pushed Eddie aside, slammed the door shut, and the car took off. Although initially he would deny it, years later Jones admitted that in addition to flashing the false summons at his captive, he held a gun on Kahahawai, the small Colt .32 automatic he had recently purchased. Whatever else he was, Jones was not foolish enough to think that the young and athletic Hawaiian, a noted boxer and football player who stood half a foot taller than Jones and outweighed him by at least forty pounds, would have gone along without being coerced.

Eddie didn't see the gun, but as he stood watching the car pull away he noticed that it turned to the right and headed up King Street before disappearing into traffic. Major Ross's office was in the armory building alongside ʻIolani Palace, just across the road. Wherever they were going, he realized, it wasn't to see Major Ross. Then he remembered what had happened to Horace Ida a few weeks earlier and he ran into the judiciary building to report what he had just witnessed.

It was not yet nine o'clock when the Buick turned off East Mānoa Road and then into Grace Fortescue's driveway, two houses down. Tommie pulled the car halfway into the garage, knowing the tall hedges of hibiscus on both sides of the house would shield them from view. Grace's roadster, with her behind the wheel and the other sailor, Edward Lord, sitting alongside, followed a few minutes later. None of Grace's neighbors on quiet Kolowalu Street—the word refers to an ancient law that safeguarded the rights of commoners—ever reported seeing anything suspicious. The next day, under questioning, several of them did acknowledge that at a little after nine they heard what sounded like a single gunshot. But they didn't know where it was coming from, and since there were no other sounds—no shouts or noise of a struggle—they quickly forgot about it.

At around 10:20 a.m. Detective George Harbottle, one of the first police officials to arrive at the Massie house on the night of September 12 following Tommie's report that Thalia had been assaulted, was standing outside his parked police car on Wai'alae Avenue. He was talking with a motorcycle officer named Thomas Kekua about Daniel Lyman, the second of the convicts who had escaped from the territorial prison on New Year's Eve and was still at large. Harbottle and Kekua were part of the dragnet that was searching for Lyman, but a short while earlier Harbottle's car radio had picked up a call from headquarters about something else. Joseph Kahahawai, one of the defendants in the recent rape trial at which Harbottle had testified, was believed to have been kidnapped. The police were told to be on the lookout for a blue Buick sedan, possibly driven by a haole man dressed as a chauffeur or by a middle-aged white woman.

That wasn't much of a description. Buick sedans were commonplace. But at just that moment, Harbottle would report, he and Officer Kekua noticed "a big sedan driven by a woman and two men in it. One of the men was sitting in the back seat on the left hand side with the left shade pulled down." The drawn shade was unusual, so Harbottle decided to investigate. He and Kekua jumped in his car and gave chase. As he pulled up behind the Buick he said he "could see through the windshield of my car the mirror of the car ahead and that the woman was watching us, and on account of this fact it aroused my suspicion all the more."

As Wai'alae Avenue headed east it eventually became Kalaniana'ole Highway, the main road that hugs the coastline leading to a dormant volcanic crater named Koko Head and a popular recreation area, Hanauma Bay. Just past the bay there is a spot known as Hālona Blowhole, an underwater lava tube at the base of the ocean cliff that has an explosive effect on waves that crash into the cliff face. As the water is forced into the narrowing tube the great pressure generated causes the water to shoot thirty or more feet into the air. The reverse is true as well. Anything sucked into the blowhole is likely never to be seen again.

The Buick picked up speed, and after several miles, as both cars approached Koko Head, Harbottle saw another police car coming from the opposite direction. He waved at it, signaling for the driver to follow him. Then he accelerated and passed the Buick, telling Officer Kekua to "look in the back seat of the sedan to see if there is anything in it." Kekua glanced over and described "something white wrapped in a bundle," Harbottle wrote in his report, "so I passed the car and stopped at the junction and hailed the approaching car to stop. Instead, they drove past me at a fast clip."

The detective pulled out his revolver and fired at the Buick several times, one of the shots taking out a taillight. Then, with the other police vehicle following the Buick closely, Harbottle got back behind the wheel and raced past both cars, finally forcing the blue sedan off the road. Gun drawn, police badge held in his other hand, Harbottle approached the car and ordered everyone out. As the rear door opened, the detective saw the "something white" that Officer Kekua had spotted earlier. It was a bedsheet, one of several, soaking wet with water and blood, and wrapped around something large. "I then noticed a human leg sticking out of the white bundle," was the way Harbottle put it in his report, "and I placed the occupants of the car under arrest."

1. The earliest known photograph of Thalia Massie, age three or four.

2. Roly Fortescue, with his young daughters, before rejoining the army for active duty in World War I. Thalia is on the left.

3. Tommie Massie, age twenty-two, and Thalia, age sixteen, at their wedding reception in Washington.

4, 5, 6. Three of the thousands of sheet music covers that filled American homes and music stores between 1915 and the early 1930s, demonstrating the romantic and suggestive images of the islands that were commonplace throughout the country.

7. Beach boys, circa 1930, entertaining Royal Hawaiian Hotel guests with the newly invented game of surfboard polo.

8, 9. Tenements for former plantation laborers on the outskirts of Hell's Half Acre.

10. Beach boys with their surfboards at Waikīkī.

11. Opening night at the Royal Hawaiian Hotel in 1927. On an island in which more than four out of five people were nonwhite, all but one of the twelve hundred guests were haoles. The exception was Princess Abigail Kawananakoa, the last link to the Hawaiian monarchy that was overthrown by American businessmen and U.S. Marines in 1893.

12. Horace Ida

13. David Takai

14. Henry Chang

15. Ben Ahakuelo

Mug shots of the young men
arrested for raping Thalia.

16. Joseph Kahahawai

17. Tommie comforting Thalia in the aftermath of the alleged assault.

18. Admiral Yates Stirling, the top U.S. military official in the islands.

19. Hawai'i's most powerful business leader, Walter F. Dillingham.

20. Territorial governor Lawrence M. Judd.

21. Princess Abigail Kawananakoa, center, surrounded by family and friends during an earlier and happier time.

22. The Territorial Judiciary Building—Aliʻiolani Hale, the "House of the Heavenly Chiefs"—setting for the two most dramatic criminal trials in the history of Hawaiʻi.

23. Defense attorney William Heen.

24. Defense attorney William Pittman.

TERITORIAL. POLICE

MAJOR ROSS, COMMANDING

25. The fake summons, prepared by Grace Fortescue as part of her plan to kidnap Joseph Kahahawai.

SUMMONS TO APPEAR

Kahahawai - Joe

Life Is a Mysterious and Exciting Affair, and Anything Can Be a Thrill if You Know How to Look for It and What to Do With Opportunity When It Comes

26. Policemen surrounding the getaway car and removing Joseph Kahahawai's body at the scene of the arrest.

27. Grace Fortescue in the police car, as she awaits transportation to police headquarters following her arrest.

28. Mug shots and arrest file of Grace Fortescue.

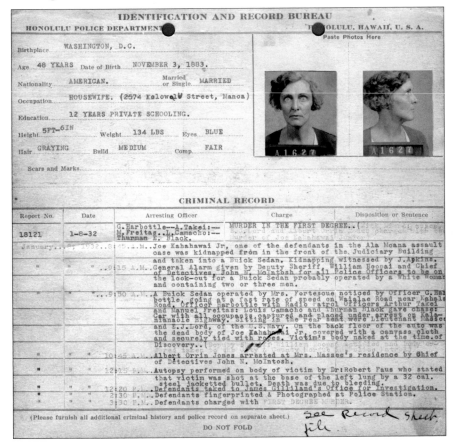

IDENTIFICATION AND RECORD BUREAU

HONOLULU POLICE DEPARTMENT   HONOLULU, HAWAII, U. S. A.

Paste Photos Here

Birthplace   WASHINGTON, D.C.

Age   48 YEARS   Date of Birth   NOVEMBER 3, 1883.

Nationality   AMERICAN.   Married or Single   MARRIED

Occupation   HOUSEWIFE. (2574 Kalowalu Street, Manoa)

Education   12 YEARS PRIVATE SCHOOLING.

Height   5FT-6IN   Weight   134 LBS   Eyes   BLUE

Hair   GRAYING   Build   MEDIUM   Comp.   FAIR

Scars and Marks.

CRIMINAL RECORD

Report No.	Date	Arresting Officer	Charge	Disposition or Sentence
18121	1-8-32	G.Harbottle--A.Takei:-- M.Freitas..L.Camacho:-- Thurman E. Black.	MURDER IN THE FIRST DEGREE..	

January.... 1932..8:45.A.M..Joe Kahahawai Jr, one of the defendants in the Ala Moana assault case was kidnapped from in the front of the Judiciary Building and taken into a Buick Sedan. Kidnapping witnessed by J.Apkins.

"   "   ..9:15 A.M..General Alarm given by Deputy Sheriff, William Hoopai and Chief of Detectives, John N. McIntosh for all Police Officers to be on the look-out for a Buick Sedan probably operated by a White Woman and containing two or three men.

"   "   ..9:30 A.M...A Buick Sedan operated by Mrs. Fortescue noticed by Officer G.Har bottle, going at a fast rate of speed on Waialae Road near Kahala Road. Officer Harbottle with Radio Patrol Officers Arthur Takei and Manuel Freitas: Louis Camacho and Thurman Black gave chase: Car with all occupants captured and placed under arrest at Hanau niaule highway. Party captured were T.H. Massie, Mrs. Fortescue and E.J.Lord, of the U.S.Navy. On the back floor of the auto was the dead body of Joe Kahahawai Jr, covered with a canvass cloth and securely tied with ropes. Victim's body naked at the time of Discovery..

"   "   10:45 A...Albert Orrin Jones arrested at Mrs. Massie's residence by Chief of Detectives John N. McIntosh.

"   "   12:15 ...Autopsy performed on body of victim by Dr.Robert Faus who stated that victim was shot at the base of the left lung by a 32 cal. steel jacketted bullet. Death was due to bleeding.

"   "   12:20 P...Defendants taken to James Gilliland's Office for investigation.

"   "   2:30 P...Defendants fingerprinted & Photographed at Police Station.

"   "   3:30 P.M..Defendants charged with FIRST DEGREE MURDER.

(Please furnish all additional criminal history and police record on separate sheet.)   *see Record sheet file.*

DO NOT FOLD

29. At Joseph Kahahawai's funeral, his mother, Esther Anito, wearing a white hat and dress, is in the middle of the crowd.

30. Kahahawai's coffin is carried to the graveyard.

31. Kahahawai's gravestone today.

BAYONETS RULE HONOLULU
AS RACES BOIL IN KILLING

Woman's Avenging Kin Held Safe on Warship

Call for White Action Made in Editorial

(Special Cable to The Press)

HONOLULU, Jan. 9.—National Guardsmen patrolled the streets of Honolulu tonight, and the entire island was virtually under martial law. The case of Mrs. Granville Fortescue, her son-in-law, Lieut. Thomas H. Massie, U. S. N., and E. J. Lord, an enlisted man, charged with the murder of Joseph Kahahawai, a native, has aroused racial feeling to the boiling point.

Throughout the island, nervous women were locking their doors in fear of intruders. Reports from reliable sources said the regular Army was ready to move troops into Honolulu.

The three accused of murdering Kahahawai had been ordered to appear in Court today, but City Attorney James Gilliland obtained a week's postponement, on grounds of obtaining more evidence.

Mrs. Fortescue, Massie and Lord are still being held aboard the U. S. S. Alton, in Pearl Harbor, for safety.

Although police announced the discovery of additional evidence tending to support

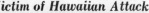

Victim of Hawaiian Attack

THE urge to kill, felt by members of the United States Navy, in order to protect their wives and sisters in Honolulu, is well explained in the following editorial from the Honolulu Times of Dec. 12, entitled "The Shame of Honolulu." It is typical of many such editorials, partisan to the whites, and calculated to whip into flame the smoldering hatreds resulting from a series of outrages on women.

In it, the editor charges:

"It is true . . . women are not safe in Honolulu . . . rape and ravishment are crimes of frequent occurrence . . . and the police do nothing." If the "lust mad youths" are punished, "the punishment is so mild as to constitute a condoning of an offense which would drive any other American community to frenzy."

Honolulu stands shamed in the eyes of the world, her reputation blackened, her good name smirched.

Word has gone out that women are not safe alone at night on the streets of our

---

BREVITIES

America's First National Tabloid Weekly

Vol. IV, No. 4   New York, February 1, 1932   Price 15 cents

HAWAIIANS
MUST BE PUNISHED!

HOTCHACHA—Page 2

Martial Law, Complete Housecleaning Necessary to Protect American Women

By L. SIMPSON
(Publisher of Brevities)

THE NEW MENACE

The melting pot of the North Pacific has boiled over and spilled its race-hatred brew into the streets of Honolulu.

An aristocratic American woman, a naval officer (the husband of her young daughter), and two enlisted men are being held on charges of murder. Race hatred swept through the streets of Honolulu. It caught up a young American girl and almost destroyed her. Then it placed the prisoners in jail.

Congress refuses to act firmly to punish the Hawaiians responsible for the situation. The Senate vacillates and in the end Washington, apparently, will wash its hands of the whole matter, hoping that the turmoil will die down.

The people of America demand justice. They cannot see their women assaulted on the streets of an island city owned by the United States without the perpetrators of the crime being punished. If it was the first offense against our women in Hawaii the matter would be serious enough. But statistics show that the recent assault against the young naval matron was one of a series carried on against white women.

Lax Law Enforcement

In most of these cases the Hawaiian authorities were lax. Punishment was not swift. It was not severe. It is now necessary that high officials step in and inflict punishment upon the criminals of our island possessions so that we can hold our own respect and that of the nations of the world.

On September 12, 1931, Mrs. Thalia Massie, 19-year-old wife of Lieutenant Thomas Massie, a submarine officer, was assaulted in the streets of Honolulu. Five men overpowered her and threw her in an automobile. She was carried to a lonely spot where the 5 men, all of mixed breed, viciously assaulted her. They bruised her body and broke her jaw. Subsequently these men were arrested and tried by a native jury. The jury disagreed and the men were freed pending further legal proceedings. Evidence was strongly against these men, but they were freed.

The brown natives gloated. They felt they

(Continued on page 13)

On cartoon sign: HAWAII'S HIDEOUS TREATMENT OF AMERICAN WOMEN

---

32. "BAYONETS RULE HONOLULU AS RACES BOIL IN KILLING"—just one of many newspaper headlines.

33. Throughout the country, in newspapers large and small, the response to the murder was the same.

34. Judge Albert M. Cristy.

35. Defense attorney Clarence Darrow and prosecutor John Kelley at their first pretrial meeting.

36. Thalia joins the murder defendants aboard the USS *Alton* as they await their trial.

37. Part of the crowd hoping to gain entry to the courtroom.

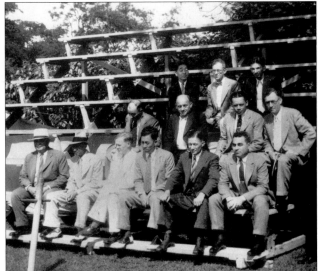

38. Murder trial jurors on a weekend break, taking in a tennis match at Kapiʻolani Park.

39. Celebrating the commutation of their sentences on the lanai of 'Iolani Palace. From left to right: Darrow, Edward Lord, Deacon Jones, Sheriff Ross, Grace (holding commutation papers), Thalia, Tommie, and George Leisure.

40. Beginning their whirlwind cross-country trip, celebrities Thalia and Tommie Massie board a plane in San Francisco for points east.

41. Dressed in black, Thalia makes the trek to Reno for her divorce in 1934.

17 Penthouse for a Prison

B y the time Admiral Stirling left for his meeting with the governor on Friday morning, newsboys on downtown street corners were hawking an extra edition of the *Advertiser* with a banner headline: "Kahahawai Kidnapped." The subhead reported that it appeared to be the work of the same men who had abducted and beaten Horace Ida. But at Pearl Harbor a rumor was spreading that the kidnappers included Lieutenant Tommie Massie. That seemed unlikely to Stirling, he recalled, given Massie's "mild and self-effacing" personality. Still, he ordered his driver to "break all the speed limits" in getting to 'Iolani Palace.

When he arrived, Stirling said, he found Governor Judd "ghastly white and shaking with emotion." Word had just reached him not only that Kahahawai had been kidnapped by Massie and his mother-in-law, Grace Fortescue, but that they had murdered him as well. Having allowed Stirling and Dillingham to dictate the government's handling of the rape accusations from the start, Judd now understood where that plan had inescapably been taking them. "They've killed one of my people," Stirling remembered Judd shouting at him, "and that's the result of encouraging a disregard of our laws."

Realizing that Judd "was attempting to connect me with the killing of Kahahawai," Stirling said, he replied: "I've been expecting something of the kind. You would insist upon letting those criminals loose instead of keeping them locked up for their own security." For his part, Judd remembered Stirling adding: "When American men find the laws will not protect their women, they take the law into their own hands. It's obvious that a degenerate sex criminal has been killed. Now what is to be done?"

Judd responded by saying that obviously the murderers would have to be tried. The admiral smiled and turned to leave, saying over his shoulder as he strode out of the room: "Well, lock up the ones that are left. It may save their lives."

■ ■ ■

Out at the cliffs overlooking Hanauma Bay things were at a standstill. Detective Harbottle and the officers who had been with him at the time of the arrest were awaiting the arrival of police backup. They had sent word that they needed a paddy wagon to transport Mrs. Fortescue, Lieutenant Massie, and the sailor, Edward Lord, to the district attorney's office. They also required a vehicle to deliver Joe Kahahawai's corpse to the morgue.

A little earlier, as the police cars had raced in pursuit of the fleeing killers, a reporter for the *Advertiser* had spotted them. He arrived on the scene as Grace was stepping out of the car, her hands raised above her head. The next day his story described the "thrill of horror" that ran through him "as the body of a man, wrapped in a sheet and bound with rope, with blood soaking through the head and left breast, the bare feet showing from the other end, was discovered in the rear of the sedan." Passing motorists who stopped to gawk were told to move on, while the apparent murderers, having been searched for weapons, were permitted to relax as they awaited the paddy wagon.

Seaman Lord stood off to the side and waited calmly, or apathetically, a spectator to everything that was happening. Tommie sat in the rear of one of the police cars, his head in his arms "as if to shut out the vision haunting him," Grace later wrote. But Grace herself had sauntered across the highway and found a place to sit on a large rock with a view of the ocean below. Dressed in a dark-colored serge suit with a white blouse, and wearing a matching cloche hat, she appeared to the reporter as someone who might be "waiting for the first race at Pimlico" or perhaps "strolling across a ballroom" at some social function. "She seemed detached," he wrote, "often looking out over the sparkling sea and saying never a word." The reporter asked for her name. Three months earlier Grace had announced her arrival in Honolulu with a press release and studio photographs for the newspapers' society pages. Now she crisply answered: "I'd rather not say."

A reporter from the *Nippu Jiji* was the first newspaperman to arrive at the scene with a photographer in tow. Seeing him, Tommie turned away, but Grace straightened, squinting into the bright sunlight, and smiled thinly at the camera. Although still refusing to speak with anyone, at this point she overheard a young man in civilian clothes engaged in conversation with the arresting officers. Grace didn't know it was Percy Bond, the policeman who had been driving the car Harbottle hailed as he was chasing the blue Buick. Not only was Bond one of the few haoles on the scene, other than Grace and Tommie and Lord, but he also spoke with a slight English accent, having been born in London thirty years earlier and raised there as a boy. Grace walked over and reached out her hand in greeting, saying he looked familiar. "Haven't I met you somewhere before?" she asked. "Didn't you come down from the coast about two months ago, the same time I did?"

Bewildered, Bond said no and turned away. Spotting Harbottle standing next to Tommie, Bond congratulated him on the capture, saying, "Good work, kid." But Tommie apparently thought the compliment was intended for him, so he smiled and grabbed his left hand in his right and began pumping it up and down as if in a handshake. "Thank you very much," he replied to Bond. Then, mimicking Grace, he said, "Hello big boy, haven't I seen you at the police station?" The two policemen looked at each other and walked off, leaving Grace and Tommie to sort out for themselves whatever was occupying their minds.

The paddy wagon showed up unaccompanied by a separate vehicle for taking Kahahawai's body to the medical examiner. But it was carrying a large rectangular wicker hamper. Lifting the corpse, still wrapped in the wet and bloodstained sheet, from the back of Grace's rented Buick turned out to be more difficult than expected. It was heavy and limp, not yet cold, and a hemp rope with a purple thread running through it was coiled from the neck to the feet of the makeshift shroud. The rope caught on the car's door handle as the police pulled. They had to roll the body over to extricate it. Then they loaded it into the hamper, covered it, and slid it into the back of the paddy wagon. The driver—Deputy Sheriff William Ho'opai, described by Grace as "a burly khaki-dressed native"—ordered Grace, Tommie, and Lord to climb in with it. It was a tight squeeze, and Grace was indignant. There was plenty of room for her in one of the other police vehicles, or in an open touring car that she noticed parked nearby. Ho'opai turned a deaf ear to her request, however, and instructed Grace to remain with her fellow arrestees in the back of the wagon.

Once they were settled, their feet propped up to provide room for the wicker casket, Ho'opai handed a large bundle to an officer who was riding with them. Found on the floor of the Buick, it contained Joe's clothes: socks, undershirt, shorts, shoes, dungarees, and a bloodied blue shirt with a bullet hole right where its wearer's heart would be. Everything was soaking wet and wrapped inside a wad of bloodstained towels.

While Detective Harbottle had been chasing the rented Buick toward Hanauma Bay, another car was moving at high speed up into the hills of Mānoa. It contained Attorney General Hewitt, Chief of Detectives McIntosh, Assistant City and County Prosecutor Griffith Wight, and a detective named Lono McCallum. Since Harbottle's police cruiser was equipped with a radio receiver but no transmitter, Hewitt and the others knew nothing of the drama then unfolding out at Hanauma Bay. But they were almost certain there was trouble in Mānoa.

Earlier, after learning that Joe Kahahawai had been kidnapped from outside the judiciary building and that Tommie Massie was rumored to be involved, Hewitt telephoned Massie at home. A woman answered and said he wasn't there. The attorney general then dialed Grace Fortescue's number.

At the Fortescue house a man answered the telephone. Hewitt asked to speak with Mrs. Fortescue. The man identified himself as Mrs. Fortescue's son-in-law, Lieutenant Massie, and said she was asleep and had left word not to be disturbed until the afternoon. Knowing this was a lie, since Hewitt had spoken with Tommie on numerous occasions and would have recognized his voice, the attorney general decided to investigate.

After hanging up the telephone at Grace's house, Deacon Jones—who had been left behind to clean up after the killing—stopped to think. Not anticipating that the others would have any trouble disposing of the body, or imagining that there was any reason for the authorities to expect there had been foul play, Jones had taken his time putting the house back in order. When the phone rang he had just finished mopping up blood from the bathroom floor, stopping from time to time for a drink of 'ōkolehao from a jug in the kitchen. There was blood in the living room as well. And the murder weapon, his .32-caliber Colt automatic, also was still in the house. If that telephone call had been an indication of trouble, he reasoned, it probably was more important to dispose of the gun than it was to finish cleaning up. Grabbing the .32, he dashed from the Fortescue bungalow, jumped into Grace's Durant roadster parked outside (she had left the key with him), and headed for the Massie house. There, Thalia and her sister Helene quickly ushered him in.

Helene volunteered to get rid of the weapon. When in boarding school she had discovered that a box of sanitary napkins made a good hiding place for all sorts of things, and that was where she put the gun. But then, realizing it might not be good enough if the police searched the house thoroughly, she took the box and drove her mother's roadster to a nearby but isolated place she had recently discovered while painting landscapes, and buried it. While she was gone, Jones remained at the Massie house, helping himself to their stock of bootleg whiskey.

When the attorney general and those with him showed up at Grace's house, no one answered the bell or their loud knocking. Though tempted, they decided against breaking in. Instead, they headed for the Massie place, a few blocks away. There they found the Durant roadster, well known to them as Grace Fortescue's car, parked in front. Detective McCallum walked over and put his hand on the hood. It was hot.

Hewitt, McIntosh, and the others were met at the door by Thalia and Deacon Jones. Visibly drunk and holding a tumbler full of whiskey, he gestured for them to come inside. When asked what he was doing there, Jones said he was guarding Thalia, and that he had been there all night. Thalia and Helene—just returned from disposing of Jones's gun—confirmed his story. In the kitchen, however, Captain McIntosh encountered Beatrice Nakamura, the Massies' maid. He asked her about Jones and she contradicted what the others had said, telling McIntosh that Jones had arrived just a little while earlier. But Beatrice did agree, as Jones and Thalia had said, that no one else had been there that morning.

Soon after they left the Massie house Hewitt and McIntosh got word on the car radio of Kahahawai's murder. McIntosh rushed out to Hanauma Bay after dropping Hewitt off downtown. The attorney general then called for a team of detectives to go up to Mānoa and enter and search Grace's bungalow. He also directed McIntosh to return to the Massies' place as soon as he was finished with the murder scene, and to bring Deacon Jones in for further questioning.

The rest of the day passed quickly, though doubtless not quickly enough for some.

At Grace's home detectives immediately discovered two handguns, an Iver Johnson .32 revolver buried inside a basket of eggs in the kitchen and, in the living room, a .45 hidden beneath a couch cushion. Under the couch was a coil of rope with an unusual purple thread running through it—the same color thread that ran through the rope wrapped around Kahahawai's body. A steel-jacketed .32-caliber bullet lay on the dining room table. Nearby, someone had tossed a man's brown cloth cap alongside a woman's purse. Inside the purse was a newspaper clipping folded to show a photograph of Joseph Kahahawai.

"I entered a bedroom and noticed the bathroom floor had been mopped recently," the lead detective's report later said. "A wet mop was in the corner, the blankets were thrown back from the beds and some of the sheets had been torn off. There were bloodstains on the floor." The closet was full of women's clothing, except for a man's shirt that was wet with perspiration and a blood-soaked towel on the floor bearing the monogram "USN." The detective opened a trunk and found "masquerade outfits, men's and women's, different kinds of makeup, black clothes."

On the floor of the bathroom another detective discovered two small buttons that had obviously been ripped from something, since a ragged piece of cloth was still attached to one of them. The buttons and the cloth would later be found to match those of Joseph Kahahawai's undershorts.

Over at the Massie house, Captain McIntosh had arrived with Commander Richard Bates of the shore patrol in tow. After announcing that Kahahawai had been murdered and that Grace, Tommie, and an enlisted man were being held for questioning, McIntosh placed Jones under arrest. He and Bates then hesitated about what to do next. Thalia and Helene were in the house with Jones. Had they been involved too? There was no direct evidence that they had, and McIntosh decided to err on the side of caution. When Bates suggested that he arrange for the two women to be taken to Pearl Harbor for safekeeping, McIntosh agreed. The commander sent for a car, and Thalia asked that it deliver them to the on-base home of a couple the Massies had befriended when they first arrived, Lieutenant Francis Old and his wife. But first she wanted to be taken to police headquarters to visit with her husband and mother.

While waiting for the navy car to arrive, Thalia and Helene packed their suitcases for an extended stay. While Thalia was arranging for a neighbor to care for her dog during her absence, the press arrived at the front door. She gave them a brief statement. "I'm sorry this man has been shot, but it was no more than he deserved," she said. As for her own safety, she was unafraid. "I have been protected at all times by the shore patrol and have carried my revolver constantly. But I do not think this town is safe for women."

Downtown at police headquarters, Joe's parents were being told the bad news. They had rushed to the station upon hearing of his kidnapping, but arrived only to find that he was dead. Too distraught to drive themselves, they were taken by police to the city morgue to identify their son. On the way they passed Joe's friends—Ben, David, Horace, and Henry—who were being brought to the city jail, where the authorities thought they would be safe. The same jail where Grace, Tommie, Edward Lord, and Deacon Jones were being questioned by police and the city prosecutor.

Leading the interrogation was Griffith Wight, who had prosecuted the rape suspects barely a month ago. In his closing argument at that time he had described the defendants as "lust-sodden beasts" and exhorted the jurors to "be men." Urging them to put themselves in Tommie's place, he had said they "would want to go down and shoot the men" who had done such a thing to "a young, vulnerable, inexperienced girl."

Except for Jones, none of the murder suspects had anything to say. Tommie and Lord were effectively silent when questioned, each providing nothing more than name, rank, and serial number. Grace, whose calm demeanor at the crime scene had slowly turned to indignation at having been arrested—"we had not broken the law," she later insisted; "we were trying to aid the law"—at first alternated between defiance and sudden memory failure when the interrogation focused on specifics. But finally, after apparently sensing that there was danger in talking at all, she ended the questioning by announcing that she would have nothing more to say, and then sat mute and unmoving. The police led her away.

Jones, on the other hand, wouldn't stop talking, repeatedly attributing his verbosity to the fact that he was drunk—"as I am two-thirds of the time"—and claiming that he didn't know what he was saying. True or not, it was an adept performance that wandered aimlessly, punctuated by repeated protests about his inebriation, and then circled back to aimlessness again. At last the police gave up and had him assigned to a segregated cell, but not before searching him and finding an empty .32-caliber shell in the watch pocket of his white uniform trousers and, inside his underwear, the magazine clip for a .32-caliber automatic. One steel-jacketed bullet was missing from the clip, and wrapped around the magazine was a folded piece of paper. It had a gold seal and a news clipping pasted onto it beneath some crudely hand-lettered words declaring it to be a summons for Joseph Kahahawai. Still, since he had not been arrested as the other three had, with Kahahawai's body in their possession, the case against Jones was more circumstantial than the case against them. For the time being, at least, the authorities decided to hold him separately.

One by one the suspects were fingerprinted and had their mug shots taken. Eddie Uli'i, Kahahawai's cousin who had accompanied him to the courthouse that morning, told police he would be able to identify the woman who pointed to Joe as they were walking out of the building and the man who had forced Joe into the car. Lineups were arranged, and Uli'i pointed out Grace and Deacon Jones as the people in question. Grace was livid at the effrontery, and even more so at the fact that the other women in the lineup, hastily gathered together from among the clerks and secretaries who worked at police headquarters, all were Hawaiian.

By midafternoon Grace, Tommie, and Lord had retained the law firm of Thompson, Beebe & Winn, the same attorneys who had assisted the prosecution in the rape trial, and provided the police with whatever formal statements they were going to give. At the city attorney's office, with the defense lawyers in attendance, Assistant Prosecutor Wight had just officially charged the trio with first-degree murder when the door to the office swung open and Admiral Yates Stirling strode into the room.

According to his own account, the first thing Stirling noticed was that the enlisted man, Lord, was in handcuffs. "Take off those irons," he demanded of the police. Wight nodded and a patrolman complied. The admiral then approached Grace and put his arm around her. "My heart went out to this brave mother," he later wrote. "She understood, and I saw a tear travel down her pallid cheek; then she looked up and smiled, and I read in her strong face that she was undefeated and would fight for justice to the end."

Stirling then demanded that the navy take custody of the prisoners. Briefly, there was confusion among the legal specialists who were present. For the past decade an informal agreement between military and territorial officials had established army and navy jurisdiction in dealing with members of the military accused of crimes other than misdemeanors. But six months earlier that agreement had been amended and an exception had been added, giving civil authorities jurisdiction in capital cases. Tommie and Seaman Lord had just been charged with first-degree murder. And Grace was a civilian, and thus not covered by any such joint arrangements.

Stirling, however, was adamant. He simply would not have one of his officers and the socialite mother of the martyred Thalia Massie spend even one night in the city and county jail. Although Grace then and in the future acknowledged that the Hawaiian police matrons at the jail had treated her with kindness, even deference, she supported the admiral in claiming that there was "a danger of mob violence" against her, Tommie, and Lord if they were held under civilian control. The prosecutor and the attorney general were indecisive. So, joined by Stirling, Sheriff Gleason, and at the last minute by Honolulu mayor George Fred Wright—they repaired to the chambers of Judge Albert Cristy for a decision.

Albert M. Cristy was one of four judges assigned to Honolulu's First Circuit Court. Prior to his appointment to the bench, each judge of the First Circuit had handled only one type of law—criminal, civil, and so on—for the duration of his term. But Cristy insisted that they rotate annually. His turn to oversee criminal cases had begun on the first of the year, only eight days earlier, so he would preside over both the forthcoming grand jury and, in the event of an indictment, the murder trial of Grace, Tommie, and the two sailors. The decision he was to make now regarding pretrial custody would send an important signal as to how he would likely handle all the rest of the proceedings to follow.

Cristy had a mixed reputation among the people of Honolulu. Very religious and a rock-ribbed Republican, he had moved to Hawai'i immediately upon graduation near the top of his class from Harvard Law School in 1914. The dean of the school had arranged a position for Cristy with the island law firm of Frear, Prosser, Anderson, and Marx. Walter Frear, the senior partner in the firm, had been chief justice of the territorial supreme court from 1900 to 1907 and had served as governor, appointed by President Teddy Roosevelt, from 1907 to 1913. For the rest of his life Frear sat on and chaired the boards of numerous banking, railroad, and agriculture corporations in the territory. Frear was twenty-six years older than Cristy, and he and his wife, a sister of business magnate Walter Dillingham, took to the young man almost as surrogate parents. When Albert married Jessamine Bowman a year after his arrival in the islands (the two had met in Cambridge several years earlier), the ceremonies were held at the Frear estate.

Under Frear's guidance and influence Cristy became secretary of the Hawaii Bar Association in 1915, a member of the territorial legislature in 1920, and, in 1926, at age thirty-seven, judge of the First Circuit Court. A staunch supporter of the death penalty, as appellate judge he had not hesitated in rejecting the insanity appeal on behalf of murderer Myles Fukunaga in 1928, condemning the obviously unbalanced teenager to death by hanging. True to his close ties with former governor Frear, Cristy's political opinions never strayed far from those of the islands' major corporate leaders.

But Cristy also had long had an interest in native Hawaiians and in their unfair treatment at the hands of haoles both before and after the toppling of their government by American sugar planters and marines. His middle name was Moses, which is rendered "Moke" in Hawaiian, and that was how he was addressed by most of the Hawaiians who knew him, beginning with Prince Jonah Kūhiō Kalaniana'ole, who from 1903 to 1922 was the islands' nonvoting delegate to the U.S. Congress. During Cristy's campaign for the legislature in 1921 Prince Kūhiō would introduce him at rallies by saying, "God did not see fit to give me a child of my blood, but He did give me a son of my heart in Albert Moke Cristy."

To be sure, the prince was a Republican who spent much of his time running interference for the islands' corporate interests, but there were other indications of Cristy's concern for Hawaiians—however paternalistic and contradictory they may often have been. He had presided over the trial of teenagers Ben Ahakuelo, Henry Chang, and several others three years earlier, when they were charged with the rape of Rose Younge. At the conclusion of the trial, although it was clear that no rape had occurred, Cristy concurred with the jury's conviction of the young men for a lesser offense—an offense they had not committed—in order to make a public statement disapproving of their consensual "multiple fornication." Then, after attacking the newspapers' overheated and unfair coverage of the trial from the bench, he had ordered the defendants brought back to his chambers. According to Ahakuelo, he then shook hands with each of them, and quietly counseled them in an almost ministerial manner, urging them to reform their lives and offering to help in any way he could.

This was something, Cristy's wife would recall, that he was in the habit of doing with almost all the men he sentenced. And perhaps that explains the standing ovation he, and only he, received from inmates at the territorial prison during a 1929 visit by the governor, the circuit court judges, and high-ranking police officials. In one interview he granted in the aftermath of the recent rape trial he said the hysteria over supposedly worsening crime conditions in Honolulu was a consequence of fabrication by the local press, and he decried what he called "the crucifying of the Hawaiian people" that had ensued.

On the other hand, as Ben Ahakuelo later recounted, during his counseling of the defendants at the conclusion of the Rose Younge case Cristy "said he would have let us go, but the society people pay too much attention." Although Albert Cristy liked to say that he tried to live according to the words his mother had written in the Bible he still kept near his bedside—"Dare to be a Daniel/Dare to stand alone/Dare to know the truth/Dare to make it known"—there was little doubt that he was not immune to the influence of public opinion.

And now he had the mayor of Honolulu, the city's sheriff and chief prosecutor, the territory's attorney general, various defense attorneys, and Admiral Yates Stirling, commander of the Fourteenth Naval District, arrayed around his desk and demanding a decision on the custody of four accused murderers. Stirling insisted that neither Grace nor the three navy men would be safe in a jail containing Hawaiian guards and prisoners. Attorney General Hewitt, who had grown to dislike and distrust Stirling in the wake of his recent public exaggerations of local crime conditions, was in no mood to defer to a man who, Hewitt and others were convinced, wanted the governor's job. But, although he doubted that anyone would attempt to carry out retribution against the defendants while they were in civilian custody, nothing would come as a surprise any longer, and Hewitt didn't want to live to regret a critical mistake in judgment.

The attorney general told Judge Cristy that he could go along with Stirling's request so long as everyone agreed that the civil authorities had jurisdiction, that the navy's custody was only temporary, and that Admiral Stirling or his designate would make the defendants available whenever requested. It was a gamble. Given Stirling's attitude, and that of the chief of naval operations, Admiral Pratt—who only three weeks earlier had made the first of his public statements seeming to justify lynching and expressing contempt for Hawai'i's elected officials—there was no guarantee that the navy would not move the prisoners to the mainland, beyond the legal authority of island courts. But Hewitt decided it was worth the risk. Cristy agreed, allowing Stirling to designate Captain Ward Wortman as his representative to be an officer of the court in charge of the defendants' custody. No bail would be necessary.

Stirling knew just the place to house the prisoners. There was a decommissioned ship in permanent dry dock at Pearl Harbor, the USS *Alton*. Built nearly fifty years earlier as the first in a succession of cruisers to be named the USS *Chicago*, it had served as a flagship to submarine forces in the Atlantic during World War I and as a submarine tender, or supply ship, to the Pacific Fleet during the 1920s. Since 1928, reconditioned and renamed the *Alton*, it had been home away from home for visiting admirals and other VIPs.

Grace would be provided with the quarters currently occupied by Commander R. W. Monroe, "a penthouse, bristling with ventilators to cool the neat single cabins within, each comparable to that on a small liner," as *Time* magazine approvingly was to describe the accommodations. A reporter for the *Honolulu Advertiser,* learning of the arrangements, rushed out to visit the *Alton,* and the newspaper published his description the next day. Beyond its polished wood and gleaming metal, there was Grace's penthouse, with its "quiet sitting room, next to a small cabin with single bunk and adjoining bathroom. On the walls were restful pictures," including one depicting "supple, shapely Polynesian girls dancing on a palm-fringed beach," while through the portholes "the sight of Hawaii's hills and valleys was enticing."

With staterooms for cells, the accused murderers of Joseph Kahahawai had available to them "books, cards, and music . . . electric fans, call bells, and all the conveniences of a modern hotel." The onboard officers' mess would provide their meals.

One unexpected inconvenience was the effusion of flowers. As word quickly spread across the ocean and around the United States about what had happened in Hawai'i, well-wishers began sending the defendants letters and radiograms of sympathy, along with floral arrangements. "Flowers by the auto load were delivered to the ship all day Saturday," the day after the killing, according the *Star-Bulletin*. The *Alton* was as long as a football field and one-third as wide. Yet, "late Saturday afternoon," according to the press report, "Marines aboard the *Alton* announced it was impossible to receive any more flowers as the ship was taxed to capacity. In every room, corridor, and even on the deck, great banks of flowers were placed."

The accused murderers were acting—and being treated—as celebrities more than as felons. Meanwhile, at Honolulu's municipal jail, the surviving men who had been charged but not found guilty of raping Thalia were being confined to cells indefinitely for their own protection and for the sake of civil order. If they wanted to eat, the sheriff informed them, their families and friends would have to provide the food.

18 Tears of Heaven

The English translation of the Hawaiian word *kanikau* is "grief chant" or "chant of mourning." But in this case the word *chant,* following common usage as a recitation performed in repetitive monotone, is a misnomer. A kanikau actually is a poem to lament the passing of a loved one, a poem that celebrates the life of the deceased, and takes the form of highly ritualized, deep, throaty wailing by someone specially trained in the art. All kanikaus are highly individualized, with the message composed specifically for the person who has died. No one who has been present when kanikaus were performed at a funeral has ever forgotten the experience.

As with everything about Hawaiian religious ceremony, kanikaus and other traditional expressions of grief were suppressed by nineteenth-century Christian missionaries. But at times of calamity—the smallpox epidemic of 1853, the banishing of leprosy victims to permanent exile later in the century—ancient funerary custom broke the bounds of imposed inhibition. To this day, upon the deaths of especially honored persons, kanikaus often embrace a sense of lamentation for the entire community as much as for those who have passed away.

That was the case in 1917, upon the death of Lili'uokalani, the last queen of Hawai'i. And it was the case on January 10, 1932, when young Joseph Kahahawai was laid to rest. Unlike the funeral of the queen, who had lain in state for a week at 'Iolani Palace and been entombed in the royal mausoleum, the rites for Kahahawai were relatively brief, and he was buried in a small graveyard in the working-class community of Kalihi. But on that day more mourners turned out, and more tears were shed, than at any funeral in the islands since that of the queen fifteen years earlier.

The bullet that killed him had been fired at close range, entering Joe's chest, passing through the lower part of his left lung, and lodging in the flesh to the right of his spine. Death was caused by massive internal bleeding. Less than thirty-six hours later, at six o'clock on Saturday night, his corpse was laid out for viewing at the chapel of the Nuuanu Funeral Parlor on School Street, a short walk from where he had grown up.

Clad in a dark suit, candles burning nearby, the body bore a crucifix on its chest and a yellow ʻilima lei. ʻIlima is a plant native to Hawaiʻi, and the traditional flower of Oʻahu. Its fragile blossoms are extremely short-lived and are so delicate that more than five hundred are needed to produce a single lei. The casket was banked with flowers, as were all the walls of the chapel and the corridors outside.

Joe's mother, Esther, and her second husband, Pascual Anito, spent the night with the body, as did his father, Joseph senior. In a steady stream, visitors began arriving early. Many stayed late. By the next morning the stream had become a floodtide. No one counted, but by the time the casket was to be moved to Our Lady of Peace Cathedral on Fort Street, newspapers were reporting that thousands had come to the mortuary to pay their respects.

The chapel was quiet during the night, apart from the sobbing of mourners and the occasional soft sounds of music played and sung by family and friends. But at ten o'clock Sunday morning, an hour before the body was to be transferred to the cathedral, an older man named David Kama appeared at the foot of the casket and delivered an unscheduled eulogy. David Kama's brother was William Kama, the policeman who had been attempting to break up a street fight when an American soldier murdered him four years earlier.

"Poor Kahahawai," Kama cried in Hawaiian, gazing into the casket and weeping as he spoke, "these haoles murdered you in cold blood. They did the same thing to my poor brother. The haoles shoot and kill us Hawaiians. We don't shoot haoles, but they treat us like this. Never mind. The truth will come out. You were not wrong. If you were, they would not catch these murderers. That is why they were caught. Thank God they were caught! Poor boy, God will keep you. We will do the rest."

Among those assembled, a phrase soon appeared on many lips, a phrase that was repeated throughout the day: Hilahila ʻole kēia poʻe haole—"The haoles are shameless." The surviving four men who had been accused by Thalia of raping her were then escorted into the room by armed police officers. Horace Ida was carrying a large bouquet of red gladioli. One by one they walked up to the casket to say a prayer and spend a few final moments with their friend, each of them breaking down and sobbing at the sight of his friend's body.

Before they were led away to return to the city jail, Joe's father addressed the mourners. Everyone knew why his son had been murdered,

Joseph senior said. Revenge. But the haole woman's accusations had been untrue. "I talked frequently with my son following his arrest," he said, "and I asked him repeatedly if he was innocent or guilty of the crime for which he was being held. He repeatedly told me he was not guilty of wrongdoing. My boy was held in jail for thirty days during the investigation of the case, and I told the police that if he was guilty that I objected to his release and that I felt he should be punished. But I questioned him again and again. . . . I asked Joseph to take an oath before God, and he said, 'Daddy, I swear before God that I never did anything wrong.'"

To some, such assertions might have mattered less than the mountain of evidence produced by defense attorneys at the rape trial. But for the people assembled in the chapel that morning, most of them Hawaiian and Catholic, there was no stronger proof of Joe's innocence than what he had sworn privately to his father.

A squad of policemen on motorcycles escorted the funeral cortege of more than a hundred cars to the cathedral. The church was filled to overflowing, while the sidewalks and streets for blocks around filled with countless numbers of people unable to get inside. Among them were teams of plainclothes officers primed to react in the event of trouble. But there was no trouble, only grief. Inside, the requiem service was performed by the pastor, Father Patrick Logan, who said the mass in Latin and closed with a quiet prayer in English. Only those standing nearby caught the prayer's closing words: ". . . and thou hast been delivered from the hands of thine enemies."

The huge procession then walked the mile or so to the cemetery. There, the crowd waiting for the burial ceremony was immense—at least another thousand people—and so densely packed that police were forced to clear a path from the road to the grave site. One newspaper estimated that three thousand people filled the cemetery. The Reverend Robert Ahuna officiated at the service, recounting what had happened on Friday morning as Kahahawai arrived for his appointment at the judiciary building, "not knowing that he would be taken out and murdered."

Referring to Joe as "the son not only of his parents, but of Hawai'i and the Hawaiians," Ahuna then recalled the fourth chapter of Genesis, on the death of Abel by the hand of Cain, a killing caused by jealousy and revenge, he said. In the same way, revenge was responsible for the murder of young Joseph Kahahawai. Nothing like this had been seen before in Hawai'i, Ahuna continued, and it must not happen again. "I call upon the Lord to pass judgment on those who committed this crime."

This was followed by a last kanikau and by the singing of several Christian hymns, including "Ka Lani Ku'u Home"—"Angel's Welcome"—and then by the Hawaiian national anthem, "Hawai'i Pono'ī," and "Aloha 'Oe," an especially haunting song among the scores composed by Queen Lili'uokalani during her lifetime. At first, wrote a reporter for the Japanese newspaper *Nippu Jiji*, the singing was "soft, and indescribably beautiful"; then it grew louder, accompanying a soaring solo by the locally famous Lena Machado, wife of the policeman who had arrested Joe and who was standing by her side. Also nearby, holding the hands of her small children, was Agnes Peeples.

One other thing was especially notable about the gathering, thousands strong, at the church and at the cemetery. Although most of the faces were those of Hawaiians, a very large number were not. Many Japanese, Chinese, and other Asians were there, along with a smaller number of whites. People would later remark on this every time they spoke about the funeral.

After the casket was lowered into the ground and the mourners were leaving the cemetery it began to rain lightly. Hawaiians call this *na waimaka o ka lani*—the "tears of heaven"—a sign that the gods are weeping in sympathy. Though little more than a mist, it was a foretaste of things to come in the weeks ahead. After a year of uncommon dryness in the islands, for day after day throughout the next month the skies opened in a deluge that caused rivers and streams to turn a deep red with runoff from the hillsides. It is called *uakoko* in Hawaiian, "blood rain."

Two days earlier, on Friday afternoon, as word of the killing rumbled across O'ahu, military and civilian police had sprung into action. Soldiers and sailors were confined to their posts, while their commanding officers were advised to avoid Honolulu. The recently mobilized territorial police, equipped with tear gas and gas masks, were joined by the local police force, the National Guard, and the navy shore patrol in deployments throughout the city, while a separate detachment was billeted at the armory awaiting emergency assignment.

Telephone lines to the governor's office jammed, forcing Governor Judd to issue newspaper and radio pleas to the public, asking that they relent and allow the government to conduct business during the emergency. One of the things people wanted to know was whether Kahahawai had been castrated. Word was circulating that his dead body had been discovered naked in the backseat of a car containing the husband of the woman Joe stood accused of raping. The husband was a navy officer and a southerner, and everyone knew what southerners did to black men that they lynched. One newspaper, reporting on the rumor, daintily described the procedure as "an act of sterilization."

Dr. Robert B. Faus, the city and county physician who performed the autopsy that day, issued several public denials. Acknowledging that the body, which was wrapped in a sheet with the identifying laundry marks cut off, had been unclothed when it was found, Faus insisted that "it was not mutilated in any way." He even called news reporters in to verify his assertion, and they filed stories confirming what he said. But few believed it to be true then, and few do to this day.

If not castrated, however, Kahahawai may not have been as quick to die as Dr. Faus indicated. Among the reporters from around the country who would soon descend on Honolulu, one from the *New York Times* claimed to have gained access to official police and other documents, now long since destroyed. They showed, he said, that the murder was especially brutal and that the victim "took a long time to die." He also questioned why none of this ever came out, since "the physician who performed the autopsy . . . must have wondered at the internal condition of Kahahawai."

Fearing civilian retaliation against military men, thirty-nine Honolulu religious leaders issued a statement counseling "against all acts which aim to take the law into private hands, and calling upon everyone to discourage with all his powers every method of direct action. Violence begets violence. It must not be tolerated." Political and religious authorities also pressured the manager of a Waikīkī movie theater to stop showing the popular Jimmy Cagney film *The Public Enemy* because of its potentially incendiary content. While protesting that the film actually carried an antigangster message, the manager reluctantly succumbed to the pressure and substituted *Shipmates,* a comedy about sailors.

Newspapers called in every available reporter and issued extra editions all day and night throughout the weekend. Everyone was poised for an explosion.

Nothing happened. The only violence occurred when Deacon Jones was walking into police headquarters after being arrested at the Massie home in Mānoa. A bystander, a young man named Perkins, broke through the crowd and took a swing at Jones. Arrested almost immediately, Perkins within hours was sentenced to serve thirty days for assault.

But that was all. There was anger. There was fear. And with the advent of interisland telephone service two months earlier, both those emotions spread quickly from Oʻahu to all the neighbor islands. Decades later, people—

especially Hawaiians—who lived in the most remote parts of Kauaʻi and Maui and the Big Island, and who were teenagers at the time, recalled the sense of deep apprehension that gripped their parents. Many adult Hawaiians had personal and bitter memories of the American military takeover of the islands, against the wishes of the majority of the people, and now they worried about what would happen next. Would the haoles who had murdered Joe Kahahawai be allowed to go free? If so, would that make it open season on Hawaiians by any military men with a notion to kill? Would the navy now seize control of the government?

The anger and fear melded into a single complex emotion for most Hawaiians, combined with sorrow over the loss of a young man's life. But there was no lashing out. Instead, throughout the weekend following the murder the mood everywhere among Hawaiians reflected the tone that on Sunday had characterized the funeral ceremonies—more smoldering indignation than raw anger, more melancholic despair than simple fear.

During that same time, from the military bases to the hills of Mānoa and other communities where the haole elite lived, a somber tension gripped everyone. Quiet descended, and held, from Friday night and all day Saturday into late Sunday evening as news of the huge funeral reached into every home in the city. But whatever the tension, there was peace.

On the mainland a different story was being told. It began early Sunday morning in New York, while the people of Hawaiʻi slept. The first newspapers to hit the streets were the tabloids, the New York Sunday News and the New York Mirror. The entire front page of the News and almost all of its opening section focused on nothing but the crisis in Hawaiʻi. "Honor Killing in Honolulu Threatens Race War," read the banner headline, placed above a wedding photograph of Thalia and Tommie and a picture of Horace Ida displaying cuts and bruises from his December beating. Inside, for page after page, the headlines all told the same story. "Melting Pot of Peril." "Hawaii Crater of Racial Hate." "Many White Women Attacked." "Bayonets Rule Honolulu As Races Boil in Killing."

With more than one and a half million readers, the News boasted the largest circulation of any newspaper in the country. Not far behind in the size of its audience, the Mirror also ran photos of Tommie and Thalia's wedding—as did most newspapers throughout the nation that day—under its own front-page headline: "Guard Honor Slayers from Hawaiian Lynch Mob." The Mirror's interior pages also were filled with stories of the "age old race war between the Occident and the Orient which threatens to envelop the Hawaiian Islands in a sea of blood." Because of the raging native mobs that had supposedly taken to the streets after the killing of one of their kind, Grace Fortescue and her murder codefendants had to be "whisked away" to a navy ship for their safety, the newspaper reported.

With remarkable consistency this was the pattern of reportage that appeared in every major newspaper in the country that day. It didn't matter whether they were tabloid scandal sheets or high-minded bastions of journalistic probity. It didn't matter whether they were in New York or Washington, Chicago or San Francisco. The story was the same everywhere. And so was the lesson to be drawn from it. As the *New York Post* put it in an editorial: President Hoover "should remove the weakling, Governor Judd," and declare martial law, while the only justice possible lay "in the deaths of the dogs who committed the crime." The crime referred to was the alleged rape of Thalia Massie, not the murder of Joe Kahahawai.

Some newspapers, including the *Chicago Tribune* and all the Hearst publications, referred to the murder as a "lynching"; others followed the *News* and the *Mirror* in calling it an "honor killing." But either way, the message was the same. In every account the murdered Hawaiian had been a denizen of what the *San Francisco Chronicle* called Honolulu's "crime nest" of "Hell's Half Acre, the slum district, near the harbor, where yellow, brown, and white men and women mix [and] whence prowling gangs emerge to prey upon defenseless women." In this case, one of those gangs of "mixed-race" thugs had kidnapped, beaten, and repeatedly raped the white wife of a United States naval officer. Now that a Honolulu jury, itself representing several races, had failed to convict the rapists—despite the woman's sworn identification of them as her assailants—her mother and her husband had properly taken matters into their own hands. They had no other choice.

The more patrician *New York Times* devoted most of its opening section, including a two-page spread of photographs, to the troubles in Honolulu. It allowed its news accounts to do the editorializing. The *Times*'s main report covered most of an entire page and ran to more than five thousand words. The attention to detail was extraordinary, asserting that more than forty rapes had occurred in Honolulu during the past year, pointing out that two of the men charged with assaulting Thalia Massie had previously been convicted of rape but served only three months, and noting that Thalia had become pregnant as a result of their raping her. The lead on the story read "Special to the New York Times," and it never mentioned the murder at all. It took a careful reader to notice that the author was Admiral Yates Stirling and

that the text was a verbatim reprint of the report he had mailed to navy headquarters in Washington on Christmas Eve.

The next day the *Times* ran another front-page story headlined "Congress
Will Act on Honolulu Crimes to Safeguard Navy." It contained a long quote
from Stirling saying that the rape of Mrs. Massie still "cries to heaven for re-
dress," yet "today the persons responsible, with the exception of the one killed
the other night, are at liberty in Honolulu." Other *Times* stories that day concerned crime conditions in Honolulu, navy efforts to have the murder trial
moved out of Hawai'i, and the deservedly pleasant conditions—"every comfort exists"—for the murder defendants being held aboard the USS *Alton*.

Admiral Stirling's Christmas Eve report was only one of two documents
that provided the background information on which virtually every newspaper in the country relied in reporting the recent events in Hawai'i. The other
one was the special "Shame of Honolulu" edition of Edward Irwin's *Honolulu
Times*. The *New York Daily News* ran Irwin's lengthy editorial from that issue
in its entirety, complete with its references to the everyday lot of Honolulu
women "if they venture forth, running the risk of being assaulted and foully
raped by gangs of lust-mad youths . . . foul, slimy creatures crawling through
the streets and attacking the innocent and the defenseless."

On the opposite coast the *San Francisco Chronicle* ran the same inflammatory editorial on Sunday—with a wedding photo of Thalia centered in the middle of the text. The following day the *Chronicle* covered most of an entire page
with reproductions of articles from Irwin's scandal sheet. The largest headline,
referring to Honolulu's "Alarming Array of Sex Crimes," was placed directly
above photos of "the five youths implicated in the latest atrocity," David Takai,
Henry Chang, Joseph Kahahawai, Horace Ida, and Ben Ahakuelo. On a reproduced front page of the *Honolulu Times* was the stamped message "Compliments of a Navy Man on Duty." An accompanying caption noted that "copies
of the publication were distributed among navy men all over the world."

The other major San Francisco newspaper was the *Examiner*, the flagship
of William Randolph Hearst's publishing empire. After buying the *Examiner*
in 1887, Hearst proceeded over the next four and a half decades to acquire
thirty-four more newspapers in New York, Chicago, Boston, Los Angeles, Atlanta, Washington, Milwaukee, Detroit, Seattle, Oakland, Rochester, Syra-
cuse, Baltimore, Fort Worth, Albany, San Antonio, Pittsburgh, and Omaha.
Nearly one in four Americans who read a newspaper in those days was reading one owned by Hearst. Although on local issues Hearst staffers largely
made their own decisions, when a major national story emerged the papers

spoke as one—with an editorial voice, a Hearst reporter once said, that sounded "like a screaming woman running down the street with her throat cut." And this was a major national story. In bold type on the front page of every Hearst paper in the country the voice of the founder thundered:

> The situation in Hawaii is deplorable. It is becoming or has become an unsafe place for white women. Outside the cities or small towns the roads go through jungles and in these remote places bands of degenerate natives or half-castes lie in wait for white women driving by. At least forty cases of such outrages have occurred and nobody has been punished. . . . The whole island should be promptly put under martial law and the perpetrators of outrages upon women promptly tried by court martial and executed. Until such drastic measures are taken, Hawaii is not a safe place for decent white women and not a very good place for self-respecting civilized men.

The unanimity of opinion was such that readers of newspapers everywhere had no place to turn for differing information had they sought it. On the contrary, with each passing day there appeared ever more reinforcement of the gruesome story. With nearly half the country's thirty million households now owning at least one radio, in early 1930 NBC had launched the first nationwide news program, starring globe-trotting reporter Floyd Gibbons, famous for his staccato delivery of more than two hundred words per minute, nearly twice as fast any other newscaster. A few months later CBS followed with Lowell Thomas as its network news announcer.

As the story from Honolulu was breaking, Gibbons was on assignment in China, covering the Japanese takeover of Manchuria. That left only Thomas—fresh from doing the voice-over narrative for a film entitled *The Blonde Captive: A Story of a White Woman Lost Among the Oldest Living Race*—to relay to radio listeners throughout America the account of what was happening in Hawai'i.

After a musical lead-in from the studio orchestra playing "The Sidewalks of New York," with its famous line about tripping the light fantastic, Thomas opened his show that night by saying "that was lightly fantastic alright, but let's go on to something fantastic and dark." He then told his millions of listeners:

> The Paradise of the Pacific is not so much of a Paradise just now. An ugly spirit of hatred and anger is brooding over the flowery islands of Hawaii. In Honolulu today white women did not venture out on the

streets alone. Navy patrols are marching through the city. An air of hush and tension prevails everywhere.

It has been declared that for some time Honolulu has been dangerous for American women. There have been a number of cases of assault by Hawaiians and Asiatics. Then came the instance in which Mrs. Massie, the wife of a young naval officer, was dragged into an automobile by a group of Hawaiians and Asiatics and carried away and maltreated, repeatedly. Arrests were made, and there was a trial. The defendants were freed. And then the affair came to a spectacular climax. The ringleader of the men accused of the attack, a young Hawaiian named Kahahawai, was kidnapped and killed. The deed is charged to Lieutenant Massie, the husband of the young woman, and to Mrs. Granville Fortescue, who is Mrs. Massie's mother.

The funeral of Kahahawai was held in spectacular fashion. Two thousand Hawaiians attended. There was music, the soft dreamy songs of Hawaii. And there was bitter denunciation, with calls for vengeance. Aboard the ship where Mrs. Fortescue is kept, the officers had to issue a command of "no more flowers." The ship was deluged by flowers sent by people who want to express their approval of the mother who killed to avenge the wrong suffered by her daughter.

Thomas closed the report by saying he doubted the accused murderers would be convicted, then followed with a news item about eight American warships and 1,600 American troops being moved from Manila to Shanghai to protect the lives and property of U.S. citizens during the ongoing international crisis in China.

For the few remaining Americans who didn't read newspapers or listen to news on the radio, but who liked to take in a motion picture from time to time, there was still no escaping the drama unfolding in distant Hawai'i. Beginning on Wednesday, January 13—five days after the killing of Kahahawai—movie theaters everywhere opened their programs with Pathe News footage of the ongoing "native uprising" in the islands. Navy warships were depicted steaming into Honolulu Harbor, followed by U.S. Marines wading ashore to rescue white settlers who were trapped in the frenzy of violence. Military airplanes circled overhead as tanks rolled through country towns and villages. Infantrymen with fixed bayonets pushed through cane fields, the excited narrator explained, in a "mopping-up" operation against the "savage natives."

It was all a pastiche of stock documentary and feature film footage. Some of the local scenes were taken from coverage of war games in the islands during 1925 and 1928. And in Honolulu most moviegoers laughed in delight when the newsreel appeared on the screen. The city fathers failed to see the humor, however, and they sought to have the film removed from circulation. Hollywood director King Vidor joined them in their outrage. Recently arrived in the islands to scout locations for his next movie, he wired protests to the Moving Picture Producers and Distributors Association and to his friend William Randolph Hearst at Hearst's castle in San Simeon, California. Insisting that the film was a "grossly unfair" portrayal, based on "exaggerated reports by selfish mainland publicity interests," Vidor said he had recently traveled all over O'ahu and he asked Hearst for "help in repairing the damage done this peaceful community." As compensation for the injustice, Vidor suggested Hearst might fund "a newsreel showing actual conditions here."

Hearst was not interested in working against the editorial interests of his own newspapers, so there would be no corrective newsreel. On the other hand, the producers and distributors association did agree to have the offending film pulled from the nation's movie houses. But not before it had shown for six weeks in most of the nation's more than twenty-two thousand theaters.

In its January 18 edition, *Time* revealed to its readers that the driving force behind the Paradise of the Pacific becoming "a restless purgatory of murder and race hatred" was miscegenation and "the lust of mixed breeds for white women." The only good news to report from that far-flung place, the magazine said, was that "if Mrs. Fortescue is ever brought to trial, few whites in Honolulu believed that she would be convicted of a part in the Kahahawai murder." Like whites on the mainland, *Time* said, most of those in Hawai'i "fully sympathized with her desperation in behalf of her daughter's honor and were ready to give her their moral support."

Those closing words were certainly true of many whites in the islands. The men who led the Big Five corporations and their wives were among those who could be trusted to lend support to Grace and the other defendants. Most other business and political leaders and their disciples could also be counted on. In a letter of January 19 to his wife, who was away on the East Coast, millionaire Walter Dillingham wrote that he could tell "from your phone message and from your recent telegram that you together with practically everyone else in the east are desperately worried lest Mrs. Fortescue and others connected with the shooting of the gangster will suffer at the hands of a jury." He hastened to assure her that "no one is to be railroaded to the gallows," and that "the serious minded group in our community is thoroughly alive to the seriousness of our situation and are working on many angles of the case."

Taking a less genteel approach was Mrs. Anne Kluegel, head of the fledgling Honolulu Citizens' Organization for Good Government. Within hours of the first newspaper reports on Kahahawai's murder, Mrs. Kluegel had announced an emergency meeting of the organization for Monday night at the roof garden of the Alexander Young Hotel. Among the topics to be discussed, she said, were the need for death as the required punishment for rape, the suppression of obscene literature and movies, and military rule in the islands. Nothing about murder was mentioned, although she did say the overall purpose of the meeting was to demonstrate the need for "rigid law enforcement."

Mrs. Kluegel had arrived in Honolulu a little over a year earlier, after spending most of her life in San Francisco and Sacramento. Her husband Harry, a Honolulu resident years before, was now a noted California political figure, recently retired as Sacramento's city manager. And in both San Francisco and Sacramento, Anne was well known as a community activist, civic leader, and indefatigable clubwoman. In the early 1920s she had campaigned enthusiastically for the election of Senator Samuel Shortridge, famous for his shrill anti-Japanese attitudes. It was he who had almost single-handedly transformed a 1924 immigration bill in Congress from one that favored northern European "old immigrants" to one that completely and deliberately excluded the Japanese. And now here was Anne Kluegel, because of her husband's insistence on returning to Honolulu, having to endure life in a place where almost 40 percent of the population was of Japanese ancestry.

According to press reports, roughly a thousand people crowded into the meeting space on Sunday night. Setting the tone with her opening address, which was greeted with a torrent of applause, Mrs. Kluegel pointed out that in Hawai'i of late "womanhood has been ravished, Christian principles outraged, and American governmental principles debased." Clearly, something had to be done. Mrs. Gertrude Damon, president of the League of Women Voters, who spoke next, said she knew where to begin—by getting the whipping-post bill, previously vetoed by the governor, enacted into law. Other speakers demanded that the federal government declare martial law in the islands or that a commission form of government be enacted until such time—perhaps ten years or so—that arrangements might be made for installing the proper people, and only the proper people, in power. The problems Hawai'i faced, it seemed, were traceable to a simple excess of democracy.

The meeting continued that way on into the night until Anne Kluegel returned to the podium and announced that it was time for adjournment. But first, she said, she had one more item of business to address. The *Star-Bulletin* reporter in attendance recorded the exchanges that followed:

"Do you know the frightful rumors now in circulation, the vile, vicious propaganda that is being circulated?" Mrs. Kluegel asked. "I don't know what to tell you about it, but it is perfectly appalling. What can we do to stop such profane and vile untruths?"

"What are the rumors?" "Tell us the stories," came cries from the audience.

"I'm not going to repeat them," Mrs. Kluegel replied.

"What's the use of trying to discuss them?" someone asked.

"You'll have to take it on the authority of those who know that vile propaganda is in our midst," she replied. "What do you want to do about it?"

William E. Miles spoke briefly, but did not disclose the stories, and the meeting was adjourned.

Soon thereafter Mrs. Anne Kluegel was hired as a syndicated columnist for the Hearst newspaper chain, specializing in the news of Hawai'i.

But the Dillinghams and the Kluegels were not the only haoles speaking out in the islands. There were others, including the irrepressible George Wright, who used his editorial page in the *Hawaii Hochi* to attack Raymond Coll of the *Advertiser,* Edward Irwin of the *Honolulu Times,* and unnamed others as "charlatans and demagogues who delight in spreading vicious slanders against the good name of Hawaii." To the local establishment, though, Wright could be dismissed as a subversive, a radical, one of the usual suspects. Others were harder to ignore, including Judge Alexander G. M. Robertson, a former member of the territorial legislature, a longtime member of the Republican National Committee, and for a number of years the chief justice of the territorial supreme court.

Robertson had been born in Honolulu in 1867, the son of a supreme court justice in the Kingdom of Hawaii. He attended the University of Virginia and Yale, where he received his law degree, returning to the islands in the 1890s to take various official positions with the all-white government that was installed following the overthrow of the monarchy. The only thing that made Judge Robertson different from some, but by no means all, of the islands' haole elite was his marriage to a Hawaiian woman, the former Ululani Papaikaniau McQuaid, of royal ancestry on her mother's side.

Ululani was similar to many other Hawaiian women who were sought after by ambitious haole men in that she was beautiful, much younger than her husband, and part of a family with large landholdings in the islands. She was unique in that she became an opera singer of some prominence, performing in Milan, Paris, and other continental venues throughout the 1920s. Especially praised for her performances in the title role of *Madama Butterfly*—"Ravishing," gushed one European review, "an artist of unusual and remarkable ability"— she debuted in Paris under the name Madame la Princesse Ululani.

As soon as he heard of the killing of Joe Kahahawai, Judge Robertson, now sixty-four years old and retired, sat down and wrote a long letter to the *Honolulu Advertiser* and the *Star-Bulletin*. "The killing of Kahahawai has put this community on trial in a manner that has not heretofore been experienced," he wrote, and "the question which the community is now called upon to decide is whether it is for or against the disgrace of lynch law. . . . If one person is to have the privilege of redressing his own wrongs others must, of course, be accorded the same privilege." He then submitted a series of rhetorical questions directed at people and groups of particular prominence in recent months:

> What is to be the attitude of the federal government? What will the admiral report with reference to the latest outrage?
>
> Will the case for the prosecution be carefully prepared so as to meet every possible defense?
>
> What about the press? Heretofore when dastardly crimes have been committed the local press has demanded vigorous prosecution and swift punishment. Will that be done now?
>
> What is the position of the Chamber of Commerce? Will a reward for evidence be offered or the prosecution otherwise financed?
>
> Will the League of Women Voters send flowers?
>
> What will the newly formed Organization for Good Government do? Is there anything more violently opposed to good government than lynch law?
>
> Will these organizations have the courage to announce a definite stand, or will they seek the cyclone cellar?
>
> The question that at present confronts the community—a question fraught with tremendous consequences—must now be answered. Some shallow-minded people will doubtless find superficial grounds for condoning the crime, but what will the answer of the community be?

The *Advertiser* declined to print the judge's letter, but the *Star-Bulletin* gave it prominence. That was no coincidence. After walking almost in lock-step with the morning paper during the months leading up to and throughout the rape trial, with the murder of Kahahawai the *Star-Bulletin* began turning in another direction. It was not because of a sudden change in political ideology; the newspaper remained under the control of former governor Wallace R. Farrington, a conservative Republican. But he, and a number of other prominent white leaders, including Governor Judd, now reasoned that the best way to cope with the damage being done to Hawai'i by the mainland news media was to take what they saw as the high road. Farrington fired off a lengthy letter to the *New York Times* and other news outlets denying that Honolulu was "either riot-ridden or race-mad," adding that Hawai'i "condones neither assaults on women nor the lynching and murder of persons in the custody of the courts."

Farrington's letter joined those sent by Judd and others to most of the nation's leading newspapers, taking the charges leveled by Admiral Stirling, item by item, and showing them to be false. The former governor went one step further, however, in raising the prospect that the five men accused of raping Thalia may well have been innocent. Pointing out that he was "in the Orient" for most of the preceding autumn, Farrington said that he returned near the end of the trial to find that "public sentiment then was all for Mrs. Massie. The attorneys for the defense, however, established an alibi that caused even trained reporters who had followed the case in its every detail to doubt whether the police had the right men. The impossibility thus far of shaking the evidence has strengthened doubt whether the right men are being held."

To the likes of Anne Kluegel and Walter Dillingham, statements like this were heresy. The *Star-Bulletin* was now "obviously in sympathy with the accused gangsters," Dillingham wrote. But both of them would have been even more alarmed to discover just how many heretics there were, speaking quietly among themselves, in the larger haole community. Louis Cain, a long-time Democratic power broker in Honolulu, originally from California, was only one of several prominent whites to write lengthy letters to U.S. senators and congressmen of their acquaintance, letters denying the picture of Hawai'i that was spreading across America and raising serious doubt as to the guilt of the five rape suspects. Others, from the chief justice of the territorial supreme court to the veteran police reporter for the *Star-Bulletin,* made their skepticism known in private interviews. So did prominent attorney Ferdinand Schnack, who told a federal interviewer that "the court reporter, court attachés, and newspaper people present at the trial all expressed doubt as to the proper identity of the defendants, and therefore the verdict seemed logical and justifiable."

But if the wall of near unity among haoles was now beginning to fracture, among nonwhites the reverse was happening. Realizing that they had key interests in common, whatever their other differences, within days of the murder leaders of the Japanese, Chinese, Filipino, and Hawaiian communities gathered together for a strategy session. Meeting at the Pan-Pacific Club in downtown Honolulu, two dozen men—with names like Akana, Aluli, Nakagawa, Hashimoto, Low, Fong, Cayetano, and Ligot—decided that their first step would be to call upon the attorney general and the governor to voice their concerns and offer their assistance in, as one of them put it, "telling our boys to keep cool, notwithstanding the present circumstances." After meeting with government officials, a spokesman for the group told a reporter, they intended to call on the city's editors and publishers to express their grievances at how the press had unfairly "stirred up feeling in Honolulu."

At the time, no one could be certain where all this was heading. Everyone in Hawai'i was too close to the action to see the emerging larger picture with any clarity. But there was no doubt that while the mainland press was flailing about in indignation and outrage, in the islands some people thought they felt the ground beginning to shift beneath their feet.

19 Grand Jury

Bird of Paradise is what the play was called. It had opened on Broadway in January of 1912, starring the voluptuous German American actress Lenore Ulric, who later specialized in playing vamps and prostitutes—at least once when made up in blackface for a play called *Lulu Belle*. This time she was cast as a Polynesian princess. A smash hit from the start, for years after its New York run ended, *Bird of Paradise* was being performed by road companies in cities and towns throughout the country. Who could resist the South Sea setting, the interracial romance, the sentimental music?

King Vidor, for one. Sometime around New Year's Day in 1932 movie mogul David O. Selznick, head of production at RKO Studios, called the famous director into his office and told him he wanted to make a movie from the play. It would star Dolores Del Rio as the dark-skinned princess and Joel McCrea as her white lover. Vidor would direct. And Selznick wanted to release it that summer.

After attempting to read the script—he couldn't make it past the first act—Vidor reported back to Selznick that it just wouldn't work. He hated it so much that he found it impossible to finish. How could he direct it? Selznick brushed his objections aside. He hadn't read it himself, he said, and he didn't care what sort of plot Vidor chose to cook up. Other than the title, all he insisted on were "three good love scenes and Del Rio jumping into a flaming volcano at the finish." Anything else to flesh things out the director was free to make up as he went along.

And that was what brought King Vidor to Honolulu in late January and February of 1932. He had gone on ahead of the cast and crew to scout locations for the filming, planning to write the script on the five-day voyage from Los Angeles. But the bad weather that had begun blowing through the islands at the time of Joe Kahahawai's funeral was now turning into a full-fledged storm. The Pacific Ocean was "on a rampage," Vidor recalled, and he was either in his berth or at the ship's rail for the entire 2,500-mile trip.

The next six weeks in Hawai'i were filled with the unexpected for the director of *Bird of Paradise*. At one point the winds blew so fiercely on the beach where he was filming that they denuded the coconut trees of their palm fronds. The next day he had a small army of local teenagers climbing the trees and nailing them back in place. But at night, when he retired to his suite at the Royal Hawaiian Hotel, the accounts he read in the newspapers of what was happening beyond his small circle, on the mainland and in Honolulu, must have seemed at least equally improbable.

While Vidor was delighted to work with hundreds of Hawaiians as members of his cast and crew, describing them in his memoirs as friendly, kind-hearted, and warm, in Washington the president was meeting with his cabinet to decide what to do about the native rampage in the islands that was said to be terrorizing white residents. Congress, in the meantime, was holding extraordinary weekend sessions to address what, because of Hawai'i's strategic importance in the Pacific, had become a national security emergency.

At a Saturday meeting of the U.S. Senate Committee on Territories and Insular Affairs, the U.S. chief of naval operations, the secretary of the navy, the secretary of war, the secretary of the interior, and the U.S. attorney general all testified on the crisis in America's most far-flung possession. Admiral William Pratt, who had recently made public his December justification of vigilante justice, asserting that American men had a right to "take matters into their own hands" when their women were violated and the law was unresponsive, told the committee that "the Hawaiian is a different sort of bird from the average American." Native men "do not know what rape is," the admiral testified, and they seem "to think pretty nearly everything is consent." Until the racial chaos in Honolulu was subdued, Pratt continued, it simply was not safe to send the fleet there. Instead, for the upcoming month-long war games, which would involve sixty-five ships and twenty-seven thousand soldiers, sailors, and marines, he had decided to have the troops lay over in Hilo on the Big Island. However, the maneuvers would still involve a feigned massive attack on O'ahu.

That was all well and good, but the senators had other matters on their mind. First, how could it have happened that the men who were arrested for the rape of Mrs. Massie, after being identified by her as the assailants, had not been convicted of the crime? And second, what was likely to happen to Mrs. Fortescue and the others who now stood accused of murder? Fearing that they might be convicted, especially since a mixed-race jury was mandated by Hawai'i law, several senators wanted to know if there was any way to get a change of venue—or simply have them removed from harm's way altogether?

Neither of those latter options was legally available, committee members were advised, but their concerns would not go unheeded. Hawai'i's delegate to Congress, Victor S. K. Houston, after being sworn in, introduced himself as a graduate of Annapolis, a former naval officer, and the son of a naval officer. He was being modest. Houston, who was born in San Francisco, had retired from the navy only five years earlier, following a thirty-year career, and his father had been an admiral. Houston proceeded to testify that all law-abiding citizens of the territory were "distressed beyond measure at the happenings that took place September last." It had been his personal belief following the arrest of "the gangsters" that they were guilty and would be convicted. Although he could not explain the failure of the jury to agree, he did say that he and others were proposing two changes in Hawai'i's rape laws that would have made a difference in the Ala Moana case. The first change would eliminate the requirement for corroboration of a rape accusation, and the second would make death the penalty for a rape conviction.

As for the difficulty that Mrs. Fortescue, Lieutenant Massie, and the others now found themselves in, Houston said, "our people realize the situation as well as anybody might . . . or perhaps more. They all sympathize with these unfortunates." In fact, he added, a change of venue would most likely increase the chances of the accused killers being convicted because in no other American community would the defendants encounter greater understanding or compassion than in the islands.

The very worst that could happen, Admiral Pratt told the committee, was a hung jury, just as had occurred with the rape trial—that is, if the defendants were even indicted in the first place. Although most of the senators appear to have found the comments of Houston and Pratt encouraging, Senator Arthur R. Robinson of Indiana remained unhappy, pointing out that a hung jury, if it came to that, would mean that "these people stand the rest of their lives as having been at least partially guilty, anyhow, to some degree." But, as Pratt responded, what would really matter in the long run was public opinion. And everyone knew that to be overwhelmingly on the side of the accused. In fact, most Americans seemed to regard them as heroes.

Satisfied that, at the least, the safety of the defendants was assured, the committee remained eager for additional information on the state of civil affairs and criminal justice in the islands. Some of its members were of a mind to introduce legislation that would change Hawai'i's territorial status and put all of its governance under the rule of an appointed commission, preferably one chaired by an admiral or a general. Toward this end, they resolved to send an investigative team to the islands that would report back to them no later than the first of June.

Headed by U.S. assistant attorney general Seth Richardson, a dozen FBI agents and Justice Department officials from Texas, Illinois, California, and Washington, D.C., set sail from San Francisco on January 29. It was, everyone knew, a potentially dangerous assignment. Honolulu, now universally viewed as a city in turmoil, was a place where white women dared not walk the streets for fear of violent assault. Even the United States Navy feared granting its enlisted men shore leave in the city.

Nevertheless, Richardson and most of the others brought their wives and children with them. It was still Hawai'i, after all.

Making rape a capital offense and doing away with the legal need for corroboration in rape cases were only two of the changes under consideration by Hawai'i's territorial legislature, meeting in special session. Others included harsh penalties for loitering, equalizing the number of peremptory challenges available to prosecution and defense attorneys, the creation of a police commission empowered to appoint and remove the chief of police, and changing the city and county prosecutor from an elected to an appointed position.

Debate on these matters dragged on as January was drawing to a close. Many legislators seemed more interested in defending Hawai'i's honor in the face of continuing attacks from mainland newspapers and politicians, attacks that portrayed the islands' capital city as an armed camp under siege. As Governor Judd later put it, "it was as if the burghers of Honolulu barricaded themselves at home every night and kept vigil with shotguns against restless natives." While most of the senators and representatives were openly antagonistic toward the men Thalia had accused of raping her, and were more than willing to accommodate Admiral Stirling and others who were calling for a major overhaul of the territory's criminal laws, they took personally some of the harsher attacks on the place they called home.

The *Boston Herald*, for instance, headlined one editorial "Barbarism in Hawaii," and that headline could well have been appended to any of numerous opinion pieces still appearing in big-city and small-town newspapers in every state. In the country's metropolitan heartland, the *Chicago Tribune* blamed everything on the indulgent "republican illusion" that had allowed nonwhites in Hawai'i to become citizens in the first place, a misguided experiment that now needed to be ended. From the *Corvallis Times* of rural Oregon came a demand that rapists in Hawai'i not merely suffer death, but "death by torture . . . burning at the stake," since that was "all that protects white women in the South." Even those sympathetic with Hawai'i, like Canada's *Vancouver Sun,* thought it unfair that the islands' "uncivilized and untaught . . . sensual and hot-blooded natives are daily made to witness the beach parades of almost nude white women. What can anyone expect of a combination like that?"

But it was the criticisms from Kentucky that most made the Hawai'i legislators' blood boil, because Kentucky was Tommie Massie's home state. The *Louisville Courier-Journal* had asked editorially what, really, could anyone have expected from a place with the "melting pot . . . racial tangle" of the islands? For its part, the *Lexington Herald* didn't ask questions, it answered them. "The men who escaped punishment" for the rape of Mrs. Massie, its editors wrote, "should have been hung without the province of law," while Mrs. Fortescue and her codefendants, faced with "being tried by a jury of yellow men for the killing of a yellow man," should be pardoned by the president and set free.

As it happened, these editorials coincided with a call from the Kentucky state legislature for President Hoover to declare martial law in Hawai'i, since its people obviously were incapable of handling their own affairs. They also coincided with the nationally reported outbreak of an interfamily feud in Laurel County, Kentucky, and a lethal duel, one county over. The feud erupted, so the Associated Press reported, when seventeen-year-old Ruby Crooks felt she was "wronged" by Willie Johnson during a mock wedding ceremony. To protect her honor Ruby's brothers Forrest and Homer felt obliged to shoot to death Willie's three brothers, Earl, "Big Henry," and "Little Henry" Johnson. This in turn required that Willie murder the Crooks brothers. In the duel, which took place in Knox County one day earlier, a man named Walter Smith and another known only as Gambrell each grasped the other's left hand and, with their right hands, emptied automatic pistols into each other. Not surprisingly, to others at least, both men died.

For people who lived in a place as backward as this to criticize Hawai'i was absurd, the island legislators said. "Why some of the dumbest people in the world come from those Southern states," claimed O'ahu senator James Jarrett in a speech on the senate floor, adding that "some of those people up there in the mountains don't even know that the Civil War is over, or that there ever was a World War." The navy was just as bad, chimed in Kaua'i senator Charles Rice. In a speech he entitled "The Rape of Hawaii by the Admirals," Rice described as "traitors" those who supported the navy call for a commission form of government, and he branded Edward Irwin of the *Honolulu Times* "the Judas of Hawaii."

But once the oratory was finished, the territorial house and senate proceeded to pass every piece of reform legislation that had been proposed and pushed by Admiral Stirling, Walter Dillingham, and Anne Kluegel's Citizens' Organization for Good Government. Stirling, Dillingham, and Kluegel also were appointed to the ten-person official welcoming committee for the U.S. Justice Department's team of investigators, as was Frank Thompson, the chief attorney representing Grace, Tommie, and the sailors Jones and Lord. As one senator put it in floor debate, the threat of martial law was so real that whatever it took to mollify Hawai'i's critics should be the island government's top priority: "We must show that we need no legislation in Washington. We must show that we can clean up our own situation."

The grand jury proceedings, to decide whether or not the murder defendants would be indicted and have to stand trial, had been delayed so that Grace's husband could travel to the islands and be at her side. But after he had fallen ill in New York on the eve of the murder, Roly's condition had taken a turn for the worse upon hearing news of her arrest. Almost two weeks had now passed and the court decided it could wait no longer. Thalia's younger sister, Helene, had been put on a ship and sent home soon after Grace was arrested. She could help look after Roly in New York. Meanwhile Grace's brother, Robert, was due to arrive in Honolulu in a day or so, and her sister and brother-in-law were on a steamship right behind him. Whatever comfort they might provide would have to suffice as Grace and the other defendants faced the grand jury.

Although it was the defense lawyers who had requested the delay, that didn't prevent them from attempting to have the murder charges dismissed on the ground that their clients had thereby been denied their constitutional right to a speedy trial. Nor did attorney Montgomery Winn's enthusiastic pleading for the motion prevent Judge Cristy from dismissing it out of hand.

The defense request was not the only pretrial matter requiring Cristy's attention. Anne Kluegel had two issues of her own that she wanted him to address. Mrs. Kluegel had been busy since the murder, giving interviews to wire-service reporters saying it would be impossible for the defendants to receive a fair trial in Honolulu because of the law prohibiting single-race—that is, entirely white—juries. She had also asked Governor Judd to bar Senator William Heen, the chair of the senate judiciary committee, from deliberating on the proposed reform legislation. Heen had raised her ire by pointing out that the two most contentious proposals—the death penalty for rape and eliminating corroboration as necessary for a rape conviction—meant, in combination, that the territory now could execute someone solely on the basis of an unsupported accusation.

Judd had not done Mrs. Kluegel's bidding on that matter, but the legislation passed anyway. Now she was formally requesting that Judge Cristy bypass the law and seat only whites on the grand jury panel. And she asked him to reserve a number of seats in the courtroom, each day of the proceedings, for her and for other officers of her Citizens' Organization for Good Government.

Cristy replied to Mrs. Kluegel in a letter that he also released to the press. Quoting from territorial and U.S. law at some length, he explained in plain language why it would be impossible for him to comply with her first request regarding the race of the grand jurors. As for the second matter, he quoted the same Sixth Amendment to the U.S. Constitution that attorneys for the defense had just employed in their effort to have charges dropped. The Sixth Amendment not only calls for a "speedy trial" but also for a "public trial," Cristy noted, which—according to precedent that he cited—prohibited him from reserving seats for spectators, no matter how important they considered themselves to be. He concluded by suggesting that it might "be more conducive to democratic equality if good citizens refrained from embarrassing the court by requests for special privileges which cannot be granted." The courtroom doors would open at 8:30 a.m., he said, for Mrs. Kluegel and for everyone else.

Walter Dillingham, meanwhile, was going about his business more quietly, although with the same general ideas in mind. No sooner had the legislature voted to create a five-man commission empowered to appoint a new police chief than Dillingham began making moves to have the commission staffed with people who would select someone he could control. The person he had in mind as police chief was Charles F. Weeber, Dillingham's personal secretary for the past eleven years and what he called his "confidential man"—his most trusted Washington lobbyist, especially on matters of anti-Japanese and antilabor legislation. The fact that Weeber had no police experience of any sort was irrelevant.

The key to getting Weeber selected as chief was having at least one strong man on the new police commission to give it direction. An especially able candidate was Edward Ellis Bodge, who, as fortune would have it, also was a member of the grand jury that had just been seated. Bodge, Dillingham knew, was adamantly opposed to finding Grace Fortescue and the other defendants guilty of anything.

Eighteen of the twenty-one men selected by the politically appointed jury commissioners to serve on the grand jury, including Edward Bodge, had European last names. Even considering the fact that some of them may have been part Hawaiian, eighteen out of twenty-one was an extraordinarily high proportion in a city where the majority of voters were nonwhite. In addition, well over half the grand jurors were employed by banks, insurance companies, or large merchant or contracting concerns that did business with the navy or with Big Five or Dillingham corporations.

Selected as the grand jury's foreman was Harry A. Franson, a fifty-six-year-old cashier and accountant for Honolulu Iron Works, a company controlled by American Factors Ltd., widely known as Amfac. Walter Dillingham was a member of Amfac's board of directors. Franson was originally from Sacramento, California, where his Swedish parents had settled in the late 1800s. Having moved to the islands at the turn of the century, Franson was best known in the community as an active and devoted member of the all-white Elks Club, of which he had been elected president—"exalted ruler" was the precise title—fourteen years earlier. About his private life very little was known.

The grand jury convened at 1:30 p.m. on Thursday, January 21. After the confirmation of the foreman and secretary, Assistant City and County Attorney Griffith Wight—the same man who had led the prosecution in the rape trial—began calling witnesses and presenting physical evidence for the territory. Court adjourned at 4:30 and reconvened at 10:15 the next morning. Wight wrapped the case up at noon on Friday.

In all, Prosecutor Wight had taken about four hours and used something in excess of a dozen witnesses to make his case, asking for indictments against the four defendants for murder in the first degree and kidnapping. By all accounts it was at best a workmanlike performance. But that is the most that is commonly necessary in grand jury proceedings because such juries are not called upon to decide guilt or innocence. Rather, all they must determine is whether there is reason to believe a crime has been committed and, if so, whether there is sufficient evidence to require that certain persons be charged and brought to trial. The accused and their attorneys are little more than witnesses to the proceedings, if that. Should the grand jury bring an indictment, all it has done is officially accuse the defendants; it has not determined that the alleged crime was in fact committed or, if it was committed, that it was committed by those who are charged.

In the case at hand, it was not difficult to determine that a crime had been committed and that those apprehended stood a good chance of being guilty. There was, of course, the dead body of Joseph Kahahawai, plus all the associated physical evidence. The only thing missing, other than a confession, was the buried murder weapon. But one of the defendants was found with an ammunition clip for a .32-caliber Colt automatic pistol, with one steel-jacketed bullet missing. The clip was wrapped inside a false police summons bearing the victim's name. Finally, in giving his lengthy instructions to the jury, the judge had explained that if they indicted one of the defendants they would have to indict them all.

After lunch on Friday afternoon, the jury began its deliberations. Edward Bodge, soon to be a member of the police commission, led the argument against indicting the defendants for anything. Less than ninety minutes of discussion passed before several jurors said they had questions for the judge and sent for him.

When Cristy entered the jury room, one juror asked about the technical definition of kidnapping: did it require evidence that force or firearms had been used? Another was concerned that the prison term for kidnapping seemed to have been lengthened in recent years. A third asked if they had to indict or fail to indict all the defendants, or might they "delete names" from an indictment?

The judge patiently answered each question, but when they were finished he decided the jury needed some further instructions on the law. The tenor of their questions made clear where the jurors were headed. Cristy explained to them again the difference between a grand jury and a trial jury. The court reporter recorded verbatim what he said:

> The primary purpose of a grand jury is, in the first instance, to prevent malicious or frivolous charges being brought against innocent people. The second part of your duty, however, and the graver responsibility, is that every person who by credible evidence has been shown to be connected with any crime . . . that those persons should be compelled to stand trial in the ordinary course of regular procedure. . . . Let me again remind you in a cool, unimpassioned fashion, without any desire to interfere with your discretion that you should [indict] no one through envy, hatred, or malice, and, on the other hand, you should leave no one [unindicted] through fear, favor, affection, gain, reward or hope therefor.

Reminding them finally, and pointedly, that they were not to "search for any fanciful defenses" for the accused, but to leave the question of their guilt or innocence to a trial jury, he left and returned to his chambers.

Within minutes, at 3:15, the jurors cast their ballots. On both first-degree murder and kidnapping the vote was nine to indict, twelve not to indict. It was over. Grace and Tommie and the two enlisted men who had served as their accomplices in killing Joe Kahahawai would go free—as they and most observers had expected—and be home in time for a celebratory dinner. As *Time* magazine drily reported, the grand jury only did what "any other panel controlled by white men from Kentucky to the Ubangi River might have done."

As instructed, the jury foreman, Harry Franson, left the jury room and went to Judge Cristy's chambers to inform him of the decision. While he was gone, the remaining twenty men began packing up their belongings and preparing to leave. Ten minutes later Franson and Cristy appeared in the doorway and the judge told them to take their seats. Apparently they still had not understood his instructions, he told them, so he would go over them once more.

And so he did, expanding on what he had said earlier about the difference between a grand jury and a trial jury, and emphasizing the gravity and seriousness of their task. The first question, he said, was "whether a crime has been committed as defined by the statutes, not as defined by individual men." And the second one was: "Has credible evidence identified those who are prima facie responsible for that crime?" It didn't matter, he continued, "whether from some inner feeling of your own you might have committed the same crime." Consider what would happen, he said, "if a crime were committed and the identity of the criminals known . . . and the grand jury for such reasons refused under their oath to present an indictment therefor. I present to you the question of anarchy in this community. Are you willing to take the responsibility for that? You know our racial structure."

Finally, Judge Cristy suggested that any juror "who cannot conscientiously carry out his oath of office should resign immediately from the grand jury." He then adjourned court for the day, excusing the jurors until the following Tuesday morning and reminding them that their deliberations were to be kept confidential.

Edward Bodge was not about to be manhandled, however. He leaped to his feet and demanded: "Do I understand you are not accepting this report?"

"There has been nothing presented to me," Cristy replied. Sitting nearby, foreman Franson said nothing. It was he who had the responsibility to convey to the judge the results of the jury's ballots, and it was he who had been sent on that mission earlier—to tell Judge Cristy that the jury had voted not to indict. Franson remained silent, not contradicting Cristy's assertion that nothing had been presented to him, as the judge stormed out of the room.

■ ■ ■

It was a long weekend, and not only for the judge, the jurors, and the murder defendants. Ben Ahakuelo, Henry Chang, David Takai, and Horace Ida were still locked up in the city and county jail—for their own protection. As one day turned into another, with no discernible end in sight, their nerves frayed, their tempers grew short. At one point, during a card game in the dayroom, Ben and David almost came to blows during an argument. This gave the police an idea. One by one, they took the men aside and grilled them again about the charge that they had beaten and raped Thalia Massie. In each case they warned the accused men that the others were on the verge of breaking and turning state's evidence against them.

An officer named D. W. Watson, who had known Ahakuelo for several years, took charge of his interrogation while a stenographer recorded it. Watson's approach was to appear friendly and sympathetic. After some small talk he warned Ben that "all the haole people on the mainland think you boys are guilty and they're blaming the Hawaiians. They're not going to let you boys off. You know what happened to Joe."

"They killed an innocent boy," Ben replied. "Joe didn't know about that case."

Watson ignored him. Wouldn't *Ben* want to kill a man if he found out he had beaten and raped his wife? Sure, Ben replied. "But Joe's not guilty of that."

"The people who killed Joe aren't dumb, Ben," Watson continued. "They were *sure* before they shot him. They were just as sure as you would be before you shot anyone. And they think the rest of you boys are guilty."

"All I know is Joe was not guilty and I am not guilty. They think Joe was dumb, but he wasn't dumb. This fellow Wight, he's a dirty guy." Ben then told the story of how the prosecutor had tried to get Joe and the others to sign statements that had been altered to suggest their guilt, but that Joe had crossed out the falsehoods before signing the document.

"I think you're hiding something from me, Ben. Why don't you tell me the truth? Why try to protect these other boys? You're the only Hawaiian left. These people shot Joe, and now there's only you, two Japanese boys, and one Chinese boy. Those other boys wouldn't help you—they're going to squeal, Ben. They're going to blame you just as sure as hell. . . . Ida is going to squawk. He's going to tell. What do you think they killed Kahahawai for? Because Ida told."

"No, I asked Ida many times and he say people tell lies. He says he never told anything." When they took him up to the Pali and threatened to kill him,

Ben said, Ida had refused to fight back and that's why they didn't kill him. Joe probably tried to resist and that's why he was murdered.

Watson wouldn't let up. "Ida wouldn't admit to you that he squealed. But those people are not killing Joe for nothing. They *know* he was guilty. That Japanese put the blame on Joe. He's a Hawaiian, Ben, and so are you."

"I know Joe is innocent and I am innocent."

"All the haoles on the mainland are blaming the Hawaiians, Ben. And these people that killed Joe blame you fellows. They got one Hawaiian and, Ben—you're going to be next. They're going to get you sure as you are alive right now. Even if it takes ten years, you'll never know when you're liable to get it. Joe got off easy. They just shot him. The next time, Ben, they're going to torture you fellows. It's going to be hell."

And on it went. In turn, all four men underwent the same kind of questioning. All insisted that they were innocent, and added that, whatever the inducements—including the five-thousand-dollar reward and reduced charges or a suspended sentence—they would not turn on the others when they knew they were innocent too. "Every known pressure and influence has been brought to bear upon each and every one of the defendants to persuade him to turn state's evidence," a disappointed Walter Dillingham wrote. But it all had been in vain.

That same weekend grand juror Edward Bodge received a phone call. It was to tell him that he had been appointed to the police commission. The commission was meeting on Tuesday afternoon, after his grand jury duties were finished. He and the other commissioners were scheduled to sit down with a man some important people thought would make an excellent police chief: Charles F. Weeber, currently Walter Dillingham's personal secretary. Mr. Dillingham would be present at the meeting.

The grand jurors returned to the courthouse to resume deliberations at 10:00 a.m. on Tuesday. Some of them were angry. Judge Albert Cristy was more than angry. Rumors about what had happened on Friday were all over town, and he had met privately with someone—no one knows who, perhaps Harry Franson—who gave him information on what had transpired in the jury room.

Before deliberations could get started, and in front of the open courtroom, with reporters and spectators present, Judge Cristy said he wanted to say a few words. First, he reported that he had received notification from the governor's office that Mr. Bodge was now an appointee to the police commission. Since it was clearly improper for someone to serve as a police commissioner and a grand juror at the same time, Cristy was relieving Bodge of his place on the jury. In fact, neither the governor nor anyone else had suggested there was any impropriety in Bodge holding down both positions. Cristy was simply asserting it—and in the process getting rid of the jury's leading voice for nonindictment. Cristy then addressed the remaining twenty men. It was his prerogative at this time to further charge and instruct the jury, and he wished to do so. He began by informing them that he had reason to believe "that one or more of you entered upon the grand jury session in the matters now pending with your minds so fixed and determined on personal views of the law and fact that you were prepared to prevent any indictment . . . notwithstanding what the evidence might be and notwithstanding what the court should advise the jury the law might be."

He assured the assembled men that he was not leveling allegations against any specific individuals among them, but said it was critical that they all be aware that "the instructions of the court as to the law are final, notwithstanding what you, as individuals, think the law is or should be." Anyone unable or unwilling to follow this rule should make that fact known immediately and excuse himself from the jury, he said. No one moved.

Then allow me to remind you, Cristy continued, that "under the laws of the Territory the taking of human life by private citizens, in the nature of a lynching or its equivalent, is prima facie murder." He went on to explain that in the case of conspiracy to commit a felony—such as kidnapping, he noted—as long as that conspiracy is still in force and a murder occurs, all the conspirators to the kidnapping are indictable for the crime of murder. There are two degrees of murder, however, first and second degree, and he informed them that the prosecutor would soon present them, for their further deliberations, an indictment for second-degree murder in addition to the earlier charges of first-degree murder and kidnapping.

But before he turned things over to the prosecutor, Cristy said he had one more thought to leave with them. "I ask you gentlemen, as representatives of the government and the community, to lay aside all race prejudice, to rise above such trivial or personal matters, and apply yourselves coolly and impartially to the question of whether this government shall exist, and how it shall exist." With that he cleared the courtroom and ordered deliberations to resume.

In the jury room, Harry Franson immediately found himself under attack. Had he properly reported to Judge Cristy the decision not to indict, the threat hanging over the territory would be ended. Their deliberations would be over, Mrs. Fortescue and the three men would be free, and the enormous outside pressure on all of them—from local business and political leaders, from the navy, from Congress, from the White House, and from the national press and public opinion everywhere—would have evaporated. As jurors, they would be celebrated for their good judgment.

Franson refused to budge. Someone called for another vote. It came out nine to indict and eleven to reject indictment. The same as on Friday, with the exception of the now absent Edward Bodge. A juror—not Franson—went to Judge Cristy's chambers and asked him to come to the jury room. When he arrived, one of the jurors told Cristy that they had voted again and the fore-man had been charged to report the vote to the court.

Cristy turned to Franson, who said, "I have no report to make."

The judge told them to go to lunch and report back at two o'clock. But first, one of the jurors said, he had a question. It was Vincent Fernandez, a vice president of the Union Trust Company and a stalwart proponent of not returning an indictment. "In case the grand jury is discharged," Fernandez asked Cristy, "has any member of the jury the right to show the records as to how he stood, as a protection for himself and the community in which he lives?"

Cristy was disgusted. He reminded Fernandez that it was a misdemeanor to divulge publicly what had transpired during their deliberations, and he said it was time for them to remember that there was more than one "commu-nity" in Honolulu, in the islands, and elsewhere.

During lunch, several of the jurors picked up a copy of that day's Star-Bulletin. It carried a prominent editorial saying the indictment of the defen-dants, in light of the evidence, was the only defensible action the grand jury could take. When the jurors reassembled after lunch, copies of the news-paper were passed around while Harry Franson held forth, elaborating on the arguments made in the editorial.

Another vote was taken. Again, no on the indictments. And again Fran-son refused to convey the result to Judge Cristy.

Someone suggested they consider voting on manslaughter, but Franson said they could vote only on the indictments already presented to them—murder in the first degree, murder in the second degree, and kidnapping. They decided to try again.

At ten minutes past three o'clock on Tuesday afternoon, Judge Cristy once more was asked to come up to the jury room. Upon his arrival, foreman Franson said he at last had something to report. By a vote of 12–8 the grand jury had voted to indict the defendants for the crime of murder in the second degree. Cristy accepted the report—and also the resignations of two out-raged jurors who had been on the losing side in the final vote.

As for Harry Franson, whether it had mattered or not in the delibera-tions, it later turned out that his wife was Hawaiian. He also soon resigned from the Elks Club.

Out at Pearl Harbor, in the Admiral's quarters of the penthouse aboard the USS *Alton*, Grace and Tommie and Jones and Lord had been waiting all after-noon for word from the grand jury. "We expected to be freed," Grace later wrote. "We had been told that fourteen of the grand jury strongly opposed any indictment." She continued:

> Three o'clock, four o'clock, five o'clock, and still we waited. No word. The sailors left for their evening meal, brought to them by a sentry from the enlisted men's mess hall on the shore. Tommie and I went down to the cabin. My daughter had been in town all day waiting in case she should be summoned before the grand jury. Just before the sunset bugle she came in. One glance at her face told the story. "You haven't heard? They indicted you—all of you! Oh, Tom-mie, Tommie!"

On Friday morning the four defendants were brought into court for the postindictment arraignment. The press duly reported on their appearance. Grace was dressed smartly in "a wine-colored felt hat, decorated with a bit of bright feather, that matched in color a tailored knitted suit," and she stepped forward "lightly, confidently . . . poise seemed as natural as breathing." In contrast, Tommie, dressed in a rumpled gray suit, slouched down in his seat, gazed at the floor, and to all appearances "did not take a direct interest in the proceedings." Lord and Jones, in uniform, sat silently and alertly as the in-dictment was read.

Judge Cristy was suspicious of what the navy and the attorneys for the defense were planning. Ever since the day the suspects were arrested, navy of-ficials in Washington had openly been seeking some way to move the trial venue outside Hawai'i. In the two days following the indictment the pres-sures had increased enormously. Admiral Stirling had wired the secretary of the navy to renew his request that a change of venue be sought, while de-fense attorney Montgomery Winn had cabled Kentucky representative Virgil Chapman, urging that he make the same appeal in Congress. Cristy didn't trust Stirling, or the Pentagon for that matter, fearing that if all else failed either or both of them might decide unilaterally to remove the defendants to the mainland—an act that, though illegal, would no doubt meet with national acclaim. In fact, Governor Judd was now thoroughly convinced, as he put it in his memoirs, "that the Navy wanted complete military rule for Hawaii."

But neither Stirling nor his superiors could steal the murder suspects away as long as they were in the city and county jail, where Cristy had placed Grace and the others until the matter of their bail was settled. He began by setting it at $50,000 for each defendant.

The defense attorneys, along with everyone else, were floored. Montgomery Winn hastened to provide an affidavit showing that Seamen Edward Lord and Albert Jones earned only $40 and $75 per month respectively, that Tommie's monthly pay was $240, and that Grace Fortescue "has no property, real or personal, or any assets whatsoever, or any income from any source other than approximately $5,000 a year." More than a few eyebrows were raised at the revelation that the Fortescues, with all their high-society pretensions, had a substantially lower income than had just been approved for the soon-to-be-appointed Honolulu prosecutor. But this was no time for Grace to put on airs. Unless she could come up with $5,000 in cash for the 10 percent a bail bondsman would require, or get the judge to lower the amount of bail, she would remain a prisoner in a city jail cell.

Judge Cristy announced that he was willing to be accommodating to the limited resources of the defendants, on one condition. He insisted that Admiral Stirling wire the Pentagon asking for a written guarantee from the highest level "that the facilities of the Navy will not be used in any way to facilitate escape." In a gentlemanly gesture to Stirling, he added: "I shall be very glad to cooperate with a lower bail upon such information being officially conveyed to me, so that Admiral Stirling shall not be in the embarrassing position of pledging his word, but subject to superior authority."

Stirling rushed off to send a cable to the secretary of the navy, seeking that guarantee. The idea that Mrs. Fortescue might be in jail for even a single night was impossible to contemplate. As it turned out, she did have to spend one night there—it took the navy secretary a day to respond with the guarantee Cristy required—but the admiral need not have worried. Rather than a jail cell, city officials allowed Grace to stay in the lockup's matron quarters, with a comfortable bed, several chairs including a rocker, various other pieces of furniture, and a pleasant adjoining bathroom.

That night the city arranged for a restaurant to supply the prisoners with whatever they wanted for dinner. Grace and Tommie had fried chicken and lima beans. The two sailors ordered sirloin steak, French fries, and apple pie. Other than the noise and "ribald songs" from the drunk tank down the hall, Grace would later say, she had a delightful time. She and the matron on duty, Jennie Mendonca, gossiped, talked about hula, and played cards for most of the night. She fell asleep reading *Women's Home Companion*. Later, Miss Mendonca would make something of a name for herself in San Francisco as a private detective.

As soon as he heard from the secretary of the navy, agreeing to the terms he had stipulated, Judge Cristy lowered the defendants' bail to $5,000 for Grace and $2,500 for each of the other three. Amfac, the Big Five corporation with Walter Dillingham on its board of directors, put up the money to have them freed, and they returned to their more comfortable quarters on the USS *Alton*.

But everything was different now. They would have to stand trial in a criminal court, with at least the remote possibility that they might be convicted. Grace remained certain that would not happen, but on the almost impossible off chance that it did, the consequences were beyond imagining. The punishment stipulated by Hawai'i law for the crime of second-degree murder was confinement at hard labor for not less than twenty years or for a greater number of years, as the court saw fit, up to life imprisonment.

By now Grace's brother, Robert Bell, had arrived, and one of the first things he told Grace was that she would have to hire a high-powered mainland attorney. Her current lawyers, Frank Thompson and Montgomery Winn, agreed: given the horrific price the defendants would pay if they lost, it would be worth every penny they could scrape up to bring in the best in the country.

What Thompson and Winn failed to say was that they wanted nothing more to do with the defendants. One of them told a *New York Times* reporter, in confidence, that "he would give five thousand dollars to be out of the case." Nor did most other local attorneys have any interest in defending the killers. Mrs. Kluegel and her crowd were still fervently in the defendants' corner, as were the military and the entire local corporate elite. But the press was growing divided, while the previously splintered nonwhite communities were coming together. And now much of the legal establishment also was beginning to turn against these haole outsiders and their imperious ways.

The day after the grand jury had finally delivered its indictments, Judge Cristy received a hand-delivered letter from Arthur Withington, the president of the Hawaii Bar Association. Noting that it was unusual to compliment a judge on the performance of his duty, Withington said he felt it was his responsibility, in this embattled time for Cristy, to express what he was certain represented the feelings of almost all island attorneys:

> To my mind the past few days have witnessed the most critical situation that has occurred in Hawaii since its admission to the United States. If the Anglo-Saxon people of these islands were to give open demonstration of the complete failure of our system of criminal jurisprudence to those of Oriental minds we would have made a confession that the keystone of the arch of our civilization had been destroyed and the collapse of our painfully established system of law and order would have been complete so far as these islands were concerned. The Ala Moana case and the killing of Kahahawai were as nothing compared with the failure of those of Anglo-Saxon blood and training to rise to the performance of their duty. It is with great pride that the Bar Association recognizes that you rose to the occasion and enforced the fundamental idea that this is a government of laws and not of men.

It may have reeked of white supremacy and been insufferable in tone as well, but one thing was certain: Withington's letter was not good news for Grace and the other defendants. They now looked forward to a trial that would be handled by a judge, Albert Cristy, who was a stalwart of the Hawaii Bar Association. No one yet knew who the replacement prosecutor would be, but attorneys Thompson and Winn were only being honest when they advised Grace that she and the others would be far better off with a top criminal defense attorney from well beyond the islands, preferably an attorney not known for adhering to the genteel niceties that bar associations held so dear.

As it turned out, one lawyer fit that description perfectly, a man universally acclaimed as the best criminal attorney the United States had ever known. His just-published autobiography was in bookstores everywhere. And he was available.

His name was Clarence Darrow. A former law partner once described him as someone whose heart held "infinite pity and mercy for the poor, the oppressed, the weak . . . all races, all colors, all creeds," and added that "the colored race" particularly regarded "with grateful hearts his heroic battles on their behalf." Clarence Darrow? Why would he agree to defend the likes of Grace Fortescue?

20   Attorney for the Damned

O ne day in the mid-1920s the young daughter of a woman with whom the married Clarence Darrow had long enjoyed a secret love affair asked the great lawyer for his autograph. When she held out her autograph book, containing the signatures of numerous important people, Darrow noticed that he would be sharing his page with Babe Ruth. Darrow was a baseball fan. Smiling, he scribbled his name beneath that of the storied slugger, then alongside it he wrote, "Pinch Hitter."

It was fortuitous that young Margaret Parton would wind up with Ruth's and Darrow's signatures on the same page of her autograph album, but it was not inappropriate. At the time, in the field of baseball, Ruth was recognized as the greatest player ever—and today, among those who know the game, many still regard him as the best ever to play it. Precisely the same thing was and is said about Darrow in the field of criminal law.

Born before the Civil War, in 1857—the same year as the Supreme Court's infamous *Dred Scott* decision denying citizenship to African Americans—by the mid-1890s Darrow already was famous for his astonishing oratorical skills, both inside and outside the courtroom. So charismatic was he that many seemed not to notice how frequently decisions went against his clients—for the same reason, perhaps, that everyone recalled Babe Ruth's home runs and not the fact that he struck out almost twice as often. In both instances the two men seemed larger than life, and when they won they won big.

Today, Darrow is most remembered for his work in the Leopold and Loeb murder case in Chicago and the "Monkey" trial in Dayton, Tennessee, when he confronted William Jennings Bryan on the teaching of evolution in public schools. The defendant in the latter case was a young man named John Thomas Scopes. He said that when he met Darrow, only a year after the lawyer had dazzled the Chicago legal establishment and brought the Leopold and Loeb trial judge to tears with his closing argument, he was wearing a straw hat and an open jacket, "in a gesture of summer casualness. It was easy to like him. He drawled comfortably and hadn't any airs . . . just an unpolished, casual country lawyer, so ordinary did he act."

That was the impression the great attorney wanted people to have of him. With his tall and lanky build, his hair always tumbling across his forehead, his clothes, as one friend described them, "fitting like a popular model from the U.S. Tent and Awning Company," and his ready smile and plain speech, Clarence Darrow presented himself as a simple man of the people. Years before John Scopes met his defense attorney, however, someone who knew Darrow far better, an old Chicago friend named W. W. Catlin—himself an odd combination of investment banker and anarchist—described the celebrated lawyer as "a strange mixture of craft and courage, generosity and penuriousness, consideration and despotism, honesty and deviousness." Still, Catlin said, "he has a big brain and a kind heart. . . . I think we should take and enjoy the good he has given us, and overlook his personal weaknesses."

Darrow campaigned for years against the death penalty, and in more than a half century of practicing law and a hundred capital cases he lost only one client to execution, in 1893. It was his first important case, one that he had not argued from the outset, but only took on a last-minute, desperate appeal. With the next big case he initiated a string of trials on behalf of organized labor, during a time when unions routinely were being crushed by corporations with the aid of government and the courts. Between 1894, when he represented the American Railway Union, led by Eugene Debs, and 1907, when he defended Big Bill Haywood of the Western Federation of Miners on a charge of murder, Darrow rose to nationwide fame for his flamboyant and aggressive courtroom demeanor.

His closing arguments became the stuff of legend, for both their duration and their emotional intensity. One of his lengthier summations (eight hours, without notes) was delivered on behalf of striking anthracite miners to a panel of federally appointed commissioners. Darrow asked the commissioners to "think of the cripples, of the orphans, of the widows, of the maimed, who are dragging their lives out on account of this business, who, if they were mules or horses would be cared for, but who are left and neglected" by mine operators who are "fighting for slavery, while we are fighting for freedom." The commissioners awarded the miners several million dollars in back pay, a 10 percent pay raise, and a shorter workday.

As early as 1901 Darrow was also speaking out publicly on behalf of African Americans. Addressing a black church congregation that year, he said he despaired over the apparent eagerness of "the white race to shoot down men in cold blood," and to carry out lesser but still degrading offenses against black people. But he urged the parishioners to remember that even if they felt "obliged many times to submit to this . . . it must always be with the mental reservation that you know you are their equal, or you know that you are their superior, and you suffer the indignity because you are compelled to suffer it, as your fathers were once compelled to do."

Twenty-five years later, Darrow was still at it, defending eleven Detroit blacks against murder charges after some of them fired guns into a threatening white mob that surrounded the house they were in, one of them killing someone in the crowd. It became known as the Sweet case, after the name of the black man who owned the house, Dr. Ossian H. Sweet. After the first trial, which ended in a hung jury, a second prosecution ended with an acquittal. The not guilty decision followed a seven-hour closing argument by Darrow that ranged from a recounting of the history of blacks in America—"captured as you capture wild beasts, torn from their homes and their kindred; loaded into slave ships, packed like sardines in a box, half of them dying on the ocean passage . . . bought and sold as slaves, to work without pay, because they were black"—to a rousing defense of a man's right to protect his home and family from the threats of an angry mob.

It was cases such as these that led Darrow himself, in one famous summation, to say that he spoke "for the poor, for the weak, for the weary, for that long line of men, who, in darkness and despair, have borne the labors of the human race." It was also cases such as these that provoked Lincoln Steffens, Darrow's friend of many years, to describe him as "the attorney for the damned." But on another occasion Steffens portrayed the great lawyer in terms that were closer to those used years earlier by W. W. Catlin. "At three o'clock he is a hero for courage, nerve, and calm judgment," Steffens wrote, "but at 3:15 he may be a coward for fear, collapse, and panicky mentality."

Catlin and Steffens were far from alone in that opinion. As time wore on many of Darrow's old radical allies in the struggle for labor and against poverty and oppression—Eugene Debs, Samuel Gompers, Jane Addams, Emma Goldman—had little good to say about him. The fact was, they never knew what stand he might take on any issue of importance that might arise. His reaction to America's entry into the First World War was only one example. Darrow had long been an ardent pacifist. But after Congress voted to enter the war it also decided to outlaw dissent. Former clients and friends of Darrow, including Eugene Debs and Big Bill Haywood, soon found themselves being carted off to prison while Darrow, having had a change of heart, was touring the country in support of America's military intervention.

It was a tendency that those around him first noticed during the early years of the century. At the very time that Darrow was rising to national prominence for his work with labor unions, he was also defending his wealthy friend William Randolph Hearst from a tort action brought by a young woman who had been seriously injured when a Hearst-owned, illegal, two-thousand-pound advertising sign crashed to the ground in downtown Chicago. Darrow lost, then appealed, and lost again, when a jury awarded the woman eight thousand dollars.

Next, he defended a group of attorneys caught bribing jurors into denying claims to plaintiffs who had been seriously injured in streetcar accidents. The attorneys, and Darrow, had been hired by Union Traction, a streetcar company owned by the famously ruthless and corrupt tycoon Charles Yerkes. A few years later Theodore Dreiser modeled a character he named Frank Cowperwood on Yerkes, using him as the personification of corporate greed in his novels *The Financier* and *The Titan*.

And when the worst disaster in Chicago's history, the Iroquois Theater fire, killed 596 people—more than four times the number who would die in New York's infamous Triangle Shirtwaist fire of 1911—Darrow put his talents to work not on behalf of the victims, but in defense of the theater owners who had illegally locked twenty-nine of the thirty emergency exit doors.

In these and similar instances, when challenged by politically progressive friends Darrow would defend himself in various ways, but his motivations clearly were money and his own personal well-being. (At one point, when it appeared that he might go to jail for bribing jurors, Darrow offered to turn state's evidence against labor leader Samuel Gompers in exchange for a light sentence for himself.) It wasn't that he didn't believe in the causes he championed, but when they conflicted with his desire for a reasonable degree of creature comfort the causes often lost out.

In 1907 Darrow turned fifty years old and longed to retire. He and his second wife, Ruby, moved into a spacious and sunny nine-room flat on the top floor of an apartment building overlooking the University of Chicago, Jackson Park, and Lake Michigan. The work for Hearst and Yerkes and the others had provided him with a sizable bankroll. But the next year a nationwide financial panic wiped out all his investments, most of which were in a gold mine in Mexico named Black Mountain. For the next twenty years he rarely again could give serious thought to retirement. And it was as those two decades were drawing to a close that he took on the cases that made him most famous, Leopold and Loeb in 1924 and the Scopes trial in 1925.

At last he retired at age seventy-one in 1928. Most of his old friends who were still living had long since absolved Darrow of his occasional past cowardice and opportunism. After all, he had also done wonderful work for important causes they held dear, and he was so charming that it was difficult not to forgive him. With a nest egg of more than three hundred thousand dollars and no debts, the old celebrity attorney and his wife could now spend their time traveling for pleasure, working on his autobiography, and from time to time hitting the lecture circuit.

Then, in the fall of 1929, the bottom fell out. The stock market crash reduced the value of the Darrows' investments from nearly a third of a million dollars to almost nothing. Worse, his son Paul had put his money into the very same stocks, and now he was not only broke, he was deeply in debt. Not wanting to return to the courtroom, Clarence decided to find other ways to earn money and help his son pay off his indebtedness.

He signed on with Universal Pictures to do a movie entitled *The Mystery of Life*. The film was designed to explain to a lay audience the scientific theory of evolution, and who was more qualified to do that than the man who had so famously argued on behalf of Darwin in the Scopes trial? When it was released Universal promoted the film to its distributors by describing the forty-two-minute four-reeler as "replete with thrilling animal scenes—countless freaks of nature—human and animal, and to top it off, the greatest magnet a marquee has ever known, Clarence Darrow's name!"

His next endeavor, barnstorming around the country and engaging in paid public debates, turned out to be even more profitable than the movies. Typically the topic was religion—Darrow was an atheist who called himself an agnostic because it was more acceptable—and his debate opponent commonly was a leading churchman in the town that was paying Darrow's fee. Officially paid five hundred dollars plus expenses for each outing (although, he later told a friend in confidence, often he received up to one thousand dollars), the great attorney became the great entertainer, speaking before crowds of 4,000 people in Columbus, Ohio, 3,000 in Houston, 3,500 in Nashville, and comparable numbers wherever he went. And while almost no one in the audience agreed with his antireligious arguments, they were delivered with so much gusto and humor that he invariably was proclaimed the winner of the debate.

But the Depression grew worse, and people began to think twice about paying admission to hear people debate onstage, especially when they could be entertained for free by performers on the radio. And if they did have some extra money to spend, the new talking pictures, starring the likes of Clark Gable and Jean Harlow, provided more excitement than a septuagenarian lawyer, no matter how famous, talking about religion. Darrow was broke again. He had spent most of the money he earned paying off his son Paul's indebtedness, which still exceeded ten thousand dollars. By Christmas of 1931 the state of Clarence and Ruby's finances was so low that they couldn't afford to buy holiday cards. Instead, Ruby made them one by one, producing what one observer called an "untidy and somewhat childlike" design. Before long, she was writing to an old friend: "Not a *thing* for Clarence and only a few spools of thread for myself for making over my old *really ragged* clothes. Have turned over my worn-out coat collars, and have not had a new hat for years, (winter and summer combined). . . . We get along with what others would not consider good enough to give away."

Then suddenly, out of the blue, a cable arrived at 1537 East 60th Street in Chicago, addressed to Clarence Darrow, Esquire. The wire was from Honolulu and the sender was inquiring as to Mr. Darrow's availability to handle the defense of Mrs. Grace Fortescue, her son-in-law, and two other men who had recently been indicted for murder. Perhaps Mr. Darrow had heard of the case.

Both the lawyer and his potential clients had a lot to think about. Darrow made it clear from the start that if he took the case—and that was a big if—his fee would be substantial. He was seventy-four years old, soon to be seventy-five, and neither his health nor his stamina were what they had once been. There also were political ramifications that he needed to mull over. He had some traveling scheduled for the next several weeks, to Florida and Kansas City, possibly New York, and he would use the travel time to read up on the case and come to a decision.

Grace's brother-in-law, Julian Ripley, was conducting the negotiations. Since Honolulu authorities had still not decided on who their new appointed prosecutor would be, Ripley told Darrow, there was ample time for him to consider the matter. In fact, there was a lot of thinking to be done on Ripley's end as well. Darrow's services would cost $40,000, plus expenses, and an additional sum for an assistant. To put that fee in perspective, it was roughly the same amount of money that Warner Brothers' latest motion picture star, Edward G. Robinson—following his success in *Little Caesar*—was now being paid for each picture in which he was featured. Gossip columnist Walter Winchell had recently described Robinson as "the hottest actor in the world." It also was a little more than half of Babe Ruth's $75,000 salary for 1932. The most Darrow previously had received for a case was the $30,000 he wound up with after the Leopold and Loeb trial.

Given his celebrity status, Darrow may not have thought $40,000 (equivalent to well over half a million dollars today for less than two months of work) an excessive sum for his services. But it was far more money than Grace could imagine being able to put together herself. Gathered in Grace's suite on the USS *Alton*, she, her brother, her sister, and her sister's husband came up with a plan. Along with the baskets of flowers from well-wishers that had filled the *Alton*'s decks in the days following the murder of Kahahawai, there were numerous cards and telegrams expressing concern for Grace's well-being. As *Time* had reported in its January 25 edition, the "heartwarming messages of sympathy and admiration" included many from Grace's "old friends in Society." Indeed they did. And some of them offered more than sympathy—they offered help. One came from Joseph Medill Patterson, the founding owner of the *New York Daily News* and a friend of Roly's from his prewar days as a correspondent in Europe. With the *News'* steady onslaught of garish headlines describing the murder of Joe Kahahawai as a justifiable "honor killing," Patterson certainly was doing his part. But there were others.

Mrs. Evalyn Walsh McLean, a longtime friend who had grown up and still lived in Washington not far from where Grace had spent her childhood, wired: "Dearest Grace, you have all my love and sympathy. If there is anything in the world I can do, don't hesitate to call on me. Devoted love." Mrs. McLean was the daughter of a fabulously wealthy rags-to-riches ex–gold miner named Thomas F. Walsh. Her husband was Edward Beale McLean, the heir to the *Washington Post* fortune. The sixty-room beaux arts mansion her father had built in the heart of the nation's capital—the most expensive residence in Washington at the time—was hers now, but she couldn't be bothered to live in it, because she preferred her husband's equally elegant home. Among her many other possessions was the 44.52-carat Hope Diamond, which was set in a tiara that she wore on special occasions. She should be able to lend a helping hand.

So, too, should Mrs. Eva Stotesbury be able to make a contribution. Her cable to Grace had read: "Dear Gracie, this brings you my love and heartiest sympathy and also my admiration and respect for your magnificent courage in this overwhelming misfortune. I would have done the same thing in your place and so would any other good mother. If there is anything I can do for you or yours, count upon me." Eva was another old friend of the family and the wife of Edward Townsend Stotesbury. At the moment she was closing up her suburban Philadelphia home—consisting of 147 rooms, forty-five baths, a bank of elevators, and a movie theater, all set within a three-hundred-acre estate—and moving with the yacht and thirty-two servants to Palm Beach. There, she and her husband would settle in for the season at their beach house, El Mirasol, often described as the grandest home ever built in Palm Beach. Several years earlier Mr. Stotesbury had estimated his net worth at a hundred million dollars, and he was known as a spendthrift. A small gift to "Gracie" would hardly be missed.

There were many others on the list that Grace and Robert drew up— including the affluent side of their own family, such as *National Geographic*'s Gilbert and Elsie Grosvenor, who had wired: "Dearest love and sympathy. How can we help?" Like Evalyn Walsh McLean and Eva Stotesbury, among others, Gilbert and Elsie would soon find out.

Not too proud to take money from wherever it might be found, Grace was delighted to learn that the enlisted men at Pearl Harbor were taking up a collection. In the end, they contributed seven thousand dollars. Brother-in-law Julian said he could kick in five thousand dollars. And although Grace did not have personal access to cash, she did have Bell Telephone Company stock left to her by her father against which she could borrow. Walter Dillingham took care of that, arranging for a loan of eleven thousand dollars, to be handled through her bank in Washington via the Bishop Trust Company in Honolulu. Dillingham was the senior vice president of Bishop Trust.

Before long most of the money Darrow wanted for his services had been gathered. Most, but not all. Dudley Field Malone, Darrow's partner during the Scopes trial along with Arthur Garfield Hays, had volunteered to serve as co-counsel again in the defense of Grace Fortescue and the others. His fee of ten thousand dollars was reasonable, but Grace didn't have it—or didn't want to part with it—and Darrow was unwilling to take it out of his forty thousand. So the famed attorney for the damned went in search of a less expensive assistant.

Through a series of contacts Darrow finally hit upon the name of George S. Leisure, a new partner in a Manhattan law firm headed by Wild Bill Donovan, who won his nickname and the Medal of Honor during World War I and would go on to establish the OSS in World War II. Leisure, it turned out, had been to Hawai'i a few years earlier as attorney for Waialua Plantation in a major civil suit, and he had also idolized Darrow for years. He agreed, following a whirlwind courtship by Darrow, to take the case for free.

Darrow wired Julian Ripley in Honolulu to tell him he would represent Grace and her codefendants. The press picked up the story and ran with it. Then, almost immediately, the great man had second thoughts. Although most of the nation's newspapers, magazines, and radio news shows were solidly, even hysterically, on the side of the accused murderers, the smaller liberal and African American press was not. The *Nation,* a magazine that Darrow read regularly and had written for, argued editorially that "lynch law in Hawaii is no more to be condoned than lynch law in Mississippi"—adding for good measure that, rather than have the military impose martial law in the islands, "every battleship, naval officer, seaman, and soldier should be recalled from the territory."

New York's African American *Amsterdam News* was even more direct. It ran a large editorial cartoon depicting the United States as a giant, menacing octopus hovering over the Hawaiian Islands, two of its tentacles labeled "automobiles" and "good roads," the others marked "lynching," "racial prejudice," "Jim Crow," and more. The *Amsterdam News* represented a constituency that Darrow strongly supported, and one that supported him.

To make matters worse, the *New York Times* had recently published a startlingly frank interview with Grace Fortescue by Pulitzer Prize–winning reporter Russell Owen. Owen described the attitude of Grace and her codefendants as "not one of indifference, but certainly not marked by trepidation or a feeling that they had done something for which they should be ashamed or sorry." In fact, Grace openly admitted that they had committed the crime, telling the reporter that she had "slept better since Friday the eighth, the day of the murder, than for a long time." The only thing she regretted was that they had botched the effort to dispose of Kahahawai's body. "I made the mistake of pulling the shade down in the car. I should not have done that. . . . Now, of course, I realize that we bungled dreadfully, although at the time I thought we were being careful."

Darrow cannot have been pleased when he read a firsthand account of one of his prospective clients admitting her guilt and treating it with nonchalance and even self-righteousness. He would have been astonished to learn that the entire text of the article had been approved in advance by the defendants' island attorneys. And he would have been outraged, and perhaps not taken the case, had Owen reported something else Grace said to him. In a subsequent account of his time in Honolulu, Owen remembered that he asked Grace "why she felt what had happened was justified, and she said that she came from the South and that in the South they had their own ways of dealing with 'niggers.' She said many other things which I will not recall now, but that one word 'niggers,' if I had ever revealed it, would have made her position much more unpleasant in Hawaii."

Darrow, meanwhile, was trying to deal with the telegrams and letters that now were arriving daily at his and Ruby's home in Chicago. They came by the bushel, from friends and from strangers who had long admired his work, asking how he could possibly consider taking on the defense of whites who had lynched a native Hawaiian. It was especially incomprehensible, some of them reminded him, in light of the fact that he had withdrawn only recently from the defense team in the Scottsboro case.

Just a year earlier, outside the town of Scottsboro, Alabama, nine black teenage boys had been arrested for the alleged rape of two white women. Their trials began twelve days later, and quickly ended in convictions and the death penalty, although as it turned out the young men were innocent. Attorneys from the International Labor Defense (ILD), a legal organization controlled by the Communist Party and devoted to the defense of people victimized by the capitalist system, visited them, as did lawyers from the National Association for the Advancement of Colored People (NAACP). Both organizations wanted to help the condemned youths, but neither of them wished to work with the other. The NAACP brought in Clarence Darrow and his colleague Arthur Hays, who together had won the important Sweet case in Detroit five years earlier, but the rancor between the two sponsors continued, and on January 4, 1932, the NAACP officially withdrew from the case. Two thousand dollars had already been paid to Darrow. He promised he would return half of that fee as soon as he was able. However, he added in apology, that day was unlikely to occur in the near future.

Then he got the telegram from Grace Fortescue's brother-in-law, Julian Ripley, asking if he would be willing to go to Honolulu and serve as defense counsel for four white people indicted as the killers of a young Hawaiian man. It was a case that had been on the front pages of all the nation's newspapers for nearly a month. It also was a case uncomfortably similar to the Scottsboro case, except this time Darrow would be working for the other side.

Among the numerous cables and letters he received after the press learned of his acceptance of the Honolulu offer, one was from a dear friend and a man he greatly admired, Harry Elmer Barnes. Barnes was much younger than Darrow, six years younger in fact than Darrow's son Paul, but Clarence and Ruby were especially close to him. In some ways, he represented all the things that Darrow had once wished for himself. Barnes had received his Ph.D. from Columbia University fourteen years earlier and had already published several important books on history, psychology, and sociology. He also was a journalist, a popular lecturer, a social reformer, and an outspoken atheist: a man after Darrow's heart. When he read that Darrow had agreed to defend the people who now, since Russell Owen's interview with

Grace had appeared in the *New York Times,* were the admitted murderers of a Hawaiian man, he wrote to Clarence, expressing his deep disappointment.

On March 5, nearly a week after he had officially and publicly accepted the case, Darrow wrote back to Barnes, saying that although he "really wanted to go," he had changed his mind and had so informed his would-be clients. After further consideration, he said, he had come to the conclusion that "anyone who tried the case could scarcely avoid discussing race conflict. I had so long and decidedly been for the Negro and all so-called 'foreigners' that I could not put myself in a position where I might be compelled to take a position. . . . The defendants are entitled to counsel who would not be handicapped by his opinions and former statements . . . so, I shall not be in the case and have so written them." Adding that the defendants should be receiving his letter of withdrawal just before Barnes opened this letter, Darrow asked him not to reveal anything he had said because it might adversely affect the trial, regardless of who would be serving as defense attorney.

What Darrow didn't mention in the letter to Barnes was that he had enclosed with his message to Julian Ripley a copy of his closing argument in the Sweet case. It had been printed in a thirty-page pamphlet and sold in bookstores after that trial ended—the trial that Darrow, at the time of his retirement four years earlier, had considered his most important case ever. He would later say that he had sent the pamphlet along as evidence for Grace and the others of his powerful commitment to the rights of people of color, thus demonstrating the inappropriateness of his representing them. And certainly, with all its attention to the horrors of African American history and the ongoing discrimination against black people, his summation in the Sweet case did that. But it also, whether intended or not, vividly demonstrated something else.

The Sweet case had presented serious difficulties for Darrow. Supporters of the accused men argued that it was a simple matter of self-defense: a black man who had just moved into a white neighborhood, or one of those helping him to move in, had fired into a white mob that was surrounding the house and threatening the man and his family. But actually it was more complicated than that. Warned that there might be violence, Dr. Sweet and the nine friends and relatives who were helping him move that day included ten guns and almost four hundred rounds of ammunition among the items they carried inside. Also, it had not been a single shot that came from the house, but a fusillade. There was genuine disagreement as to how large and how menacing the gathering of white people outside the house had been, but in any case, although rocks had been thrown, there was no evidence of immediate or life-threatening provocation. And finally, the dead man, who was sitting down across the street and smoking a pipe at the time of the shooting, was discovered to have been shot in the back.

Added to all this, the jury was local and entirely white, while the city of Detroit bristled with racial hostility. On the facts available, and the technicalities of the law, the defense was in trouble. But Darrow was a past master of a legal technique known as jury nullification. As described by a more recent practitioner, William Kunstler—defense attorney for black radicals and antiwar activists in the 1960s and 1970s—jury nullification advocates do not maintain "that men are free to pick and choose with impunity what laws they will or will not obey." What they do assert, however, is the right to "let juries in on the closely guarded secret that they are, in the final analysis, the consciences of their communities and, as such, are free to acquit those who . . . under ordinary circumstances, are indeed guilty of breaking the law in question."

Or, as Darrow put it in his Sweet trial summation: "Gentlemen, these black men shot. Whether any bullets from their guns hit Breiner [the victim], I do not care. I will not discuss it. . . . There are bigger issues in this case than that. The right to defend your home, the right to defend your person, is as sacred a right as any human being could fight for, and as sacred a cause as any jury could sustain." There are, in short, "unwritten laws" that from time to time should take precedence over laws defined by legislatures—or so Darrow and others like him have argued in America since the eighteenth century. And when they have convinced jurors to follow those unwritten laws instead of the ones printed in statute books, fugitive slaves have been freed, executions have been averted, political prosecutions have been derailed, civil liberties have been sustained. And, for the better part of a century, Southern lynch mobs operated with impunity. Nullification is a double-edged sword.

Upon reading the material Darrow had sent them, Grace Fortescue and Julian Ripley fired back a telegram. In a letter to Barnes, written a week after his first letter, Darrow reported the contents of that telegram: "They thought I was right in my position on the race question, and they wanted that attitude maintained in court." As a result, he concluded, "there was nothing for me to do but go." Later, in an autobiographical essay on the trial, Darrow would say that he took the case because he was bored, broke, and eager to see Hawai'i, "the only place I ever visited that turned out to be better than I expected."

As for Ruby, who described herself as "anxious not to offend" her husband "in my old-fashioned wifely way," she tried to put the best face on things. Writing to Barnes herself while Clarence was out of town for two days, she said she hoped that by going to Honolulu "CD," as she called him, "would establish a bridge between the white and brown folk, a new understanding, a better code of conduct on the part of the white people, and on the part of the brown people, back and forth, a lessening of that element termed 'color-line' in the minds of both." Clarence might even "do a *great kindness* to the natives by going," she continued, "and by doing the job *his way* and thus preventing some lawyer of the other 'school'—or what is it?—from going there and stirring up a worse hatred between the two kinds of people." Finally, she admitted, "I feel dreadfully uncomfortable about it all!"

The conservative *Los Angeles Times* had a different opinion. It wrote that taking the Massie case was the first respectable thing Clarence Darrow had ever done.

In a matter of days, Ruby and Darrow, joined by George Leisure, Darrow's new assistant, and his wife, were aboard a train heading from Chicago to San Francisco. It could have been a political whistle-stop campaign. At various cities and towns along the way Darrow held rousing press conferences with reporters from the surrounding areas, regaling them with his opinions on everything except the murder trial in Honolulu. He did flirt with it, though. In Reno, when asked about so-called honor killings, he admitted that he didn't know of any that had ever resulted in conviction. And when he was about to board the ship for the islands, with reporters clamoring for an opinion on the case, he smiled and said, "You never see a good looking, intelligent woman convicted of murder, manslaughter, or refused alimony." That was it. As for Prohibition, he was opposed, calling it "sadistic." The death penalty? Against that too. Religion? Same answer. Capitalism? Anything but. Further questions about the upcoming Massie case, however, were off limits.

As a matter of fact, the subject of the trial was so off limits that Darrow wouldn't even discuss it with Leisure. That worried the young attorney. Both on the train and aboard the ship that spent five days voyaging to Hawai'i, he tried to inquire about their strategy. Darrow waved him away. Leisure wondered about the facts in the case, and what their clients were like. Darrow said he knew very little.

But the old courtroom warrior had no doubt that they would win. What, after all, were they up against? Some newly appointed prosecutor, hailing from one of those little islands out there. A low-paid county attorney who would be taking on his very first case. They had nothing to worry about.

21   A Copper Miner's Son

The month of March was a busy time for lei sellers in Honolulu. After a blustery six weeks of filming *Bird of Paradise,* King Vidor decided to pack up and finish the movie in Hollywood. A "native village" was being built for him there. A year later the same set would be used for *King Kong.*

No sooner had the cruise ship carrying that cast and crew departed from Honolulu Harbor, with hundreds of leis tossed from the deck into the surrounding water as custom dictated, than another group of actors arrived to receive the equally customary lei greeting. They included Bela Lugosi and Warner Oland—known to movie fans everywhere from a previous role in *The Mysterious Dr. Fu Manchu*—and they were in Hawai'i to film *The Black Camel,* a Charlie Chan movie, at the Royal Hawaiian Hotel.

The Black Camel opened in New York three months later, and *Variety* loved it. When it showed up in Waikīkī, Chang Apana, the policeman whose exploits had been the model for the fictitious detective, went with a group of fellow officers to see it. They, too, were impressed, although his friends may have wondered why, if that was supposed to be Apana up on the screen, he never uttered such immortal lines as "Alibi have habit of disappearing like hole in water" or "Always harder to keep murder secret than for egg to bounce on sidewalk."

Real-life criminal investigators came and went from Honolulu that month as well. The team of U.S. Justice Department investigators headed by Seth Richardson had finished its work and was on its way back to Washington to file its report. And finally, on March 24, Clarence Darrow and his retinue arrived, to bigger headlines and a larger crowd at the dock than all previous celebrities combined. Other than perhaps hurting some feelings when he insisted on removing the leis that had been draped around his neck—"Let's get rid of these jingle bells," he complained; "I feel like a decorated hat rack"—Darrow charmed everyone who was gathered to greet him. At least at first.

One person remarked that the great attorney would be happy to find his autobiography was on sale in local bookstores. He furrowed his brow in a mock frown. "On sale still? I thought they would be sold out by this time." After more joking with reporters, saying at one point that he might decide to become a beach boy as soon as the trial was over, he mentioned that he would be seeking a continuance of a week or so. The trial was scheduled to begin in a few days, but he needed more time to meet with the defendants and various witnesses.

As he was leaving, someone asked Darrow what he thought about the new law in Hawai'i establishing the death penalty for the crime of rape. Any legislature that passed such a law was a legislature made up of "damned fools," he replied: "A man committing rape will get the same punishment under this law that he will get for murder, so he might as well go the whole way and remove the evidence." And beyond that, he said, "I have an abiding conviction that the law should apply equally to all persons. They have those laws in the South and I don't remember any white men being executed under them."

Well then, a reporter asked, what about the other new law allowing conviction in rape cases solely on the uncorroborated testimony of the complaining witness? "More bunk," Darrow replied. "Such a law opens the way for blackmail, and rape accusations may be brought for spite or for money. Rape is a difficult charge for a man to disprove. If laws such as that continue to be enacted, no man will be safe unless he's in jail." With that he strode off.

The bewildered reporters turned to his wife, Ruby, and asked her why he had taken the case. Smiling sweetly, she replied that she hadn't the slightest idea. "You ask him and then tell me," she said. "I'd like to know myself."

Apart from one or two minor hitches, Walter Dillingham thought things were going wonderfully. The indictment of Grace Fortescue and the others had been unexpected and troubling, but not only was Clarence Darrow now on board, they had disposed of Judge Albert Cristy. On behalf of the defendants, attorneys Thompson and Winn had filed affidavits charging him with personal bias and prejudice, as evidenced by his allegedly ordering the grand jurors to vote for indictment, and they asked that he remove himself from further involvement with the case.

Four days earlier Thompson and Winn had sought to quash the indictments altogether on the same grounds of judicial coercion. Cristy dismissed that effort after suggesting that the attorneys read the entire grand jury transcript, not merely "isolated quotations as the devil may do with Scripture."

He also restated his position that "the errors of jurors who take the law into their own hands would bring on a state of anarchy in any civilized community." The judge did not mention the praise for his actions from the Hawaii Bar Association, nor the fact that he had sought and received support from a national legal research bureau on the propriety of what he had done.

However, in response to a follow-up request that he disqualify himself from serving as judge at the criminal trial, Cristy agreed to step aside. At the end of a thirteen-page point-by-point rebuttal of the defense attorneys' allegations, he concluded that the crucial question was not whether he actually was biased against the defendants—which he asserted he was not—but that they believed him to be prejudiced. In order to prevent further speculation about the fairness and impartiality of the upcoming trial, he agreed to transfer the case to Judge Charles S. Davis.

Davis was the same age as Cristy, forty-two, but he had grown up in Honolulu before going away to college and law school at Cornell, Harvard, and Stanford. Though conservative—he had been a prosecutor for a number of years and considered the upper echelon of the police department to be riddled with corruption—he had a far less volatile personality than Cristy. His reputation among attorneys was one of quiet fairness.

Dillingham could live with that, especially with Darrow now coming in to handle the defense. And it gave him a breather to catch up on his correspondence. In a letter written on the same day that newspapers were reporting Judge Cristy would be stepping down from the forthcoming murder trial, he regaled his old friend Army Major George S. Patton with tales of what his daily life was like. He had been "spending ninety percent" of his time on the hubbub caused by the rape and murder trials, he wrote, and the fact was that all the news stories about crime in Honolulu were much ado about nothing. "If half they said were true I would not have dared to go out of the house other than armed." But at least the uproar had given him cover to take care of some "political and social house cleaning." In his reply, Patton wrote: "It seems to me that what the Honolulu Rapers need is some quick hangings. It is better for a few inoscent [sic] natives to hang than for the reputation of a great City to suffer. Don't quote me in that but you probably agree."

Dillingham did agree, although he would not have expressed the thought so crudely, at least in writing. In a private letter he would soon circulate among friends and colleagues, he acknowledged the "considerable doubt" that he and others had long had as to the guilt of the accused rapists. But the fact was that the turmoil had been a catalyst that led to what he regarded as long overdue administrative and legal reforms. His own man—"my faithful

Weeber," he described him to friends—was now the chief of police, Hawaiʻi's criminal law statutes had been thoroughly overhauled, and instead of selecting the city and county prosecutor at the ballot box, making the process a popularity contest, the office had now been made an appointive one. On this last matter, however, Dillingham did have some lingering reservations.

During the legislature's debates on converting the prosecutor's job from an elective to an appointive position, Dillingham had pressed to have the territorial governor and attorney general make the appointment. Others argued that, since it was a city and county post, the decision should be up to Honolulu's mayor and board of supervisors. Dillingham, in a letter to his cousin Ike in Boston, described himself as "worked up to a high pitch of fury" over the matter. That was because he had much more influence with the governor's office than with that of the mayor, and he wanted to be absolutely certain the right sort of man was chosen. In all the news and correspondence he was receiving from the mainland about the murder defendants, he wrote, "there is a sweeping feeling that these people should be let off without punishment and some of my letters carried the thought that they should be decorated." He agreed with that sentiment, and since the new prosecutor's first case would be the murder trial, the man chosen had to be someone Dillingham could control.

He wasn't. After being turned down by several nominees, including Alva Steadman, the now retired judge in the rape trial, the bar association had recommended forty-six-year-old attorney John Carlton Kelley for the $7,500-a-year post. The legislature had finally settled on granting power of appointment to the mayor, with the consent of the board of supervisors. At the time, the mayor and six of the seven supervisors were Republicans. So was John Kelley. And, although not the sort of Republican Dillingham and his supporters had in mind for the job, he sailed through the approval process.

Kelley's reputation was well known in the city. He was an exceptionally smart and hardworking lawyer, a bulldog in the courtroom who rarely lost a case. He was also known as a straight talker. Although many people regarded this trait as admirable, it hadn't helped when he ran for the elective prosecutor's position in 1926. Maybe he had simply pushed the straight talking too far when he declared his candidacy by saying: "I have no promises to make. I have no undated resignations to tender. To handle the legal affairs of the city and county promptly and efficiently . . . and to suppress vigorously and prosecute vice and crime will be my aim. My record is open to the public. My hat is in the ring." At a time when political campaigns in the islands were extravagant affairs, with candidates giving long and grandiloquent speeches at colorful lū'aus in their honor, complete with hula dancers and music well into the late-night and early-morning hours, Kelley's terseness was unusual. It also was no surprise to anyone when he lost.

But, Republican or not, Kelley was just the kind of man William Heen and Norman Godbold, both of them leaders of the Democratic Party, wanted on their side in a courtroom. They made him a partner in the firm of Heen, Godbold, and Kelley. And they didn't ask too many questions about his past, which was just as well.

Kelley had been born in 1885 in Butte, Montana, a city noted for its "appalling surface barrenness," one writer observed, the air thick with "sulphur and arsenic fumes from ore roasted in the open or belching from smelters." Butte was copper country, tough, hardscrabble, and very Irish. At the turn of the century it had almost three hundred saloons, open twenty-four hours a day. Gambling, crime, and violence were the essence of Butte, with Silver Bow County regularly providing the Montana state penitentiary and the state hospital with at least half their inmates and patients.

Marcus Daly, the copper baron and founder of the Anaconda Company, ran Butte with a paternalistic attitude and an iron fist. One of Daly's best buddies was Jeremiah Kelley, a miner he had met at the Comstock Lode in Nevada. Kelley followed Daly to Montana in 1881 and eventually moved up the ranks to become a mine supervisor. It was an axiom in Butte that when an Irish boy finished school he was handed a lunch bucket, a company work slip, and directions to the nearest mine shaft. Any man or boy who didn't work in a mine was derided as a "capon," a castrated chicken. But Marcus Daly took an interest in Jeremiah Kelley's two sons, John and Cornelius, and paid their way through college and law school at the University of Michigan.

John was only thirteen when Cornelius (known as Con) returned home after law school and took a job with Anaconda's legal department. In no time Con made his name by crushing local farmers who were complaining that pollution from the smelters was damaging their crops, water, and livestock. Con Kelley not only used all the power of the corporation to destroy the farmers' claims in court; he also saw to it that a scientist who testified on their behalf lost his job at the state university. After Daly's death, Con carefully plotted his way up the company's corporate ladder.

In contrast to Cornelius, when John returned home from law school, he let it be known that he wanted nothing to do with Anaconda. Just one state over, at that very moment, something far more interesting was happening: the great Clarence Darrow was defending Big Bill Haywood of the Western Federation of Miners on a murder charge. John and his older brother fought all the time, and finally John was kicked out of the house and went to live with distant relatives in Dublin Gulch. Although he did practice some law, John had developed a serious drinking problem—"in the bottle all the time, a terrible drunk," recalled a cousin years later—and because of that and his opposition to Con's autocratic behavior, no member of the family wanted anything to do with him.

Years later it was hard for anyone to recall exactly when it happened, but one day John just packed up and left Montana for good. He had some money put aside and wanted to get as far away as possible. He wound up in China. Then Australia. Then Fiji. And, finally, he came ashore in Hawai'i. It was as different from Butte as a place could be, and that suited him fine. While his brother, Con, now was a prominent Democrat in Montana known for his union busting, John became a Republican in the islands—and loved to show people his union card from the days when he worked as a meatpacker in an Australian slaughterhouse.

The one thing he could never entirely leave behind was the alcohol. When other attorneys and judges were asked about him as he was being considered for the prosecutor's post in early 1932, the sole criticism any of them had concerned his drinking. They all either mentioned it directly or alluded to it. Judge Cristy, speaking in confidence, described Kelley as an honest man, politically independent, with a great deal of trial experience. About Kelley's "personal habits," he said he preferred to express no opinion. Judge Steadman also said Kelley was honest and politically "unobligated," that he was aggressive, forceful, intelligent, and possessed of excellent legal skills, but that "he goes on occasional benders." The local United States attorney preferred to call them "sprees," although he too said Kelley was one of the best trial lawyers he had ever seen, with a terrific "jury personality" when he was sober.

As soon as Kelley was hired for the new position, his name and face appeared on newspaper front pages throughout the country. He was the man slated to do battle with Clarence Darrow in America's most explosive murder trial in recent memory. For someone who had his own personal demons to conquer, the pressure would prove to be enormous. Whatever mental toughness he had acquired growing up in one of America's most squalid and violent cities would be needed now.

Darrow and Kelley met privately soon after the defense team arrived in town. Photographs were taken of the meeting before reporters were ushered away, and the physical contrast between the two men was striking. Kelley—round faced, pink cheeked, and bald, with piercing blue eyes—was wearing a light-weight tropical sport jacket, a casual variation on his trademark white linen suit. Darrow, almost thirty years older, also looked as he always did—tall and shambling, with a sallow complexion, rumpled hair, and the lined face and furrowed brow of an old courtroom warhorse, wearing an ill-fitting and dark woolen jacket and trousers.

Even their wives were a study in dissimilarity. Ruby Darrow was a quiet, possessive woman who worshipped Clarence and unhappily tolerated his re-peated dalliances with other women. When Lincoln Steffens once asked how they were getting along, Darrow replied: "Fine, because Ruby and me, we both like Darrow." While in Honolulu, after a meeting on trial strategy that Ruby sat in on, Clarence turned to Tommie Massie and said, in her presence, "You know, she doesn't understand a thing we've said all evening."

Kelley would never have dared say such a thing to his wife, Nan. A year earlier, while on vacation in San Francisco and attending a movie with a fe-male friend, the "pretty brunette," as the press described her, claimed that a man sitting next to her had put his hand on her knee. She stood up, removed the belt from her leather coat, and beat him with the buckle, chasing him out of the theater into the arms of the police. At his arraignment, however, she declined to prosecute, saying the man had suffered enough.

But for all their differences, there were traits the two attorneys had in common: a stubbornness to have their way and an unwillingness to back down from a fight. That would become evident within minutes of the trial's opening, now scheduled for Monday, April 4. First, however, some prelimi-nary matters required attention.

Although he had welcomed reporters to his meeting with Kelley and had invited photographers to take his picture standing on Waikīkī Beach with famed Olympic swimming champion Duke Kahanamoku (Darrow still dressed in his dark winter suit and fedora), in less public moments the attorney for the defense was meeting with Walter Dillingham, Admiral Stirling, and others, in-cluding Thalia's navy physician, Dr. John Porter.

In late January, just prior to Darrow's being asked to take the case, Admiral Stirling had written to a friend in San Francisco named Joseph C. Thompson, a retired navy commander and physician now making his living as a psychoana-lyst. Stirling was seeking information about a possible insanity defense for the accused murderers, although none of them currently was manifesting what to his eye were psychopathic symptoms. Thompson replied in a longhand letter marked "Confidential," writing that such a defense was quite possible, and that

Stirling should not worry about the defendants' present state of mind. "I hasten to make clear to you a view point," Dr. Thompson wrote:

The four who are in trouble may be today in a perfectly normal mental state. But I believe that the defense runs the risk of missing a forensic point of paramount value unless they have deeply sown into the record full testimony as to the probability of human rage having been raised to the point of a temporary abandon of the elements of normal reason. This will require a trained psychiatrist, one expert in court procedure.

As it turned out, at almost precisely that moment an especially grisly murder case was going to trial at the Maricopa County Courthouse in Phoenix, Arizona, and receiving national attention. The defendant was Winnie Ruth Judd, accused of killing two people, hacking them to pieces, stuffing the remains into two trunks, and shipping them to herself in Los Angeles. Two psychiatrists, still commonly known in those days as "alienists," were called for the defense, Dr. Thomas Orbison and Dr. Edward Huntington Williams. Not surprisingly, since insanity defenses were rarely successful at that time, their testimony did not convince the jury that Judd was insane (although, independent of them, she later was saved from execution and committed to an asylum). But whether or not juries were resistant to the plea of insanity, Stirling had it on trustworthy authority that such a defense was possible and, handled properly, might well work in what people everywhere now referred to as the Massie case.

Soon after meeting with Stirling, Darrow huddled with Grace and Tommie and told them they needed to raise more money, quickly—not for him, but for two psychiatrists he now wanted to bring in from the mainland. They must, however, keep the matter in the strictest confidence. Grace immediately wired her friend Eva Stotesbury in Palm Beach for another three thousand dollars, and within days Drs. Thomas Orbison and Edward Huntington Williams were boarding a ship in San Francisco that was headed for the islands.

Kelley, meanwhile, was wrestling with his own trial problems. At his meeting with Darrow they had casually discussed the possibility of an insanity plea, and the defense attorney had dismissed it. Although the press was full of speculation that Darrow would claim for his clients a form of temporary emotional breakdown then known as "alarm clock" insanity to relieve them of criminal responsibility, his rejection of the idea made sense to Kelley.

In his autobiography, which Kelley had read, Darrow claimed to be "a fairly close student of psychology," and of one thing he was certain, he wrote: "There is no way of determining who is sane or who is insane."

In fact, only once in half a century of trying cases had Darrow hired psychiatric experts. That was eight years earlier, in the Leopold and Loeb "thrill killing" case—and it was a failure. At that trial he had pleaded his clients guilty, but sought to avoid the death penalty by introducing evidence that they were, if not insane, "mentally diseased." The judge didn't buy the argument. What mattered, he said, was what the law defined as insanity, and Darrow's clients didn't meet that standard. It was Darrow's emotional closing argument, not the psychiatric testimony, that saved Leopold and Loeb from the gallows.

If there was a trial in Darrow's background that was at all similar to the Massie case, Kelley knew it was the Sweet case, not Leopold and Loeb. In both instances several people were on trial, none of whom would confess to firing the weapon that did the killing. There also were no independent witnesses to either murder, and the weapons used had never been found. In the Sweet case the bullet had passed through the victim and could not be located to match up with a gun; in the Massie case a bullet existed, but the gun had disappeared. Kelley would have to build his case on circumstantial evidence. There was plenty of it, but Darrow was a master of indirection and courtroom sleight of hand, distracting jurors from the matter of evidence and leading them to think about what the law should be, rather than what it was.

He had displayed that ability on many occasions—including his own trial for bribery—but in the Sweet case Darrow succeeded in large part by asking the jury to empathize with the defendants, to understand their fears and their reasons for acting as they had. "Put yourselves in their place. Make yourselves colored for a little while," Darrow had admonished the all-white jury:

> It won't hurt. You can wash it off. They can't, but you can; just make yourselves black for a little while; long enough, gentlemen, to judge them, and before any of you would want to be judged, you would want your juror to put himself in your place. . . . What would you have done? [Send them to the penitentiary if you wish], but if you do, gentlemen, if you should ever look into the face of your own boy, or your own brother, or look into your own heart, you will regret it in sackcloth and ashes.

Kelley was convinced that Darrow would use a comparable plea in the present case, that he planned to put on an "honor killing" defense, contending that the "unwritten law" protecting a man's right to avenge an assault on his wife justified the murder of the young Hawaiian man. As at the Sweet trial, the defense would ask jurors to put themselves in the place of Thalia's mother or husband and have them imagine what they would have wanted to do in the same situation. The only way to compete with that, the prosecutor decided, was to insist on the rule of law as essential to social order and to make the evidence so overwhelming and graphic that it would compel the jury to vote for conviction.

Assisting Kelley was a slim and wiry middle-aged attorney named Barry Ulrich, an unassuming but intense and intelligent man, and yet another Harvard Law graduate who had made his way to the islands. After asking around about him, the *Times*'s Russell Owen reported that Ulrich's reputation as a lawyer was one of being "cold, suave, and relentless in his tactics." During the aftermath of the hung jury in the rape trial, the chamber of commerce had hired Ulrich to work privately as a special assistant in the prosecutor's office, pursuing leads that might culminate in a successful prosecution at the second trial.

Kelley was happy to have Ulrich's support when he was appointed as prosecutor, but upon learning that the first case on the calendar would be the murder trial and not the retrial of the rape suspects, the chamber's officers decided to cut off their funding of Ulrich. The *Hawaii Hochi* was the only newspaper to recognize (or care) what was happening and to point out in an editorial that obviously "the business men of the community are not really anxious to have Hawaii put up a vigorous prosecution in the [murder] case." For a time, Governor Judd said he would try to locate replacement funding, but then he too suddenly ran out of money. Ulrich decided to stay on anyway, assisting Kelley in an unofficial capacity.

As the two sides prepared their cases, newsmen from outside the islands were arriving by ship almost daily. The first to show up, back in January, had been Philip Kinsley of the *Chicago Tribune,* accompanied by his wife. When they disembarked he told local reporters that it had been very cold in Chicago and he "was glad something happened in Honolulu to give me an assignment here." Before long he was earning his keep, writing long feature articles for the *Tribune* on the background to the murder and saying such things as "the Massie case ranks with drama of the Electra type and stands as one of the great criminal cases of modern times."

Kinsley was followed by Harry Carr of the *Los Angeles Times* and then by Russell Owen of the *New York Times*. After that, the floodgates opened, and journalists began pouring in from throughout the country and as far away as

London, while the story was appearing in newspapers from Budapest to Sydney. Most of them had never been to Hawai'i before, and they were alternately amused and entranced by its exoticism. Kinsley and Owen, however, were among the nation's leading and most experienced journalists. They had both covered the Scopes trial in Dayton, Tennessee, and they were less interested in recreational distraction than in the courtroom fireworks that lay just ahead.

Technology also was doing its part to bring Hawai'i closer to the rest of the world. At the beginning of March direct radio phone service had opened between Honolulu, Europe, and South America. But foreign reporters who wanted to file their stories by telephone would have to learn to speak quickly, since rates to Great Britain and Brazil were fifteen dollars a minute—a week's wages in some jobs during the Depression—with costs higher to other locales.

Nowhere in the city was pretrial activity more frenzied than at the Judiciary Building. Traffic would be routed away from the streets on each side of the courthouse while the trial was in session, and signs and roadblocks were being set up in advance. A large room adjacent to the main courtroom was being outfitted with desks, typewriters, and telephones for the visiting journalists, while the noise of hammering and sawing rang out from the uppermost reaches of the building's rotunda. There, a spiral staircase was being installed that led to a newly constructed lounge with kitchenette and powder room. An appeal to authorities had convinced them that requiring Mrs. Fortescue to use public facilities during the time of her trial was unseemly. So a suite was being built for her private use at a cost to the territory of $3,007.50.

Then word began leaking out that the U.S. Justice Department investigation of crime conditions in Hawai'i, soon to be known in shorthand as the Richardson Report, was complete and would be filed on Monday, simultaneous with the start of the trial. Would it call for martial law? For a commission form of government? What would it say about race and criminality in the islands, or about the "shame of Honolulu," the alleged epidemic of rape and the widely broadcast fear that women had of walking the streets day or night?

It was hard to say which of the two events Honolulu residents were anticipating more, the opening of the trial or the release of the report. But as Monday dawned, not much of anything else was on people's minds.

22 Territory of Hawaii v. Fortescue et al.

When Mrs. Anne Kluegel and the other officers of her Citizens' Organization for Good Government showed up Monday morning for the trial, they were flabbergasted. People wishing to be spectators at the opening session had been lining up all night. There was not a chance that she or the others in her party would be admitted. Even her plea that she was now a special correspondent for the Hearst newspapers fell on deaf ears. She was too late, the policemen on the scene informed her as they turned her and hundreds of others away.

Inside the courtroom Tommie, according to the *New York Times,* couldn't stop "nervously working his mouth, as if chewing." One entire wall of the large chamber was lined with press representatives from big-city dailies on down to what one reporter disapprovingly characterized as "the *Rural Herald,* the *Rustic City News,* the *Squeedunk Journal,* and the *Toonerville Tribune.*" Elsewhere in the room, attorneys and other court personnel filled designated places at long, polished tables.

Grace glanced around at the spectators who had taken seats. She appeared very unhappy. Most of those who had come to watch the proceedings, and had shown up early enough to be admitted, were Hawaiian or Asian, including a large and somber-looking man named Joseph Kahahawai Sr. The most prominent exception to the racial makeup of the spectators was Mrs. Louise Dillingham, Walter Dillingham's wife. As Walter noted in a letter to his cousin Ike in Boston, "Louise has been honored with the bailiff's seat so that I have not been deprived of her company during the time she would otherwise have had to stand in line."

After preliminary court details were out of the way, the first order of business was jury selection or voir dire. As in so much else, Clarence Darrow for years had been well ahead of his colleagues in recognizing the importance of this phase of any trial. It has been joked that in England a trial starts when jury selection is complete, whereas in America when jury selection is complete the trial is over. Darrow would not have considered that to be much of an exaggeration. And like professional jury consultants today, he had his own rigorous set of guidelines, although he distilled them into a kind of folk wisdom.

The judge at the Sweet trial, a man named Frank Murphy, once asked the defense attorney why he liked Irish Catholic jurors so much. "Because I never met an Irish Catholic yet who didn't think that someday he might be in trouble himself," Darrow answered. He was only half joking. Darrow carried in his head an elaborate typology of juror types, based largely on religion and nationality, that he associated with proprosecution or prodefense tendencies. Proprosecution jurors had strong religious attitudes toward sin and punishment—primarily Lutherans, Baptists, and Presbyterians—and he especially tried to avoid Scandinavians. Ideal prodefense jurors, conversely, were religious skeptics—or, if religious, were Unitarians, Congregationalists, or Jews—as well as Irish Catholics.

None of this was any help at all, however, when, at nine o'clock Monday morning, Darrow and his co-counsel, George Leisure, glanced at the list of names in the jury pool from which they would try to select veniremen most favorable to their clients. Of the first twenty-one persons called, ten were named Auyong, Imada, Wong, Yap, Ching, Awana, Akana, Sunnu, Teixeira, and Kaleiwahea. To make matters worse for the defense, or so they surmised, a number of the remaining potential jurors with names more familiar to Darrow and Leisure—people named Renton, White, Waterhouse, and Strohlin— may well have been part Hawaiian in ancestry. Or they might have had nonblood kinship that the defense would find objectionable, as was the case with one haole who was a brother-in-law of Princess Kawananakoa. The only way to find out was to ask them or to rely on background checks that had been conducted by attorneys Thompson and Winn.

The last trial in America that had riveted this much of the nation's attention was the Scopes trial seven years earlier. The men in that jury pool were eager to serve on the panel, it was said, because it was the only way to guarantee a front-row seat for the legal circus to follow. In Honolulu almost no one wanted to serve. Between family, friends, and business associates, potential jurors realized they were bound to offend someone, whichever way they voted. And given the intensity of emotion surrounding the case, the way they decided might mean they would be balancing the prospect of lost friendships against unemployment. It seemed best to avoid serving altogether. Thus, from the start, one after another potential juror who was called and sworn announced that he had a fixed opinion on the guilt or innocence of the defendants, and that he would be unable to change that opinion whatever the evidence.

If that effort failed, there were other approaches to take. After unsuccessfully claiming that he didn't understand English, a Japanese fisherman named Eugene Mioi pleaded that the traps he had laid at sea were filling up and all the fish would die if he couldn't tend to them. He was excused. A well-known orchestra leader, Johnny Noble, decided to feign deafness. Whatever the attorneys or the judge said to him was received with a blank stare and the words "I'm sorry, I can't hear a word you say." Robert Kin Heu said he had a firm opinion regarding the defendants that could not be changed no matter what. Suspicious, Darrow asked when he had formed that opinion. "Night before last," Heu answered, "right after being summoned."

When Willy Beyer, a German who made and sold potato chips for a living, took the stand he said he didn't understand English well enough to serve. "Do you know the meaning of 'doubt'?" the judge asked him. "I looked it up in the dictionary but I forgot." "Do you know what it is to be 'guilty'?" Yes, Beyer conceded. "It means you're wrong. I was fined one time for speeding and that's how I know." Darrow liked Germans and he liked people who had been in trouble with the law. Beyer remained on the jury. That night, on his national radio show, Lowell Thomas jokingly referred to the exchange, but he changed a few things. "In the Honolulu courtroom where the trial of the 'honor slayers' is taking place," he said, "a Chinaman was dismissed from the jury because he couldn't define the meaning of the word innocence."

There were exceptions to the rule that no one wished to serve on the panel. One man who did want to be on the jury, but who found himself excused, was a Hawaiian named William Huihui. A background investigation by the defense had revealed him to be strongly biased against their clients and to have told people that on several occasions. "Did you ever tell anyone you thought the defendants should be hanged?" Darrow asked him. "No," Huihui replied. Darrow hesitated, checked his notes, then asked: "Did you ever tell a Mrs. Wood what you thought ought to be done with these people?" "Yes," he answered, "I said they ought to be shot." Huihui was excused.

For what appeared to be good reason—one that was underlined by Huihui's questioning—the defense went out of its way to avoid Hawaiian jurors, challenging more Hawaiians than members of any other group. However, some veteran observers of the courts in Honolulu speculated that this might have been a mistake. As a senior U.S. district judge named William Lymer observed, Hawaiians as a group were intelligent, thoughtful, ethical, and in general "ideal jurors in every case," but he faulted their susceptibility to appeals for mercy. "The Hawaiian has something of an emotional nature," he said in an interview, "and they are a very forgiving and gentle people. They do not like to insist on penalties which seem harsh, and for that reason they are rather inclined to be an acquitting juror." Precisely the sort of jurors Darrow ordinarily craved.

The first day of jury selection ended at noon, as would every day of the trial except the last. This was in deference to Clarence Darrow's advanced age and presumably frail health. That was fine with Darrow, since, in theory at least, it gave him, Leisure, and the rest of the defense team time to catch up on a backlog of trial preparation. But there were those who thought it an unnecessary kindness. This opinion especially gained ground among people who spotted Darrow in the afternoon at Waikīkī Beach, in a bathing suit, splashing in the waves and getting instructions on canoe paddling from Duke Kahanamoku and other beach boys.

Besides jury selection, everyone's attention that night was on the just-released Richardson Report. The bulldog edition of Tuesday's *Advertiser* gave the story a front-page banner headline, as did the *Star-Bulletin,* both of them saying the study called for "drastic changes" in the islands' governance, including a battery of new "federal controls." Leading the report's recommendations, said the newspapers, were proposals for a territorywide police force, on the order of state police, that would be headed by a man appointed by the U.S. president. In addition, the report's main author, Seth Richardson, suggested that the president be empowered to appoint an attorney general who would have "exclusive charge of prosecutions" throughout all the islands.

But the layouts, headlines, and subheads of the articles in both papers implied a far more draconian report, one apparently filled with calls for a federal near takeover of the government, than close attention to the articles or the report itself revealed. Only after following the front-page jumps into the newspapers' interior pages would readers discover that the federal investigators "were not impressed with the seriousness of alleged bad conditions at the public beaches" or with "public reports regarding the alleged proclivity of members of the Hawaiian race to sexual crime." On the contrary, the articles finally quoted the report, "investigations we made and tabulations we prepared do not show that crime, including sexual crime, in the Islands can properly be laid at the door of the Hawaiian."

The report, in fact, was a remarkable piece of work on many levels. Quantitatively, it actually was astonishing. The investigators had interviewed a multiracial collection of more than four hundred lawyers, judges, businesspeople, politicians, newspaper editors and reporters, prison officials, police officials, clergy, and various independently prominent men and women. The transcripts of those interviews filled 3,380 pages of typescript in fifteen unpublished volumes. The investigators had also combed through a huge body of government documents and statistical analyses of criminal and judicial data. The volume on conclusions and recommendations, separate from the interview volumes, was more than three hundred pages long, and it included scores of charts, tables, and exhibits. All of this was completed and released two months to the day after the investigative team arrived in Honolulu.

After sifting through all this information the Justice Department began its report with the statement: "We found in Hawaii no organized crime, no important criminal class, and no criminal rackets. We did not find substantial evidence that a crime wave, so called, was in existence in Honolulu, either disproportionate with the increase in the population or when viewed in comparison with crime records in cities of similar size on the mainland." Law enforcement conditions were "in good order," Richardson's executive summary concluded, "persons and property are reasonably safe," and "serious crimes . . . seem few in number and wholly sporadic." Finally, the U.S. assistant attorney general found "no evidence of the supposed racial turmoil that has filled countless mainland newspaper headlines for the past three months."

It was only after this preface that the Justice Department study suggested certain changes in the territory's police, court, and prison administrations. And even then it did so while admitting to a "lack of consistency" in "the mainland [asking] of Hawaii more law observance than it itself presents." Richardson's offered justification for the dual standard was that "the Territory's position as a military and naval post of great importance requires a higher degree of law enforcement in order to avoid embarrassment of the military and naval force." But none of the changes suggested in the report so much as hinted at martial law, while its conclusion firmly agreed with "the great majority of the citizens of the Territory [who] are opposed to a commission government."

In the end it was not any unusual level of crime or racial antagonism that was cause for concern, the report said, but rather "the violent partisanship [now] existing in the islands with respect to the pending rape and murder cases." In recognition of this social climate, Richardson wrote that he had "grave doubts" that the legislature did the right thing in eliminating the corroboration requirement in rape cases, especially in combination with its making rape a capital offense.

It took some days for the full report to reach Honolulu, and for readers of it to discover not only the material not reported in the press but, nearly two hundred pages into the document and among its appendixes, a long letter to the investigators from Admiral Yates Stirling. The letter was a ringing call for a change in Hawai'i's governmental structure to one of "limited suffrage" extended to "men primarily of the Caucasian race," under a federal commission including high-ranking U.S. Army and Navy officers. This hybrid of a political oligarchy and a military junta was justified by the admiral's contention that the islands should be governed not in a fashion similar to that of states on the mainland, but rather in the way that "ships of war" are ruled on the high seas. He found additional justification in the fact that the population of the islands included many potentially traitorous "orientals . . . [who] could be fanned into active race hatred in time of war," and mixed-race people who "are of a lower moral and mental caliber than the pure-blooded types of each race." Continued interbreeding, which now seemed inevitable, would only lead to ever "lower intellect and increasing degeneracy."

The fact that the federal investigators had rejected Stirling's inflammatory pronouncements and proposals may have been heartening to some nonwhite island residents. The fact that Stirling had made them was not. Hawaiian and Asian political leaders seethed, some of them openly expressing outrage, while the most powerful businessman in the islands, Walter Dillingham, took what he believed was a moderate position on the issue. Writing to the admiral's superiors in Washington, he said that the time might come for such a "radical change in government," but not yet. As for Stirling's racial views, Dillingham said, it remained "a debatable question whether from now on we should treat the children of Asiatic parents as enemies of the United States and deny them any of the privileges of citizenship."

But there was something else revealed by the split between Stirling's opinions and those of the Justice Department. Stirling's perspective was consonant with that of the outraged American media, most of Congress and the military, popular opinion throughout the United States, and Hawai'i's old-guard haole elite. The Justice Department's views, reflecting statistical data and extensive interviews with hundreds of island residents, were those of people looking closely at the evidence before them.

The rest of the week in court was taken up with continued jury selection. Slowly, one by one, jurors were found who agreed to serve and who were acceptable to both sides. But early in the morning on the initial day of voir dire Kelley and Darrow had sparred on a subject that continued to hover over the entire proceeding. It was fundamental to the trial to come.

When examining a prospective juror named Kenneth Bankston, Kelley asked: "Are you willing to return a verdict, understanding that the guilt or innocence of Joseph Kahahawai in the Ala Moana case has nothing to do with this present trial?"

Before Bankston could answer, Darrow was on his feet, his head thrust forward and his long arm pointing at the prosecutor. "If I have anything to do with it, the Ala Moana case will certainly have something to do with this trial," he interrupted. "I hardly think counsel should ask the jurors to ignore that matter."

"Wrong," Kelley snapped back. "As a matter of law, Joseph Kahahawai could be as guilty as any man could be, and still that does not provide an excuse for killing him." Darrow warned that the defense would not relent in resisting any effort to bar discussion of the Ala Moana case.

For his part, Darrow reversed matters. He insisted on asking prospective jurors questions about the rape case, with Kelley repeatedly objecting. And finally Barry Ulrich drew Darrow's wrath by taking it upon himself to instruct one man, Shadford Waterhouse, that the ultimate decision regarding the defendants' guilt or innocence "must rest on evidence, regardless of whether you think the crime was justified." If allowed to stand, this pronouncement would be a dagger in the heart of any defense strategy that appealed to a higher law, an "unwritten" law—that is, to a strategy of jury nullification. When Darrow objected, Ulrich turned to the bench and said: "May it please the court, this jury should be selected on the assurance that no appeal can be made to anything but the law itself."

"That isn't the law," Darrow angrily insisted. As with his earlier objections, Darrow's claimed legal principle was crucial to the defense he intended to mount, but protecting this particular juror from dismissal was another reason for the defense lawyer's heated criticism of Ulrich's flat declaration. Waterhouse's roots traced back to haole settlers in the mid-nineteenth century who had risen to prominence in white society, and both he and his father were officers of the Bishop First National Bank. His uncle John Waterhouse had been an officer of the bank as well before taking over as vice president and manager of Alexander & Baldwin, one of the Big Five corporations. Also like his father and his uncle, the twenty-seven-year-old Waterhouse was a graduate of Princeton.

If worse came to worst, it would take only one negative vote to prevent the jury from convicting Grace Fortescue and the others. To the defense team, Shadford Waterhouse looked like a person who could be trusted to do that. And the young man obviously was eager to be on the jury. In this, Waterhouse was typical of those on the jury panel who shared his elevated social and economic status. Counter to the general rule in most trials, in this case people with the most privileged backgrounds seemed far more willing to serve than did those who were less privileged.

Judge Davis said he would rule later on the dispute between Ulrich and Darrow regarding the freedom of a juror to follow his conscience if it conflicted with the law. But he suggested that the prosecution tread lightly. Ulrich resumed, converting his assertion into a question. "If, after all the evidence is in," he asked the prospective juror, "will you vote for conviction if you are convinced the crime was committed according to the law, regardless of your opinion of the rightness or wrongness of that law?" Darrow fumed, but did not object. Waterhouse said yes. The assistant prosecutor continued, asking if he would be able to convict an individual who was shown to be part of a conspiracy even if that person did not actually fire the fatal shot. Waterhouse said yes again. And finally, Ulrich asked if he would be able to convict Grace Fortescue for the crime of murder. After prefacing his question by saying that it was unfortunate a woman of such refinement and culture had found herself in this difficult predicament, he continued, "If you believe her guilty, regardless of your emotional reaction to the situation, will you vote for her conviction?" One last time, Waterhouse answered affirmatively.

And so it went. Under the recently revised legislation on court procedure, the defense and the prosecution now had an equal number of peremptory challenges, six for each defendant or a total of twenty-four. By the end of the second day each side had used eight. For attorneys who were on hand to watch, and for seasoned court observers, it became a fascinating tactical tug-of-war. But to the evidently weary wire-service reporters and other journalists who had traveled from afar to watch sparks fly, all that seemed to matter was how many whites and how many nonwhites were being seated. The rest was tedium.

Other spectators who had waited in line through the night for the first two sessions were growing restless and bored as well. This was hardly what they had expected. After two days of voir dire fewer casual observers showed up, while Mrs. Kluegel and her friends had devised a strategy for getting in. Police were handing out what were called "barber shop numbers," in order of appearance, to those who got in line early. Women with servants began routinely sending a maid or a gardener down to the courthouse in the middle of the night to get a number, which would then be surrendered to the employers, who arrived just before court opened. Women without servants, but with money to spare, let it be known that they were willing to buy low-number tickets for five dollars (Dillingham said up to ten dollars) each day.

Since five dollars could purchase a hundred balcony tickets to a movie matinee in Waikīkī (or in New York, two tickets to the latest Broadway musical), they had no shortage of takers.

By the end of the week almost the entire spectator section of the courtroom was filled with well-to-do white women who had come to show their support for Grace. In dozens of cities across the country where a Hearst newspaper was published, people read about the change. "No longer do the spectators consist of sullen rows of brown and yellow faces, with hard, unfriendly eyes," the Hearst wire story announced. "Today, white women, a whole delegation of them . . . were on hand to tender aid through their sustaining presence." Grace turned and smiled at her advocates, the account continued, "wanting the women of her own race to understand that she appreciated the strength of their presence."

The *Hawaii Hochi's* George Wright had a different response. Throughout the night "most of those who wait are yard boys or servants," he wrote, "but just before the doors open there is a swift change. High society dames arrive in silks and satins unruffled by exposure to the night elements and slip into the places that have been secured for them by accommodating servants who have endured the hardships in order that milady might enjoy her beauty sleep and still be assured of an opportunity to sate her morbid curiosity as she listens with twitching lips to the sordid story of a tragedy."

On Thursday, with an abruptness that surprised everyone, both sides moved to stop the skirmishing and wrap up jury selection. Perhaps it was the mood established that morning by a would-be juror named Walter Napoleon.

More than a hundred prospective jurors had been examined and each side had exhausted most of its peremptory challenges when the man, appearing to be in his early thirties and identifying himself as a meat cutter and manager for the Piggly Wiggly Market, took the stand. He made it clear from the beginning that he wanted no part of jury service. Judge Davis asked him why. Because he received a 30 percent commission on the meat he sold, Napoleon answered, and some of his customers were in the military. "I've met people on both sides of this case and if I formed an opinion it would hurt my business," he said. "That's why I'm not interested."

The forthrightness of his answer amused some spectators and interested the attorneys for both the prosecution and the defense. Judge Davis pressed on, suggesting that Napoleon consider that service on juries was an obligation of American citizenship. Napoleon said he hadn't thought of it that way. Attorney Winn stepped forward. He had supervised the background check on the venireman.

"You served in the Navy during the war, didn't you?" Winn asked. Napoleon acknowledged that he had. "And you're a member of the Mormon Church, aren't you?" Yes, he was. Speaking honestly, as a patriot and a religious person, had he formed any opinion regarding the guilt or innocence of the defendants? "No," Napoleon replied, "except that I felt that if anyone wanted to go out and commit a crime it was their business."

As courtroom spectators laughed, Winn asked the young man if he had any children. Of course he did, he was a good Mormon. How many? Seven, he answered. "Boys or girls?" Winn inquired. "Half and half," Napoleon answered, and everyone, including the attorneys and the judge, collapsed in laughter.

Finally Darrow stood and asked the meat cutter about his ethnicity. It was complicated, Napoleon said. He was an American, of course, but also a mixture of Hawaiian, Tahitian, French, Scotch, and Irish. And he spoke Japanese and Hawaiian, in addition to English. Dumbfounded—as was the *San Francisco Examiner* the next day, headlining a story "Juror Belongs to Six Races!"—Darrow asked what that made him, in terms of nationality. "League of Nations," Napoleon answered.

The defense and the prosecution each decided he would be fine on the jury. And before long the panel was complete.

Which side had won this initial round in the trial was open to question. For mainland newspapers that still found it difficult to accept a jury containing nonwhites, the fact that three men on the panel were Chinese and two more were Hawaiian seemed ominous. A disgusted Admiral Stirling said such a racially tainted group was little more than "a forum of the Orient," although he did concede that "the defendants could count upon the white men on the jury to vote not guilty." Less pessimistic supporters of the accused killers regarded the presence of seven whites on the jury, including one Portuguese, as a clear victory for Darrow. That's what *Time* thought, since "the final mottled jury . . . has a white element preponderantly higher than the average population of Hawaii."

But for local observers, who looked past the racial identifications, there was more important information available on the men who would decide the fate of the defendants. Of the twelve jurors on the panel, half had attended or graduated from college, including Princeton and Stanford—at a time when only about one in eight young Americans was pursuing higher education. Four were employees of Big Five corporations. Two more worked for enterprises owned by Walter Dillingham. And one was employed by a company that contracted its legal services to Thompson, Beebe & Winn, which had two of its partners seated at the defense table alongside Clarence Darrow and George Leisure. The foreman selected was John F. Stone, a forty-three-year-old mainland college graduate and an executive employee of Castle & Cooke Ltd., one of the Big Five.

In terms of social class and occupational affiliation, this was a jury far more closely allied with the defendants than with the victim, which no doubt is why Darrow later praised its collective intelligence. Equally important, as far as the defense was concerned, it would take only one of them to block a guilty verdict, assuming the vote wasn't unanimous for outright acquittal. And if it did turn out to be a hung jury—as Grace and almost everyone in Hawai'i and throughout the country expected—the territory would likely have no desire to try the case again. The defendants would walk free.

As they filed their stories on Thursday about jury selection being completed, many reporters commented on the openly amicable relationship that had developed between the prosecutor and the lead defense counsel, despite the intensity of their disagreements before the bench. At the close of that day's session the two men and their wives chatted about Darrow's autobiography, which Mrs. Kelley said she was then reading, and other matters of interest beyond the courtroom. "Astonishingly little acrimony has been shown in the case thus far," the New York Times's Russell Owen wrote, "and both sides seem willing to meet each other half way. One of Mr. Kelley's opponents said today: 'He is the most dangerous sort of prosecutor, because he is fair.'"

Most newspapers also mentioned in passing some new information that was circulating. The Times carried it in a small story under the headline "Alienists to Aid in Trial":

Honolulu, April 7. Two alienists who figured in notorious murder trials of Southern California and Arizona, arrived here tonight to confer with Clarence Darrow, the Chicago lawyer who heads the defense counsel for Mrs. Granville Fortescue and three naval men on trial for second degree murder. Defense counsel declined to comment upon the arrival of the alienists, Dr. Edward Huntington Williams and Dr. Thomas Orbison. Both physicians remained aboard the steamship Malolo on which they arrived. They were expected to confer with Mr. Darrow tomorrow.

When he picked up the newspapers the next day John Kelley exploded. He was furious, not with Darrow, but with himself. Clarence Darrow, the old fox, had sandbagged him. And he, the small-town rube, had fallen for it. Darrow had been under no obligation to tell Kelley about his plan to bring in psychiatrists when Kelley had asked him about an insanity plea the first time they met, but when Darrow had discounted the idea, the prosecutor, naively, had believed him.

Kelley called in the press, complaining publicly and threatening to delay the trial until he was able to bring in comparable experts to rebut those Darrow planned to use. Honolulu had its share of psychologists, of course, including several at the university. And there were any number of men around town who claimed to be in the mental health business. But there was no one within 2,500 miles—almost a week away—who could be expected to counterbalance the celebrated expertise of Darrow's two psychiatrists. In addition, the prosecution had no money in its budget to hire top-notch people even if it could find any and arrange for them to arrive in time to testify. Kelley could see the case slipping away before he had even delivered his opening statement.

Finally, the prosecutor became convinced that his public tirade was only making matters worse and that there was no way to delay the trial. The jury already was sequestered at the Alexander Young Hotel, the same hotel where the defense team had its rooms, and the judge could not now permit them to go home. Nor would he allow them to remain virtual prisoners during a court recess while the prosecution sought out its own psychiatric experts. Judge Davis would say, quite properly, that Kelley should have thought of bringing in mainland experts earlier. But there still might be time, if the money could be found and if he acted quickly.

Monday, April 11, was a warm day, filled with sunshine that poured through the open courtroom windows. With only a light breeze moving among the two hundred people in the large chamber—Admiral Stirling and Walter Dillingham seated themselves in the coolest spot beneath a window—spectators fanned themselves as Prosecutor Kelley rose to address the jury. He was dressed in a crisp and spotless white tropical suit, set off with a bright red necktie. Some court watchers said the tie was an homage to a famous Chicago prosecutor Darrow would have known, an Irishman nicknamed "Red Tie" O'Brien for his habit of wearing such distinctive haberdashery when trying murder cases. Others said it was intended to remind Darrow of

Robert E. Crowe, the prosecutor in the Leopold and Loeb case. Either way, reported the *New York Times,* Kelley "presented a marked contrast to the grimly angular form of Clarence Darrow, whose hair was strewn over his head in what Mrs. Darrow calls a wind blown swirl."

It was 9:01 a.m. Speaking without notes, Kelley approached the jury box and leaned on the rail, surveying the twelve men seated in front of him. "Gentlemen of the jury," he began, "these defendants are charged with the crime of murder in the second degree." He read the indictment, then said: "In order that you may follow the course of the evidence, I will outline briefly what the Territory will endeavor to prove to you."

For the next forty-seven minutes the prosecutor briskly and systematically laid out the case against the defendants, striding back and forth before the jurors, one hand occasionally in his jacket pocket while the other gestured for emphasis. He began with the morning of January 8, when "Joseph Kahahawai came to this building . . . according to Judge Steadman's orders. On that last journey he was accompanied by Edward Uli'i, his cousin. As they approached this building three persons were outside who soon would put into action forces that would end Kahahawai's life." Kelley turned and pointed out Deacon Jones, Tommie Massie, and Grace Fortescue. After Kahahawai and Uli'i left the building, he continued, "and arrived almost to the statue of Kamehameha, under the shadow of its outstretched hand, the finger of doom pointed at one of the members of that king's people. That finger was pointed by Mrs. Fortescue."

Step by step, sometimes minute by minute, Kelley took the jury through every detail of what had occurred that January morning, painting a sequence of vivid images with his words. He told them of the false summons, and of Uli'i attempting to join Kahahawai in the getaway car before being pushed away. The prosecutor then jumped ahead in time, to the police pursuit of the car carrying Kahahawai's dead body. He described the capture of the defendants and their demeanor. He described the condition of the body. He told of the police finding the victim's clothes in the car, and he dwelt upon the rope that bound the body, a distinctive hemp cord with a purple thread running through it. He told them of the authorities' encounter with Deacon Jones at the Massie house, "which by a twist of fate is on Kahawai Street," and of the police later finding, concealed in Jones's trousers, the false summons that had been used to lure Kahahawai.

Then Kelley described for the jury what had been discovered in Grace Fortescue's rented cottage, including two guns, a .45- and a .32-caliber revolver, several steel-jacketed bullets, and Mrs. Fortescue's purse "with Kahahawai's picture so placed that it could always be seen when the purse was opened." They also found a damp towel with blood on it, blood on the floor, and a coil of rope identical to the one that had been wrapped around the body. It was a type of rope, the prosecutor noted, that could not be purchased in Honolulu, but was commonly in use at the Pearl Harbor Naval Base.

As he carefully and systematically previewed the evidence he would soon present, Kelley was doing more than demonstrating the responsibility of the defendants for Joe Kahahawai's death. He was directing everything toward two key conclusions. First, he argued, the murder was premeditated. Second, the killing was cold-blooded and not done in self-defense.

When Kelley finished his opening statement, saying that after all the evidence was presented he was confident the jury would find the defendants guilty as charged, Judge Davis turned to Darrow. The defense attorney said he would reserve his opening until completion of the prosecution's case. So Kelley began, calling as his first witness Edward Uli'i.

Uli'i testified to the abduction of his cousin, identifying Deacon Jones and Grace Fortescue as the people he recognized from the scene of the kidnapping. Grace never got over the indignity of having "the insignificant native . . . fix his hard black eyes on me, slowly raising his hand with a pointing finger," she wrote later. Uli'i's cross-examination by the defense was only cursory, but Kelley had used the occasion to introduce his first exhibits: the fake summons; Jones's gold dragon ring; photographs and diagrams of the Judiciary Building and the place of the abduction; and then, piece by piece, Kahahawai's clothing, including his bloodstained blue shirt with a bullet hole through the left breast.

His next witness was the probation officer Kahahawai had seen that morning. He was followed by the arresting officers and by a photographer who had taken pictures of the defendants and the arrest scene on the cliff near Hanauma Bay. All described what they had witnessed, in conformity with what Kelley had promised in his opening. As before, cross-examination was either passed or was done briefly and without consequence. And with each new witness Kelley introduced more physical evidence. At one point, referring back to Kahahawai's clothing, he picked up the undershorts, blue and white, with a pattern of small black diamond shapes and with the buttons ripped off. And, again, the blood-spattered shirt containing the bullet hole. He held them aloft, pausing silently, and then handed them to the jury for their examination. More than one juror turned and looked away. Grace Fortescue, according to a reporter, visibly flinched. And Joseph Kahahawai's mother, Esther Anito, began to sob.

Darrow stood and asked that the victim's mother be removed from the courtroom. Judge Davis denied the request. Hesitating for a moment, Kelley decided this was an exchange he wanted the jurors to remember. It was 12:23 p.m. He asked for, and was granted, adjournment for the day.

On Tuesday, April 12, the courtroom was as warm and as crowded as the day before. The press reported that the lineup for seats had begun well before 5:00 a.m., with many hopeful spectators bringing folding chairs and sandwiches and thermoses filled with coffee. Kelley picked up where he had left off, swearing in another police officer from the scene of the arrest and introducing more physical evidence—in this case, the twenty-foot length of rope that had bound Kahahawai's body. With this and with the succeeding witness, Darrow halfheartedly cross-examined for a combined total of less than three minutes, eliciting nothing of consequence.

The third witness of the day was Dr. Robert B. Faus, the city and county physician who had performed the autopsy on the victim. Kelley's direct examination took just over half an hour, during which time he introduced photographs of blood spots on the floor of the Fortescue cottage, the .32-caliber steel-jacketed bullet that had been removed from Joe Kahahawai's body, and a government-issue hand towel stained with blood and bearing the letters "USN" in blue. As Kelley held up the towel the courtroom grew silent, with one reporter writing the next day that the blood and the initials of the U.S. Navy seemed to symbolize the entire trial. Then, in succession, Kelley introduced Kahahawai's wristwatch and his class ring from St. Louis High School, both of which had been removed from the naked body by the coroner.

The prosecutor asked Dr. Faus to describe the victim. He was a well-built young Hawaiian male, Faus said, about six feet tall and perhaps 190 pounds, with especially muscular shoulders and upper torso. Kelley referred to a Red Cross medical chart and asked the physician to trace the path of the bullet and describe the cause of death. The shot had been fired from the front and off to one side, the doctor said, with the bullet following a downward course into the left side of the victim's chest, two or three inches above his nipple, and finally lodging to the right of the seventh dorsal vertebra. "The chest was filled with blood, four or five liters," Faus testified, "and the cause of death was hemorrhage from a bullet wound penetrating the left pulmonary artery." There were no other signs of injury.

Kelley then passed a photograph to the jurors showing Joe Kahahawai's dead body, marked to indicate where the bullet had entered the chest. With no other injuries apparent, on his body or on those of the defendants, it was clear that there had not been a struggle. And the pathway of the bullet, fired from above, left no doubt that Kahahawai had been sitting down, and his killer standing, when the murder took place.

For the first time, Darrow conducted a cross-examination that was more than perfunctory. He asked precisely where the bullet had lodged, and whether or not it had touched the spine. Was there water in the victim's lungs? How old did the bloodstains on the floor of the house appear to be? Might they have been there for some time before the day in question? Then back to the exact location of the bullet that the doctor had removed. And again to the matter of water in the lungs. The questioning lasted less than ten minutes and accomplished little. But it probably was not intended to do more than interrupt the momentum and emotional force that the prosecution's case was now developing.

Throughout the rest of that day and all of the next the parade of witnesses continued: the detectives who examined the cottage, two neighbors who heard the gunshot, the rental-car clerks who identified the defendants, a police matron who had searched Grace and reported discovering in her coat pocket two long strips of cloth containing laundry marks. And with each witness Kelley added more physical evidence: photographs of Grace Fortescue's bed with its sheets removed, the fake summons used to lure the victim into the rented car, receipts for the purchase of two guns and several boxes of .32-caliber bullets, the pearl buttons that had been ripped from Kahahawai's undershorts, and more.

For many the most riveting moment occurred when the prosecution called to the stand Vasco Rosa, who had sold Deacon Jones the gun that was now missing. As the witness waited, Kelley carefully placed in front of him the cartridge clip, with one bullet missing, that had been found concealed in Jones's clothing. Next to that he put the empty shell that also had been found on Jones's person, and alongside it he stood on end an unfired bullet found in the house where the killing occurred. The witness testified that the bullet was identical to those in the clip, and the empty shell matched the others as well.

Then the prosecutor opened an envelope marked "Exhibit 18" and removed the slug that the coroner had taken out of Joe Kahahawai's body. It was clean and hardly marked, having only passed through tissue without making contact with bone. Kelley added that to the row of items now in front of the witness. After a pause, as he walked away from the witness, giving the courtroom time to fall into silence, Kelley asked Rosa to pick up the slug that had been removed from the victim's body and try to insert it into the empty cartridge that had been found on Jones. It fit perfectly.

The next day's press reports described the prosecution's case as overwhelming. Even the Hearst papers, despite their lengthy articles and editorials thick with unabashed support for the defendants, could not help but describe Kelley's presentation as powerful and skilled. That did not prevent their reporters from complaining about "the unnecessary display" of physical evidence that sometimes sent a "shudder through the white women who came to the courtroom to give their moral support to the patrician mother and her three co-defendants." An especially objectionable moment of this sort occurred, one Hearst story said, when Kelley instructed a policeman to hold up the sheets in which Kahahawai's body had been wrapped, with their "dark stains of blood, apparent to everyone in court, [causing] a chilling hush to settle upon the spectators."

Darrow's restraint in cross-examination at first puzzled the press. Then, with a rush of unanimity, reporters decided that it was part of an overall master plan. It was only a matter of time, the Hearst news service reported, before "the wily leader in many spectacular defensive court fights will seize upon testimony . . . to free the four Americans." Describing the unfolding scenes as "an almost unbelievable fantasy, with all the plot and setting of a good detective story," the *Chicago Tribune* described the defense as "waiting to spring a story of justification which now can only be guessed at." Whatever Darrow had planned, the *Tribune* writer assured his readers, "the stage is set for one of the most dramatic courtroom plays ever enacted."

Actually, the reason for Darrow's restraint was much simpler: he wanted the damaging testimony to end as quickly as possible. There was no benefit to be derived from prolonging the floodtide of incriminating evidence with lengthy objections or cross-examinations. As Darrow later wrote in his memoirs, "All the attorneys for the prosecution, and those for the defense, as well as the judge, knew that legally my clients were guilty of murder." Darrow had no desire to challenge vainly Kelley's seamless narrative. Instead, he planned to tell a different story, a counternarrative.

And now, after three days and twenty-six witnesses, the prosecution was about to wrap things up. It was Thursday morning, April 14, and Kelley announced that he had just one final witness to call: Mrs. Esther Anito, Joseph Kahahawai's mother.

Darrow had attempted to derail this testimony earlier, meeting in Judge Davis's chambers with Kelley and arguing that it was unnecessary and could be prejudicial to his clients. Davis disagreed. Now, in the courtroom, Darrow preferred not to object openly to the testimony, sensing that his effort two days earlier to have Mrs. Anito ejected for weeping had not been received well by the jurors. But the last thing he wanted, as Kelley well knew, was emotional prosecution testimony just before he was to begin putting on his own case. So he gave it a last try and had one of the local attorneys, Montgomery Winn, attempt to prevent her from taking the stand.

Winn stood as the witness's name was called and asked: "What is the purpose of this testimony?" To have the victim's mother identify her son's clothing, Kelley said, the clothing he wore on the day he was murdered. "The defense will stipulate that the clothing entered as evidence is the clothing worn by the deceased man on the day he died," the defense attorney replied. Kelley said he preferred to have Mrs. Anito identify the individual items. Judge Davis told him to go ahead.

Esther Anito was a large but graceful middle-aged woman, dressed in a white *kīkepa*—a Hawaiian version of the sarong that in Tahiti is called a *pareau*—and a white *lau hala,* or woven pandanus-leaf hat. Several newspaper correspondents were struck by her reserved and formal bearing, not knowing that since her divorce from Joseph's father and the onset of the Depression she had worked sewing burlap bags at a fertilizer factory in Pālama. After hesitating before the bench as the attorneys argued about the necessity of her testifying, she took the witness stand when the judge nodded for her to do so.

Mrs. Anito's testimony was brief, barely ten minutes, and for the duration it seemed as though no one in the courtroom moved. Kelley asked about her marriage to Joe's father and about any other children they had. She and Joseph Kahahawai Sr. were divorced now, she said. They had had four children, she continued, but two of them died at an early age. "Only two are now living, Joseph and Lillian."

"Is Joseph alive?" a surprised Kelley asked, but before he could finish Mrs. Anito realized her error and said: "No. No—he is dead." Her voice came out "like a faint wail," wrote the *Times*'s Russell Owen. "She did not become hysterical or cry noisily," then or later, he reported, "but held herself with dignity and sometimes used her handkerchief to dry her eyes." When did she last see him? At the undertaker's, she said, before he was buried.

Had Joseph been living with her until the time of his death? Yes, she answered, with her and her second husband. When did she last see her son alive? Early on the morning of January 8, when he left home for his appointment at the courthouse. She began looking down as she spoke, dabbing at her eyes, and the judge asked her to lift her head so that the jurors and the court reporter could hear her testimony.

Then, piece by piece, the prosecutor handed Mrs. Anito the clothing her son had worn on the day he was shot. She affirmed that those were the clothes he had on that day. The shoes, the socks, the dungarees, the shorts, the cap found by police in Grace Fortescue's home, the bloody shirt with its bullet hole. She had washed and mended everything the night before, she said. And no, there had been no buttons missing when he left that morning.

The prosecution rested.

One emotionally moved veteran attorney was quoted in the press as saying, "If these were not white people and Navy people, there would be a hanging here."

Indeed, every newspaper reporter covering the trial agreed that Kelley's prosecution had been devastating. Only one question remained unanswered. Which of the four defendants had pulled the trigger and actually committed the murder? From the start the prosecution had argued that it was a question without relevance, since all the defendants had conspired in the abduction and thus were equally guilty of the killing. But to Clarence Darrow nothing in the entire case was more important than that question because of the way he intended to answer it.

23 Dementia Americana

At the outset of the trial Judge Davis had banned smoking and cameras from his courtroom. Soon, in response to threats on John Kelley's life, he added guns to the list of prohibited items.

Hate mail from throughout the United States and addressed to Kelley began showing up at his office as soon as it was announced that he would be prosecuting the murder case. Most letters were one variation or another on the theme that he was "not only a disgrace to American manhood but a reproach to the entire WHITE race, a stench in the nostrils of ALL right thinking people," to cite one carefully typed message from San Francisco. But others, invariably unsigned, threatened violence or death, so Judge Davis decided to err on the side of caution. Everyone entering the courthouse, including Kelley and Darrow, was required to be searched for weapons.

Judge Davis called the court to order following the morning recess, and the old Chicago lawyer rose from his chair. Emotions in the crowd had remained high after the quietly tearful testimony of Joe Kahahawai's mother. And now Darrow was expected to unfurl a powerful rhetorical argument for the defense. Instead, for the second time, he waived his opening. "The defense calls Lieutenant Thomas H. Massie." A rumble of surprise and disappointment passed through the courtroom among those expecting a dramatic opening speech. But it quickly quieted as the slight and pale-complexioned navy lieutenant made his way to the stand.

Tommie was dressed in a dark gray civilian suit, white shirt, and beige tie. He appeared to be very nervous and had difficulty controlling the tone and volume of his voice as he was sworn in and began answering the first questions about his name, his age, his profession, his place of birth, his education. But Darrow was soothing, his arms folded, head bowed, shoulders hunched forward as he asked the questions in a soft voice. Gradually, he brought the young officer to that September evening seven months earlier, and to his attendance with his wife at a party and dance at the Ala Wai Inn.

Immediately, prosecutor Kelley interrupted with a question. "We wish to offer no unnecessary objections to this line of testimony," he said, "but if counsel intends to go into the Ala Moana case . . . there are only certain conditions under which it can be admitted." He was, he said, referring to an insanity defense. For the past two days the psychiatric experts hired by the defense had been sitting in the courtroom.

Darrow replied that he did indeed "expect to raise the question of insanity" regarding "the one who shot the pistol."

Judge Davis said he thought that answered Kelley's question, but the prosecutor replied that it addressed only part of it. He objected to any further testimony from Lieutenant Massie on the subject of the Ala Moana case unless Darrow specifically named him as, in the defense attorney's words, "the one who shot the pistol" and therefore the one on whose behalf the insanity plea would be entered.

This was the first direct mention of a key matter at the core of both the prosecution and the defense cases. Which of the defendants had actually killed Joseph Kahahawai? The murder weapon had not been recovered, but he had been shot with a steel-jacketed bullet from a .32-caliber automatic, and only one such gun was known to have been in the possession of the defendants and never found—the one purchased and owned by Deacon Jones. Kelley took the position that it didn't matter which of the defendants had fired the gun. If any one of them had pulled the trigger, he contended, all of them were equally guilty. But an insanity defense could complicate the matter.

Well aware of this, Darrow, smiling broadly, now turned the prosecution's argument back against itself, pointing out to Kelley and the court that if the one who shot the pistol was to be found not guilty by reason of insanity, then all the defendants were equally innocent and should go free. After all, it would not make legal sense or common sense to convict as accomplices people who had not fired the gun while acquitting the one who had fired it. But Kelley was not satisfied, with the law or with the logic supporting Darrow's claim or with the defense attorney's refusal to answer his question. "We have the right to know which defendant this plea is going to be presented for," he said, so that psychiatric experts for the prosecution could have an opportunity to examine that person. After exerting all the political pressure on the governor that he could muster, Kelley had received funding to hire outside psychiatrists: the same two men who had bested Darrow's experts when they testified at the Winnie Judd trial two months earlier. They were preparing to board a ship headed for Honolulu at that moment.

With a gesture of magnanimity, the defense attorney said he would be happy to have physicians come to court and observe—from the spectator section—any and all witnesses called for the defense. But he certainly would not allow direct psychiatric examination by the prosecution's experts of Lieutenant Massie or any of Darrow's other clients. The prosecution's opportunity to do that had passed long ago.

And Darrow was right. The prosecution had rested its case. Any psychiatric experts it now called would be rebuttal witnesses, and the law did not require that the defendants be made available to them. If the prosecution had wanted them examined it should have done so prior to the trial. Of course, for most of that time Kelley had not been the prosecutor and the defendants had not been easily accessible, since they were being held under navy custody on the USS *Alton*. But it would not have been impossible to examine them, and Kelley knew that. He was still paying for his gullibility when Darrow had casually dismissed the option of an insanity defense on the day they first met.

Judge Davis ruled that Darrow should proceed. For the next hour, following the defense attorney's gentle prodding, Tommie Massie unfolded a tale of agony and bitter torment. It was the same story that Thalia had told the jurors at the previous trial, differing only in detail and perspective. The altered detail concerned Joe Kahahawai: in Thalia's testimony—prior to Kahahawai's murder—he had been but one of the five men she said had raped her, while in Tommie's telling he was the brutal leader of the gang. As for the difference in perspective, while it was Thalia who had been physically assaulted, it was Tommie who had been forced to bear an especially crushing psychological burden—the burden of having failed to protect his wife.

In describing Thalia's appearance upon his arrival home on the fateful night when the men had "beaten her and taken her to a place and ravished her," Tommie spoke of blood pouring from her nose and mouth, her lips "crushed and bruised," her eyes swollen from the violence. As he took her in his arms she cried, "I want to die! I hope to die!" And he was helpless as "she just stayed there in my arms and cried and sobbed. She was completely broken." Upon being admitted to the hospital the next day, he said, the physicians described her as in "critical condition."

Still, he testified, when the authorities "brought four of the assailants in for identification," Thalia mustered the strength and courage to identify them—concentrating, he said, on Kahahawai. Not wanting to have innocent men unfairly accused of a crime, Tommie recalled, he "leaned over the bed" and urged his wife, "Please, darling, don't let there be any doubt in your mind, because you know what that means." And then "the tears came into her eyes and she said, 'Don't you know if there was any doubt in my mind I couldn't ever draw an easy breath as long as I live?'" The words were coming smoothly and easily now as Tommie confidently settled into his testimony.

Because he had so little money after paying the hospital bills, Tommie said, he could not afford the twenty-four-hour home nursing care that Thalia needed for weeks following the assault. "So I got a day nurse and acted as night nurse myself." During those long and sleepless nights as he watched over her, Thalia would bolt into wakefulness, screaming, "Don't let him get me! Don't let him get me!" He would hold her and say, "It's all right, darling, nobody is here but me," and she would reply that there was someone else there: "Kahahawai." Although on those occasions Tommie said he knew that Thalia had been dreaming, on another night he himself heard footsteps outside their window. He rushed outside with a gun. "I didn't see anyone, but I know someone was there."

For a month after the attack, Tommie testified, he hardly slept at all, lost his appetite, and began growing thinner than he had ever been before. It was then, he said, that Dr. Porter, Thalia's physician, "explained that we would have to expect two things that were possible, disease and conception. Those were the things that preyed on my mind every minute of the day—worse than anything I could imagine."

In reply to a question from Darrow, Tommie continued: "After Mrs. Massie's mother came we knew that an operation would be necessary to prevent pregnancy. That had a strange effect on my mind."

"Was it done, the operation?"

"Yes, I took her to the hospital and Dr. Withington performed the operation."

"Did you know or did she know that the pregnancy was due to you or not?"

"There couldn't be any doubt that it wasn't."

Darrow glanced at the clock. It was 12:37. The tragedy of Thalia's aborted pregnancy—and the "strange effect" it had on Tommie's mind—was a perfect note on which to end the day's testimony. He asked for and was granted adjournment until 9:00 a.m. on Friday.

Throughout the courtroom, the press reported, many women were openly weeping. Grace Fortescue was sitting stiffly with tears rolling down her cheeks, never raising a hand or a handkerchief to brush them away. Thalia had not yet attended any court sessions, but as Tommie stepped down from the witness chair Grace took him by the arm affectionately and led him away to where she said Thalia was waiting for them.

The women who had endured an all-night vigil to be certain they would be admitted to the courtroom that day had been amply rewarded for their perseverance. They promptly marched back outside and opened their folding chairs on the lawn so as to guarantee that they would be the first people in line for Friday's session, nearly twenty hours away.

Other than the trial, few topics could hold most people's attention for very long that day or night, not even the arrests of two men for sexually assaulting two girls, aged fourteen and five. But the men were white and the girls were not, and as one wire story put it: "Only for a short time did the arrest of the whites on sex charges serve to divert attention from the drama that has been unfolding in the historic 'House of the Chiefs.'"

Understandably, Clarence Darrow was delighted with the way the day had gone. Tommie's performance on the witness stand had been superb and especially welcome after the daily parade of prosecution witnesses all week. In fact, so pleased was Darrow with his morning's work that he spent the greater part of that night in his hotel suite with a gathering of mainland newsmen, drinking 'ōkolehao and talking. As the evening and the alcohol flowed on, he wound up describing with anticipatory triumph his strategy for the rest of the trial.

That strategy, several correspondents reported the next day—without citing their source or the conditions under which the information was gathered—included having Tommie confess to killing Kahahawai while in a state of profound distress. Darrow "will develop that the spark that touched off the explosion in Lieutenant Massie's brain was a statement made by the half-caste native after he was kidnapped," said the Hearst wire service account. "It is reported that Kahahawai was brazen, defiant, that he laughed at his captors, taunted them, and was even boastful. Darrow feels confident that no jury would convict anyone after hearing Lieutenant Massie's story, the basis of which is 'alarm clock' insanity."

To prove Tommie's insanity, the defense would rely on its two psychiatric experts. And just to tie everything up and end with a flourish, tens of millions of Americans read in their newspapers the next day, Darrow planned to call the navy officer's young wife, Thalia, to the stand.

But not quite yet. On Friday morning Darrow was too hung over to attend court. He pleaded an attack of gastritis, and that day's session was canceled.

On Thursday, when the prosecution had rested and the defense opened its case, a local reporter had called attention to the presence of some recognizable people in the crowd who had not attended previous sessions. One was the British consul. Another was a University of Hawai'i professor named E. Lowell Kelly. The reporter knew only that Kelly was a psychologist. He was unaware that the young professor had examined Thalia the previous summer, a month or so before the eventful night in Waikīkī. After going through several counseling sessions, and having her fill out an extensive case history questionnaire, Kelly had decided that Thalia was seriously in need of psychiatric help.

During the fall of 1931 Kelly had kept up with the assault trial in the same way that most haoles in Honolulu did, by reading the *Advertiser* and *Star-Bulletin*. Those two newspapers, unlike the *Hawaii Hochi*, refused to print the name of the alleged rape victim in the case. It was only after the murder of Joe Kahahawai that Professor Kelly, along with many of the city's residents, learned that the accuser of Kahahawai and his four friends was a young navy officer's wife named Thalia Massie. "On discovering that Mrs. Massie was the plaintiff in the rape trial," he wrote years later in a letter to Governor Judd, "I could not but doubt the validity of her accusations. But since my doubts were based on information which I had obtained while counseling with her about her emotional problems, I was in a quandary as to whether I should communicate my doubts to anyone else."

In search of advice, Kelly turned to a friend on the university staff, Dr. Robert Faus—the same Dr. Faus who, in his other post as city and county physician, had performed the autopsy on Kahahawai. Kelly was especially conflicted over possible use of the case history questionnaire in a retrial of the rape case. He was convinced that Thalia's accusations were false and that the documents in his file would establish that likelihood by undermining her credibility. But he also was concerned about the privileged nature of the information Thalia had given him. Faus advised Kelly that, in his opinion, the information was not legally privileged because Kelly was not a physician—he was a psychologist, not a psychiatrist—and the materials therefore would be subject to subpoena.

Kelly was now torn. One man had already been murdered because of what he believed to be Thalia's fabricated story, while the four remaining defendants might well be convicted in a second trial and given life sentences unless he came forward with what he knew. But he also was unconvinced by the legal opinion Dr. Faus had given him. Regardless of what the law said, Kelly felt it professionally improper to violate the privacy of someone he had counseled.

Two days after Kelly's appearance at the trial a deputy attorney general named Harold Kay showed up at the office of the university president, David L. Crawford. Professor Kelly was on Maui, Kay said, and authorities urgently needed some materials of his. President Crawford went to Kelly's office, removed the file on Mrs. Thalia Massie, and gave it to the deputy attorney general.

The trial was moving at a snail's pace. With both sides' concurrence, Judge Davis announced that from then on court would be held six days a week, and so on Saturday, April 16, the trial resumed after a one-day hiatus. Darrow looked refreshed. Tommie was back on the stand.

Darrow opened the morning by stating that he wished to clarify something. Although still insisting that the prosecution was incorrect in arguing that he was obligated to say in advance whether it was Lieutenant Massie who had fired the shot that killed Kahahawai, Darrow announced that he was willing to provide the requested information anyway. "The evidence will show," he announced, "that the defendant Massie, now on the stand, held the gun in his hand from which the fatal shot was fired in this case."

It was an oddly evasive locution, phrased passively, but Kelley and Judge Davis took it to mean that Tommie had killed Kahahawai. After more of the same sort of jousting that had interrupted the start of the preceding day's testimony on the technicalities of the insanity defense, Darrow decided to clarify his earlier clarification. Addressing the judge, he said: "Your Honor, we expect the evidence to show that this defendant was insane. I did not say that he would testify that he killed the deceased. We will show that the gun was in his hand when the shot was fired, but that the question as to whether he knew what he was doing at the time is another question."

Kelley and his assistant, Barry Ulrich, then took turns in saying they wanted to know, since the defense was prepared to demonstrate that Massie had once been insane, whether it also was able to demonstrate that he presently was sane. If not, then he wasn't qualified to testify. They also wished for Darrow to explain what type of insanity Massie had been—and perhaps still was—laboring under, so that psychiatrists for the prosecution might properly address the question. Darrow, uncharacteristically, became flustered. Neither he nor "anybody on earth" could say precisely what type of mental illness someone was suffering from in the past, he said: "There are so many different kinds and so many different doctors disagree among themselves as to what class they fall in. It is quite impossible."

Kelley smiled and said, "I quite agree with counsel in that respect."

Judge Davis told them to move on. Within minutes Darrow had Tommie recounting the effects that the mistrial in the rape case had had on him. He was "confused and perplexed," Tommie said. And what other difficulties had followed in the wake of the verdict? The "vile and low" rumors that had been spreading prior to the trial now escalated, Massie testified, rumors claiming that he and Thalia were getting a divorce. Rumors that he knew she had lied about the rape and hadn't attended the trial for that reason. Rumors that what really happened on the night of September 12 was his returning home to find Thalia in bed with another naval officer, causing him to beat her up. Rumors that Thalia "had never been assaulted at all and was simply a seeker of notoriety who wanted to get into the headlines."

It was then, Tommie said, that he had gone to see attorney Eugene Beebe, who informed him that nothing less than a confession was likely to result in a conviction of the rape defendants. But, Tommie said, Beebe cautioned that "no force was to be used and no marks should show"—which was why anything that Horace Ida might have said during his beating was inadmissible.

From this point on, to the surprise of many in the courtroom, Tommie's recounting of Kahahawai's abduction was identical to what the prosecution had spent the better part of its case describing. The only difference was on the matter of the false mustache Edward Uli'i said Massie had been wearing when disguising himself as a chauffeur. Tommie insisted that he had not worn one.

The admissions continued with Tommie describing the four murder defendants bringing Kahahawai into Grace Fortescue's cottage and seating him in the living room. At that point, Tommie said, after removing his gloves and hat and dark glasses, he picked up Deacon Jones's .32 automatic, "pulled back the catch and let it flip in place. I wanted to scare him as much as possible."

There then followed, Tommie testified, a lengthy interrogation during which he, Kahahawai, Seaman Lord, and Grace were present. Grace had told Deacon Jones to wait outside. Tommie, seated across from Kahahawai, repeatedly accused the young Hawaiian of kidnapping, beating, and raping his wife. Kahahawai denied it again and again. Finally, Grace spoke up. "There's no use fooling around with him any longer," Tommie quoted her as saying. "He will just sit there and lie all day. Let's carry out our other plan." The other plan, as Tommie said he explained it to Kahahawai, was to have Lord and Jones, along with a fictitious gang of sailors supposedly waiting outside the house, come in and "beat him to ribbons." What they had done to Horace Ida was nothing compared to what they would do to him, Tommie recalled telling Kahahawai.

Then suddenly, he said, Kahahawai blurted out, "Yes, we done it." And that was all Tommie remembered until the police were taking him, Grace, and Lord into custody an hour or so later. At that time "a bunch of people, some of them were in uniform . . . talked about a body," he testified. "I remember that word" but nothing else. He did not recall firing any shots or traveling in the rented car to the scene of the arrest, he claimed. He also had no idea what became of the gun. Darrow, after a long pause, quietly asked, "Do you know what became of you?" And Tommie answered, "No, sir."

"That is all," Darrow told the court.

As *Time* magazine noted, alongside photographs of Kelley and Darrow, the situation might have come "straight out of Greek drama," were not "the husband a Kentuckian and the ravisher a brown-skinned buck."

After a fifteen-minute recess, the trial resumed with cross-examination. Kelley strode quickly to the witness box and asked Tommie if he had ever entertained thoughts of killing Kahahawai. Tommie said no.

Never? Not even when he was at the hospital with Thalia and she identified Kahahawai and three of the other defendants? The navy officer, unruffled, admitted that he might have "felt like it" at that time, "but I never thought of it. I knew that was no way."

For an hour Kelley hammered away in a fruitless effort to erode the defendant's composure. By having Tommie admit in advance to almost everything for which there was evidence in the prosecution's case, Darrow had left Kelley with little else to do. It was a disarming, if risky, defense.

After failing to get Tommie to admit that he had considered killing Kahahawai in the days and weeks immediately following the attack on Thalia, Kelley tried another, more oblique approach. He inquired as to where Tommie was born, and when the defendant said Kentucky the prosecutor asked if he was proud to be a southerner. Darrow immediately objected, asking what the purpose of that question was. "I don't know. I just want to find out," Kelley answered. "Well I do know," Darrow said, "and the purpose of the question is to create prejudice," fully aware that the prosecutor was preparing to embark on a discussion of racism and lynching.

"We are concerned here with a man who claims he killed a man by reason of insanity," Kelley countered. "On the motivating impulses that led this man to become insane, we can trace them back to the cradle, and we so desire to do that." It is those impulses, born of youthful experience in a particular social environment, he added, that "create a condition of mind."

Judge Davis said he tended to agree with that general principle, but not with the contention "that the witness's pride has any bearing on the issues in this case," so he sustained the objection.

Kelley continued on, trying to find a way in. He attempted to show premeditation by the presence in Grace's cottage of the rope from the navy shipyard that had bound Kahahawai's body. Tommie said he had brought it home months earlier to tie up his dog and he had no idea what it was doing in Mrs. Fortescue's home.

The prosecutor asked why he had used Jones's .32 to frighten Kahahawai and not his own "more impressive" .45, which was found in the house. Tommie shrugged: "A gun is a gun to me."

Kelley brought up the matter of Admiral Pratt's widely publicized cable on the eve of the murder that appeared to justify lynching. The defendant said he recalled hearing some reference to those words, but only long after the killing. The prosecutor asked about Grace's interview with the *New York Times* in which she expressed no remorse and, by saying they had "bungled" the job by lowering the shade in their car and calling attention to themselves, in effect admitted that the killing was planned. Massie said he hadn't read the article and knew nothing about its contents.

Although by asking these questions Kelley at least was able to put Admiral Pratt's and Grace's compromising statements before the jury, nothing Kelley asked Tommie got the prosecutor anywhere with the well-coached defendant. After Kahahawai supposedly said, "Yes, we done it," Tommie insisted repeatedly, he had no memory of anything for the next hour. And he was well prepared for every trick the prosecutor employed in trying to uncover an inconsistency. Time and again, while discussing other matters, Kelley would switch back to the moment of the killing and its aftermath, seeking to elicit from the defendant some detail that would give the lie to his alleged memory loss. But with the exception of one or two near slips, Tommie stuck to his story.

The *Chicago Tribune*'s Philip Kinsley had watched Darrow in court for years and he recognized the handiwork. "Massie kept himself well under control," he wrote the next day, describing the testimony as "perfectly staged, timed, and presented by that master showman of criminal trials, Darrow."

Over the weekend Kelley met informally with reporters in his office and openly described as "bunk" the claim that Tommie had pulled the trigger but couldn't remember doing so. In fact, the prosecutor said, he was certain Tommie had not even done the killing, but was covering up for someone else. He didn't explicitly add—not yet, at least—that Tommie was accepting responsibility for "holding the gun in his hand from which the fatal shot was fired" because, as Thalia's husband, he had the strongest claim to moral outrage and temporary insanity in response to Kahahawai's alleged confession.

Kelley had a long list of reasons for suspecting that the killer was Jones. It was his gun, though still missing, that had presumably fired the fatal shot, and he had been found with an empty shell hidden on his person that matched the bullet lodged inside Kahahawai's body. "You get used to a gun, like a wrist watch or other personal equipment," the prosecutor told the newsmen, and "Massie admits that he brought his own gun to the Fortescue house that morning." If Tommie had done the killing, he would have used the weapon he was used to, Kelley said. And the murder clearly was premeditated, he added: "If they didn't plan to kill Kahahawai when they took him to the Fortescue house, they had made all the preparations to do it."

It was one thing to say all this to reporters in his office, but come Monday morning—which was Darrow's seventy-fifth birthday—Kelley was faced with the same calm, composed, and intransigent Tommie Massie that he had been unable to break two days earlier. As it turned out, the only headway Kelley made on this second day of cross-examination occurred when he abruptly shifted gears and asked if Massie had "ever been implicated in a kidnapping plot."

"No, sir," Tommie answered.

"Are you sure?"

"Quite sure."

Then, very slowly, question by question, Kelley dragged out of the reluctant young officer the story of the time he and Thalia had taken a baby from the lobby of a movie theater near the Roosevelt estate in Long Island. It had all been a mistake, Tommie finally insisted. But whether that was true or not, at least some courtroom observers thought Massie's credibility had suffered a blow when he denied the accusation at first, and then resisted at every step as the prosecutor pulled the story out of him.

If it is true that tarnishing a witness's credibility is what most cross-examinations are all about, then Kelley may at last have scored some points. But it wasn't much to brag about. On the contrary, one reporter observed, "Lieutenant Massie is proving that he is every inch a man." Mrs. Kluegel, in her Hearst column, wrote that she had "never before seen a greater demonstration of manhood, honor, bravery, and truth" than that demonstrated by Massie, who now "can take his place with other great heroes in naval history for defending true American womanhood."

At 11:00 a.m. Kelley finally let the lieutenant go. All told, he had cross-examined Tommie for three hours, far longer than Darrow's direct examination, and had come up with very little. Whatever the jurors may have thought of the young navy officer's performance, throughout the United States few press outlets would disagree with a syndicated Hearst editorial claiming that "every man can understand how Massie's mental lapse would come." The "slaying of the half-caste" was far less about Kahahawai's individual crime, the editorial continued, than it was "a defense of womanhood . . . before the ravages of the hoodlums of mixed races that infest the 'Paradise of the Pacific.' From that 'paradise' the serpent had to be banished, the evil element had to be evicted . . . womanhood must be protected."

For the rest of Monday morning and the beginning of the next day's session Darrow and Kelley took turns building up and knocking down a series of minor witnesses called by the defense. Then, at 10:00 on Tuesday, the nineteenth, Darrow called the first of his two psychiatric experts, Dr. Thomas J. Orbison.

As a successful criminal defense tactic, the claim that a man's violated sexual honor could cause a bout of temporary insanity, or *mania transitoria,* was almost as old as Darrow himself. In the first noteworthy jury verdict of its kind, in 1859 a U.S. congressman named Daniel Sickles was acquitted on a murder charge after he momentarily became "frenzied" and fatally emptied the contents of two revolvers into a man who had been sleeping with his wife. But the most famous incident, and the one on many minds while Tommie Massie was giving his testimony, occurred in the spring of 1907. A man named Harry Thaw, the fabulously wealthy son of a Pennsylvania industrialist, stood trial in New York for the murder of a man who had allegedly forced himself upon Thaw's young wife prior to their marriage. The wife was Evelyn Nesbit, a beautiful former dancer and Broadway "Floradora girl," while the man said to have raped her was the famous architect Stanford White. Although Nesbit had been White's (and John Barrymore's) mistress for several years, soon after her marriage to Thaw she explained her nonvirginity to her new husband by saying that White had once plied her with champagne and then taken advantage of her after she passed out.

Outraged and then, for more than a year, haunted by the story, Thaw finally confronted White at a gala event in Manhattan's Madison Square Garden, which White had designed, and shot him to death in the presence of hundreds of witnesses. The ensuing murder trial was noted for two especially compelling moments. The first, following medical testimony regarding Thaw's claimed exculpatory irrationality—a sudden "brainstorm" had overtaken him, one physician said—was the alleged rape victim's emotional account of her tragic seduction by White, an account that shocked the courtroom and brought many listeners to tears. The second key element was her celebrity lawyer's closing argument. In it, California attorney Delphin Delmas reminded the jurors and spectators of their own emotional reactions to Evelyn's story and asked them to put themselves in Thaw's place, to consider how they would have felt if they had been the lovely Evelyn's husband.

The fact was, Delmas contended, Thaw had gone temporarily insane when he encountered White. It was a condition he labeled "Dementia Americana," describing it as "that species of insanity that persuades an American that whoever violates the sanctity of his home or the purity of his wife or daughter has forfeited the protection of the laws of this state or any other state." And as a victim of that episodic mental disease, the attorney argued, Harry Thaw was entitled to go free.

The jury was unable to reach a decision. A second jury, however, found Thaw not guilty by reason of insanity. Dementia Americana entered the lexicon.

Could a similar defense succeed in the trial of those who had killed Joseph Kahahawai? As Philip Kinsley wrote in the *Chicago Tribune* the day after Tommie Massie left the witness stand: "This is Honolulu, where 'Dementia Americana' and insanity defenses are something new and the result cannot be predicted." Perhaps not, but Darrow believed he had much more going for him than had the colorful defense attorney in the Thaw case.

Dr. Thomas Orbison took the stand. Round-faced and ruddy complexioned, wearing eyeglasses and a hearing aid, Dr. Orbison proudly listed his current affiliations with the Los Angeles General Hospital, the Whittier State Institution for Delinquent Boys and Girls, and the Los Angeles County Lunacy Commission. After examining Lieutenant Massie for five or six hours, Orbison said, he had concluded that at the time of the murder the defendant was suffering from "delirium with ambulatory automatism." This was a rather common condition originating "in the internal glandular apparatus," the doctor said, specifically the suprarenal glands: "Fear, hate, rage, and stress are known to be due to the activity of the suprarenal glands. A protracted worry may bring out an actively irritated condition, resulting in pouring a secretion into the blood which may cause a nervous condition."

At any time, once this outwardly invisible pathology has settled into its host, almost anything might set it off, Orbison said, from typhoid fever to, in this case, hearing someone admit that he has raped your wife. At that point, "when the bomb explodes," the carrier of the affliction "is liable to do anything," yet have no memory of what he has done. In fact, the doctor revealed, "most cases of insanity are temporary, many so short that they're never heard of." But this time it was just as well that the bomb went off when it did, Orbison said, because "if something had not relieved the pressure on his mind I think there was a good chance of him going permanently insane."

Darrow appeared to be enthralled by all this, much more so than the jury, at least to gauge from the way they had taken to turning and whispering with one another, drawing glares from Dr. Orbison as he droned on. After almost an hour of testimony, Darrow decided it was time to cut to the chase. Referring to the interviews the doctor had conducted with Massie, the defense attorney asked: "From all he told you, you can say he was insane at the time of the shooting?" Yes, Orbison replied: "He was insane and didn't know what he was doing."

The prosecution team had decided to let Barry Ulrich conduct the cross-examinations of the psychiatric experts, and that was a good idea. Kelley was not temperamentally suited to this sort of dialogue, but it was perfect for the more tolerant Harvard graduate, who, detractors said, loved hearing nothing more than the sound of his own resonant voice when engaged in subtle and clever repartee. In this case, however, Ulrich did not hesitate in getting to the point.

"You have testified that Lieutenant Massie was insane when he fired the shot," the prosecutor began. "I am interested to know how much your opinion was based on your observation and how much on what he told you. Is it not true that you have expressed the opinion that he did not know what he was doing because he told you he did not know?" Orbison said that was not true, that he had based his opinion on what Tommie had told him in addition to "information from outside parties and evidence that has been brought out in this trial." Who those outside parties were and what they had told the doctor was never revealed, nor was the relevant trial information, but Ulrich did not press the point. He was less interested in the content of the alienist's testimony than in the circularity of his logic, causing the witness at one point to complain that a question was "so mean that I don't care to answer it." The jury, according to all accounts, found this far more interesting than it had the scientific intricacies of delirium with ambulatory automatism.

Several lengthy exchanges followed in which Ulrich pursued such matters as the technical difference between a sane person's "irresistible impulse" and the legal definition of insanity. But time and again the attorney returned to what many courtroom observers were coming to see as a dispute between Ulrich's common sense and Orbison's insistence that he should be believed because he said so.

"You don't think a sane man's emotions can overcome his reason to this extent?" the prosecutor asked.

"It's possible, but in this case highly improbable. I don't believe it," Orbison replied, without disclosing the reasons for his disbelief.

"How can you assume the condition of his mind?"

"It's a typical condition that nobody who knew about it could fake."

"It's odd that he happened to say [to you] the only thing on which you base your opinion. . . . You recognize that there would be every motive to invent this story?"

"I do, but this man told the detailed truth, and money wouldn't buy my opinion."

Finally, believing that he was speaking for everyone in the room, Judge Davis interceded. "Did I understand that the defendant became insane at the last words of Kahahawai?"

"No," Orbison explained, "the mental picture of his wife set him off."

Ulrich thanked the judge and the witness and said he was through. Even one of the Hearst chain's most popular columnists, Annie Laurie, wondered, if it was the image of his wife being attacked that triggered Tommie's insanity, "why did the dementia take so long, and do people with dementia take a mother-in-law and two sailors along as a usual thing?"

Darrow's second psychiatric expert, Dr. Edward H. Williams, now was sworn in. Perhaps because of what had just happened, combined with his own frequently stated belief that there was no way to tell the difference between sanity and insanity, Darrow had his assistant, George Leisure, conduct the direct examination.

Dr. Williams was tall and thin, with a narrow face and a gray goatee and mustache. Although physically almost the exact opposite of Dr. Orbison, what he said differed not at all from his colleague's presentation. When asked about his credentials, Williams gave a ten-minute chronological recitation that one enterprising reporter discovered was an expanded version of his entry in *Who's Who in America*. As he appeared to be nearing the end of his curriculum vitae, defense attorney Leisure deftly interrupted by saying, "Which briefly brings your work down to the present," while from the nearby prosecutor's table John Kelley snapped, "Briefly!"

In fact, under Leisure's guidance, Dr. Williams's testimony was quite succinct, lasting less than half an hour. It confirmed Dr. Orbison's previous conclusions regarding the importance of glands. "You hear in a joking way about monkey glands," he said, "but it isn't a joke, it's the most serious thing in the world. If I could have tested Lieutenant Massie's blood at the time this thing happened it would have shown the gland secretions were deficient. This man carried about him a bomb. He was in an automatic condition." Summing up, Williams described Tommie's condition at the moment of the murder and for an hour or so after as "shock amnesia," similar to what happens to a boxer who goes "out on his feet."

On cross-examination Barry Ulrich said he had come to regard as fascinating this business of glands and insanity. Recalling that Dr. Williams and Dr. Orbison had just recently testified for the defense in the Winnie Judd trial, which ended in her conviction, he asked Williams about the condition of Mrs. Judd's glands. Defense attorney Leisure instantly objected to the prosecution's bringing in a wholly different case. Ulrich countered that he simply wished to find out if the witness still agreed with his testimony in that trial. Darrow then joined the objection, and as Judge Davis started to say that he thought the question might have relevancy, Ulrich withdrew the question. By informing the jury that another famous murder case jury had found against the testimony of these same two defense psychiatrists only two months earlier, he had accomplished all that he intended.

With few further preliminaries, the prosecutor then zeroed in on what would be the centerpiece of his cross-examination, asking the witness: "Have you not written a book in which you stated that in most cases insanity pleas are spurious?" Williams indignantly denied that he had. Ulrich then picked up a volume from the prosecution table, reading aloud the title, *Crime, Abnormal Minds, and the Law*, by Ernest Bryan Hoag and Edward Huntington Williams. Was he not the same Edward Huntington Williams who had coauthored that book? The psychiatrist agreed that he was.

"Well, reading from page seventy-four . . ." As Ulrich turned the pages to find what he was seeking, Darrow shifted in his chair, as if to object, then stood and approached, asking to look at the book. After glancing at it he returned to his seat. "Here," the prosecuting attorney continued once he had found his place. "I quote: 'Under the present system in force in most states, Justice Wilbur of the Supreme Court of California has recently stated, most pleas of insanity are made by sane people, who frequently go free, while most insane criminals make no insanity plea and are duly convicted and sentenced.'"

Williams proceeded to confuse most of the nonlawyers in attendance with his enigmatic phrasing. "As I understand it," he said, "that is to introduce testimony that otherwise could not be."

Ulrich understood exactly what the doctor was saying. "Then they are faked cases?"

"No," Williams quickly countered, "I don't like the word 'fake.' People may think they have been insane."

But Ulrich had everything right where he wanted it. Whatever happened with the insanity plea in this case, the defense had been allowed to introduce highly emotional testimony related to Thalia's rape accusation that would never have been admissible except for its purported relevance to an insanity defense. It was that ploy that Kelley and Darrow had argued over from the first day of the trial.

"But isn't it true," Ulrich said, pursuing the point, "that insanity pleas are interposed to introduce evidence that could not be brought in otherwise?"

Darrow was on his feet, heatedly objecting.

"Overruled," the judge said.

Bristling, the psychiatrist answered: "Yes, it is true" that such tactics are sometimes employed, he admitted, but not by alienists, "by lawyers!"

Ulrich turned and looked at the defense table. "As in this case," he said.

"This case doesn't come into the argument at all," Darrow fairly shouted.

Unperturbed, Ulrich returned to the book in his hand, leafing through more pages until he found what he was after. "Didn't you write in your book on page one hundred," he asked the witness, "and I quote: 'According to our present methods, such testimony is largely unscientific, partisan, and undignified, and tends to discredit both the medical and legal professions, and it frequently totally fails to serve the ends of justice, as already indicated.'"

Dr. Williams shifted in his seat, preparing to answer as the attorney paused. But Ulrich raised his hand to hold him off, and continued to read: "According to methods now in vogue, medical experts are employed both by the prosecution and the defense, thus, in the very beginning tending to make the whole procedure, from the examination of the patient to the testimony given before the jury, a purely partisan affair rather than an impartial scientific attempt to arrive at a correct diagnosis. This is the antithesis of the method employed by reputable medical men in their usual attempts in the diagnosis of disease."

The witness was now allowed to answer. He explained that his words were in support of legislation, now finally in place in California, that discouraged attorneys from privately hiring psychiatrists to say whatever they were paid to say. Instead, the new law empowered judges to appoint truly independent experts. Silently, Ulrich nodded. Glancing from the psychiatrist to Darrow, he noted: "That is not the case in Hawaii."

Across the street, on the lawn of 'Iolani Palace, the sounds of the Royal Hawaiian Band's noontime concert had incongruously begun to filter into the courtroom. Philip Kinsley of the *Chicago Tribune* recognized the music. He informed his readers that "strains of 'Swanee River,' 'Massa's in de Cold, Cold Ground,' and other old songs floated in through the open windows."

24 "Everybody Knows I Love You!"

C all Mrs. Massie," Darrow announced, and Thalia, who had been sitting between her husband and her mother, holding their hands in her lap, got to her feet and walked slowly to the witness box. She was dressed demurely, her hair tied back, her manner hesitant and tentative. Since this was her first day in the courtroom for the murder trial, most people on hand had never seen Thalia in person, and they murmured about how young and fragile she seemed. Every major newspaper in the country later mentioned how she looked like "a school girl" or "a hurt child," so "winsome and childlike" were her demeanor and appearance.

Darrow was more than half a century Thalia's senior, old enough to be her grandfather, and that was the tone he assumed as he guided her gently but firmly through her testimony. He asked her where and when she was born, went to school, and was married. Thalia replied very softly, in a low voice, nervously twisting a handkerchief in her hands.

The defense attorney's questions brought her to the night of September 12, when she and Tommie and the others had gone to the dance at the Ala Wai Inn. Almost immediately, John Kelley stood and objected. "We are not retrying the Ala Moana case," he complained. Since the stated purpose of examining this witness was to elicit information on Lieutenant Massie's mental condition during the morning in which he apparently shot to death Joseph Kahahawai, the prosecutor said, Mrs. Massie should be limited in her testimony to things she said to her husband that might have affected his state of mind. Judge Davis sustained the objection and Darrow reframed his last question. It concerned the time when she next saw Tommie after leaving the inn to go for a walk, and as Thalia answered she began to cry, silently bowing her head and holding the handkerchief to her eyes. When she looked up her face was streaked with tears.

Darrow asked the question again, and she started to answer: "I saw him about one o'clock. He telephoned. I asked him to come home right away, that something terrible . . ." But she couldn't go on, and again she buried her face in her handkerchief as her entire body shook convulsively with sobbing.

Grace got to her feet and brought a paper cup filled with water to the defense table. George Leisure took it from her and gave it to Thalia. After she composed herself and lifted her head, her cheeks remained wet, her face contorted with what looked like innocent despair. It was an especially hot and muggy morning, the courtroom packed with dozens more spectators than had been allowed on any previous day. Throughout the room the faces of the women who had so faithfully attended each session in support of Grace—Mrs. Dillingham, Mrs. Kluegel, Mrs. Stirling, and all the others—mirrored Thalia's tragic distress. Tommie also began to weep.

But Darrow would not let up. For the next hour he elicited from the young woman a tearful version of the same tale she had told on another witness stand in this same building five months earlier, but this time as seen from the perspective of what she had said to Tommie. How she told him about the men who had grabbed her, punched her—especially Kahahawai—and, after driving to a lonely spot, ravished her repeatedly as she struggled to be free. How she remembered the license plate number of the car her assailants had been driving, and how she had identified the men over the course of the next two days. How she had suffered in the hospital and at home. How she had undergone "an operation to stop pregnancy."

"Was it due to Tommie?" Darrow asked.

"I knew it wasn't."

At one point Kelley became frustrated with Darrow's patent abuse of the latitude the court had granted. He rose and said, "I don't want to keep interjecting objections, but . . ."

"You shouldn't!" Darrow snapped at him.

"I think I should have objected much more." But the judge cut him off and overruled the objection before he even heard it.

During a short recess in the middle of the testimony Thalia seemed too enervated to get to her feet. As she groped for the railing to pull herself up, Tommie hurriedly pushed his way through the crowd in her direction. She reached out to him and collapsed in his arms. Throughout the break the couple sat quietly together, her head nestled against his shoulder, his hand stroking and comforting her.

When the examination resumed, Thalia had composed herself, but sat stiffly, as if trying consciously to control her trembling—anxiously twisting and wrapping her soaked handkerchief around her fingers. She told of how kind Tommie had been during her long ordeal upon returning home from the hospital. "He never complained about the many times I would wake him at night. He was wonderful," she said. But in the midst of his selfless nurturing, rumors had begun to spread—rumors about them getting a divorce because he didn't believe her, about his catching her in bed with another navy officer and beating up both of them. They tried to ignore the gossip, she said, but it obviously was taking its toll on him. He lost weight "and used to walk up and down, get up in the night and go into the living room, and walk up and down and smoke. When I got so I could cook, I would prepare tempting dishes for him, but he wouldn't eat. He would get up and smoke a cigarette."

After taking her through the rape trial, Darrow drew out of Thalia how the hung jury had troubled Tommie deeply and caused him to wish there were some way to pry a confession from one of the men. His deep and protective love of his wife combined with an increasing obsession to see justice done. At last she reached the morning of January 8, when Deacon Jones showed up at her home, "excited and pale." He handed her a gun, she testified, and said, "Here, take this, Kahahawai has been killed."

A few moments later Darrow ended his direct examination. At least half the courtroom was in tears. The reporter for the Hearst syndicate wrote that "even some men in the courtroom sobbed. The mixed-blood jury, every member of which is a husband, listened attentively to the story which in almost any court in America would win immediate acquittal for the four white defendants on trial." A more skeptical correspondent, who had interviewed Thalia and some friends of hers weeks earlier and described her as "bovine and calculating at the same time," as someone who "talks about the assault as if it happened to someone else," now found himself suffused with emotion and entirely won over:

> There was no reservation of doubt left in that courtroom that Mrs. Massie's story of rape by Kahahawai and four other hoodlums of a mixed race on the night of last September 12th was all too true. It was torn from her in agony today as she went to the defense of her mother and her husband to save them from prison, but she did more than this. She embroidered her story with such details that no one could doubt the overwrought condition of Massie's mind when he shot Kahahawai. And the plea of insanity, which was relegated to second place in the defense, was given support, if such support was needed, by her story of the tender care Massie gave her and his progressive weakness under the strain.

Prosecutor Kelley began his cross-examination in pursuit of minor and only peripherally significant information. Almost as if his failure to break her husband's testimony had drained his sense of purpose, Kelley's questioning of

Thalia bordered on indifference, rarely pursuing follow-ups to her confident answers. He asked about her maid, Beatrice Nakamura, and inquired as to the time Beatrice arrived at Thalia's home on the day of the killing. He asked about the number of drinks Deacon Jones had poured for himself that morning after he showed up on her doorstep with a gun in his hand. He asked about some phone calls she and Jones had made. Thalia was alert and crisp with her responses, no longer the forlorn waif she had appeared to be under Darrow's examination. In contrast, Kelley's questions seemed almost aimless.

Using the same unthreatening tone, the prosecutor then asked if Tommie was always as kind to her as the two of them had testified. Of course he was, she said, her eyes following his hand as it reached into a breast pocket and removed a folded piece of paper.

While slowly opening the document, and now standing only a few feet from Thalia, he asked: "Did you have a psychopathic examination at the university last summer?"

"Yes. I went to see Professor Kelly," she answered warily.

"Is this your handwriting?" Kelley reached out and handed Thalia the paper.

In that instant, reported the *New York Times* the next day, "there came a transformation from the pathetic looking figure into a woman who, with low voice but blazing face, turned on the prosecutor." Her face coloring, her voice cold with rage, Thalia demanded: "Where did you get this?"

"I'm asking the questions, not answering them," Kelley snapped, his mood changing as abruptly as hers. Then, with a hard edge to his voice, he repeated his first question: "Has your husband always been kind to you?"

Not answering the inquiry, Thalia cried out: "Don't you know this is a confidential communication between doctor and patient? You have no right to bring this into the courtroom." And as she spoke, Thalia slowly tore the paper in half. Then, more rapidly, she tore it again and again, speaking quickly in a harsh, angry tone: "I refuse to say whether that is my handwriting or not."

The prosecutor stood silently, apparently stunned by what Thalia was doing. The piece of paper was in shreds, some of it falling to the floor, some of it balled up in her fist. One person in the room began to clap. Soon the entire courtroom was filled with applause. All the society women joined in, as did the defendants, including Tommie, who leaned forward in his chair, smiling, and making theatrically long, rapid, sweeping movements with his arms before slapping his hands together.

Judge Davis banged his gavel, angrily demanding that the demonstration be stopped or he would clear the court. As the noise died down, Kelley loudly but calmly said: "Thank you, Mrs. Massie, at last you have shown yourself in your true colors."

At that, Darrow was on his feet. "I object to the words of counsel."

The judge agreed, saying to Kelley: "Your language is objectionable. It may be stricken."

Kelley paused, then announced that he was through with the witness and walked away. Thalia lurched from the stand, bent at the waist as if in pain, and stumbled toward Tommie, who was rushing to catch her. "Throwing her arms around him," the *New York Times* would report, "she cried loudly and hysterically: 'What right has he got to say that I don't love you? Everybody knows I love you!'"

Thalia's cross-examination had lasted only eight minutes. Darrow announced that the defense was resting its case.

The next day, Thursday the twenty-first, opened with Kelley and Darrow agreeing for the record that the page from the psychological inventory that Thalia destroyed on the stand was not a privileged communication under the laws of the territory. The board of the Hawaii Medical Association concurred. When asked if he might wish to submit a replacement of the document as an exhibit, Kelley brushed the question aside and said it was the only copy he had. During a recess both lead attorneys spoke with newsmen, laughing about the previous day's incident. Shaking his head, Darrow said it was the most dramatic thing he had ever seen in a courtroom. "I never saw anything like it," he continued. "I've seen some pretty good court scenes, but nothing like that one. I was pretty limp when it was all over. I couldn't sleep when I went to bed last night."

The prosecution's two psychiatric experts had just arrived from California, Kelley informed Judge Davis as the court was called back to order. One of those witnesses would be ready to testify on Saturday, the other on Monday. If it was acceptable to the defense, he was therefore requesting a continuance, with the trial to resume at nine o'clock Saturday morning. Darrow found that eminently acceptable, saying: "Well, so long as we have to stay somewhere on this earth as long as we live, I can't think of any better place to stay than in Honolulu."

After no court activity the rest of Thursday or all day Friday, Saturday turned out to be a short session. One prosecution witness was called to support previous testimony that Tommie Massie had appeared calm, composed, and sane at the time of his arrest. Then Dr. Faus, the city and county physician, who revealed that he had taken some psychiatric training at the University of Chicago, and Dr. Paul E. Bowers of California testified. In their judgment there was no good evidence to support the defense's contention that Tommie had experienced temporary insanity at the time of the killing. Darrow's cross-examinations were brief. With Faus, he elicited the fact that his psychiatric training had lasted less than a year and that psychiatry had never been his specialty. Of Dr. Bowers he only asked if he was being paid for his testimony. Bowers said yes and he was excused. The court adjourned just before 11:00 a.m. That afternoon many of the trial's principals assembled outside the courthouse to be filmed by a Paramount crew from Hollywood that had just arrived.

The prosecution and defense huddled separately on Saturday and Sunday to prepare their summations, which were expected to begin on Tuesday, and to draw up last-minute proposed jury instructions for Judge Davis to consider. Time was allotted by each group for beach parties on Sunday afternoon, however, and that morning prosecutor Kelley spent some time with his final two witnesses, Dr. Joseph Catton, another California psychiatrist, and— once again—Dr. Faus. There was a final piece of evidence that Kelley wanted Faus to introduce in rebuttal.

On Monday morning almost everyone noticed an entirely different mood in the courtroom, one that was lighter, friendlier, more informal than before. Perhaps it was due to the short vacation everyone had just enjoyed. The defense expected Monday's session to go as smoothly and easily and quickly as Saturday's had, since the witness lineup was almost identical: Dr. Faus once again, and another California alienist. Like Dr. Bowers on Saturday, neither of today's witnesses had even spoken with Tommie, as per Darrow's insistence. But the defense was in for a surprise when Dr. Catton took the stand at 9:04 a.m.

In his early forties, Catton was considerably younger than any of the other three imported psychiatrists. Tall, slim, and relaxed, he also had a knack for describing arcane medical conditions and procedures in terms easily understandable to laypersons without sounding condescending. Over the weekend Kelley had coached him in the correct pronunciation of Hawaiian phrases and names, in contrast to the defense experts who had blithely mangled every Hawaiian word they could not avoid having to say. The Californian was far from perfect, but local spectators appeared to appreciate the effort.

After Catton briefly presented his bona fides—associate professor of medicine at Stanford University Medical School and consulting psychiatrist to the San Francisco City and County Hospital—Barry Ulrich started to ask about the last trial at which he had testified, the Winnie Judd "Trunk Murder" case in Arizona. But Darrow was on his feet objecting before the doctor could reply. The court sustained the objection.

Next, Ulrich asked Catton if he had examined any of the defendants directly. Catton replied that he had requested an opportunity to examine them but had been rebuffed by the defense. Again Darrow objected, insisting that it was sufficient to say that he had not examined the defendants. Judge Davis sustained the objection, but the prosecution's point had been made.

What had he done in preparation to testify, then, Ulrich asked, and had he been able to reach a conclusion as to Lieutenant Massie's sanity at the time of the killing? Catton said he had read the documentation that was available, including the entire transcript of the trial thus far—listing the names of all the key witnesses without referring to notes—and he had reached a very definite conclusion. But before stating his finding, he went on, it was necessary for him to provide the facts upon which it was based. The psychiatrist then set out to recount the sequence of events leading up to the murder, beginning with Tommie's childhood, his education and military training, his marriage, his transfer to Pearl Harbor, his and Thalia's penchant for going home separately from parties, the gathering at the Ala Wai Inn on September 12 of the preceding year, and the details of what had transpired at the inn—from the number of drinks people said they had consumed to the number of times they had danced.

At that point, Darrow exploded in frustration. "I object to the whole recital of this testimony," he told the court. "The jury have heard it, and it has no special bearing on this case—all these details, that he had a drink here or had a drink there or how old Mrs. Massie was. It is almost a verbatim recital of the testimony that has taken days to put on."

Judge Davis asked Ulrich if he intended to have the witness continue to describe with such meticulousness the facts on which he had based his clinical opinion. The prosecutor said yes. Not only was such detail essential to understanding the foundation for the doctor's conclusion, but the defense had successfully argued earlier in the trial that Thalia's account of Tommie's ordeal from September on into January was required if the jury was to comprehend his state of mind on the day Kahahawai was killed. The same was true regarding Dr. Catton's testimony. Darrow again interjected: "This witness has said he read every word of testimony. Does he need to tell the jury every word or just the fact that he has read it? To have him recite here again this long story is not at all necessary." Ulrich replied that Catton was not reciting the entirety of the preceding testimony, but only those portions pertinent to the conclusion he had reached. In that case, the judge said, he might continue.

And he did. For the better part of the next hour the Stanford psychiatrist treated the courtroom to what must have sounded to some like an undergraduate lecture, but one that grew more interesting as it proceeded. At first the jurors fidgeted in their seats, mumbled to one another behind their hands, and craned their necks to stare at the ceiling in boredom. But as Catton's recitation continued they became still, some leaning forward to catch his words. Courtroom spectators did the same.

Part of the reason Catton was able to engage the jurors' attention was his manner: he turned in his seat and addressed them directly, making eye contact and speaking plainly. He also performed an astonishing feat of recollection: without referring to any written material, he was weaving together a summation of events—including names, dates, and other details—that flowed in perfectly logical order. But most important of all, he was telling the story dispassionately, in a way no one before him in the courtroom had done. Thus, the Massies' emotional laments over the vicious and vile rumors that had been spread about them appeared in Dr. Catton's account merely as evidence that many people in Honolulu did not believe Thalia's charges. Also, when referring to the rape he insisted on calling it the "alleged" assault, thereby triggering the only moments in the entire trial when Grace Fortescue audibly wept and moaned.

Throughout Catton's testimony Darrow was more animated than at any previous time, constantly standing to object and angrily joust with opposing counsel and with the witness. The doctor refused to be rattled. When the defense attorney objected to the use of the word "alleged," Catton agreed to amend his language by saying that "some people believed there had been no assault." When Darrow objected to the way Catton addressed the jury and his use of his hands in explaining things, the doctor said he would make an effort to restrain himself, "but part of my speech comes out through my hands as well as my tongue."

"Then you might put them in your pockets," Darrow snapped.

"No, sir," Catton replied, "that is not a habit of mine, to put them into the pocket. May I have the last question, please?"

And so it went. By the time he was finished, the witness had described and characterized Tommie's behavior on the day of the murder as that of a perfectly sane but extremely angry man. The anger derived from "his own belief that Kahahawai was the real assailant" being in conflict with that of a "public divided as to whether Kahahawai was the assailant, or whether there had been any assault at all." In this context, "believing that he could not depend on the forces of law and order to work out the case the way he believed it should be worked out . . . he chose himself to become the agent who would deal with Kahahawai." Catton then listed the sequence of events immediately preceding the murder that had been carefully and rationally worked out by Massie and the others.

Turning then to the aftermath of the killing, the psychiatrist referred to the testimony of police and other eyewitnesses who had described Tommie at the time of his arrest as pale from fright, hiding his head in shame, and asking a policeman for a cigarette. None of these were behaviors symptomatic of delirium, psychosis, automatism, or amnesia, he said. In fact, the only shred of evidence suggesting that Tommie had suffered a memory lapse was the uncorroborated, self-serving testimony of the defendant himself. Darrow was free to put the other defendants on the stand to substantiate Tommie's claim, of course, but that would expose them to cross-examination, a predictable disaster in the case of Grace and Deacon Jones.

Darrow's cross-examination of Dr. Catton was, at least at first, by far his most aggressive at any point in the trial, but it accomplished little. He got the witness to acknowledge that he testified quite a bit in murder cases and that he sometimes had testified for the defense. That meant little, however, and before long their exchanges had evolved into a superficially philosophical discussion in which both men acknowledged, as Catton put it, that "we would agree on a lot of things if we were not in the trial of a case."

During a recess following the cross-examination reporters noticed with surprise that Darrow and Catton were engaging in friendly and animated banter. Standing nearby was Dr. Thomas Orbison, one of the two psychiatric witnesses for the defense. Smiling and shaking his head, he was overheard to say: "That's what's known as crossing 'em up."

At 11:15 Monday morning the trial's final witness was called. Dr. Robert Faus, the city and county physician, took the stand for the third time. His testimony lasted three minutes. In answer to questions from prosecutor Kelley, he testified that after Joseph Kahahawai was shot he most likely remained conscious for up to five minutes and it may have been twenty minutes before he actually died.

Those in the courtroom sat in stunned silence.

25 Where Is Kahahawai?

There would be four closing arguments, two from each side. On Tuesday, Barry Ulrich was to open for the prosecution, to be followed by George Leisure for the defense. On Wednesday the order would be reversed, with Darrow speaking first and then Kelley. When asked by reporters how long they expected to speak, all the attorneys' estimates ranged from one to two hours. Except for Darrow. He said he might hold forth for three or four hours. "Who knows? A lawyer can go on arguing this case for hours and hours," he replied. "I don't know another case like it."

Neither did the nation's press. Throughout the past two weeks celebrity journalists had been arriving in Honolulu with increasing frequency. On Tuesday they included Frazier Hunt, longtime *Chicago Tribune* war correspondent and now a syndicated writer for dozens of newspapers and magazines. With everyone else, Hunt said, he had come "to hear the old lion, Clarence Darrow, roar." He squeezed into a space in the courtroom's press section, more crowded now than on any previous day, all on hand to witness the summations. First there would be the two opening acts, and then what certainly was to be the final closing argument of Darrow's storied career. Like the other journalists, Hunt was impressed with the number of spectators and their makeup: "The proportion of women attending continues to be at the rate of at least ten to one," one of them wrote. "Here and there a man appeared," added another, "looking a little like a commercial traveler strayed into a convention of women's clubs."

Associate prosecutor Ulrich had arranged for a small table to be set before the jury box, and on the table he placed a blue-bound copy of the trial transcript and a box filled with evidence exhibits to which he would refer, including photographs of Joseph Kahahawai's dead body. This was a trial for murder, and with all the defense's distractions of late Ulrich was determined to not let the jurors forget that fact.

"Gentlemen of the jury," he began, "we approach the end of this trial, I am sure, with some relief." He expressed appreciation for the jurors' ordeal of sequestration, but said the duties they were entrusted with were "vital to the Territory," as it faced "the greatest crisis in all its history. Far more hangs on this trial than the fate of these four defendants. Our power of self-government is being questioned. You jurors, the judge, the people of this Territory are on trial, charged with not being able to govern ourselves. No twelve people in the Territory are charged with a greater responsibility than you."

All the jurors knew exactly what he was talking about. But, Ulrich said, if you allow "your emotions . . . your feelings" to govern your judgment, "it will be the end of the administration of justice in this Territory. It is your duty only to find the fact, not to estimate the worth of the law." Referring to the defense argument that two of the people on trial, Lieutenant Massie and Mrs. Fortescue, had suffered greatly because a court failed to deliver a verdict in the rape case, Ulrich said that was a topic outside the jury's purview. "No man may take the law into his own hands, and no amount of suffering or injury will justify taking the life of another. And the fact—if it were a fact— that the deceased committed an assault upon the wife of one of these defendants, is no justification under the law for the crime with which they are charged. . . . You cannot make Hawaii safe against rape by licensing murder."

It was the associate prosecutor's job to lay out with precision the case against the defendants and to preempt the anticipated pleadings of Leisure and Darrow. For the next two hours that is what he did.

Believing that in the battle of the alienists it was the prosecution that had prevailed, Ulrich came close to mocking the insanity defense. Reminding the jurors that "the only witness as to what occurred is a man who says his mind went blank and he doesn't know what happened," the prosecutor asked them to use their common sense. The test they should apply to all the defense's claims was a simple one, he said. Just ask: "Does that sound reasonable?"

In fact, nothing sounded reasonable in the defendants' account of what had happened, Ulrich said, including their description of the killing. He then took the jurors step by step through the preparations for Kahahawai's abduction, including the placement in Mrs. Fortescue's cottage of the coiled rope that was used to bind the body and the fact that "they had a veritable arsenal up there—not one, but three guns, all loaded." Everything they did before the killing, Ulrich said, pointed directly to premeditation: "They plotted a plan that might place a life in jeopardy—and persons engaged in an undertaking that places a life in jeopardy are responsible for the loss of that life if it occurs."

And what happened after Kahahawai was shot? Reminding the jurors that

Dr. Faus had said the victim remained conscious for up to five minutes and alive for perhaps twenty minutes, Ulrich said, "Obviously, the defendants had no way of knowing he was going to die—that the bullet had pierced a vital spot. They had a telephone. There are plenty of doctors in town. Why didn't they do something if they didn't want him to die? They let him die because they wanted him to die. The defense has told you a lot about the presumption of innocence. What presumption of innocence did they give that Hawaiian boy?"

Returning then to the insanity defense, Ulrich called it a sham, "just a peg to hang a verdict on." But without insanity, what did the defense have? Nothing. "The defendants are guilty. It is a plain and obvious fact. They not only admit it—they proclaim it. The eyes of the world are upon Hawaii, and you must answer that challenge. We ask you to convict these four defendants of murder in the second degree."

After a fifteen-minute recess, the court reconvened and George Leisure addressed the jury on behalf of the defendants. He would take barely a half-hour to present his argument. Although Darrow had decided that the insanity defense was unlikely to carry the day, it seemed at least worth mentioning, if only as an entry point for repeated reference to what Leisure called "the greatest crime that can be committed: the ravishing of a man's mother, his wife, his sister, his daughter." It also allowed defense counsel to attack the prosecution's psychiatric witnesses. Referring to Darrow's single question to Dr. Bowers, the first prosecution psychiatrist—"Was he being paid for his testimony?"— Leisure observed that "if he had been testifying for the defense, he probably would have found Massie insane." This, of course was precisely the point Ulrich had raised with the defense psychiatrist, Dr. Williams, except in reverse.

As for Dr. Catton, who had mesmerized the courtroom the day before: "He rode in like Sheridan at the battle of Shiloh—to win the battle after it had been lost. Mrs. Massie can be ravished," Leisure said, "but Catton must win his case so that he can go back to California and tell them he got another verdict. He couldn't trust his own prosecution lawyers. He had to be the lawyer, the judge, and the jury." And speaking of Shiloh—the biblical Shiloh—afforded the attorney a segue to scripture. Leisure quoted Deuteronomy 22:25–27: "But if a man find a betrothed damsel in the field, and the man force her, and lie with her, then the man only that lay with her shall die. But unto the damsel thou shalt do nothing . . . for he found her in the field and the betrothed damsel cried, and there was none to save her."

At this point Darrow, perhaps wishing that he hadn't settled for unpaid assistance, began scribbling a note. Leisure continued—attacking prosecutor Kelley for bringing up the kidnapping incident in Long Island, celebrating the defendants as "young sailors in the service of their country," and returning to Dr. Catton, who "was in his diapers" when the older defense psychiatrists were practicing medicine. Darrow slipped the note to his young assistant and Leisure began to wrap up. But not before openly celebrating the murder—bluntly saying that Joseph Kahahawai had deserved to be killed, not only for what he had done, but also for what he most certainly would have continued to do if not stopped by the defendants:

> Not long ago the body identified as that of a man who criminally as-saulted the wife of one of your neighbors was found. His death was as just under the laws of God and as direct a consequence of his own acts as if he had leaped from your historic Pali. Do you suppose the cruel appetite of this man would have been satiated by one drunken debauch? No. His next victim might have been your wife or sister.

Finally, saying that he had no doubt the court would deal fairly with the defense, having "read some of the charges and instructions of Judge Davis in previous cases and finding them to be outstanding in the history of American jurisprudence," Leisure told the jury: "I won't take your time going through all this evidence that you have already heard." Instead, he announced that he would close now, having kept his remarks brief—"I say 'brief,' because any extended argument, as I am to be followed by Mr. Darrow, might be consid-ered presumptuous on my part."

And then he sat down. His boss would have to pick up the pieces.

Writing about the magnetic appeal of courtroom drama, Clarence Darrow once said: "The audience that storms the box-office of the theater to gain en-trance to a sensational show is small and sleepy compared with the throng that crashes the courthouse door when something concerning real life and death is to be laid bare to the public. Everyone knows that the best portrayals of life are tame and sickly when matched with the realities."

This sense of the law as theater had been at the heart of Darrow's legal technique for nearly half a century. He could be a brilliant courtroom tacti-cian, although he hated what he called "hair-splitting lawyers and ponderous judges quibbling over nothing," but his fabled success was rooted in his ability to connect with a jury. From a distance, some of his speeches read like bombast, but in the heat of the courtroom—and, like this one in Honolulu, many of the courtrooms in which he performed seem to have been sweltering—Darrow rarely failed to move judges and jurors to sustained periods of intense emotion.

At the core of Darrow's courtroom technique was his insistence that a rigidly narrow-minded and punitive approach to the law was foolish and cruel, that true justice demanded an understanding of the facts as they appeared to the defendants at the time they did whatever it was they were accused of doing. Darrow's friend and partner in several famous cases, Arthur Garfield Hays, once described Darrow's classic strategy more pithily than Darrow ever would. As Hays put it in his opening statement at the Sweet murder trial: "We will show not only what happened in the house, but we shall attempt a far more difficult task—that of reproducing in the cool atmosphere of a courtroom, a state of mind—the state of mind of these defendants, worried, distrustful, tortured, and apparently trapped."

As he entered Honolulu's Judiciary Building on Wednesday morning, April 27, that once again was the task Darrow had given himself. The courtroom had been filled to capacity the day before. But today, the *New York Times* reported, "it seemed as if double that number" were on hand. Almost everyone was white. The press reported that apart from Joe Kahahawai's parents, no more than a dozen Hawaiians or Asians had made it inside. People were sitting on laps, standing pressed along walls and against one another. Spectators with influence sat within the railing and next to the attorneys' tables or the jury box. Some, ducking out of the judge's sight, ensconced themselves behind the jury platform. When the defendants entered, accompanied by Thalia for the only time other than the day of her testimony, they discovered there was no room for them. People stood and squeezed aside to make places, but the two sailors, Jones and Lord, wound up sitting at the counsel table. Ruby Darrow somehow lost her seat and settled for a folding chair in a corner. The morning air was hot and still, but it was the hundreds of bodies jammed together that turned the courtroom into an oven.

Throughout the trial, radio stations across the country had broadcast staged reenactments of the day's courtroom events. But this morning Darrow's closing argument would be carried live. Three days earlier Americans on the mainland had turned their clocks ahead for daylight saving time. It was now lunch hour on the West Coast and midafternoon in the East as people huddled around radios throughout the nation to hear the great Clarence Darrow's voice, most of them for the first and last time.

On the only occasion since he arrived in Honolulu, Darrow showed up in a lightweight, pale gray tropical suit. It was brand-new, with horizontal creases still evident in the trousers. His hair, temporarily, was slicked down. Long before he was finished it would be typically askew, falling over his forehead, and his suit would be as rumpled as those he had brought from Chicago. The courtroom windows were wide open, electric fans humming and turning slowly overhead. When the legendary attorney stood and approached the jury to deliver his final words, someone sneaked into his seat.

"This case illustrates the working of human destiny more than any other case I have handled," Darrow began. "It illustrates the effect of sorrow and mishap on human minds and lives, and shows us how weak and powerless human beings are in the hands of relentless powers."

Only eight months earlier, Darrow said, Lieutenant Massie—"respected, courageous, and intelligent"—and his young wife—"handsome and attractive, known and respected and admired by the community"—were living their quiet lives in the tree-shaded hills above Honolulu. Now, however, "they are here today in the criminal court. What has befallen this family in this short space of time?"

What had befallen them was the brutal rape of Mrs. Massie. About this, the defense attorney asserted, "there is no question." He then recounted the assault on Thalia in horrifying detail, concluding again that "no one has raised even a doubt about this story . . . or placed their finger upon a single fact to contradict the saddest tale that was ever brought to a husband." It was a story terrible enough "to unsettle any man's mind," Darrow told the jury, challenging them to put themselves in Tommie's place: "Suppose you'd heard it? What effect would it have had on your mind? What effect would it have had on anybody's mind?"

He returned to the narrative. "The doctor orders an operation to prevent pregnancy. Here's a man and his wife, and she's carrying inside of her the germ of whom? Not of him, but of some one of the ruffians who raped her and destroyed a home—a home that you will be asked to further destroy. Is this not a foundation for insanity?"

Although, in his entire summation, he never once mentioned his own alienists, Darrow now tore into Dr. Catton. The most compelling medical testimony before the jury, laid out with exactitude by the Stanford professor, was that Tommie Massie clearly was sane at the time Kahahawai was killed. That had to be undermined. The only way to do it was with the same ridicule and rhetoric that had been used against his own experts.

"Dr. Catton is an honorable fellow," Darrow said, "sitting at his door as a spider sits in its web, watching for flies. He is impartial. The first one is taken in. All that is necessary is to get there first. In this case they got there first, although we might have, I suppose.

"Gentlemen," Darrow asked, "I wonder what fate has against this family, anyhow? And I wonder when it will get through taking its toll and leave them to go in peace, to try to make their own life in comfort for the rest of their days? I wonder." Consider Mrs. Fortescue.

> Numerous poems and rhymes have been written about mothers. . . .
> To them there is one all-important thing, and that is the child that they carried in their womb. [Grace Fortescue] acted as every mother acts. She felt as your mothers have felt, because the family is the preservation of life. Everything else is forgotten in the emotion that carries her back to the time when her child was a little baby in her arms, which she bore and loved. Your mother was that way, and my mother.
>
> And here she is in this courtroom, waiting to go to the penitentiary. All right gentlemen, go to it! If this husband and this mother and these faithful boys go to the penitentiary, it won't be the first time a penitentiary has been sanctified by its inmates. But when people come to your beautiful islands, no matter when, one of the first places they will wish to see is the prison where the mother and the husband are confined—and confined only because they moved under emotion! When that happens, if it does happen, that prison will be the most conspicuous building on this island, and men will wonder how it happened, and will marvel at the injustice and cruelty, and will pity the inmate and blame fate for the persecution and sorrow that has followed this family.

Walking forward and leaning over the jury box railing, Darrow looked each of the jurors in the eye and asked: "Would you . . . and you . . . and you . . . and you . . . if any of you had been caught in the hands of fate— would you have done differently? No, life doesn't come that way. It comes from a devotion of mothers, of husbands—and when that dies in the human heart, then this world will be desolate and cold and will take its lonely course around the sun alone. Every instinct that moves human beings, every feeling that is within you, every feeling that moves in the mother is with us in this case. You can't fight against it. If you do you will fight against nature."

It was not yet 10:30. Darrow had been arguing for barely an hour but he clearly was exhausted. So were the spectators, many of them openly weeping. He asked for a recess and fell into his chair. George Leisure shook his hand in congratulations, but then John Kelley was at his side, worried. Darrow appeared to be on the verge of collapse. There seemed to be no air left in the room. It was hot and suffocating, and people pressed in to look at the old man. Kelley and Darrow leaned in close and spoke softly, Kelley patting his arm, Darrow smiling.

Then he was back on his feet, picking up where he had left off and continuing uninterrupted for another ninety minutes. He talked about his fifty long years in courtrooms and of the "sorrow and distress" that reside there: "I have seen men on their way to the gallows. I have seen them tired and confused, led into the doors of dungeons." Justice is not about laws, he told the jury, it is about "feeling," it is about "instinct," and "since the earliest man it has existed independent of laws, independent of rules that often destroy it."

He circled back to the night of the rape and its aftermath, pursuing now the rumors that began to spread about Thalia. Pointing to Tommie, Darrow asked: "What effect could it have but the effect that it did have on the mind of this defendant? Gentlemen, it was bad enough that the wife was raped and these vile stories circulated, causing great anxiety and agony. But now you ask that they must spend the rest of their lives in prison!" As before, he threatened that putting the defendants in the penitentiary "would place a blot upon the fair name of these islands that all the Pacific seas would never wash away." But the threat was balanced with his trust in the jurors' humanity. There was within them, Darrow said he was certain, as there was within every good person, "somewhere deep in the feelings and instincts . . . a yearning for justice, an idea of what is right and wrong, of what is fair between man and man, that came before the first law was written and will abide after the last one is dead."

On and on he went. "At times the old master's voice was as soft as a woman's," the Hearst newspapers reported the next day. "At others its roar was like thunder. He was dramatic. He was impressive in his rages, as his body crouched and bent, lean arms thrashing through the air. Now and then he brushed away a tear when dwelling upon some tragic part of the evidence." After once again repeating the tale of the Massies' misfortunes, Darrow cried out:

> My God! Gentlemen, am I dreaming? Is it possible that here in this court are twelve men honestly deliberating whether they should put this man Massie, the husband of this woman, and the mother of this afflicted woman, in prison for life on account of the circumstances that have surrounded this case? All right, gentlemen, I don't believe you can do it. I have seen too many jurors and know too many peo-

ple to believe that anywhere on this wide earth you can find twelve men so lacking in human qualities, in kindness, and in understanding. How could you sleep, hearing the words of Massie, picturing the tear-stained face of Massie's wife?

At noon, Darrow asked for another recess. Judge Davis gave everyone an hour and a half for lunch and people began filing out. Grace Fortescue remained seated, waiting for the courtroom to empty, her eyes on the departing jurors. "The stoical Oriental faces betrayed no emotion," she later wrote. "Ethnologically and traditionally, white and yellow and brown races are apart. How could such a plea appeal to the six men to whom the white man's code is a mystery?"

After the lunch break, through which he slept, Darrow returned to court refreshed and ready to continue his plea for compassion. Although his speech was elaborately decked out in rhetorical finery—patriotism, religion, psychology, and more—in the end all those themes were braided about a simple core: mercy. Darrow wanted the jurors to believe that Tommie had blacked out, and he repeatedly hammered away at the pressure the young naval officer was under and how any of them would have succumbed to it as he had. But even if they didn't believe the temporary-insanity plea, hadn't the husband and mother of the innocent young woman who had been beaten and raped suffered enough? What good could possibly come from imprisoning them? "I can't understand it!" Darrow shouted as he neared the end of his oration. "On top of all they have suffered, is it possible that anyone should say that the black gates of a prison should close upon them? Are they that type? Tell me, what have they done? Would they steal? Would they forge? Do they *look* like any sort of criminal type?"

During his entire time in Honolulu, after his early session with prosecutor Kelley, Darrow never spoke seriously or at length with anyone other than his clients, the press, and powerful members of the white business and military communities. As he later wrote in his autobiography, Darrow was puzzled by the few nonwhites he did encounter, recalling that "it was not easy to guess what they were thinking about, if anything at all." However, he had it on the authority of his haole friends that whites possessed absolutely no racial prejudice against nonwhites. Alas, the reverse was not true. "I knew that the white men had no prejudice against the brown ones," he wrote, "nevertheless the brown men were prejudiced against the white." It was true, he admitted, that nonwhites believed they had grievances. The Hawaiians had lost their land to the haoles and resented it, and "the new-comers, the Japanese and the Chinese, have accumulated little property . . . even though the white planters meant to be fair." But whatever the cause, the antipathy of nonwhites for whites was something he decided he had to address.

After telling the jurors how much he had enjoyed his stay "in this beautiful land, this fairy land . . . with its green mountains, its ocean waves that turn to every hue of the rainbow, its flower-scented breath, its kindly dispositioned people," Darrow turned briefly to the matter of race. He began by asserting that he had "never had any prejudice against any race on earth" and had "no racial feeling against the four or five men who committed this crime against Mrs. Massie. To me they are all alike." He continued:

> I ask every man in this jury to forget race and look upon this as a *human* case. As it affects the Massies, so it affects you and it affects me. Take this case as you would take one of your own. Ask what is right and I'll be content with your verdict. Take it gentlemen. You have in your hands not only the fate but the life of these poor people. What is there for them if you pronounce a sentence of doom upon them? What have they done? You are in a position to heal. You are not a people to take and destroy. I ask you to be kind, understanding, considerate, both to the living and to the dead.

It was 2:23 in the afternoon when Darrow finished—5:23 on the West Coast, 8:23 in the East. The first assessments of his performance were heard immediately on radio newscasts, while print reporters on the scene were preparing to wire their stories across the Pacific. On CBS Lowell Thomas intoned his opinion, calling Darrow "that veteran bulldog of murder trials" and describing his closing argument as "one of the most sensational efforts of his long and extraordinary career as defense counsel, and as the greatest showman at the American bar. The jury of seven white men, three Hawaiian half-castes, and two Chinese, showed more symptoms of interest in the proceedings today than at any other period in the trial."

In the courtroom, meanwhile, awaiting the prosecution's summation, Russell Owen of the *New York Times* scribbled the opening sentences of the story he would be filing that evening: "The years have not touched Clarence Darrow's power. With a vigor which belied his age, with sweeping gestures and flashing eyes, he held entranced a packed courtroom as he pleaded

Wednesday for an end to the suffering of those involved in the Fortescue-Massie murder trial."

Judge Davis called a fifteen-minute recess. The microphones were removed and across the country people turned off their radios or tuned to the regular programming.

At 2:38 John Kelley stood to deliver the prosecution's closing words. Somehow, despite the sultry atmosphere of the courtroom, his white suit remained crisp and unwrinkled. His cherry red tie appeared new. Telling the jurors that he suspected they were nearing a point that "the experts might call conversation amnesia," he promised to be brief. His position, he said, was simple. "I stand before you for the law—and opposed to those who have violated it. The facts are unrefuted. The defendants killed Kahahawai." Looking over at the defense table, he then added: "Are you going to decide the case on the plea of a man who for fifty years has stood before the bar of justice—which he belittles today—or are you going to decide this case on the law?"

Contrary to the heroic and compassionate portrait of Tommie Massie that Darrow had painted, Kelley described him as "a conceited, vain, egotistical individual who is responsible for everything that has happened since the night last September when he insisted that his wife go to a party that she did not want to attend." Ever since then, when he wasn't trying to "hide behind the skirts of his mother-in-law," the prosecutor said, Massie was lying about everything, including "the trances the doctors give such funny names to. Ever since the case of Harry Thaw that defense has been the screen for the rich and influential, so they could get liars and experts to put on a defense of insanity—as in this case. But this defense is not insanity. It is sympathy."

Later, Lowell Thomas would tell America that prosecutor Kelley's address was given "with a zeal amounting almost to ferocity." The *Chicago Tribune's* Philip Kinsley, a complete convert to the defense since the morning of Thalia's testimony, compared the two closing arguments, calling Darrow's "masterful" and Kelley's "vitriolic." In any case, it was the opposite of what everyone had heard all morning and most of the afternoon thus far.

Kelley provided examples of where Tommie had slipped while giving his testimony on the witness stand, betraying recollections of things he shouldn't have known during the time he claimed to have been blacked out. "If he remembers that, he remembers everything—and their insanity plea, like the dove of peace, flies out the window." If Leisure and Darrow could refer to God's will, so could he, Kelley decided, reminding the jurors that "they almost got away with it. Another five minutes. A shade up on the left side of that car, and the body of Joseph Kahahawai would have been consigned to the deep forever. But an omnipotent God prevented that, saying 'Thou shalt not kill—and get away with it.' Three able men and a cold, calculating woman let that man bleed to death in front of them, inch by inch. They let him die. They dragged him into the bathroom like a dog and let him die."

He went on to note that while anyone might confess to anything at gunpoint, he doubted that Kahahawai had, pointing out that Massie didn't even have the local dialect correct in his recounting of what supposedly were the victim's last words. But even if he had confessed—even, in fact, if he had committed the crime, although to this day, in his grave, he remained innocent—that did not give the defendants the right to kill him. And for that killing they must be punished. Eight years earlier, Kelley said, in representing the murder defendants Nathan Leopold and Richard Loeb, Darrow had admitted—here he quoted Darrow—that "there is no excuse for killing," and "if to hang these two boys would bring the victim back to life, I would say let them hang." But it wouldn't have brought him back to life and so Darrow asked the court to "grant these boys mercy by spending the rest of their lives in prison." Turning to look at Darrow, he asked: "What has transpired since then to change Mr. Darrow's ideas and now argue that killing may be justified?"

Perhaps the explanation for the defense attorney's change of heart could be summed up in the same word Darrow used to explain away Dr. Catton's testimony, Kelley said. And that word, "only multiplied several hundreds of times," was "pay." Like a psychiatrist, "a lawyer doesn't work without something on the line."

The Leopold and Loeb case was not the only trial of Darrow's that Kelley had apparently studied. He now paraphrased a line from the closing argument in the Sweet trial, though only he and Darrow probably knew it. Darrow had asked that jury to imagine what would have happened if a group of white men had killed a black man while protecting their home from a black mob. "Why they would have been given medals!" Darrow said. Kelley's version was: "What will happen if you give Lieutenant Massie a walk-away ticket in this case? Why they'll make him an admiral! They'll make him chief of staff! He and Admiral Pratt are of the same mind—they believe in lynch law. And if one man is allowed to take the law into his own hands, others will do so. I tell you, if the serpent of lynch law is allowed to raise its head in these islands, watch out. Watch out!"

Kelley's tone suddenly turned to disgust as he glanced across the room to where Tommie was sitting. "The best you can say for Massie is that he lied like a gentleman and had a very convenient memory. The defense must take you for a bunch of morons. Is there going to be one law for strangers in our midst and another for you and me?"

He was winding up now, pacing back and forth, then approaching the jurors and speaking to each of them by name. "I say to you Mr. Stone, and you Mr. Waterhouse, and you Mr. Sorenson, and you Mr. McIntyre, and you Mr. Chang"—and so on down the line—"that each of you has the most vital duty to perform of any twelve men who ever sat in a jury box under the American flag. And as long as that flag flies on its staff without an admiral's pennant over it, you must regard the Constitution and the law."

Referring to the title of a recent magazine article by a famous retired marine major general—and knowing well the jurors' fears for their livelihoods and for the political status of the islands—Kelley then added: "Pay no heed to what the admirals say. With General Smedley Butler, I say, 'To hell with the admirals!' Do what is right. You will have nothing to fear. Your families, your loved ones will have nothing to fear.

"Mr. Darrow has spoken of mother-love. Repeatedly, he has spoken of Mrs. Fortescue as 'the mother' in this courtroom. Well, there is another mother in this courtroom. Has Mrs. Fortescue lost her daughter? Has Massie lost his wife?" Kelley glanced over to where the parents of the murder victim were seated, and he paused, then asked: "Where is Kahahawai?"

26   The Unwritten Law

I t all came down to the "unwritten law," Clarence Darrow said later. "While it could not be found in the statutes," he wrote after returning with Ruby to Chicago, "it was indelibly written in the feelings and thoughts of people in general." Darrow was correct. The unwritten law, the belief that a man has a right to kill another man who has assaulted his wife, was still widely subscribed to by Americans, especially when the rape victim was white and the rapist was not. The unwritten law had been a silent but undeniable presence in the courtroom throughout the trial.

Judge Davis was not a believer in vigilante justice. He also knew that Judge Steadman's jury instructions in the Ala Moana trial had come in for after-the-fact criticism. It was unwarranted criticism—his instructions had actually been quite fair—but some people searching for a way to explain that jury's inability to reach a decision had focused on what they regarded as imprecise legal language by Steadman in his charge to the jurors. Davis would not make that error.

For thirty-five minutes the judge read his instructions aloud. He explained in detail the meaning of presumption of innocence, of reasonable doubt, of burden of proof. He defined insanity according to the law, and he noted that when a defense of insanity is introduced, "the burden of proof rests upon the Territory to prove the defendant sane beyond all reasonable doubt." He told jurors the difference between murder in the first degree, which requires premeditation; murder in the second degree, which requires malice aforethought, though not premeditation; and manslaughter, which does not require premeditation or malice aforethought, but is killing without authority, justification, or extenuation by law.

Assuming that any unanimous decision could be reached by the jury, for three of the defendants—Fortescue, Jones, and Lord—the possible verdicts were guilty of second-degree murder, guilty of manslaughter, or not guilty. Added to those options for Massie was not guilty by reason of insanity.

Judge Davis also instructed those who would be deciding the case that "the guilt or innocence of the deceased, Joseph Kahahawai, Jr., of the crime of rape upon the person of Thalia Massie cannot be considered by you or enter into your deliberations upon the guilt or innocence of the defendants." That, no one doubted, was the law. But as Darrow knew better than anyone, it was one thing to prohibit people from entertaining thoughts and quite another to enforce the prohibition.

Then there was the matter of public opinion. Long before being selected for the jury, all twelve men had known what a guilty decision in this trial could mean. The call for martial law in Hawai'i, or at the least a military-led commission government, had become a daily drumbeat in the national press. Media celebrity Floyd Gibbons had taken it on as a personal campaign, traveling to Washington to push the agenda with senators and congressmen, hammering away on the theme in his newspaper columns and radio commentaries, which reached tens of millions of people.

Even now, as the jurors were preparing to begin deliberations, in New York Gibbons was polling editors and publishers at the annual meeting of the American Publishers' Association. As he would report with delight four days later, there was overwhelming support among the hundreds of newspapers represented for putting the army and navy in sole political control of the islands. As a front-page headline in Hearst's Sunday *San Francisco Examiner* would read: "Leaders of Nation's Press Back Move to Save Hawaii for U.S. and End Asiatic Misrule."

In addition to the political repercussions, all the jurors would be affected personally by the final vote. Despite prosecutor Kelley's assurance that they and their families had nothing to fear if they voted to convict, each of them knew that was untrue. Jobs, businesses, friendships, hung in the balance. Nor is it likely that they were ever fully sealed off from the outside world while sequestered. It was now three weeks since the trial began, the hotel where the jurors were staying was thick with newsmen, and the twelve men had spent numerous afternoons and evenings attending movies and sporting events under the easygoing island-style supervision of court bailiffs.

Deliberations began at 4:30 on Wednesday afternoon. After an hour of preliminary talk, then nearly two hours for dinner, they returned for further discussion between 7:30 and 10:00 p.m. In wagering among newsmen and others the odds favoring a hung jury were prohibitive. It seemed certain that the vote would deadlock at seven for acquittal and five for conviction—the same as the proportion of whites to nonwhites among the jurors.

Following extensive discussion, and just before retiring for the night, the first round of ballots was cast. The vote was seven to five for acquittal.

. . .

By mid-morning on Thursday the press had discovered that adjoining the jury room there was a balcony that overlooked a park at the rear of the courthouse. Reporters began gathering in the park to watch for signs of juror unity or discord. Throughout the day the sounds of angry exchanges floated out through the open windows. From time to time small clusters of men would leave the room and stand on the balcony, smoking and talking. Observing closely from across the way, the *Chicago Tribune*'s Philip Kinsley wrote: "The first manifestation that the jurors were deadlocked came late this afternoon, when the seven Caucasian members came out of the jury room and stood on the balcony in the light rain. Their five colleagues, of Oriental and native strain, stayed inside."

That night, signs of a shift in the voting were rumored. In his nationwide news broadcast, Lowell Thomas said his sources confirmed the speculation. "The latest from Honolulu is that the jury is still deadlocked," he told his listeners. "Some reports now have it that the jury is ten to two for acquittal—others that the figures are eleven to one."

As lunchtime approached on Friday, the jury had been out nearly forty-four hours. Judge Davis called Kelley and Darrow to his chambers. Upon his arrival at the courthouse, Darrow cheerfully greeted the gathered newsmen, asking them how they thought things looked. Delighted with their replies, he asked: "I wonder if I can get the prosecution to agree to leave the verdict to you?"

Judge Davis was in a far less happy mood. He was close to deciding that he should call a halt to deliberations, but he informed the attorneys that he first planned to summon the jurors in the afternoon to light a fire under them. If they did not believe it was possible to reach a verdict, he would call an end to things before the weekend. Darrow was the only attorney to protest. He did not want a hung jury, with the possibility of a retrial, when it was common knowledge that the jurors were so close to outright acquittal.

At 4:00 p.m. the judge called the jurors to the courtroom. He addressed the jury foreman, John Stone, saying: "Mr. Foreman, this case has been in your hands for forty-seven hours. Answer this question 'yes' or 'no': Have you arrived at a verdict?"

"No," the foreman replied.

"Answer this question 'yes' or 'no,'" Davis continued: "Is there any prospect of your reaching a verdict?"

The foreman began to explain, but the judge cut him off. "Yes or no," he said sharply.

"Yes," Stone said. Then, after a pause: "I think so."

Everyone in the room was stunned.

In her memoirs, Grace Fortescue recalled the moment vividly. "The words startled me," she wrote. "Even though we believed the jury stood ten to two for acquittal, still I had harbored little hope of a verdict. Confident, we returned to the hotel. An hour elapsed. Again word came summoning us to the courthouse."

Apart from the reporters who now seemed to be living in the courthouse pressroom, a beaming Clarence Darrow was the first to arrive after the judge's call went out. "How did you get here so soon?" one correspondent asked him. "I flew," replied the old attorney. "Fifty years in the game and I still get excited!"

Next door in the pressroom, the wire-service equipment was being made ready. In addition, the local telephone company president had arranged for direct phone lines to be connected through to Roly Fortescue in New York; Tommie's mother in Winchester, Kentucky; and Deacon Jones's mother in New Bedford, Massachusetts.

It was nearly 5:30, the jury was assembled, the judge was on the bench, the attorneys' tables and the spectator gallery were full. All that was missing was the prosecutor, John Kelley. Everyone waited. Several minutes passed, and then the courtroom door flew open and Kelley, remembering at the last moment to snatch his white Panama hat from his head, rushed to take his place.

The judge asked the defendants to please rise. They did, and with them stood Thalia, brightly dressed in a pale blue summer dress with a small white turban on her head. A bailiff motioned for her to sit. Looking confused, Thalia reluctantly returned to her seat.

"Gentlemen, have you arrived at a verdict?"

"We have, Your Honor," foreman Stone replied.

A clerk took the jury's ballot sheets from the foreman and delivered them to the judge. He flipped through them, then handed them back to the clerk to read aloud.

The clerk appeared more nervous than the defendants. His hands trembled and his voice cracked. There would be four separate verdicts. The first was Tommie.

"We, the jury, find the defendant, Thomas H. Massie, guilty of manslaughter. Leniency recommended.

"We, the jury, find the defendant, Mrs. Grace Fortescue, guilty of manslaughter. Leniency recommended."

After the decision on Tommie was announced, he flinched and began working his jaw nervously. But Thalia shrieked, then collapsed into loud sobs, then wails. Many spectators were unable to hear the clerk's reading of the verdict on Grace, Jones, or Lord. But a look at their faces told all that was necessary. Each of them had been found guilty of the same crime, manslaughter, and for each the jury had recommended leniency.

But the lawyers in the room, unlike the jurors, knew that Judge Davis had little room for discretion in imposing prison time. Under the law governing manslaughter, he was required to sentence the defendants to the maximum of ten years at hard labor. Only after the first few months of incarceration could the inmates appeal to a prison board that, in consultation with the judge, might decide to reduce their sentences.

Clarence Darrow almost fell into his chair after all four verdicts were read. Later, in speaking with reporters who described him as looking much older than he had upon entering the courtroom, he said: "I couldn't believe it. I couldn't think or understand how anybody could be that cruel."

Following brief confusion and angry words between Kelley and Captain Wortman regarding custody of the defendants, Judge Davis set formal sentencing for the following Friday, May 6, exactly one week away. The now convicted felons were escorted from the courthouse, with Thalia, still in tears, turning to lash out at the prosecutor as she passed. Thalia's sobbing had become contagious. All over the courtroom people were crying. But not Grace. She walked head high and dry eyed to face a cluster of newsmen waiting outside for a comment.

Next door, the telephone calls to the defendants' relatives had gone through. When told of the verdict, Roly said: "What?" Then he hung up. In Kentucky, Mrs. Massie replied: "Manslaughter? What does that mean?" And in Massachusetts, Mrs. Jones sadly said: "There just doesn't seem to be any justice."

Grace agreed with Deacon Jones's mother. "I expected it," Grace told the gathering of reporters. "I felt all along that we would be unable to get a fair and just trial in Honolulu. American womanhood means nothing even to white people in Hawaii." That was the quote the Hearst newspapers, and all the others that subscribed to the Hearst wire service, led with. But it wasn't true. Grace later admitted that the verdict had taken her completely by surprise, just as it had everyone else. As she subsequently wrote: "There were six

white men on that jury who, it was rumored, in the first ballot voted for acquittal. If so, what caused those men to reverse their decisions?"

It was a question on the minds of many. The next day the *Chicago Tribune*,
with especially good access to Darrow, expressed the puzzlement shared by
most people who had been following the trial closely. "The lawyers for the
defense are still stunned by the verdict," its front-page story reported. "Conviction was regarded by them as almost impossible. . . . Racial lines were
obliterated by the jury's verdict, and the Hawaiian race cannot be in any way
held responsible for this decision. The Caucasian members of the jury could
have blocked the verdict. . . . The greatest business houses in the Territory
were represented on that jury."

Several jurors stepped forward, happy to explain what had happened,
although only one—Theodore Char, a young accountant with his own
business—agreed to be identified by name. At first, they said, the racial split in
the jury was almost exactly as predicted. During deliberations on the first
night and for most of the next day, the six haoles had held out firmly in favor
of acquittal. George McIntyre, a part-Hawaiian juror, joined them. A graduate
of Kamehameha High School, a quasi-missionary institution for Hawaiian
youth, McIntyre was employed as a clerk by the Matson steamship company.
Equally adamant in their opposition to the majority, and insisting on a guilty
verdict for second-degree murder, were the other Hawaiian juror, the Portuguese juror, and the three Chinese jurors.

On Thursday afternoon, after having been out more than twenty hours,
several of the haole jurors announced that further discussion was pointless.
They would never vote for conviction on the murder charge, they said, because they did not believe the defendants had possessed "malice aforethought," as explained to them by the judge. But they—and, as it turned out,
everyone else in the room—also were not convinced by the claim that Tommie had gone temporarily insane at the moment he pulled the trigger. In fact,
few of the jurors believed that he was the one who had pulled the trigger at
all, and most of them thought it extremely unlikely that Kahahawai had confessed to anything. But even if he had, no one regarded that as defensible
grounds for killing him, whichever of the defendants may have fired the gun.

In sum, neither of the defense's main strategies, the insanity defense or
the implied "unwritten law" that would have justified an honor killing, had
been successful in swaying the jurors. But the majority simply would not vote
to convict the defendants of murder. On the other hand, those most
adamantly in favor of a murder conviction believed with the others that

Thalia had been raped—perhaps by Kahahawai, perhaps not—and expressed sympathy for the Massies' ordeal.

Following separate caucuses an hour or so prior to dinner on Thursday, the jurors who supported conviction for second-degree murder suggested reducing the charge to manslaughter as a path to a compromise agreement. That reopened discussion because, as juror Char explained, regardless of their sympathies for the defendants, "Kahahawai was killed . . . and we could not allow ourselves to be swayed by emotions. Law and order must prevail for the sake of the best interests of Hawaii."

One by one, for the rest of Thursday afternoon and throughout the evening, the haoles began changing their votes. When they went to bed Thursday night, only two jurors still held out for acquittal: Willy Beyer, the German who made and sold potato chips for a living, and the Hawaiian, George McIntyre. Subsequent rumors in the press that the voting Thursday night stood at 10–2 were correct—but it was 10–2 for conviction on manslaughter, not 10–2 for acquittal.

On Friday morning, Willy Beyer joined the others. That left only McIntyre insisting on a not guilty verdict when they broke for lunch. He was still holding out, but appeared to be wavering, when Judge Davis called them in at four o'clock to ask if a verdict seemed possible. After returning to the jury room, the Hawaiian said he would support a guilty verdict if they all agreed to append to the decision a plea for leniency in sentencing. That sealed the vote. In the end, Char said, they all agreed that "no other verdict was possible. . . . We had to do our duty as we saw it."

As for Clarence Darrow's emotional four-hour closing appeal to them, another juror said: "He talked to us like a bunch of farmers. That stuff may go over big in the Middle West, but not here."

The verdict was announced at 5:38 p.m. on Friday, April 29. It was payday for the military, and that night Honolulu was filled with soldiers and sailors out for a good time. Every available police officer was put on emergency duty. The National Guard was on alert. Police in squad cars equipped with mounted machine guns escorted the jurors to their homes, and guards were posted outside. Thalia's alleged rapists were brought into police headquarters and locked up once again for their own safety. But the evening passed peacefully. News of the verdict hadn't had time to circulate, officials worried. The silence was ominous. The explosion would come Saturday night.

But Saturday was the start of the May Day weekend, and in Hawai'i for the past five years May Day had been celebrated as "Lei Day," a time for singing and dancing, pageants with honorary kings and queens, and the decoration of everything in sight with all manner of flowers and leis. On Saturday morning and afternoon the only gathering of military men and civilians occurred at the Honolulu Stadium, where army and navy marching bands performed while a celebrity baseball game was in progress. That night, at a public dance, a few sailors in attendance were said to have made loud and derogatory remarks about Hawaiians, but everyone ignored them—and soon a downpour as ferocious as a monsoon sent everyone scurrying home. On Sunday, again, the city was peaceful.

Some of the press did its best to stir up or to locate trouble. The *Advertiser* ran an editorial saying that even if Lieutenant Massie wasn't non compos mentis, prosecutor Kelley appeared to be so when, in his closing argument, he "lost his head and let loose a tirade" against the military. The *Honolulu Times* called Kelley's summation "a vicious and dangerous appeal to hate" and attacked the verdict, saying the defendants should have been "commended, not convicted" for what they did. And out at Pearl Harbor some navy men and their wives expressed their anger to reporters, one woman going so far as to vow never to eat another pineapple for as long as she lived.

Then there was Anne Kluegel. She was still getting a prominent by-line in the Hearst newspapers, and the day after the verdict was announced she called for a boycott of every company that employed the men who had served as jurors, beginning with the Piggly Wiggly store where Walter Napoleon worked. She also announced a mass rally, to which only white women were invited. The rally was sparsely attended, and John O'Loughlin, Napoleon's boss, confirmed that he had received an anonymous threat claiming that more than two hundred people would stop shopping at the Piggly Wiggly unless he fired the young Hawaiian meat cutter. O'Loughlin said the boycotters were free to take their business elsewhere, but Walter Napoleon would stay, and he did.

Philip Kinsley, the veteran reporter for the *Chicago Tribune,* had been the first mainland reporter to arrive in Honolulu to cover the case. By now he had been in town for a little over three months, and in a front-page story on Sunday, May 1, he observed that among a surprising number of people "the verdict is regarded as in strict conformance with the law, perfectly supported by the evidence, and the best thing that could happen in the islands. The situation goes fundamentally into the new attitude toward race and sex crimes that has developed here. Nowhere on the mainland perhaps could there have been aroused such a wide questioning and distrust of the story told by Mrs.

Massie. That was a result of the new interracial consciousness, which the Navy people have never been able to understand."

Kinsley was not alone in remarking that there appeared to have been a shift in racial attitudes during the past several months. Before more commentators on this topic were heard from, however, another crisis would loom.

In her quarters on the berthed ship USS *Alton,* Grace Fortescue was seething. Walter Dillingham had just sent her a huge bouquet of flowers and his condolences. She didn't want flowers. As she told one visitor, they had killed the wrong person. Instead of Kahahawai, she should have shot William Heen and William Pittman, the two attorneys most responsible for the failure to convict the accused rapists. Darrow said he wasn't through with trying to work his magic, for all that it had been worth so far. He told Grace and everyone else who was listening that they would seek a new trial, appeal to a higher court, ask for a pardon from the governor, and whatever else needed to be done. But in reality he knew his options were limited. "We could appeal to another court," he later recalled thinking. "This one can always do, and then be beaten again." If anyone was going to rescue Grace and the others, it would not be Darrow.

"I am astounded! Shocked!" So began Floyd Gibbons's Hearst column on Saturday morning, barely twelve hours after the guilty verdict was announced in Judge Davis's courtroom. "The Fortescue-Massie case verdict is legal mockery," he continued, suggesting that America "take the scales out of the hand of Lady Justice and give her a gun." But who was at fault for this outrage, this atrocity? None other than "every politician in Washington" who has refused the call for a "complete militarization of all the islands under a military commission." Because of their "refusal, negligence, or stupidity . . . Washington politicians have sacrificed American womanhood and decency in Hawaii."

Hard on the heels of this column, Gibbons followed with radio addresses and another, more lengthy, article that also was splashed across scores of front pages from coast to coast. "Are we no longer Americans? No longer free and white? Are all the mainland millions of us in a class with those seven white men of the Massie jury who let five yellow and brown men swing a verdict directly against the sympathies of the whole civilized world?"

The questions, of course, were rhetorical. But Gibbons answered them anyway. "I don't think so," he cried. "I won't think so! Maybe you don't want white American rule in Hawaii. I do!" He then called upon everyone willing "to line up on the side of right and decency" to "write or wire your representatives in the Senate and the House to do what they can, not only to knock down that verdict, but to make life safe for our American women in Hawaii."

For those who might be at a loss for words, every Hearst newspaper carried two boldfaced and boxed messages—one condemning the "Hawaiian rabble" and another to be cut out and mailed to Washington. With blank spaces for the sender to fill in the name of a senator or congressman, along with the sender's own name and address, the coupon contained a message urging the nation's leaders "to take immediate action to afford the protection of the United States government to American women in Hawaii . . . and to force respect in Hawaii for the American flag and its defenders." Soon reports out of the nation's capital said the volume of mail and cable messages on this issue was greater than on any subject since the end of World War I.

But Congress wasn't waiting to be told. A chorus of voices from the Senate and the House began calling upon President Hoover to pardon the convicted killers. It was answered by a Justice Department opinion saying the president didn't have that power, only Hawai'i's governor did. So a petition quickly circulated on Capitol Hill demanding that Governor Judd take action. At the time there was an almost perfect balance between Republicans and Democrats in the House of Representatives, each side equally obstructionist and—particularly since it was an election year—unable to accomplish much of anything. But within hours more than a hundred congressmen from both parties had signed the petition. They represented thirty states, from every region of the country, and they included the House majority and minority leaders as well as the chairmen of the committees on appropriations, military affairs, ways and means, and foreign affairs. The message, which was conveyed in a cable to Judd containing the names and titles of each signatory, expressed Congress's "deep concern for the welfare of Hawaii" and warned that only "the prompt and unconditional pardon of Lieutenant Massie and his associates" would assure the continuation of that concern.

In Hawai'i, Judd displayed his characteristic political acumen by describing the message as "a thinly veiled threat." It wasn't the only one. Within twenty-four hours more than a hundred cables arrived at his office in 'Iolani Palace, some from everyday citizens, many from government officials, including the secretary of the interior and Hawai'i's delegate to Congress. All of them urged immediate pardons before Judge Davis was forced to sentence the defendants to prison on Friday. The Hawaiian Sugar Planters' Association weighed in as well, with its Washington representative telephoning a frantic message suggesting that economic disaster was a certainty if the governor didn't—as Judd later recalled the words—"appease mainland sentiment."

Behind the scenes, as always, Walter Dillingham was wheeling and dealing. Darrow's assistant counsel, George Leisure, would soon describe Dillingham, who had not graduated from college, as the best lawyer among the bunch of them. Among Dillingham's many friends and acquaintances was Herbert Hoover, the president of the United States. A year earlier, at Hoover's urging, he had traveled 14,000 miles on an economic and political mission. During that time, he also had met with the president at the White House on several occasions.

Across the mainland pressure continued to build. The Hearst empire represented only part of the media assault on Hawai'i. Small-town newspapers piled on as well. It was not surprising that Tommie Massie's hometown *Winchester Sun* would rail against the "Japs, the Chinese, the Filipinos, and the Hawaiians with their different views of womanhood," claiming that in "any American state there would have been a prompt acquittal." But such editorials were typical everywhere that newspaper presses were rolling. Salem, Oregon, for one, was almost as distant from the South as it was possible to go on the continent. Its *Capital Journal* decried the conviction of the "honor lynchers," contending that the absence of the "unwritten law" in Hawai'i only demonstrated the islands' lamentable lack of "a code of morality as exists in Christian lands." That white men on the jury would vote to convict the killers of Joe Kahahawai only showed that "they have gone native and lost their racial pride."

Back in Washington, meanwhile, senators and congressmen were lining up to introduce a flood of legislation designed to punish Hawai'i. Even Lowell Thomas, on his nightly news broadcast, was led to comment that "some of these bills, if the truth were known, bear symptoms of the hysteria that always comes at such a time." And Will Rogers, trying for levity, as usual saw more deeply than most. "Well, about all you can see in the papers is Honolulu," he noted in his syndicated newspaper column. "Of course, I guess I'm all wet, but I have never seen any reason why the U.S. or any nation should hold under subjection any kind of islands or country outside of our own. We say we have it to protect the Pacific. Why don't we have the Azores to protect the Atlantic? Let's all come home and let every nation have its own surfboard, play its own ukuleles, and commit their devilment on their own race."

For almost forty years, since the toppling of their government by Americans, most Hawaiians had thought much the same thing. And that was why Lawrence Judd hesitated to do what the most powerful forces in the country were demanding of him. Pardoning Grace Fortescue and the others might placate Washington, but what message would that send to people in the islands—especially those who weren't white?

This wasn't mere paternalism. It was Dillingham who best put Judd's dilemma into words. "Unless one has lived in this community," he wrote in a memorandum to a wide circle of acquaintances, "one cannot appreciate the importance of the example to the people that they have no right to take the law into their own hands. While this may be condoned under conditions which prevail where whites are in the majority, it would be a hazardous thing to give any such recognition of lynch law in our community where it is vital to stress the necessity of abiding by the laws of the country." In other words, it's fine to lynch—so long as you don't give ideas to the wrong people.

Judd called together his kitchen cabinet, the heads of Hawai'i's largest corporations, and he consulted as well with others whose judgment he trusted. What should he do? The answers were mixed, even among top executives of the Big Five. Those who opposed unconditional pardons were as adamant as those who supported them were. Governor Judd was on his own.

And then, so some people at the heart of the case later said—although Judd always denied it—he got a call from the White House.

27   Case Closed

The first Monday of May opened with Governor Judd trying to deal with the torrent of messages he was receiving, as well as a carefully timed visit to his home from Clarence Darrow. Across the street from Judd's office at 'Iolani Palace the city and county prosecutor, John Kelley, already was back in court. Having been on hand for the sentencing of Grace Fortescue and the others Friday evening, on Monday morning he was beginning voir dire in a new case. In idle moments he was also catching up on a huge backlog of correspondence.

Most of it was hate mail, ranging from carefully typed letters with Park Avenue and Beverly Hills return addresses to scrawled messages in dull pencil on brown paper from cities and small towns throughout the country. Some, such as one on St. Moritz Hotel stationery, were relatively polite, merely describing Kelley as "one of the most slimy and loathsome characters in the world." Others referred to him as a skunk, a louse, a rat, a rodent, a dirty dog, a cur, a mongrel, a beast, a snake, a degenerate, a bastard, a cad, a son of a bitch, "a nigger turned inside out," and more. A number of letters, including one from a Kentucky chapter of the Ku Klux Klan, threatened to kill or to maim him.

A handful of correspondents, mostly lawyers, supported the prosecutor. The National Bar Association, organized seven years earlier as the leading organization of African American attorneys, passed a resolution praising Kelley's "performance of his duties unflinchingly and without fear or hesitancy." And one note, praising his courage and wishing "more power to your kind," came from William Pickens, the field secretary of the NAACP. Prominently featured on his letterhead was the name Clarence Darrow, a member of the organization's board of directors.

On Tuesday evening, May 3, Kelley received a telephone call at home from the territory's attorney general, Harry Hewitt. He wanted to meet with the prosecutor as soon as possible. It was important. There had been a new development in the Massie-Fortescue case.

A few newspapermen and a small group of attorneys were the only people on hand in Judge Davis's courtroom when, at three minutes before ten o'clock on Wednesday morning, a large U.S. Navy sedan pulled up at the rear of the Judiciary Building. Out of it stepped Grace Fortescue, Tommie and Thalia Massie, and the other two defendants.

Judge Davis called the session to order, announcing to those assembled that sentencing in the case of *Territory of Hawaii v. Fortescue et al.* was being conducted two days earlier than planned. Prosecutor Kelley stood and formally moved that sentence be pronounced. One by one, beginning with Deacon Jones, the defendants were called to the bar. "It is the judgment and sentence of the court," Davis announced, "that you, Albert O. Jones, be confined in Oahu Prison, at hard labor, for the term of not more than ten years. Costs remitted. Mittimus"—meaning the warrant of commitment to prison—"forthwith." Davis asked the prisoner if he had anything to say. Jones said no and sat down.

So it went, next with Lord, then Massie, and finally Grace Fortescue. At that point the new high sheriff of Honolulu, Gordon Ross, entered the room to take custody of the convicts. Newsmen were directed to leave, exchanging puzzled words with one another as they did so, because all the defendants—now sentenced to ten years at hard labor—were beaming with obvious pleasure. Thalia, who was dressed in a bright blue summer dress as though prepared to attend a party, seemed the happiest of all. Kelley quietly suggested to the reporters that they remain outside the building, but some of them headed across the street toward 'Iolani Palace. Governor Judd had announced earlier that morning that he would be holding an important press conference at 11:00 a.m.

Soon the doors to the courtroom opened and the sheriff led his prisoners away. After a stop at the attorney general's office, they were taken to Governor Judd's private chambers, where they stood by as their attorneys presented the governor with a petition for commutation. Darrow and Judd had agreed upon the language in advance. It wasn't a request for a pardon, which would have overturned the guilty verdict. Instead the petition sought only a reduction in sentence. Judd signed it, then left the defendants in his office, "strolling about, scanning the portraits of Hawaiian kings," wrote one observer, as he headed for the news conference.

Judd walked into his large outer office alone and read a brief announcement to the assembled press corps and other curiosity seekers:

> The four defendants in the so-called Fortescue case were sentenced this morning in accordance with Territorial law to ten years in prison. Acting on a petition of the four defendants, joined by counsel for the

defendants and in view of the recommendations of the jury, I am commuting the sentence to one hour in custody of the High Sheriff.

Since the warrant ordering the incarceration of the prisoners had been read at 10:30, their sixty-minute sentence was now due to expire at 11:30, about twenty minutes from then. Judd left, and the prisoners filed through his office and out onto the palace lanai to have their photographs taken and to supply reporters with their thoughts on all that had happened. Thalia said she was "thrilled and happy." Grace thanked her "friends back on the mainland, especially those who made it possible for Mr. Darrow to come out here." And Darrow told the press that he was satisfied. Of course, appreciation was due the governor, the judge, and the attorneys who had assisted him, he said. But most of his gratitude was reserved for "the newspapers that have given this case wide publicity, so that it went before a jury of 100,000,000 people, most of whom are not hampered by absurd rules of law and do not believe statutes are better than human beings."

Someone tapped Darrow on the shoulder. He was wanted on the telephone. The *London Times* was calling.

That night the defendants and their attorneys and supporters went out for a large celebratory dinner at a Chinese restaurant in Honolulu. The next night Walter Dillingham had them and two dozen others to a gathering at La Pietra, his Waikīkī estate. Following dinner, Dillingham, Darrow, George Leisure, Admiral Stirling, Admiral Pettengill, and Police Chief Weeber retired to the games room for cigars and brandy. They remained there until midnight, discussing a few loose ends that still required attention.

The biggest piece of unfinished business was the Ala Moana rape case that had ended in a hung jury five months earlier. Prosecutor Kelley had just announced that he planned to retry the case in a matter of weeks, but that meant Thalia would have to be available and willing to testify once again. Darrow's advice to her was that she pack her bags and get out of town immediately.

Publicly, Darrow said his urging Thalia to avoid a retrial was intended to save her from further trauma, and "for the peace of the island that I had learned to love." What he didn't say was that he had developed a very close friendship with Thalia's doctor, John Porter, referred to in Darrow's memoirs only as "a genial and wise physician." It was to Porter's beachfront home that the attorney often "stole away from the stress and strain of court to rest and talk about the endless problems that have ever been too deep and complicated for the minds of men." Darrow didn't say, but those deep and complicated concerns may well have included Thalia's reasons for making the rape accusation in the first place. Dr. Porter seriously doubted that she had ever been raped, and he knew that even if she had been, she could not have identified her assailants on a dark and moonless night.

But Walter Dillingham was adamant that Thalia remain in the islands to carry through with a second trial. Although on several occasions Dillingham, like Dr. Porter and many others, had expressed private doubts about the guilt of the accused men, he wanted Thalia to "complete her heroic stand," he said, "and not give those who have been vicious an opportunity to say further unkind things." He also wanted to satisfy the navy, with which he had a collection of multimillion-dollar contracts.

Darrow's recommendation won out. On Sunday, four days after the commutation of their sentences, Grace and Tommie—who was being transferred by the navy to another assignment—along with Thalia and Clarence and Ruby Darrow, boarded the ocean liner *Malolo* for the journey to San Francisco. Jones and Lord were leaving the next day on a navy vessel. Honolulu authorities insisted that Thalia remain for the rape retrial, and they announced their intention to use legal means to keep her in the islands. The result was a minor comedy of subterfuge and frustration. Thalia and the others were brought alongside the ship in a navy minesweeper and sneaked aboard through a cargo bay while Captain Wortman wrestled with a police officer, successfully preventing him from serving Thalia with a subpoena.

For the next five days, as the *Malolo* steamed east, wire-service reporters and photographers on board sent news and images of the ship's most celebrated passengers to an eager public on the mainland. Thalia and Tommie and Grace were now famous. Clarence Darrow always had been. Everything they did was considered interesting. Darrow played the ship's horse race game, the Associated Press reported, but lost and decided to quit. Thalia started out taking her meals in her cabin, an observant Hearst correspondent wrote, but after the second day she began eating in the ship's dining room. Grace announced that she would campaign against Prohibition. Even Thalia and Tommie's dog was photographed snuggling up with the two of them as they sat in deck chairs, wrapped in blankets, smiling for the camera. The wirephoto flashed around the world. Anyone might have thought they were movie stars.

Back in Honolulu, Governor Judd was under fire from every direction. Almost no one approved of his commutation of the prisoners' sentences. Hawaiians were especially outraged. Princess Kawananakoa spoke for most of them when she observed that for months all the talk in the white press had been about "the laxity of conditions for law enforcement in Honolulu" and the need for "strict law enforcement." But as soon as a group of haoles was convicted of a crime, what happened? "With this commutation," she said, "the verdict of a jury composed of men with intelligence, sound judgment, and good character, with the facts and the law before them, becomes a farce. And the truth, as brought out by the prosecution, becomes a travesty. Are we to infer from the governor's act that there are two sets of laws in Hawaii— one for the favored few and another for the people generally?"

That, said the *Hawaii Hochi*, representing a largely Japanese constituency, was exactly what should be inferred. Reminding its readers of the Fukunaga case a few years earlier, the *Hochi* explicitly approved the Hawaiian princess's words and added: "When a thousand Honolulu mothers petitioned Governor Judd for commutation of the death sentence to life imprisonment, in behalf of an insane Japanese boy who had killed the son of a prominent banker, he turned a deaf ear to their pleas. But when a few powerful influences are brought to bear in behalf of society people who killed a Hawaiian youth the Governor is eager to grant the favor." That put him on record, in racially select instances, as "condoning crime, abrogating law and order, [and] justifying private vengeance."

Even the more conservative Japanese press joined the *Hochi* on this issue. A spokesman for the moderate *Nippu Jiji* took to the radio in a denunciation of haoles and American justice so "inflammatory and intemperate," wrote the *Hochi*'s editor, that he publicly disassociated himself from it.

More restrained, but no less important, the haole-owned *Star-Bulletin* joined the Japanese press. The jury's finding of guilt was the only possible verdict "unless our whole structure of government, the foundation of our liberties, and our civilization are to be set aside," it wrote. Among individual whites, retired territorial supreme court chief justice Alexander Robertson, preparing to leave in a few days as one of Hawai'i's two delegates to the Republican National Convention in Chicago, perhaps commanded the most attention. The guilty verdict rendered by the jury "was fully justified by the evidence and a victory for law and order," he said. "The immediate commutation of the sentence, however, renders the victory a hollow one." Anticipating criticism from the other side, he added: "A pardon would condone lynch law and set a disastrous precedent."

The two most ardently promilitary and probusiness newspapers in the city attacked from the opposite direction—the governor had not gone far enough. By commuting the sentences of the four defendants but not pardoning them, the governor had been "evasive and ungenerous," wrote the *Advertiser*. Since the opinion of the entire nation had favored a pardon, Judd's halfway measure "vitiated the spirit of clemency by inflicting on the defendants a stigma" and thereby again "placed Hawaii in an unenviable light before the nation." The failure of a complete pardon by the governor also unfairly left "a blot on [the defendants'] records," said the *Honolulu Times,* adding that everyone knew Lieutenant Massie only "acted as any decent, self-respecting man might."

But these comments were mild compared with the demands for a pardon made in Washington by senators and congressmen, and around the country by angry editorial writers. Floyd Gibbons quickly expressed his outrage that Judd's action left the defendants "branded as convicts," and called for another outpouring of letters to pressure Washington into forcing Hawai'i's governor to extend full pardons. And, whether carrying Gibbons on the front page or hammering away with its own editorials and editorial cartoons, the Hearst press, as always, led the way. Lest there be any doubt that William Randolph Hearst endorsed his editors' views, Hearst signed a two-column front-page Sunday editorial in all his newspapers referring to the islands as dominated by cowardly, incompetent, and corrupt "mongrels" who must be placed under total military control for the sake of U.S. security. But first, the convicted killers must be pardoned.

Across the nation, contrary opinions were hard to find. One was voiced by the small-circulation liberal weekly the *New Republic.* In an editorial it suggested that the conclusion to the Massie case had revealed an unpleasant truth about America's "master race" and the legal system that protected it. To bring the nation's formal and implied legal codes into alignment, the magazine's editors proposed adding "an amendment to the criminal law as follows: 'No white person shall be guilty of murder if he kills a member of another race, believing him guilty of a crime of violence against a member of the killer's family.'"

The *New Republic*'s proposal was intended as sarcasm, although many—perhaps most—white Americans would have supported it. One who with his words would not have, but with his deeds did, was Clarence Darrow. As promised to Grace, he soon filed an application with Governor Judd for a full pardon for his clients. The logic was pure Darrow. Since the governor had demonstrated with his commutation of the sentences that the killing of Joseph Kahahawai was no more serious a matter than "the mildest misdemeanor," Darrow said, it was "absurd" to burden his clients with a lifetime of lost voting privileges as felons. The commutation itself provided the grounds for a pardon, he claimed—and the slate should simply be wiped clean.

For once in his life Lawrence Judd held firm. It took him many years to admit it, but in his memoirs Judd said that he felt deeply guilty for "granting commutation in the face of threats" and wanted to "scrub my hands afterwards." Elsewhere, he said: "Had I possessed facts of which I learned later, I doubt that I would have commuted the sentences." Subsequent action and inaction on Judd's part make that last claim improbable, but even with what he knew then, Darrow's insulting application for a pardon was the last straw.

In a lengthy statement explaining his denial of the pardon request, the governor praised the prosecution and the jury, "which yielded every indulgence in favor of the defendants," and he excoriated the defendants for criminal recklessness and their attorneys for dishonesty in the presentation of their case. As the jury requested, he had extended mercy to the defendants, Judd wrote. But that was all he would do. "By their verdict the jury has built a monument upon which it is inscribed that lynch law will not be tolerated in Hawaii, and for the public good I propose to do nothing which would in any way tear down or destroy that monument."

Following this, Judd fired off a five-page letter to the secretary of the interior. In it, he said local navy officials, especially Admiral Stirling and Captain Wortman, had publicly lied about conditions in Honolulu in the aftermath of the first trial in December. They had also expressed contempt for police authority on numerous occasions, ranging from their evident support for the kidnapping and beating of Horace Ida to interference with efforts to serve a lawful subpoena on Mrs. Massie. Most important, however, was the navy's openly racist contempt for native Hawaiians. Judd said that Admiral Stirling had admitted in his presence that he and "practically all of the Southern officers in the Navy consider the Hawaiians or any dark-skinned person" to be deserving of the same treatment whites accorded blacks in the South. In light of all this, Judd wrote, he was requesting that Admiral Stirling and Captain Wortman be assigned elsewhere. Their replacements, he added, should be instructed that Hawaiians "are entitled to the same consideration, respect, and courtesy as any other American citizen."

Almost immediately, Wortman was shipped to another post. Stirling was transferred within the year.

■ ■ ■

Since early March, a month before the murder trial had begun, another sensational news story had been simmering in the pages of the country's newspapers, the kidnapping of the Lindbergh baby. Then, on May 12, one week after Judd signed the commutation order, the child's decomposed corpse was discovered and removed from a shallow grave less than five miles from the Lindbergh home. Headlines screamed with news of the tragic event. Eight days later Amelia Earhart, nicknamed "Lady Lindy," took off on a solo flight across the Atlantic that would make her the first person to accomplish the feat since Charles Lindbergh five years earlier. Meanwhile, Washington was filling up with thousands of World War I veterans living in tents and demanding payment of past-due cash bonuses. Elsewhere, the president of France and the Japanese premier were assassinated, and in Germany the chancellor resigned and a ban on Nazi storm troopers was lifted.

The Massies and Hawai'i quickly faded from public view. When, in late May, both the navy and the War Department formally declared their opposition to a military takeover of the islands, the bills in Congress seeking to impose martial law or a commission government collapsed. Lowell Thomas reported to his listeners that even Admiral Pratt, the chief of naval operations and the man who first publicly proclaimed the navy's right to lynch law in Hawai'i, said he was against a military takeover. When asked for his reasons, the admiral cryptically explained that "there are too many big outside interests."

The rest of the country may now have turned its attention to other matters, but in Honolulu John Kelley remained determined to retry the Ala Moana case. If the surviving four men were guilty of raping Mrs. Massie, they deserved to be punished, he said. If they were not guilty, they deserved to be acquitted and not left carrying the burden of public suspicion for the rest of their lives. An editorial in the *Hawaii Hochi* suggested that the four men were seeking a retrial.

Kelley knew Thalia's absence might make another trial impossible. But he was seeking advice on the legality of introducing Thalia's sworn testimony from the previous trial. A judge was likely to rule her earlier testimony inadmissible as hearsay, but hearsay exceptions were not impossible, especially in cases where a key witness was unavailable.

Kelley told the governor of his resolve to see the Ala Moana case retried, but after carefully reviewing the investigative reports and the trial record, he was convinced that the entire prosecution was tainted. A new investigation was required, one that would go over the same ground as before, including reinterviewing witnesses, but one that also looked in places that had previously gone unexplored. Moreover, this investigation would have to be conducted by an independent agency from outside Hawai'i, an agency that could not subsequently be accused of bias on behalf of the defendants—as the navy, the Dillingham coterie, and most of the national press had done regarding the first prosecution. Judd agreed with Kelley, and told him he had already asked the FBI to conduct just such an inquiry, but the Bureau had refused.

Kelley suggested bringing in the oldest and largest private detective firm in the United States, New York's Pinkerton National Detective Agency. For the past eighty-two years the Pinkerton Agency (which coined the term "private eye") had built an estimable reputation for coast-to-coast domestic espionage, crime fighting, and labor union subversion. Its agents had warred with Jesse James, infiltrated the Molly Maguires, and served as union-busting enforcers for railroads and mining corporations. If there was any partiality associated with the firm, it was one that would be favorable to those seeking a no-holds-barred prosecution. Whatever its agents uncovered and concluded, they could never be accused of a whitewash. And if the case was to be retried, Kelley—unlike his predecessor—would go to court with solid evidence.

Judd and Honolulu's mayor prevailed on the territorial legislature and the city's board of supervisors to fund the investigation. On June 9, Judd met in San Francisco with a senior Pinkerton agent named J. C. Fraser, who would be in charge of the inquiry. For the next three months both open and undercover Pinkerton agents interviewed scores of people, witnesses and nonwitnesses, in Honolulu, Los Angeles, Portland, Washington, Boston, and New York. They dug into the backgrounds of the accuser and the accused, studied police and hospital reports, retraced with stopwatches the steps of all parties on the night of September 12, and pursued leads suggesting that other men may have been responsible for the assault. One locally contracted detective who spoke Hawaiian interviewed and filed reports on dozens of men in pool halls and saloons expressly to dig up rumors and leads that would have eluded police investigators.

On October 3rd Kelley, Judd, and Attorney General Hewitt met in New York with Asher Rossetter, the General Manager of Pinkerton, who provided them with a draft of the final report. It was exhaustive, nearly three hundred pages in length, not counting interview transcripts, and it was devastating. Adding everything up, it concluded that "it is impossible to escape the conviction that the kidnapping and assault was *not* caused by those accused." A mountain of evidence showed that the five men "had no opportunity to commit the kidnapping and the rape." Those words were in the summary. The real bombshell came sixty-seven pages later: "We have found nothing in the record of this case, nor have we through our own efforts been able to find what in our estimation would be sufficient corroboration of the statements of Mrs. Massie to establish the occurrence of rape upon her."

Someone at the agency had leaked the results of the investigation to the press, and when Judd, Kelley, and Hewitt emerged from Pinkerton headquarters reporters were waiting for them. Judd refused to comment and left town as quickly as possible—but not before calling his office and dictating a formal letter to prosecutor Kelley and Attorney General Hewitt, ordering them to say nothing to the press about the report. Although he, the governor of Hawai'i, was the signatory to the letter, Judd said in it that he "had been directed by competent authority to do everything possible to keep the case out of the papers."

Back in the islands none of the three men would say anything about their meetings in New York or about the report, but before long the legislature and the board of supervisors began turning up the heat. By mid-November a rising chorus of political voices was saying publicly that the taxpayers had funded the report, as well as the men's trip, and they had a right to know the results.

Adding to the burden on Judd was revived pressure from the navy—and now the White House—for him to grant a blanket pardon to Tommie Massie and the other defendants. In late November the secretary of the interior, Ray Lyman Wilbur, sent Judd a cable in code demanding that he suppress the Pinkerton report, inasmuch as its conclusions were "unfavorable to the action sought"—meaning the pardons. Unspecified in the cable, but obvious, was another reason for keeping the Pinkerton findings under wraps: Washington's fear of embarrassment should it be revealed that five innocent men had been arrested and tried—and one of them murdered—for a rape that had never occurred. Judd replied to Wilbur that he was finding it increasingly difficult to justify withholding the report from territorial and city officials who had appropriated the money to commission it. Moreover, he now more than ever was not inclined to grant pardons.

Along with his response to Secretary Wilbur, Judd enclosed a lengthy memorandum prepared by the Honolulu law firm of Robertson & Castle. Robertson was the retired territorial supreme court chief justice who had spoken out critically several times during the past year on the matter of a whitewash in the murder trial. And Castle, as Judd informed Wilbur, was the brother of the current U.S. undersecretary of state for European affairs and a member of a prominent missionary and Big Five family. Their memorandum strongly supported the findings of the Pinkerton report, noting that its conclusion came as no surprise to members of the Honolulu bar who had followed the case closely. Contrary to "the commonly accepted and entirely mistaken view on the mainland," it said, everything in the rape case pointed to the innocence of the accused men and to the improbability of Mrs. Massie's claim that she had been raped. "The feeling is quite general," the memorandum added, "that the real story as to what happened to Mrs. Massie that night has never been told."

What Governor Judd appears not to have known was the extent to which Walter Dillingham was also making his views known to the White House and the Pentagon. Through direct contacts with the secretary of the navy, and by way of paid lobbyists to top officials in the executive branch, Dillingham was pushing Washington to demand suppression of the Pinkerton report and the granting of full pardons for Massie, Fortescue, Jones, and Lord. In his correspondence Dillingham did not deny the findings of the report regarding the innocence of the accused men or the fact that Thalia's rape, as he put it, may well have been "faked," but his larger concern was "the rotten publicity" that would inevitably follow upon the report's release. That was the same reason he gave for his advocacy on behalf of the pardons. As if to underline his fear of publicity, the Associated Press then declared the Massie case one of the top international news stories of the year.

But the local pressure on Judd was as intense as that coming from Washington. John Kelley joined in at last, reminding the governor that he had to do something soon about either retrying the rape case or dropping the charges. Since a retrial was now out of the question, Kelley had to give the court some reason for abandoning the case. And in doing so he had no intention of failing to mention the fact that the accused men clearly were not guilty, and that there had not been much of a case for their prosecution in the first place.

That, finally, was how a summary of the report, but not the report itself, was released. On February 13, 1933—the eve of Thalia's twenty-second birthday—Kelley entered a courtroom at the Judiciary Building and quietly took a seat. A trial was in progress, with Judge Charles Davis presiding. At 11:00 a.m. Judge Davis recessed the proceedings and asked Kelley if he had business with the court. Kelley approached the bench, holding a sheaf of papers in his hand, and said he did. "With the consent and permission of the court, I ask leave to file this motion for nolle prosequi"—the dropping of charges—"as to all the defendants in this case upon the grounds stated in this motion with which your honor is familiar."

Davis took the papers from the prosecutor, glanced through them, and said: "The nolle prosequi may be entered, the defendants discharged, and their bonds cancelled."

And that was that. None of the defendants or their attorneys were present. Attached to Kelley's motion was a detailed summary of the Pinkerton Agency's and his own findings in the case. All of it was printed in the newspapers the following day. Also printed was a story quoting Clarence Darrow to the effect that although he had not read the report, he rejected it. "I still firmly believe that the persons Mrs. Massie identified as her attackers were the guilty ones."

Thalia resurfaced as well. Since the moment of the first leaks regarding the report back in October, she had been calling the press from her home in suburban Philadelphia, close to where Tommie was now stationed, claiming the findings were rigged and making new allegations. The Pinkerton Agency obviously was just doing what it was told to do by Honolulu authorities wanting to avoid a retrial, she told reporters. All anyone in Honolulu cared about was protecting the surviving men who had raped her, she claimed: "The four Hawaiians are under the protection of a very wealthy halfbreed Hawaiian woman, a haole-hater whose influence upon public officials there is common knowledge."

As for her hiding from a subpoena server and her flight from Honolulu, she said that had all been a charade "to satisfy the natives who were angered when we were given our freedom." She had wanted to stay, she claimed, but local authorities coerced her into leaving by making the sentence reductions conditional upon her not testifying. She had, she said, been forced to trade the justice she sought for the freedom of her husband and her mother. To which a disgusted John Kelley, said: "Pure bunk."

Thalia also claimed that there had been eyewitnesses to her abduction and assault that the first prosecutor, Griffith Wight, had refused to subpoena. Wight, whose prosecution had been so aggressive and dishonest that he risked charges of planting evidence and suborning perjury, issued a bewildered denial. But Thalia vowed not to let the matter drop. "I sent an important cablegram to Honolulu today," she told the Associated Press on February 14. Declining to reveal the contents of the message or its addressee, she added that she "may have something startling to say when I receive a reply." The next day she called reporters again to tell them she had been the recipient of "a very satisfactory reply" to her cable, willing to identify the sender only as "an authoritative source." However, she was awaiting word from two other people she had contacted, she said, before she would make public her promised revelation.

In Hawai'i, no one knew what she was talking about. No public officials or prominent private citizens had received any cables from Thalia, including her strongest supporters, Admiral Stirling, Walter Dillingham, Anne Kluegel, or the editors of the *Honolulu Advertiser* or the *Honolulu Times*. Within days the mainland press lost interest in Thalia's obviously contrived stories. Honolulu's newspapers let them die them as well. Even before her latest headline chasing, Dillingham had met with the publishers of both the *Advertiser* and the *Star-Bulletin,* getting them to agree, he reported privately and with understatement, "that it was much to be desired that the matter be closed."

Only sporadically in the months ahead did anything noteworthy about the Massie case turn up in the press anywhere. One of the few instances occurred in early May when Illinois congressman Oscar DePriest referred to Tommie in a speech on the floor of the House of Representatives. DePriest was the first African American elected to the U.S. Congress in the twentieth century, and the only black congressman at that time. His speech concerned the ongoing trials of the African American "Scottsboro Boys," falsely accused of gang raping two white women in Alabama.

One of the defendants in the Scottsboro case, Haywood Patterson, had just been convicted and sentenced to death. Congressman DePriest contrasted Patterson's treatment by the Alabama court, based on dubious evidence, with that of Lieutenant Thomas Massie, the acknowledged and convicted killer of a young native Hawaiian. Not only was Lieutenant Massie free, but he remained a member in good standing of the United States Navy. Apparently, DePriest said, murdering a Hawaiian did not even rise to the level of "conduct unbecoming an officer and a gentleman."

28 Prelude to Revolution

Beginning in the late 1930s and continuing for years thereafter, the Hawaiian Room at Manhattan's Lexington Hotel was one of the nation's top venues for island entertainers. With its Polynesian decor and music and dancing it also became a favorite haunt of gossip columnists and, wrote one reviewer, anyone else seeking "relief from the noisy swing music and jazz entertainment reigning in many other places throughout the city." One night, former Hawai'i governor Lawrence Judd found himself there in the company of retired navy admiral Yates Stirling. Although, Judd recalled, their early friendship had deteriorated badly during the time of the Massie case almost a decade earlier, he invited the admiral to join his party at an after-dinner gathering in his suite.

Following some small talk the conversation inevitably drifted back to those months of turmoil in 1931 and 1932. Clarence Darrow and John Kelley had both died in early 1938. Darrow's death, at age eighty and after a lengthy bout of ill health, was not unexpected. Thousands attended his funeral in Chicago. The *New York Times* carried his obituary on its front page, the headline listing his three most memorable trials: Leopold and Loeb, the Scopes "Monkey" trial, and the Massie case. Ruby was overwhelmed with letters of condolence from politicians, attorneys, businessmen, journalists, actors, authors, and former clients—some still in prison. One telegram, carrying the return address "Wireless via Tropical Radio, Nassau," said, "Deepest Sympathy, Thalia."

Kelley's death, in contrast, was sudden and unexpected. He was fifty-two years old, and the cause was heart failure. In the years since the conclusion of the Massie-Fortescue trial Kelley had had a stormy tenure as Honolulu prosecutor, continuing to war with the haole establishment. Not surprisingly, the pallbearers at his funeral and those who attended the graveside service represented every race and nationality in the islands. In an irony that he would have appreciated, the *Star-Bulletin* chose to run a laudatory review of his professional life—"an able attorney, a fearless and remarkably resourceful prosecutor"—alongside an editorial concerning a federal antilynching bill that had recently been introduced in Congress. The newspaper was opposed to the legislation, saying it was an attack on states' rights and thus one more indication of America's turn toward totalitarianism. And it claimed a privileged and objective point of view on the subject, since Hawai'i, the paper said, was fortunate in having no history of serious racial trouble, violence, or lynching.

That night in New York, however, Admiral Stirling was less interested in talking about Darrow or Kelley than he was in pursuing some conjectures regarding Grace Fortescue. His autobiography, *Sea Duty: The Memoirs of a Fighting Admiral,* had just been published, and in it Stirling speculated about Joe Kahahawai's murder. After assuring his readers that Kahahawai was "a great brown athlete and beast" whose life was "not worth saving," he said that Anne Kluegel, the founder of the Honolulu Citizens' Organization for Good Government, believed that her friend Grace Fortescue, not Tommie, had done the killing. Stirling said he hoped she was right, because a mother more than anyone else would have a right to pull the trigger when her daughter's "confessed ravisher stood before her, saying: 'Yes, I done it.'"

The admiral's published hope had since become a conviction, and now Stirling was eager to know if Judd shared it, asking him, "Who do you think killed him?" Judd reported that he was lighting a cigar at the time and he brushed off the question by saying, "Admiral, when I don't know, I don't think." He and Stirling never spoke again.

But at least four people did know who killed Joe Kahahawai, and in time one of them admitted to having fired the fatal shot. It was neither Tommie nor Grace, but the sailor Deacon Jones. And Jones didn't do it because Kahahawai had confessed to the rape. He hadn't confessed, or spoken about much of anything, Jones recalled.

In an interview with a *Look* magazine writer in the early 1960s, Jones said that after the kidnapping, and immediately upon entering Grace's bungalow, he and Tommie had forced Kahahawai to sit down. Tommie was not carrying a gun—he had given his .45 to the other sailor, Edward Lord—but Jones was holding the elusive .32 automatic and was pointing it at Kahahawai. Grace and Lord had not yet arrived from the courthouse. So "here we are," Jones recalled; "we got a nigger sitting right there and I got a gun." Tommie began asking questions about the rape.

Initially Kahahawai appeared frightened, Jones said, "but then he started getting his nerve back . . . you could almost see that in his attitude. I suppose he was thinking what he would do to either one of us if he could get us alone." Then the young Hawaiian moved. At first Jones said he "lunged," but then the ex-sailor corrected himself, admitting that "somebody else might say he just leaned forward." So Jones shot him. He didn't hate "the black bastard," he said in response to a question. But when Kahahawai shifted in his seat, Jones regarded it as "a challenge," he explained. And in the end, he said, "I had no use for him."

At this point, "just as we killed this joker," Grace and Lord arrived. "I guess there was maybe a lapse of a minute at the most," Jones estimated. After momentary panic, the three men dragged Kahahawai into the bathroom, put him in the tub, turned on the water, and began removing his clothes. Jones had no explanation for this, other than to say they were frightened and that, on reflection, it now seemed an "asinine" idea.

A half hour or so passed—a little more than the time the medical examiner estimated it had taken Kahahawai to die—and then the three men wrapped the body in sheets Grace had given them and lugged the corpse out to the car. According to Jones, Tommie was a full and active participant in everything other than the murder itself, even ordering him to remain behind while the other three drove off to dispose of the body.

So who came up with the plan to say that Tommie had done the shooting after Kahahawai's supposed confession, and with the claim that he had blacked out just before pulling the trigger? "It was Mr. Darrow's idea to let Tommie take the rap," Jones said. "Tommie had a motive and the reason. After all, it was his wife."

Jones was not the most credible of witnesses, on this or anything else. But his story matched at critical points what Edward Lord had said in a previous independent interview. It was also what John Kelley had openly suspected all along. And not only Kelley. Other attorneys on hand during the murder trial said the same thing. Beyond the fact that the defense admitted the killing had been done with Jones's gun, Jones had been arrested with a cartridge clip minus one bullet hidden in his trousers, along with an empty shell matching the slug that was removed from the victim's chest. Jones also was said to have reacted nervously in court, visibly flushing during Tommie's testimony when he discussed holding the gun on Kahahawai and supposedly blacking out.

Legally, of course, none of it now mattered. Jones had been convicted of manslaughter along with the other three and had served his time, such as it was. Nothing more could be done to him. He was jaunty and seemed delighted with himself as he spoke.

After an initial honeymoon with the public upon their return from Hawai'i, the same would rarely be said of Tommie or Thalia.

· · ■

Back in May of 1932, as the *Malolo* was passing through the Golden Gate, San Francisco and the country waited to embrace the recently freed killers on board. A speedboat was sent to meet the ship so that Grace could make the initial connection for her cross-country trip to New York. A navy destroyer carrying Jones and Lord took them to the Mare Island Naval Base. And admirers joined reporters in mobbing the Massies and the Darrows as they made their way down the gangplank.

At an impromptu press conference on the pier, Thalia delighted the press with a humorous imitation of her tearing up the document prosecutor Kelley had handed her on the witness stand. "I don't think I ever saw anyone as mad as Kelley," she chortled. "My! He was just boiling!" While she spoke, Tommie was going from reporter to reporter, asking each of them to autograph his new copy of Darrow's autobiography. He also confirmed, said the Associated Press, that he had turned down "numerous stage contracts and other commercial offers" since being freed.

Standing nearby, waiting for Tommie and Thalia, was an automobile with a uniformed chauffeur. Admiral W. C. Cole, commandant of the Twelfth Naval District, had informed the press that he was putting a staff car and a driver at Lieutenant Massie's disposal for as long as he wished to stay in San Francisco, beginning with delivery to whatever hotel he selected.

Two weeks later, at the wheel of a newly purchased Auburn sedan, Tommie drove into his hometown of Winchester, Kentucky, Thalia seated by his side. In early May, when news came that his sentence for manslaughter had been commuted to a single hour in the company of the sheriff, a huge demonstration had broken out in Winchester. "The fifty-piece high school band led a parade of more than 100 cars, while many persons on foot carried torches," reported the *Winchester Sun*. "Whistles and bells over the city sounded a salute to the four Americans implicated in the 'honor slaying.'"

After nine days of parties, luncheons, and polo matches—plus a Women's Club fete for Thalia, a "stag dinner" for Tommie, and a nostalgic visit to the Millersburg Academy, where Tommie's military education had begun—the couple headed east again, first to Washington and then New York. Thalia spent the summer with her parents on Long Island, while Tommie reported for duty in Philadelphia. It was just like old times for Thalia. Before her visit was over she was arrested for speeding and driving recklessly through Bayport. The story told around town was that she became abusive with the arresting officer, who proceeded to tell her—before hauling her off to court—that she might be able to get away with murder in Honolulu, but Bayport was different.

Soon after she rejoined Tommie in Philadelphia, the findings of the Pinkerton investigation were leaked to the press. Thalia's bizarre phone calls to reporters and her imaginary cables to Honolulu were only external reflections of a private life that was now back to where she and Tommie had left it before that September night in 1931. Before long, Tommie was transferred to San Diego, but he went alone. Thalia moved in with her grandmother in Washington and let it be known—two days after attending a White House reception—that she and Tommie would soon be getting a divorce.

Meeting with the press on the eve of her departure for Reno, then the divorce capital of the country, she said: "The divorce is entirely Lieutenant Massie's desire. He feels the ties of marriage irksome and would rather be free. I have never believed in divorce, but my husband wants it so I will give it to him. . . . I'm terribly fond of him, and whatever he wants me to do I will do, gladly, because he wants it."

On February 23, 1934, Thalia appeared before Judge Benjamin Curler of the Reno District Court. Dressed entirely in black, as though she were a widow, Thalia filed the necessary paperwork claiming she was the victim of extreme mental cruelty. The divorce was granted in less than ten minutes.

Six weeks later, on the cruise ship *Roma* outside Genoa, Thalia slashed both wrists with a razor blade. After that failed to have its intended effect, she rushed to the railing of the ship's upper deck and threatened to leap, but other passengers pulled her away and had her taken to the ship's infirmary. When the *Roma* docked in Genoa, Thalia was admitted to a mental hospital, where she was found to be suffering from both "lapsus melancholia" and "nervous vibrations."

On board the ship Thalia had explained that she had tried to kill herself because she was despondent over her unwanted divorce. While resting in the Genoa hospital, however, she received a cabled message of sympathy from Tommie and said she had no intention of answering it. "He has ceased to exist for me," she told the press. As for whether she intended to attempt suicide again, she alternated her answers from day to day. But of one thing she was certain: "I shall never return to the United States." Within a month she was back in Washington.

By this time Grace's inheritance from her father had cleared all the complications that had kept her dependent on her stepmother during her stay in Honolulu. At last, she—and Roly—were rich. They bought a home in the Bahamas, naming it "Stonehaven," then moved to Palm Beach and supplied

Thalia with an allowance as she traveled from place to place, trying to find herself. As the years passed, she appeared in court periodically, usually on charges of public drunkenness. In 1950, while living in Los Angeles as Thalia Massie Bell, she was sued for beating and causing serious injury to her pregnant landlady after drinking wine for five hours. At the time she said she was a part-time student at Los Angeles City College, having been unemployed for the past three years. During that period she had been arrested several times for drunk driving.

Finally, Thalia married again. But it didn't last long. She divorced her husband and moved to Palm Beach to be close to her mother. Roly had died in 1952 and Grace was now living alone. Thalia took an apartment two miles away from where Grace lived, and on July 2, 1963, she was found dead in her bedroom, having swallowed an overdose of barbiturates.

By this time, Tommie had remarried twice and long since left the navy behind. But he had served eight more years following his transfer from Pearl Harbor. After the divorce from Thalia he was moved from one duty station to another—the USS *New Mexico,* the USS *Oklahoma,* the USS *Wright,* the USS *Tulsa,* and various navy yards from Puget Sound to the Philippines. But, despite his constant requests, none of his assignments were connected in any way with submarines. In 1938 he once again appeared, briefly, in the national press. While he was stationed in Shanghai, Tommie's new wife, Florence, had a run-in with a Japanese sentry, who slapped her face. Both Japanese and American authorities quickly intervened to prevent the matter from becoming an international incident.

Two years later, while assigned to the USS *Texas,* Tommie began behaving strangely. Both at home and aboard ship he would erupt in fits of rage, throwing dishes and other objects around. He showed up for work unkempt and unshaven, speaking incoherently and claiming that he could will himself to die at any moment if he cared to do so. He carried a small empty bottle with him everywhere, telling people that as soon as he filled it with the correct fluids it would bring him amazing powers. He could hear "pretty music" in his head, he told people, music that sounded like his thoughts being sung aloud, and he was convinced that he was under the guidance of supernatural forces.

After becoming violent at home one night, Tommie was taken to the Norfolk Naval Hospital in Portsmouth, Virginia, for observation. There, the same symptoms persisted—"ideas of grandeur and mental superiority," the medical reports read, "hallucinations, delusions, definite paranoid traits." Schizophrenia (or in the language of the time, "dementia praecox") was the preliminary assessment. From the Norfolk hospital he was transferred to the U.S. Naval Hospital in Washington, where psychiatrists confirmed the diagnosis, adding that he was "actively psychotic." Then he was moved again, to St. Elizabeth's Hospital, also in the nation's capital.

Following two months of observation and testing, Tommie was found to be suffering from "manic depressive psychosis, manic type." And, the diagnosis continued, "it is believed that this condition has existed over a period of years and has been responsible for many of his difficulties in the past." While under treatment at St. Elizabeth's, his medical report said, "much of the silly, bizarre, and unusual conduct began to subside and the patient settled into a mild hypo-manic state [which] it is believed is approximately his normal state."

On July 9, 1940, Tommie was discharged from the navy, the examining board having determined that "Lieutenant (junior grade) Thomas H. Massie"—the same rank he had held for the past ten years—"is incapacitated for active service by reason of psychosis, manic depressive. His incapacity is permanent, and is the result of an incident in the service."

For the next forty-seven years Tommie lived in San Diego on his disability pension, supplemented by jobs at General Dynamics, Convair, and other arms manufacturers. He also worked for a time as a real estate agent. On January 8, 1987—the fifty-fifth anniversary of Joseph Kahahawai's murder—Tommie died at home, following a prolonged illness. He was two months shy of his eighty-second birthday.

Of the major protagonists in the Honolulu tragedy, only Grace truly thrived in the years to follow. Within days after leaving Honolulu in mid-May of 1932, she told reporters that she would like to return to Hawai'i sometime. "Why not?" she said. "The climate is the best in the world, and I have many dear friends there." Grace never did return. But she did the next best thing. She had an architect design a special home for her in Palm Beach, calling it "Isle Home," a residence "that captures the glamorous flavor of Hawaii," wrote an admiring society columnist in the *Palm Beach Post*. The house, overlooking Lake Worth, was built around a swimming pool, with the interior furnishings and draperies all done in a Hawaiian motif. "Gorgeous sunsets and moonlit nights" were an integral part of the island feeling, the *Post* writer said.

At age seventy-five Grace took up waterskiing. At eighty-seven, on a visit to Acapulco, she tried parasailing. She lived in apparent contentment until age ninety-five, playing bridge and other favorite games up to the very end.

■ ■ ■

In Hawai'i, resentment smoldered. The Pinkerton report was placed in Governor Judd's papers at the territorial archives. Years later a noncirculating copy was made available to the university library. Few people read the report, or even knew it existed. The day after John Kelley announced he was dropping charges against the surviving defendants, newspaper coverage was extensive. But with the intervention of Walter Dillingham and the publishers of Honolulu's two leading dailies, it was short-lived. For the next thirty years those two papers, combined, produced barely a dozen stories related to the Massie case. Most people in the islands were left to rely on gossip or their memories to determine the actual guilt or innocence of the five young men Thalia had accused of raping her.

The four surviving suspects refused to speak publicly about the matter after the charges against them were dropped. Ida, Takai, and Chang did their best to melt anonymously into the community. Only Ben Ahakuelo, who continued to box for several years, remained a public figure. He again won the Hawai'i amateur championship, this time as a welterweight, but AAU officials prohibited him from returning to Madison Square Garden because they feared for his safety outside the ring in New York. "They might kill me there," he recalled being told. So he turned professional in 1935, finally retiring in 1938. Thirty years later he became the only one of the four men to break their self-imposed silence, giving a single brief interview to a reporter who had stopped him on the street.

They married, had families, and worked for decades in a range of jobs—stevedore, janitor, taxi driver, fireman, and more. Henry Chang was the only one to have further trouble with the law. But the stigma never left them. It haunted their marriages. Their children returned home from school to ask if the stories being told about their fathers on the playgrounds were true. At least one was urged on his deathbed to tell the truth about what really happened. Even Joseph Kahahawai, who had been murdered, could not escape. Some members of his family changed their last name because of a lingering sense of shame.

In the immediate aftermath of the affair, one thing the accused men had in common with directors of the Big Five and leaders of the tourist industry was a desire for public forgetfulness. Throughout 1932 fearsome images of native rapists lying in wait for white women remained a staple of most American newspapers. During the next twelve months the imprint of those fantasies on the American consciousness lingered, and tourism in Hawai'i remained stuck at its lowest level in more than a decade. But the lure of the islands would not die that easily, especially when it gradually became apparent that the tale told by Thalia Massie—even if true—was an aberration.

In 1934, although more than one in five Americans remained out of work, tourist arrivals jumped by more than 50 percent and continued to climb for the rest of the decade. The new president, Franklin Roosevelt, visited. The kings and queens of Hollywood also returned. But as far as Hawai'i's image was concerned, Clark Gable, Bing Crosby, Carole Lombard, and all the rest couldn't hold a candle to seven-year-old Shirley Temple—the biggest box-office draw in the country—who made a hugely publicized visit in 1935. Even the bartender at the Royal Hawaiian Hotel was inspired to name a nonalcoholic drink in her honor. The next year more tourists showed up than ever before.

By then, as crowded luxury liners once more sailed into Honolulu Harbor, their passengers greeted by musicians, dancers, and smiling Hawaiians with armloads of flower leis, it seemed as though old times—the glamorous halcyon days of the 1920s—had returned. But it wasn't old times. It would never be old times again.

In late August of 1927, while sixteen-year-old Thalia and her young naval academy beau Tommie were falling in love at the Roosevelt estate on Long Island, the Italian anarchists Nicola Sacco and Bartolomeo Vanzetti were electrocuted in Massachusetts. To this day, no one knows for certain whether or not they were guilty of murdering a paymaster and his guard at a shoe factory in South Braintree. But there is no question that their trial was a fraud and that the executions changed America by exposing the gross partisanship of a judiciary in the grip of that era's Red Scare.

A year later, in a letter to a friend, the literary and cultural critic Edmund Wilson said that the Sacco and Vanzetti case had "revealed the whole anatomy of American life, with all its classes, professions, and points of view, and all their relations, and it raised almost every fundamental question of our political and social system. It did this, furthermore, in an unexpectedly dramatic fashion."

Small incidents, from time to time, have a way of doing that, whether or not precisely what transpired is ever known in detail. Twenty-eight years to the day after the executions of Sacco and Vanzetti a fourteen-year-old black youth named Emmett Till slept his last night in a small town in the Mississippi Delta. The next day, August 24 of 1955, the beaten and mutilated corpse of that eighth grader was thrown into the Tallahatchie River. Was it two men who killed him? Or was it ten? Even today, half a century later, that question is being revisited. But, as with the executions of Sacco and Vanzetti, there is little doubt that public revulsion against the lynching of Emmett Till helped to transform American society.

So, too, in Hawai'i, with the Massie case and the unpunished murder of Joseph Kahahawai. The Pinkerton detectives in 1932 and various other investigators since then have tried to determine exactly what happened to Thalia on the night of September 12, 1931. Who was the white man seen following her and possibly forcing her into a car? Was it "Red" Rigby, the only navy man at the Ala Wai party who possibly fit the description of her stalker or companion? Or was it Rudolph Fink, the man known as "Red Fig," who spent nights and weekends with her when Tommie was away? Was it someone else? And why were her facial injuries apparently more serious after she returned home than when she was picked up on Ala Moana Road?

For what it was worth, Tommie's best friends, the Pringles, later said they thought Thalia "told the story of rape to excite sympathy from her husband, and having told the story stuck to it, believing that her husband, who is a Southerner, would not leave her under such conditions." The only thing known for certain is that the truth was far more prosaic than the story she cooked up. Someone took Thalia for a ride and punched her. Perhaps Tommie added to her injuries before calling the police, perhaps not. But she was not raped. And the men she accused had never seen her before and had nothing to do with her at all.

But what Thalia unleashed changed Hawai'i—permanently. Beneath the glitter of the 1920s, life for most nonwhites in the islands had been a nightmare, especially for those laboring on the plantations or locked away in the slums, pitted against one another as they struggled to survive. In the midst of the Massie-Fortescue turmoil, however, and especially after the killing of Joe Kahahawai, cracks started to appear in what for years had been a monolithic social order. Prominent haoles in the legal community, in the press, and in politics began to speak out against the arrogance of the long-standing white oligarchy. At the same time, Hawaiian, Japanese, Chinese, and Filipino community leaders began meeting and finding more common ground than ever before. Even Admiral Stirling, in characteristic fashion, noticed what was happening, observing that the trials caused "the whites [to be] divided against themselves," while ensuing events "produced sinister forces in that polyglot community."

The changes in consciousness that had begun to emerge during the upheavals of late 1931 and early 1932 would not succumb to the media's after-the-fact suppression of the truth. Some of what the future had in store was quickly and readily discernible, beginning with election day in November of 1932, six months after Thalia and the others had left the islands. More than 90 percent of registered voters showed up at the polls. That was a higher figure than at any time in the previous twenty years and a greater proportion than would turn out for another election until statehood in 1959. Two years earlier, in the elections of 1930, Republicans had swept both houses of the territorial legislature with the same landslides to which they had grown accustomed since 1912. Republicans in 1930 captured forty-two out of forty-five seats, a ratio of fourteen to one. But in 1932 that majority was cut to three to one, as Democrats more than quadrupled their representation in both houses.

Even more striking was the change in the Honolulu Board of Supervisors. Voters turned the board upside down, transforming a six-to-one Republican majority into a three-to-one Democratic advantage. It was the Honolulu Democrats' greatest victory in twenty years. Outside observers might have attributed these shifts in political allegiance to the coattails of Franklin Roosevelt, who won the election to the presidency by capturing 58 percent of the national vote. But politics in Hawai'i was limited to local matters and local candidates. Voters couldn't cast ballots even for their own governor. The big issue in 1932 was the Massie case, and Republicans were identified with navy interests and with allowing Joseph Kahahawai's murderers to go free.

Among those swept into seats on the Board of Supervisors was Louis Cain, widely known to have lobbied Congress during the peak of the murder trial's national outrage, assuring his Washington contacts that the accused rapists were almost certainly not guilty. Also elected to the seven-member board was William Pittman, co-counsel for the defense at the Ala Moana trial less than a year earlier. His extraordinary closing argument—accusing the police and prosecutor of criminal malpractice and condemning upper-middle-class haoles as "rabble" and "servile sycophants" of the Big Five and the navy—still echoed in the public mind. Pittman would go on to serve as attorney general of the territory, and following his death in 1936 the bar association praised his courage in defending Joseph Kahahawai and the other accused men. "In a day of public hysteria, when others faltered," its resolution said, "he represented, with determined resoluteness, the causes of his fellow men."

The most prominent public office up for grabs every two years was that of delegate to Congress. In the election for that post in 1930 Republican Victor Houston had easily defeated the Democratic candidate, Lincoln

McCandless. It was the eighth time that the same hapless Democrat had run for the seat and lost. But in 1932 McCandless finally won, defeating the incumbent Houston handily.

McCandless, who was haole, made the Massie case the keystone of his campaign. In one speech, before a crowd of more than five thousand people in 'A'ala Park—once famed for its labor rallies—McCandless boomed: "Victor Houston wired the governor to pardon those people who murdered that innocent boy, a boy who had never been convicted of committing a crime. Houston wanted to have vigilantes here in Hawaii. Does that sound as if he had the best interests of Hawaii at heart?" It became his punch line, and it was a winner.

Two months later, as Walter Dillingham continued his efforts to have the Pinkerton report suppressed, he complained to his chief Washington lobbyist about the dangerous election results. "McCandless was elected, in my judgment," he wrote, "on his statements that he believed the boys innocent and that he never would have consented to a commutation of sentence for the Navy group." Local newspaper commentators agreed, one of them noting that the new congressional delegate had captured the post because of "mass Hawaiian defections and the help of Japanese votes."

Sweeping into office with McCandless, Pittman, Cain, and an unprecedented number of other Democrats, was an equally unprecedented number of Asians, including four Japanese and three Chinese members of the Territorial House of Representatives. And in contrast to 1930, when Hawaiians complained about the first Japanese to be elected, in 1932 Hawaiians—who voted in larger numbers than ever—were crucial to the success of the Japanese, who still represented a small minority of registered voters.

In elections to follow throughout the 1930s nothing was ever again so clear-cut. The Democrats began squabbling among themselves over other issues, while many Japanese candidates still cautiously ran as Republicans. But the 1932 vote was just the visible surface of what was developing into a deep-rooted structural shift in Hawai'i's politics and culture. Other examples included the subsequent appointment of Robert Murakami, the third member of the Ala Moana trial's defense team, to a federal court judgeship—the first Japanese American to serve in that position. And Albert Cristy, reviled by the haole elite and threatened with disbarment after refusing to accept the grand jury's votes to free Grace and Tommie and the other murder defendants, instead of losing his job was later elevated to the territorial Supreme Court. Different signals of change, however, were detectable only by looking beneath the surface of things—at everyday language, for instance.

In Hawai'i, as elsewhere, referring to a person as a "local" had always meant that he or she was a longtime resident of the islands. It had nothing to do with race or nationality. Ethnic characteristics were ascribed using conventional terminology appropriate to each individual group—Japanese, Hawaiian, Portuguese, and so on. But beginning in the fall of 1931, people of color in Hawai'i took to describing the accused young men—who individually were Hawaiian, Japanese, and Chinese—by the collective term "local" to distinguish them from their haole accuser and her supporters.

At first it was a convenience, nothing more. But as the tempest continued, haole commentators both inside and outside Hawai'i, from Admiral Stirling to William Randolph Hearst, from the *Honolulu Times* to *Time* magazine, lumped nonwhites in the islands into catchall categories with noxious characteristics: "savages," "mongrels," "half-castes," "mixed breeds," and more. Proposals were made to disenfranchise nonwhites, to make them subject to all-white military rule. In response, the term "local" took on expanded and more potent meaning. Locals became, and to this day still are, natives and longtime Pacific Islander and Asian residents. Haoles could be many things, both good and bad, but in the new parlance of the islands they could never be local. A line was being drawn that signaled an emerging interracial and interethnic unity of consciousness among Hawai'i's various people of color whose mutual antagonisms, initially bestowed on them and nurtured by plantation overseers, had for so long kept them apart.

If a new sense of nonwhite solidarity was making itself known through the ballot box and the language of the streets in Honolulu, a related shift was occurring in rural areas and on the outer islands. For more than half a century immigrant workers from different nations, brought to the islands to labor on plantations, had created what linguists at the time called "makeshift languages," ethnically distinct blends of ancestral tongues with English. These were creole dialects, "pidgin English," that permitted a modicum of communication with English-speaking overseers but remained different from one another. Thus, there were separate Japanese, Chinese, Korean, and other creole dialects.

But recently, especially during and after the time the Massie case was playing itself out, those dialects had begun merging into a single panethnic creole that linguistically united the disparate groups. This dramatic shift was first written about by a young man named John Reinecke, who had started teaching school in the remote plantation community of Honoka'a on the Big Island in 1931, just when Thalia made her sensational accusations.

Reinecke, who followed the Massie case closely, remained in Honoka'a for four years, later using his observations there as the foundation for a master's thesis and then a doctoral dissertation at Yale. During that time he witnessed, among the younger generation of Hawaiians and Asians, the rapid evolution of their diverse ethnic creoles into a single dialect. Accompanying that change was the emergence of "a strong emotional bond [and] a consciousness of kind" among the nonwhite speakers of the new dialect, he wrote. The new mode of expression was "a class dialect and a local dialect in one" that served as "a mark of a large we-group of racial and class origin."

Reinecke worried that although what he was observing was "valuable in unifying the majority group of the island population," meaning all non-whites, it also was "a disruptive force between this group and the haoles." The same thing would be said of the new use of the word "local" on the streets of Honolulu. But that was precisely what some people—a young generation of labor organizers in particular—thought might be needed at that moment. The last two serious plantation strike efforts had occurred in the early 1920s. Each of them had represented the efforts of a single nationality, Japanese in one case and Filipinos in the other. Both had been disasters for the strikers. Since then, reported a federal study in 1931, labor activism had been virtually nonexistent.

Now, however, with their growing sense of multiethnic solidarity, union organizers of all racial and national backgrounds, especially Hawaiian and Japanese, began appearing on the outskirts of plantations and in the hangouts for stevedores and other workers near the docks. The new labor leaders' ancestries were evident in their names, including "Silent Jack" Kawano, Harry Takashita, Fred Kamahoahoa, "Benny Big Nose" Kaha'awinui—and, a classic of mixed racial parentage, Marcus "Maxie" Kamakanaikaouiliokalani Weisbarth. They also recruited haole union representatives from California and elsewhere to help them, and one of the first things the new arrivals suggested was the publication of a weekly newspaper.

From its very first issue the *Voice of Labor,* as it was called, had a single guiding principle: "Although they may not have a common origin racially, all men have a greater thing in common, the need to earn a living by the sweat of their brows." It was a theme hammered home, week after week, as groups of local laborers sent and received messages of support linking them with racially integrated unions on the mainland. At one point, recalling Clarence Darrow's performance in Hawai'i, the *Voice* noted that in a recent essay Darrow had written, "There is no such thing as justice either in or out of court." The newspaper's comment was "Clarence ought to know."

As early as the summer of 1933—only a year after the outrage over the freeing of Joe Kahahawai's killers—confidential navy intelligence reports were warning of growing interracial solidarity in even the most remote parts of the outer islands. The injustices of the Massie affair had provided the catalyst, but transforming the attitudes of Hawai'i's ethnically divided and intimidated workforce took time. That there would be no going back, however, became clear on a summer morning in 1938 when two hundred nonstriking workers in Hilo, on the Big Island, gathered to march in an expression of support for strikers on O'ahu. At one point, police opened fire on them. The *Voice of Labor* printed the spoken words of the leader of the demonstration, a Hawaiian named Harry Kamoku: "They shot us down like a herd of sheep. We didn't have a chance. The firing kept up for about five minutes. . . . They shot men in the back as they ran. They ripped their bodies with bayonets. It was just plain slaughter."

But in contrast to the failed strikes of 1920 and 1924—and every other strike prior to then—this time the marchers were not all of one nationality. They were Chinese, Japanese, Portuguese, Filipino, Hawaiian, and haole. And instead of the violence routing the demonstrators, by nightfall up to three thousand people were gathered in a nearby park to hear labor leaders denounce what had happened and call on those present to send letters of protest to Washington and continue the struggle. Obviously, workers had a long way to go. And, clearly, they would be resisted violently every step of the way. But now the entire field of battle had changed.

Two days after the jury in the Massie-Fortescue murder trial had returned its verdict, the *Chicago Tribune*'s Philip Kinsley wrote at length about "the new interracial consciousness" that people in Honolulu were talking about. That consciousness had grown throughout the 1930s, but after December 7, 1941, it would be tested as never before.

The Japanese bombing of Pearl Harbor killed and wounded thousands, including many civilians. An anti-Japanese panic swept the United States, and in barely two months President Roosevelt was signing Executive Order 9066. Although it ostensibly only empowered the secretary of war to "prescribe military areas . . . from which any and all persons may be excluded," in reality the order meant the internment of the entire Japanese American population of California, Oregon, and Washington, more than 110,000 people. That most of these people were American citizens, born in the United States, meant nothing. As the *Los Angeles Times* editorialized: "A viper is nonetheless a viper wherever the egg is hatched—so a Japanese American, born of Japanese parents, grows up to be Japanese, not an American."

If those Japanese Americans on the mainland were considered too dangerous to remain free, what of the larger number, and far greater proportion of the population, who lived in Hawai'i? In fact, less than two weeks after the attack and the declaration of martial law in the islands, the president's cabinet unanimously endorsed a plan to move all Hawai'i residents of Japanese ancestry from the major island of O'ahu to a remote and isolated locale.

But it never happened. In the end, less than 1 percent of Hawai'i's Japanese population was interned, only a third of whom were citizens. The conventional explanation for that relatively small number was that the Japanese represented such a large part of the population, almost 40 percent, that moving them would have been close to impossible. Moreover, they were needed to fill civilian jobs. All this is true.

What often is overlooked, however, is that in the islands, in stark contrast to what occurred on the mainland, an exceptionally aggressive anti-internment movement arose among non-Japanese. Not surprisingly, in light of the multiracial union and political struggles that had emerged during the past decade, this movement included Hawaiians and other nonwhites. But it also counted among its members what an army intelligence report referred to as anti-internment haole "zealots." And although the *Honolulu Advertiser* generally reflected the views of its second largest stockholder, Walter Dillingham, who dismissed talk of "the rights of American citizens" as so much "hooey that nobody cares a damn about," the *Star-Bulletin* campaigned editorially for the release of locally held internees.

The most telling examples of how people of non-Japanese ancestry felt about their Japanese neighbors, however, are found not in the records of what people said, but in the small things that they did. For one example among many, just as the War Relocation Authority was concluding its roundup of all West Coast Japanese Americans, in Hawai'i, on the island of Kaua'i, the citizenry reelected four Japanese incumbents to the territorial legislature and the county board of supervisors. Only after a national uproar, initiated by the *New York Daily News*, did the four step down, whereupon Hawai'i's governor congratulated them for their patriotism.

On O'ahu, meanwhile, the civilian population was being submerged in a rising tide of soldiers and sailors—almost 200,000 by 1943, more than 400,000 one year later. Most streetcar drivers were of Japanese ancestry, having been fired from federal jobs at Pearl Harbor, and they were constantly being ha-

rassed, especially late at night, by inebriated military men. As one driver recalled years later, it was commonplace for haole soldiers and sailors "to
threaten the small Oriental drivers, push them, call them 'slant eye' and 'Jap'
and give them a bad time." Then one night, unsolicited and unknown to the
drivers, groups of what he called "roving protectionists," large and powerfully built Hawaiians, boarded the streetcars. "They rode on the car," the former driver remembered. "They just stayed with some small drivers to see
that they were okay. No problem . . . 'cause these guys protected us."

Many local Japanese gave as well as they got when it came to supporting
victims of discrimination, especially African American soldiers and sailors,
most of whom were experiencing poor morale because of mistreatments by
white officers and enlisted men. Japanese streetcar drivers were known to
wait with their doors closed as brawls between blacks and whites played
themselves out on street corners, opening the doors only if it became necessary for the blacks to escape. "The relationship between the local people, local men and black men was close," recalled one African American veteran.
"There was what you would call an empathy from the local people as to what
the black people had endured." That was why, once the war ended, the black
civilian population of the islands increased tenfold.

Concerned and suspicious, military intelligence officials devoted one
fourth of a confidential 1943 report entitled *The Negro Problem in the Fourteenth Naval District* to the friendliness of the Japanese. The report noted that
some Japanese families were known to invite black military men to their
homes, sometimes as often as three or four nights a week. The pastor of the
Harris Memorial Church, the Reverend Harry Shigeo Komuro, came under
scrutiny for sponsoring social activities for African American soldiers and
sailors. Wilfred Mitsuji Oka was doing the same thing under the auspices of
the YMCA, and he was of particular concern because he was rumored to
have once met with officials of the NAACP in New York. (The report failed to
mention that he also was a longtime labor organizer.) Specific cafés and
dance halls were worrisome too, because "the Japanese, Chinese-Hawaiian,
and Filipino girls at these establishments have at times reminded the colored
boys of the discrimination by white people against other races, and they have
adopted a sympathetic attitude toward the Negroes."

Despite their efforts, the counterintelligence officers who prepared the
report were unable to find nefarious designs in these and numerous other
worrisome interracial activities. "While there is evidence indicating a genuine and legitimate common interest among Japanese and Negro leaders in
the advancement of minority groups generally," the report concluded, "the

motives actuating Japanese leaders remain obscure." If Japanese families caused concern by inviting black soldiers and sailors into their homes, however, one especially prominent Hawaiian leader provoked outright astonishment. Princess Abigail Kawananakoa moved out of both her houses, the mansion in which she had entertained royalty and her country home on the beach, and invited military men and women of all races to use them for dances and recreation until the war was over.

The fact was, Hawai'i was different. For more than a decade now, many people of color in the islands, along with supportive haoles, had consciously sought to overcome their differences in the interest of breaking down the white oligarchy that continued to control politics and the economy. In the process they had also begun to undermine exclusionary racial attitudes throughout the population at large.

With the end of the war, the power of Hawai'i's labor movement soared. Between December 1941 and October 1944 the islands had been under martial law, which prohibited labor unions. Immediately upon the lifting of military rule, however, certification drives began. Within fifteen months a hundred unions were certified, and the number continued to grow. One union in particular exploded in size. The International Longshoremen's and Warehousemen's Union (ILWU) increased its Hawai'i enrollment from 900 in late 1944 to 30,000 by 1947, expanding its reach well beyond the docks and into the vast agricultural industry.

The ILWU had a strictly enforced policy of nondiscrimination and racial inclusion. When its first postwar strike against the sugar industry resulted in a contract providing even more than the union originally had sought, the announcement was printed in all the languages of Hawai'i's multiracial workforce. The islands, one labor leader wrote at the time, had finally ceased to be "a feudal colony." Another labor and political activist noted the close ties between the union and the Democratic Party, its ranks swelling with Asian and Hawaiian veterans returning from the war and determined to at last take control of island politics from the Big Five and the Republicans. It was becoming a matter of "whether the Democratic Party was a part of the ILWU or the ILWU was a part of the Democratic Party," he said.

But when a dockworkers' strike in 1949 shut down the port for six months, causing food shortages and bankrupting businesses that were dependent on shipping, the Big Five and the Republicans struck back, accusing the union leadership of communism. At first, the rank and file brushed off the charges. As one member later put it, "Most of the boys didn't know communism from rheumatism, but they did hate the bosses." By the late 1940s and early 1950s, however, red-baiting had become the ultimate political weapon in America. And on June 4, 1951, the U.S. Supreme Court gave its approval to the Smith Act, which made it illegal to advocate the violent overthrow of the government. Less than three months later agents from the FBI's Honolulu field office arrested six men and one woman for violating the Smith Act. All but one of them were either Japanese or had a Japanese spouse, and all were connected in one way or another to the ILWU. They quickly became known as the "Hawaii Seven."

The transparently trumped-up nature of the charges, the racial character of the prosecution, and the familiarity of some of the names of the people pushing for conviction—including Walter Dillingham and the *Advertiser*'s editor, Raymond Coll—reminded observers throughout the country of the events of 1931–32. "Not since the celebrated Massie case twenty years earlier has any trial commanded such wide interest in these islands," reported the *Chicago Daily News*. Dillingham even tried to revive the old proposal for a federal takeover of the island government. But times had changed.

One of the accused men was John Reinecke, the linguistics scholar who, as a schoolteacher on the Big Island in the early 1930s, had first noticed the changing language patterns of nonwhites that signaled an emerging multiracial solidarity. In recent years he had written articles for a small Japanese-owned newspaper, the *Honolulu Record*, recalling the Massie case and comparing it with a then ongoing trial involving two Hawaiian men facing the death penalty for rape and murder. As before, the haole press had convicted the men prior to trial—raising the specter of a "crime wave" and referring to the "blood lust" and "savagery" of the defendants—and as before, the evidence was less than compelling. Eventually the men were convicted, and then pardoned. But now, under indictment as a suspected enemy agent and thus writing anonymously, Reinecke used the *Record*'s press to produce a thirty-seven-page pamphlet that suddenly seemed to be everywhere.

The title of the pamphlet was *The Navy and the Massie-Kahahawai Case: A Timely Account of a Dark Page in Hawaiian History*. It was timely not only because of the present murder trial—which Reinecke compared with the continued framing and execution of black men in the South as well as with the Massie case—but because it linked the white supremacy and political tyranny of the Big Five with racial doctrines that had been discredited in World War II. On its first page, the pamphlet observed that nearly everyone in Hawai'i had heard of the Massie case, but few people knew just how much of a sham the rape charges had been. And that was because the Pinkerton report, which established that fact beyond doubt, had been suppressed by the very same people who were behind both the railroading of the presently accused murderers and the defendants in the Smith Act trial.

At the time, all across America, people who were being hauled before courts and congressional committees on charges of communism quickly found themselves without jobs or friends, pariahs in their communities. In contrast, when the FBI asked Alva Steadman—the conservative judge in the Massie rape trial and now president of the Cooke Trust Company—to testify in the Hawaii Seven trial, he agreed. But he said he would testify for the other side. They didn't call him. However, fifty others did testify—as Steadman had intended to do—for the defense. One of them was John Henry Wilson, the mayor of Honolulu.

Wilson had been the head of the Democratic Party in the islands twenty years earlier. During the national convention in Chicago that summer of 1932 he gave a rousing speech informing his listeners that everything they had heard in the press and from Clarence Darrow about the Massie case was wrong. Now eighty years old, in the autumn of 1952, the Hawaiian-Tahitian-haole mayor publicly described Jack Hall, the principal labor leader among the Smith Act defendants—and, in fact, a member of the Communist Party—as an eminently loyal American and not a subversive at all. Moreover, he added, Hall had accomplished what the mayor had been trying to do since 1911, organize laborers of all racial ancestry, "so I take my hat off to him." The same attitude was expressed by John Burns, then the chairman of the Democratic Party and soon to become Hawai'i's governor.

None of this prevented the defendants from being convicted. But they won their case on appeal, and years later the Hawai'i legislature voted to award John Reinecke and his wife a quarter of a million dollars in compensation for the loss of their jobs and the injustice they had suffered. By then, however, Hawai'i was a state, the sitting governor was of Japanese ancestry, and the legislature was both multiracial and overwhelmingly Democratic.

The final turnaround had happened in 1954, a little more than a year after the Hawaii Seven trials. And the political transformation has thus far been permanent. So stunning was the Democratic success at the polls that year—with a coalition of Hawaiians, Asians, and labor-friendly haoles taking two thirds of the seats in both the House and the Senate—that it has been known ever since in the islands as "The Revolution of 1954." Among those reelected that year was Senator William Heen, chief counsel for the defense at the Ala

Moana trial more than two decades earlier. The longest continuously serving legislator in Hawai'i's history, Heen received more votes than any Senate candidate ever had, despite being unable to campaign because of illness.

Years later, Theon Wright, a courtroom reporter who had covered the 1932 murder trial for the *Advertiser*—and the son of George Wright, editor of the English-language section of the *Hawaii Hochi*—attributed the massive political shift of the 1950s directly to the Massie case. The rape and murder trials "widened the gap between the ruling oligarchy and those whom they regarded as second-class citizens," he wrote, thus leaving "the missionary–sugar planter faction exposed in all its totalitarian nakedness." The Massie case was, "in the long term," he said, "prelude to the revolution."

It is not unusual for revolutions to be short-lived. Unfortunately for Hawaiians, this one was no exception. Within five years of the oligarchy's ouster from dominance in the territorial legislature, the U.S. Congress approved statehood for Hawai'i, opening the floodgates of tourism and immigration. During the 1960s and 1970s the number of visitors to the islands increased from 250,000 to 4,000,000 annually, while tourist expenditures soared from $130 million to $3 billion per year. Residential population also grew rapidly, but it was driven far more by in-migration than by births. As the years passed, fewer and fewer islanders had been born in Hawai'i or had any sense of its tumultuous history, including the past struggles of Asians and Hawaiians for freedom from oppression.

Moreover, many people who should have remembered found it convenient to forget. Wealth and power in Hawai'i have always been synonymous with land. That was the case under the Hawaiian monarchy, under the reign of the plantation oligarchy, and in the years since statehood. Tourism and inmigration drove up land prices for both resort and residential development, and those who were in a position to take advantage of the situation, and were inclined to do so, did. Overwhelmingly, they were well-placed Democrats of Japanese and haole ancestry. With few exceptions, they were not Hawaiians.

The Japanese and other Asians who put down roots in the islands, rather than returning to their homelands or moving to the West Coast after leaving the plantations, became settlers in what, during the territorial period, was an American colony. As victims of racism, like the Hawaiians, they fought alongside the native people and against oppression from the 1930s through the mid-1950s. But when victory was achieved, and opportunities for material gain presented themselves, the disparity between the Hawaiians and everyone else, whatever their race or ethnicity, became manifest.

That should not be surprising. Settlers from afar, whether Asian or haole, understandably viewed the islands as a place where they might better their lives, and statehood provided newfound and seemingly limitless prospects for personal success. In contrast—and equally understandably—Hawaiians had not forgotten the U.S. seizure of their government and land, or the suppression of their language and culture, and to many of them statehood promised an opening to use long-denied democratic processes to right wrongs and protect what remained of their ancestral traditions. Rather than join the rush for individual prosperity, most Hawaiians devoted their post-statehood energies to protecting the land from further military expansion and from rampant commercial development. As with American Indians and other indigenous peoples throughout the world, to Hawaiians land and culture—a culture that predates the fall of Rome—remain inseparable.

But now, at the dawn of the twenty-first century, Hawaiians find themselves relatively no better off—and politically worse off—than they were a hundred years ago. Like indigenous peoples everywhere, Hawaiians today are the most ill housed and impoverished people in the islands. They have far and away the worst health and the shortest life expectancy of any ethnic group. In some categories their quality-of-life profiles are indistinguishable from what prevails in much of the Third World.

The crossroad Hawaiians face today is far different from that of their former allies in the battle against white supremacy and political oppression. And they are not the only ones who recognize that fact. At least a remnant of the non-Hawaiians who participated in that fight has been equally critical of what happened to Hawai'i's native people after the overthrow of the white oligarchy in the 1950s. One former stalwart in the struggle, born in the islands of Japanese parents in 1924, put it well in a letter to the author of a book on the Japanese success story. "If we are to be credited for what once was a noble cause forty years ago," Yugo Okubo wrote, "let us [also] be credited today for our unquestioning of the status quo, our blindness to injustice, and our ignoring of the victims of society."

In terms of civil rights and civil liberties, as well as the affability of everyday interracial relationships, Hawai'i remains well ahead of most of the rest of the country. But many of those achievements are legacies of an earlier time, when a semblance still remained of the idealism and solidarity that emerged following confrontations with raw, white power during the tumultuous rape and murder trials of 1931–32. The details of how and why that spirit declined are complicated—another story for another time. But unless it can be recovered, a rare and precious historical moment, one for which people gave their lives, may have been wasted.

Acknowledgments

This book began with a conversation I had with Susan Rabiner four years ago, while in New York on other business. Susan had been the editor of my first two books many years earlier, when she was at Oxford University Press. Since that time we have remained friends, as she went on to other publishing houses before founding her own literary agency and I moved five thousand miles away to my present home in Hawai'i. It is impossible for me to thank her adequately for all the support she has provided over the years—and especially with this book—without sounding maudlin. So, instead, I have dedicated the book to her.

One of the things Susan told me as contract negotiations were proceeding was that I would be extremely fortunate to have Wendy Wolf as my editor. As always, Susan was right. Wendy has been so enthusiastic and supportive of the project, and so charming and insightful, that I hardly noticed when her scalpel left page after page of an overlong manuscript on the cutting room floor. Actually, I did notice, and nearly wept on occasion, but it's a far better book because of her. Assistant editor Hilary Redmon has been a great help on several fronts, and has never failed to be diplomatic, even when she had good reason not to be. Adam Goldberger's copyediting was at once both precise and sensitive, a rare combination.

In Hawai'i, Haunani-Kay Trask read the manuscript with care and a wealth of knowledge. The Trask family has been a part of Hawai'i politics for almost a century. Her grandfather David Kaukaohu Trask was deeply immersed in the Massie affair; he acted as Ben Ahakuelo's attorney during Ahakuelo's first brush with injustice in 1929 and served as one of prosecutor John Kelley's pallbearers in 1938. Elected to numerous political offices, and a vociferous critic of Admiral Stirling and the plutocrats of the Big Five, he demanded an apology from *Honolulu Times* editor Edward Irwin for one of his characteristically racist editorials and wound up in a fistfight with him on the floor of the Territorial Senate. The Trasks continue to be on the political front lines, and Haunani's insights were invaluable.

Two other people in Hawai'i provided extraordinary support. For almost three years Ka'iulani Akamine worked as my research assistant, with the generous support of Manu Ka'iama, director of the University of Hawai'i's Native Hawaiian Leadership Project. Whether it was drudge work, such as plowing through and reproducing thousands of pages of microfilmed newspaper stories and other reports, or more creative detective work in the Bishop Museum and First Circuit Court Archives, Ka'iulani was never less than superb. As the end of the writing drew near, my dear friend Eiko Kosasa took time out from her own busy writing and teaching schedule to read the manuscript with inordinate care. She is an expert on local Japanese politics and culture, and her insights and corrections proved invaluable.

One day, while pressing ahead with the latter stages of writing, I received a telephone call from Mark Zwonitzer of Hidden Hill Productions in New York. He had been contracted to produce and direct a documentary film on the Massie case for WGBH and the PBS series *The American Experience*. Wary of having my hard-won research used by a likely competitor—whose film almost certainly would be released before my book was published—I was less than enthusiastic when he asked me to appear in the film and talk about my findings. I did agree to have dinner with him, however, when he arrived in Honolulu to do research. Out of that dinner's conversation came one of the most fruitful collaborations I have ever enjoyed—with one of the most intelligent and thoughtful people I have ever met. Rather than compete with one another, Mark and I spent the better part of the next year openly sharing ideas, information, documents, interviews, and photographs—becoming friends in the process. It has been a delight to work with him and with Jamila Wignot and Yuka Nishino, his extraordinarily engaging and talented associates. Without Jamila's assistance, in fact, this book would not contain most of the photographs that it does. We were even able to arrange things so that the publication of the book and the initial airing of the film—*The Massie Affair*—occurred on the same day.

Many other people were generous with their time and suggestions on specific matters, including Floyd Matson, Dennis Ogawa, Michael Forman, Momi Kamahele, and Karl Kim of the University of Hawai'i, and Roland Tharp of the University of California at Santa Cruz. Eddie Croom, curator of the Honolulu Police Department Museum, provided me with documents and an afternoon of good conversation. Stephanie Kelly donated a rich collection of Hawaiian and hapa-haole sheet music, while Malcolm Rockwell shared his extensive knowledge of that music and much more.

Several people with intimate knowledge of central figures in the case graciously provided information that would not have been available elsewhere, including Queenie Cavaco and Deena Ahakuelo (Ben Ahakuelo's daughter and niece, respectively), Ellen Hyer (Agnes Peeples's daughter), Nanette Purnell (juror Walter Napoleon's granddaughter), James Whiton (grand jury foreman Harry Franson's grandson), James Valuckas (Judge Albert Cristy's grandson), and others who asked that their names not be mentioned. Wilfred Mitsuji Oka, who grew up with the men accused of rape, spent several long afternoons with me, discussing his friends and the world they inhabited. Others with memories from that time included Gladys 'Ainoa Brandt, Judge Sam King, Dr. George Schnack, Dr. Rodney T. West, and Arthur Trask. Shirley Tavares Wetzel faxed me a copy of an important document not otherwise available, while Joseph R. Svinth, Curtis Narimatsu, and Francis Hoʻokano provided further information. In addition, Mark Zwonitzer shared with me transcripts of interviews he conducted with Ruthie Judd, Kay Napoleon, Ah Quon McElrath, and Judge Ronald Moon.

The heart of a project such as this resides, of course, in libraries. I have benefited from the extraordinary expertise and generosity of numerous people, beginning with Lynn Davis, head of the Preservation Department at the University of Hawaiʻi's Hamilton Library; Dore Minatodani of the Hawaiʻi-Pacific Collection at the same library; and De Soto Brown of the Bishop Museum Archives in Honolulu. Luella Kurkjian, the exceptionally knowledgeable chief of the Historical Records Branch of the Hawaiʻi State Archives, went out of her way to be helpful, as did archivist Patricia Lai. Marlene Paʻahao and Sandra Harms, also at the Hawaiʻi State Archives, were very helpful as well. Mary Ellen Rogin, archivist in the Theater Collection at the New York Public Library for the Performing Arts at Lincoln Center, and Nancy Sensil of the University of Denver's Westminster Law Library provided access to the radio scripts of Walter Winchell and Lowell Thomas.

At the National Archives and Records Administration, Pacific Region, Robert Glass was a generous, genial, and expert host, guiding me to materials I never would have located without him. Lynda Corey Claassen, director of the Mandeville Special Collections Library at the University of California, San Diego, went out of her way to provide access to essential volumes of the Richardson Report that were not readily available elsewhere. Melanie Francis of the American Heritage Center at the University of Wyoming Library helped locate letters of Clarence and Ruby Darrow in the Harry Elmer Barnes Collection, while the staffs overseeing the Darrow Collection at the Library of Congress and the newspaper and photograph collections at the San Francisco Public Library were unfailingly helpful with all my requests. At the Murray Research Center of the Radcliffe Institute for Advanced Study, Harvard University, research assistant Kathleen Ferguson located and copied for me E. Lowell Kelly's decades-old questionnaires on personality and marriage.

On Long Island, Gary Kerstetter of the Bayport–Blue Point Public Library steered me toward Mark H. Rothenberg of the Patchogue-Medford Public Library—who dug out everything he could find on the Fortescues and the Massies. John Bartosek of the *Palm Beach Post* did the same for items contained in his newspaper. And Deanna L. LaBonge, reference librarian for the Nevada State Library and Archives, located newspaper clippings from Reno related to Thalia and Tommie Massie's divorce. My apologies to anyone I have overlooked.

Notes

Three years after Thalia Massie's death in 1963, the first nonfiction books on the Massie case were published: Robert Packer and Bob Thomas' *The Massie Case,* Peter Van Slingerland's *Something Terrible Has Happened,* and Theon Wright's *Rape in Paradise.* A fourth book, Cobey Black's *Hawaii Scandal,* was published in 2002. All of them are competent journalistic accounts, and the volumes by Van Slingerland, Wright, and Black each contain information not available to the other authors.

Van Slingerland, a senior editor at *Look* magazine, interviewed Tommie Massie, Deacon Jones, Eddie Lord, and Thalia's physician, Dr. John Porter. Wright—whose father, George Williams Wright, was the editor of the English-language section of the newspaper *Hawaii Hochi* during the 1920s and 1930s—had covered the murder trial as a reporter for the *Honolulu Advertiser.* In his book he drew upon personal contacts he had made at the time. Black had access to navy materials that the others didn't, and her account has fewer factual errors than the previous books. Overall, however, they tell the same story.

This book is different from the others in several ways, at once both much narrower and far broader in scope than those that precede it. It is narrower in that it explores in detail the intimate lives of the central characters, demonstrating that they were not at all what previous authors thought them to be. It is broader in that it places the narrative within a thick historical context—reaching back more than a century and extending forward to the present. The Massie case was more than a true-crime drama. It was a pivotal moment in the history of Hawai'i, one that exposed a white supremacist social order (both locally and nationwide) and that provided the seedbed for subsequent change throughout the islands.

By and large, the written sources for previous accounts were local newspaper stories and an occasional reference to the summary pages of a report produced in late 1932 by the Pinkerton National Detective Agency. Neither the report itself nor the extraordinarily detailed and extensive field notes of Pinkerton's investigators—scores of interviews conducted in Honolulu, Los Angeles, Washington, New York, Boston, and Oregon—were used to any extent by previous writers. It is here, as well as in Tommie Massie's navy personnel and medical records, that much of the previously hidden information on the Fortescues and the Massies is found. The notes, typed and unpaginated, are on fragile onionskin paper in folders within the Judd Papers at the Hawai'i State Archives. Listed in the following pages as "Pinkerton Report," the field notes are cited here by the interviewees' names because of the absence of pagination.

Other large and unpublished caches of documents that have never before been explored include the fifteen-volume study *Law Enforcement in the Territory of Hawaii,* carried out under the direction of U.S. Assistant Attorney General Seth W. Richardson. It presents the findings of a team of Justice Department investigators sent to the islands in early 1932 to determine the reality underlying the crime wave hysteria that had recently leapt onto the front pages of newspapers throughout the country. The first 315-page volume analyzes the group's findings on everything from criminal activity and police force competence to the court system and the influence of "immoral and degenerate motion pictures" on Hawai'i's "youthful polyglot population." But at least as important are the succeeding fourteen volumes, composed entirely of interview transcripts with more than four hundred Honolulu businessmen, police officers, "prominent women," attorneys, ministers, journalists, and other citizens. Listed in the notes as "Richardson Report," by volume and page number, the study exists in hard copy at the Library of Congress and the Mandeville Special Collections Library of the University of California at San Diego. The University of Hawai'i's Hamilton Library lists the collection on three reels of microfilm, but the second reel (containing crucial volumes of interviews with journalists, attorneys, and police officials) is missing.

In addition to these archival materials, a dozen volumes of interviews produced by the University of Hawai'i Oral History Project, cited in the bibliography, provided important insight into attitudes of local people from the late 1920s through World War II. The Hawai'i-Pacific Collection of the University of Hawai'i's Hamilton Library also has relevant oral history documents gathered by Lawrence Fuchs for his book *Hawaii Pono* and other historical interviews conducted for the Watumull Foundation. These sources were supplemented with numerous interviews conducted specifically for this book. The Preservation Department of Hamilton Library has a number of exceptionally detailed annotated maps of Honolulu from the late 1920s and early 1930s that were drawn up by the sociologist Andrew Lind; they are very helpful in pinpointing neighborhoods in terms of race, ethnicity, crime rates, disease, and much more.

A good deal of valuable information was gleaned also from the diverse historical records of the Fourteenth Naval District Headquarters at Pearl Harbor, which kept close tabs on the Massie case; the records are on file at the West Coast branch of the National Archives in San Bruno, California. The Clarence Darrow Collection at the Library of Congress and the Harry Elmer Barnes Collection at the University of Wyoming provided insight into Darrow's state of mind at the time he agreed to represent the murder defendants. Scripts for Lowell Thomas's radio commentaries, heard by tens of millions of people at the time, are available on microfiche at the University of Denver's Westminster Law Library. Walter Winchell's scripts (which proved less valuable for this project) are on microfilm at the New York Public Library for the Performing Arts at Lincoln Center.

Archival materials in Honolulu include the Lawrence M. Judd Papers, the John C. Kelley Papers, and the Victor Houston Papers at the Hawai'i State Archives, as well as the extensive but not fully catalogued Walter F. Dillingham Collection at the Bishop Museum. Personal letters, memoirs, and other family materials regarding Judge Albert M. Cristy were graciously provided by Judge Cristy's grandson, James Valuckas.

Part of the confusion found in some previous writings on the case is attributable to the authors' reliance on newspaper accounts of the two trials, rather than official transcripts. A particularly interesting transcript of the first trial, in the Hawai'i State Archives, contains numerous handwritten comments in the margins. Although the author of the notes is not identified, several first-person references make it clear that they are the work of the prosecutor, Griffith Wight. They are revealing of his state of mind, both in what they say and what they don't say, especially when he is being accused in court of professional misconduct. No similarly complete transcript of the murder trial is available (access to many of that trial's documents is restricted until January 31, 2013), but most of it can be pieced together with materials from the state archives and the archives of the First Circuit Court—including partial transcripts and a minute-by-minute trial summary. The First Circuit also has a detailed record of the controversial grand jury session and its aftermath.

In addition to the material in the two leading Honolulu daily newspapers, the *Advertiser* and the *Star-Bulletin*, important information and opinions are sometimes found in the *Honolulu Times, Hawaii Hochi*, and to a lesser extent *Nippu Jiji*. At particularly controversial junctures I have also consulted such local newspapers as the *Hawaii-Chinese News, The New Freedom*, the *Hilo Tribune-Herald*, and the *Maui News*. A half dozen mainland newspapers were followed for the duration of events, while others were consulted for specific issues. They are listed in the bibliography and sometimes, but not always, in the notes. This is because the source notes that follow are designed to provide researchers with the information they need to pursue work on the case, without burdening the general reader with unnecessary detail. Where the events and narrative of the moment are uncontested and well covered in previous books, I have tried to avoid redundancy by not citing the obvious.

Similarly, I have cited newspaper accounts and editorials only when noteworthy and not otherwise obvious from the chronological context. The alternative would be to fill page upon page with unexceptional daily newspaper references as the narrative proceeds—providing information that researchers will already have and that general readers will not require. Most of the notes that follow, then, refer only to information beyond what is provided in earlier books or to data and/or interpretations that differ from what has been said in the past.

Introduction

The Patton quotation on Jews is from his journal, dated September 15, 1945, and cited in Eizenstat, *Imperfect Justice*, p. 11. His favorable comment on dictatorship is from a letter to Walter Dillingham, dated July 11, 1932, in the Walter F. Dillingham Papers (Box 24, Folder 553). Dillingham's congressional testimony is quoted in Duus, *The Japanese Conspiracy*, p. 273. The first of the two quotations comparing the lot of Hawai'i's plantation laborers with slaves comes from the U.S. Department of the Interior, Bureau of Education, *Survey of Education in Hawaii*, cited in Okihiro, *Cane Fires*, p. 141. The second is from a report by the National Labor Relations Board's Western Regional Director, Elwyn J. Eagen, "Report on the Hawaiian Islands," quoted in Zalburg, *A Spark Is Struck*, p. 16. For citations showing that such views date back to the nineteenth century, see Beechert, *Working in Hawai'i*, pp. 80–81. The comments of John Francis Neylan are from a letter to Walter Dillingham dated August 24, 1932, in the Dillingham Papers (Box 49). The statistics on executions are in Theroux, "A Short History of Hawaiian Executions," pp. 156–58.

All but one of the listed social and political characteristics of contemporary Hawai'i are factual matters of public record. The exception, as the only one subject to interpretation, concerns state tax fairness and equity; on this, see the detailed analysis entitled "The Way We Tax: A 50-State Report," in *Governing: The Magazine of States and Localities*, February 2003.

Newspaper and radio accounts of the 1932 trial, alluded to here, are given detailed citation in chapters 18 and 22–26. For cited examples of international coverage, see the *Times* of London and *Sydney Morning Herald*, January 11–12, 1932. The *Chicago Tribune*'s reference to the case as "one of the great criminal trials of modern times" appears in a front-page story on March 6, 1932. The Associated Press executive editor Charles B. Honce reported the vote of his editors on the top stories of 1932 in a wire-service story that was carried in the *Honolulu Star-Bulletin* on January 2, 1933. The "Hawaiian Horror" issue of *True Detective* (complete with a full-page cover illustration of a terrified, bound-and-gagged white woman) was its May 1932 edition.

The *Recorder* editorial appeared in its edition of May 4, 1932. The cited *New York*

Times reference to Clarence Darrow and the Massie case appears in the *Times*' obituary for Darrow on March 14, 1938, while the quoted clipping saved by Darrow is Kahn's 1933 article "Clarence Darrow Looks at America," in the magazine *Real America*. The clipping is part of the Darrow collection at the Library of Congress. Also in that collection is the special May 1938 issue of *Unity*, published to commemorate Darrow's life and work. It contains tributes from James Weldon Johnson, Arthur Garfield Hays, Harry Elmer Barnes, Clarence True Wilson, and others praising the legendary attorney's decades of labor on behalf of the underprivileged and the victimized. Not one refers to his last case, in defense of Joseph Kahahawai's killers. The phrase quoted from *Time* comes from its edition of October 7, 1966.

Chapter 1: Nothing but Trouble

The testimony of the people who were stopped by Thalia on Ala Moana Road is discussed at the end of chapter 3, where it is treated in more detail. On Roly Fortescue's paternity and his father's character, see Miller, *Theodore Roosevelt*, p. 51, and McCulloch, *Mornings on Horseback*, pp. 21–22. His college exploits were treated in a profile in the *Chicago Tribune* on January 10, 1932. For the extent of Roly's war injury, see Roosevelt, *The Rough Riders*, pp. 152, 249. Contrasting conditions aboard ship for the different classes of the Rough Riders are discussed by Samuels in *Teddy Roosevelt at San Juan*, esp. pp. 85–86. TR's reference to "savage tribes" is quoted in Drinnon, *Facing West*, p. 291, and Roly's opinion of the Japanese is mentioned in one of Teddy's letters collected in Morison, ed., *The Letters of Theodore Roosevelt*, vol. 4, p. 1115.

The Taggart divorce case was "a sensational scandal that rocked the nation in 1905," as one wire-service story recalled years later, during the Massie turbulence (see "Love Scandal Recalled by Lynching," *San Francisco Call Bulletin*, January 13, 1932); although the divorce was covered in newspapers throughout the country, the most accessible account now is the *New York Times*, esp. February 3, 1905; August 5–29, 1905; and October 13, 1905. On Roly's hunting and other White House activities involving Teddy, as well as Teddy's assessments of Roly, see Dalton, *Theodore Roosevelt*, p. 273, and Morison's *Letters of Theodore Roosevelt*, vol. 3, pp. 683, 689, and vol. 4, pp. 724, 732, 1086, and 1160–61. Also, see the *New York Times*, November 26, 1904, for TR's using Roly as a punching bag, and November 18, 1905, for Roly's resignation from the army. Roly's life following the Taggart scandal, from his first days as a war correspondent through his and Grace's World War I exploits in Europe, is recounted in his memoirs, *Front Line and Deadline*, esp. pp. 9–10, 24–25, 32–33, 181–85.

For Grace Bell Fortescue's brief engagement to Gaston de Ramaix, see the *New York Times*, August 23, 1908, and June 3, 1910 (mentioned as part of a story on her wedding to Roly). Grace's childhood and her life with Roly became the subject of newspaper feature stories during the events of 1931–32 and in her later years, when she lived in Palm Beach. See a wire-service story, "All Loyal to Mrs. Fortescue, Friends Praise Goodness," published in the *Honolulu Advertiser*, January 31, 1932, and an article on Queen Lili'uokalani's visit to the Hubbard estate in the same newspaper's December 20, 1931, edition. Other profiles appeared in the *Palm Beach Post* on May 7, 1965, and August 1, 1974. See also an unnamed Pinkerton agent's interview with reporters for Patchogue, Long Island's, *Island News & Eagle* and the assistant editor of the *Suffolk County News* in the Pinkerton Report's "New York Interviews" file. In that same file, for information on Roly and Grace's financial situation and style of life, see especially the comments of Mr. and Mrs. Emil Anderson, Mr. and Mrs. Ernest Bouché, Mrs. Warner, Mr. George Egner, and Colonel M. C. Buckey.

The Pinkerton "New York Interviews" file also contains information on Thalia and her sisters as children and teenagers; in particular, see the above-cited interviews with George Egner, the Andersons, and the Bouchés, as well as those with the Lincoln School's Mrs. Meyer, Mrs. Louise Henderson, Mr. Charles Fairchild, Mr. Gustave Johnson, and Mr. Robert B. Thurber. The diagnosis of Thalia with thyroid disease and its early symptoms are reported by the principal of the Hillside School, Mrs. Margaret Brendlinger, and the school's physician, Dr. George G. Fawcett, both again in the Pinkerton "New York Interviews" file. Thalia's extreme near-sightedness is reported in Van Slingerland, *Something Terrible Has Happened,* pp. 41, 97. Van Slingerland cites an interview with Thalia's military physician, Dr. John Porter, as the source of his information on Thalia's "drastically reduced visual acuity" and her near-inability, in Dr. Porter's words, even to "see in the daytime" without her glasses. (According to Van Slingerland, Porter attributed this to preeclampsia, but visual problems from that gynecological condition would most likely have been temporary.) Compounding Thalia's problem of near-sightedness were her difficulties with depth perception, a consequence of the strabismus that is evident in many extant photographs of her.

The American Thyroid Association kindly supplied information on hyperthyroidism and Graves' disease, while the *Oxford Textbook of Medicine,* vol. 1, sec. 10, pp. 40–45, provides historical details, including the fact that prior to the availability of radioiodine treatment the symptoms of Graves' disease were known, in some patients, to come and go and be "self-limiting." In addition to the entire range of symptoms that Thalia exhibited, the diagnosis of Graves' disease is supported by two basic facts: she had been medically diagnosed with thyroid disease, and the symptoms clearly indicate hyperthyroidism, not hypothyroidism; and she was afflicted with exophthalmos, which, among people with hyperthyroidism, appears only among those who have Graves' disease.

The first of the *Palm Beach Post* articles (see above) and several undated clippings from its files (and one dated September 7, 1934) discuss the activities and career of Thalia's sister Helene. Tommie and Thalia's summer kidnapping prank was reported in Long Island's *Suffolk County News* and the *Patchogue Advance* on August 26, 1927. Their engagement was announced in the *New York Times* on September 26, 1927, and their wedding was covered by the *Washington Post* on November 25 and 27, 1927.

America's economic and social conditions during the 1920s are well known. For some of the specific information cited in this chapter, however, see the following: Kurtz, *The Challenging of America, 1920–1945,* pp. 55–56; McElvaine, *The Great Depression,* pp. 37–39; Phillips, *Wealth and Democracy,* pp. 60–68, 79; MacLean, *Behind the Mask of Chivalry;* Susman, *Culture as History,* pp. 122–49; Lears, "From Salvation to Self-Realization," pp. 30–34; and Epstein, *Sister Aimee,* pp. 236, 252, 282–314. On Robert Roosevelt Jr., see the Pinkerton Report's "New York Interviews" with George Egner, Mr. and Mrs. Bouché, and Louise Henderson.

Chapter 2: Paradise of the Pacific

Thalia's failed pregnancy is reported in the Pinkerton Report's "New York Interviews" file by Mrs. Louise Henderson and Mrs. Emil Anderson. According to an interview with Dr. David Liu, in the report's "Honolulu Interviews" file, and the Ala Moana trial transcript testimony of Dr. John Porter, it is likely that the child was born dead, rather than having been miscarried. The cited rumors regarding Thalia's behavior in Panama, and her alleged stay in a sanatorium, come from interviews with Robert B. Thurber in Pinkerton's "New York Interviews" file and Nelson P. Pringle in its "Honolulu Interviews" file. One among many exuberant descriptions of Hawai'i from this era that refers to the islands as the "Paradise of the Pacific"—this one calling Honolulu in 1929 nothing less than the most beautiful city in the world—is Faris's travel book *The Paradise of the Pacific*. That was also the name of the publication that was the precursor to today's *Honolulu* magazine.

Schickel provides the box office information regarding *The Birth of a Nation* in his *D. W. Griffith: An American Life*, pp. 267, 281. On San Francisco's Panama-Pacific International Exposition, see Rydell, *All the World's a Fair*, pp. 209–33. For Hawai'i's participation and the American fascination with the 'ukulele, see Crampton, "Hawai'i's Visitor Industry," pp. 234–36; Beloff, *The Ukulele*, pp. 17–18; and Kanahele, *Hawaiian Music and Musicians*, pp. 290–92, 394–403. The quoted comment on most of the "Hawaiian" singers being Italian is from a letter cited in the *Honolulu Advertiser*, December 1, 1916, "Ukuleles Turned Out Like Wooden Nutmegs," while the reference to the sales of Hawaiian-style recordings is in Kanahele, *Hawaiian Music and Musicians*, p. 292. I am grateful to Stephanie Kelly for sharing with me her remarkable collection of Hawaiian sheet music from this era, and to Malcolm Rockwell for providing me with a wealth of background material on Hawaiian and hapa-haole music.

On the general topic of Waikīkī at this time, see Brown, "Beautiful, Romantic Hawai'i," and, for a more critical treatment, Wood, *Displacing Natives*, esp. chaps. 5 and 6, and Desmond, *Staging Tourism*, pt. 1. For an annotated list of films shot in and about Hawai'i from the late teens to the early thirties, see Schmitt, *Hawaii in the Movies*, pp. 22–37. The distinguished Hawaiian matron quoted on white women and beach boys is Princess Abigail Kawananakoa, from an interview in the Richardson Report, vol. 3, p. 495. Reference to the nineteenth-century requirement that single female visitors testify to their good intentions is in Porteus, *A Century of Social Thinking in Hawaii*, pp. 114–15. On the beachboys, see Timmons, *Waikiki Beachboy* (cited references on p. 138), and interviews with Fred Paoa and Louis Ko'oliko Kahanamoku in "Waikiki, 1900–1985," vol. 2, pp. 555–75, 853–82.

There is an enormous body of material on the making and marketing of Hawai'i—and especially Waikīkī—as a paradise during this time. Corporate-sponsored but informed and illustrated works include Berry and Lee, *Waikiki in the Wake of Dreams*, and Cohen, the *Pink Palace*, on the Royal Hawaiian Hotel and the *Malolo*. (The Mary Pickford and Alfred Bloomingdale references come from Berry and Lee, pp. 61, 79; opening night at the Royal is described in Cohen, pp. 42–49, and Desmond, pp. 88–94.) On the *Malolo*, see also Landauer, *Pearl*, p. 216. The price range for a room at the Royal in the late 1920s was listed in the naval commandant's "Living Conditions in Hawaiian Islands," no doubt as a warning, since no other hotel was even half as costly; see the same source (in correspondence files of Commandant, Fourteenth Naval District) for the advice for incoming officers on the "servant problem" and more. Statistics on tourist arrivals and expenditures during the 1920s and 1930s, cited here and elsewhere, are in Schmitt, *Historical Statistics of Hawaii*, p. 273, Table 11.7. See p. 660, Table 26.2, of the same volume for the decade-by-decade military population.

On open discussions among Japanese military leaders about an invasion of Hawai'i, see Stephan, *Hawaii Under the Rising Sun*, pp. 59-63. The quotation from the southern recent arrival is in Smith, "The Hybrid in Hawaii as a Marginal Man," p. 462. On Hawai'i and Tahiti as paradise, see Smith, *European Vision and the South Pacific*, and Forbes, *Encounters with Paradise*.

The reporter's description of Mānoa's homes appeared in the *Chicago Tribune* on March 13, 1932. Bennett's observations regarding Mānoa come from his book *Narrative of a Whaling Voyage*, pp. 203–4. The Hawaiian legend of Kahalaopuna exists in many versions; an abbreviated but convenient one can be found in Beckwith, *Hawaiian Mythology*, p. 152. The Maugham quotation is from "Honolulu" in *The Trembling of a Leaf*, pp. 207–8. Racial covenants in Mānoa real estate transactions, and those of other elite white

Honolulu neighborhoods during the 1920s, are mentioned in Johnson, *The City and County of Honolulu,* p. 309. The quoted *Star-Bulletin* editor was Bill Ewing, from an interview with Lawrence Fuchs for his book *Hawaii Pono,* University of Hawai'i Hamilton Library, Hawai'i-Pacific Collection. A very revealing demographic survey of Mānoa was conducted at the start of the 1930s; see Coulter and Serrao, "Manoa Valley, Honolulu." Annual tourism numbers are listed in Schmitt, *Historical Statistics of Hawaii,* p. 273. For business and bank failures, see Watkins, *The Great Depression,* p. 55. Information on the New York hotel scene in 1931 comes from Thurber's *Fortune* article, "New York in the Third Winter," and personal contact with the Essex House.

The Pinkerton file of "Honolulu Interviews" contains numerous personal recollections of the Massies' fractious initial year in Honolulu. Those whose comments are here cited are Mrs. Derek Perry, Dr. Paul Withington, Mr. Marcus R. Monsarrat, Miss Beatrice Nakamura, Mr. David L. Olson, Mr. J. V. Melim, Mr. and Mrs. Nelson Pringle, Detective Samuel C. Lau, Mr. J. K. Atcherley, and—from the Pinkerton "Los Angeles Interviews" file—Mr. and Mrs. H. O. Pfaender, who had been neighbors of the Massies before moving to the West Coast. The Ruthie Judd interview was conducted by Mark Zwonitzer for his film *The Massie Affair;* I am grateful to him for sharing it with me. On the frequent late-night police calls to quiet down activities at the Massie house (including his own visits in that capacity), see the interview with police officer William K. Simerson in the Pinkerton "Honolulu Interviews" file. See p. 167 of Blanding's *Hula Moons* for the quoted passage.

I am grateful to Karl E. Kim, former vice president for academic affairs at the University of Hawai'i, for information on Thalia's academic career at the university. Her sonnet "On Approaching Blindness" was published in *The Troubadour,* a University of Hawai'i student publication in May 1931; it and another poem of hers are quoted at length in the *Chicago Tribune,* April 2, 1932. Tommie mentioned his failed attempt as an actor in his trial testimony of April 18, 1932. Thalia's 1931 pregnancy is mentioned in the Atcherley interview cited above and is discussed in Van Slingerland, *Something Terrible Has Happened,* pp. 13, 39, 41.

Dr. E. Lowell Kelly's detailed account of his counseling sessions with Thalia, and his use of the case history questionnaire, is contained in letters to former governor Lawrence M. Judd, dated February 20 and March 9, 1967. See the Judd correspondence file in the Hawai'i State Archives; also, University of Hawai'i Board of Regents minutes for April 22, 1932. For background information on Kelly's work and his longitudinal study, I am grateful to Professor Roland Tharp of the University of California at Santa Cruz, one of Kelly's last doctoral students. Kelly's questionnaires are on file at the Murray Research Center of the Radcliffe Institute for Advanced Study, Harvard University; for help in locating them I am grateful to Kathleen Ferguson.

The "probation" agreement drawn up by Tommie is discussed in the Pringle interview, cited above. The quotation from Al Capone appeared in an approving *Honolulu Star-Bulletin* editorial on September 22, 1931, while the Mackaill passage can be found in LaSalle's *Complicated Women,* pp. 76, 189. LaSalle's book also contains detailed discussions of the films of Shearer, Bennett, and others during Hollywood's pre-Code era.

Chapter 3: Something Awful Has Happened

For the phase of the moon and other meteorological information regarding the night of September 12, see the testimony of U.S. Weather Bureau chief J. F. Voorhees in the Ala Moana trial transcripts. Information on the gathering at the Massie home and the trip to the Ala Wai Inn was provided by the Bransons and the Browns in interviews with the city and county attorney on September 23, 1931; the transcripts are on file in the Hawai'i State Archives. Annapolis class standings for Massie and Branson are listed in the U.S. Naval Academy Merit Roll, Graduating Class of 1927. The inventory of Thalia's clothing and accessories for the night of September 12 is from the Honolulu Police Department's examination of them; see the summary volume of the Pinkerton Report, pp. 62–64. Minor details in the text regarding Thalia's dress and the Ala Wai Inn come from the Pinkerton "Honolulu Interviews" with U. Uyeno, I. Uyechi, K. Shima, Tokuko Inouye, Yoshito Kifune.

The best discussion of the Ala Wai Canal is in Nakamura, "The Story of Waikiki and the 'Reclamation Project.'" For the quotation on attitudes of U.S. military personnel toward nonwhites in Hawai'i, see *Harper's*, October 1932, for Symes's "What About Hawaii?" A brief account of the F-4's sinking, in the context of the history of Pearl Harbor, is found in Landauer, *Pearl*, pp. 203–5. More generally, see Gray, *Few Survived*, and Maas, *The Terrible Hours*. On O'ahu having the largest concentration of U.S. military personnel anywhere in the world at the time, see Richardson Report summary volume, p. 12.

Mrs. Stogsdall's interview with Pinkerton agents, in the "Honolulu Interviews" file, provides the best description of Thalia's encounter with Lt. Stogsdall, along with background information. See also her previous interview (and those of two dozen others who were at the Inn) with the city and county attorney, in the Hawai'i State Archives. Thalia's first formal police interview, discussed more fully in ch. 6, contains her statement that she left the Ala Wai Inn "around twelve midnight." This timing is confirmed by her statement that there was no music playing at Waikiki Park when she passed by, and by the testimony of Mr. and Mrs. Goeas and Alice Aramaki, who placed her on John Ena Road at 12:10 or 12:15 a.m. Thalia's interviews on these points are excerpted in the Pinkerton Report's summary volume, pp. 18–20, 24; the testimony of the Goeases and Aramaki appear on pp. 95–121, including George Goeas's expressed regret at having seen Thalia. For personal memories of Aloha Amusement Park/Waikiki Park—and the surrounding area, including "Submarine Alley"—see "Waikiki, 1900–1985: Oral Histories," esp. vol. 2, pp. 549–50, 653–54, 969–70; vol. 3, pp. 1191–95, 1224–25, 1492–98; and vol. 4, pp. 1604–5, 1838. See the Richardson Report interviews, vol. 7, p. 1376, for the quotation from Honolulu attorney W. B. Pittman. The definitive history of rape in the islands is Nelligan, "Social Change and Rape Law in Hawai'i."

The relevant testimony of the Clarks and the Bellingers is in the Pinkerton Report's summary volume, pp. 3–7, and in their trial testimony. The George W. Clark Jr. interview, in the Pinkerton "Honolulu Interviews," is a matter of consequence because originally he had placed the time of the encounter with Thalia at about ten minutes past 1:00, and the delivery of Thalia to her home at roughly 1:40. After speaking with the others who were with him that night—all of whom put both times at twenty minutes or so earlier—he corrected his estimate. A Pinkerton reenactment confirmed the time they picked up Thalia as 12:50. Tommie Massie's account of his telephone call to Thalia and other quoted remarks are contained in his police statement, excerpted in the Pinkerton Report summary volume, pp. 168–69, and his testimony during the second trial. In the first instance he quotes Thalia as saying "something awful has happened," while in the second he has her saying "something terrible has happened"—which accounts for the different renderings of that exclamation by subsequent authors.

Chapter 4: Thalia's Story

The state of the Honolulu Police Department, and of crime in Honolulu, is the principal subject of scrutiny in the Richardson Report. See also Report of the Governor's Advisory Committee on Crime, February 9, 1931, esp. pp. 7–8, 22–24, and, for a general overview, Straus, *The Honolulu Police Department,* esp. pp. 18–28. Chang Apana's obituaries appeared in most major newspapers on December 10, 1933. The quotations from the Richardson Report on the characteristics of Hawaiian and other policemen appear in the summary volume, pp. 86–89; for the cited statistics on criminal convictions during 1930–31, see the same volume, p. 200, Exhibit No. 13, Table II. Mrs. Agnes Peeples's police report is quoted in the Pinkerton Report, summary volume, pp. 82–83. See also her courtroom testimony in the Ala Moana trial transcript.

Personal background information on police officers and detectives in this and the following chapter comes from interviews with them in volumes 10 and 11 of the Richardson Report. Additional information on John Jardine, including his actions on the night in question, can be found in his autobiography, *Detective Jardine,* esp. pp. 3–13, 58–81. Captain Kashiwabara's description of the telephone call from Tommie is in his Ala Moana trial courtroom testimony. The account of subsequent police activity that night, including the interviews with Thalia at her home, is taken from courtroom testimony and from interviews with the subjects conducted by Pinkerton agents. The prosecution did not want this information introduced as evidence, so the only testimony from the officers who interrogated Thalia that appears in the Ala Moana trial transcript came from those individuals called by the defense—Frank M. Bettencourt, William Furtado, George Harbottle, John Jardine, and George Nakea. For a fuller picture, this testimony should be read alongside the Pinkerton "Honolulu Interviews" with Nakea, Furtado, Bettencourt, William A. Gomes, C. A. Rickard, and William K. Simerson. Jardine's *Detective Jardine* also contains a retrospective view, including (p. 66) the then-generic nature of the local nickname "Bull," but Jardine's account is filled with minor factual errors and must be used with care.

Chapter 5: Hell's Half Acre

Greer's "Cunha's Alley" provides some nineteenth-century background on this area. See Kirch, *Feathered Gods and Fishhooks,* pp. 211–14, and Culliney, *Islands in a Far Sea,* pp. 227–29, for an overview discussion of Hawaiian fishponds. The population of Hawai'i at the time of Western contact and its subsequent collapse are the subject of Stannard, *Before the Horror* and "Disease and Infertility." On Hawai'i at the moment of initial European contact, see Beaglehole, ed., *The Journals of Captain James Cook,* which includes lengthy excerpts from the writings of Clerke, Samwell, and other officers and crewmen. The specific passages quoted are from vol. 3, pt. 1, pp. 591–96 (Clerke); and vol. 3, pt. 2, pp. 1158–59, 1170–71, 1178–82, 1562 (Samwell).

On sugar production and plantation labor, see Takaki, *Pau Hana.* The growth of the immigrant labor force is plotted in Nordyke, *The Peopling of Hawai'i,* pp. 178–79, Table 3–1. Reinecke, *Feigned Necessity,* p. 47, is the source of the quotation from the executive secretary of the Hawaiian Sugar Planters' Association. The most recent general account of the U.S. overthrow and annexation of the Hawaiian government is Coffman, *Nation Within.* On the extraordinary and prolonged efforts of Hawaiians to convince Washington to undo those actions, see Silva, *Aloha Betrayed.* The post-annexation Hawaiian-haole alliance is described in Fuchs, *Hawaii Pono,* pp. 153–62.

The Chinatown fire is the subject of Iwamoto's "The Plague and Fire of 1899–1900 in Honolulu." The cited newspaper exposés of slum life appeared in the *Honolulu Star-Bulletin* on January 2, 1920, and April 26, 1922. The 1911 report was Ray Stannard Baker's "Wonderful Hawaii," while the later sociological investigations were led by Andrew Lind; see citations in bibliography. On taxi dancing, see Lord and Lee, "The Taxi Dance Hall in Honolulu." See also the recollections of former residents in the oral history volumes, "Kalihi: Place of Transition"; "Reflections of Palama Settlement"; and "Remembering Kaka'ako: 1910–1950." I am also very grateful for information provided in several lengthy interviews by Wilfred Oka, who was born in 1910, grew up in these neighborhoods, and in time became a well-known community activist and labor organizer. The long-forgotten film *Hell's Half Acre* was a Republic Picture, starring Wendell Corey and Evelyn Keyes.

On the near-absence of unionization in the islands at this time, see Beechert, *Working in Hawai'i*, pp. 248–49. For annual inventories of increasing pineapple and sugar production, see Robert C. Schmitt, *Historical Statistics of Hawai'i*, p. 414, Table 16.4; and p. 419, Table 16.6. A statistical chart listing rates of voter registration, per capita property holdings, and much more data by race and ethnicity for the year 1928 is contained in the Fourteenth Naval District Headquarters Classified Correspondence, 1912–1941, under "Characteristics of Population, Territory of Hawai'i, by Nationalities." See also Lind, *An Island Community*, pp. 245–74 and 298–327, for additional statistical data. For detailed lists of Japanese employment data, Japanese radicals to be watched, and discussion of the need to eliminate language schools and undermine Japanese influence in the islands, see the lengthy unpublished document "Japanese Affairs: Survey of the Situation," in Dillingham Papers, Box 14.314. On the press and the attack on language schools, see Chapin, *Shaping History*, pp. 140–48.

Tensions among Chinese and Japanese are discussed briefly in Stephan, *Hawaii Under the Rising Sun*, pp. 15, 36, while alarm over potential Japanese voting strength among haoles and Hawaiians is discussed in Fuchs, *Hawaii Pono*, pp. 177–81. See also the Fuchs interview with Donald K. Mitchell of Kamehameha Schools in his notes on file at the University of Hawai'i's Hamilton Library, Hawai'i-Pacific Collection, and Princess Kawananakoa's interview with Seth Richardson, Richardson Report, vol. 3, esp. pp. 477–78. The Richardson Report's summary volume also is the source of the quotation on "loiterers and hoodlums," pp. 69–70. Data and insight on the ghettoes and slums of Honolulu, with emphasis on crime and interracial cooperation, are found in two articles by Andrew Lind, "The Ghetto and the Slum" and "Some Ecological Patterns of Community Disorganization in Honolulu."

Chapter 6: Arrest

Among his colleagues, according to the Richardson Report interviews, Detective John Cluney's reputation for veracity was not high, and it would fall to a new low by the time the present investigation was concluded. Typically, his different descriptions of the arrest of Horace Ida varied from one telling to the next. Since his is the only extant account of what happened at the Ida house that night—and since the details do not bear significantly on the case—I have constructed the most plausible rendition from his courtroom testimony and his Pinkerton interviews. The account of what happened at the hospital is based on courtroom testimony and Pinkerton interviews with C. A. Rickard, William Seymour, A. W. McKechnie, John Jardine, Monte Rigby, Agnes Fawcett, and Dr. David Liu.

John McIntosh's family background, and his service with the South African Constabulary, the New Zealand National Police Force, and the 'Ewa Plantation are from his Justice Department interview in the Richardson Report, vol. 10, esp. pp. 2208–9. On the Boer War and New Zealand's police force, see Judd and Surridge, *The Boer War*, esp. pp. 187–96, and Belich, *The New Zealand Wars*. The story of the Irish volunteers who fought against the British in the Boer War is told by McCracken in *Macbride's Brigade*.

For accounts of the 1920 and 1924 strikes, including the quotations cited in the text, see Takaki, *Pau Hana*, pp. 164–76, and Okihiro, *Cane Fires*, pp. 65–81. Ray Stannard Baker's extraordinary three-part report on early-twentieth-century Hawai'i was published in *The American Magazine* in November and December of 1911 and January of 1912. The quoted passage is from pt. 3, p. 331.

See Sheriff Patrick Gleason's comments on McIntosh in his Richardson Report interview, vol. 10, esp. pp. 2132–33. The latter portion of vol. 10 and all of vol. 11 are given over to interviews with policemen and detectives, most of whom have strong feelings one way or the other regarding Gleason, McIntosh, and each other. On McIntosh's habitual mispronunciation of Hawaiian names, see his own comment on the topic in the transcript of his testimony at the Ala Moana trial. McIntosh's comments on his being hired by "the business interests" and his thoughts regarding the competence of his officers and detectives are in his Richardson Report interview, vol. 10, pp. 2216–23. The interview with Detective George Nakea, the senior detective during the initial interview with Thalia, was so filled with invective regarding McIntosh—charging the captain with inefficiency, incompetence, and drunkenness, among other things—that the interview was cut short (vol. 11, pp. 2495–96).

The events at police headquarters are derived from courtroom testimony, Richardson Report interviews, and Pinkerton Report interviews with the following: John Cluney, Cecil Rickard, John McIntosh, Claude Benton, Percy Bond, and Horace Ida.

Chapter 7: Rush to Judgment

For Jardine on the interrogation of Ida, see his *Detective Jardine*, p. 69. Sheriff Gleason's comments on Machado are in the Richardson Report, vol. 10, p. 2133; Machado's comments on Gleason and McIntosh are in vol. 11, pp. 2483–86. On boxing and barefoot football in the 1920s and early 1930s, see the recollections in "Kalihi: Place of Transition," esp. vol. 1, pp. 159–66, 206–12, 225–35, 310–16; vol. 2, pp. 480–81; vol. 3, pp. 770–72, 837–40; and "Remembering Kaka'ako," vol. 1, pp. 69–101, 515–17, 522–23; vol. 2, pp. 672–82, 718–24, 734, 930–41, 1081–84. Also see Svinth et al., "Western Boxing in Hawaii."

The activities of Tommie Massie, Captain McIntosh, Officer Sato, Dr. Porter, and Detectives Machado, Finnegan, and Stagbar on Sunday morning and afternoon are reported by them in trial transcripts (in Massie's instance, the transcript of the second trial) and, with the exception of Massie and McIntosh, in their Pinkerton Report interviews. See also the Pinkerton interviews with Henry Chang and David Takai. The Pinkerton Report interview with Beatrice Nakamura is the source for the description of her brief time at the Massie house that day. I am grateful to information from the Model T Ford Club of America for information on the Model T and the Model A. On Takai's youth, see Pinkerton interview with Harold Godfrey. Joe Kahahawai's reputation among his National Guard colleagues is reported by Sergeant George Cypher, of the same Guard Company, in his Pinkerton Report interview; Curtis Iaukea is the source for the comment on the prosecutor in Kahahawai's robbery trial (Richardson Report, vol. 3, p. 524). The murder of William Kama and the subsequent military trial were covered extensively in the *Advertiser* and *Star-Bulletin* between October 5 and November 15, 1928. For military documents on the case, see United States v. Private Chester Nagle (Military Justice C.M. 184854), Office of Judge Advocate General, National Archives.

Deacon Jones was the sailor who, three decades after the fact, recalled what he and the other sailors thought had happened to Thalia; see Van Slingerland, *Something Terrible Has Happened*, p. 312. The quotes from Admiral Stirling, along with other recollections of that Sunday morning, are contained in his memoir, *Sea Duty*, pp. 79, 230–34, 241, 245–48, 269. Capsule accounts of the cited rapes of Hawaiian women appear in the

Richardson Report's summary volume, pp. 222 and 225, under perpetrator names Costello and Cooke. On Governor Judd, see his autobiography, *Lawrence M. Judd and Hawaii,* esp. pp. 73–90, 102–27, 138–40. On the Judd family and the Māhele, see Kame'eleihiwa, *Native Land and Foreign Desires,* esp. pp. 180–98. The evolution and eventual power of the sugar factors is discussed in Beechert, *Working in Hawai'i,* pp. 79–80, 178–79. An extraordinarily detailed chart of Hawai'i's interlocking corporate directorates is provided in the summary volume of the Richardson Report. The statistics on forthcoming navy construction expenditures were reported in a November 9, 1931, editorial in the *Honolulu Advertiser.* Sheriff Patrick Gleason's comment that the prosecution of the suspects was premature appears in his Richardson Report interview, vol. 10, pp. 2143–44. The sentence quoted from Governor Judd is in his autobiography, p. 166.

Chapter 8: Making News

Ahakuelo's recollection of his arrest is in an interview with him in the *Honolulu Advertiser* on June 14, 1968. The *New York Herald Tribune* article on Ahakuelo appeared on January 10, 1932. The Rose Younge case was front-page news in both the *Advertiser* and the *Star-Bulletin* between March 27 and April 29, 1929. See also correspondence from Governor Judd and Judge Cristy in Richardson Report, summary volume, pp. 195–96, confirming the innocence of Ahakuelo and the other defendants. For post-trial statistical studies, see Territorial Conference on Social Work, "Delinquency and Crime in Hawaii," pp. 3–8, 25; and Territory of Hawaii, "Report of Governor's Advisory Committee on Crime," pp. 7–8.

Information on Raymond Coll is found in articles written about him at the time of his death, especially in the *Honolulu Advertiser,* on April 10, 1962. For some of Coll's cited opinions and attitudes, see his Richardson Report interview, vol. 7, pp. 1256–64. Nan Coll's recollections of her husband and of Honolulu in the 1920s and later are in the 1972 oral history interview with her cited in the bibliography under Annie Towzey Coll. See also Chaplin, *Presstime in Paradise,* pp. 159–63; the quotation on Dillingham, Thurston, and the Japanese is on p. 239. Cited articles and editorials are from the *Bisbee Daily Review,* April 14 and 18, 1906, and the *Douglas Daily Dispatch,* August 4, October 28, and November 19–29, 1908. For general information on Bisbee and Douglas at this time, see Gordon, *The Great Arizona Orphan Abduction,* esp. pp. 30–31, 48, 100–102, 180–81. The antics of MacArthur and Patton, and their concern with the "Orange Race," are described in Hirshon, *General Patton,* pp. 174–216. The first of the two trials to come was stopped to retrieve police reports at the *Advertiser* during the testimony of Officer Claude Benton. The reports sought were prepared by Officer Benton and Officers Harbottle, Furtado, Machado, Nakea, and Hoapili.

Chapter 9: Alibis and Accusations

The bulk of this chapter is based on interviews with police officials and the defendants Chang, Ida, and Takai in "Pinkerton Honolulu Interviews," and on testimony during the rape trial. Ida's family background is the subject of an article in the *Star-Bulletin* on December 15, 1931. His youthful experiences, and those of the others, are discussed in a Pinkerton interview with Mrs. Joseph Tyssowski, who ran the Kauluwela Mission in the 1920s. For providing me with additional information on the defendants and juvenile social life at that time, I am grateful to Wilfred Oka, who attended school with the accused men. In addition, his 1935 master's thesis, "A Study of Japanese Social Institutions in Hawaii," helped me to understand the world of the geisha, teahouses, and other immigrant social relationships. I am also grateful to Ellen Hyer, Agnes Peeples's daughter, for granting me an extended interview. For background information on Fred Makino, see Duus, *The Japanese Conspiracy*, pp. 101–8; on Wright, see Reinecke, *Feigned Necessity*, pp. 176–77 and 514 (for quote on his "white man's intelligence").

Chapter 10: Taking Sides

Regarding the traditional obligations of ali'i for maka'āinana, see Trask, "Cultures in Collision," esp. pp. 98–106. A brief biography of Princess Kawananakoa appears in Peterson, *Notable Women of Hawai'i*, pp. 209–11; her lengthy interview in the Richardson Report appears in vol. 3, pp. 475–523. For background on Heen and Pittman, see brief biographies in Nellist, *The Story of Hawaii and Its Builders*, pp. 502, 702–3, and Richardson Report, vol. 7, pp. 1335, 1371. Dillingham's personal and family history is the subject of Melendy's *Walter Francis Dillingham*, but no reference is made there to his affiliation with the American Defense Society. For that, see Reinecke, *Feigned Necessity*, pp. 365–66, and items in Dillingham Papers, Box 7, Files 183–84. On the ADS, see Higham, *Strangers in the Land*, pp. 208 and 374, n. 35. See Kühl, *The Nazi Connection*, for information on relations between Nazi scientists and Grant, among others.

On the meeting called by the Chamber of Commerce, and on other pretrial arrangements by navy and business leaders, see Stirling, *Sea Duty*, pp. 248–49; Judd, *Lawrence M. Judd*, pp. 169–72; Judd Papers, Box 6, File 104, p. 151; and Dillingham, "A Memorandum," pp. 3–4. (At least one previous author, Wright, has used Dillingham's "Memorandum," believing it to be, as Dillingham suggested, a confidential document. In fact, the preliminary distribution list—see Dillingham Papers, Box 49—contains eighty-nine names, ranging from General Douglas MacArthur to Adolph Ochs, the owner and publisher of the *New York Times*.) Also see letters to Dillingham of October 13 and 27, 1931, from Frank Thompson in Dillingham Letters, Box 24, Folder 565, and "Memorandum for Rear Admiral Pettengill" from Harry S. Hayward of the Chamber of Commerce, Dillingham Letters, Box 22, Folder 526. For Thompson's extracurricular activities, see Okihiro, *Cane Fires*, pp. 71, 178.

Chapter 11: Grace and Tommie

Beatrice Nakamura's observations on the Massie household throughout this chapter are found in her Pinkerton interviews. Grace makes reference to the Dillinghams receiving her at their home in a letter of May 11, 1932, in the Dillingham Papers, Box 49. Another letter detailing her activities, including the necessity of finding a place of her own to rent—and Tommie's mental health, mentioned later—was written to her stepmother, but never sent; it is in the Kelley Papers at the Hawai'i State Archives. The account of Thalia's stay in the maternity hospital comes from a Pinkerton interview with nurse Helene Tromlitz; see also Pinkerton Report, p. 56, for a copy of the hospital report. Grace's dealings with Mrs. Koloa'amakai'i are discussed in Bouslog et al., *Mānoa*, pp. 148–51. Her racial comments to a newspaper reporter are in Owen, "Hot Lands and Cold," p. 222; Owen also is the source for the recollections of "one of Honolulu's prominent businessmen," p. 219.

The 1919 brawl was reported in the *Honolulu Advertiser* on July 6, 1919. See the op ed page of the *New York Herald Tribune* on January 14, 1932, for the cited piece by a former Honolulu Advertiser editor. Ida Knudson von Holt is quoted in the Richardson Report, vol. 3, p. 610. See Nelligan, "Social Change and Rape Law in Hawai'i," for numerous instances of white men raping Hawaiian and Asian women and girls. Tommie's background is part of his naval academy record. The other Millersburg student quoted is

Grover Sales, in his memoir, "All the Wrong Notes," p. 2. Discussion of the lynchings of Grant Smith and David Walker and a name-by-name list of Kentucky lynch mob victims are in Wright, *Racial Violence in Kentucky, 1860–1940*, pp. 114, 123–24, and 307–23. For the ratio of black victims per 100,000 black population, by state, see Tolnay and Beck, *A Festival of Violence*, p. 38, Table 2-3. The Little Rock editorial is quoted in Litwack, *Trouble in Mind*, p. 306. The quotation from Walter White is in his *Rope and Faggot*, p. 6. Again, Tommie's naval personnel file is the source for his efforts to become a pilot. Dr. Porter's advice to Tommie is noted in Van Slingerland, *Something Terrible Has Happened*, p. 82; his doubts about Thalia's story are noted on p. 290. Tommie discussed the rumors then in the air during his opening testimony at the murder trial.

Chapter 12: On Trial

The exchange between the governor and the admiral is recounted in Judd's autobiography, pp. 171–72. Judge Steadman's background is sketched in the Richardson Report, vol. 2, pp. 390–91; his comment on whites as natural leaders is on p. 395. The Fukunaga case can be followed in the local newspapers beginning on September 18, 1928. Dillingham's favorable judgment of Steadman is in his "Memorandum," p. 5. The law regarding the race of jurors is in sec. 83 of "Act of Congress Organizing Hawaii into a Territory," in Thurston, ed., *The Fundamental Law of Hawaii*, pp. 282–83. For a discussion of the tendencies of single-race juries in rape cases during the pre-territorial era, see Nelligan, "Social Change and Rape Law in Hawai'i," pp. 110–26. The corroboration requirement was in Section 4156 of Rev. Laws of Hawaii (1925), stating that "no person shall be convicted of rape . . . upon the mere testimony of the female uncorroborated by other evidence direct or circumstantial." Heen's quoted comments are from his interview with Pinkerton agents, in their "Honolulu Interviews" file. The remainder of this chapter is based upon the transcript of the trial, filed in the Hawai'i State Archives. Since the unpaginated transcript is approximately 1,500 pages long, encompassing sixty-four witnesses called over a period of almost two weeks, testimony obviously has had to be compressed. Newspaper references correspond to the dates of the trial.

Chapter 13: For the Defense

This chapter is based entirely on the trial transcript and on press reporting.

Chapter 14: "Lust-Sodden Beasts"

Most of this chapter is based on the trial transcript. See also the brief discussion of Detective Jardine's involvement with surprise witnesses in his *Detective Jardine*, pp. 74–76. The trial transcript does not contain the attorneys' closing arguments. For them, I have relied upon extensive newspaper accounts and minor additional citations from the notes of *Advertiser* reporter Theon Wright, as summarized in his book *Rape in Paradise*, pp. 178–79.

Chapter 15: "The Shame of Honolulu"

Steadman's comments regarding his hopes for a guilty verdict, as well as his other quoted statements on the trial cited in this chapter, are contained in his Richardson Report interview, vol. 2, pp. 401–2. On Admiral Stirling's reactions to the hung jury and his meetings with territorial officials, see *Sea Duty*, pp. 250, 254. Grace Fortescue's quoted comments on the trial, and on her meetings with Steadman and Stirling, are in her article "The Honolulu Martyrdom," pt. 1, pp. 6–7. On Dillingham and details of the post-trial Chamber of Commerce meetings, see the lengthy letter to the membership from the chamber's board of directors dated January 16, 1932, in Dillingham Papers, Box 22, Folder 526. On Dillingham and "reasonable doubt" about the defendants' guilt, see his "Memorandum," p. 5.

Edward P. Irwin's background is discussed in Chaplin, *Presstime in Paradise*, pp. 151–54. His work for Dillingham is mentioned in Reinecke, *Feigned Necessity*, pp. 184, 230, and his opinions quoted in the text are from his lengthy interview in the Richardson Report, vol. 7, pp. 1269–96. For the cited example of Irwin's published racial views, see his article "Ed Irwin More Than Suggests That We Should Not Try to 'Americanize' Orientals in Hawaii." Steffens recounts his invented crime wave on pp. 285–91 of *The Autobiography of Lincoln Steffens; Time's* quoted review appeared in its May 4, 1931, edition.

The day-to-day events for the remainder of this chapter draw upon daily press reports. *Time's* "Lust in Paradise" article appeared in its edition of December 28, 1931. Cobey Black's *Hawaii Scandal* is strong on the military at this point (pp. 119–34), quoting at length several previously unpublished cables. The Judd-Stirling encounter is treated in Judd's *Lawrence M. Judd and Hawaii*, pp. 177, 182. See also Judd's personal papers (M-420, Box 6, File 104) in the Hawai'i State Archives. Deacon Jones's physical description comes from his subsequent Honolulu Police Department arrest file and booking report. Grace's comments on him are from her article "The Honolulu Martyrdom," pt. 1, p. 6. Jones's comments on Grace and on Thalia, in addition to discussion of the gun purchases, appear in his interview with Van Slingerland, *Something Terrible Has Happened*, pp. 313–15.

Chapter 16: A Death in the Islands

Grace's letter to her stepmother was in her possession when she was arrested. It was never mailed and is in the Kelley Papers at the Hawai'i State Archives. The navy New Year's Eve party is described in Van Slingerland, *Something Terrible Has Happened*, p. 135; the description appears to have been based on an interview with Tommie Massie. The goings-on at the governor's mansion are described in Judd's autobiography, pp. 178–81. For the commentaries of Judd and Kuykendall, see Richardson Report, vol. 1, pp. 1–45. The planning for and execution of Kahahawai's kidnapping is well covered in Van Slingerland, *Something Terrible Has Happened*, pp. 138–48, based on interviews with Tommie; Grace also discusses it in "The Honolulu Martyrdom," pt. 1, pp. 7–10, although on the killing she follows the line invented by Darrow for the murder trial. For Grace's efforts to enlist *Advertiser* editor Raymond Coll in the enterprise, see Watumull Foundation interview with Coll's wife, Annie Towzey Coll, in the University of Hawai'i Hamilton Library, Hawai'i-Pacific Collection. The account of the capture and arrest of the killers is based on Detective Harbottle's description in the local press. On some details it is at odds with—but more credible than—the first official police reports.

Chapter 17: Penthouse for a Prison

The Judd and Stirling accounts of their meeting are in Judd, *Lawrence M. Judd*, pp. 185–86, and Stirling, *Sea Duty*, pp. 255–56. In addition to the extensive newspaper coverage of the arrest and its aftermath, supplementary information on the scene at Hanauma Bay is provided in the murder trial testimony of Dr. Joseph Catton and the arresting officers; also in a brief interview with Detective Harbottle (aka Von Arnswalt) in the Richardson

Report, vol. 11, p. 2572. Grace Fortescue discusses it as well, with indignation, in "The Honolulu Martyrdom," pt. 2, pp. 10–12.

Newspaper reports and courtroom testimony provide the bulk of information on the scene at the Fortescue and Massie homes following the murder, but for details regarding Jones's drinking and related matters, see Beatrice Nakamura's Pinkerton interviews. On Helene Fortescue's disposal of the murder weapon, see Van Slingerland's interview with Jones in *Something Terrible Has Happened,* pp. 320–21. Stirling's self-serving account of the encounter in the city attorney's office is in his *Sea Duty,* p. 257. For a brief background on Judge Cristy, see the biographical sketch in Nellist, *The Story of Hawaii and its Builders,* p. 382. More information was provided by Cristy's grandson, James Valuckas, in the form of clippings, correspondence, and a short, unpublished biography written by Cristy's widow, Jessamine Bowman Cristy. Cristy's interview in the Richardson Report is unusually revealing of his personal attitudes; see vol. 2, pp. 285–302. The quoted *Time* article, "Murder in Paradise, Cont'd," appeared on January 25, 1932.

Chapter 18: Tears of Heaven

Joseph Kahahawai's funeral was covered in all the local newspapers, but the best reporting is found in *Hawaii Hochi* and *Nippu Jiji.* The other events described at the start of this chapter derive from newspaper accounts, except the citation from the *New York Times* reporter. That comes from Owen, "Hot Lands and Cold," p. 219. The mainland newspaper coverage cited in the aftermath of the murder all appeared between January 9 and January 18, 1932, while the quoted Hearst reporter on that newspaper chain's editorial voice is from Tierney, *Darrow,* p. 198. Lowell Thomas's quoted news broadcast appears on microfiche 3, January 1932, in Thomas transcripts at the University of Denver.

The Dillingham letter of January 19, 1932, is in the Dillingham Papers, Box 21, File 503. The other letters mentioned (to and from Jack Frost and I. Townsend Burden) are in the Dillingham correspondence file, Box 49. On Judge Robertson, see Nellist, *The Story of Hawaii and Its Builders,* p. 736, and on his wife see Hall, "Two Hawaiian Careers in Grand Opera." On Farrington, see Chaplin, *Presstime in Paradise,* pp. 101–4; Nellist, *The Story of Hawaii and Its Builders,* pp. 433–34; and the Richardson Report, vol. 1, pp. 46–80. I am grateful to Shirley Tavares Wetzel for sending me a copy of one of Louis Cain's letters to Washington officials. The cited Supreme Court Chief Justice was Antonio Perry, and the *Star-Bulletin* reporter was Harry Stroup. For their remarks, and those of attorney Ferdinand Schnack, see the Richardson Report, vol. 2, pp. 375–78, and vol. 7, pp. 1321, 1396.

Chapter 19: Grand Jury

King Vidor's experience in Hawai'i with *Bird of Paradise* is recounted in Dowd and Shepard, eds., *King Vidor,* pp. 129–33, and in Vidor, *A Tree Is a Tree,* pp. 192–201. The cited U.S. Senate committee meeting took place on January 16, 1932. Quoted material appears in Hearing Before the Committee on Territories and Insular Affairs, Seventy-second Congress, First Session on Senate Joint Resolution 81, pp. 38–46. Summaries of the reform legislation appear in the Richardson Report summary volume, pp. 24–27.

The controversial grand jury proceedings were carried extensively in the local press. Because of the confidentiality of the proceedings, however, much was withheld from reporters that can be followed only by examining the court documents. For the names, addresses, and occupations of the jurors, see subpoenas on file in the Circuit Court of the

First Circuit, Territory of Hawaii, in the matter of *Territory of Hawaii v. Grace Fortescue et al.* Judge Cristy's lengthy admonitions to the jury are on file in the same location under Supplemental Instructions Given to Territorial Grand Jury on Friday, January 22, 1932. These instructions became part of the record in the defense attorneys' subsequent effort to quash the indictments, and it is in these documents that a virtual narrative of events unfolds. See especially Affidavit of Montgomery E. Winn, filed with the First Circuit Court on January 28, 1932, and accompanying Offer of Proof. Judge Cristy's ruling, denying the motion, is also on file, dated January 29, 1932.

For background on the grand jury's foreman, Harry Franson, I am grateful for an interview with his grandson, James Whiton, and for a follow-up interview with Colleen Howard, librarian of the Honolulu Elks Club. The transcript of the interrogation of Ben Ahakuelo at police headquarters on January 30, 1932, is filed as "Conversations Between D. W. Watson and Ben Ahakuelo" in the Judd Papers, Hawai'i State Archives. The reactions of Thalia and the others to news of the indictment are contained in Grace's "The Honolulu Martyrdom," pt. 2, p. 13.

The matter of bail for the murder defendants is the subject of correspondence and cables among Admiral Stirling, Judge Cristy, and the Secretary of the Navy, between January 27 and 30, 1932, all on file with the First Circuit Court. It is Russell Owen, in "Hot Lands and Cold," p. 222, who reports on the eagerness of the defense attorneys to be rid of the case. A copy of the congratulatory letter from the Hawaii Bar Association's Arthur Withington to Judge Cristy was provided to me by Cristy's grandson. The comment on Darrow was made at his funeral by a former law partner, William Holly; see Stone, *Clarence Darrow for the Defense,* p. 518.

Chapter 20: Attorney for the Damned

Darrow's autograph episode is reported in Weinberg, *Clarence Darrow,* p. 158; his speech to a black church congregation is quoted on pp. 84–85. The quotation from John Scopes appears in Larson, *Summer for the Gods,* p. 136. For the "Tent and Awning" quotation, see Tierney, *Darrow,* p. 140, while the Catlin quotation is in Cowan, *The People v. Clarence Darrow,* p. 61. See Cowan also for summaries of Darrow's dealings with Hearst, his handling of the Union Traction and Iroquois Theater cases, and his willingness to turn state's evidence against Samuel Gompers, pp. 50–51, 502. Cowan's book is the definitive work on Darrow's bribery trial. See Lucas, *Big Trouble,* esp. pp. 288–345, on labor and general background; Darrow's famous "I speak for the poor" speech, from the "Big Bill" Haywood trial, is quoted on p. 711. An edited version of Darrow's summation on behalf of the anthracite miners is printed in Weinberg, *Attorney for the Damned,* pp. 327–409. For differing views on aspects of the Sweet case, see Tierney, *Darrow,* pp. 374–85, and Boyle, *Arc of Justice.* The Depression's effect on Darrow and his response are covered in Tierney, *Darrow,* pp. 386-402; for his Leopold and Loeb fee, see p. 350 and Higdon, *Leopold and Loeb,* p. 326. Robinson's contract with Warner Brothers is cited in Schatz, *The Genius of the System,* p. 138; Winchell's comment was made on his radio show of March 1, 1932.

The cited Universal Pictures' description of Darrow is in a July 6, 1932, letter to district managers, now in the Darrow Papers, Library of Congress. The early date for negotiations between Darrow and Julian Ripley is noted in an affidavit of March 2, 1932, filed by Frank Thompson and Montgomery Winn with the First Circuit in Honolulu seeking a trial delay. Letters from Darrow to Barnes discussing planned travels and Darrow's decision to turn down the Honolulu case are dated February 8 and March 5, 1932, in the Harry Elmer Barnes Collection (Accession 745), University of Wyoming Library;

see also the letter from Barnes to Darrow of February 21 in the Darrow Papers, Library of Congress. Also see an undated letter from Ruby Darrow to Barnes, expressing her financial concerns, in the Barnes Collection.

On the McLeans and the Stotesburys, see McLean, *Father Struck It Rich*, and Maher, *The Twilight of Splendor*. Dillingham's arrangements for a loan to Grace are the subject of a February 27, 1932, letter from him to the president of the Bishop Trust Company; see also Grace's March 4 note of appreciation. Both items are in the Dillingham Correspondence, Box 49. On Darrow's search for an associate and the trip to Honolulu, see Tierney, *Darrow*, pp. 414–16; Tierney interviewed both Tommie Massie and George Leisure. Leisure is quoted on the subject in Stone, *Clarence Darrow for the Defense*, pp. 503–4. The fact that Leisure worked for free, and even paid his own expenses, is confirmed by a notation made by Ruby Darrow on a telegram from the Leisures sent on April 18, 1940; in the Darrow Papers, Library of Congress. The *Nation* editorial appeared in its January 27, 1932, edition. The Owen interview with Grace appeared in the *New York Times* on February 8, 1932; his follow-up comments are in his "Hot Lands and Cold," pp. 221–22. A contemporary account of Darrow's involvement in the Scottsboro case, including the cited reference to his fee, appeared in *The Crisis* of March, 1932, pp. 81–83; a copy can be found in the Darrow Papers, Library of Congress.

The quotation from William Kunstler appears in Conrad, *Jury Nullification*, pp. 137–38. Darrow's Sweet trial closing argument is reprinted, in part, in Weinberg, *Attorney for the Damned*, pp. 229–63. Ruby's letter to Barnes is dated March 7, 1932, while Darrow's letter explaining his reasons for agreeing to defend Grace Fortescue and the others is dated March 12, 1932; both are in the Barnes Collection.

Chapter 21: A Copper Miner's Son

Reports of the comings and goings of the movie crews, the Darrows, and the Richardson Report investigators appeared in the local press frequently in late March and early April. Chang Apana's local fame as the model for Charlie Chan (and his and his friends' delight in it) led to a sly article on the topic by Earl Derr Biggers after the release of *The Black Camel*; see *Honolulu Advertiser*, September 11, 1932. Cristy's agreement to step aside is detailed in his Decision on Request of Defense Counsel to Transfer Case, dated March 17, 1932, First Circuit Court. For a brief background on Judge Davis, see the Richardson Report, vol. 2, pp. 315–19.

The cited exchanges between Dillingham and Patton are dated March 10 and March 22, in the Dillingham Papers, Box 24, Folder 553. On Walter Dillingham's pleasure in having "my faithful Weeber" appointed as chief of police, and his efforts to control the prosecutor appointment, see the letter from Dillingham to his cousin Ike, dated January 29, 1932, in the Dillingham Papers, Box 21, File 504. Kelley's 1926 speech is quoted in *Honolulu Advertiser*, May 22, 1926.

General background on Kelley is derived from obituaries and articles about him at the time of his death in early January 1938. See also the article on him by Jan Jabulka in *Advertiser*, April 17, 1936. For Butte during the time of Kelley's life there, see Emmons, *The Butte Irish*, esp. pp. 20–22, 61–93, 268–75, 378–83, and Mercier, *Anaconda*, esp. ch. 1. For the Kelley family in Butte, see Marcosson, *Anaconda*, pp. 27–29, 68–77, 102–10. On Jack Kelley as a young man, especially on his heavy drinking, I am grateful to Mark Zwonitzer for sharing his interview with Tom Kelly, a distant relative of the prosecutor who appeared in Zwonitzer's film *The Irish in America*. For the cited comments on Kelley by Cristy, Steadman, and the U.S. Attorney, William Z. Fairbanks, see the Richardson Report, vol. 2, pp. 298, 399–400, and 448–49.

On Ruby Darrow, the quotation from Lincoln Steffens, and Darrow's comment to Tommie Massie, see Tierney, *Darrow*, pp. 181–82. Nan Kelley's assault on a "masher" was the subject of two Associated Press stories carried in the *Honolulu Star-Bulletin* on January 7 and 9, 1931. The letter to Stirling from Dr. Thompson of San Francisco is in the Fourteenth Naval District Headquarters, Pearl Harbor, T. H. Commandant's Office Classified Correspondence, 1912–1941, EG 12 (1). The appeal for additional money to hire psychiatrists is discussed in Van Slingerland, *Something Terrible Has Happened*, p. 228. For the quotations from Darrow on psychology and insanity, see his *Story of My Life*, pp. 242, 337. The quoted passage from Darrow's Sweet trial summation is in Weinberg, *Attorney for the Damned*, pp. 252–53, 261–62. The presence of Kinsley and Owen at the Scopes trial is noted in Larson, *Summer for the Gods*, p. 148. The story of the spiral staircase (including photograph and cost statement) was provided by retired Hawaiʻi Supreme Court Chief Justice Ronald Moon in an interview with Mark Zwonitzer.

Chapter 22: Territory of Hawaii v. Fortescue et al.

Dillingham's letter on the crowded conditions in the courtroom, including the scalping prices for seats and Mrs. Dillingham's special treatment, was sent to his cousin Ike on April 18, 1932, and is in the Dillingham Papers, Box 21, File 504. Darrow's comment on Irish jurors to Judge Murphy is quoted in Tierney, *Darrow*, p. 381. For Darrow's general ideas regarding the inclinations of jurors from different national and religious backgrounds, see his "Attorney for the Defense." On the desire to serve on the Scopes trial jury, see Larson, *Summer for the Gods*, p. 153. In seeking to avoid serving, the Honolulu jurors were acting more like the jurors in the racially charged Sweet trial; see Boyle, *Arc of Justice*, pp. 260–61, 384. Since the official transcript for this trial is incomplete, and what exists does not contain the voir dire exchanges or the examinations of the prosecution's opening witnesses, I have combined all newspaper reports (the local papers carried their own transcripts), the detailed trial summary from the First Circuit Court, and the court's exhibits list and juror subpoenas—providing names, addresses, and occupations—to reconstruct the part of the trial reported in this chapter.

The comment by Judge Lymer on Hawaiians as jurors is from his Richardson Report interview, vol. 2, pp. 327–28. Admiral Stirling's quoted letter to Richardson appears on pp. 197–99 of the report's summary volume. The Dillingham letter on "a radical change in government" and "Asiatic citizenship" was sent to Admiral Brooks Upham, Commander in Chief of the U.S. Asiatic Fleet, on June 15, 1932; in Dillingham Letters, Box 24, Folder 565. The Lowell Thomas report comes from microfiche 2 for April, 1932, in his collected scripts. Stirling's "forum of the Orient" remark is from *Sea Duty*, p. 262. The quoted words from *Time* were in its article "Mottled Jury," of April 18, 1932.

Darrow's quoted comment on jury selection at the Sweet trial is in Stone, *Clarence Darrow for the Defense*, p. 478. Most Darrow biographers take note of Darrow's habit of attacking prosecutors and prosecution witnesses personally; for a succinct summary on this point, see Tierney, *Darrow*, pp. 342–43. Darrow's admission that his clients were guilty of murder is in *The Story of My Life*, pp. 468, 476.

Chapter 23: Dementia Americana

The hate mail to Kelley is in his file at the Hawaiʻi State Archives. Official trial transcripts, available at the archives, begin with Tommie Massie's testimony and continue through that of Irving Blom, Eugene Beebe, and Gordon C. Ross. The bulk of this chapter draws upon that testimony and upon newspaper reports.

That Darrow's illness was a hangover is confirmed by Van Slingerland, *Something Terrible Has Happened*, p. 244, and Tierney, *Darrow*, pp. 417–18; both men had interviewed Darrow's co-counsel, Leisure. The information on Professor E. Lowell Kelly derives from letters to Lawrence Judd of February 20 and March 9, 1967; "Correction" in *True* magazine, April 1969; and memorandum from Kelly on libel suit, dated November 15, 1969, all in the Judd Papers, Hawai'i State Archives. Also, see Board of Regents, University of Hawai'i, minutes of the April 22, 1932, meeting on "exposing confidential records." The *Time* quotation is from its article "Horror, Rumor, Trigger," of April 25, 1932. On the Thaw trial and "Dementia Americana," see Mooney, *Evelyn Nesbit and Stanford White*, pp. 244–75.

Chapter 24: "Everybody Knows I Love You!"

This chapter is based almost entirely on trial transcripts from the Hawai'i State Archives and the First Circuit Court. The cited "skeptical correspondent" was Kinsley. Darrow's comments on Thalia's performance were reported in all press reports; for more, see his reflections in *The Story of My Life*, pp. 474–75. The weekend beach parties are mentioned in an undated letter to Kelley from prosecution psychiatrist Catton, in Kelley Papers, Hawai'i State Archives.

Chapter 25: Where Is Kahahawai?

As with the Ala Moana trial, there is no official transcript of closing arguments in the murder trial. A partial transcript of Darrow's summation is in Weinberg, *Attorney for the Damned*, pp. 104–18, but it is based on a newspaper account. There were many such accounts. They were detailed and extensive, and they are the source for the closing arguments as recounted in this chapter. Darrow's quoted words on trials as theater are at the opening of his essay on jury selection, "Attorney for the Defense." Hays's opening statement at the Sweet trial is excerpted in his book *Let Freedom Ring*, pp. 214–18. The Grace Fortescue quotation is from her "Honolulu Martyrdom," pt. 3, p. 16. Darrow's claim that Hawai'i's whites were unprejudiced is in *The Story of My Life*, pp. 470–71. Thomas's radio broadcast script is on microfiche 7 for April, 1932, University of Denver Law Library.

Chapter 26: The Unwritten Law

Darrow's comments on the "unwritten law" are in *The Story of My Life*, p. 468. Like "Dementia Americana," the unwritten law was then a commonplace notion and references to it were everywhere in the national press during the trial. For background, see Ireland, "Insanity and the Unwritten Law," and Hartog, "Lawyering, Husbands' Rights, and 'the Unwritten Law.'" This chapter draws on local and national news reports for most of its material. Theodore Char's inside account of jury deliberations was published in the Hearst press, including the *San Francisco Examiner*. On Dillingham's flowers for Grace, see her note to him of April 30, 1932, in Dillingham Correspondence, Box 49. Grace's comment on wishing she had shot Heen and Pittman was made to her friend J. Webb Saffold, who conveyed it to Dillingham in a letter of May 13, 1932. He also says she told him the "story of the shooting," public knowledge of which would only "add to their embarrassment." See Dillingham Letters, Box 24, Folder 561.

A copy of the congressional petition is in the Judd Papers, Hawai'i State Archives. Judd discusses his deliberations and consultations with various people in *Lawrence M. Judd*, pp. 200–3. Dillingham reports Leisure's compliment in a letter to his sons, Lowell and Ben, on May 6, 1932; see Dillingham Letters, Box 21, Folder 505. On Dillingham's relationship with Hoover, see Melendy, *Walter Francis Dillingham*, pp. 200–3. Thomas's radio commentary is on microfiche 1 for May, 1932, University of Denver Law Library. Dillingham's thoughts on lynching are in his "Memorandum," p. 9. Grace Fortescue, in her "Honolulu Martyrdom," was among those in the know who said that the president telephoned Judd.

Chapter 27: Case Closed

Darrow's visit with Judd is mentioned in Judd's autobiography, *Lawrence M. Judd*, p. 203; unless otherwise noted, additional personal references to the governor's actions during this time derive from the same source, pp. 201–14. About two hundred letters, postcards, and telegrams regarding the trial, almost all of them abusive, are in Kelley's correspondence file in the Hawai'i State Archives. The events in and around court that day are drawn from local and national newspaper reports, other than the dinner and meeting at La Pietra, which is described by Dillingham in the above-cited letter of May 6, 1932, to his sons Lowell and Ben. Dillingham's efforts to convince Thalia to remain in Honolulu for a retrial of the rape case are the subject of a May 11–12 exchange of notes between him and Helen Ripley (Dillingham Correspondence, Box 49). Darrow explains his position on the matter, and mentions his friendship with "a genial and wise physician," in *The Story of My Life*, pp. 480–83; Porter is identified as that physician in Van Slingerland, *Something Terrible Has Happened*, pp. 226–27, and in Tierney, *Darrow*, p. 423.

Cited reactions in the local and national press appeared in the days immediately following May 4; the *New Republic* editorial is from its edition of May 18, 1932. In addition to his belated expression of regret in his memoirs over commuting the sentences, see Judd's comments on having been pressured to do so in a *Honolulu Star-Bulletin* article of February 13, 1967. A copy of Judd's detailed rejection of the pardon request is in his papers, Hawai'i State Archives, as is his letter, dated May 17, 1932, to Ray Lyman Wilbur, the secretary of the interior (Dole Gov 7, Box 28). The Lowell Thomas commentary is on microfiche 6 for May 1932. Admiral Pratt's remarks, quoted by Thomas, were seconded by Admiral Brooks Upham in the postscript of a letter to Dillingham dated June 4, 1932; see, Dillingham Letters, Box 24, Folder 565.

Judd's effort to enlist the FBI is noted in a comment initialed by him on p. 324 of his personal copy of Van Slingerland, *Something Terrible Has Happened* (Judd Papers, Hawai'i State Archives). The findings of the Pinkerton Report are the subject of letters to Judd from the company's vice president and general manager, Asher Rossetter, dated October 3 and October 14, 1932, and bound with the report on file in the archives. Other key materials include letters from Judd to Attorney General Hewitt and prosecutor Kelley dated October 9, 1932; a cable from the Secretary of the Interior Wilbur to Judd of November 26, 1932; a return cable from Judd to Wilbur, dated December 10, 1932; and a letter to Wilbur from Judd dated December 15, 1932, enclosing an analysis of the case by A. G. W. Robertson—all in the Judd Papers, as cited above.

Dillingham's attempts to destroy or suppress the report, and to quash local news coverage, can be followed in a series of exchanges with his chief Washington lobbyist, Lee P. Warren, dated December 1, 1932; December 15, 1932; December 28, 1932; January 25, 1933; and February 3, 1933. See also a note to Warren from the Secretary of the Navy dated February 1, 1933, and a letter from Dillingham to Lawrence Reifsnider dated February 14, 1933. All this correspondence is contained in the Dillingham Papers, Box 22, Files 511–12, and Letters, Box 24, Folder 559.

The Associated Press article ranking the Massie case among the world's top ten stories of 1932 was filed and carried by most newspapers on January 2, 1933. Kelley's dropping of rape charges against the surviving defendants is detailed in the *Advertiser* and *Star-Bulletin* on February 13–14, 1933. Thalia's attempts to recapture attention by attacking the Pinkerton Report and threatening to return to Hawai'i were covered by local and national newspapers on October 4, 1932, and February 14–16, 1933. Congressman DePriest's speech linking the Scottsboro and Massie cases was reported by wire services and was carried in the *Star-Bulletin* on May 5, 1933.

Chapter 28: Prelude to Revolution

Former governor Judd discussed his New York meeting with Stirling in his autobiography, *Lawrence M. Judd and Hawaii*, pp. 215–16. On the Hawaiian Room generally, see Imada, "Hawaiians on Tour," esp. pp. 126–34. On Darrow's death, see *New York Times*, March 14, 1938; on Kelley's, see the *Honolulu Advertiser* and *Star-Bulletin*, January 7, 1938. Stirling's comments on Kahahawai are in his *Sea Duty*, pp. 259, 264. Thalia's telegram is in the Darrow Papers at the Library of Congress. The *Look* magazine writer was Peter Van Slingerland; the interviews with Lord and Jones are reprinted in his book *Something Terrible Has Happened*, pp. 307–22. One who recalled Jones's courtroom demeanor was former Territorial Supreme Court Chief Justice Robertson; see his account, attached to Judd's letter to Secretary of the Interior Wilbur on December 15, 1932, in the Judd Papers.

The Massies' arrival in San Francisco and subsequent trip across the country were covered in most major newspapers, but see especially the Honolulu dailies and the *San Francisco Chronicle* and *Examiner* for the period of May 13–25, 1932. See also the *Winchester Sun* from May 5 (for the town's celebration) through June 1, 1932 (the day of the Massies' departure from Winchester). Thalia's summer in Bayport and her arrest for speeding are discussed in the Pinkerton "New York Interviews" with Louise Henderson and others. The Massies' divorce proceeding is most closely covered in the *Reno Evening Gazette*, February 23–28, 1934, while Thalia's suicide attempt, hospitalization in Italy, and return to the United States were reported by all major wire services and newspapers between April 6 and May 23, 1934. The Los Angeles assault charge against Thalia, with information on her other recent activities, was reported in a United Press story carried widely on February 2, 1950, as was her death on July 2, 1963.

The incident involving Tommie's second wife in Shanghai was carried by the wire services in most newspapers on June 25, 1938. His navy fitness reports, medical records, and retirement documents are included in his file, Proceedings of Naval and Marine Examining Boards, 1929–41. The detailed mental health diagnoses begin with the report from the Norfolk Naval Hospital on April 2, 1940, and conclude with the St. Elizabeth's Hospital report of June 7, 1940. His later life is covered briefly in his obituary in *Shipmate*, May 1987. On Grace's life in Palm Beach, see articles in the *Palm Beach Post* dated September 16, 1956; May 7, 1965; August 1, 1974; see also her obituary on June 25, 1979.

The interview with Ben Ahakuelo appeared in the *Honolulu Advertiser* on June 4, 1968. Information on the lives of the surviving Ala Moana trial defendants derives from interviews with family and friends, including Deena Ahakuelo, Queenie Cavaco, and Wilfred Oka. The Edmund Wilson quotation comes from his *Letters on Literature and Politics*, p. 154. Public interest in the number of men responsible for killing Emmett Till was revived by the documentary film *The Untold Story of Emmett Louis Till* (2003). The Pringles' reflections on the rape accusation are from their Pinkerton interviews. Stirling's comments on the white and "polyglot" communities are in *Sea Duty*, p. 267.

The 1932 election data are from several sources, including Schmitt, *Historical Statis-*

tics of Hawaii, pp. 603–7; Johnson, *The City and County of Honolulu*, pp. 128–31; and the *Honolulu Star-Bulletin*, October 1, 1932 (for McCandless's speech) and the *Star-Bulletin* and the *Advertiser* for November 9–11 (for election coverage). The Dillingham reference to McCandless is in a letter to Lee Warren dated December 1, 1932; on the elections in general, see his letter to Admiral Brooks Upham of December 16, 1932 (Dillingham Papers, Box 22, File 512 and Letters, Box 24, Folder 565). The judgeships of Murakami and Cristy, as well as the bar association resolution on Pittman, are discussed in Marumoto, "The Ala Moana Case and the Massie-Fortescue Case," pp. 274, 278.

On the transformation of the word "local" during the time of the Massie case, see Rosa, "Local Story," especially text and citations on pp. 5–6. The quoted passages from Reinecke are in his *Language and Dialect in Hawaii*, pp. 173–74, 190; see also Reinecke, *A Man Must Stand Up*, pp. 20–21, on the Massie case. The continued relationship between language and ethnic politics first noted by Reinecke is discussed in Sato, "Linguistic Inequality in Hawaii," esp. pp. 265–66. On the early labor movement of the 1930s, see Beechert, *Working in Hawai'i*, pp. 248–69, and Zalburg, *A Spark Is Struck*, pp. 4–31. Quotes from the *Voice of Labor* appeared in the issues of November 4, 1935; July 8, 1936; and August 4, 1938. For the navy intelligence reports, see classified correspondence files for this time period under Commandant, Fourteenth Naval District, in bibliography. On the violence in Hilo, see Puette, *The Hilo Massacre*.

Much has been written on the Japanese internment, but the material cited here is found in Takaki, *Strangers from a Different Shore*, pp. 379–89, and Okihiro, *Cane Fires*, pp. 234–37, 269–70. See also Chaplin, *Presstime in Paradise*, pp. 200–10, and Chapin, *Shaping History*, pp. 171–89. For a wealth of personal testimony, Center for Oral History, *An Era of Change: Oral Histories of Civilians in World War Two Hawaii*, is invaluable. For quoted material, see also Bailey and Farber, *The First Strange Place*, pp. 161–64; District Intelligence Office, Fourteenth Naval District, *The Negro Problem*, pp. 4–20; and, on Princess Kawananakoa, see the *Honolulu Advertiser* and *Star-Bulletin*, February 24, 1942; January 1, 1943; and May 25, 1945.

The postwar labor movement, Smith Act trial, and election of 1954 are discussed in Fuchs, *Hawaii Pono*, pp. 308–22, 354–76; Beechert, *Working in Hawai'i*, pp. 296–322; Zalburg, *A Spark Is Struck*, esp. pp. xiv–xv and 324–65, for Hall's Communist Party membership; and Boylan and Holmes, *John A. Burns*, pp. 90–127. Wilson's 1932 speech in Chicago is mentioned in Krauss, *Johnny Wilson*, p. 221, while the *Chicago Daily News* is quoted in Zalburg, *A Spark Is Struck*, p. 343. The passage quoted from Theon Wright is in *The Disenchanted Isles*, p. 83. For tourist and population growth data during the 1960s and 1970s, see Nordyke, *The Peopling of Hawai'i*, pp. 236, 259–60. The post-statehood economic boom is treated in great detail in Cooper and Daws, *Land and Power in Hawai'i*; see esp. pp. 452–59 for discussion of its ethnic and racial dimensions. For a summary of contemporary Hawaiian economic, health, and other demographic conditions, see Stannard, "The Hawaiians," *Cultural Survival Quarterly* (Spring 2000). Yugo Okubo is quoted in Odo, *No Sword to Bury*, pp. 272–73.

Bibliography

Unpublished Materials

Barnes, Harry Elmer. Papers. University of Wyoming Library, American Heritage Center.

Coll, Annie Towzey. Interview. Watumull Foundation Oral History Project. University of Hawai'i, Hamilton Library, Hawai'i-Pacific Collection.

Commandant, Fourteenth Naval District, Pearl Harbor, T.H. Commandant's Office Correspondence, Classified and Unclassified, 1912–1941, EG 12 (1). In National Archives, San Bruno, California.

Crampon, L. J. "Hawaii's Visitor Industry: Its Growth and Development." Unpublished bound manuscript in University of Hawai'i, Hamilton Library, Hawai'i-Pacific Collection.

Darrow, Clarence. Papers and Correspondence. Library of Congress, Washington, D.C.

Dillingham, Walter F. "A Memorandum." University of Hawai'i, Hamilton Library, Hawai'i-Pacific Collection.

———. Papers and Correspondence. Bishop Museum Archives, Bernice P. Bishop Museum, Honolulu, Hawai'i.

District Intelligence Office, Fourteenth Naval District. "The Negro Problem in the Fourteenth Naval District." National Archives, San Bruno, California.

"An Era of Change: Oral Histories of Civilians in World War Two Hawai'i." Social Science Research Institute, Center for Oral History, 3 vols. University of Hawai'i, Hamilton Library.

Fuchs, Lawrence H. Interview Transcripts for *Hawai'i Pono*, 1958–59. University of Hawai'i, Hamilton Library, Hawai'i-Pacific Collection.

Grand Jury Transcripts and Documents and Transcripts and Documents for Massie Fortescue Case (partial). Archives of the Circuit Court, First Circuit, Honolulu, Hawai'i.

Houston, Victor. Papers. Hawai'i State Archives.

Judd, Lawrence M. Papers. Hawai'i State Archives.

"Kalihi: Place of Transition." University of Hawai'i Social Science Research Institute, Ethnic Studies Oral History Project, 3 vol. University of Hawai'i, Hamilton Library.

Kelley, John C. Papers. Hawai'i State Archives.

Kelly, E. Lowell. Research Questionnaires on Personality and Marriage. Murray Research Center, Radcliffe Institute for Advanced Study, Harvard University.

Pinkerton National Detective Agency, Inc. Investigation and Report on Ala Moana Case, Summary Volume (paginated) and Addendum Interview Files (unpaginated). Honolulu, Los Angeles, New York, 1932. Hawai'i State Archives, Papers of Governor Lawrence M. Judd. Referred to in notes as Pinkerton Report.

Proceedings of Naval and Marine Examining Boards, 1929-1941, RG 125. Thomas Massie File, Naval Retiring Board, July 9, 1940. Navy Department, Washington, D.C.

"Reflections of Palama Settlement." University of Hawai'i Social Science Research Institute, Center for Oral History, 2 vol. University of Hawai'i, Hamilton Library.

"Remembering Kaka'ako, 1910–1950." University of Hawai'i Ethnic Studies Program Oral History Project, 2 vol. University of Hawai'i, Hamilton Library.

Territorial Conference on Social Work. "Delinquency and Crime in Hawaii," July 11–13, 1929. University of Hawai'i, Hamilton Library.

Territory of Hawaii. "Report of Governor's Advisory Committee on Crime," February 9, 1931. University of Hawai'i, Hamilton Library, Hawai'i-Pacific Collection.

Thomas, Lowell. Radio Scripts, December 1931–June 1932. University of Denver, Westminster Law Library.

Trial Transcripts of Ala Moana Case and Massie-Fortescue Case (partial). Hawai'i State Archives, Papers of Governor Lawrence M. Judd.

United States Department of Justice. "Investigation Concerning Law Enforcement and Crime Conditions in the Territory of Hawaii." Submitted by Seth W. Richardson, Assistant Attorney General of the United States, April 4, 1932. 16 vol. Library of Congress and Library of University of California, San Diego. Partial collection in University of Hawai'i, Hamilton Library, on microfilm. Referred to in notes as Richardson Report.

United States Senate, Seventy-second Congress, Committee on Territories and Insular Affairs. Hearings on Joint Resolution 81 (1932).

United States v. Private Chester C. Nagle (Military Justice C. M. 184854), Office of the Judge Advocate General. National Archives, Washington, D.C.

University of Hawai'i Board of Regents. Minutes. April 22, 1932.

"Waikiki, 1900–1985: Oral Histories." University of Hawai'i Social Science Research Institute, Oral History Project, 4 vols. University of Hawai'i, Hamilton Library.

Winchell, Walter. Radio Scripts, December 1931–June 1932. New York Public Library for the Performing Arts at Lincoln Center, Billy Rose Collection.

Newspapers

Bisbee Daily Review (Arizona)
Chicago Tribune
Douglas Daily Dispatch (Arizona)
Hawaii-Chinese News
Hawaii Hochi
Hilo Tribune Herald
Honolulu Advertiser
Honolulu Star-Bulletin
Honolulu Times
Maui Times
New Freedom (Honolulu)
New York Daily Mirror
New York Daily News
New York Herald Tribune

New York Times
Nippu Jiji (Honolulu)
Palm Beach Post
Patchogue Advance (New York)
Reno Evening Gazette
San Francisco Call-Bulletin
San Francisco Chronicle
San Francisco Examiner
Sydney Morning Herald
Times (London)
Voice of Labor (Honolulu)
Washington Post
Winchester Sun (Kentucky)

Books, Articles, Dissertations

Bailey, Beth, and David Farber. The First Strange Place: Race and Sex in World War II Hawaii. Baltimore: Johns Hopkins University Press, 1994.

Baker, Ray Stannard. "Wonderful Hawaii: A World Experiment Station." Three-part series in *The American Magazine:* November 1911 (pp. 28–38); December 1911 (pp. 201–14); January 1912 (pp. 328–39).

Baldwin, Hanson W., and Shepard Stone, eds. *We Saw It Happen: The News Behind the News That's Fit to Print.* New York: Simon and Schuster, 1938.

Beaglehole, J. C., ed. *The Journals of Captain James Cook,* vol. 3, parts one and two. Cambridge, England: Hakluyt Society, 1967.

Beckwith, Martha. *Hawaiian Mythology.* Honolulu: University of Hawai'i Press, 1970.

Beechert, Edward D. *Working in Hawai'i: A Labor History.* Honolulu: University of Hawai'i Press, 1985.

Belich, James. *The New Zealand Wars.* Auckland: Auckland University Press, 1986.

Beloff, Jim. *The Ukulele: A Visual History.* San Francisco: Backbeat Books, 2003.

Bennett, Frederick Debell. *Narrative of a Whaling Voyage Round the Globe, from the Year 1833 to 1836.* London: Richard Bentley, 1840.

Berry, Paul, and Edgy Lee. *Waikiki in the Wake of Dreams.* Honolulu: Filmworks Press, 2000.

Bingham, Hiram. *A Residence of Twenty-one Years in the Sandwich Islands.* Hartford, Conn.: Hezekiah Huntington, 1849.

Black, Cobey. *Hawaii Scandal.* Honolulu: Island Heritage, 2002.

Blanding, Don. *Hula Moons.* New York: Dodd, Mead, 1930.

Bouslog, Charles, et al. *Manoa: The Story of a Valley.* Honolulu: Mutual Publishing, 1994.

Boylan, Dan, and T. Michael Holmes. *John A. Burns: The Man and His Times.* Honolulu: University of Hawai'i Press, 2000.

Boyle, Kevin. *Arc of Justice: A Saga of Race, Civil Rights, and Murder in the Jazz Age.* New York: Henry Holt, 2004.

Brown, DeSoto. "Beautiful, Romantic Hawai'i: How the Fantasy Image Came to Be," *Journal of Decorative and Propaganda Arts* 20 (1994).

Chapin, Helen Geracimos. *Shaping History: The Role of Newspapers in Hawai'i.* Honolulu: University of Hawai'i Press, 1996.

Chaplin, George. *Presstime in Paradise: The Life and Times of the Honolulu Advertiser, 1856–1995.* Honolulu: University of Hawai'i Press, 1998.

Coffman, Tom. *Nation Within: The Story of America's Annexation of the Nation of Hawai'i.* Honolulu: Epicenter Books, 1998.

Cohen, Stan. *The Pink Palace.* Missoula, Mont.: Pictorial Histories, 1986.

Conrad, Clay S. *Jury Nullification: The Evolution of a Doctrine.* Durham, NC: Carolina Academic Press, 1998.

Cooper, George, and Gavan Daws. *Land and Power in Hawai'i.* Honolulu: University of Hawai'i Press, 1990.

Coulter, John W., and Alfred G. Serrao. "Manoa Valley, Honolulu: A Study in Economic and Social Geography." *Bulletin of the Geographical Society of Philadelphia* 30 (1932).

Cowan, Geoffrey. *The People v. Clarence Darrow: The Bribery Trial of America's Greatest Lawyer.* New York: Times Books, 1993.

Culliney, John L. *Islands in a Far Sea: Nature and Man in Hawaii.* San Francisco: Sierra Club Books, 1988.

Dalton, Kathleen. *Theodore Roosevelt: A Strenuous Life.* New York: Knopf, 2002.

Darrow, Clarence. "Attorney for the Defense." *Esquire,* May 1936.

———. *The Story of My Life.* New York: Da Capo Press, 1996.

Desmond, Jane C. *Staging Tourism: Bodies on Display from Waikiki to Sea World.* Chicago: University of Chicago Press, 1999.

Dowd, Nancy, and David Shepard, eds. *King Vidor.* London: Scarecrow Press, 1988.

Drinnon, Richard. *Facing West: The Metaphysics of Indian Hating and Empire Building.* Minneapolis: University of Minnesota Press, 1980.

Duus, Masayo Umezawa. *The Japanese Conspiracy: The Oʻahu Sugar Strike of 1920.* Berkeley: University of California Press, 1999.

Eizenstat, Stuart E. *Imperfect Justice: Looted Assets, Slave Labor, and the Unfinished Business of World War II.* New York: Public Affairs, 2003.

Emmons, David M. *The Butte Irish: Class and Ethnicity in an American Mining Town, 1875–1925.* Urbana: University of Illinois Press, 1989.

Epstein, Daniel Mark. *Sister Aimee: The Life of Aimee Semple McPherson.* New York: Harcourt Brace, 1993.

Faris, John T. *The Paradise of the Pacific.* New York: Doubleday, 1929.

Forbes, David W. *Encounters with Paradise: Views of Hawaiʻi and Its People, 1778–1941.* Honolulu: University of Hawaiʻi Press, 1992.

Fortescue, Grace. "The Honolulu Martyrdom." *Liberty,* July 30, August 6, and August 13, 1932.

Fortescue, Granville. *Front Line and Deadline: The Experiences of a War Correspondent.* New York: G. P. Putnam's Sons, 1937.

Fuchs, Lawrence H. *Hawaii Pono: A Social History.* New York: Harcourt Brace, 1961.

Gordon, Linda. *The Great Arizona Orphan Abduction.* Cambridge, MA: Harvard University Press, 1999.

Gray, Edwin. *Few Survived: A Comprehensive Survey of Submarine Accidents and Disasters.* Philadelphia: Trans-Atlantic Publications, 1999.

Greer, Richard A. "Cunha's Alley: The Anatomy of a Landmark," *Hawaiian Journal of History* 2 (1968): 148–50.

Hall, Dale E. "Two Hawaiian Careers in Grand Opera." *Hawaiian Journal of History* 26 (1992).

Hartog, Hendrik. "Lawyering, Husbands' Rights, and 'the Unwritten Law' in Nineteenth-Century America." *Journal of American History* 84: 1 (1997): 67–96.

Hays, Arthur Garfield. *Let Freedom Ring.* New York: Liverwright Publishing, 1937.

Higdon, Hal. *Leopold and Loeb: The Crime of the Century.* Urbana: University of Illinois Press, 1999.

Higham, John. *Strangers in the Land: Patterns of American Nativism, 1860–1925.* New York: Atheneum, 1968.

Hirshon, Stanley P. *General Patton: A Soldier's Life.* New York: HarperCollins, 2002.

Imada, Adria L. "Hawaiians on Tour: Hula Circuits Through the American Empire." *American Quarterly* 56:1 (2004), 111–49.

Ireland, Robert M. "Insanity and the Unwritten Law." *American Journal of Legal History* 32 (1988).

Iwamoto, Lana. "The Plague and Fire of 1899–1900 in Honolulu," in *Hawaii Historical Review: Selected Readings,* ed. Richard A. Greer. Honolulu: Hawaiian Historical Society, 1969.

Jardine, John. *Detective Jardine: Crimes in Honolulu.* Honolulu: University of Hawaiʻi Press, 1984.

Johnson, Donald D. *The City and County of Honolulu: A Governmental Chronicle.* Honolulu: University of Hawaiʻi Press, 1991.

Judd, Denis, and Keith Surridge. *The Boer War.* New York: Palgrave, 2003.

Judd, Lawrence M. *Lawrence M. Judd and Hawaii: An Autobiography.* Rutland, VT: Charles E. Tuttle, 1971.

Kahn, Clarence M. "Clarence Darrow Looks at America." *Real America* 1: 2 (April 1933).

Kameʻeleihiwa, Lilikalā. *Native Land and Foreign Desires.* Honolulu: Bishop Museum Press, 1992.

Kanahele, George. *Hawaiian Music and Musicians.* Honolulu: University of Hawaiʻi Press, 1979.

Kirch, Patrick Vinton. *Feathered Gods and Fishhooks: An Introduction to Hawaiian Archaeology and Prehistory.* Honolulu: University of Hawaiʻi Press, 1985.

Krauss, Bob. *Johnny Wilson: First Hawaiian Democrat.* Honolulu: University of Hawaiʻi Press, 1994.

Kühl, Stefan. *The Nazi Connection: Eugenics, American Racism, and German National Socialism.* New York: Oxford University Press, 1994.

Kurtz, Michael L. *The Challenging of America, 1920–1945.* Arlington Heights, IL: Forum Press, 1986.

Landauer, Lyndall and Donald. *Pearl: The History of the United States Navy in Pearl Harbor.* Lake Tahoe, CA: Institute for Marine Information, 1999.

Larson, Edward J. *Summer for the Gods: The Scopes Trial and America's Continuing Debate over Science and Religion.* Cambridge, MA: Harvard University Press, 1998.

LaSalle, Mick. *Complicated Women: Sex and Power in Pre-Code Hollywood.* New York: St. Martin's, 2000.

Lears, T. J. Jackson. "From Salvation to Self-Realization: Advertising and the Therapeutic Roots of the Consumer Culture, 1880–1930," in *The Culture of Consumption*, ed. Richard Wightman Fox and T. J. Jackson Lears. New York: Pantheon Books, 1983.

Lind, Andrew W. "The Ghetto and the Slum." *Social Forces* 9: 2 (1930): 206–15.

———. *An Island Community: Ecological Succession in Hawaiʻi.* Chicago: University of Chicago Press, 1938.

———. "Some Ecological Patterns of Community Disorganization in Honolulu." *American Journal of Sociology* 36: 2 (1930): 206–20.

Litwack, Leon F. *Trouble in Mind: Black Southerners in the Age of Jim Crow.* New York: Alfred A. Knopf, 1998.

Lord, Virginia, and Alice Lee. "The Taxi Dance Hall in Honolulu." *Social Process in Hawaii* 2 (1936): 46–50.

Lowry, Donal, ed. *The South African War Reappraised.* Manchester: Manchester University Press, 2000.

Lucas, J. Anthony. *Big Trouble: A Murder in a Small Western Town Sets Off a Struggle for the Soul of America.* New York: Simon and Schuster, 1997.

Maas, Peter. *The Terrible Hours: The Man Behind the Greatest Submarine Rescue in History.* New York: HarperCollins, 1999.

MacLean, Nancy. *Behind the Mask of Chivalry: The Making of the Second Ku Klux Klan.* New York: Oxford University Press, 1994.

Maher, James T. *The Twilight of Splendor.* Boston: Little, Brown and Company, 1975.

Marcosson, Isaac F. *Anaconda.* New York: Dodd, Mead and Company, 1957.

Marumoto, Masaji. "The Ala Moana Case and the Massie-Fortescue Case Revisited." *University of Hawaiʻi Law Review* 5: 2 (1983): 271–87.

Maugham, W. Somerset. *The Trembling of a Leaf.* New York: Doubleday, 1921.

McCracken, Donal P. *Macbride's Brigade: Irish Commandos in the Anglo-Boer War.* London: Four Courts Press, 1999.

McCullough, David. *Mornings on Horseback.* New York: Simon and Schuster, 1981.

McElvaine, Robert S. *The Great Depression: America, 1929–1941.* New York: Times Books, 1993.

McLean, Evalyn Walsh. *Father Struck It Rich.* Boston: Little, Brown and Company, 1936.

Melendy, H. Brett. *Walter Francis Dillingham, 1875–1963: Hawaiian Entrepreneur and Statesman.* Lewiston, NY: Edwin Mellen Press, 1996.

Mercier, Laurie. *Anaconda: Labor, Community, and Culture in Montana's Smelter City.* Urbana: University of Illinois Press, 2001.

Miller, Nathan. *Theodore Roosevelt: A Life.* New York: William Morrow, 1992.

Mooney, Michael M. *Evelyn Nesbit and Stanford White: Love and Death in the Gilded Age.* New York: William Morrow, 1976.

Morison, Elting E., ed. *The Letters of Theodore Roosevelt.* vols. 3 and 4. Cambridge, MA: Harvard University Press, 1951.

Nakamura, Barry Seichi. "The Story of Waikiki and the 'Reclamation Project.'" Master's Thesis, University of Hawai'i, 1979.

Nelligan, Peter J. "Social Change and Rape Law in Hawai'i." Doctoral Dissertation, University of Hawai'i, 1983.

Nellist, George F. *The Story of Hawaii and Its Builders.* Honolulu: Honolulu Star-Bulletin, 1925.

Nordyke, Eleanor C. *The Peopling of Hawai'i,* second ed. Honolulu: University of Hawai'i Press, 1989.

Odo, Franklin. *No Sword to Bury: Japanese Americans in Hawai'i During World War II.* Philadelphia: Temple University Press, 2004.

Oka, Wilfred Mitsuji. "A Study of Japanese Social Institutions in Hawaii." Master's Thesis, Springfield College, Massachusetts, 1935.

Okihiro, Gary Y. *Cane Fires: The Anti-Japanese Movement in Hawai'i, 1865–1945.* Philadelphia: Temple University Press, 1991.

Owen, Russell. "Hot Lands and Cold," in *We Saw It Happen: The News Behind the News That's Fit to Print,* eds. Hanson W. Baldwin and Shepard Stone. New York: World Publishing, 1938.

Packer, Robert, and Bob Thomas. *The Massie Case.* New York: Bantam Books, 1966.

Peterson, Barbara Bennett. *Notable Women of Hawai'i.* Honolulu: University of Hawai'i Press, 1984.

Phillips, Kevin. *Wealth and Democracy: A Political History of the American Rich.* New York: Broadway Books, 2002.

Porteus, Stanley D. *A Century of Social Thinking in Hawaii.* Palo Alto, CA: Pacific Books, 1962.

Puette, William J. *The Hilo Massacre: Hawai'i's Bloody Monday.* Honolulu: Center for Labor Education and Research, 1988.

Reinecke, John E. *Feigned Necessity: Hawaii's Attempt to Obtain Chinese Contract Labor, 1921–23.* San Francisco: Chinese Materials Center, 1979.

———. *Language and Dialect in Hawaii: A Sociolinguistic History to 1935.* Honolulu: University of Hawai'i Press, 1969.

———. *A Man Must Stand Up.* Honolulu: University of Hawai'i Press, 1993.

Renehan, Edward J., Jr. *The Lion's Pride: Theodore Roosevelt and His Family in Peace and War.* New York: Oxford University Press, 1998.

Roosevelt, Theodore. *The Rough Riders.* New York: Charles Scribner's Sons, 1899.

Rosa, John Patrick. "Local Story: The Massie Case and the Politics of Local Identity in Hawai'i." Doctoral Dissertation, University of California at Irvine, 1999.

Rydell, Robert W. *All the World's a Fair: Visions of Empire at American International Expositions, 1876–1916.* Chicago: University of Chicago Press, 1984.

Sales, Grover. "All the Wrong Notes," in *Anderson Valley.net* (www.andersonvalley.net/blues.htm), January 2001.

Samuels, Peggy and Harold. *Teddy Roosevelt at San Juan: The Making of a President.* College Station: Texas A&M University Press, 1997.

Sato, Charlene J. "Linguistic Inequality in Hawaii: The Post-Creole Dilemma," in *Language of Inequality,* eds. Nessa Wolfson and Joan Manes. Berlin: Mouton, 1985.

Schatz, Thomas. *The Genius of the System: Hollywood Filmmaking in the Studio Era.* New York: Pantheon Books, 1988.

Schickel, Richard. *D. W. Griffith: An American Life.* New York: Simon and Schuster, 1984.

Schmitt, Robert C. *Demographic Statistics of Hawaii, 1778–1965.* Honolulu: University of Hawai'i Press, 1968.

———. *Hawaii in the Movies, 1898–1959.* Honolulu: Hawaiian Historical Society, 1988.

———. *Historical Statistics of Hawaii.* Honolulu: University of Hawai'i Press, 1977.

———. "Statistics on Income in Hawaii, 1825–1966," in *Hawaii Historical Review: Selected Readings,* ed. Richard A. Greer. Honolulu: Hawaiian Historical Society, 1969.

Silva, Noenoe. *Aloha Betrayed: Native Hawaiian Resistance to American Colonialism.* Durham, NC: Duke University Press, 2004.

Smith, Bernard. *European Vision and the South Pacific,* second ed. New Haven, Conn.: Yale University Press, 1988.

Smith, William C. "The Hybrid in Hawaii as a Marginal Man." *American Journal of Sociology* 39: 4 (1934): 459–68.

Stannard, David E. *Before the Horror: The Population of Hawai'i on the Eve of Western Contact.* Honolulu: University of Hawai'i Press, 1989.

———. "Disease and Infertility: A New Look at the Demographic Collapse of Native Populations in the Wake of Western Contact." *Journal of American Studies* 24 (1990).

———. "The Hawaiians: Health, Justice, and Sovereignty." *Cultural Survival Quarterly,* Spring 2000.

Steffens, Lincoln. *The Autobiography of Lincoln Steffens.* New York: Harcourt Brace and Company, 1931.

Stephan, John J. *Hawaii Under the Rising Sun: Japan's Plans for Conquest After Pearl Harbor.* Honolulu: University of Hawai'i Press, 1984.

Stirling, Yates. *Sea Duty: The Memoirs of a Fighting Admiral.* New York: G. P. Putnam's Sons, 1938.

Straus, Leon. *The Honolulu Police Department: A Brief History.* Honolulu: The 200 Club, 1978.

Stone, Irving. *Clarence Darrow for the Defense.* New York: Doubleday, 1941.

Susman, Warren I. *Culture as History: The Transformation of American Society in the Twentieth Century.* New York: Pantheon Books, 1984.

Svinth, Joseph R., Curtis Narimatsu, Paul Lou, and Charles Johnston. "Western Boxing in Hawai'i: The Bootleg Era, 1893–1929." *Journal of Combative Sport,* March 2003.

Symes, Lillian. "What About Hawaii?" *Harper's Monthly Magazine,* October 1932.

Takaki, Ronald. *Pau Hana: Plantation Life and Labor in Hawai'i.* Honolulu: University of Hawai'i Press, 1983.

———. *Strangers from a Different Shore: A History of Asian Americans.* Boston: Little, Brown and Company, 1989.

Theroux, Joseph. "A Short History of Hawaiian Executions, 1826–1947." *Hawaiian Journal of History* 25 (1991): 147–59.

Thurber, James. "New York in the Third Winter." *Fortune,* January 1932.

Thurston, Lorrin A., ed. *The Fundamental Law of Hawaii.* Honolulu: Hawaiian Gazette, 1904.

Thurston, Lucy. *Life and Times of Mrs. Lucy G. Thurston.* Ann Arbor, MI: S. C. Andrews, 1882.

Tierney, Kevin. *Darrow: A Biography.* New York: Thomas Y. Crowell, 1979.

Timmons, Grady. *Waikiki Beachboy.* Honolulu: Editions Limited, 1989.

Tolnay, Stewart E., and E. M. Beck. *A Festival of Violence: An Analysis of Southern Lynchings, 1882–1930.* Urbana: University of Illinois Press, 1995.

Trask, Haunani-Kay. "Cultures in Collision: Hawai'i and England, 1778." *Pacific Studies* 7 (1983).

Unity 121: 6 (May 16, 1938). Special issue on Clarence Darrow.

Van Slingerland, Peter. *Something Terrible Has Happened.* New York: Harper and Row, 1966.

Vidor, King. *A Tree Is a Tree.* Hollywood: Samuel French, 1981.

Watkins, T. H. *The Great Depression: America in the 1930s.* Boston: Little, Brown and Company, 1993.

Weinberg, Arthur. *Attorney for the Damned: Clarence Darrow in the Courtroom.* Chicago: University of Chicago Press, 1989.

Weinberg, Arthur and Lila. *Clarence Darrow: A Sentimental Rebel.* New York: G. P. Putnam's Sons, 1980.

White, Walter. *Rope and Faggot.* New York: Arno Press, 1969.

Wilson, Edmund. *Letters on Literature and Politics, 1912–1972.* New York: Farrar, Straus and Giroux, 1977.

Wood, Houston. *Displacing Natives: The Rhetorical Production of Hawai'i.* Lanham, MD: Rowman and Littlefield, 1999.

Wright, George C. *Racial Violence in Kentucky, 1865–1940: Lynchings, Mob Rule, and "Legal Lynchings."* Baton Rouge: Louisiana State University Press, 1990.

Wright, Theon. *The Disenchanted Isles: The Story of the Second Revolution in Hawaii.* New York: Dial Press, 1972.

———. *Rape in Paradise.* New York: Hawthorn Books, 1966.

Zalburg, Sanford. *A Spark Is Struck: Jack Hall and the ILWU in Hawaii.* Honolulu: University of Hawai'i Press, 1979.

Index

Kahahawai, Joseph, Sr., 243, 252, 260–61, 317, 334
Kahanamoku, Duke, 94, 312, 320
Kaikapu, Lui, 238
Kaʻiulani, Victoria, 12
Kalākaua, David Laʻamea, 51
Kalanianaʻole, Jonah Kūhiō, 255–56
Kama, David, 260
Kama, William, 100, 260
Kamoku, Harry, 415
Kashiwabara, Hans, 58–59, 203
Kawananakoa, Abigail, 78, 138–41, 227, 317, 391–92, 417–18
Kekua, Thomas, 245–46
Kelley, Cornelius, 310–11
Kelley, Jeremiah, 310
Kelley, John Carlton, 309–15, 322, 327–39, 342–47, 354–58, 370, 373–75, 377, 379, 383, 388–89, 395–99, 401–2, 408
Kelley, Nan, 312, 327
Kelly, E. Lowell, 39–40, 340–41, 357
Kentucky, lynching and violence in, 154–55, 279
Kewalo Inn, 7, 53
Kinsley, Philip, 315–16, 345, 348, 353, 373, 383–84, 415
Kluegel, Ann, 270–71, 273, 280–81, 291, 317, 324, 346, 383, 400, 402
Komuru, Harry Shigeo, 417
Koreans in Hawaiʻi, 3, 72, 75, 87
Ku Klux Klan, 19, 388
Kunstler, William, 304
Kuykendall, Ralph, 239

labor unions in Hawaiʻi, 75–76, 86–88, 414–15, 418–20
Lau, Samuel, 133, 196
Leisure, George S., 300, 305, 318, 350, 363, 365, 369, 373, 386, 390
Leopold and Loeb trial, 5, 296, 298, 314, 374, 401
Lewis, Sinclair, 21
Liliʻuokalani, 12, 69, 139, 259, 262
Lindbergh, Charles A., 4, 20, 395
Liu, David, 83–85, 198
Liu, Roger, 200
Lombard, Carole, 41, 409
London Daily Telegraph, 11, 13

London Times, 389
Lord, Edward J., 241–44, 248, 253–54, 289–90, 343, 367, 389, 391, 402–3
Los Angeles Times, 305, 315, 415
Louisville Courier-Journal, 279
Low, James, 200–201
Lugosi, Bela, 306
Lyman, Daniel, 245
Lymer, William, 319
lynching, 154–56, 264–65, 304

MacArthur, Douglas, 118
Machado, Lena, 93, 262
Machado, Luciano, 93–95, 98, 100–101, 198, 205
Mackaill, Dorothy, 41–42
Makino, Kinzaburo (Fred), 135
Malone, Dudley Field, 300
Manchuria, 4, 19, 29, 267
Mānoa Valley, 31–32
Marconi, Guglielmo, 228
Massie, Thalia, 7–8, 13–23, 35–55, 60–64, 83–85, 89–92, 97–98, 101–3, 130–31, 149–51, 212, 232–35, 240–41, 338–39, 346, 367–72, 377, 380, 389–91, 399–401, 404–6; Graves' disease and, 16–17, 22; murder trial testimony, 354–58; pregnancies, 22, 38–39; rape trial testimony, 166–72, 189; vision, 16–17, 38
Massie, Thomas Hedges (Tommie), 17–23, 35–40, 43–50, 55, 59, 61–64, 95–97, 130, 149–50, 153–58, 232–35, 240–44, 248–49, 252–54, 289–91, 329, 355, 364, 367–72, 374, 376, 379–80, 383, 389, 391, 400, 403, 406–7; murder trial testimony, 336–40, 342–46
Matsumoto, Tatsumi, 126, 128, 190–91
Maugham, W. Somerset, 33
McCandless, Lincoln, 411–12
McClellan, George, 208–9
McClellan, Ramona, 208–10
McCrea, Joel, 275
McIntosh, John, 62, 85–92, 97–98, 101, 121, 127, 130, 133, 145, 167, 186–89, 193, 205, 239, 249, 251–52
McIntyre, George, 381–82
McKechnie, A. W. ("Doc"), 63–64, 156
McKinley, William, 233